T0366555

# MAGNIFICENCE
## AND PRINCELY SPLENDOUR
## IN THE MIDDLE AGES

# RICHARD BARBER

# MAGNIFICENCE

## AND PRINCELY SPLENDOUR IN THE MIDDLE AGES

THE BOYDELL PRESS

© Richard Barber 2020

All Rights Reserved. Except as permitted under current legislation
no part of this work may be photocopied, stored in a retrieval system,
published, performed in public, adapted, broadcast,
transmitted, recorded or reproduced in any form or by any means,
without the prior permission of the copyright owner

The rights of Richard Barber to be identified as
the author of this work have been asserted in accordance with
sections 77 and 78 of the Copyright, Designs and Patents Act 1988

First published 2020
The Boydell Press, Woodbridge

ISBN 9781783274710

The Boydell Press is an imprint of Boydell & Brewer Ltd
PO Box 9, Woodbridge, Suffolk IP12 3DF, UK
and of Boydell & Brewer Inc.
668 Mt Hope Avenue, Rochester, NY 14620–2731, USA
website: www.boydellandbrewer.com

*Frontispiece*
The month of January, from the calendar in *Les Très Riches Heures du duc de Berry*.
Jean, duke of Berry, is shown welcoming guests. It has traditionally been interpreted
as the beginning of a feast, but in the light of recent work on New Year's gifts at
this period, it could well be that the visitors are bringing their offerings for the traditional
exchange of gifts on New Year's day.

Background to title page: design from fifteenth century textile in the Victoria and
Albert Museum, used by Liberty for a velvet material c.1890, and redesigned as wallpaper
in 1990. © Richard Barber

A catalogue record for this book is available
from the British Library

Designed by Simon Loxley
Printed by Gomer Press

# ✳ CONTENTS

## INTRODUCTION

◆ *The coronation of king Arthur: an imagined festival* ◆ *The festival at Mainz, 1184* ◆ *Defining princely splendour*

# PART ONE

## PRINCELY SPLENDOUR

◆ *The status of a king* ◆ *'A substitute for long hair'* ◆ *The king in his court* ◆ *The ceremonies of kingship* ◆ *Crown-wearings* ◆ *Crowns*

◆ *Sicily: creating a royal culture* ◆ *Palermo as a royal capital* ◆ *Friedrich II: recreating the past, exploring the future* ◆ *The arch at Capua* ◆ *Friedrich as builder: Castel del Monte and Castello Maniace* ◆ *St Louis and Henry III* ◆ *Paris* ◆ *London* ◆ *Royal mausoleums*

# PART TWO

## MAGNIFICENCE

◆ *Popes, emperors and kings* ◆ *Philip IV and the Church* ◆ *Aristotle and the* Nicomachean Ethics ◆ On the Government of Princes

# PART THREE

## THE MANAGEMENT OF MAGNIFICENCE

# ✳ LIST OF ILLUSTRATIONS

## LINE ILLUSTRATIONS IN TEXT

To my colleagues past and present at Boydell & Brewer, with thanks for fifty years of support and friendship.

# ✦ PREFACE

The word 'magnificence' has a good deal of history to it. We can trace it from its first appearance in Greek philosophy in about 320 BC to royal propaganda in the fourteenth and fifteenth centuries. The idea behind it evolved over the centuries, but at the end of the thirteenth century, the rediscovery of Greek texts gave a new meaning to 'magnificence'. This made it into a personal virtue which all kings should possess. The central theme of this book is the part that this new idea of magnificence played in justifying or encouraging the behaviour of kings and princes in the middle ages.

The subject is enormously wide-ranging, across a range of languages and literatures, involving enough different princes to need a cast list (which follows), a wonderful variety of contemporary voices. It is a book about people: not just ambitious princes, but artists, craftsmen and musicians of all kinds and the personnel of the court, from cooks and showmen to scribes and clerks. Indeed there have been encounters with unexpected characters who scarcely figure in English histories of Europe.

It is also a book about the dazzling objects that were produced to promote magnificence, and the illustrations are an essential part of it. It was not uncommon for the king to restrict the right to wear rich silken and embroidered clothing to himself and his family. His jewellery, particularly his crowns, were the most dramatic pieces made by goldsmiths, and he surrounded himself with other opulent creations, culminating in the outstanding illuminated manuscripts of the late fifteenth century. The royal collections also included remarkable collections of relics, themselves enclosed in exquisite gold casings, and vast quantities of loose jewels, rings, badges and other ornaments. The king's rooms were hung with tapestries which proclaimed his lineage in their bright heraldic patterns. And the setting for the king and his court were palaces and castles which were the most imposing secular buildings in the realm.

MAGNIFICENCE WAS IN ESSENCE reliant on publicity, on the royal events or appearances being reported by chroniclers or letter-writers. We are so used to the ready availability of all types of news in the media that it is difficult to imagine a world where communications were slow and where news was shared with only a handful of people. For the twelfth and thirteenth centuries, the sources are erratic and quite sparse, so that a great event which happens to come to the attention of a diligent and eloquent writer will assume an importance that it may not deserve. Furthermore, there is little in the way of official records to back up such descriptions. By the fifteenth century the opposite is true: for a major festival we may have two or three separate eyewitness accounts, full expenditure details from the treasury, and even a memoir from the man who organised it.

Overall, in England and Burgundy both narratives and financial details are very full. In France the financial details are sparse; in Spain and Germany they are more erratic. For the intriguing period when French kings ruled in eastern Europe, there is very little detail, and I have in any case had to rely on secondary sources for material in Hungarian, Czech and Polish.

What may seem another bias is that the majority of the protagonists are male. The records for queen consorts are very variable, because they often had their own households and finances, but records of these were not kept by the central administration, and have rarely survived. Only a handful of women were queens in their own right, or ruled in the name of their sons, usually in times of political turbulence.

AS TO THE SECOND PART of this book's title, what do we mean when we write of 'medieval Europe'? The term the 'Middle Ages' is first suggested by the fifteenth-century humanists, who saw a 'middle time' between the end of the Roman empire and their own revival of classical ideals; the phrase 'middle time' first appears in 1468, and 'Middle Ages' in 1518. *Medium aevum*, from which our word medieval derives, is first recorded in 1604, but became the standard phrase only in the late seventeenth century. The concept of a barbarian interval between the decline of classical civilization and its revival was central to the rationalist thinking of the eighteenth century, and the period was now precisely defined: Chambers' Encyclopaedia in 1753 equates the Middle Ages with the centuries between the reign of Constantine and the taking of Constantinople, and the accepted dates soon became from c.500 to c.1500 AD. 'Medieval', an invented word, is first found a century later. An invented word for an invented period? Most historians would agree. The 'fall' of the Roman empire took centuries; the Renaissance, the supposed rebirth of that same civilization, also took centuries. Many writers use the term for the period from the coronation of Charlemagne to the troubled time at the end of the fourteenth century when the whole of western Europe seemed subject to anarchy and sudden change, and which arguably represents the crucial moment of transition from the old idea of Europe and Christendom as an entity to the modem, narrower ideal of the nation-state.

It is important to remember that for most of world history, there is no such thing as the 'Middle Ages', and that 'medieval' always implies Europe as the subject under discussion. Even then, it is Europe in a limited sense, best defined as Western Christendom, those countries that recognised the pope as the head of the church (with varying degrees of respect and obedience). Its border was defined to the east by the territories that owed allegiance to the Orthodox church, and to the north-east by the pagan lands around the Baltic. The Atlantic and the Mediterranean were its western and southern limits, except in Spain, where there was a Muslim presence until 1492. In secular terms, Western Christendom formed a relatively close cultural entity, particularly at the level of society which will principally concern us, that of the royal and princely courts.

# ✶ THE RULERS OF EUROPE 1100–1500

## Kings of France and their Descendants

Paris was the greatest city in Europe in the period with which we are most concerned, the thirteenth to fifteenth centuries, and it is therefore our starting point. Until 1328, the French kings were all direct descendants of Hugh Capet, crowned in 987. LOUIS IX, who came to the throne in 1226, is better known to us as St Louis. He figures here not for his personal splendour – he was modest in his dress – or for his tireless crusading efforts, but as a great builder and collector of relics, culminating in the installation of the crown of thorns, said to have been worn by Jesus at the crucifixion, in the Sainte-Chapelle.

His grandson, PHILIP IV (1285–1314), was a very different character, a ruthless politician who was largely responsible for the downfall of the great crusading order of the Templars. In a sense, he is the pivotal figure in this book, for it is in the handbook on government written for his education by a philosopher from the university of Paris that the medieval definition of magnificence first appears. Philip IV's sons all died without heirs, and the kingdom passed to the house of Valois when PHILIP VI became king in 1328. Philip's claim to the throne was challenged by Edward III of England, who was the senior descendant of St Louis. Edward's claim was through his mother, and was therefore invalid, according to the Parisian lawyers.

The aggressive efforts of the English kings to enforce this claim was the reason for the long period of misery for France known as the Hundred Years' War. Yet the two countries were linked not only by royal marriages but also by a shared French culture. And the wealth of France itself was far greater than that of England: one of the most luxurious periods of French art of all kinds took place at the end of the fourteenth century, despite the military defeats at Crécy in 1346 and Poitiers in 1356. JEAN (John) II (1350–1364), son of Philip VI, was captured in the second of these battles, and a massive ransom was paid. Despite this, CHARLES V, Jean's successor (1364–1380), was able to rebuild both French finances and the administrative structure of France. He was a scholar and a collector of manuscripts and jewellery; his son, CHARLES VI (1380–1422), was more warlike, but was afflicted by madness in 1392 at the age of twenty-three, and the government of the kingdom passed into the hands of his mother, Isabeau of Bavaria, and his uncles, the hugely powerful dukes whose territories covered much of France. Jean duke of Berry, another great collector, was immensely wealthy, and continued to spend lavishly on the arts and on luxuries, while the dukes of Anjou and Burgundy were both ambitious to compete as independent magnates.

Yet it was precisely at this time that French artistic work reached the pinnacle of luxury and display. Almost all the magnificent – truly magnificent – Parisian jewellery of this period has disappeared, some of it being melted down to pay for the costs of the war in 1422. On the death of Charles VI in that year, the succession passed to HENRY VI of England and CHARLES VII (1422–1461) became a claimant to the throne, exiled from Paris. The royal finances only began to recover after the effective end of English rule in 1435.

THE BROTHERS OF THE FRENCH KINGS were remarkably successful in establishing themselves as kings and princes. In the thirteenth century, the brothers of St Louis were the first group to do so, and CHARLES, the youngest, acquired the title of king of SICILY, ruling both Sicily and southern Italy, from the Pope after he had defeated Friedrich II's grandson Conradin with the Pope's encouragement in 1266. After the revolt of Sicily in 1282, the famous 'Sicilian Vespers', he lost Sicily itself, and Naples became a separate kingdom. He acquired the nominal title of king of Jerusalem by purchase in 1277. His descendants ruled NAPLES for the next century: ROBERT (1309–1343) was the most distinguished of these.

In 1382, his granddaughter JOANNA I was murdered, having reigned for nearly forty years. She had named as her heir a distant relative, Louis duke of Anjou, brother of Charles V of France. However, he was unable to claim the kingdom, as Joanna's cousin CHARLES OF DURAZZO (1382–1386), who had had her murdered in order to succeed her, held the kingdom for several years and was able to pass it to his son LADISLAUS (1386–1390, 1399–1414). At this point, the crowns of Hungary, Aragon and Naples become intertwined. The upshot was that Charles's daughter JOANNA II (1414–1435) briefly adopted Alfonso V of Aragon as her heir, quarrelled with him, and named Louis of Anjou's grandson RENÉ D'ANJOU (1435–1442) as her successor instead. René was driven out by Alfonso V of Aragon, who already held Sicily, and retired to France where he died in 1480. In his time he had claimed the kingdoms of Naples, Sicily, Aragon and Jerusalem.

The youngest brother of Charles V, PHILIP DUKE OF BURGUNDY, married Margaret, daughter and heir of Louis count of Flanders, in 1369, and on the death of Louis in 1384 Burgundy and Flanders were effectively united. The combination of the wealth of the Flemish trading towns with the rich Burgundian territories, immediately to the south created a state almost as rich and powerful as France itself. Although Burgundy was technically part of France, and the counts of Flanders were French vassals, Philip, known as 'the Bold', and his successors pursued an independent policy. Under JEAN (John) THE FEARLESS, vicious infighting between the royal dukes developed: 'ruthless' might have been a better nickname for him. He had his uncle Louis duke of Orléans assassinated in 1407, but was in turn assassinated by supporters of Louis' son Charles d'Orléans in 1419. It was under Jean's son PHILIP THE GOOD that the Burgundian court became the most lavish in Europe, with the creation of the Order of the Golden Fleece and immensely spectacular feasts. He was succeeded by his son CHARLES THE BOLD, called in French 'le téméraire', which can be translated as either bold or rash. 'Rash' is probably more appropriate, as it was his decision to attack a strong force of Swiss pikemen with inadequate troops that led to his death in battle at Nancy in 1477. Four years earlier, he had made formal approaches to the emperor Friedrich III to be granted a kingdom within the empire. They met at Trier, but Charles's hopes were disappointed after weeks of discussion and the ancient kingdom of Burgundy was not revived. His death meant that his rich and extensive domains went to his son-in-law Maximilian who succeeded Friedrich as emperor. Burgundy was absorbed into the Austrian realms.

## Kings of England

Compared with the convoluted genealogy of the house of Anjou, the line of English kings with whom we have to deal is extremely simple. From a previous holder of the title count of Anjou, HENRY II (1154–1189), until RICHARD II, the throne passes from father to son: first JOHN, then HENRY III (1217–1272), EDWARD I (1272–1307), EDWARD II

(1307–1327), EDWARD III (1327–1377) and RICHARD II (1377–1400). Henry III, Edward III and Richard II all figure largely in what follows. The fifteenth century kings are less prominent, as the defeats in France and the Wars of the Roses take their toll on English resources.

# Kings of Aragon

Aragon appears on modern maps as an inland province in northern Spain, yet it was at one time the most powerful kingdom in the Mediterranean. In the medieval period, Aragon was originally a kingdom in northern Spain, which became a kind of federation of lands under one ruler, sometimes called the 'Crown of Aragon'. This included the modern Catalonia and Valencia on the Spanish mainland, and the kingdom of Majorca. From 1282, the kings of Aragon also ruled Sicily, and in 1442 they conquered Naples, which had once been part of the Sicilian kingdom. At its greatest extent, their territories included Sardinia and Corsica as well. The first king of Aragon of interest to us is PETER III (1276–1285), in whose reign Sicily was acquired; the second is ALFONSO V (1416–1458) who made good his claim to the other part of the Norman kingdom of Sicily, and whose court in Naples bridged both medieval and Renaissance culture.

# Kings of Castile

Castile is more or less identical with the modern Spanish province of that name. Although it had links to both England and France in the fourteenth century, only two kings are of interest to us: ALFONSO X (1252–1284), known as 'the Wise' because of his extensive writings rather than his singular lack of success as a ruler, is the most important; his law code is actually a wonderful portrait of life in Spain in the thirteenth century as well as a landmark in legal history. His great-grandson ALFONSO XI (1312–1350), by contrast, was a succesful military leader, and founded one of the earliest secular orders of knighthood.

# Kings of Sicily

The kingdom of Sicily was created by the Pope for the Norman conquerors of the island of Sicily, but included extensive lands in southern Italy. These became a separate kingdom in 1282, after Sicily rebelled against the French successors of the original Norman dynasty. Sicilian culture was a remarkable fusion of Norman, Greek and Arab customs and languages. The first king was ROGER II (count 1105–1130, king 1130–1154); the formal creation of the kingdom, subject to the Pope as overlord, was proclaimed in 1130. He and his grandson WILLIAM II (1166–1189) were responsible for most of the splendid palaces and visual imagery which enriched Palermo before the dynasty collapsed early in the next century. However, much of Sicily's intellectual and artistic heritage reappears in the court of the emperor Friedrich II, whose mother Constance was the queen of Sicily from 1194 to 1198.

Later Sicilian kings were Charles I of Anjou and his successors, replaced by the kings of Aragon after 1282.

## Kings of Hungary

From 1300 onwards, the Hungarian kings were related to western European princely families: KÁROLY (Charles, 1301–1342) was the brother of Robert the Wise of Naples and introduced western European customs to the country. These included one of the earliest secular orders of knighthood, that of St George, founded in 1326. LOUIS THE GREAT (1342–1382) inherited Poland from his uncle, and his lands formed a small empire in central Europe, but it was largely personal to him, and on his death Poland and Hungary separated once more.

## Kings of Bohemia

JEAN (John) (1310–1346) count of Luxembourg married Elisabeth, heiress of Bohemia in 1310, and deposed the reigning king of that kingdom, a descendant of Friedrich II, in the same year. His father was a minor French noble, and he was brought up at the French court. As king of Bohemia, he spent more time on chivalric pursuits and imperial politics than on his kingdom, and was regarded as an alien by the Czech lords. He lost his sight on crusade in Prussia in 1336; the sequel is the famous scene at the battle of Crécy, portrayed by Froissart, of the blind king being led into battle by his knights, to die in the fighting.

KARL (Karel, Charles) (1346–1378) was both king of Bohemia and the fourth Emperor of the Holy Roman Empire with that name. He is probably the most imposing figure in this book, a truly international statesman, deeply religious, and very conscious of appearances, settings, rituals and presentation.

## The Holy Roman Empire

Voltaire simply described the Holy Roman Empire as 'in no way holy, nor Roman, nor an empire', He was using the words in their eighteenth century meaning; the original Latin meaning of the phrase 'Sacrum Imperium Romanum' describes an institution that involves consecration, power and a link to the Roman papacy. It is an organisation with no real parallel. In terms of territory, it was vast, and its tentacles reached out into the Low Countries and the Rhine and Rhone valleys. It included most of modern Germany, Austria, northern Italy, Switzerland, Savoy, parts of Burgundy and the Low Countries. The impact of imperial rule depended very much on the personality of the emperor and the strength of his own power base.

By the mid-thirteenth century, there were three archbishops and four princes as electors, and this remained the case to the end of our period. The initial election was to the office of 'King of the Romans', who was in effect an emperor in waiting, though he did not always become emperor depending on changes in the political situations. Theoretically, the electors could choose among a wide range of princes, and there was no commitment to any one family. However, in practice, the emperors were chosen from just five families from 1125 to 1440: three Hohenstaufen, one Welf, three Luxembourg, one Wittelsbach, and finally the first of the Habsburgs, who held the office for the next four centuries. The Hohenstaufens, FRIEDRICH BARBAROSSA (1155 1190) and FRIEDRICH II (1220–1250), his grandson, together with KARL IV (1346–1378) from the Luxembourg family made the most impression on their contemporaries. We shall also encounter SIGISMUND of Luxembourg (1433–1437) and the Habsburg FRIEDRICH III (1440–1493).

# Counts of Savoy and Northern Italy

Savoy was part of the ancient kingdom of Arles, an almost fictional institution by the mid thirteenth century because so many areas had been sold or transferred to other powers, chiefly to the French kings. After 1365, Savoy became a separate county. AMADEUS VI (1343–1383), nicknamed the 'Green Count', was a successful military and political leader, while at the same time renowned for the feasts and rituals at his court at Chambéry. The tradition continued under his hospitable son, Amadeus VII and his grandson AMADEUS VIII (1391–1440), who commissioned his cook Master Chiquart to set down his knowledge of cookery and of the organisation of great festivals.

The northern Italian cities were also technically under the jurisdiction of the Holy Roman Emperor. The greatest of these was Milan, Venice being an independent republic. Milan was often very hostile to the emperor, and at its apogee had as grand a court as any in Europe. They were immensely rich, and it is here that the modern concept of princely magnificence, as reshaped by the Renaissance, first appears.

# ✳ NAMES AND COINAGE

## Names

Writing about the rulers throughout Christian Europe, is fraught with problems. There are a plethora of them, and many of them have the same names: there are rulers called Charles in France, Germany, Hungary, Naples, Sicily, Navarre, Bohemia, and Flanders. To confuse the reader further, Charles I of Bohemia is also the emperor Charles IV, and Charles I of Navarre becomes Charles IV of France. There is no really satisfactory way of separating out these individuals so that the reader knows instantly which prince is meant. I have therefore adopted the convenient, if inconsistent, system used by my old tutor at Cambridge, Richard Vaughan, whose four superb volumes on the dukes of Burgundy have been among the chief sources for the present book. Broadly speaking, where a name only occurs in one context, I have used the English version: thus, *Philip* rather than *Philippe*. On the other hand, the confusion of Charleses is resolved by using the native versions of their name: *Charles* in France, Flanders and Navarre, *Karl* in Germany and Bohemia, *Károly* in Hungary, *Carlo* in Naples and Sicily. The index cross-references from the English equivalent to the names used in the text.

## Coinage

Even with the help of Peter Spufford's massive *Handbook of Medieval Exchange*, it is very difficult to translate values either into a single coinage of the time, or to give meaningful modern equivalents. The value of coins depended on the amount of silver they contained, which tended to diminish over time: a ruler could make a quick profit by reducing the percentage of the metal used in each coin, while retaining its face value. The basic coin was the silver penny, used under different names across Europe. It was silver to which the values of gold coins of varying sizes were related: a silver standard rather than the twentieth century 'gold standard'. Thus the English gold coin called the noble was worth 33.33 silver pennies. However, if the exchange rate between silver and gold varied, it was the weight of the gold coin which changed, not that of the silver pennies.

The chief accounting currencies were the pound in England, for which I have used the familiar £ sign. The French currency was also in *livres* or pounds, for which I have used l. Many Italian cities used florins, named after their origin in Florence.

There are various online resources for those curious enough to want modern values for particular sums: the best is probably that at the National Archives website, http://www.nationalarchives.gov.uk/currency-converter/. But there is no simple exchange rate between medieval and modern money.

# ✳ EUROPEAN KINGDOMS IN THE FOURTEENTH CENTURY

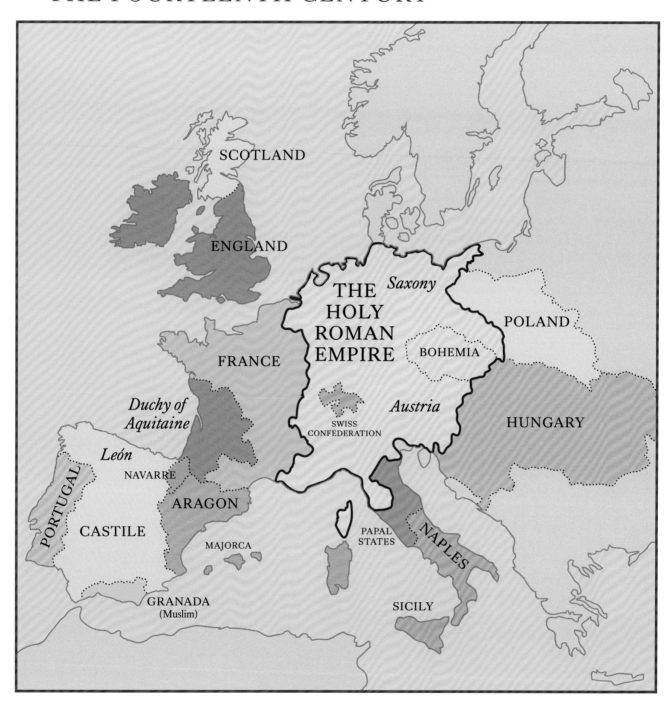

SCOTLAND

ENGLAND

*Saxony*

POLAND

THE HOLY ROMAN EMPIRE

BOHEMIA

FRANCE

*Austria*

HUNGARY

*Duchy of Aquitaine*

SWISS CONFEDERATION

*León*

NAVARRE

PORTUGAL

ARAGON

CASTILE

MAJORCA

PAPAL STATES

NAPLES

GRANADA (Muslim)

SICILY

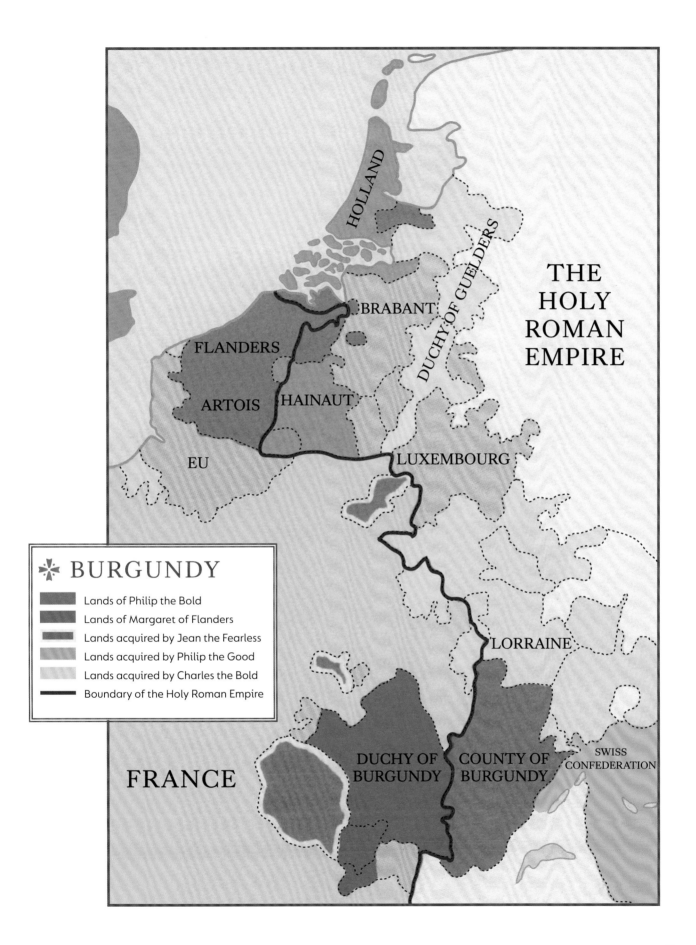

THE
HOLY
ROMAN
EMPIRE

HOLLAND

BRABANT

DUCHY OF GUELDERS

FLANDERS

ARTOIS

HAINAUT

EU

LUXEMBOURG

## ✳ BURGUNDY

| | |
|---|---|
| | Lands of Philip the Bold |
| | Lands of Margaret of Flanders |
| | Lands acquired by Jean the Fearless |
| | Lands acquired by Philip the Good |
| | Lands acquired by Charles the Bold |
| ▬ | Boundary of the Holy Roman Empire |

LORRAINE

SWISS
CONFEDERATION

FRANCE

DUCHY OF
BURGUNDY

COUNTY OF
BURGUNDY

**1.** The crown of the Holy Roman Empire, probably made in AD 962 or AD 967 for the coronation of the emperor Otto the Great or his son. The octagonal form is common to many medieval crowns, and the panels are linked by pins. The arch and cross were added in the eleventh century. There are four enamel plaques, showing Christ and three Old Testament kings, which are in the Byzantine style of the period.

# INTRODUCTION

*…aspects are within us; and who seems*
*Most kingly is the king.*

THOMAS HARDY

# 1 | SPLENDOUR AND MAGNIFICENCE

K INGS WERE NOT ALWAYS EXPECTED to be splendid or magnificent. When kingship, which had been the norm among the tribal societies which preceded the Roman Empire, emerged again when new tribes invaded and conquered the Roman territories, the king was leader of a warband. Such a king might take the lion's share of the plunder, and display his gold and treasure, but his own appearance was not of importance. By the sixth century, there are early forms of regalia which distinguish the king on ceremonial occasions, yet men remembered the days when the king was known by his long hair and by the ox-cart in which he travelled. Splendour came later, as the king became ruler of a settled people and trade began to revive. The idea of personal adornment of a special kind which distinguishes the king gradually extends to his family, his entourage and his surroundings.

*Splendour*

This first stage I would describe as 'splendour', and is covered in the three chapters that follow. The Norman kingdom in Sicily in the twelfth century, drawing on Greek and Arab culture as well as that of the Christian West, created monuments of remarkable originality and beauty. Friedrich II inherited Sicily and was at the same time ruler of Italy and Germany as Holy Roman Emperor. He is the first of the extraordinary personalities in this book, invoking the imagery of ancient Rome to show his authority, while at the same time corresponding in Arabic with the sultan of Egypt and investigating the new scientific discoveries of his time.

When Frederick died in 1250, the succession to the Empire was disputed. Soon afterwards the popes, who claimed authority over both the Empire and the kings of Europe, were driven out of Rome into exile at Avignon. It was at this moment that the French kings made their bid for independence from pope and emperor.

*The word 'magnificence'*

MAGNIFICENCE IS A WORD RARELY USED before the end of the thirteenth century. When Philip III of France commissioned a handbook on the 'government of princes' for his son, the future Philip IV. Giles of Rome, who wrote it, proclaimed that 'magnificence', an idea from Greek philosophy, was not an option but both a virtue and a royal duty. 'A king should be magnificent' as God's representative on earth, and he was bound to dress and to act in a way which was appropriate to his high office. Magnificence was to become the hallmark of royalty, and the visual expression of the king's right to rule over his subjects. Giles boldly applied this new idea to everything the king did. His appearance, above all, should be magnificent, and Alfonso the Learned, king of Castile agreed with him: 'Kings should wear garments of silk, adorned with gold and jewels', in order that men might know them as soon as they saw them.

Giles's book *On the Government of Princes* was endlessly copied and translated, and read by kings, or perhaps more frequently, by their tutors and advisers. The word magnificence itself is suddenly everywhere. Two centuries after Giles wrote, a courtier who wanted to celebrate Charles the Bold of Burgundy, who had just died in battle, recorded his 'magnificences' as his memorial. After 1300, the king's demonstration of magnificence projects the idea that he is the rightful king. Kings themselves had rejected the authorities which had vouched for their legitimacy in the past. They were no long elected (as the Holy Roman Emperor continued to be), they no longer looked to the pope as their superior who could vouch for them, and they no longer considered themselves under the emperor's jurisdiction. Instead, the kings and would-be kings of western Christendom employed an astonishing variety of means to persuade both their subjects and their enemies that they possessed the kingly virtue of 'magnificence'. Put succinctly, 'How is it that rulers, humans like the rest of us, are able to hold sway? What kind of fictions are in place to enable some to command the allegiance, even the worship, of others?'[1] The world that we are about to enter is one where material appearance is everything, both for ruler and subject. It is epitomised by the quotation from Thomas Hardy which is our epigraph. Indeed, we could define magnificence as the ultimate weapon in the effort to 'seem most kingly'. *Kingly virtue*

Magnificence was applied to everything to do with the ruler: his person, his family, his entourage, his court, the artists, musicians and architects he employed. Above all, it was on show in his public appearances, his feasts and ceremonies. And it was also what inspired the great collections of jewels, manuscripts and holy relics, admission to which was limited to a handful of favoured visitors. Those visitors also had to be entertained, and royal feasts, with their elaborate etiquette, developed into an amazing form of performance art.

All this is explored in the pages which follow, covering the whole of western Europe, centring on France, the wealthiest of the kingdoms, members of whose extended royal family were at different times kings of Poland, Hungary, Naples, Jerusalem, England and, most spectacularly, dukes of Burgundy. The court of Burgundy was the most splendid in Europe in the mid fifteenth century, and when Charles the Bold tried to persuade the then Holy Roman Emperor to grant him a kingdom in 1473, he did so by arriving for the negotiations in a style so magnificent that onlookers were lost for words.

Patronage was a vital element of magnificence. We meet the artists, such as Barthélemy van Eyck, whose room was next to the chamber of René d'Anjou, his patron, so that they could work together on the marvellous illuminated manuscripts for which the king wrote the text. The musicians range from the 'kings of minstrels' who turn out to be gangmasters *Patronage* providing the required quantity of musicians for a feast to the great composers of the fifteenth century who moved from court to court. And there are the contractors, like John of Cologne, armourer and supplier of embroidery, costumes and disguises for English royal entertainments.

Magnificence was also reflected by the royal castles and palaces, and the royal chapels and cathedrals. We watch Henry III of England and the Holy Roman Emperor Karl IV touring the wonders of Paris, and comparing them with their own buildings at Westminster *Architecture* and Prague. The great cities were the settings for royal processions, the formal entry of the sovereign into a city which could match him for wealth. Here display was everything: elaborate tableaux and theatrical effects were nothing new.

By the fifteenth century, royal magnificence was imitated by those princes and dukes who aspired to rival the king. The dukes of Burgundy, whose revenues were as great as those of most kings, mounted a series of deliberately 'magnificent' occasions, particularly feasts, which seem to us today to have been sheer extravagance. In fact, there was a powerful *Princes and dukes* political agenda behind this magnificence, which began after 1440. Burgundy was at peace with both France and England, and Philip the Good had reorganised the government of his territories into a single system. He was now free to enhance Burgundian prestige and influence by the use of magnificence, with the ultimate aim of transforming his duchy into a kingdom: and he spent royally in the pursuit of his objective.

All this is portrayed through contemporary, often eyewitness, descriptions, and in royal and princely accounts and inventories. The chroniclers may give us the overall picture, but the dry records fill in details which would otherwise have been lost. One of Edward III's clerks wrote a full description of the exotic embroidered gown that the king had worn at a royal entertainment, as a change from simply entering the amount paid for it. Inventories describe named jewels and the long-vanished masterpieces of the Parisian goldsmiths, melted down to pay bills or to create new works of art. The entries are often astonishing in what they reveal about techniques, materials and even working conditions: John of Cologne's workmen doing overtime by candlelight; Chinese dragon and cloud patterned silk being bought for Joan, daughter of Edward III; Kathelot producing hats with tiny figures on them for the French princes.

As I worked through the colour and brilliance of the feasts and ceremonies, I grew increasingly interested in the logistics of all this: how did you organise a medieval feast or run a tournament or a civic entry? How did you plan such an occasion, and find the artists and performers? Apart from the artists and architects, there were the administrators at court. Olivier de la Marche in Burgundy sent a hundred pages of description of a wedding he had organised to his counterpart in the service of the duke of Brittany, as it would be a help to him for a similar occasion. Perhaps most unexpected of all is the cook Master Chiquart, whose employer, the duke of Savoy, ordered him to write down his skills. Chiquart, despite protesting that he did not know how to write a book, left us a wonderfully vivid picture of the challenges of ensuring the success of a great feast.

And finally, there is the dramatic end of the duchy of Burgundy, at a time when its magnificence reflected high political ambitions. The list of the twelve magnificences of the last duke made shortly before he died brings down the curtain on this highly theatrical world.

## The Coronation of King Arthur: An Imagined Festival

MEDIEVAL FESTIVALS ARE THE HIGH POINTS of both splendour and magnificence; but what were they like? There are hundreds of descriptions of such occasions in the chronicles and memoirs of the period, and we begin with three samples. There was often a basis of established ritual, as at a coronation or a knighting, but beyond that lies a huge variety of creative approaches. Our first example, which predates almost all the historical descriptions of festivities, is from one of the most popular books of the period, Geoffrey of Monmouth's *History of the Kings of Britain*, and is a highly imaginative account of the coronation of king Arthur: even though it was written about 1135, when the ideas of courtly behaviour and courtly love were real novelties, and before tournaments were other than military exercises, it has all the elements that we shall find in court festivals for the next three centuries:

> When they had all arrived at Caerleon, on the day of the festival the archbishops were led to the palace to place the royal diadem upon the king's head. Undertaking this duty because the court was being held in his diocese, Dubricius performed the act. After the coronation, the king was duly escorted to the metropolitan cathedral. He was flanked to right and left by two archbishops; four kings, of Scotland, Cornwall, Demetia and Venedotia, walked before him, bearing four golden swords, as was their right; a choir of clergy of all stations sang before him. From the other direction the archbishops and prelates led the queen, wearing her own regalia, to the convent church of the nuns; as

was the custom, the queens of the four kings already mentioned bore four white doves before her; all the women attending followed her with great joy. After the parade there was such music and singing in both churches that the knights who were taking part were too captivated to decide which to enter first. They rushed in crowds from one to the other and would not have felt bored even if the ceremony had lasted all day. When at last the religious services in each church were over, the king and queen removed their crowns and put on lighter robes, and the king went with the men to dine at his palace, the queen to another with the women; for the Britons used to observe the old Trojan custom that men and women should celebrate feastdays separately. After they had all been seated according to their rank, Kaius the steward, dressed in ermine, and with him a thousand nobles similarly attired, served them courses. Opposite, a thousand men dressed in vair followed Beduerus the butler, similarly attired, offering various drinks of every sort in goblets. In the queen's palace numerous attendants in various liveries were also doing service and performing their roles; if I were to describe it all in detail, my history would become too wordy. So noble was Britain then that it surpassed other kingdoms in its stores of wealth, the ostentation of its dress and the sophistication of its inhabitants. All its doughty knights wore clothes and armour of a single colour. Its elegant ladies, similarly dressed, spurned the love of any man who had not proved himself three times in battle. So the ladies were chaste and better women, whilst the knights conducted themselves more virtuously for the sake of their love.

When at last they had had their fill at the banquets, they separated to visit the fields outside the city and indulge in varied sports. The knights exercised on horseback, feigning battle. The ladies, watching from the battlements, playfully fanned the flames in the knights' hearts into furious passion. Then they peacefully passed the remainder of the day in various games, some contending with boxing gloves, some with spears, some in tossing heavy stones, some at chess, and others with dice. Arthur rewarded all those who had been victorious with liberal gifts.[2]

Geoffrey's account draws on an interesting range of sources. The separate churches for men and women existed in Byzantium at the time, while the games at the wedding are derived from the description of the funeral of Anchises, Aeneas' father in Virgil's *Aeneid*, which in turn goes back to Homer and the funeral of Patroclus in the *Iliad*. The rites of the coronation are an elaboration of contemporary ceremonies. Overall, however, his fictional celebration might almost be a template for the ideal medieval festival.

# The Festival at Mainz, 1184

OUR NEXT EXAMPLE IS PROBABLY the first full description of princely splendour in action at this period. In the spring of 1184, Friedrich Barbarossa, ruler of the Holy Roman Empire, the greatest state in Europe, sent out messengers to announce that he would hold an imperial council at Whitsun in Mainz, on the eastern border of his domains. It was an ancient city, once the Roman Moguntium, and lay on the river Rhine; it was well placed for Friedrich's magnates to answer the emperor's summons, and this was to be no ordinary event. The gathering at Mainz was to be in honour of the knighting of his sons Heinrich, later the emperor Heinrich VI, and Friedrich, who became duke of Swabia. Messengers went out to all the princes of the empire, whether 'French, German, Slav, Italian, from Illyria to Spain'.[3]

Mainz's crowded houses and streets did not have room to accommodate the anticipated multitudes, and the citizens watched in astonishment as the imperial officers organised the building of a new 'city' on the level plain between the town and the Rhine. A palace with a very large chapel for the emperor's use was built of wood; around it there were numerous wooden houses for his men, all in a style befitting the imperial dignity. Seventy or more princes and lords arrived, bringing huge retinues with them, in such numbers that the medieval chroniclers were quite unable to tell how many there were. The best guess is that over 10,000 arrived. (For comparison, London, at the beginning of the twelfth century, had about 15,000 inhabitants.) Of those who came to Mainz, many were knights, each with their own attendants, who served in the retinues of the magnates of the empire. The duke of Bohemia appeared with the largest number, estimated at two thousand, while the emperor's brother Conrad and the landgrave of Thuringia both came with more than a thousand, Leopold of Austria with five hundred. Gilbert of Mons, who was with the retinue of Baldwin count of Hainault, claims that 'everyone in Bavaria, Saxony, Swabia, Franconia, Austria, Bohemia, Burgundy and Lorraine' had been invited, while another chronicler noted that there were visitors from many kingdoms outside the emperor's territories. The crowds that came to Mainz were on a scale that had not been seen since the days of the Roman Empire.

*A new city*

Each contingent brought its own tents, multi-coloured pavilions of painted canvas lined with silk and other rich fabrics, whose owners vied with each other to produce the most beautiful effects. Gilbert naturally claims that in the vivid panoply of the city of tents pitched round the imperial village those of the count of Hainault were the finest. The tents were carefully arranged by the emperor in a circle, so that there should be no question of precedence. There was the same rivalry in terms of arms and equipment, of lavish displays of table silver and of rich furnishings in exotic materials. Arnold of Lübeck, who was also an eyewitness, was so overwhelmed by what he saw that he could only attempt to give an idea of the scale of proceedings by taking a rather strange example:

*The finest tents*

> What shall I say of the abundance, indeed of the superfluity of victuals, which were gathered from every land, that it was inestimable, and could not be told by any man's tongue. There was copious wine beyond measure, brought from upstream and downstream along the Rhine, as in Ahasuerus' feast, that could be drawn for every possibility and wish. I quote just one small example, so that you can see how impossible it would be to describe the greater matters. There were two large and spacious houses built with perches everywhere, which were filled from top to bottom with cocks and hens, so that no-one could go in there suspiciously; many wondered at them, for they scarcely believed that so many hens existed in all that country.[4]

The festival began on the Sunday, with the crown-wearing. This was a ritual, enacted at the great feasts of the Church, Christmas, Easter and Whitsun, which was designed to impress the special status of the emperor on the assembled lords who were subject to him. After a service held in the wooden chapel, the emperor and empress processed in full imperial regalia to the hall where their thrones stood. They were preceded by the count of Hainault bearing the imperial sword, and were acclaimed by the assembled nobles. Heinrich, who as heir to the empire, was already consecrated king of the Romans, also appeared with crown and regalia.

On the Monday after the festival, the emperor's sons were ceremonially knighted, and Arnold noted that 'they and all the princes and other nobles gave poor knights and those who had taken vows to go on crusade, and to travelling players (male and female) horses, precious garments, gold and silver', in honour of the occasion and to enhance their own reputation. This was followed by equestrian games over the next two days, which the writer describes as a tournament without arms, and which was part of the imperial tradition. On the Tuesday evening proceedings were disrupted by a sudden storm which destroyed several buildings, including the church, killing five men trapped in the ruins. This brought the festivities to an early end. There seem to have been plans for a real tournament, with full armour and weapons, at the nearby town of Ingelheim, but this was abandoned.

This is the first recorded court festival to attract wide attention in terms of participants and of reactions to it. It is the earliest example of the kind of great gathering which was to be typical of European courts for the next three centuries. The Mainz festival made a considerable impression on contemporaries. Chroniclers could not find enough superlatives to describe it (as Arnold of Lübeck's attempt demonstrates), and poets used it as the exemplar for the most magnificent of all courts. Heinrich von Veldeke, in his German version of the *Aeneid*, declared that the feast was so splendid that stories would be told about it until Judgement Day, while Guiot de Provins, writing in northwest France, compared it to the courts of Arthur, Alexander and Julius Caesar, declaring that Friedrich's court had no rival.

# Defining Princely Splendour

IN THE TWELFTH CENTURY PEOPLE expected a prince to be splendid, to appear with a great entourage which displayed his wealth and his special status. The best illustration of this is from the life of a king who was notorious for his dislike of grand occasions and rich garments, Henry II of England. In 1158, he was negotiating with Louis VII of France about a marriage between his son Henry and Louis's daughter Margaret. He sent Thomas Becket, who was then his chancellor, to open the talks that summer, and on Henry's instructions

the Chancellor prepared to display and lavish the wealth and resources of England, so that in all things and before all men the person of his liege lord might be honoured in his envoy, and that of the envoy in himself. He had about two hundred of his own household mounted on horseback, including knights, clerks, stewards, serjeants, squires and sons of nobles bearing arms in his service, and all in fit array. These and all their train were resplendent in new and festive attire, each according to his rank. He himself had four-and-twenty changes of raiment, 'whose texture mocks the purple dyes of Tyre', many garments of silk – almost all of which were to be given away and left overseas – every kind of fur, miniver and skins, cloaks and carpets, too, like those which customarily adorn the chamber and bed of a bishop. He had with him hounds and birds of every kind, such as kings and rich men keep.

In his equipage he had also eight waggons, each drawn by five horses, in size and strength like chargers. Each horse had its appointed groom, young and strong, girt in a new tunic and walking beside the waggon, and each waggon had its driver and guard. Two waggons bore nothing but beer, made by a decoction of water from the strength of corn and carried in iron-hooped barrels, to be given to the French, who admire liquor of this sort, for it is certainly a wholesome drink, clear, of the colour of wine and of superior flavour. One waggon was used for the furniture of the chancellor's chapel, one for his chamber, one for his bursary and another for his kitchen. Others carried different kinds of meat and drink, others cushions, bags containing nightgowns, bundles of clothes and baggage. Twelve pack-horses and eight chests carried the Chancellor's gold and silver plate, his cups, platters, goblets, pitchers, basins, saltcellars, salvers and dishes.

Other coffers and packing-cases contained his money – more than enough for his daily expenses and presents – his clothes, some books and similar articles. One packhorse, in the van of the others, bore the sacred vessels of the chapel and the ornaments and books of the altar. Each pack-horse had its own groom fitly provided. Each waggon had a dog chained to it, large, fierce and terrible, capable, it seemed, of subduing a lion or a bear. And on the back of each horse was a monkey or 'ape that mocked the human face'. At his entry into the French villages and castles first came the footmen, 'born to eat up the land', about two hundred and fifty of them, proceeding six or ten or more abreast, singing something in their own tongue, after the fashion of their country. There followed at a short distance hounds in pairs and greyhounds in leash with their keepers and attendants. A little behind there rattled over the paved streets iron-bound waggons, covered in with great hides of animals sewn together, and yet further back the pack-horses ridden by their grooms with their knees pressing on the horses' flanks. Some Frenchmen rushed out of their houses when they heard the din, asking who it was and whose the equipage. They were told it was the Chancellor of the English king going on embassy to the king of France. Then said the French, 'What a marvellous man the king of England must be, if his Chancellor travels thus, in such great pomp!'[5]

*A lesson in propaganda* The expectation was of course that Becket's master would be even grander when he himself appeared. But Henry refused to play the 'marvellous man' whom the French expected, and thereby created an even greater impression. He himself followed in September, travelling in striking simplicity, with a modest retinue and even refusing the lavish feasts which were offered to him: all of which impressed the Parisians and the French court far more than another show of splendour would have done. The Parisians were said to have danced with joy at his arrival, and it was reported that he 'behaved magnificently and bountifully' to everyone, particularly to churches and to the poor.[6] Henry's careful calculation of the propaganda value of an unexpected subversion of the normal rituals only serves to emphasise the way in which the psychology of princely splendour worked. He was very conscious of his audience, and this understanding of the effect of display is a fundamental element of what follows.

IN ALL THREE EXAMPLES, the king or emperor is the central figure around which the rituals and celebrations revolve. We take the king in history for granted, and forget that it is an office that evolved over centuries. To understand the background to the ideas of splendour and magnificence, we have to move back in time and look at the evolution of the central figure of the king.

# PART ONE

# PRINCELY SPLENDOUR

# 2 | DYNASTIES, KINGS AND COURTS

◆ *The status of a king* ◆ *'A substitute for long hair'* ◆ *The king in his court*
◆ *The ceremonies of kingship* ◆ *Crown-wearings* ◆ *Crowns*

DYNASTIES WERE ALL-IMPORTANT in the medieval world. The first dynasty to dominate Europe after the fall of Rome was that of Charlemagne, who crowned himself emperor in AD 800. Charlemagne modelled his empire on that of Rome, although it was much smaller and centred on France, Germany and Italy. It fell apart shortly after his death in 814: France became a kingdom, while his German and Italian lands retained the title of empire, later known as the Holy Roman Empire. It was an empire where the ruler did not inherit his title: instead, from the thirteenth century onwards, he was chosen by seven electors, the great secular and religious princes of Germany. The realm of the Anglo-Norman kings, which at its greatest extent included England, Ireland, Normandy and Aquitaine, was a more ephemeral affair. Created in 1154 by the marriage of Henry II and Eleanor of Aquitaine; it was largely reduced to the British Isles and parts of Gascony by 1216.

In Spain, the huge Muslim presence which had once threatened Charlemagne's empire was slowly reduced and replaced by a number of small kingdoms. These gradually merged until Castile and Aragon were united in 1479. The last Muslim kingdom, at Granada, was conquered in 1492. The spectacular success of the Norman rulers in Sicily and southern Italy, was also shortlived: the Norman duke Roger I was promoted to kingship by the pope in 1130, and the last king in the direct male line died in 1204. Aragon, the modern Catalonia, was the centre of a sea-borne empire which came to include Sicily and Naples.

*The Empire and kingdoms*

The most stable dynasties were in France, where the house of Capet and the house of Valois ruled for the entire period under discussion. In the Holy Roman Empire, a succession of dynasties was established, despite the fact that the office of emperor was never actually hereditary. Three families predominated between 1100 and 1450. These were the Hohenstaufens, the house of Luxembourg and the Habsburgs, with a chaotic interregnum from 1254 to 1347 when there were sometimes two rival emperors.

*Succession*

LEADERSHIP IN WAR was an essential function for a medieval king, and there was therefore a very strong prejudice against allowing a child or a woman to succeed. The 'Salic law' in France supposedly debarred women from the succession: in fact, it was a legal tradition rather than an actual statute. If no male candidate of full age from the ruling family was available, this often led to a change of dynasty. In France, there was a direct succession to the throne through the male line until 1316, at which point a general assembly of nobles and bishops declared that women could not inherit the throne. Philip V became king as a result, as a great-grandson of St Louis by male descent. In 1328, when the same problem recurred on the death of Philip V's brother and successor, the claim of Edward III of England, through his mother Isabella and grandfather Philip IV, was rejected by the French, though the question as to whether women could pass on the right of inheritance without being able to exercise it themselves had never been formally debated. On both occasions, political practicalities were the real reason for the decision.

Each dynasty had as its base formal territorial units, a kingdom or principality. In addition, dynasties had links through marriage and through younger sons who became kings and founded their own dynasties, who retained links to their original family. A modest dynasty with modest origins might have widespread influence. Sometimes the family trees of medieval Europe seem to resemble the network of links produced by the marriages of the children of Queen Victoria in the nineteenth century. The most spectacular of these, probably unfamiliar to the English-speaking reader, is the house of Anjou. This clan is not to be confused with the first house of Anjou, Henry II and his sons, the Angevin rulers of Normandy and England. When the county of Anjou was conquered by the French in 1205, it was incorporated into the titles of the French king, but forty years later it was given by St Louis to his brother Charles, who was already count of Provence. His descendants established themselves around the boundaries of Western Christendom. In the mid fourteenth century there were Angevin rulers in Provence, Sicily, Naples, Hungary and Poland and nominally in Jerusalem.

*Marriage alliances*
See p. xviii

Furthermore, the Holy Roman emperors for most of the fourteenth century were French by origin. The emperor Heinrich VII, elected in 1308 as a compromise candidate to end the long interregnum since the death of Friedrich II in 1250, was the son of the count of Luxembourg. He had been brought up at the French court, as was his son Jean, king of Bohemia.* Jean's son Charles was also brought up at the French court. He was christened Wenceslaus, but took the name Charles when he was confirmed. He then became Holy Roman Emperor, and in what follows he appears as Karl IV, king of Bohemia and emperor.

If France predominates in this book, it is for two reasons: French kings were the wealthiest in this world for much of the period we are discussing, and dynasties closely linked with France ruled from England to Hungary and Poland. Each individual country had its own cultural variants, and the status of rulers ranged from the Holy Roman Emperor, whose title all too often was at odds with his real power, to the lords of Italian towns, where few dynasties maintained their prestige for as much as a century.

*French dominance*

# The Status of a King

KINGS ARE THE CENTRAL FIGURES in this book, and we need to have some idea of what it meant to be a medieval king. The nature and status of kingship between the fifth and ninth centuries is, like so many things from that period, elusive and difficult to define. Nonetheless, there are certain factors which stand out as defining a king. A king is a military leader, and has an army at his command. He is supported and sometimes specifically chosen by the aristocracy. And he rules over one or more identifiable peoples. The boundaries of his power are fluid, and the authority by which he holds his office is far from clear. There is a degree of election or at least assent about his accession to the throne, and increasingly there is a view of kingship as something which is more than just a secular leadership.

The history of the Merovingian dynasty of kings in France is a good example of the conflicting ideas about kingship in the eighth century. The first of the Merovingians appears as a Frankish commander in the Roman army in Gaul in the fourth century AD.

*The Merovingians*

* Charles IV had married Elizabeth, the sister of king Jean of Bohemia.

His descendant Clovis was the real founder of the dynasty, leading his men against the Romans, and breaking their hold on northern France in 486. Twenty years later, he fought off the invading Visigoths and established a kingdom which his descendants ruled until 751. By this time, however, power had gradually ebbed away from the kings to their chief administrators, the 'mayors of the palace'. It was Charles Martel, as mayor of the palace, who led the Frankish troops at the pivotal battle of Tours in 732, which halted a Moorish invasion of France and prevented the extension of the Moslem kingdoms of Spain beyond the Pyrenees. When the Frankish king Theuderic IV died in 737, Charles did not trouble to appoint another king. Pepin, his son, succeeded him as mayor, and the historian Einhard, writing a century later, describes the last of the Merovingian kings as the merest puppets:

> All that was left to the King was that, content with his royal title, he should sit on the throne, with his hair long and his beard flowing, giving audience to the ambassadors who arrived from foreign parts ... Whenever he needed to travel, he went in a cart which was drawn in country style by yoked oxen, with a cowherd to drive them.[1]

Einhard may have mocked these rustic customs, but they were in fact echoes of a distant past. Both long hair and a carriage drawn by oxen had once been symbols of kingship.

## *'A substitute for long hair'*[2]

THE CONFUSED AND VIOLENT HISTORY of the Merovingian kings of France is wonderfully recorded by Gregory, bishop of Tours, in his contemporary chronicle. He was an active participant in the political world in the last half of the sixth century, and had no illusions about the problems of kingship in this period. Writing of the assassination of the king of the Visigoths in Spain in 554, he notes drily that 'the Goths had adopted the reprehensible habit of killing out of hand any king who displeased them'.[3] In 584 King Guntram was involved in a quarrel with his rival Childebert. A peace conference was arranged: it ended with both sides hurling insults at each other, and Childebert's supporters warned Guntram that 'the axe is still ready and waiting which split open the heads of your brothers. One day it will split open your head, too.'[4]

*The dangers of kingship*

In 751, Pepin decided that since he exercised the royal power, he should become king. With the consent of the Frankish nobles, he went to the pope for approval. Once this was obtained he was 'elevated into the kingdom' by being elected by 'all the Franks', with the support of the bishops and lay magnates. Election to the kingship was also part of 'the rules of ancient tradition'. What was new was the role that the pope played in this ritual.

We know little of the religious involvement in the ceremonies surrounding the succession of a new king among the peoples who invaded the Roman empire in the West from the fourth century AD onwards. The genealogies of the Anglo-Saxon kings were traced back in some cases to Woden, implying that in pagan times there was a connection between royalty and divinity. As the gradual process of conversion to Christianity continued, the Church claimed its place in the appointment of a ruler. Initially, as with knighthood, this may have been no more than a blessing, but by Pepin's day the involvement was much closer. Three years after he became king, he, his wife Bertrada and their sons Charles (Charlemagne) and Carloman were anointed by the pope; the pope's letters on the occasion spoke of a royal priesthood, an idea which was later taken up by the kings themselves.

*Kingship rituals*

However, the idea that the king was in some way set apart and sacred took a long while to evolve, and it is only in the tenth century that the formal rituals for coronation and consecration begin to come into use. The two were originally quite separate: a ceremony

**2.** The throne of Dagobert king of the Franks, seventh century. The model for this is a Roman ceremonial chair. It may be genuine, or it may have been produced a century later under Charlemagne, when Roman architectural forms were being revived.

**3.** The royal sceptre of France, made for the coronation of Charles V, with a statue of Charlemagne at the top and decorated with scenes from Charlemagne's life. Sceptres were a symbol of the king's authority, appearing in Greece and Etruria from the earliest times.

of anointment with holy oil was used for bishops before it was used for kings, and the use of a crown in the inauguration of a new king appears about the same time in 838 in the French kingdom of Charlemagne's son Charles. This slow process of formalising the rituals of coronation resulted in the creation of an order of service for such occasions in both France and England, an order which is still reflected in English coronations today.

The intervention of the Church into kingship is paralleled by the development of services for the blessing of the newly made knight and indeed for humbler trades and vocations. These were general blessings, while the king's coronation was designed to make him a *The king's evil* unique figure, and eventually led to the idea that he had special powers. For example, it was believed that a properly consecrated and rightful king had the ability to cure scrofula, known as the king's evil, by touching the sufferer: Guibert of Nogent, in the early years of the eleventh century, claims to have seen Louis VI of France heal a man with this disfiguring skin disease, by touching him on the affected area on his neck, adding that Philip I, Louis's father had lost his ability to effect such cures because of his sinful lifestyle. He also observed that no English king had, to his knowledge, carried out such a cure.[5]

Once this was established as a royal attribute, the ability to touch for scrofula becomes a test of true kingship. In a letter from around 1182, Peter of Blois, an important figure in the court of Henry II, took this idea a step further. He declared that 'there is something holy about serving the lord king, for the king is indeed holy and the anointed of the Lord. The sacrament of unction at his coronation was not an empty gift. Its virtue, if there is anyone who is unaware of it or calls it in question, will be most amply proved by the disappearance of the disease which attacks the groin and the cure of scrofulas.'[6]

It was remarkably difficult to overthrow an established dynasty, or even a single king within that dynasty. The long struggle between France and England which stemmed from Henry II's creation of a power in France much greater than that of the king, Louis VII, *Established* is a good illustration of this. At first, the question was largely one of feudal law: the king *dynasties* of England was a vassal of the French king in respect of his French lands – an awkward situation, with its inevitable tensions. It was the feudal relationship which enabled French kings such as Philip Augustus in the early thirteenth century and Philip IV at the end of the century to erode English power by declaring their lands forfeit for infringements of feudal contracts. It is possible to see Edward III's pursuit of his claim to the French throne itself as a way to resolve this conflict; yet despite his military superiority and the very strong legal basis of his case, he was unable to enforce what he saw as his rights. The French kings were among the first to be anointed, and the sacred nature of kingship was part of their credo. Equally important was that in 1328, when the last of the Capetian dynasty died, Philip of Valois, Edward's rival for the throne, was seen as French at a time when national feeling was becoming important; Edward was only half-French. Moreover, Philip had been anointed king by the time Edward put forward his claim.

The identity of king and nation, harking back to the old identity of the kings of the post-Roman period with their tribes, was even more sharply in evidence after 1422. By the treaty of Troyes, signed after the English victory at Agincourt in 1415, the succession *Identity of king* was to pass to the heirs of Henry V, who had married Catherine, daughter of Charles VI of *and nation* France. Henry VI was therefore, like Edward III, half-French; but even with the installation of Henry's government in Paris, the national support for Charles VII, son of the late king, was a latent force. Brought into focus by Joan of Arc, who emphatically declared Charles to be the 'true king', the change of dynasty failed, and the English were removed from all of France – bar Calais – within thirty years.

Even in Sicily and southern Italy attachment to the dynasty remained. Sicily changed hands twice within twenty years after Manfred the last of the Hohenstaufen kings was killed in battle in 1266. Charles of Anjou, the victor, was crowned king by the pope. But resentment at the imposition of a French ruler led to the 'Sicilian Vespers' of 1282. This rebellion resulted in Charles's eviction from Sicily in favour of the king of Aragon, Peter III, nephew of Manfred. The Angevin kings continued to rule southern Italy, which became the kingdom of Naples, but when Queen Joanna II, who was childless, selected her heir in 1414, she promised it to Alfonso V of Aragon, thus reuniting the two parts of the old Sicilian kingdom. She later changed her mind, and reverted to one of her Angevin relations, René d'Anjou. He failed to make good his claim, and was ejected by Alfonso V. It is noticeable that throughout the extraordinarily tangled web of kings and would-be kings of Sicily and Naples, the descendants of the Hohenstaufen and the descendants of Charles of Anjou were the only contenders. Ironically, it was the pope who had originally granted the kingship in both cases.

*Naples and Sicily*

If we look at the deposition of rulers, the doubts and hesitations expressed by the agents of their downfall are revealing. The two outstanding cases in the later Middle Ages are both English, Edward II and Richard II.[7] In the case of Edward II, the strategy of a forced abdication of the throne was adopted, which respected his status as king, and allowed the transfer of power to Edward III. There was never a formal act of deposition. When it came to Richard II, there was nothing in Edward II's case which would serve as a precedent. There was, however, a papal example. In 1245 the pope had declared the deposition of Friedrich II as ruler of the Holy Roman Empire, over which the popes claimed a hotly-contested jurisdiction. The chronicler Adam of Usk tells us that the committee of legal advisers who deliberated on the matter in Richard II's case had a copy of the papal document of 1245, and as a result, as Richard's biographer Nigel Saul points out, 'the case against Richard was essentially one that had its basis in canon law'. After a week of increasing pressure, Richard finally agreed, though he insisted that his anointment with holy oil at his coronation had been a sacred act, and could not be cancelled. When he surrendered the crown, he placed it on the ground, saying that 'he resigned his right to God', thus maintaining his insistence that kingship was an office not of this world. In this he echoed the words of an anonymous Norman cleric two centuries earlier who, at the height of the dispute over the pope's authority over secular rulers, had written that the sacrament of coronation by which the king was 'dedicated to God' was unique. As 'the Lord's anointed', 'he is the supreme ruler, the chief shepherd, master, defender and instructor of holy Church, lord over his brethren'.[8] This was an extreme and deliberately provocative statement. Yet it is indicative of how powerful the idea of a divine element in kingship could be.

*Deposing the king*

# The King in his Court

WHEN CHARLEMAGNE INHERITED half the Frankish kingdom in 768, he spent the early years of his reign in an endless succession of military campaigns. The business of government was transacted wherever he happened to be, though he had inherited a number of palaces which formed a kind of network. These provided him with accommodation on his travels and had a small permanent staff of officials. This was in sharp contrast to Byzantium, the static capital of the eastern Empire. The medieval courts of western Europe were to remain peripatetic for centuries to come. Charlemagne himself ruled a much more extensive area than any of his medieval successors, and therefore spent a huge amount of time travelling. It was only in 794 that the palace at Aachen began

*A king on the move*

to develop into a kind of capital, from which his whole empire was administered. The emperor's cousin, Adalhard of Corbie was said to have written at the end of his reign that 'officials of sufficient number and type ... should never be missing from the palace; at all times the palace was to be adorned with worthy councillors'.[9] In the past, such men would have been on the road with Charlemagne himself.

*The court at Aachen*

As Charlemagne's empire expanded, he needed to be able to communicate with, and assert his authority over, the medley of different peoples within it. Latin was to be the common language of his subjects; Latin teachers and education were essential. To this end he brought scholars from England and Ireland, from Spain and Italy, to join his own Frankish scholars, to ensure that a proper curriculum of teaching was established. Their students would serve not only the church, but also the emperor, for his officials were almost all clerics. A by-product of this emphasis on education was the emergence of a distinctive court culture at Aachen itself, where the scholars formed a group of surprising importance. The men who attended Charlemagne in person most of the time, and therefore formed what we would call his court, naturally included the heads of the various parts of his government and military establishment. The men in charge of his household offices, the seneschal, the constable and the marshal, were in effect his ministers. At a personal level, however, the emperor's chosen companions were the outstanding men of letters who were behind his educational programme. The chief among these was Alcuin, who had been in Charlemagne's entourage since the 780s, and had taught both the emperor and his children. Charlemagne himself loved learning, though he was never able to write properly. He studied Latin to good effect, and Alcuin taught him a little Greek as well, a rare accomplishment in the West. His interest in the past led him to collect old songs in German which told of the deeds of the German kings, and he even tried to produce a grammar of Frankish.

'COURT', CONFUSINGLY, HAS A double meaning throughout the medieval period. It is both an occasion, a formal gathering when the ruler 'held court', often at the great religious festivals of the year; and it is also used of the group of people who attended the prince, his household, counsellors and close associates. These are the courtiers, and men

*Defining the medieval court*

judged the prince by their reputation and behaviour. When the troubadour Bertran de Born came to the court of Henry II and Eleanor of Aquitaine in Normandy in the autumn of 1182, he was accustomed to the small courts of nobles in Aquitaine, where music and poetry predominated. In the intellectual world of Henry's courtiers, he was deeply disappointed by the atmosphere: 'A court is never complete without joking and laughter; a court without gifts is a mere mockery of barons! And the boredom and vulgarity of Argentan nearly killed me ...'[10] We shall come to the question of courtly culture, and courtly literature, which was Bertran's natural habitat. But others praised Henry's court for its learning and serious discussions. It is the cultural and social aspect of the court, rather than its political and administrative side, with which we are concerned.

Henry's grandfather, Henry I, was famous for his learning, and Henry himself had been brought up in the entourage of his uncle, Robert of Gloucester, where scholars such as William of Malmesbury, historian of the English, Geoffrey of Monmouth, author of the legendary history of Britain, and Adelard of Bath, one of the first English scientists, were to be found. Because Henry's interests were largely in law and government, his companions were men such as John of Salisbury, Walter Map and Peter of Blois, all of whom have left accounts of the energetic, sometimes chaotic, nature of the royal court. If Henry relaxed, it was when he retreated to his chamber to read.

*The English court*

Essentially, the core of the prince's court in the twelfth century was a group of men, trained by the church, who were the king's chief counsellors and servants. But their work for the king was not religious. Peter of Blois called the courtiers of Henry II's court *professores mundi*,[11] using profession in the medieval religious sense as when a monk made a public declaration of faith on entering a monastery. These were men who had declared for the world, with all the spiritual perils that entailed. Peter addressed a general letter to the courtiers, questioning whether the court is a proper place for men in holy orders, and paints a vivid picture of the miseries endured by the courtiers, very different from the leisured and cultured society reflected in courtly literature. And he concludes, having left the court himself, that 'even you, my dearest friends, will think over your life, which you have wasted at court, in bitterness of spirit'.[12] It is a splendid diatribe on the evils of court life; but Peter later returned to the court and offered a partial retraction, acknowledging that 'It is no slight praise to have pleased the princes of men.'

*The profession of courtier*

In the case of Henry, the court was not only the centre of royal government, but also the place where his ideas and policies were shaped in discussion. Henry was a formidable figure, both physically and intellectually. He was a natural linguist, said to know something of all the languages used in Christendom. He was widely read and 'he had a keen and enquiring mind: in his household, every day was like a school, and there was constant discussion of difficult questions', points of law or problems of administration: his passion was the establishment of peace and justice within his realms. He was the most learned of kings, yet he was always approachable, and people thronged round him: he would deal with them patiently, and when he had had enough would retire to his chamber, where no one dared to disturb him. He also had a formidable memory for faces and conversations, and never forgot anyone with whom he had been in close contact.

*'School every day'*

The court of the kings of Sicily is another example of this intellectual activity around the king. Peter of Blois was tutor to William I of Sicily, and there were other links between the English and Sicilian courts at this period: the gardens at Henry's palatial hunting-lodge at Woodstock seem to have been based on Sicilian ideas. Roger II, William's father, began a tradition of interest in learning similar to that in the Plantagenet court, but with access to far wider resources. He himself explored topics such as mathematics and geography. The Arab traveller and scholar al-Idrisi became Roger's close friend. And the books of the Greek philosophers, almost unobtainable in western Europe, were to be found here, in a court where French, Latin, Greek and Arabic were current languages. Artistically, this was the high point of the Sicilian kingdom, when the royal palace and its chapel were decorated with the mosaics which are the best records of the splendour of the Sicilian court. The court rituals and the titles of the court officials reflect the influence of Byzantium and the imperial style which the Norman kings sought to emulate: their officials were in many cases Greek.

*Sicily: the learning of west and east*

# The Ceremonies of Kingship
## *Crown-wearings*

*William I*

CROWN-WEARING WAS AN OCCASION in most of western Europe, a vital ritual for reinforcing the king's claim to royal status. For example, when William I was anxious to establish his right to rule in England after the conquest, he instituted a formal court which took place at Christmas at Gloucester, Easter at Winchester and Whitsun at Westminster. At these courts, he was enthroned wearing his crown. It seems to have been observed more frequently towards the end of his reign, and only happened if William was in England: in Normandy he was only duke, and such a court would have been out of place. By the time he died, the anonymous writer of the Anglo-Saxon Chronicle thought that it was always held on these dates, and at these places. But the idea of kingship was alien to the Norman barons, descended from the Vikings and already disrespectful of the French kings who were their overlords. This same ambivalent attitude is probably behind a story told in the biography of Lanfranc, archbishop of Canterbury in William's reign:

> It was one of those three great festivals on which the king, wearing his crown, is accustomed to hold his court. On the day of the festival, when the king was seated at table adorned in crown and royal robes, and Lanfranc beside him, a certain jester, seeing the king resplendent in gold and jewels, cried out in the hall in great tones of adulation: 'Behold! I see God! Behold! I see God!' Lanfranc, turning to the king, said: 'Don't allow such things to be said of you ... Order that fellow to be severely flogged, so that he never dares to say such things again.'[13]

Lanfranc, a churchman for whom kingship was a divine office, failed to see the jester's point: that William, who as duke of Normandy was simply one of the great lords of that country, had now elevated himself to a higher status. Many of the barons would have laughed with the jester, and William might have joined in.

These were occasions when the great affairs of the realm were transacted, and foreign visitors were received: they were marked by sumptuous and magnificent feasts, and the king put on his royal regalia. The Anglo-Saxon kings had held courts on the same festival days, but they had not affirmed their kingship by using their regalia. And it is possible that at the Norman festivals, the king not only wore the regalia in the great hall, but also at mass on those days. He may have appeared in public as well: it has been suggested that a balcony on the west front of Winchester cathedral may have been used for this purpose, and that there was a procession from the cathedral to the hall.[14]

*Henry II*

As time wore on, and the idea of kingship was generally accepted, the crown-wearing of the English kings both became accepted and far less frequent: it had served its purpose. At Worcester in 1158, Henry II and Eleanor laid their crowns on the altar and swore never to wear them again. This may well reflect Henry's dislike of ceremony, but the French kings were also abandoning crown-wearings at about the same time.[15] They were, however, used when a king's title to the throne had been undermined in some way, particularly if he had been in captivity. This was the case with Stephen in 1141, who was effectively recrowned when he was released following his capture at the battle of Lincoln. Likewise, when Richard I returned from crusade, he held a solemn crown-wearing which was evidently intended as a reaffirmation of his kingship after his imprisonment in Austria. In the fifteenth century, Edward IV, on regaining the throne in 1471, was both recrowned and wore his crown in public processions afterwards; the following Christmas he held a crown-wearing at the feast. When Richard III was crowned in 1483, he wore his crown in a procession at York shortly

**4.** (above) Iron Crown of Lombardy. This is probably in part from the eleventh century, but cannot be dated precisely. It is made of six curved hinged panels, and contains an iron band said to be made of one of the nails used at the Crucifixion.

**5.** (left) Crown of Saint Wenceslas. This was made for the coronation of Karl IV of Bohemia in 1347, and is kept in a vault beneath St Vitus Cathedral in Prague. It was originally placed on the effigy of St Wenceslas in his chapel in the cathedral, and was only removed for the coronations of the Bohemian kings.

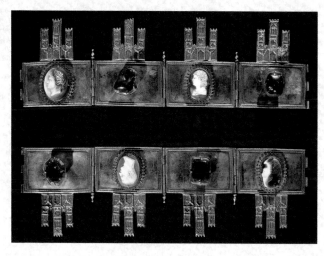

**6.** Crown of Sancho IV. Sancho IV reigned from 1284 to 1295. His crown is unusual in that the imagery is almost entirely secular, with castle towers and antique Roman cameos: the castles represent his kingdom of Castile.

afterwards. And it is arguable that the most extreme style of crown-wearing ceremonies, that of Richard II described below, also has to do with his insecurity about his position as king in the face of rebellious lords. The true king, it seems, expected to be recognised by the magnificence of his appearance as a crowned monarch.[16]

*The Holy Roman Empire*

Crown-wearings were also important in the Holy Roman Empire. The imperial government was very much an itinerant institution, and assemblies were held throughout the empire. As elsewhere, they were usually held on the major feasts of the Church – Easter in particular, but also at Whitsun and Christmas and occasionally on other feast days – and were hosted by a regular pattern of bishops or archbishops at the great religious centres of the empire. On these occasions, from the tenth century or earlier onwards, the bishop or archbishop would solemnly place the crown on the emperor's head (and similarly on that of his empress) in one of their churches.[17] Wearing their crowns, they would lead a solemn procession to the cathedral or church where Mass was to be celebrated, preceded by one of the imperial princes as sword-bearer; and from there, they would continue into the hall to begin the feast.[18]

*Political gathering*

Crown-wearing could mark important political gatherings. In 986, the emperor Otto III held a crown-wearing at Quedlinburg, the centre of his personal domains, as a demonstration of his power over the empire, with a feast at which he was attended by its great princes. He was served by Henry duke of Bavaria as seneschal, Conrad duke of Swabia as chamberlain, Henry duke of Carinthia as butler, and Bernard duke of Saxony as marshal, showing both their recognition of the emperor and their willingness to serve him in those functions in the future.[19] Friedrich Barbarossa is recorded as wearing his crown at Merseburg, which was one of his most important palaces with a large staff, in 1152, when he declared Sven the rightful king of Denmark and crowned him. During his 35 year reign, Friedrich held other crown-wearings in about sixty different places, both in Germany and northern Italy.[20]

*A brilliant occasion*

We began with the festival at Mainz in 1184, which was probably the greatest of the crown-wearing festivals. These events were essentially a public relations exercise for the ruler; it was not a required ritual, to be regularly observed at set intervals, but when it did take place it was often in a context where the splendour of the ceremony had political overtones and the brilliance of the occasion was therefore very important. In 1199 Philip of Swabia, second son of Friedrich Barbarossa and since 1198 king of the Romans, held a solemn crown-wearing at Christmas, with his wife Irene, the daughter of Emperor Isaac II of Byzantium. It was probably an assertion of Philip's title, as a rival king had been elected at about the same time. It was masterminded by his chancellor to ensure the maximum effect, with the duke of Saxony carrying the imperial sword ahead of the king, and an escort of nobles and their ladies, while the bishops walked on either side of the royal couple. Walther von der Vogelweide, the greatest poet of the age, was evidently at the ceremony, and was impressed by the appearance of the couple:

> King Philip strode out in all his splendour. There went an emperor's brother and an emperor's son, three persons in one costume. He bore the Empire's sceptre and its crown. He walked with measured pace, followed modestly by the noble queen, rose without thorn, dove without gall. Nowhere was there such a presence as his.[21]

The men of Saxony and Thuringia, too, were impressed. if we are to believe another eye-witness, they cheered and applauded, showing their pleasure in the occasion which they followed to the very end. The crown-wearing had achieved its object, and had made the king appear as an exceptional, powerful figure, worthy of loyalty and reverence.

# Crowns

CROWNS TODAY ARE TAKEN AS THE ultimate symbol of kingship; but this was not always the case. Before the barbarian invasions, crowns were not specifically associated with royalty, and we shall see that they were used by high-ranking members of royal families as well as the king in the later Middle Ages. Rulers in classical Antiquity used a diadem rather than a crown as a sign of status. Early Christian royal crowns were little more than circlets of gold, embellished with inset jewels. The so-called Iron Crown of Lombardy, which was once believed to have been used by Charlemagne when he was crowned king of Lombardy, is the earliest surviving example, kept at the cathedral at Monza in northern Italy. Its date, despite intensive study, is uncertain: it may have elements from as early as the fourth century incorporated in it. Its name comes from the inner band which reinforces it, which recent chemical analysis has shown to be silver. The gold work is relatively unsophisticated, set against a green enamel ground with stylised flowers. Its form is that of the type of diadem adopted by the emperor Constantine in the early fourth century, and used by all later Byzantine emperors.[22] The Byzantine emperors themselves did not use crowns until the tenth century in their coronation ceremonies.

*The Iron Crown of Lombardy*

**4**, p.19

The crown of the Holy Roman Empire, used to crown the future emperor after he had been elected, but before his coronation by the pope, was much more elaborate than any of its predecessors.[23] It was made in the late tenth or eleventh century, and consists of eight plaques of heavily bejewelled 22-carat gold, originally fastened by pins, so the crown could be packed flat to avoid damage to the central hoop, which was obviously vulnerable. Enamelled scenes from Scripture alternate with the jewelled plates, which are much more intricate and with far more stones than the Iron Crown. The fine filigree work in which the jewels are mounted is the work of a skilful goldsmith, as are the patterns of pearls on the hoop. The hoop enhances the effect of the crown by making it much more prominent than the simple circlet. There is a tradition that the large sapphire at the top of the front panel is a replacement for a stone known as the 'orphan', which was regarded as unique, both in its beauty and in the light which it reflected. Such a stone, called 'orphanos' in Greek, was present in the Byzantine imperial crown, and it has been argued that the crown now in Vienna is not the crown described by medieval writers, including the poet Walther von der Vogelweide and the encyclopaedist Albertus Magnus. The latter describes it in about 1250 as being of the colour of a delicate red wine, and reflecting a brilliant white light. It may have been a garnet of exceptional quality or a rare red zircon, the stone called 'hyacinth' by Wolfram von Eschenbach. It was last recorded in 1350. Either it was replaced after that date, or the medieval descriptions apply to a different crown altogether. But the idea of a spectacular central jewel glowing above the emperor's forehead is an image that is entirely appropriate to magnificence.

*The Imperial Crown*

**1**, p.xxiv

The crown of Charlemagne himself does not survive. There is a drawing of it from before the French Revolution, when it was destroyed, which shows it as a 'lily crown', with four *fleurs-de-lis*. A crown of this form, dating from the end of the tenth or beginning of the eleventh century, is in the cathedral at Essen. It was once thought to be the crown used for the emperor Otto I when he was crowned as a child in 983, but its style is nearer to that of early eleventh-century crowns. Equally, the crown attributed to Charlemagne at the abbey of Saint-Denis in the eighteenth century was probably from that period, and it is a pattern which can be seen in many manuscript miniatures of kings.

*The crown of Charlemagne*

The Hungarian royal crown, known as the crown of St Stephen, who was the first king of Hungary, is very probably a late twelfth-century reworking of an eleventh-century

*The crown of Castile*

**6**, p.19

circlet. This simple form was used in Byzantium; here it is combined with a double hoop in the Latin style. It seems to have been made up from parts of one or more crowns in the mid twelfth century, and includes enamels which may have been given to King Geza I in the 1070s. Crowns were both ornaments and relics, and their antiquity was very important, giving extra legitimacy to the king who was crowned with them. On the other hand, we find designs which reflect the political situation at a given date. An example is the crown of Sancho IV of Castile, which is almost certainly that of his predecessor Alfonso VIII. It is made of eight plates, each of which is surmounted by a castle, and by Sancho's day Castile had been united with León. The absence of the arms of León would mean that it must be dated before 1217, and hence to Alfonso's reign. Around the crown, antique cameos alternate with sapphires on plain gold rectangles. It is the first crown with armorial bearings, a crown whose design makes it specific to one kingdom.

# THE CULTURE OF KINGSHIP

3

*◆ Sicily: Creating a royal culture ◆ Palermo as a royal capital*
*◆ Friedrich II: Recreating the past, exploring the future ◆ The arch at*
*Capua ◆ Friedrich as builder: Castel del Monte and Castello Maniace*
*◆ St Louis and Henry III ◆ Paris ◆ London ◆ Royal mausoleums*

A KING WAS DISTINGUISHED BY HIS status and title, and also by the context in which he lived and moved. Early medieval kings were constantly on the move, like Charlemagne, and even in the fourteenth century it was rare for them to spend more than a few weeks in the same place.

Until the middle of the twelfth century, the king had to live off his lands, because so much of his revenue was paid in kind, or was produced on his domains. Charlemagne created a network of twenty-five major and 125 minor royal palaces designed to receive him and his entourage as they travelled through his territories. In the tenth century, some palaces began to be fortified and were an important sign of the continuity of the empire: when the citizens of Pavia tore down the imperial palace there in 1024 on the death of the emperor Henry II, his successor Conrad II rounded on them, fiercely proclaiming that 'even if the king had died, the kingdom remained, just as the ship whose steersman falls remains. They were state, not private buildings; they were under another law, not yours.' In the increasingly troubled times after Charlemagne's death, fortifications became critical, and kings, princes and lords alike fortified the towns where their principal residences stood. Cash to pay for the workmen and materials was scarce until the middle of the twelfth century, when the gradual emergence of a sufficient store of coin made a cash economy possible. By the end of the century, 'money fiefs', where the dues from tenant to lord were paid in cash rather than produce, were to be found in France, the Low Countries, England and Germany. The growth of towns and the establishment of capital cities, where both the kings and great lords spent much of their cash, followed. The trading centres of the Low Countries, essential for the luxury goods which were needed for princely splendour, developed in the thirteenth century and moved on to the next stage of development with the emergence of a banking system which linked most of Europe.[1]

*The rise of the castle*

In these conditions, Paris and London became true capital cities, rather than the largest towns in the realm, and the king's peripatetic government gradually became fixed here as well. Sicily was a special case, and is in many ways the most interesting. The Norman conquerors of Sicily rapidly built a centralised administration in their relatively small island. Administration was a particular skill of the Norman peoples, and when the dukes of Sicily became kings, they were able to create a capital in a relatively short time. Palermo became a spectacular place, mixing the gardens of Arab cities with the panoply of Byzantine decorative skills, funded by a generally well organised government.

*Capital cities*

In each of these cities the dominant features are the king's palace and the royal church relating to that palace. The design and decoration of these buildings characterise them as royal property, and are a public statement of the king's wealth and power. New styles of architecture and the absence of restrictions that the need for a defensive residence imposed meant that the interiors of these royal palaces became spacious and well-lit, suitable for royal display of wealth and power. Great halls designed for public occasions appear: Westminster Hall, built in the late eleventh century, remained one of the largest such spaces in Europe until the end of the fifteenth century.* Public audiences and receptions of ambassadors became possible, and new spaces for feasting and ceremonial were now available. Kings looked enviously at what their counterparts were doing, partly from curiosity and partly with a view to rivalry. At the beginning of the eleventh century, there was no very great difference – other than size – between the royal castles and those of his most powerful subjects. With the emergence of the capital and its new buildings, princely splendour begins to be a distinct and impressive style.

*Great halls*

## Sicily: Creating a Royal Culture

THE NORMAN CONQUEST OF SOUTHERN Italy and Sicily in the last half of the eleventh century brought to power adventurers who had little cultural baggage of their own. The dukes, and later kings, of Sicily were the sons of lords in Normandy who had barely been in France for two generations: their great-grandfathers were effectively Vikings from Scandinavia. In many ways, the Normans were chameleons, taking on the hue of the peoples they conquered – French, English, Sicilian, and Arab. When they invaded Sicily in 1061, they found themselves in a multi-cultural society. The island had once been subject to Byzantium, but more recently had been fought over by Arab emirs nominally allied to a caliph in north Africa. The Byzantine presence and civilisation in Sicily had never been eradicated by the Arabs, and the Normans, tolerant in their treatment of the conquered Arabs and Greeks alike, created one of the most cultured and open societies in western Europe.

*The Normans in Sicily*

The Byzantine artistic legacy was strong, and it was curiously reinforced by the political situation, which brought about its adoption by the new rulers of the island. Robert Guiscard was duke of Sicily thanks to the pope; Nicholas II had invested him with the title in 1059, and when Roger, his nephew, became king, again by the pope's authority, in 1130, he was appointed papal legate at the same time. He was thus invested with the pope's power, which could not be used against him. The image of Roger being crowned by Christ at the church of La Martorana in Palermo shows him wearing priestly garments as legate. But other elements of the portrait tellingly echo the traditions of imperial costume and style at Byzantium. The long stole, or *loros*, is the hallmark of imperial Byzantine dress of the most exalted kind, restricted to the emperor's family and close associates, and the crown which Christ holds is equally Byzantine. Roger also used the Byzantine emperor's title of 'basileus'. The implication was that Roger's kingship was a divine appointment, merely confirmed by papal decree.

*Byzantine art in Sicily*

This shows how deeply the Byzantine world penetrated Norman Sicily. When the Normans took Palermo by storm in 1071, they were delighted to take possession of 'the palaces and the things that they found outside the city, ... the pleasure gardens full of fruit and water ... a terrestrial paradise'.[2] The new palaces created by the Sicilian kings were the work of native craftsmen, the most skilled of whom were Greek and Arab.

---

* Westminster Hall is longer than the Palais de la Cité in Paris, but narrower; there is little difference in the total area.

## Palermo as a royal capital

AS KING, ROGER NEEDED TO CREATE a royal capital, with a palace and a cathedral on a suitably impressive scale. He chose to rebuild the castle which dominated the city, his existing residence. Its core was a castle built in the Grecian period in Sicily around 500 BC, as part of the walls of the fortified town. When Roger II decided to create his palace in the early twelfth century, one tower of this survived. Al-Idrisi, an Arab geographer who worked for eighteen years at Roger's court, describes how the king had recently built a palace of 'very hard cut stone, which was covered with inscriptions of surprising skill and admirable ornaments'.[3] Ibn Jubayr, a Muslim from Valencia who had been secretary to the governor of Granada, came to Palermo in December 1184, and was taken to the palace to be interviewed by the royal officials, as was the custom with such visitors.

> Over esplanades, through doors and across royal courts they led us, gazing at the towering palaces, well-set piazzas and gardens ... Among other things we observed was a hall set in a large court enclosed by a garden and flanked by colonnades. The hall occupied the whole length of that court, and we marvelled at its length and the height of its colonnades. We understood that it was the dining-hall of the king and his companions ...[4]

By the time of their visit, Roger II's son William I had completed the decorative works inside the palace. Ibn Jubayr saw it at its most splendid moment. From then on its fate was linked entirely with the vagaries of Sicilian history, and most of the original decor has disappeared.

The marvels which so impressed twelfth-century visitors can only be seen today in the Cappella Palatina and in the so-called Sala del Ruggero, whose mosaics of leopards and palm trees have become a kind of visual shorthand for the glories of Norman Sicily. The Cappella Palatina survives largely intact, a measure of the awe that this dazzling interior arouses. It is embedded in the palace buildings and the exterior is no longer visible. By sheer good fortune, I happened to be in Sicily while the restoration of 2009 was in progress, and wanted to see it again. It was officially closed, but a friend who lived in Palermo told me that it was possible to tour the restoration work, with an English guide, by prior arrangement. The next day, four of us found ourselves standing on the scaffolding immediately below the carved ceiling of the chapel, so close to it that we had to remove the hard hats we were wearing to avoid touching it. The intricate work of the Muslim craftsmen had been almost impossible to decipher from ground level. Centuries of alternate damp and drying out had loosened the paint and removed much of the gilding. Seen at close quarters, the drinkers, dancers and musicians in the lively scenes from court life and the episodes from the bestiary, the Christian equivalent of Aesop's fables, were sharp and clear again. I remember a lively discussion with the guide about the bestiary scenes, standing in the cramped space with the images all around us on the forest of pendants which make up the ceiling.

In any other building, the roof would be marvel enough. Here its intricate workmanship yields to the mosaics, almost perfectly preserved. These have been recognised since they were first created as the finest since classical times: the pope himself was among those who praised them.[5] The workmen were probably local artists; the designs have a strong Byzantine streak, and it is very likely that Greek masters were brought in to carry out the huge programme of mosaics of which the Cappella Palatina is, so to speak, the second instalment. The cathedral at Cefalù, along the coast from Palermo, was intended as a royal mausoleum and was the first of the buildings to be decorated in this style: the third is the cathedral at Monreale, to which we shall come next.

**7.** West end of the Cappella Palatina in the Norman royal castle in Palermo. This space at the west end of the chapel would have held the throne of Roger II, below the mosaic of Christ in Majesty. The whole programme of mosaics commemorates his coronation as first king of Sicily.

Medieval Sicily was the place where the cultural legacies of classical antiquity, filtered through the Byzantine empire, met with Arabic civilisation and the newly emerging art of Christian Europe. Its rulers were still in touch with France, partly because of the crusades. In 1149 a ship carrying Eleanor of Aquitaine, returning with her husband Louis VII from crusade, was blown off course almost to north Africa. It landed eventually in Palermo, and Roger II escorted her to Calabria where she was reunited with Louis.[6] Roger II had another important French contact, Abbot Suger of Saint-Denis, whom Louis had left in charge of the French kingdom during his absence. The ideas about kingship which underlie the imagery of the mosaics owe much to contemporary French attitudes: there are echoes of Saint-Denis at both Cefalù and the Cappella Palatina. The Sicilian kings studied the 'customs of other kings and peoples very diligently'[7] and adopted anything which they felt would be appropriate. Although the visual style is unquestionably Byzantine, the magnificence to which Roger II aspired is that of a western monarch.

The entrance to the Cappella Palatina is through two doorways in the west wall, which flank the royal dais on which Roger's throne was placed, and the programme of the mosaics is subtly adapted to his viewpoint. From where he sat, he would have seen Biblical episodes and texts echoing his kingly position. It is also a reminder that this is a dynastic foundation. The charter dated 1140 establishing the chapel says that it is a thanksgiving for the creation of the Sicilian kingdom. Royalty, and the splendour of royalty, is the driving force behind it. As a private royal chapel, it is the place where the king would most frequently appear in the midst of his court, and to which only privileged visitors would be admitted. The west end was also designed to act as an audience hall, and forms a separate section within the church. This arrangement was also used in imperial chapels in Byzantium.

All three of the Sicilian royal churches have the same dominant image on the curved roof of the apse, that of Christ 'Pantocrator', 'ruler of all'. At the Capella Palatina, the image of the king is placed in exact counterpoise to the divine ruler, at the west end, as a mosaic above the throne. Around the walls, the overwhelming impression is of a glittering surface on which the symbolic figures and biblical narratives are placed. The use of gold and silver glass tesserae to reflect light in a space which is inherently dark, with small windows, and the refusal to leave undecorated an inch of the surface above the level of the pillars, gives a rich depth to the whole of the mosaic work, with its proliferation of images. Below the line of the pillars, which are reused classical columns, the style is totally different: for the most part, it consists of large marble panels with patterned borders. And there are inscriptions everywhere, drawn from both Greek and Latin litanies: this is a chapel for a literate and sophisticated congregation. It has been argued that behind all this lie the ideas attributed to St Denis, who was believed to have written a treatise entitled *On the Celestial Hierarchy*, much discussed by scholars at just this time. Hence the numerous angels, and the emphasis on light: 'evidently Roger, like [Abbot] Suger, believed that material brilliance "should brighten the minds so that they may travel, through the true lights, to the True Light, where Christ is the door".'[8] Suger had used stained glass extensively for the first time when he rebuilt St Denis to provide colour and light; here, the reflections of the tesserae are the source of that light.

The French writer Guy de Maupassant called the Cappella Palatina 'the most surprising jewel ever imagined by human thought'.[9] This complex, glorious space, despite the unfamiliarity of its imagery and the welter of inscriptions in Greek and Latin, is one of the best surviving examples of medieval splendour, surrounding the prince and assuring him of his position on earth, and hopefully in heaven as well.

MONREALE IS THE SEQUEL TO the Cappella Palatina, spacious where the Cappella is confined, and set on the hills above Palermo because the king had – to say the least – an uneasy relationship with the archbishop of Palermo, an Englishman named Walter Offamilo. This had led William II, grandson of Roger II, to decide to build a new royal abbey with a cathedral church 13 kilometres outside the city, which would serve as the dynastic mausoleum. This arrangement is paralleled at Westminster and at Saint-Denis, so was by no means unusual. What was unusual was that, due to the way in which the Sicilian kingdom had been created by the papacy, William II was also the pope's legate in Sicily, and able to grant himself permission to create the abbey. Equally remarkable was the speed with which it was built, beginning in 1174 and completed in a mere four years.

Monreale is therefore no ordinary abbey church. It was designed from the start as a place for royal ceremonial, and that accounts for the huge space within, 40 metres by 102 metres. The monks of the abbey were Cluniac, and all their services were conducted in the sanctuary. The interior is totally at odds with the Cluniac condemnation of ornament in churches, and is entirely devoted to creating a magnificent backdrop for royal pomp and circumstance. The richness of the mosaics, which are Byzantine in general style but quite unlike any contemporary work in Byzantium itself, would seem to be the work of local craftsmen, or at least craftsmen who had worked in the south of Italy. The subjects that cover walls and ceiling are on a grand scale: they tell the story of the Bible from Genesis to the Resurrection and Pentecost, and the royal imagery is a very small element in the whole. But it is present, and carefully positioned. The royal throne is at the entrance to the sanctuary: looking towards the altar, the scene is dominated by a figure of Christ Pantocrator in the apse as at the Cappella Palatina and the old royal cathedral at Cefalù. This is not simply the largest, but is the most sophisticated and striking of the three. William II's throne would have been 'at the right hand of God', facing that of the abbot-archbishop.

Above the throne, Christ is shown crowning William, in a grander version of the other mosaic on this theme: the crowning of Roger II in the church of La Martorana in the heart of Palermo. The Martorana mosaic is a much simpler composition, with the majestic standing figure of Christ and the king inclining his head towards him as the crown is placed on it. The earlier image is less grand and more powerful: Roger's kingship was not acknowledged by much of Europe, as the pope who granted it was not recognised either in the Holy Roman Empire or in France. Roger seems to stand alone, while William II at Monreale is surrounded by angels and is crowned by a magnificently enthroned Christ. On the facing wall, William II presents the church to the Virgin Mary, in a pictorial theme familiar throughout western Christendom; it is repeated on a capital at the entrance to the cloister.

The Sicilian kings stand slightly apart from the other European princes. Their history is a microcosm of princely concerns, the struggle to establish and maintain a dynasty, the reconciliation of different traditions and influences, and the rise and fall of the house of Hauteville in the space of less than a century. Yet they were linked in one way or another to France, England and the Holy Roman Empire: they had come from France, one of them had married an English princess, and Englishmen were often at their court, and their inheritance eventually passed to the German emperor Friedrich II, William's first cousin. Their style was one of the few real links between that of the Byzantine court and the West. The trappings of Sicilian magnificence are reflected in the inheritance of Friedrich II.

8. Coronation of Roger II by Christ. Roger was crowned before any of the royal churches in Palermo had been completed. This mosaic is in the small church of the Martorana, built by his chief minister George of Antioch and finished in 1151.

9. William II offers his new cathedral of Monreale to the Virgin Mary. Dedication images of this kind are not uncommon, though this is on a much larger scale than usual. It is part of a huge cycle of mosaics which are of exceptional quality, executed by Greek workmen from Sicily who had seen contemporary Byzantine work.

# Friedrich II: Recreating the Past, Exploring the Future

FRIEDRICH II, HOLY ROMAN EMPEROR from 1220 to 1250, is one of the most intriguing figures that we shall encounter in this book. Endlessly energetic, he is an elusive character. Each new biographer seems to find a new interpretation, and despite monumental tomes devoted to him, it seems that he is too protean to be contained within the covers of a single volume. He inherited both Sicily and the Holy Roman Empire from his parents: his mother Constance was the great-granddaughter of Roger II, and the emperor Heinrich VI his father. He saw himself as successor to the Roman emperors, looking back beyond Charlemagne and taking them directly as his models. But he was also in touch with the latest developments in philosophy and science, including the rediscovery of works of Aristotle. His own famous treatise on falconry, *On the art of hunting with birds*, is based on his own skill as a falconer; it also relies on the value of observation of the natural world which shaped Aristotle's books on zoology. He corresponded with the sultan of Egypt, and was deeply interested in the civilisation of the Arab world. To the pope, he was a dangerous heretic, supporter of the radical Franciscan order, and dabbling in unorthodox philosophy, as well as a political opponent to the papacy's worldly ambitions. The moment in his career which encapsulates these contradictions is his success in regaining Jerusalem for the Christian world in 1229, while he was under sentence of excommunication by the pope.

Friedrich II had a very keen sense of the past and of his position as the modern heir to the Roman emperors. He deliberately attempted to reinvent himself as a Roman emperor, and there are three monuments which speak to us directly of his vision. All survive only as *Friedrich II:* fragments, chiefly of the statues and inscriptions. The earliest, the castle at Foggia northwest *Foggia* of Bari, begun in 1223, in an area which is peppered with Friedrich's buildings, was one of his favourite residences. He was only in his thirties when he put up the proud inscription above the arch of the doorway, which begins:

THUS CAESAR ORDERED THIS WORK TO BE MADE
THUS BARTHOLOMEW BUILT THAT WORK

In the text which follows, the emphasis is on his imperial titles – 'emperor of the Romans', 'Caesar', and, most tellingly, '*Semper Augustus*', the official title used by the Roman emperors.

Foggia was the nearest that Friedrich, the most peripatetic of all rulers of the Holy Roman Empire, came to having as his capital residence. He spent several months each year there, usually in the winter, except for the years 1236–1239 when he was occupied with the struggle for Lombardy. After his victory over the rebellious city of Milan at Cortenuova in 1237, he ordered that some of the captives should be taken to see Foggia, to witness his imperial power.[10]

## The arch at Capua

THE MOST IMPOSING of these classical monuments was the triumphal gateway Friedrich created at Capua, north of Naples, in 1234. This was a project in which he took a close personal interest, and he may even have had a hand in the design.[11] It stands at the end of a bridge, and consists of two massive towers, of which only the bases remain. Above the arch which spans the roadway between the towers, a screen wall was decorated with antique pillars and with a central statue of Friedrich himself, clad in a toga. Around him

I. A reconstruction of Friedrich II's gateway in the classical style at Capua, built 1234–40.

*Friedrich II: Capua*

were busts, both antique and modern, all in the classical style, a number of them *spolia*, originals from the Roman period incorporated into the new work. It was a deliberate echo of the ancient gates of Rome itself, very similar to the Porta Appia (now the Porta San Sebastiano). When Capua was besieged thirty years later after the defeat of Friedrich's son Manfred, one of the besiegers, Andrew of Hungary, was awe-struck by the massive monument, estimating that it must have cost 'twenty thousand ounces of pure gold'. He called the statue of Friedrich 'an eternal and imperishable memorial', and describes the figure as stretching out its arms and pointing towards the onlooker, as if to warn him, in the words of the inscription below, that only the just may enter in safety; the wicked will be punished, and the infidels imprisoned.[12]

An even more intriguing witness to Friedrich's adoption of the mantle of the Roman emperors is now no more than a handful of fragments. In 1237 Friedrich had been faced by a serious revolt among the cities of Lombardy, led by the Milanese, and at the end of November he lured them out of a very strong fortified position outside the city of Brescia by pretending that he was retreating to his winter quarters at Cremona. The ruse worked, and the Milanese army was annihilated, its leaders captured. The precious standard-chariot or *carroccio* of Milan, surmounted by a cross with a sacred relic, fell into Friderich's hands. It was a major victory, and he celebrated it with a triumph in the antique Roman style. One of his highest officials, Piero della Vigna, published an account of the occasion in a letter addressed to the faithful of the Empire. This described how the *carroccio*, with the Milanese leader chained to the front of it and the standard trailing in the dust, was tied behind the emperor's elephant and hauled through the streets of Cremona.[13] Friedrich later presented the *carroccio* to the senate of Rome, a pointed gesture aimed both at the pope, who had supported the Milanese, and at echoing his imperial forebears. It was mounted on the Capitol, with an inscription which the rulers of classical Rome would have instantly recognised:[14]

*The Milanese* carroccio

FROM THE AUGUST CAESAR FRIDERICUS THE SECOND
RECEIVE, O ROME, THIS CARROCCIO, ETERNAL ORNAMENT OF THE CITY
CAPTURED AT THE DEFEAT OF MILAN, TROPHY OF CAESAR'S TRIUMPH,
IT COMES AS A NOBLE PRIZE.
IT WILL STAND TO SHAME THE ENEMY AND HONOUR THE CITY
REVERENCE FOR THE  CITY IMPELLED HIM TO SEND IT.

Even Roman art, rarely prized by Christian monarchs, was precious to Friedrich.[15] In 1240, and again in 1242, he ordered classical statues to be taken to his castle at Lucera, 154 kilometres northwest of Bari. Here he had created a Moslem town: faced with religious rebellion in Sicily, he had moved the insurgents out of the island and had offered them special privileges to ensure their future loyalty. (There was admittedly a certain irony in decorating the castle with statues which the inhabitants would have found sacrilegious.) We have Friedrich's instructions for transporting two stone figures from the castle at Naples, which were to be carried very carefully on the porters' shoulders. Friedrich also prized Roman jewellery in the form of cameos, both original and contemporary work in the classical style. His successor Conrad IV sold no less than 987 pieces of jewellery to a Genoese merchant, among which were seventy-seven unmounted and fifty gold-mounted cameos. And we can add to this list the design of his gold coinage of 1231 struck in Sicily, which shows him with the traditional laurel wreath of the emperors rather than with a crown, in profile. Finally, there is the massive sarcophagus made of imperial porphyry in which he was buried at Palermo in 1250.[16]

FRIEDRICH'S SUCCESSORS IN THE KINGDOM of Naples, the Angevin dynasty of the late thirteenth century, continued to look to Rome as a model. There is a striking series of statues in a pose similar to that of Friedrich on the Capuan gate, beginning with Arnolfo di Cambio's figure of Charles I of Anjou. This shows the king as a Roman senator, rather than as an emperor. Charles was elected to the senate in 1263, and the statue was carved from a huge block of antique marble in 1277, just before he had to retire from the post. He became a senator again in 1281, and its creation may have had something to do with these manoeuvres. Charles is shown in traditional senatorial robes, holding a scroll, rather than in the commanding gesture of Friedrich's image. The tombs of later Angevin kings have figures in royal regalia in a similar fashion, as part of massive cenotaphs which stand behind the high altars of Neapolitan churches. But it is not until the mid fifteenth century under Alfonso V of Aragon that Roman triumphs on the scale of that of Friedrich II are seen again in Naples.

*Arnolfo di Cambio*

## *Friedrich as Builder: Castel del Monte and Castello Maniace*

THE CHRONICLER OF THE ABBEY of Santa Giustina in Padua wrote eloquently of Friedrich II as a builder of both palaces and castles.[17] The emperor, he recorded, 'had palaces built with incomparable fervor and of such beauty and proportions as though he was going to be able to live forever'. Not content with this, he 'raised fortresses and towers on the tops of the mountains and in the cities as though he was afraid of being besieged by his enemies from one moment to the other'. As to Friedrich's purpose, he declared, 'All this he made to demonstrate his power, by inciting fear and admiration, and thus impressing his name so profoundly in the memory of men that nothing would ever be able to cancel it.'[18] Two examples of his activity will have to suffice.

*'to demonstrate his power'*

CASTEL DEL MONTE IN APULIA is the most famous of Friedrich's Italian castles. It stands in a relatively sparsely populated landscape on the eastern side of a ridge of hills some 50 kilometres west of Bari. When I first caught a glimpse of it in the distance, I mistook it for a massive modern building in a totally incongruous setting. To the medieval traveller it would have seemed even more gigantic, lowering and hostile, partly screened by forest. However, when at close quarters, it is a subtle and elegant building of extraordinary symmetry and beauty. That symmetry is the essence of the architecture. Seen from the air, the plan of Castel del Monte is remarkable. It is a perfect octagon, and around the octagonal centre are eight smaller, equally perfect octagons, mounted at its angles. At its heart, there is an octagonal courtyard. Given the tools available to a medieval builder, the basic structure of the building is in itself a major feat.[19] Computer analysis reveals that the design has a highly complex mathematical origin. It has the beauty inherent in so many complex geometric patterns, enhanced by the play of light and shade in the dazzling Italian sunlight. It was almost certainly achieved, together with other aspects of the castle, by means of geometrical skills derived from Arabic scientists.

*Castel del Monte*

**10**, p.37

What we see today are the bare bones of the building. The outer façade is weathered, and apart from the loss of the tops of the octagonal towers, little altered. Within, however, there are the merest traces of the original appearance. Just as with medieval churches, a riot of colour has vanished. The one place where we can see something of the original is the main outer doorway, with its classical pediment and surround in coralline breccia, which is similar to marble; the same stone was used to frame the window openings. Inside, however, it was used to face the walls of the rooms on the ground floor. The lower floor is dark, and the imperial rooms on the first floor, including what was probably a throne room, have distinctive windows which admit much more light. One particularly elaborate window looks down towards the city of Andria, which had a very personal significance for Friedrich. His second wife, Isabella of Brienne, heiress to the kingdom of Jerusalem, was buried at Andria in 1228 to be followed by his third wife, Isabella of England, whom he married in 1234, and who died in 1241.

*Castel del Monte: symmetry*

It is not only the wall facings that are missing, of course. Many of the marble columns have gone, and there are only traces of sculptural decoration. In one room there are the remains of an elaborate octagonal mosaic. We need to imagine an interior with a play of light and shade, with plants in the courtyard, and with rich furnishings. There are no traces of wall mosaics like those in the Sicilian palaces at Palermo, though the Cistercian vaulting of the ground floor might imply a rather more ascetic northern approach to decoration. There is no doubt, however, that this was a building designed to overawe the visitor from the moment they approached it.

*Castel del Monte: décor*

Another feature is highly personal, and relates to Friedrich's skill in falconry. In one of the towers there is a carefully constructed eyrie above the vaulting, accessible only by a ladder from the room below, with a staircase leading to the roof. Falconry, too, was a symbol of royal prestige. The eyrie would have contained hawks appropriate to Friedrich's imperial rank, probably both peregrines from the Mediterranean and the much-prized gerfalcons from the Nordic world. The emperor's enthusiasm for astronomy and astrology may explain the octagonal shape of the castle. But first a word of warning. What we have here is a castle that was never completed, and which Friedrich II may never have inhabited. There is a still unresolved scholarly debate about fundamental points, such as the planning and building of the castle, let alone its undocumented purposes, so what follows needs to be treated with caution. Having waded through the vast literature on it in Italian and German, I can only say that what follows seems to make sense to me.

*Friedrich II and science*

Friedrich was deeply involved with the emerging scientific world of his time, which prized observation of natural phenomena as equal or even superior to Christian tradition, to the Church's dismay. He used this close observation in his book on falconry, but his knowledge of science derived in large part from contact with the Arab intellectual world. The result is visible in the mathematical and geometrical plan of the building. The philosopher Michael Scot was at Friedrich's court from about 1220 until 1236, the year of his death. He was renowned for his learning, and particularly his knowledge of Arabic science including astronomy, and, indivisible from it in the medieval period, astrology, subjects which he certainly discussed with the emperor. Friedrich also owned a planetarium given to him by the sultan of Damascus, with 'figures of the sun and moon, indicating the hours of the day and night in their determined movements', and he himself corresponded with an Arab scholar about astronomy.[20] Furthermore he had met the sultan of Egypt in 1229 and corresponded with him about astrology.

The main entrance of the castle is placed precisely east, which was the only easily calculated compass point before the magnetic compass was refined enough to give an accurate reading. The octagon is therefore a perfect compass rose, with the towers marking the cardinal points. For the astrologer, who needed to observe the sky with the greatest precision possible, this meant that, on the roof, the central octagon could be used to give exact positions. The size of the opening is such that one degree of the compass is represented by a space of roughly 10 cm. Given the accurate construction of the building, the whole castle could act as an excellent observatory. Because there were no common standards of time, an almanac for any given place depended on recording the basic data over a period of a year or more to establish the necessary tables. And Arabic astronomers aimed to record the data they needed for astrology, rather than to investigate the theoretical side.

*Castello Maniace*

CASTELLO MANIACE AT SYRACUSE guards the superb harbour which gave the city its importance from classical times onwards. It lies at the eastern end of the island of Ortigia, behind fortifications which have grown more massive with each century. It was rebuilt by Friedrich II between 1232 and 1240, and here the palatial interior survives, at least in part. The ground floor consisted of a massive hall, 50 metres by 50 metres, with five rows of five columns supporting vaults which rise to at least twice the height of the columns themselves. The impression is of an immense roof, dwarfing the human beings below. The castle was heavily damaged when it was still an important fort – an earthquake in 1693 and an explosion in the powder magazine in 1704 – and over half the central structure has virtually disappeared. Only two rows of the columns have been restored, but they are enough to allow us to imagine the effect of the original.

The central vault of the hall was open to the sky, and formed a small inner courtyard flanked by four triple columns; there was almost certainly a fountain there. Apart from this, the light was from just two windows and the main door, giving a strong contrast between the cool darkness inside and the brilliant sunlight reflected from the sea outside.

The visitor would have entered by the portal flanked by two bronze rams in the classical style, one of which survives. The arcade leading to the doorway itself uses a combination of black and grey marble and a stone which appears almost gilded when set against these colours. This is almost all that we have of the décor, which has almost entirely vanished. Castello Maniace is in a sense a palace built within massive outer fortifications which were already in place.

These were the works of a man who, in the eyes of the chronicler, intended to inspire 'fear and admiration'.[21] His contemporaries called him '*immutator mundi*' and '*stupor mundi*', both a transformer of the world and its wonder. The transformation, a permanent establishment of a new Roman empire, eluded him, and all we are left with is the wonder, a precursor of the 'magnificence' that Giles of Rome defined thirty years after his death.

*'immutator mundi'*

# St Louis and Henry III
## *Paris*

IN 1254 HENRY III CAME TO PARIS to visit St Louis, almost as a tourist. Matthew Paris, whose monastery at St Albans was in close contact with the royal court, and who knew Henry personally, says that he was eager to see 'the cities, churches, manners and clothes of the French, and the most noble chapel of the kings of France which is in Paris, as well as the incomparable relics which were in it'.[22] Henry had just overseen the reburial of his mother Queen Isabella at Fontevraud, where Henry II, Eleanor and Richard were buried. He came by way of Orléans to meet Louis at Chartres. Louis ordered that all towns through which Henry was to pass should be cleansed and decorated with cloths, branches and flowers and other ornaments, and that the royal visitor should be reverently and joyfully received with suitable music and ceremonial. The kings went on to Paris, where the other members of the French royal family greeted Henry. The English scholars studying at the university appeared in festive robes, with musicians, for a celebration which lasted throughout the night and the following day. Henry lodged outside the walls in the headquarters of the Templars, because his retinue was so large, before visiting the Sainte-Chapelle the next day.

*Henry III visits Paris*

Henry gave a banquet at the Templar establishment in Paris. Here the hall was hung with shields, 'as is the fashion abroad', among them that of Richard I. Henry's jester said to the king, 'Are you inviting the French here? If they see that shield they will be too frightened to eat!' Matthew Paris gives a full list of the guests, including not only the great clerics and nobles, but also the oldest inhabitants of the city. The kings spent eight days together; Henry admired the elegant plastered houses of Paris with many rooms, followed by crowds of the citizens eager to catch sight of him. The kings, according to Matthew Paris, had very friendly conversations – their wives were sisters – and got on very well at a personal level. Matthew claims that Louis told Henry that 'if only the twelve peers of France and my barons would agree to it, we would be inseparable friends', a neat reminder that the personal warmth of the meeting was unlikely to produce political results.[23]

## PALAIS DE LA CITÉ

After the banquet at the Temple, Henry went for the night to Louis's main palace in Paris, on the Ile de la Cité. This site was a natural stronghold, and had been fortified since the fourth century AD. Under the first Capetian kings of France, descendants of Hugh Capet who had been elected king of the Franks in 987, Paris became their power base and the effective capital city of the kingdom. The buildings there were gradually remodelled as the Palais de la Cité over the next two centuries. Under Louis VII in the twelfth century the palace was enlarged by the great royal hall, a massive defensive tower, royal lodgings and a chapel, the essential elements of a medieval palace. Here his son Philip Augustus, at the beginning of the thirteenth century, established the new administrative offices of the kingdom, including a law court and the king's chamber. Furthermore, he built a new city wall round Paris, so that the defensive aspect of the Palais became less important.

*The Ile de la Cité*

Philip's successor, St Louis, added further government offices to the Palais, including the repository of royal charters and the accounting chamber. His most spectacular creation was the Sainte-Chapelle at the heart of the palace. From the detailed chronicles of his reign we learn a good deal about the rooms and buildings and who occupied them, including the king's private chambers and dining room to the west of the old fortified area, and the Sainte-Chapelle and the residences of its clergy to the south. Within the enclosed space, there were still gardens, notably that next to the royal law court, where St Louis famously dispensed justice in the open air. On the north side, a smaller ceremonial hall, the Salle sur l'Eau, was added: it was intended for those royal occasions when crowds would not be present.

*The creation of the Sainte-Chapelle*

By 1285, when Philip IV came to the throne, the royal law court had been moved elsewhere. During the next decade, Philip's centralisation of the government departments changed the nature of the Palais de la Cité. From 1298 until his death in 1314, he and his architect, Enguerrand de Marigny, rebuilt it accordingly. The semi-official chronicle written at the abbey of Saint-Denis called it 'a new palace of marvellous and costly work, more beautiful than anyone in France had ever seen'.[24] A new entrance, the Great Staircase, was created, with a steep flight of steps leading to an ante-chamber giving access to the main rooms of the palace. This was placed so that when the king came to a ceremonial occasion in the most impressive of the new rooms, the platform at the head of the staircase became the point where spectators gathered in the main court would see him, before he crossed the courtyard into the Grand'Salle.[25] This hall was one of the largest in Europe, 63 metres long and 27 metres wide, with a barrel vaulted wooden roof above. At the west end a huge black marble table, made of nine slabs, took up almost the whole width of the hall. There was a massive row of central pillars which, with the corresponding arch pillars on the walls, carried polychrome statues of the French kings, reputedly very lifelike. These were the forerunners of the dynastic portraits at the Karlstejn in Prague, intended to reinforce the idea that the Capetian kings were the true heirs of Charlemagne rather than newcomers in the tenth century. Hence the series of statues began with the mythical king Pharamond and his shadowy semi-historical successors before going on to Charlemagne and the supposed Capetian connection to him.

*'a new palace of costly work'*

**13**, p.39

This remarkable space was at once a dining hall and a space for theatrical and spectacular performance. It was destroyed in a fire in 1618; only the lower hall survives, which served as a refectory for the palace staff, numbering almost two thousand. It was slightly larger in area, though shorter in length than Westminster Hall in London, at 1,785 square metres. The Grand'Salle could probably have seated nearly a thousand for a feast. It will appear in later chapters as the scene of some of the greatest displays of the period. It also served as the place where the king's justice was administered, as was the case with Westminster Hall.

**10.** Castel del Monte in Apulia, near Bari. Considered the most remarkable of Friedrich II's multitude of castles, it dominates the surrounding landscape. Its octagonal form, with octagonal towers, is built to a remarkable degree of geometric accuracy. Friedrich never stayed there, as the castle remained unfinished at his death.

**11.** Henry III brings the relics of the Passion to Westminster, a contemporary drawing by Matthew Paris, artist and chronicler.

**12.** The Crown of Thorns. Originally the focal point of the Sainte-Chapelle, it was transferred to Notre-Dame. The gold casing is modern, but it has always been encrusted with gold and jewels. It is displayed on Good Friday each year.

## THE SAINTE-CHAPELLE

The modern aspect of the Palais de la Cité in Paris from the street is that of a fairly ordinary nineteenth-century office building. Only a spire soaring behind the façade gives any hint of the extraordinary reliquary in its inner court. For the Sainte-Chapelle is exactly that, built by St Louis to house one of the greatest relics in Christendom, the crown of thorns reputed to have been worn by Christ at the crucifixion.[26] The building itself is in the form of the jewelled chests in which such relics were often kept, and was originally as brilliantly coloured as any goldsmith's work. It was created and decorated in a mere five years, from 1243 to 1248, and although the painting has been much restored, the contemporary effect of highly coloured surfaces contrasting with the light shed by the superb, soaring windows is still a stunning experience. The ceiling was deep blue, spangled with stars, an effect often copied in later churches in the apse; here it ran through the whole length of the nave as well. There is very little wall space, simply the narrow pillars that support the roof and frame the windows, and their base, a wall which is perhaps a sixth of their height. Here carved and gilded sculpted arcading surrounded spaces decorated with glass inset into a silver ground, reflecting the shafts of coloured light from above. In London, the buildings which corresponded to the Palais de la Cité and Saint-Denis were on the same site, outside the city walls in the village of Westminster. Here the royal burial place was Westminster Abbey, flanked by the centre of royal administration at the palace of Westminster. This is how it struck a medieval observer, Jean de Jandun, writing seventy-five years after its completion:

> But also that most beautiful of chapels, the chapel of the king, most fittingly situated within the walls of the king's house, enjoys a complete and indissoluble structure of most solid stone. The most select colors of the pictures, the precious gilding of the images, the beautiful transparency of the gleaming windows on all sides, the most beautiful cloths of the altars, the wondrous merits of the sanctuaries, the figured work on the reliquaries externally adorned with dazzling gems, bestow such a hyperbolic beauty on that house of prayer, that, in going into it from below, one understandably believes one self, as if rapt to heaven, to be entering one of the best chambers of Paradise.[27]

## London

IN LONDON, THE BUILDINGS which corresponded to the Palais de la Cité and Saint-Denis were both on one site, outside the city walls in the village of Westminster. Here the royal burial place was Westminster Abbey, flanked by the centre of royal adminstration at the palace of Westminster.

## WESTMINSTER ABBEY

The reasons for Edward the Confessor's decision to build a monumental new church at the relatively obscure monastery of Westminster at an unknown date, probably not long after he came to the throne in 1042, are quite simply unknown. He had spent twenty-four years in exile in Normandy, and the building he commissioned seems to have been on the lines of the abbey at Jumièges, with its massive twin towers at the west end. But in size 'it far exceeded any of the eleventh century churches of Normandy which have survived'.[28] The church, largely completed, was consecrated on 28 December 1065. A week later, Edward was the first king to be buried there. His ill-fated successor Harold was the first king to be crowned there, on the same day.

Edward was canonised in 1161, and his body was translated to a new shrine in 1163. Westminster remained important as the place of coronation. Henry III had been crowned

**13.** The month of June, from the calendar in *Les Très Riches Heures du duc de Berry*. In the background is the Palais de la Cité, on an island in the Seine. There are gardens within its walls with bowers and pergolas, and a great staircase behind. The Sainte-Chapelle, without its spire, is inside the first line of roofs.

at Gloucester as a matter of urgency after the death of his father John in 1216, but this was regarded as a temporary measure. He was crowned again at Westminster in 1220. Yet just as Edward's original decision to create a monumental church at the abbey is obscure, so is the reason for Henry III's decision to tear down that church and rebuild it in the latest French style. One of his motives may well have been rivalry with his brother-in-law St Louis of France, who had not yet begun the Sainte-Chapelle in his palace in Paris when Henry began to spend money at Westminster. Matthew Paris attributes the choice of Westminster to a personal enthusiasm on Henry's part for St Edward, and this seems persuasive.[29] As to the style, Edward the Confessor would have known the Norman Romanesque churches from his years of exile, whereas in 1225 Henry III had never been to Paris and its surrounding cathedral towns, the scene of the latest fashion in Gothic architecture which he now adopted for Westminster Abbey. However, his architect, Henri de Reyns, was a Frenchman who had trained at Reims. This was the coronation church of the French kings and had recently been rebuilt. He was therefore well placed to offer Henry ideas which related to the latest grand style in French architecture, and there is undoubtedly a link at some level between the buildings at Reims and Westminster.[30] Equally, Henry was too far advanced with his work on the Abbey for there to be any question of reshaping St Stephen's Chapel in the Palace of Westminster, technically the equivalent of the Sainte-Chapelle. When he saw the latter in 1254, Henry is said to have been so enthusiastic that if he could have put it on a handcart and taken it home with him, he would have done so.[31]

*Henry III and Westminster*

One very distinctive feature at Westminster Abbey may be due to the long shadow of the Roman empire. This is Henry's choice of Italian artists to embellish his new church. The mosaic floors created by the Cosmati family from Rome are in the tradition of imperial splendour, using scarce porphyry, semi-precious stones and glass to create a depth of colour and form unrivalled in Europe. They worked extensively in their home town, and to a lesser extent in other central Italian towns, but nothing like this was to be seen in Paris or northern France. The Cosmati team was led by a man who is named in the inscriptions as Odoricus, and the design of the pavement in the sanctuary is to be found in contemporary work by the Cosmati in Rome, though not on this scale. The layout of the east end of the church allows this floor to be much more extensive, and the coronation ritual which is performed there more spacious and impressive.[32]

*The Cosmati pavement*

The shrine of the Confessor himself was also the work of the Cosmati, who were only just beginning to undertake such commissions in their Italian homeland. Its actual design is not Italian, but typical of English pilgrim shrines, with spaces below for pilgrims to get as close as they could to the magical relics within. This type of mosaic, by flickering candlelight, has a life of its own which modern lighting does not evoke: the tomb would have been a glittering focal point within the church. The saint's remains were housed in a rich iron feretory demolished at the Reformation; our knowledge of this comes from the document by which Henry III, crucially short of funds in the late 1260s, had to pawn the statues on it, a dozen or so in all including St Peter holding a model of the church and a Virgin and Child.

Henry III, as a devout prince, collected relics, and received gifts of them with enthusiasm. As nephew of Richard I, the only king to have campaigned successfully in the East since the conquest of Jerusalem in 1099, he was a particular target for such blandishments. It is only through the chance survival of a list of gifts he received in 1234/5 that we know that the Knights Hospitaller had sent him a choice selection of relics from the Holy Land.

In 1247, Henry III acquired his own special relic of the Passion, a phial of the Holy Blood sent to him by the emperor Heraclius, which had been authenticated by the patriarch of Jerusalem and the Knights Templar. Relics of the Holy Blood were far from uncommon – one scholar has listed over 220 in all – but the provenance of this, and the fact that the patriarch had sent it, made it especially precious to Henry. It also gave him the chance to promote Westminster to an equal standing with the Sainte-Chapelle. The relic was therefore presented to the world at large in the most dramatic way possible.

*Henry III and the Passion relic*

Henry concealed the fact that it was being sent to him until the day of the ceremony, and then announced the arrival of the precious gift in the presence of Matthew Paris. Matthew Paris not only describes the event, having been ordered by the king 'to write a plain and full account of all these events', but also provides a drawing of the procession from St Paul's to Westminster, with the king walking under a canopy as if going to his coronation. He confirms the suspicion that rivalry with France was one aspect of the celebration, claiming that the bishop of Norwich had preached a sermon in which he said that the Crown of Thorns was made holy by its contact with the body of Christ, and declared that 'more holy is the blood of Christ' because it is the blood which sanctifies the other relics. It is sometimes claimed that Henry was trying to make Westminster a place of pilgrimage. However Edward the Confessor was nothing like such a draw as Thomas Becket at Canterbury. Henry did amass a considerable collection of remains of saints here, but a series of indulgences for separate activities at the abbey issued by the pope are not necessarily evidence for this. We shall find similar indulgences* issued at Karlstejn near Prague, again in connection with a royal collection of relics, and this was probably the true character of Henry's efforts. The Westminster chronicler confirms this, claiming that 'the church of Westminster was richer in royal treasure than all the churches north of the Alps, and indeed than those beyond the Alps as well'.[33]

**11**, p.37

## THE PALACE OF WESTMINSTER

It was under Henry III that Westminster was established both as the centre of the administration and as a true royal palace. Work on the palace began in the 1220s, and continued during the rebuilding of the abbey, in tandem with the latter, but on a smaller scale. Edward the Confessor had built a palace next to Westminster Abbey in the years before the Norman Conquest, and this continued to be used under William I, though we know little about it. In 1097 his son William Rufus started to rebuild it on a massive scale, and held his Whitsun crown-wearing there two years later. It was the precursor of a series of such great halls. We have noted the Grand'Salle in Paris, but these two remained the prime examples. Even the huge Vladislav Hall in the palace at Prague, a late Gothic creation from the beginning of the sixteenth century, is slightly shorter, and only two thirds of the width. The hall of the royal palace of Aragon in Barcelona was rebuilt by Peter the Ceremonious in 1359 and is visually more dramatic, though smaller, with a perspective of round arches, 18 metres in width, which are the largest of their type in the Middle Ages.

*Westminster Hall*

What there was apart from the hall at Westminster is not clear, as the kings seem to have been there only for ceremonial purposes or for sizeable assemblies: it was certainly not a major residence until Henry II's reign, and even then we know very little about it, apart from the holding of royal crown-wearings there. Thomas Becket as chancellor was responsible for restoring it rapidly from a half-ruined state, and there were by his time chambers for the king and queen and offices for the royal exchequer, which is recorded as meeting here in 1165.[34] By 1167 a new hall had been added. The main royal treasury, which had been at

---

* Indulgences were issued to pilgrims and promised that they would be spared time in purgatory after they died in return for their pilgrimage.

Winchester since Anglo-Saxon times, was moved here at some time in the early thirteenth century, during John's reign.

*The Painted Chamber*

The palace's most remarkable feature, the Painted Chamber, and the other wall paintings are discussed in chapter 7 below. These were only part of the décor: the floors were of glazed tiles. It is possible that there were resplendent Cosmati pavements within the palace like the 'Great Pavement' before the high altar in the Abbey, but no trace or record of them survives. English tiles of the period are quite sophisticated, and surviving examples from Clarendon Palace near Salisbury and Chertsey Abbey show the kinds of patterns and pictorial scenes that would have been used. Indeed, the Chertsey tiles with their illustrations of Richard I jousting against Saladin are more secular than religious. The mouldings of the windows were gilded and coloured, and plaster with coloured glass embedded in it used on wall spaces not occupied by paintings. Westminster Hall was at some point before 1253 provided with a massive marble table at the south end, and a marble throne with the traditional lions supporting it was added soon afterwards.

Edward I continued to have work done on the buildings of the palace. Builders and painters were still at work in 1297 when finances ran out. This was followed by a fire which caused considerable damage in 1298, and the palace was temporarily abandoned. When Edward II came to the throne in July 1307, he had urgent reasons to repair the damage, as his coronation was planned for the following February, after his wedding in Paris to Isabella of France in January. The wedding would obviously be a splendid affair, given the wealth of the French monarchy, and to present his new bride with a ruinous palace would be a serious loss of face. By spending about £3000, the buildings were made presentable, and temporary buildings for the coronation itself were erected. Thereafter the palace was simply maintained, and annual expenditure dropped to almost nothing.

*Richard II remodels Westminster Hall*

In 1393 Richard II set in train the remodelling of Westminster Hall, which despite its huge size compared unfavourably with the Grand'Salle in the French king's Palais de la Cité in Paris, with its much greater height. Hugh Herland, the king's master carpenter, devised a roof of the latest design, a startling and striking 'double hammerbeam', which, combined with work to raise the walls, produced a height in proportion to the width of the building. This space was now lit by Gothic windows in the new Perpendicular style along the walls, with a window worthy of a cathedral façade at the north end.* All that remained of the old hall were the original Norman walls, as the base of the new structure. A set of statues of the kings of England from Edward the Confessor to Richard II were ordered, evidently in imitation of those of the French kings in the Palais de la Cité and the royal dynasty in the Karlstejn. Only six were placed in the hall, the rest seemed to have been stored pending a decision as to where to put them. Ironically, the hall was still incomplete in 1399 when Richard was deposed. The first major ceremony to take place in a setting designed to fit in with the grandiose idea of kingship which Richard favoured in the last years of his reign was the assembly which recognised his nemesis, Henry IV, as king.[35]

* This is now overshadowed by Charles Barry's Victorian buildings.

# Royal Mausoleums

D YNASTY WAS A CRITICAL CONCEPT for a medieval prince. The panoply of his ancestors vouched for his legitimacy as a ruler, and added glory to his own person as the descendant of great men. If those forebears could include a royal saint, so much the better. The royal mausoleum was usually in an abbey with close royal links, or, less usually, in the cathedral of the capital city. The presence of a royal saint was also a factor, even if the genealogical link was tenuous: in England it was Edward the Confessor at Westminster. In France, the situation was different, because Saint-Denis was the dynastic mausoleum before St Louis was canonised. In the fourteenth century Karl IV established the royal burial place at St Vitus' cathedral because of the presence of the tomb of St Wenceslas.

THE KINGDOM OF LEÓN BECAME A separate state when the kingdom of Galicia was divided among the sons of Alfonso III in 910. The church of St Isidore, patron saint of the kingdom, became a royal monastery for both men and women, under the jurisdiction of an abbess who was always a princess of León. The church itself was built in brick on the ruins of a building destroyed in a Moorish raid in 998, and rebuilt in stone after 1050 by King Fernando and his queen, Sancha. San Isidoro was dedicated in 1063, when the body of St Isidore, exacted as tribute from the Moorish ruler of Seville by Fernando, was brought here.

The pantheon was added afterwards towards the end of the eleventh century by Urraca, daughter of Alfonso VI who ruled as queen from 1109 until 1126.[36] The succession and continuation of the dynasty were seriously in question at this point. Her predecessors, the kings of Asturias, had a similar pantheon at Oviedo, in the beautiful temple-like church of Santa Maria on the edge of the city, founded early in the ninth century, where there were numerous royal graves.[37] In 911, the capital was moved to León, and the kingdom acquired its new name.

*Urraca, queen of León*

The pantheon at León is a free-standing chapel, in the precincts of the basilica of San Isidoro, and is small by contrast with most of the princely buildings we have looked at: only three bays wide, it measures 8 metres square. Immediately after it was built, the bodies of four kings were exhumed and brought here for burial in the pantheon. In all, eleven kings, twelve queens and nine of their children are buried here. The tombs were destroyed in the war of independence in 1808, and for the most part only the epitaphs remain.[38]

*The pantheon of San Isidoro*

The interior has been called 'the Sistine Chapel of Romanesque art', in the sense that it is the most complete Romanesque interior to survive, almost untouched and never 'restored'. It shows what passed for splendour in the mid twelfth century. There is a frescoed cycle of New Testament pictures on the life of Christ, painted by an unknown master. There is a crucifixion on the end wall, and the figure of Christ and the makers of the four gospels over the central vault.[39] These were completed by 1160, and were in the local Leónese style, perhaps with some Byzantine influences. The kings of León claimed the title 'Emperor of Spain', and although the Pantheon is very small, the quality of the paintings is exceptional. A portion of the library, including books produced by the scribes here dating as far back as 940, is still in place. A richly jewelled chalice given by queen Urraca is a reminder of the treasures which the monastery contained.[40] Ironically, the pantheon itself probably survived because the imperial ambitions of the kings came to nothing: León was merged with Castile in 1301, and the city ceased to be the capital. Castile had nothing to rival this concentration of royal burials: even the monastery of Las Huelgas at Burgos has only the tombs of two kings and five queens.

**14**, p.45

CONRAD II WAS THE FOUNDER OF the dynasty of Salian rulers of the Holy Roman Empire, and one of his first acts was to order the rebuilding of the cathedral at Speyer. Emperors were elected and although in practice dynastic succession was the norm, there was never a single imperial city. The only major group of imperial tombs are here, at the centre of Conrad's own rather modest territory as count of Speyer. Work began in 1030 and the scale of the project was highly ambitious, ranking alongside the cathedrals at Santiago de Compostela and Durham and the abbey church at Cluny. Conrad himself was buried there before the work was completed; by 1041 the imperial mausoleum in the crypt was consecrated, and his successor, Heinrich III, the first of the Salian emperors, was buried there.[41] Heinrich III found their simple gravestones 'far too small and narrow', and although he is said to have had them altered, he too was given a simple slab. The graves of all the Salian emperors, ending with Heinrich V, were reshaped as a monumental block, with the names of those buried there on six marble plaques. Subsequent graves were placed outside the block, and in 1291 the first effigy was placed, on the grave of Rudolf of Habsburg. A second set of burials ended with Albert of Austria in 1308. In 1689, the graves were destroyed by invading French troops and the grave goods plundered, and it was only between 1900 and 1906 that the bodies were exhumed again, sorted and separated, and the present layout established.

The cathedral itself, rather than the imperial tombs, is the monument to the aspirations of the early emperors. It was altered to its present form with an entirely vaulted roof and a semi-circular apse by Heinrich IV at the end of the eleventh century, and the architectural ornamentation was made more elaborate with arcading and galleries. The vault itself, with a span of fourteen metres, and a height of over thirty metres, was the largest of its kind in Europe. Classical-style sculptural details were added, which derive directly from Roman originals, particularly the Corinthian capitals and the acanthus foliage. At its zenith in 1310, when Elizabeth, daughter of the emperor Heinrich VII married Jean of Luxembourg, later king of Bohemia, here, it was a monumental visual representation of the emperors' power.

SAINT-DENIS IS NOW A SUBURB of Paris, but it was once a proud independent abbey obedient only to the king lying outside its walls. Before the French Revolution the abbey contained the greatest surviving collection of royal tombs anywhere in Europe. It was built on the site where St Denis, the first bishop of Paris, was said to have been buried after his martyrdom in AD 250. It had been patronised by the Merovingian kings of France. When Charles Martel, Charlemagne's grandfather, decided to be buried there in 741, it was partly out of personal devotion to the cult of St Denis, and partly for political reasons. The Carolingian mayors of the palace were on the point of displacing the last of the Merovingian puppet kings whom they supposedly served, and burial there linked him to the last true Merovingian ruler, Dagobert. Charlemagne clearly expressed his wish to be buried there, although his new capital was at Aachen: his wishes were ignored, and his tomb is at Aachen. When the last Carolingians were replaced by a new dynasty, the first king, Eudes, was again buried at St Denis. With the accession of the Capetian kings in 987, the abbey regained its status. After Hugh, the first of the dynasty, was interred there in 996, only three French kings were not buried there until the Revolution, a span of eight hundred years.[42]

Suger, who was abbot of Saint-Denis from 1122 until 1151, found that the anniversary services for the kings buried there were seriously neglected, and ensured that these were revived. He embarked on a complete rebuilding of the abbey church in the latest style. It was a precursor of the new Gothic fashion for light and spacious buildings rather than the

14. (above) The rich ceiling paintings of the Panteon de los Reyes at the Basilica of San Isidoro, León. The tombs of the kings of León were assembled here by queen Urraca in the early twelfth century, and the decoration dates from the same period.

15. Tomb of the Holy Roman Emperor Friedrich II in the cathedral at Palermo. Porphyry was associated with the Roman and Byzantine emperors. By the time this monument was built, it was no longer available from any source, and was obtained by reusing the small stock of available Roman materials.

earlier monumental and dimly lit Romanesque interior. It might have been expected that he would emphasise the abbey's royal connections by also rearranging the royal tombs and replacing plain slabs with the kind of sepulchres which were just becoming the custom for such burials. However, when Louis VI wished to be buried in a place where earlier tombs would have to be moved, Suger responded that it was 'neither proper nor customary to exhume the bodies of kings'.[43]

*St Louis reburies the kings*

Nonetheless, Saint-Denis was so intimately connected with the kings that a thirteenth-century monk forged a charter showing that Charlemagne had given the kingdom of France to the abbey as a fief, and that the king himself was its vassal. Naturally, it was not accepted, even by St Louis, who might have been expected to be sympathetic to such a claim. St Louis's attitude to reburials was the opposite of Suger's a century earlier and he was determined to establish the abbey visibly as the royal burial place. The monks made a search for all such burials that had already taken place in the church, presumably with his encouragement. The earliest was that of Clovis II, dating from 664, and fourteen were discovered in all. The tombs were adorned with rather routine standard effigies in thirteenth-century clothing. Their layout was designed to emphasise the continuity of the succession to the French throne. Hugh Capet had been elected to the throne in 987 in somewhat doubtful circumstances, and had succeeded in getting his son Robert crowned in his lifetime to ensure that the kingship would remain in the family for the next generation.[44] This manoeuvre unexpectedly established a dynasty which was to last for three and a half centuries, the envy of all other European monarchs of the period.

*Les Grandes Chroniques*

When St Louis died in 1270, he was buried at Saint-Denis. However, on his canonisation in 1298, his grandson Philip IV wanted to transfer his remains to the Sainte-Chapelle. This was resisted by the monks of Saint-Denis, who by now regarded themselves as guardians of the royal traditions. Around the time of the reburial of the kings at their monastery, the monks had also become the official recorders of French history for the royal court. *Les Grandes Chroniques* was compiled from earlier histories kept by monks of Saint-Denis, and originally ended in 1223. It was soon extended up to the death of St Louis in 1270, and continued to be revised until the end of the fourteenth century, bridging the painful transition from the Capetian dynasty, after the death of all Philip IV's sons without male heirs, to the new Valois kings in 1328. The final version of the chronicle ended with the death of Charles V in 1380.

IN ENGLAND, A SIMILAR PROCESS OF proclaiming dynastic magnificence through the establishment of a splendid royal burial place took place at Westminster Abbey, where Henry III rebuilt the church and made its focal point the cult of Edward the Confessor, canonised in 1161, to whom the king was particularly devoted. In 1246, he decided to be buried next to the resplendent shrine he had built for the saint, rather than in the Temple Church, 'on account of reverence for the most glorious king Edward'. There was no fixed burial place for the English kings: since the Conquest, their graves had been as far afield as Fontévrault in Anjou, Gloucester, Caen and Worcester, despite Henry I's plans for Reading Abbey as a possible royal necropolis. As at Saint-Denis, there was a desire for continuity. Henry III was imitating Edward the Confessor himself, whose refounding and rebuilding at Westminster had begun some time after 1040. By doing so he was linking himself with the Anglo-Saxon rulers of England, as their legitimate successor, and indeed as their descendant, through Henry I's wife, granddaughter of the Anglo-Saxon prince Edward the Aetheling.

*Westminster Abbey as royal mausoleum*

Westminster was intended by Henry III to be the royal mausoleum, and he himself was buried there. All the Plantagenet kings except Edward II followed him. It was only in the fifteenth century that Windsor became an alternative, and the Tudors returned to Westminster in the sixteenth century. Ironically, Richard II was an ardent patron of the cult of Edward the Confessor. At the critical moment of the rebellion of 1381, he went with his supporters, the nobles and the citizens of London 'to supplicate at the shrine of the sainted king for divine aid where human counsel was altogether wanting'.[45] He commissioned the double tomb for himself and his first wife, Anne of Bohemia, soon after her death in 1394, modelling the effigies on that of his grandfather Edward III which had been installed at the beginning of his reign. The tombs of Henry III's successors filled the spaces between the pillars surrounding the high altar, and the burial of Henry VI at Windsor may in part have been due to the fact that there was no appropriate place for him. Henry VII solved the problem by building the superlative chapel which bears his name, and which enabled Westminster to continue as a royal mausoleum until the Civil War in the seventeenth century.

THE NORMAN KINGS OF SICILY and their five tombs of imperial porphyry present a different case. The royal burial place was never properly established, although Friedrich II deliberately reassembled the tombs of his ancestors, and Palermo Cathedral would have filled that role if the dynasty had not failed after Friedrich's death in 1250.

Over a century earlier, in imitation of the Greek emperors, Roger II acquired two sarcophagi made of porphyry, a rare stone, which, like lapis lazuli, is only found in one remote place, in this case in the eastern Egyptian desert. Working at the quarry seems to have ended in the early fourth century, and all the porphyry used since then has been *Imperial porphyry* recycled from classical buildings. There are stones similar to the imperial porphyry, but these are prone to weathering and lack its dense grain. In Byzantium, porphyry was a symbol of empire, used in special places in the imperial palaces. The Frankish emperor Charles the Bald had been buried at Saint-Denis in an antique porphyry sarcophagus.

Roger sent these two impressive sarcophagi to Cefalù, at that point the royal burial place, but in the end he himself was buried at Palermo Cathedral, in a tomb made of thin slabs of porphyry, probably because nothing better could be obtained. William II tried to establish his new cathedral at Monreale as the royal burial place, and planned unsuccessfully to have Roger's tomb moved there. He did, however, move the body of his father, William I, from the Cappella Palatina to Monreale, and a new porphyry tomb was made from such blocks of antique porphyry as could be found, to create something resembling the two original sarcophagi. Similarly the last of the tombs to be made, that of Friedrich's mother the empress Constance, had to be cobbled together from fourteen separate pieces of porphyry, indicating how difficult it was becoming to find the precious material.

When Friedrich II became king of Sicily, he transferred the sarcophagi from Cefalù to Palermo as the tombs of his father, Heinrich VI, and himself. Above each tomb he placed a canopy supported on porphyry pillars, creating four miniature temples. These canopies were a novelty, derived from surviving Christian tombs in Rome; they were generally used **15**, p.45 above altars rather than graves. Here they emphasise the status of the royal burials, as another sacred place within the church. The effect is massive, simple and deeply moving: there are no images, no sweeping triumphal ornaments, and only the briefest of inscriptions, yet they convey all Friedrich's imperial and dynastic ambition. That ambition was never to be fulfilled, as his son Conrad died four years after his father, having lost Sicily to a papal army. It was the pope, as overlord of Sicily, who invited the French prince, Charles of Anjou, to be the new ruler of the island.

Miniature showing Henri de Gauchi presenting his French translation of *De regimine principum* to Philip IV of France. The text is one of a group of nine moral and philosophical treatises copied for the library of Charles V in 1372. It was lost from the royal library at some time between 1413 and 1424, but evidently remained in France.

# PART TWO

---
---

# MAGNIFICENCE

---
---

# 4 | DEFINING MAGNIFICENCE

*◆ Popes, emperors and kings ◆ Philip IV and the Church ◆ Aristotle and the* Nicomachean Ethics *◆ On the Government of Princes*

## Popes, Emperors and Kings

THE TWO GREAT POWERS OF EARLY medieval Europe, the Church and the Holy Roman Empire, both claimed that national kings were under their authority. In the pope's view, he was also the emperor's overlord, and there had been bitter quarrels over the papal attempts to enforce the Church's authority. The pope's power of excommunicating his enemies was a hugely powerful weapon, as it excluded them from all contact with Christian society. The emperor's view was that he and the pope represented the secular and spiritual realms, and were effectively equal in status. The pope had created the kingdom of Sicily for Roger II in 1130, and was his overlord. Pope Innocent III used the most formidable of all papal weapons in 1208. During a quarrel with King John he issued an interdict forbidding all church services in England: John himself was excommunicated the following year. This forced King John to submit and become the pope's vassal. But papal use of these powers did not always work: Friedrich II defied the pope and recovered Jerusalem for Christianity while excommunicated.

*Church and Empire*

The power of church and empire began to be challenged in the early thirteenth century, at a time when the title to the Holy Roman Empire was disputed by rival claimants. Lawyers were faced with the reality that the emperor no longer had any authority over kingdoms such as France. At first they invented a new category of kingdom, which was exempt from the emperor's overlordship in real terms though theoretically subject to the empire. There was never any question of the emperor having spiritual authority over kings: 'in temporal matters all peoples and all kinds are subject to the emperor, just as they are in spiritual matters to the pope'.[1]

*French claims to independence*

THE FRENCH KINGS HAD BEEN THE FIRST to explore the idea that there was justification in canon law and theology for the idea of 'kings not recognising a superior'.[2] In 1254, St Louis declared that Roman law was to be applied in France as he did not want to change the existing customary use of it. However, he made it clear that this edict excluded the idea in Roman law that kings were subject to the emperor, as France was an exception to this rule. A little later, a French writer who discussed the issue claimed that the kings of France 'for more than a hundred years had recognised no superior save God'.[3] No emperor ever directly challenged the French claim to independence. However, when in 1312 the emperor Heinrich VII tried to claim that the kingdom of Naples was subject to him, its ruler, Robert of Anjou, the great-nephew of St Louis, was able to defy the condemnation for treason which resulted from his resistance to the emperor's claim. This was all part of a series of disasters for the claims of both pope and emperor to have jurisdiction over the kingdoms of western Christendom.

The political tide therefore favoured the kings towards the end of the thirteenth century. Their economic position was also increasingly strong, with a sharp rise in purchasing power in the previous hundred years.[4] In addition, the transition to a cash economy which had underpinned the creation of capital cities had also enabled kings to raise taxes in money. Now the bankers of the Italian towns would lend against this revenue. Sovereign debt, as we would now call it, was a risky business, but it was the bankers, not the king, who shouldered this risk. The English kings alone were responsible for the collapse of at least two Florentine banks. But the confidence of kings in their new-found wealth and status coincided with the possibility of claiming independence from higher authority.

# Philip IV and the Church

PHILIP IV, GRANDSON OF ST LOUIS, came to the French throne in 1285. His reign was marked by an aggressive policy towards his vassals, and he attacked both the count of Flanders and Edward I as duke of Aquitaine in order to strengthen his hold over their territories. In the course of a quarrel which originated in an argument about the status of clergy and the question of whether the pope had jurisdiction over monarchs, Philip convened a council at Paris in 1297 to condemn the pope, Boniface VIII. This was at the instigation of two cardinals from the powerful Roman family of the Colonnas. The Colonnas had been antagonised by the pope's attempts to promote his own family, the Caetani, who were less powerful than the Colonna clan, at the expense of the latter. The dispute between Philip and Boniface led to a French invasion of Rome during which Boniface was severely beaten when the French tried to arrest him. He died a month later. The outcome was that, far from the pope gaining authority over kings, the papacy left Rome and moved to Avignon, where the French kings were able to exert influence over it.

*Philip IV and the papacy*

The idea of magnificence as a particular virtue of kings has its origin in the French court, in exactly this context of identifying the ruler as set apart from ordinary mortals. When Philip III wanted a set of secular guidelines for the education of his son, he turned to the University of Paris. Giles of Rome,* who wrote *On the Government of Princes* for the future Philip of France at some time between 1281 and 1285, belonged to the Augustinian order. He had been a teacher in Paris since 1260. He had a great reputation, was immensely well read, and indeed was hailed as 'the founder of learning'.[5]

*Philip III commissions Giles of Rome*

Giles's treatise was written at a time of intellectual and political turbulence in the church. Much of the intellectual ferment arose from the rediscovery of the works of the Greek philosopher Aristotle, and particularly from the recently completed translation of Aristotle's *Nicomachean Ethics*. Greek culture lies at the heart of European civilisation, particularly secular thought and secular institutions. Many ideas that we simply take for granted can be traced back to the great Athenian thinkers, and of these Aristotle was – and is – the most influential. His ideas derive from the work of the extraordinary generations of philosophers who taught in Athens during the fourth century BC. His master Plato was a visionary who dealt with the wide philosophical concepts which he had in turn learnt from Socrates. Plato looked upwards, to the ultimate questions of the mind or soul and its place in the eternal order of things. Aristotle, by contrast, wrote for the rulers of Athens about the practical virtues which they need in order to govern well, and presented them with a 'philosophy of human affairs'.

*The rediscovery of Aristotle*

Greece had been incorporated into the Roman empire after the battle of Corinth in 146 BC, and the Romans adopted the values of the Athenian philosophers into their culture.

---

* He is also known as Aegidio Colonna; the connection with the Colonna family in Rome is doubtful. See Appendix.

Latin authors found the pragmatic approach of Aristotle more congenial than Plato's more spiritual ideas, and, given the absence of any real code of conduct other than that of their laws, seized on Aristotle as a guide to ethics and read what we would call his scientific works with enthusiasm. Where Plato was interested in speculation, Aristotle loved observation, and wrote the first scientific accounts of the natural world. He was concerned with the perception of tangible objects, and even his discussion of abstract ideas continually invokes images from the real world. The surviving texts by Aristotle can be divided into those about the presentation of ideas (logic and rhetoric), about concepts (metaphysics and ethics), about practical affairs (politics and economics) and about what we would now call science (broadly speaking, physics and zoology, biology and psychology).

## Aristotle and the *Nicomachean Ethics*

IT IS IN ONE OF ARISTOTLE'S WORKS entitled *Nicomachean Ethics* that we encounter his views on magnificence. Here it is one of the four cardinal virtues, concerned with the getting and giving of large sums of money. This is how he defines it:

> [Magnificence] ... seems to be a certain virtue pertaining to money ... a fitting expenditure on a great thing. ... The magnificent person ... is able to contemplate what is fitting and to spend great amounts in a suitable way ...
>
> Of expenditures, we say that some kinds are honorable, such as those that concern the gods – votive offerings, sacred buildings, and sacrifices – and similarly those that concern the entire divine realm and are proper objects of ambition in common affairs: for example, if people should suppose that they ought to endow a chorus splendidly or outfit a trireme or even provide a feast for the city. But in *all* cases ... the expenditure must be fitting ... not only to the work but also to the person producing it. Hence a poor man could not be magnificent.[6]

*Magnificence defined*

We have to remember that Aristotle was writing for the Athenians, and was outlining the virtues which the rulers of Athens should possess. The city was governed by an elected body of five hundred men, who served in rotation on the council which met daily, and Aristotle sees magnificence as an ideal which the leaders of this council – if they could afford it – should pursue.

When the Romans came to study Aristotle, rather different conditions applied from those in Aristotle's native Athens. Politics at Rome in the time of the Roman republic, which lasted from around 509 BC to 27 BC, focussed much more on personalities. The Roman orator and statesman Cicero, in his essay *On invention*, begins by echoing Aristotle, and defining magnificence as an element in the virtue of fortitude. However, he describes fortitude in much more general terms, while at the same time making magnificence a question of an individual's character:

*Cicero on magnificence*

> [Fortitude is] ... a deliberate encountering of danger and enduring of labour. Its parts are magnificence, confidence, patience, and perseverance. Magnificence is the consideration and management of important and sublime matters with a certain wide seeing and splendid determination of mind.[7]

Magnificence has become an active virtue, the undertaking of great enterprises of any kind, whereas Aristotle seems to have had in mind the specific activity of public works for the good of citizens. And the meaning of the word shifted further in Roman times,

'Magnificentia' was used as a formal mode of address in the *Codex Theodosianus*, the great compilation of the laws of the Christian emperors from 312 to 439, which was in force in the Byzantine territories in Italy. For example, an edict dated AD 389 from the three ruling emperors addresses the count of the privy purse as 'Your Magnificence',[8] and this usage for officials and others lasts into the twelfth century. In western Europe, the pope addressed kings in this way.

THE LONG SHADOW OF THE ROMAN EMPIRE lies over western Christendom in the millennium after its fall. Roman rule was a remembered time of stability and prosperity, embodying Virgil's concept of the golden age; a possible model for ambitious rulers; a ruined legacy of monumental buildings which the Anglo-Saxons saw as the work of giants; and, more immediately, the root of medieval learning in the shape of the continuing use of Latin. The heritage of Latin literature was not just the famous classics translated and retold today. Alongside Virgil, Ovid and Horace, there was a vast array of books on all kinds of topics, some of which survived and were far better known than the Roman literature which we revere today. Because medieval teaching in cathedrals and in monasteries was so firmly based in the classical tradition, texts in Latin were preserved as exemplars irrespective of their content. Ancient manuscripts were kept because they were rare, even if their contents were beyond the ability of the teachers or pupils to read them. As a result, at the end of the first millennium, secular texts in Latin survived in monasteries, as specimens of the language, or as models for the different scripts in which they were written. Greek manuscripts survived in much smaller quantities, because only a very small number of scholars could read them. The shelves of a large monastic library might contain works which their guardians would have found immoral, heretical and downright dangerous if they had known what was in them.

*The survival of Latin and Greek learning*

By the twelfth century, there were a number of cathedral schools throughout Europe which existed to train the clergy. At Paris, which was the foremost intellectual centre in Europe, there were three schools, one at the cathedral, and others at the church of Ste Geneviève and at the monastery of St Victor. At the same time, in Italy, there were municipal schools run by laymen entirely outside the framework of church discipline: these were for the study of Roman law, also an inheritance of the classical past.

*The cathedral schools*

As these schools developed, adventurous scholars began to look at the obscurer books on their shelves, and, dangerously, began to think for themselves. I learnt about this intriguing time from one of the most charismatic teachers I have ever had the good fortune to encounter, David Knowles. He was theoretically a member of the Benedictine enclosed order at Downside, but had by then become professor of medieval history at Cambridge. A slight, quizzical figure, he lectured in his Benedictine habit, and it seemed as he talked that we inhabited for a while another world.

What he conveyed vividly was the sheer excitement of the eleventh and twelfth century, when the classical writings were being rediscovered, and new ideas – so often anathema to the medieval church authorities – were being proposed in the most daring fashion. He explained how the schools gradually focussed on grammar and rhetoric alone, and by the tenth century created an entirely secular syllabus based on literature, ostensibly so that the language of the church should be as eloquent as possible.

What changed in the revival of learning in the eleventh century was that scholars regained their confidence in the capacity of the human mind, and began to explore again the powers of logic. For instance, at the beginning of the twelfth century, St Anselm, archbishop of Canterbury, proposed a definition of God which depended on entirely logical reasoning,

*The new learning*

rather than invoking belief. For traditional churchmen, this was a bombshell. Reason was a creature of God, and could not be used to define its maker. Anselm's argument still resonates today in the debate between science and religion.

*Translating Aristotle*

The numerous works of Aristotle were largely unknown, and only his books on logic were available in Latin. Scholars now began to explore what else he had written, because the Greek texts had survived, unread for centuries. It was not until the mid thirteenth century, once all Aristotle's scientific works had been translated, that Robert Grosseteste, bishop of Lincoln, tackled Aristotle's *Nicomachean Ethics*. This offered a secular system of ethics, and was almost a direct challenge to the church's monopoly of moral judgements. St Thomas Aquinas reconciled Christian and Aristotelian logic and ethics in his masterpiece, the *Summa Theologica*, of which David Knowles wrote that its 'design, the symmetry, the sublimity and the beauty flow from the genius of Aquinas; the basis upon which the soaring structure rests is in the main the work of Aristotle'.[9] Aquinas had worked in the faculty of arts at the University of Paris, which came under the jurisdiction of the archbishop of Paris, Étienne Tempier. Tempier was conservative in his views, and in 1270 issued the first of a series of condemnations of doctrines which derived from Aquinas's teachings. The most sweeping of these was in 1277, when 219 propositions were listed as unacceptable and condemned as heretical.

Among these propositions were many put forward by Giles of Rome, who had been a pupil of Aquinas. He was forced to leave the university when his works were banned, and we do not know where he went; the next known record of him is in Italy in 1281. In 1285, the condemnations were reviewed and quashed, and he returned to teaching. What we do know, however, is that at some time during this exile, Giles wrote *On the Government of Princes*.

## On the Government of Princes

*Mirrors for princes*

GILES'S WORK IS ONE OF THE SO-CALLED 'mirrors for princes', a genre extraordinarily neglected – because somewhat dull! – by all but a handful of specialists. Yet it was a prodigious success: it survives in no less than 326 surviving manuscripts.[10] This success was at least due in part because it offered rulers a secular code of conduct, not always in line with the Church's teachings. More importantly, Giles portrayed the princes as they may have wished to be seen. There is no modern edition of the original; the sheer number of copies has proved an obstacle to producing a definitive text, and only preliminary studies of the manuscripts have appeared. Anyone wishing to tackle this erstwhile bestseller has to use one of the printed editions of the sixteenth century, the first of which appeared at Augsburg in 1473.

Giles of Rome advises Philip that 'magnificence is principally concerned with works for God and for the common good – and therefore with worthy persons and with oneself'. He is not an easy writer to read, as I discovered when wrestling with the passage below. I was reassured to find that I was by no means the first to find Giles difficult. In March 1403, Jacobinus, an Italian scribe working at Chioggia, ended his copy of Giles of Rome as follows:

> Here ends Brother Giles's book On the Rule of Princes, clearer and briefer than its exemplar, but in no way mutilated. Herein are all the chapters and all the arguments, with not a little of the chaff removed.

**16.** Giles of Rome presents *On the Government of Princes* to Philip IV, from a French translation of his book, possibly copied in England around 1310.

**17.** This illustration of a feast is headed 'Magnificentia', and is from a fourteenth century version of Aristotle. It shows how royal display of all kinds was now classed as magnificence.

I have done my best to abbreviate his wonderfully prolix and leisurely repetitions, but have reluctantly put the full text into an appendix.[11] Here are Giles's most important arguments:

*The king and magnificence*

> Since therefore the king is head of the kingdom and a person of honour, revered and a public figure, and it is his task to distribute the goods of the kingdom, it is absolutely fitting for the king himself to be a magnificent man.
>
> For because the king is head of the kingdom, and in this treads in the footsteps of God who is head and chief of the universe, it is absolutely necessary for the king to show himself to be a person of magnificence in respect of holy temples and in preparations of the things of God.
>
> Because the king is a public person under whom the whole community and the whole kingdom is ordered, it is crucial for him to show magnificence in works for the common good which affect the whole kingdom. Further, because he has the chief responsibility for distributing the kingdoms' goods, it is completely fitting for him to show magnificence towards worthy persons, to whom good things worthily belong. Moreover (as we said above), the king's person should be revered and worthy of honour, and it is the king's task to show magnificence towards his own person and towards the persons close to him such as his wife and sons, finding them honourable dwellings, making good marriages for them, and training them for the top army posts.
>
> ... it is right for kings themselves to have all the qualities of the magnificent man but more fully and more perfectly. And so the Philosopher in Ethics book 4 wants to say that not everybody is able to be magnificent, because not everybody is capable of great expenditure. But, as is said in the same place, such people have to be noble and famous. Therefore the nobler a man is than others, the more it behoves him to exhibit magnificent things and to have the qualities of the magnificent man.[12]

*The popularity of* On the Government of Princes

The immense popularity of *On the Government of Princes* meant that this praise of magnificence must have reached a very wide potential audience. Even if kings themselves did not read it, their advisers very probably did. There are translations into Latin, French and English. Robert, the Angevin king of Naples, had a copy made in 1310;[13] Richard II's tutor and close adviser Simon Burley owned a French copy, and seven copies can be traced in Oxford alone in the late fourteenth century.[14] Charles V and the dukes of France all probably had their copies, though there were many imitations, and a book noted in a medieval library catalogue as 'On the government of princes' is not necessarily by Giles of Rome. Its influence was everywhere. In the 1470s, the manual for the household of Edward IV, known as The Black Book, opens with a grand preamble on the history of the royal establishment, and includes a section on 'the magnificence of the king's house' which is taken from Giles of Rome.[15]

Giles writes in a stiff and rather repetitive style. He eschews the citations from classical authors and the anecdotes illustrating the argument which other writers use. This approach seems to derive from Aristotle himself. He is following the principles laid down in Aristotle's *Rhetoric*, on which he had written a commentary at about the same time. Rhetoric, in his view, was the best way of actually influencing the person who was being addressed, and achieving a practical result. 'His was a work which would confine itself to the general and the typical in an attempt to persuade both ruler and populace of the benefits of leading a life of virtue.'[16]

The crucial difference between Aristotle's definition of magnificence as a virtue and Giles of Rome's text is that the objective of magnificence is transferred from the *impersonal*, performing magnificent deeds, to the *personal*, being magnificent. Aristotle sees magnificence as the action of a virtuous man, the correct spending of wealth in honour of the gods and **17**, p.55 for the benefit of the public. Instead, Giles focusses immediately on the *person* of the ruler himself, his appearance and his entourage. In his view, this is where magnificence should start, whereas Aristotle offers no encouragement for personal splendour. The magnificent man, for the Greek philosopher, is known by his actions. For Giles, he is known firstly for his person, and secondly for his actions.

By a curious reversal, Giles's ideas influenced the reading of Aristotle's *Ethics* by the early fourteenth century. Another work that uses Aristotle as its basis, delightfully entitled *The Art of Love, Virtue and Good Living*, is in many places a close version of his original text. It is heavily illustrated, and at least two copies of it hold a real surprise. The chapter on magnificence is headed by a miniature portraying a feast, immediately below the rubric 'This chapter is on magnificence'.[17]

'IT IS ABSOLUTELY FITTING FOR THE KING himself to be a magnificent man', according to Giles. We use the word magnificence freely, but to Giles's readers this would have been something strange and new. Magnificence to us means splendour and wealth which everyone admires. We have seen – of course – that princes and kings were splendid *How to be* and wealthy before Giles's day. The difference is this: Giles defines magnificence as a virtue, *magnificent* while splendour and wealth are open to accusations of extravagance and pride. What might be seen as a negative and selfish display becomes a prerequisite of kingly behaviour.

Rulers – princes as well as kings – nonetheless needed reassurance that they ruled legitimately. Election by acclamation had been one of the original ways by which kings were chosen. Now there was no such interaction between the king and his people, and the king needed to show that he and his dynasty were the rightful lords. When Giles wrote his book *On the Government of Princes*, he was telling the future Philip IV what he wanted to hear: that kings were a race apart, and that this new idea of magnificence was a natural virtue of kingship, which kings should demonstrate.

For example, Giles recommended that in order to be magnificent, the king must dress in the finest garments. This was by no means a novelty: in the twelfth century Henry II had been criticised for preferring the practical clothing of a man of action to royal robes. Henry was one of those rare kings able to project a royal image without adopting the style expected of the ruler of a kingdom. Lesser men needed reassurance, a means of showing that they were the legitimate king, the true representative of the royal dynasty, should it be called in question. Giles provides the theoretical justification for royal splendour, at the same time rechristening it as the virtue of magnificence.

It is a staging point in the gradual changes of approach which mean that by the end of the fifteenth century a great occasion or a great building sends a different kind of message to a different kind of audience. That audience will understand magnificence as a vital part of what is presented to them.

# 5 | THE IMAGE AND PERSON OF THE PRINCE

◆ *The prince in person: appearances* ◆ *Coins and seals* ◆ *The prince's dress*
◆ *Materials* ◆ *Opulence: embroidery,* opus anglicanum ◆ *Fashion*
◆ *The prince's crowns* ◆ *The prince's jewels* ◆ *Gems and jewels*
◆ *The prince's armour* ◆ *The prince's portraits*

## The Prince in Person: Appearances

'WHAT DOES YOUR PRINCE LOOK LIKE?' That is a question that few people before the sixteenth century would have been able to answer. Magnificence is essentially a visual concept, centring on the image of the prince himself, and that image was only familiar to a handful of people, the close associates of the prince, who had seen him in person. For most of the population, their ruler would have been a remote figure, irrelevant to their daily lives: even the world of castle and court was a mystery to them. If their prince had suddenly appeared to them in full state, their reaction might well have been that of Perceval in Chrétien de Troyes's French romance of that name, written in around 1180. Perceval, brought up in remote surroundings, reacts to his first encounter with a fully armed and mounted knight by falling to his knees, and saying to the knight 'Are you God?'. The world of castle and court scarcely existed for most people.

### Coins and seals

THE PORTRAIT OF THE PRINCE MOST VISIBLE to his subjects was of course that on his coinage. Until the fourteenth century the silver penny or its equivalent was almost the only coin in general circulation, and the crude crowned head roughly engraved in a die and struck into silver with a hammer was hardly a likeness. Gold coins, which would only be seen by the wealthiest and most influential of the king's subjects, were a different matter. In 1231, Friedrich II issued a gold coin in Sicily, showing him as a Roman emperor, with a stylish profile head probably taken from the antique. His successor as king of Sicily two decades later, Charles of Anjou, has a recognisable portrait, again in profile, on a much cruder coin minted on his accession in 1266. In France, England and Flanders there was *The war of* fierce competition to issue the largest and most valuable coin. Philip IV's coinage of 1296 *the coins* began the series, and established the model for subsequent coinages until the end of the fourteenth century. On the largest coin the king is shown enthroned with regalia and royal robes against an architectural background, with the French lilies on a shield or as an overall pattern. This pattern was repeated by Philip VI and Charles V of France, and when Edward III introduced the first English gold coinage in 1344, he too used an image of himself enthroned, inscribing it 'Edward king of England and France' in accordance with his claim to the French title. But his florin was noticeably larger than the French example, weighing half as much again. Partly because of this, and a miscalculation of the ratio between the new English gold coins and the existing silver coins, the issue was not a success. However,

**18.** The emperor as successor to imperial Rome: gold augustalis of Friedrich II.

**19.** Edward III commemorates his victory over the French fleet at Sluys in 1340.

**20.** Jean II portrays himself as a knight on horseback.

**21.** Edward prince of Wales and Aquitaine marks his victory at Poitiers, where he fought on foot.

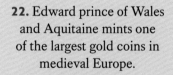

**22.** Edward prince of Wales and Aquitaine mints one of the largest gold coins in medieval Europe.

**23.** Charles VII as duke of Aquitaine portrays himself as Samson, slaying the English lion.

its replacement, a gold 'noble', was larger still, and bore a defiant portrait of the king armed and on board ship, a stark reminder of the English domination of the seas since Edward's destruction of the French fleet at Sluys in 1340.

The war of the coins continued in the duchy of Aquitaine, where Edward issued an almost exact imitation of the French 'enthroned' coins, also in 1344. These were replaced with a warlike image of the king, marching in full armour, in 1361, a riposte to Jean II's gold 'franc' showing him armed and on horseback issued the previous year: the English had won the battle of Poitiers by fighting dismounted. However, when Edward conferred the duchy of Aquitaine on his son, the Black Prince, in 1362 the prince reverted to the 'enthroned' image, on coins heavier than those of the French kings. Charles, dauphin of France, produced a new propaganda image when he became duke of Aquitaine after the English had been defeated, in the shape of a gold coin issued in 1469, on which he was shown as Samson fighting a lion and forcing its jaws apart.[1]

These pieces were largely 'money of account', handled only by great merchants, bankers and of course the royal exchequers. Of all the pieces, the noble of Edward III probably had the widest circulation because of the extensive English trading connections with Scotland, Flanders and the Hanse towns in Germany and the Baltic.[2] The gold noble in England was minted in large quantities from 1351 onwards; the triumphant image of the king on shipboard would have struck a chord with merchants and the nobility who followed eagerly the newsletters which reported the English victories at Crécy – possibly the most widely reported battle in the medieval period – and Poitiers.

PRINCELY SEALS WERE ONLY SEEN BY a very limited audience, far smaller than even the relatively select group who handled gold coins. Seals had been used to authenticate documents since Roman times, and the idea of closing a letter with a piece of wax impressed with the writer's fingerprint can be traced back to China in the fourth century BC. The Romans used seals with a personal emblem, but medieval seals use heraldry as a means of identification. Small seals were used to close letters, but major legal enactments and charters were public documents – 'letters patent' is the technical term – and the document would be sealed at the foot, with the seal on a ribbon attached to the parchment. They might be displayed in certain circumstances, such as civic ceremonies, but they were largely kept carefully in private or civic archives, and only produced if required by a lawsuit. Nonetheless, they had to be of suitable appearance to match the status of the person using them.

*Types of seal*

Lead seals were more durable than wax, which had to be protected by a wooden case or by a silk or cloth bag, sometimes embroidered. Lead seals first appear in Charlemagne's time, in the ninth century, and by the late eleventh century the German emperors were using gold seals. The golden seal of Karl IV was affixed to a decree in 1356 which set out the regulations for imperial elections, which remained in force with minor amendments until the end of the Holy Roman Empire in 1806. These spectacular objects were exclusive to the emperors; even the popes used lead seals on their documents. Red wax was the most common medium, as in the impressive seal of Rudolf IV of Habsburg, which is simply a very large and beautifully executed example of a knightly seal, showing him on horseback, fully armed, with a display of heraldic shields around the border. Green wax was used by French kings as a symbol of acts which were to be permanently valid. In England both red and green wax were used; red came to be reserved for the king's personal seals in the fourteenth century. Within the small circle of high ranking officials and nobles who were concerned with such matters, the prince's seal was a special aspect of his image. Rulers often had more than one seal during their reign, reflecting changing circumstances and ambitions. The most dramatic of these changes is the alteration in Edward III's seals (and, in this case, coinage) when he claimed the throne of France in 1338, and added 'king of France' to his titles.

In the mid fourteenth century, the most important documents which were sent out under the great seal sometimes included elaborate initials in which there were miniature portraits of the ruler. One of the finest likenesses of Charles V is a pen drawing on a charter of 1366 relating to a grant to his uncle, the duke of Orléans, a small but striking sketch evidently from the life.[3] Similarly, the best contemporary depiction of Edward III and his son prince Edward is on the massive parchment which records the king's grant of the duchy of Aquitaine to Prince Edward in 1361.

*Portrait initials*

Portraits, coins and seals were the official representations of the prince, seen by many people who would never encounter him in person. His appearance and manner, however, would be remarked on and recorded by the chroniclers who came in contact with the court, either directly or through courtiers who attended it. Even in an age of limited communications, this was probably the most vital element in the establishment of his reputation.

# The Prince's Dress

IN THE THIRTEENTH CENTURY ALFONSO X of Castile, called 'the Wise', declared in his great law code known as the *Siete Partidas*, which is a kind of encyclopaedia of medieval life in Spain, that 'a king should dress with great elegance'. The reasons he gave were these:

> Dress has much to do with causing men to be recognized either as noble, or servile.
> The ancient sages established the rule that kings should wear garments of silk, adorned
> with gold and jewels, in order that men might know them as soon as they saw them,
> without inquiring for them; and the bridles and saddles with which they ride, should be
> ornamented with gold, silver and precious stones. Moreover, on grand holidays, when
> they assemble their court, they should wear crowns of gold, richly ornamented with
> gold, silver and precious stones.[4]

This was to be done 'in order to indicate the splendour of Our Lord God, whose position they occupy on earth'. The king's attire, as described by Alfonso X, has nothing to do with fashion. It is simply a richer, more elaborate version of the dress of the period, using the public display of treasure to underline the king's prestige. Alfonso and his successors ensured that this display remained unique to the king and his family by a series of regulations forbidding the wearing of such materials in public by anyone else. In 1348, Alfonso XI collected and confirmed these laws in a single ordinance.[5]

Early medieval costume was essentially simple, with relatively little distinction between rich and poor other than in the quality of the materials used. In 808 Charlemagne, in one of the many ordinances issued for his imperial estates, specified the material from which the peasants' clothing should be made, and a gradual difference according to rank begins to appear. Nobles wore a short cloak pinned at the neck over a tunic ending above the knee, and linen hose. This was the costume preferred by Charlemagne. It was modified in the tenth and eleventh century, when both the cloak and tunic became longer, with an undergarment of linen. Short tunics were still worn, with the addition of leggings. These garments were

*Early medieval costume*

**24.** The Coronation Mantle, made for Roger II. The two lions are attacking camels, symbolic of the Norman conquest of Arab Sicily. At the top the enamel stars of the clasp are Byzantine in style, with cosmogram patterns symbolising the relationship of heaven and earth from near Eastern art. It is a reminder that Sicily still had a large Arab population: the cloak was made and signed by Arab embroiderers in the service of the king.

**25.** (top) Star mantle of Heinrich II given to Bamberg cathedral soon after 1020. Based on a contemporary poem on the constellations, it has inscriptions praising the emperor.

**26.** (bottom right) The 'Eagle Dalmatic' c.1330–1340. Probably made for the emperor Ludwig IV, it is covered with imperial eagle badges, and medallions with kings and emperors on the hem. It seems to be a secular garment rather than an ecclesiastical one.

**27.** (bottom left) Henry II and Matilda from the *Gospels of Henry the Lion*, written for St Blaise's Abbey, Brunswick, around 1188. Henry is shown in the style fashionable in Germany, standing behind Matilda who is being crowned. Henry is unlikely to have worn anything of this kind, but the artist imagines him as he thinks a king should be.

modest, since cloth was mostly locally produced, and there was little international trade in more luxurious materials at this time.

The exception to this simplicity was in the ecclesiastical world, where liturgical dress, colour-coded for festivals, emerged by the twelfth century, and grew increasingly elaborate. Vestments also reflected the rank of the wearer, and we learn from critics of the luxury of these items that silk robes were in use by the fifth century AD. Even after the schism between Byzantium and Rome, papal and episcopal vestments were probably the richest that were to be seen in the West. Most of the fragments of clothing that we possess dating from before 1300 come from religious sources, such as the vestments found in the tomb of St Cuthbert, placed there after the original burial in 698, but certainly no later than 1104, which are imports from Byzantium or the Muslim world.

The splendour of church vestments undoubtedly influenced princely dress; the religious aspects of lordship linked the prince to the church hierarchy. At their coronations and on state occasions rulers wore garments which were essentially ecclesiastical in style: in the fifteenth century, at the coronation of Henry VI of England, the king was robed as a bishop during the ceremony. In 1149 the rulers of the Holy Roman Empire were granted by the pope the privilege of actually wearing full liturgical vestments, as used by priests in holy orders, on the occasion of their crowning:[6] one of these vestments was the *pluviale*, the mantle worn over the shoulders. Several of these royal and imperial mantles survive in treasuries, some in a remarkable state of preservation. The earliest date from the eleventh century and, like so many of the objects we shall discuss, come from the art of the Arab world.

The treasury at Bamberg contains three eleventh-century royal mantles, of which the most famous is that known as the star mantle of the emperor Heinrich II. This has been heavily restored, and the blue silk which makes it so striking is not original: the pieces of gold embroidery have been cut out and mounted onto it. It was given to the emperor by a certain 'Ishmahel', who was created duke of Apulia in 1020, and the presentation probably took place at that time. Heinrich then presented it to the cathedral, and an inscription to that effect was added; but it was originally designed as a secular and imperial garment. Laid flat, its impact is reduced. When it is draped on the wearer's body the effect is of a kind of vertical reflection of the heavens, appropriate to the status of the Holy Roman Emperor.[7]

The mantle of Roger II of Sicily, now in the imperial treasury at Vienna, is the most famous example of these ecclesiastical trappings of royalty, a cape of scarlet silk embroidered with the pair of facing lions which appears frequently in twelfth century Sicilian art. It is the most precious and spectacular of all surviving medieval costumes. He was crowned in 1130, and this is often described as his coronation mantle. It was actually made for a later occasion, since there is an Arabic inscription dated 1133–4 on the curved edge. This reads:

> This work was carried out in the flourishing royal workshop, with happiness
> and honour, zeal and perfection, power and efficiency, approval and good fortune,
> generosity and exaltation, glory and beauty, completing desires and hopes,
> propitious days and nights, without pausing or intervals, with honour and care,
> watchfulness and safeguard, prosperity and integrity, triumph and skill, in the
> capital of Sicily.[8]

Sewn within the inner lining of the mantle was a strip of linen, first discovered in 1980, with another Arabic inscription, which named those who had undertaken the work: Marzuq, Ali and Mahmud had embroidered it, under the supervision of Damyan, and Tumas, probably a tailor, had assembled it. The design is remarkable, and has a strong political message; it

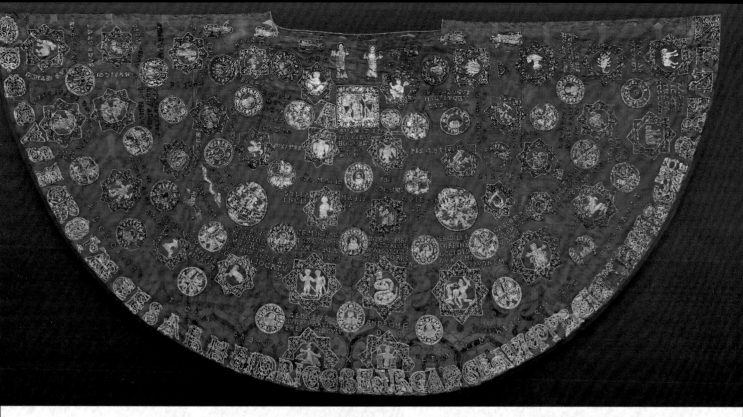

appears in several places in Palermo at this time, in the palace chapel and the so-called Hall of Roger, in the Zisa palace and in the church of the Martorana. The two lions, who appear elsewhere simply facing each other, are here both engaged in attacking a camel, having pounced on its back.*[9] It is symbolic of the Norman conquest of the Arab rulers of Sicily. When Roger put it on, the embattled beasts would have appeared on the front, fastened by two eight-pointed stars in *cloisonné* enamel just above the lions' heads. These stars, if not from Byzantium itself, were made by craftsmen trained there. The superimposed squares that form the stars symbolise the relation of the heavens and the earth, and are 'cosmograms', found in Near Eastern art for more than a millennium. The gold and patterning of pearls seem astonishingly fresh: this is delicate work for all its grandeur. Thousands of seed pearls were strung and then stitched down to create the white outlines of the creatures and the pattern of the border. The mantle was first used for the coronation of Friedrich II at Rome, and was then taken before his death to the imperial treasury at Trifels in the Rhineland with other Sicilian vestments. During the succeeding centuries it was one of the great symbolic garments of the Holy Roman Empire, used at imperial coronations. It was held by the emperors and taken with them as part of their personal treasure, until it found a permanent home at Nuremberg in 1424. It was later taken to Vienna, just before Napoleon reached Nuremberg in 1796, and has been in the imperial treasury since then. At imperial coronations from the seventeenth century, a copy of the mantle was used, which accounts for the superb condition in which we see it today.

When Arab textiles were not available, imperial robes were less dramatic. For example, a mantle which was probably used by Otto IV at his coronation has much smaller figures, which seem almost insignificant. The striking outlines on Roger's mantle are replaced by a scattering of images, including the leopard of England as a reminder that Otto was Henry II's grandson, figures of the Virgin and child, imperial eagles and stars and moons. A knowledgeable observer would have known how splendid a piece it was despite its relatively low-key decoration.[10] Another vestment in the Vienna Treasury, the 'Eagle Dalmatic', would have been worn under a cloak and may have been made for the emperor Ludwig of Bavaria in about 1320. It has embroidered badges of the German imperial eagle, in black and gold with black glass edges. However, these are sewn on to a splendid Chinese silk damask with a traditional cloud pattern, and give a much more impressive result than the plain red silk used for Otto's mantle. The neck and sleeves and hem are edged with embroidery, including the figures of thirty-four kings.[11]

IT IS ONLY IN THE TWELFTH CENTURY that we begin to find an expectation that rulers should dress splendidly in a secular setting as well. With the rise of the towns and the extended trade of the twelfth century, costume became more varied, initially through the use of dyes and patterns, and then through the import of luxury fabrics from Byzantium and, in Spain, from the Arab world.

One of the milder critical comments about Henry II of England was that he would not dress in appropriate pomp. His clothes were simple, without any regard to fashion: his boots were plain, his caps had no decoration, and he even preferred the old short tunic to the normal long cloak: hence his nickname 'Curtmantle'. Royal splendour was not his style, yet observers noted that he exuded a royal dignity even in his simple garments. However, people who did not know him automatically assumed he would wear royal robes.[12] In 1168, his daughter Matilda married Henry the Lion, duke of Saxony, one of the most powerful figures

---

* There is an Arab saying from this period that lions pray to God for strength before attacking a camel.

in the Holy Roman Empire. The gospel book which they presented to St Blaise's Abbey in Brunswick still survives. It was sold for the first time in 1983 for over £8 million, and was bought by the German government as a national treasure. It contains fifty miniatures, and is in almost perfect condition. In a picture illustrating the coronation of Matilda, she and her husband are shown with their ancestors: Henry II stands to the right of Matilda, next to another Matilda, his mother, who had been empress of the Holy Roman Empire. Henry's robes and crown are particularly splendid, because the artist envisaged him as the empress's son, and had never seen him in the flesh.

## Materials

THE IMAGE OF HENRY IN *Gospels of Henry the Lion* looks very much like the mosaic of Roger II of Sicily in his coronation robes in the Martorana at Palermo, dating from around 1150. It is in the countries bordering the Muslim world, Spain and Sicily, where the materials which were to be the staple of princely clothing from the twelfth century onwards first appear. Silk, mentioned specifically by Alfonso X as appropriate to a king, is the most 'magnificent' of all. Silk was known to the Romans as an import from China. It was cultivated in southern Spain and Sicily from the end of the ninth century onwards. By the twelfth century, it was also produced in northern Italy. The great Italian trading houses dealt in bulk in silk from that period onwards, particularly the merchants from Lucca and Florence: Lucca was pre-eminent for quality up to the fourteenth century; the city was sacked in 1314, and an exodus of its weavers began.[13] Genoa became an important centre by the late thirteenth century, famous for the variety of silk weaves that it produced. 'Silk fever' raged in the Italian towns in the fourteenth century, and Italy alone could not meet the demand for silk. It continued to be imported from further afield, from the Near East and from the Islamic world. The superior quality of the Chinese silk thread meant that imports from the Far East, rare since Roman times, were now resumed.

Silk came in various forms: plain silk, satin – originally produced in Zaitun, now Quanzhou, in China – and velvet. Velvet weaving required a special process involving an extra weave which was passed over rods, and was then cut to form the velvet pile. It probably originated in the Mongol kingdoms of central Asia, and was very rare in the West until the fourteenth century, when the silk weavers at Lucca in Italy began to produce it.[14] Damask, a silk with striking patterns formed by dull and shiny surfaces integral to the woven material, was imported from China; an early form of it has been found in London in a context which dates it to 1325–50. Satin, valued for its sheen and smooth surface, was created by using more threads in the warp or vertical threads on the loom, and passing them over four or five weft threads rather than over and under each individual weft. It was a more delicate fabric, but it is surprising that in a medieval environment, where clothes were much more exposed to damage, that any of the silks were practical for clothing. When the prince and his consort appeared in immaculate satin or velvet, the impression would have been all the greater. *Silk in western Europe*

The range of different materials available is shown in a remarkable list of the cloth bought for Edward III's coronation in 1327. Some of the items seem to have come from as far afield as China and the Mongol empire, silk brocades called 'nak', including a few with gold patterns. There were three hundred metres of the next category, figured silks woven in damask. The largest expenditure was on 'diasper' silk, which seems to have been of outstanding quality and strength, with a great deal of gold and silver thread, woven to very high technical standards. We know something of the patterns on the silks from the account *A variety of materials* of items 'furtively' taken from the wardrobe at night at some time in the following year. The descriptions of the missing pieces talk of dragons, monkeys, peacocks and falcons, with details picked out in gold. French princes held similar amounts of precious textile. A list of the cloth in the household of Charles V when he was duke of Normandy in 1363 includes thirty-six pieces of *camacas*, a fine silken material with rich patterning probably made in Italy which imitated the 'Tartar' silks, with a wide variety of patterns, typically of birds or foliage, in all kinds of colours, including one the colour of peach flowers and another with peach-coloured leaves.[15]

*Relative costs*

As to the relative costs, the finest woollen cloths from the Low Countries were often very expensive. The best cloth was woven at Brussels; light and of a fine weave. A complete set of robes and clothing for Edward III in 1349 required 250 metres of cloth, costing £75, the price of a very expensive warhorse.[16] These costly fabrics were dyed using highly expensive ingredients: scarlet dye came from the Mediterranean, and was such a byword for luxury that any costly cloth was known as a 'scarlet' cloth, and 'scarlets' ranging from black to peacock blue are entered in the accounts. Linen came from Paris and Reims. In 1343 the English royal accounts give prices for a wide range of materials.[17] Velvet with gold stripes bought in Bruges cost about £7 for a piece 8 metres long, while other velvets bought in London were never less than half that price. Cloth of gold silks cost the same as ordinary velvet, and plain silks went for £1 for 8 metres. Occasionally the design on the material was so impressive that it was specified in the bill, as with the cloth of gold on which dragons and serpents writhed on a blue background provided for the marriage of Edward's daughter Joan in 1348.[18] This sounds as if it was a piece of *raccamacas*, a heavy cloth of gold from Lucca. A close analogy would seem to be the extraordinary blue and gold silk worn by St Edmund on the famous Wilton Diptych: this depicts pairs of cranes, their throats encircled by crowns and with fanning tail feathers.

**30**, p.70

*Samite*

As an example of the use of such cloths, let us look at the fabric called samite, a fabric with a glossy sheen which was highly prized. White and single-coloured samite was originally reserved almost exclusively for priests: Henry III gave numerous pieces of samite to the clergy, and rarely ordered it for himself. He did so on the occasion of his eldest daughter Margaret's marriage to Alexander of Scotland on Christmas Day 1251: the king's robe was to be of the 'best violet samite that was to be got', with three leopards on the front and back.[19] There seems to be a tradition of using it for knighting ceremonies: it is found in that connection in England in 1306.[20] In France white samite was specified for the new knights of the short-lived Order of the Star in 1361.[21] And at the coronation of Louis II of Anjou as king of Sicily at Avignon in 1389, the young prince was clad in white samite as a symbol of purity, and the robe was lined with ermine as a mark of his status.

*Furs*

For winter clothing, furs were needed, sometimes to make whole garments, but more often to trim the clothes, sourced from the Baltic and from Russia. These too could be very luxurious, and there was a strict hierarchy according to rank which governed their use. Miniver was made from the winter belly fur of red squirrels trimmed down so that only the white was used. It was then sewn together into large pieces, and was bought in large quantities. The most sought-after fur was ermine, the white winter pelt of the stoat with a black tip to the tail. Furs supplied by the royal tailor in 1347–8 included over twenty thousand pieces of miniver, but only twenty of ermine: it was in effect reserved for the king and queen.[22] Similarly, when the first assembly and feast of the Order of the Star, founded by Jean II of France while he was still dauphin, was held at Epiphany (6 January) 1352, thousands of miniver furs were used for the knights' clothing. The princes who were knighted on the occasion were given ermine trimmings marking their royal status, at the huge cost of 240 Paris pounds for three pieces used to trim their cloth-of-gold mantles and coats.

## Opulence: embroidery, opus anglicanum

THE RICHEST GARMENTS OF ALL WERE produced by using embroidered designs. These were supplemented from the late thirteenth century onwards by the use of gold thread and jewels. The women of Anglo-Saxon England were renowned for their skill in embroidery; in later centuries, *opus anglicanum*, 'English work', was regarded as the finest available. It is not so much a specific technique or style as a generic term for English embroidery. Among the pieces taken from the tomb of St Cuthbert at Durham in 1827 were pieces of embroidery which included among the figures an inscription dating them to 909–916, and naming queen Aelflaed, wife of Edward the Elder, as the person who commissioned them. Shortly after the Norman Conquest an Italian bishop from Benevento at the council of Bari in 1098 is recorded as having an English cope 'exceedingly valuable, adorned all round with a gold fringe', grander than that worn by the pope himself on the same occasion.[23] The embroidery produced in England dominated the market for this type of dazzling costume until the mid fourteenth century, chiefly for religious purposes. The vogue for it was such that in 1246 Pope Innocent IV demanded that the Cistercian abbots in England should send him such vestments, 'if possible free of charge'.[24] Because most of the surviving examples of these great works of art are in the treasuries of cathedrals and churches across Europe, it might appear to have been largely restricted to religious vestments.[25] However, the existence of a very large number of secular vestments is attested by the English royal accounts from the late thirteenth century onwards. In the last decade of the thirteenth century, demand for it at the English court was such that a group of women seem to have been working on it in the Queen's Chamber. Among the names is that of Christiana of Enfield, who helped to create the 2,800 French *fleurs-de-lis* and English 'leopards'* for Margaret, the French wife of Edward I, which were to be used on her chamber hangings while she was in France.[26]

Opus anglicanum

Embroiderers were employed at the English court well into the fifteenth century; their apogee was probably during the reign of Edward III, when we have a large number of records of their work in the account rolls. Edward III's clothing for festivals kept them extremely busy. For instance, he appeared at the Christmas games at Guildford in 1337 in the most fantastic of all the costumes of which we have descriptions. He wore a dramatic piece of headgear, a hood covered in gold and silver ornaments, embroidered with

*Embroidery for Edward III*

> tigers holding court made from pearls and embossed with silver and gold, and decorated on another edge with the image of a certain castle made of pearls with a mounted man riding towards the castle on a horse made of pearls, and, moreover, between each tiger a tree of pearls and a tree of gold ...[27]

His costume, which was copied for his cousin Henry of Grosmont and his closest friend William Montagu, was

> decorated with the image of a castle made of silk and trimmed with gold, displaying towers, halls, chambers, walls and other pertinent things around it, and within the walls divers trees of gold, while on the breast of each tunic an embroidered figure in

* The 'leopards' in strict heraldic terminology are lions passant guardant, i.e. walking forward and looking at the viewer.

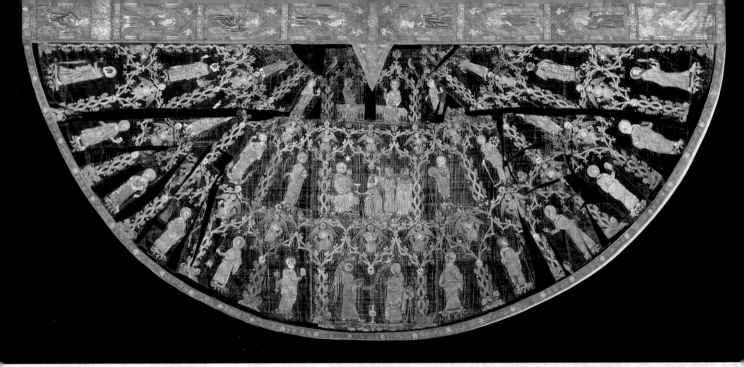

**28.** (above) The Butler Bowdon cope, based on the Gothic architecture of the mid-fourteenth century, and one of the finest examples of English embroidery (*opus anglicanum*) of the period.

**29.** (right) King Roboam from the Jesse cope, 1310–1325. The king is shown wearing a sumptuous robe with a dramatic yellow and green pattern, with a mantle whose pattern is similar to that of the cloth of the cope.

**30.** (left) In this detail from the Wilton Diptych, St Edmund is wearing a garment of blue and gold silk patterned with pairs of cranes, their necks encircled by crowns.

gold standing under a canopy on the battlements, whereas the hems of these tunics are designed in such a way in green cloth as to resemble the moats and ditches of this castle surrounded by a green field.[28]

The tunics and mantles of the king and queen and of William Montagu were trimmed with 228 golden clouds. These were clothes for a private occasion, but one which would have been witnessed by most of the courtiers; and the clerk who wrote out the description of them in the royal accounts seems to have been mightily impressed by all this.

The English court was obviously not alone in the use of these spectacular garments, but there is no real evidence of export of English embroidery to European courts. The French embroiderers were regulated by the authorities in Paris as early as 1303, and the documents list over two hundred workers plying their trade in the French capital.[29] These regulations tell us much about the organisation of the trade, but sadly very little of their work survives. Among the rules is a prohibition of the use of candles, even to supplement daylight: but pressure from royal customers caused this to be withdrawn in 1316. In both French and English accounts, there are records of additional payments made for producing garments to a tight deadline, and for candles and food for those who worked on such projects.[30]

Among the few surviving details of French embroidery is a blue velvet surcoat made for the dauphin Charles in 1352 which had on it flowering trees, with flowers picked out in pearls, and what are described as 'panthers of various kinds', also worked in pearls, forming a circle round each of the 131 trees, which cost 660 *livres* in Paris money.[31] And still the search for even richer effects went on: the finishing touch might be gold leaf stamped onto the garments, which could be used to pattern them with heraldic arms.

*French embroidery*

We can gain some idea of what thirteenth-century royal garments were actually like from the extraordinary assembly of textiles recovered from the tombs in the monastery of Las Huelgas in Burgos. Here, in what is justly called a 'pantheon' of the royal house, the Spanish kings, who were Alfonso X's immediate predecessors, lie under the banner carried at the great victory over the Muslims at Las Navas de Tolosa in 1212. The tomb of Alfonso VIII, the victor in the battle, who died in 1214, revealed that he was buried in a quite exceptional set of clothing, clothing which was to set the pattern for other European monarchs of the period, notably Henry III and St Louis.[32]

*Spanish royal garments*

The reason for the presence of such robes in the tomb was a particularly Spanish tradition. In the law code of his great-grandson, Alfonso X, it was specified that 'neither rich clothes nor valuable ornaments, such as gold or silver, could be put aside for the dead, except for a very few people like the King or the Queen or their children.'[33] What distinguished the rich clothes of the princely family was not just the fact that they were silk, but the dramatic use of colour. Alfonso VIII was buried in a cape and tunic of a very bright blue. The dye was probably indigo, a luxury available through Spanish contacts with the Arab world. It was ornamented with simple gold stripes, a classic colour combination which would have been both striking and unfamiliar at that time. Blue was normally obtained from woad, which did not produce this brilliant colour, and it had become associated with the image of the Virgin Mary, whose cult came into prominence in the twelfth century. By the mid thirteenth century we find both St Louis and Henry III dressing in blue robes. This colour was specifically reserved for royalty by Alfonso X in 1267, when he instructed the people of Murcia that they could dye with any colour they wished, except for indigo blue and three specific shades of red, including crimson (kermes), which, like indigo, was Arabic in origin.[34] A similar 'reserved' colour was the imperial purple of the Byzantine empire, made from the shell

**31-34**, p.73

of a sea-snail; the dye varied widely in colour, but was valued for its sheen and its resistance to fading.

The patterned weaves which decorate twelfth-century robes, as in the examples of Roger II and Henry II, began to include heraldic devices by the beginning of the thirteenth century: Alfonso VIII's coffin was lined with a green cloth with red shields on it. The clothing of Fernando de la Cerda, who died in 1275, eldest son of Alfonso X, has similar heraldic patterning, on his mantle, his *pellote*, and his beret. His sword and embroidered belt were also found in his tomb, and give an almost complete picture of the civilian dress of a prince of the mid thirteenth century.

## Fashion

FASHION IS VERY MUCH A MATTER for the court in the early middle ages. Clothing styles were simple, and the basic cut of the upper garment was a T shape, made of two pieces of cloth sewn back to back. Complaints about outrageous costume date back to the eleventh century. It is only after the introduction of the sleeves, cut separately and sewn on, that close-fitting tailored garments appear. Buttons were also a real novelty, first recorded in England in 1337.[35] These tight garments are in evidence in court circles from about 1320 onwards, and miniatures in manuscripts show the new styles. There was still wariness about the innovation; a dramatic change occurred after the onset of the disaster of the Black Death in 1348–9. Gilles le Muisit, abbot of Tournai, tells us that both men and women abandoned the extreme fashions they had worn, and the women gave up their extravagant hairstyles. Furthermore, trade was severely disrupted for a time, and the imported fabrics on which the tailors depended for their new creations were difficult to obtain.

Beginning in 1361, there are renewed complaints about new-fangled fashions. In England, the chronicler at Malmesbury Abbey declared that 'the whole of English society' was plunged into a 'fury of pride' over new styles of clothing. Men wore 'gowns' which no longer opened down the front and hung loose at the back, but were tight and made them look like women from the back. Their hoods were also tight, and worse still, they were buttoned and covered with gold and silver embroidery and precious stones, with liripipes down to their heels, as if they were jesters. And there was a silk garment called a paltok: to these their multi-coloured hose were attached by ties. All this cost a fortune, and the wearers of these monstrosities were victims of every kind of vice and weakness. For all this, the monk concludes, 'it is to be feared that a dire punishment from God will follow'. When the plague broke out again in 1365, the chronicler at Reading Abbey declared that the outbreak of the 'pokkes' was directly related to these fashions. In France, in the same year, Jean de Venette noted that beaked shoes were all the rage, and that both Charles V and the pope had issued edicts against the new fashions. He is quite right about the edicts, but the shoes are only a variant on those described in Milan in 1340 and indeed by Orderic Vitalis two centuries before that.[36]

Yet court fashions continued to move on, despite the jeremiads of the chroniclers. We might expect tirades from the clergy about 'magnificence', but the acceptance of the idea that the king should dress splendidly seems to have precluded this. Christine de Pizan describes Jeanne de Bourbon, wife of Charles V, at one of the annual court feasts, perhaps Christmas or Easter,

> crowned or adorned with a great richness of jewels, clothed in royal robes, long, wide and flowing ... or in royal cloaks made of the most costly cloth of gold or silk, adorned

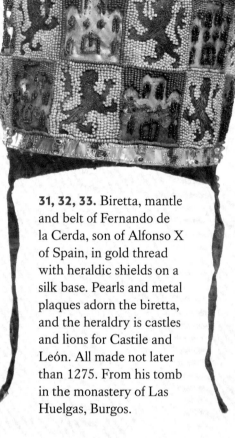

**31, 32, 33.** Biretta, mantle and belt of Fernando de la Cerda, son of Alfonso X of Spain, in gold thread with heraldic shields on a silk base. Pearls and metal plaques adorn the biretta, and the heraldry is castles and lions for Castile and León. All made not later than 1275. From his tomb in the monastery of Las Huelgas, Burgos.

**34.** (below) Overgown of Eleanor of Castile, queen of Aragon. Silk embroidered with designs and lettering of Arab origin, made not later than 1244.

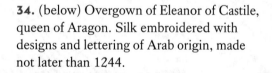

with a splendour of rich stones and precious pearls with belts, buttons and straps; these clothes she changed according to the different times of day, as is the custom of kings and popes, so that it was a marvel to see the queen on such occasions.[37]

For the knighting of the princes of Anjou in 1389,[38] the royal accounts show that the two princes, their two younger brothers and two cousins were all provided with vermilion tunics and cloaks trimmed with miniver or squirrel fur. There is also a list of the clothes provided for the eldest son, Louis for the various stages of the ceremony, which his brothers probably also received. Firstly there was a brown robe trimmed with lamb fur for use at the start, while he was still a squire – probably the flowing gown in an antique style described by the chronicler – and an outfit of fine violet cloth for the preliminaries of knighting. Then, for the knighting itself, there were both the vermilion tunic and cloak and a tunic and mantle in cloth-of-gold trimmed with ermine. And there are three more robes, trimmed with miniver, in different colours, including two shades of green. Finally, there are two dancing suits for the evening. The way in which princes changed their clothing during the day of the festival was designed to impress the onlookers with the sheer richness of the royal court.

*Clothes for a knighting ceremony*

To cap it all, there were magnificent hats, of which the French were particularly fond. Perhaps the most extravagant creation was the velvet 'parade' hat made by Kathelot the hatter for the wedding of Blanche of Bourbon to the king of Castile in 1352, on which embroidered gold figures of children keeping pigs under oak-trees 'as if they were alive' formed the main theme, with flowers, pearls and other ornaments.[39] For the knighting of the princes of Anjou in 1389, hats embroidered in gold and green with flowers and foliage of broom, the royal device, were supplied.[40]

*Kathelot's hats*

A very few pieces from this period survive. After Edward prince of Wales died in 1376 his funeral achievements were placed above his tomb. They include a very richly embroidered heraldic jupon, which would have been worn in processions and at tournaments. It is a ceremonial garment that was worn over armour, and it displays the prince's arms, which are the royal arms of England, with a 'label for difference' which indicates that he is the king's eldest son. It is currently being restored for the second time, as it has been in the open in the cathedral for over six hundred years, with no real protection. A replica is being created, which will give much more of an impression of what this heraldic jacket was really like. From France there are two *pourpoints* from the 1370s, also called *jaques*, which are immediately recognisable as the forerunner of the jacket of today. That in the museum at Lyons belonged to Charles of Blois; it is cut from twenty-six pieces of oriental cloth of gold, and has thirty-four buttons down the front. It is very much a tailored and designed garment, the sharpest possible contrast to the draped clothing of the beginning of the century.[41]

In the 1360s, a long overgarment with flared sleeves and a trailing skirt called the *houppelande* in France and the *goun* in England, made its appearance, and this remained fashionable for much of the next century. It was sometimes open at the front, and showed an expensive gown beneath. We have details of the thirty-six *houppelandes* of Philip the Bold and of the young Jean the Fearless, and these show how the explosion of fashionable styles ended with a return to something nearer the early fourteenth-century robes. Instead of the shaping of the garments, it was now the ornament that predominated again. Philip ran the gamut of princely colours, gold, scarlets, crimson and every kind of red, often in velvet. On these were embroidered his badges, 'wreaths of broom with pearls and suns within', usually on the sleeves. Other examples had four oak branches from the waist to the shoulders, or thorns and daisies (*marguerites*) with the letters P and M to celebrate his marriage to Marguerite duchess of Flanders. The most spectacular was a *houppelande* ordered by Philip for the festival held to welcome Jean back from captivity in Turkey in 1398: this was of cloth-of-gold, with seven spiral ribbons of different colours running round the body. Such costumes required vast amounts of cloth: for just one of the *houppelandes* 14 metres of cloth-of-gold was ordered. And as a finishing touch, quantities of the most expensive fur were used to trim the cuffs and collar.[42]

For Marguerite and her daughters, there is little mention of *houppelandes*, which were only later worn by women: instead they have *cotes* and *corsets*, tight-fitting tunics. These, like the prince's garments, were made of very rich material, and often embroidered. In 1392, Philip gave Marguerite 278 gold letters P and M and hawthorn and trefoil leaves to sew onto a sleeve, traditionally the left sleeve, for one of her tunics. This passion for patterns based on plants is something that is general in both art and architecture of the period: the tracery of late Gothic buildings and the pages of illuminated manuscripts are both enriched by this kind of decoration. Jean the Fearless in his youth adopted the hop as his device, the most rampant of all plants, and embroideries were ordered accordingly, often on a black background. Black was to become the hallmark of the Burgundian dukes, partly as symbolic mourning for the violent death of Jean the Fearless himself, but also as a fashion statement, a deliberate turning away from the riotous colours of the last years of Charles VI and his court. Dark colours could also be a statement of princely magnificence, and all the Burgundian dukes wore them for their portraits: Philip the Bold is shown in dark purple, while his successors are all in black. Even Charles the Bold, famed for his love of cloth-of-gold, is portrayed in this colour.

*Designs and devices*

THE MOST REMARKABLE FEATURE of the dress of great ladies of the late fourteenth and fifteenth century is their headdresses. Hairstyles had become quite distinctive in the 1350s, as shown in the effigy of Philippa of Hainault, with the careful framing of the face in plaits. By the end of the century, the current fashion was for increasingly complicated hair-dressing, which the poet Eustache Deschamps nicknamed 'harribouras'. Rich coifs for the hair were the support for a whole structure of cloth, gold embroidery and jewels, with a padded *bourrelet* or *cornette* at the core of it. The *bourrelet* was said to have been introduced by Queen Isabeau of France and was a circlet of rich material stuffed with cloth, forming a kind of coronet raised at each side.[43] This headdress grew into the *hennin* by 1429, which could be as much as 60 cm high, and consisted of two 'horns' around which a veil was coiled, falling freely down the wearer's back. Moralists, as usual, had something to say about this. Monstrelet tells us that a Carmelite preacher made children run after their wearers, crying 'Au hennin', rather as in Victorian England children would shout 'Beaver!' at a bearded man.[44] Headdresses of various kinds form a large part of Marguerite's jewels; they were described as being 'the new fashion' in 1408, so Marguerite was evidently a leader in this respect.[45]

*Headdresses and hairstyles*

# The Prince's Crowns

'MOREOVER, ON GRAND HOLIDAYS, WHEN they assemble their court, they should wear crowns of gold, richly ornamented with gold, silver and precious stones', declares Alfonso X after he has described the prince's dress.[46] Sixty years later, in 1344, Edward III held a festival at which he announced his intention to found an Order of the Round Table. Edward deliberately invited not only knights but also wealthy citizens from London to an impressive gathering at Windsor. In particular, he invited ladies, who filled the great hall for the feast on Sunday 19 January. Three days of jousting followed, and on the Wednesday night

> the king had it proclaimed that no lord or lady should presume to depart, but should stay until morning, to learn the king's pleasure. When the morning of Thursday came, at about nine o'clock the king caused himself to be solemnly arrayed in his most royal and festive attire; his outer mantle was of very precious velvet and the royal crown was placed upon his head. The queen was likewise dressed in most noble fashion.

When mass had ended, the congregation gathered outside, where the king

> was presented with the Bible, and laying his hand on the Gospels, swore a solemn oath that he himself at a certain time, provided that he had the necessary means, would begin a Round Table, in the same manner and condition as Arthur, formerly king of England, established it, namely to the number of 300 knights, and would cherish it and maintain it according to his power, always adding to the number of knights.[47]

See p.282
Edward had had to solve an embarrassing problem before he could hold this ceremony, because he had pawned his great crown in Flanders in 1339 when he was in desperate need of funds to pay his allies. His agents succeeded in getting it returned in time, and were well rewarded.

Very few crowns survive from the later Middle Ages: they were often remodelled to keep up with fashion, while others were melted down in times of financial stress. Martí I of Aragon, like his predecessors since its conquest in 1282, was also king of Sicily, and his crown, now in Barcelona, has been identified as Sicilian. Its form, with arches supporting a cross and a double ring, goes back to Byzantine origins; the lower ring is at the opposite extreme, in the latest Gothic style. Even more striking is his throne, also at Barcelona: sadly, this is used as the display shelf or *ostensorium* for a large monstrance[48] which I can only describe as an eyesore. The magnificence of his throne has to be recreated from an old photograph by modern technology.

*Charles V's crowns*
Inventories drawn up by the royal treasuries tell us a good deal about what has been lost, and some of them list the crowns in a complete hierarchy. At the head of these lists are the great crowns. In 1363, an inventory drawn up for the future Charles V, then duke of Normandy, starts with a crown made for his father Jean II to wear at the inauguration of the French chivalric Order of the Star in 1352. It is followed by another of the same weight made by the order of the duke which had a mass of jewels on it. There were eight *fleurs-de-lis* round it, with nine rubies, three sapphires, twenty pearls and twelve diamonds mounted on the main *fleur-de-lis* alone. In 1400, it was described as 'the king's best crown', and does not seem to have been surpassed by any subsequent crown.[49]

When Charles V died in 1380, he owned forty-seven crowns, coronets, chaplets and circlets, including those intended for use by his family. This compares with Richard II's total of twenty-two in 1399.[50] Charles had commissioned two other crowns, on a less grand scale than the best crown: one of these was called the 'crown with long emeralds', on which the less valuable emeralds replaced the sapphires of the best crown. It was nonetheless highly regarded: when the emperor Karl IV visited the king in 1378, he asked to see it, and it was brought specially from the chateau of Beauté outside Paris. The third new crown was that containing a thorn from the relic of the crown of thorns, for which St Louis had built the Sainte-Chapelle; thorns from it were occasionally given to favoured fellow-monarchs. Many of the smaller crowns, it was noted, had been partly dismembered to supply jewels for the new crowns. Among the total of seven great crowns were the pieces of the crown of the

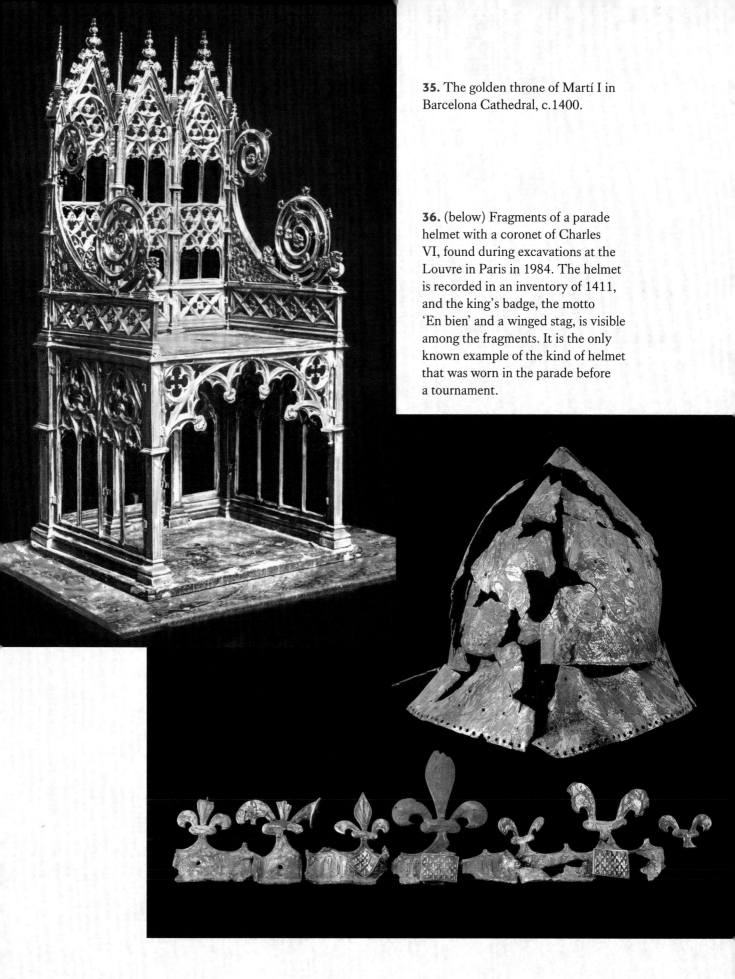

**35.** The golden throne of Martí I in Barcelona Cathedral, c.1400.

**36.** (below) Fragments of a parade helmet with a coronet of Charles VI, found during excavations at the Louvre in Paris in 1984. The helmet is recorded in an inventory of 1411, and the king's badge, the motto 'En bien' and a winged stag, is visible among the fragments. It is the only known example of the kind of helmet that was worn in the parade before a tournament.

Order of the Star, which, the clerk notes, had been taken apart in Jean II's reign. The great crown of Charles's wife Jeanne de Bourbon was also included in the list.[51]

*The inventory of Richard II's treasure*

A very full inventory of Richard II's treasure was drawn up by Henry IV's clerks soon after the latter seized the throne in 1399. It was rumoured to amount to a massive hoard of cash, jewels and plate, and when the document was rediscovered in the early 1990s, it confirmed Richard II's pre-eminent reputation for magnificence among English medieval kings.[52] The first section of the roll lists eleven crowns, of which one survives. The most costly of them is called a 'great crown', and is valued at a total of £33,584, possibly the highest figure put on any object in a medieval inventory. Of this amount only £251 was ascribed to the gold content of the piece, the gems and pearls being estimated at the round figure of 50,000 marks or £33,333. In a document recording it as being in Edward III's possession in 1339, it is called 'the hereditary and preeminent crown of England'.[53] Its history before Edward III's reign is not clear, but it may originally have been created for King John and subsequently remodelled. It was probably embellished with additional jewels over a period of time, though the direct relationship of the 1339 loan to the 1399 valuation – the loan is exactly half the latter figure – implies that it was unchanged during the reigns of both Edward III and Richard II. Its function was as the great coronation crown, and it was used in 1344 when Edward III revived the defunct Anglo-Norman tradition of crown-wearing.[54] He continued this practice after the Windsor festival, wearing crowns for great feasts, as an account of the keeper of the Tower armouries for 1353–60 shows: the crowns were taken, with other plate, 'for the king's feasts at Christmas, Easter, St George's, Pentecost and All Saints, to Windsor, Woodstock, Marlborough, Hampstead Marshall, Reading and Eltham at a total cost of £10 8s. 6d.'.[55]

In France, we find great nobles in possession of crowns, which are probably what we would now call coronets. When Raoul de Nesle, constable of France, was killed in the great disaster of the battle of the Golden Spurs in 1302, the inventory of his possessions included five crowns, the most expensive of which was valued at 450 *livres*.[56] Interestingly, the document specifies that they were made up of separate pieces, ranging from twelve to eighteen; the crown of Anne of Bohemia, discussed below, shows how this was done. Even when taken apart, crowns were liable to damage: Yolande duchess of Bar paid to have a crown repaired which was missing two fleurons, two sapphire, one balas ruby, and one emerald (which she still had).[57]

## The Prince's Jewels

*Gold resources in western Europe*

THE RESTRICTION OF THE USE OF GOLD and jewellery of the highest quality to the royal family and its entourage was fairly consistent throughout the medieval period. Furthermore, it was the male members of this group who wore the most resplendent pieces. Gold and jewels were an essential part of the king's distinctive appearance, worn as ornaments, decorating his clothing and his horse's harness. Gold was scarce in the Middle Ages, as the few active gold mines in western Europe produced relatively little. So when it started to be used for coinage from the thirteenth century onwards, partly as a symbol of princely prestige, the stocks rapidly diminished. Gold and silver coin was often 'exported' in return for goods from the East, and since the Islamic world bought little from Europe, this reduced the money in circulation in the West. The discovery of substantial gold mines in Hungary, at Kremnica, in about 1320, provided temporary relief, but the search for new sources of gold was to be one of the driving forces behind the voyages of exploration at the end of the Middle Ages.[58] In Castile, the export of gold was frequently forbidden, and the ability of rulers to maintain a gold coinage was often a problem. The tenuous nature of the gold supply is underlined by the effect of one battle: when Alfonso XI defeated Abu Hassan, king of Morocco, at Salado in 1340, and seized his camp, so much bullion was among the booty that the price of gold and silver in Castile is said to have fallen by a sixth.[59]

## Gems and jewels

> Carbuncle and moonstone, balas and gagathromeus, onyx and chalcedony, coral and bestion, union and ophthalmite, ceraunite and epistites, hierachite and heliotrope, pantherus and androdragma, prasine and sagda, hæmatite and dionise, agate and celidony, sardonyx and chalcophonite, cornelian and jasper, aetites and iris, gagate and ligurite, asbestos and cegolite, galactite and hyacinth, orites and enhydrite, absist and alabandine, chrysolectrus and hyæna, emerald and loadstone, sapphire and pyrites. Here and there stood also turquoise and liparite, chrysolite, ruby, paleise and sardine, diamond and chrysoprase, malachite and diadochite, peanites and medusite, beryl and topaz.[60]

THIS EXTRAORDINARY LIST of gemstones conveys something of the medieval fascination with jewels, which were not only valued for their rarity and beauty, but played a part in medicine and alchemy, each having its own particular qualities. Wolfram von Eschenbach wrote his romance about Parzival and his quest for the Grail in the early thirteenth century. He names these stones as the ornaments and protective magic on the bedspread under which Amfortas, the wounded Grail king, lies, the most royal of rulers and yet the most tormented by sickness. The ambon* in the cathedral at Aachen, with its frontal studded with precious stones and large pieces of agate and rock crystal, shows how jewels were used in eleventh-century Germany. Very few precious stones are found in Europe, they had to be imported from the East. Stones were not cut in the modern style until the late fourteenth century; instead, they were polished into *cabochons*, more or less regular oval shapes, which were then mounted, usually on gold. The size of the stones was probably more important than the setting, as the *cabochon* finish made it difficult to create the kind of highly stylised montage of patterns characteristic of modern jewellery.

*The Grail king's jewels*

Cut stones are mentioned in the records of the guild of jewellers in Paris in 1381, when it was reported that a German workman swore on oath that he could cut diamonds.[61] Soon afterwards, we hear of squared (*quarre*) gems, and both pictures and inventories bear witness to cut stones. By 1416 diamonds are being cut in the shape of hearts. Because diamonds benefit most from cutting and facetting, mentions of other stones, such as sapphires, being cut are rare, though in modern jewellery this is how they are usually presented. Portraits by the van Eyck brothers and other Burgundian court painters depict the mixture of *cabochon* and cut stones which resulted.

Stones were often named: the best-known example is the Black Prince's balas ruby, which is in fact a red spinel rather than a true ruby. He accepted it in part payment of his fee for restoring Pedro II to the Spanish throne in 1367. It is possible that it was incorporated into the so-called 'Spanish crown' which was inherited by Richard II in 1377 (and pledged immediately for a loan).[62] It remains part of the English coronation regalia to this day. The greatest connoisseur of the late fourteenth century, Jean duke of Berry, collected jewels in the same way that he amassed illuminated manuscripts. He and his brothers, Philip

*Collecting gemstones*

* The place from which the gospel was read during services.

of Burgundy and Louis of Anjou, accumulated extraordinary hoards of jewels in the last quarter of the fourteenth century, despite the disastrous state of France under Charles VI, their nephew – who also amassed his own hoard.[63]

In more favourable times these objects were very much part of the prince's splendour. Jean de Berry had about thirty stones of such quality that they were named.[64] Twenty-four of these were either true rubies (rubies of Alexandria) or the less colourful balas rubies or red spinels. Small sapphires were quite common, but larger stones seem to have been rarer or less fashionable than rubies. And good pearls were scarce. All the rubies were mounted in rings, which was the typical way in which men wore jewels. None of the balas rubies seem to have been used in this way. Even though they are named, they are all part of objects such as crosses. One of the sapphires, both diamonds and the emerald are also in rings. The one exception is the Great Sapphire of Burgundy, once the property of Jean's brother Philip of Burgundy, which 'used to be in a golden collar', and seems to have been an intaglio or gemstone carved in the antique style.

*Pearls*

Pearls, which were used to outline figures and patterns on costumes, were bought in very large quantities. The quantities of pearls used were very high. In 1298, Elisabeth, the bride of Albert I, king of the Germans and heir to the Holy Roman Emperor, had a dress embroidered with six thousand gilded pearls, six thousand corals, three strings of multi-coloured pearls and five ounces of white pearls.[65] In 1343, 165 large pearls and two thousand small pearls were bought for the English royal family. This kind of level of use across Europe led to shortages, in the absence of the cultivated pearls of today. The French were particularly fond of pearls. In 1338 Raoul I duke of Eu, constable of the royal household, had a cloak decorated in gold and pearls, showing three ladies in a ship fishing for hearts, and another with a knight hawking for rabbits, very much in the manner of Edward's garments the previous year.[66] In 1351, an account for the king of Navarre (who was a member of the French royal family) notes that a velvet robe intended for the queen of France could not be completed because the necessary pearls were not to be found. And in 1356, a chronicler remarked that the use of pearls in the new fashions had resulted in a steep rise in price.[67] Charles d'Orléans once wore a robe whose sleeves were embroidered with 568 pearls arranged to depict the music for a song he had composed in his lady's honour.[68]

*Badges and belts*

Other forms of ornament were enamel plaques and paste jewels sewn onto garments, and also 'wafers', very thin gold plaques, often in the shape of coins or even of the badge of an order of knighthood such as the Garter. No less than a pound of gold was supplied for two gowns made for Edward's daughter Joan for her bridal trousseau in 1348. The account for the inauguration of the Order of the Star gives a very detailed list of jewellery for the same purpose. Fifty gold settings with small rubies and emeralds were supplied to be sewn onto garments; a small gold chaplet was to be broken up and eleven groups of pearls on it and ten rubies were to be reused, and the gold to be returned to the treasury. Eight more rubies and a large pearl were needed to make up four badges of the Star for the French royal princes, while the dauphin's badge took six rubies and six groups of pearls.[69] In 1389, the gifts at the knighting of the princes included two gold belts, one on a green backing with eleven rubies, nine sapphires and ninety-eight pearls, the other on a red backing studded with gold nails and a clasp with six pearls and a sapphire. Resplendent belts such as these were a particular feature of later fourteenth-century costume, and attracted much hostile comment from chroniclers.[70] After the 1389 jousts, actual gold coins removed from doublets which had been made for the duke of Burgundy for the occasion were valued at over a thousand francs.[71]

DESIGNS ON CLOTHING OFTEN HAD a message to convey, sometimes personal, as in the case of Charles d'Orléans's embroidered pearls, and sometimes more in the nature of propaganda. Such designs needed to be drawn up specifically for the occasion. Even small items could be incredibly rich. The dauphin had a pair of slippers made in 1353 with 110 large pearls, with gold fretwork and gold leaves, and lions framed by the fretwork, all worked in Cyprus gold thread.[72] And the hem of one of queen Philippa's corsets or jackets in the 1360s imitated the fashion for ribbons bordering a garment: in this case, the ribbon was of plate gold, with an untranslatable motto ('Ich wyndemuthe') embroidered on it in coloured silk, gold and pearls.

Jewels fashioned as collars were worn both by men and women, and the prominence of such objects made them a popular way of indicating allegiance or friendship: when Richard II and Charles VI met at Ardres near Calais in 1396 to negotiate Richard's marriage to Isabella of France, they exchanged collars, which probably bore their respective heraldic emblems, the white hart and the badge of broom. In 1399, Richard II owned eighteen such collars, and the French badge recurs on five of these. It is from this period that the widespread use of collars of this kind dates. At the same time, the use of expensively wrought brooches, which had become fashionable for women, now became equally popular for men as well. Their original purpose had been to fasten garments; now they decorated hats and were worn prominently on dress. Again, the heraldic element was important, and symbols of personal significance, such as Richard II's white hart, or of the new monarchical orders of knighthood such as the Order of the Garter, were frequent, though many were simply decorative. Two Garter badges are listed in the inventory of his goods made in 1399 after his death; one of these weighed nearly a kilo and was among the most valuable items.

*Collars*

Besides these, there were also a wide variety of lesser ornaments, belts, buckles and clasps. Ornamented buckles have a very long history; some of the most splendid items in the seventh-century Sutton Hoo treasure are buckles and clasps, and when fashion changed in the fourteenth century and belts became prominent again, the jewelled buckles reappear. Richard II had an enormously expensive set of buttons, valued at £852, representing eagles set with sapphires, balas rubies and pearls. These were evidently intended for use with a matching silk belt with an eagle of pearls to wear at a tournament 'when he was armed'.[73] Richard rarely participated in tournaments, and the most likely occasion for these to have been used is in a parade at the great Smithfield tournament of 1390.

*Buckles and buttons*

The royal inventories, which survive from the early fourteenth century onwards throughout Europe, tell us a great deal about the possession of jewels and jewelled objects. Their underlying purpose is to record the king's assets, and gold and jewels were the most immediate financial reserve on which medieval princes could draw. Quite apart from when such documents reveal that 'treasure' had to be used for financial purposes, as we have already noted, there was a steady process of breaking up old-fashioned pieces, and turning them into new and fashionable forms. In March 1382, more than six hundred pearls and precious stones were sent to the jeweller Jean Duvivier on Charles V's orders to be made into a new piece as instructed by the duke of Burgundy.[74]

Wearing such jewels in public was one way of establishing the prince's magnificence. What is really interesting is that the actual contents of the princely treasury were displayed to important visitors. When the emperor Karl IV visited his nephew Charles V of France in 1377, all the treasures of the French king's collection were shown, from relics to manuscripts as well as the jewels. Charles had been an ardent seeker of such things from an early age. At fourteen, he had his treasure taken from Paris to Montereau, 92 kilometres away, where he was lying sick, so that he could distract himself by looking at it. Seven years later, in 1357,

*Viewing the king's treasure*

while his father was in captivity in England, Charles's uncle the duke of Anjou reprimanded him for his lavish expenditure on gold and jewels.[75]

An account of the travels of Leo of Rozmital, the brother-in-law of George king of Bohemia, in 1466 makes it clear that exhibiting princely treasures was a regular occurrence for a privileged few. Rozmital's secretary relates that after the visitors had dined with Charles the Bold they were sent to see his private menagerie, and then

> the duke caused his treasures and jewels to be shown to my lord which are beyond measure precious ... It is said that nowhere in the world were such costly treasures, if only because of the hundred thousand pound weight of beaten gold and silver-gilt vessels which we saw in many cabinets, and which were so abundant that we never thought to see the like. I have indicated the principal objects so far as I was able to see them.
>
> *Item*, twelve little tunics, none worth less than 40,000 crowns
> *Item*, the hat which he wears, worth 60,000 crowns ...
> *Item*, an ostrich feather on his hat,* 50,000 ...
> *Item*, a great golden cross, wherein is one of the nails, 60,000 gulden...
> *Item*, so many costly jewels that they could not be shown to us, for the keeper of the jewels said he could not show them in [less than] three days. He told us that his lord had so many jewels that he had not seen them all in many years and indeed did not know where they were.[76]

# The Prince's Armour

IN JOHN BOORMAN'S FILM *EXCALIBUR*, Mordred, Arthur's treacherous bastard son, appears in dazzling golden armour which substitutes a face mask for a helm, a piece of deliberately anachronistic magnificence which is based on the resplendent armour of the Italian renaissance. Royal and princely armour at the beginning of the twelfth century was far less distinctive, and it is only through pictorial evidence that we can see how the ruler, as leader of the army, was identified on the battlefield. The seals of thirteenth-century kings such as Alfonso X of Castile, his brother-in-law Edward I of England, and Robert the Bruce as king of Scotland, show them with a crown on their helmet, and their arms displayed on their shields and horse trappers. This contrasts with the image of the ruler enthroned with his crown and sceptre as markers of his status which was common in the twelfth century, and which the French kings continued to use. Henry III of England combined the two styles on his seal, which portrayed him enthroned on the obverse and with a crowned helmet on the reverse. The gold franc issued by Jean II of France in 1360 to pay his ransom after his capture at the battle of Poitiers shows him in a crowned helmet and striking a proud warlike pose despite his defeat. Miniatures in manuscripts confirm the idea that the crowned helmet was usual as royal armour by 1250: the great picture Bible, now in the Pierpont Morgan Library in New York, produced in Paris at about that time shows all the Old Testament kings wearing them.

Only one actual crowned helmet survived into modern times, that of Casimir the Great of Poland, and its whereabouts is currently unknown.[77] This may be because crowns were easily separated from the helmet, and were sometimes much more valuable than the helmet

---

* Presumably a jewelled badge in the form of an ostrich feather. The nail in the golden cross is one of the nails from the Crucifixion.

itself. Some crowns were firmly attached to the helmet, as in the case of a helmet made for Jean II of France in 1352; the receipt specifies that it was nailed with studs enamelled with crosses. Thirty years later, Charles VI bought two helms with visors, one with a crown and one without, which implies that the crown was a fixed one.[78] Again, there is a record of a new coronet for Henry IV's bascinet in 1402, but this does not tell us whether it was fixed or not.[79] About the same time, Charles VI is depicted on the image of the Virgin known as the *Goldenes Rössl* accompanied by a squire holding a crowned helmet. If we are to believe the miniature painters from the thirteenth century onwards, the king always wore a crowned helmet; but this is likely to be their visual shorthand for portraying a king with his army, and is not reliable evidence as to what happened on the battlefield. Furthermore, in terms of visual effect, the crown was much less prominent than the display of princely heraldry on the surcoat and horse trapper.

*Crowned helmets*

The king needed to be identified by his own men in the thick of the fight, but it also meant that he was an obvious target for the enemy. Deceptions were sometimes practised, and Froissart claims that at the battle of Poitiers 'king Jean was armed in royal manner, and twenty others like him' to confuse his attackers.[80] Equally, if a king's army was put to flight, he needed to remove his surcoat and trapper to avoid capture. At Mons-en-Pévèle in 1304, when the Flemish routed the French army, the bodyguard of Philip IV tore off his surcoat, and he was able to escape unharmed. Likewise, if the commander was wounded or needed to rest, someone might impersonate him so that the army was not disheartened: this happened at Courtrai two years earlier, when the Flemish leader William count of Jülich withdrew from the battle to recover.[81]

Battlefield armour remained practical and relatively plain until the fifteenth century. Display was much more important in the tournament, and in the early thirteenth century an extraordinary menagerie and mixture of objects began to appear as crests surmounting a plain helmet. These became part of the sport, in that the crest was targeted deliberately: to remove an opponent's crest deftly with the point of the lance was regarded as one of the most telling blows in an encounter in the lists. The collection of German love poetry known as the Manesse manuscript, written in Zurich about 1300 and added to up to 1340, has powerful full-page images of the poets, many of them of knightly status, wearing such crests. Surviving examples are rare: the horned helmet of the Prankh family, dating from about 1450 and now in the armoury at Vienna, is the most spectacular. More modest helms, such as that in the treasury of the Teutonic Knights, also in Vienna, showing a figure holding what appear to be two drinking horns, are also extremely rare.

**98**, p.271

Towards the end of the fourteenth century, parade armour, so called because it might only be worn during the processions to and from the lists at a tournament, begins to appear. A helmet excavated at the Louvre may have been made for a court ceremony in 1410, when Jean the Fearless of Burgundy became tutor to the future Charles VII. It is made of gilded copper, chased, sculpted and enamelled, with the king's motto 'En Bien' and his device of a winged stag, and was probably matched by a breastplate in the same style. It was found in pieces; there was no defensive purpose for it, and it was lightly constructed.[82]

*Parade armour*

**36**, p.77

Armour used for ceremonial purposes could be highly decorated and bejewelled. Ornamental swords are recorded from the fourteenth century onwards, and Philip the Bold had 'a little sword, called the sword of St George, inlaid with white silver and with a jasper pommel' at his death in 1405. Five years later, Jehan Mainfroy was commissioned to adorn armour, daggers and swords for Jean the Fearless and his son Philip at a total cost of 1,727 *livres*. In 1443, Philip set out to conquer Luxembourg, the title to which he had acquired

**37.** (above left) Portrait of Robert of Anjou, king of Naples, from Simone Martini's *St. Louis of Toulouse Altarpiece*, 1317. The kneeling donor is clearly identifiable, by its correspondence to other known portraits of him, as Robert d'Anjou.

**38.** (left) Portrait of Jean II. Claimed as the oldest portrait to have been painted in France, the sitter has traditionally been named as Jean II. The artist could have studied at Avignon under Simone Martini in the 1340s.

**39.** (above) This realistic portrait of Charles V is from a bible commissioned in 1371–2 by Jean Vaudetar for presentation to the king.

from his aunt, and left Dijon in splendid array for the beginning of the campaign. Olivier de la Marche describes the occasion in his memoirs:

> With the duke were eighteen horses identically caparisoned with black velvet embroidered with his emblems, which were steels with flints causing sparks, and over the velvet were large studs of gold enamelled with steels, which cost a great deal to make. His pages were richly decked out and wore various head-armours decorated with pearls, diamonds and balas rubies, marvellously ornate. One sallet alone was estimated to be worth 100,000 gold crowns. The duke himself was armed richly and nobly, with vambraces and leg-harness, and these, together with his horse's chanfron, were decorated all over with large jewels which were worth a fortune. I speak of this as one who was then a page of the duke ...[83]

## The Prince's Portraits

THE EARLIEST ACTUAL PORTRAITS (in the modern sense) that we have were intended to be seen by a very small group of people. Surprisingly, such pictures were mostly the private possessions of royalty rather than public images. The first painted likeness that we can verify is that of Robert of Anjou, king of Naples, where we have three separate depictions of him which are clearly of the same man, and in each of which the artist is attempting to 'counterfeit' life, not in our modern sense of forgery, but in the medieval sense of 'making lifelike'. None of these is a portrait as subject of a painting: there is an effigy, and the other two are a miniature in a manuscript and part of an altarpiece by the Italian master Simone Martini.[84] Simone Martini is known to have painted portraits of individuals in the 1330s and 1340s, and it is possible that the first surviving princely portrait, that of Jean II of France, was the work of an Italian artist working at Avignon in 1349.[85] Jean II's son, Charles V, had a portrait of his father in his private rooms in 1380. It is unlikely to have been the portrait which survives in the Louvre today, because it was part of a set of four paintings which were designed as folding panels. They are listed as a single item: 'a picture [made] of wood, of four pieces, on which are painted the present king, the emperor his uncle, his father Jean and Edward king of England'. It was kept in a small room off his main study, in which only four items were listed in the inventory of his possessions.[86]

Karl, king of Bohemia and later ruler of the Holy Roman Empire as Karl IV, had spent seven years at the court in Paris, from 1323 to 1330. He was therefore very familiar with the style and fashion of French royalty. Unlike the French kings, Karl IV regarded portraits of himself as a crucial part of the propaganda he used to project his status as Holy Roman Emperor. A remarkable total of seventy such images survive. Both the evidence of Matteo Villani, the Florentine chronicler, who had met Karl and describes him, and the reconstruction of his face from his skull, suggest that the portraits are remarkably realistic.*[87] It also draws on two apparently separate traditions. The often very realistic portrait busts of the Roman emperors were familiar to pilgrims to Rome throughout the Middle Ages. These were imitated by the emperor Friedrich II when he built his great triumphal arch at Capua in the 1230s. Karl IV was well aware of antique imperial images; the poet Petrarch met him at Mantua in 1354, and in the course of the conversation presented him with

*The portraits of Karl IV*

---

* Given the rarity of portraits in France and England, the enormous number of pictures of the emperor suggests a very determined campaign to make the emperor's face familiar to his subjects.

**40.** Statues of Margrave Eckard II and his wife Uta in Naumburg Cathedral, c.1250. These are highly realistic and individual statues, amounting to true images of contemporary sitters. However, they are not portraits of the people they are said to represent, who lived c. AD 1000.

some gold and silver coins bearing the portraits of our ancient rulers and inscriptions in tiny and ancient lettering, coins that I treasured, and among them was the head of Caesar Augustus, who almost appeared to be breathing. 'Here, O Caesar,' I said, 'are the men whom you have succeeded, here are those whom you must try to imitate and admire, whose ways and character you should emulate: I would have given these coins to no other save yourself.'[88]

For Karl IV, the echoes of ancient Rome were perhaps less important than those of Charlemagne. He was christened Wenceslaus at his baptism, but when he was confirmed at the age of seven, his godfather, Charles IV of France, changed this, and once the Bohemian king had become emperor, he invoked the first Holy Roman Empire in his charters and elsewhere. Interestingly, when he was portrayed in fifteenth-century French manuscripts, the artists showed him as a venerable bearded figure, exactly like the contemporary depictions of Charlemagne.

What is most remarkable in contemporary portraits of Karl is their immediacy and realism. He was evidently no beauty: even the depiction of him at the heart of Karlstejn Castle, in the chapel dedicated to the Virgin Mary where the holiest relics were kept, shows him with a prominent nose – which is positively bulbous in other portraits – and full cheeks, with a receding chin concealed by his beard. There is no attempt to soften his features into a bland elegance. Anyone who had seen pictures of the Holy Roman Emperor would be able

**41.** Contemporary portrait of Richard II at Westminster Abbey, by an unknown artist, in many ways the most direct image of regal magnificence.

to recognise him. The same is true of his uncle, Charles V of France. Charles is consistently shown with a 'long nose, thin face, high cheekbones and shoulder-length hair',[89] and his biographer, Christine de Pizan, also describes him in similar terms. Again, there is no surviving portrait painting, but a wide range of images – from a statue which probably came from his palace at the Louvre to numerous miniatures in the books which were dedicated to him and formed part of his famous library. Jean Bandol painted the most engaging of these, showing him receiving an illustrated Bible from a member of his royal council.

*Sets of dynastic portraits*

BY THE END OF THE FOURTEENTH CENTURY, the idea of realistic portraiture was firmly established, and princely portraits were of great interest to an increasingly wide public. The idea of sets of portraits of ancestors was another vital element in the panoply of the prince. Medieval sculpture was often idealised and bland, but sculptors of such sets of forebears had already successfully adopted a realistic approach. These figures begin to appear from the thirteenth century onwards, sometimes portraying ancestors in contemporary dress. The finest of these are the figures of the founders in the cathedral at Naumburg in Germany. The west choir of the church, with its elegant light-filled apse in the best early Gothic style, is dedicated to the Virgin Mary, and it is surrounded by twelve life-size statues, described in 1249 as being those 'of the first founders of our church'.[90] They represent members of the families of the local dukes from the eleventh and twelfth centuries, but were created long after the last of those portrayed had died. They are therefore entirely fictional; but, like the best fiction, they are nonetheless extremely lifelike. The Gothic statues of northern France had broken away from the formulaic style of late Romanesque art, but here at Naumburg, the elegance of French gothic is combined with a new reality. The most striking pair are Duke Ekkehard II of Meissen, who died in 1046, and his consort Ute. He is shown in civilian costume – of the thirteenth rather than the eleventh century – but with his hand on the hilt of a massive sword, while in the other hand he holds his shield by the strap. His face is expressive: boldness tempered by the cares of state would be a fair reading of it. More important for present purposes, this is a face we would instantly recognise if we met him in the street. Likewise, Ute is dressed in a long heavy cloak, which she has gathered up with her left arm, at the same time clasping it to her throat with her right hand, as if to protect herself against a cold wind. Her gaze is level but hesitant, and once again she is entirely recognisable, an extraordinarily appealing image.

One of the first royal or imperial sets of portraits of ancestors is, not surprisingly, that created by the emperor Karl IV at Karlstejn. In 1414, Edmund de Dynter was sent as ambassador from Anthony of Burgundy, duke of Brabant, to Prague on a mission to the imperial court. He found the emperor Wenceslaus at Karlstejn, and after he had conducted his diplomatic business, Wenceslaus led de Dynter 'by the hand' to a gallery where 'precious images of all the dukes of Brabant down to Jean III were painted, which the emperor Karl, his forebear, had had painted there. He told me that this was his genealogy, because he was descended from the Trojans ...' Wenceslaus explained that his grandmother had been the daughter of Jean I of Brabant.[91] Wenceslaus himself was married to the heiress of Jean III. The pictures are lost, but survive in sixteenth-century copies; the originals were life-size, and numbered around sixty in all, possibly arranged in two tiers around the hall. Like so many royal family trees in the medieval period, that of Karl IV was largely fictional. It made the traditional claim to Biblical and classical forebears, in this case Noah and king Priam – a suitable adjunct to the image of his magnificence. In this plethora of figures, only the image of Karl himself can claim to be a realistic likeness. Even that seems to have been reinterpreted by the sixteenth-century copyist, perhaps because by then it had deteriorated.[92]

**42.** The monumental tomb of king Robert of Anjou, overshadowing the altar of Santa Chiara church, Naples. The figure of the king is based on the statue of Charles of Anjou by Arnolfo di Cambio in the Capitol at Rome.

These images may be a clue to the origin of the most dramatic of all surviving royal portraits of the later Middle Ages, that of Richard II at Westminster Abbey. Much restored, and moved from the unknown setting for which it was designed, this almost lifesize figure now looms over the nave in Westminster Abbey. Richard is shown in full state, formally enthroned; the face, though impassive, seems to be a genuine portrait. It feels as if it belongs in a palace rather than a church, and this may well have been the case. It is tempting to see in this somewhat sinister but magnificent image the king who at crown-wearing ceremonies ordered a throne to be prepared for him in his chamber, on which he sat ostentatiously from after dinner until vespers, 'talking to no-one but watching everyone; and when his eye fell on anyone ... that person had to bend his knee to the king'.[93]

*Tomb of Robert, king of Naples*

TOMB EFFIGIES ARE PORTRAITS, and often realistic, but they are not of living rulers, and their only value in terms of magnificence is as part of the dynastic display that legitimates the prince. There are however two remarkable exceptions in the kingdom of Naples, where the effigy of a past ruler dominates the church, and is a positive proclamation of his successor's magnificence. In the church of Santa Chiara in Naples stands, half-ruined, what was once the apotheosis of all medieval royal tombs, that of King Robert, who died in 1343. The monument dominates the church, once attached to a nunnery, because it is placed behind the high altar, and becomes the focal point for both the priest celebrating mass and the congregation. The king is enthroned above the crucifixion and above his own tomb, in the place where we would expect to see God the Father. The pose is that of Friedrich II on the gate at Capua or the statue of his forebear Charles on the Capitol at Rome: the king as judge, a second Solomon.[94]

THIS THEN, IS THE PRINCE, in pride of person, decked out in the richest jewels, the finest materials, the latest fashions, a figure of unmistakable distinction, ideally with a consort at his side, who was almost – but not quite his equal in attire. We now turn to the queen and her part in royal magnificence.

# QUEENS AND PRINCESSES 6

♦ *The queen as monarch* ♦ *The queen as the king's consort* ♦ *Weddings and dowries* ♦ *Crowns for queens and princesses* ♦ *Dowries* ♦ *The inventory of a duchess* ♦ *The tragedy of Isabella of Aragon*

## The Queen as Monarch

'THERE WAS ALMOST NO PLACE for reigning queens in twelfth century Western society. The queens of that age were the wives of kings, or kings' daughters transmitting an inheritance. If, after the death of a ruler, a female heir wielded the sceptre, it was normally for a very brief period, until a suitable husband could be found to wear the crown in his wife's right, or a young son reached an age to be associated with his mother in government.'[1] This was how the distinguished historian of Anglo-Norman England, Marjorie Chibnall, began her biography of the Empress Matilda, daughter and heir of Henry I.

The medieval queen regnant is an exceptional figure. The destiny of most princely women was to be a pawn in diplomatic manoeuvres, as the willing or unwilling partner in a marriage alliance.[2] Nor did the situation change until the sixteenth century. It was partly to do with attitudes, and partly a matter of practicality. To her contemporaries Joan of Arc was shocking and unnatural in that she both led an army and fought in battles. One of the most important functions of a ruler was to do exactly that, and no medieval queen actually fulfilled that role: 'Europe never produced a race of Amazons'.[3] This was why the problem was so often resolved by making her consort co-ruler, although the degree to which there was an effective transfer of power to her husband varied considerably. Among the higher nobility, duchesses in their own right, not at all uncommon in the Low Countries, were similarly constrained by their marriages to men of their own status, with their own territories. This was the case with Margaret of Flanders and Philip of Burgundy in the late fourteenth century.

Nonetheless, the idea *per se* of a queen succeeding to the throne with full powers and duly crowned was never regarded as impossible, and even the supposed clause in the Salic law of France barring queens from the succession was highly debatable: the ban was declared to be an ancient custom, 'from time immemorial' and since the question of female succession had not arisen for over three hundred years, it was difficult to prove otherwise.[4]

*Queens regnant*

Female emperors had ruled in eleventh-century Byzantium, and in 1109 Urraca became queen of León and Castile, using the style 'Empress of all the Spains' in some of her documents. There was no bar to female succession in these kingdoms, and there is little doubt that Urraca was the ultimate authority in the kingdom throughout her reign, relying on favoured counsellors but taking the final decisions herself.[5] Although her charters survive, we have no records of her treasury and very little in the chronicles about her personal life, other than the very chequered tale of her marriages, lovers, and finally death in childbirth in 1126: there is simply no surviving information outside the sparse chronicles of the period. We have already pointed to her creation of the mausoleum of the kings of León at San Isidoro, a celebration of her dynasty and a regal act.

If queens were rarely sovereign in their own territories, we do find princely figures among duchesses and countesses who were genuinely independent, and who played a more considerable part in politics than many of the rulers whom they nominally served. In the eleventh century, Urraca's contemporary, Matilda, countess of Tuscany from 1076 to 1115, was a political figure of international importance. She was a key figure in the struggle between Pope Gregory VII and the emperor Heinrich V over the appointment of high-ranking clergy on whom the emperor depended for his administrative personnel, the so-called 'Investiture Contest'. Matilda was also a military commander of genius who defeated the imperial armies on more than one occasion. Her vast domains in northern Italy effectively formed a barrier between the Holy Roman Empire and Rome, and she was reputed to have founded a hundred churches, many of which had hospices for pilgrims making their way to the papal city. But we know little of her personal life apart from the usual scandalous stories which monkish chroniclers loved to invent about queens. We have extensive information about her military activities,[6] but little knowledge of her court.

*Matilda of Tuscany*

The Matilda with whom this chapter opened is an equally striking figure. She used the title 'Lady of the English' rather than queen of England, because she never attained the power which she sought. She was by 1125, at the age of twenty-three, the widow of the emperor Heinrich V of Germany, and was generally known as 'the empress Matilda'. She married again in 1128, taking Geoffrey count of Anjou as her husband. Her father, Henry I, had named her as his heir. But although his barons had sworn to accept her, her cousin Stephen seized the throne in her absence overseas when Henry died in 1135. Matilda did not land in England until 1139, though her chief supporter, Robert of Gloucester, had upheld her cause in the meanwhile. Even though her forces captured Stephen at Lincoln in 1141, this was nullified by the capture of Robert of Gloucester by the king's men. Matilda was generally found overbearing and distant, and she was driven out of London by the citizens who disliked her and were in any case supporters of Stephen: without London, she could not be crowned. She fought on until 1147, when Robert of Gloucester died, and she then retired to Normandy, leaving it to her son Henry to establish his claim to the throne six years later.

*The empress Matilda*

Margaret I of Denmark was as important a figure in her way as Matilda of Tuscany. In the course of a long and complex career, she was able to rule as queen in all but name of the kingdoms of Denmark, Norway and Sweden. Although Danish custom did not allow for female succession, she was given the title of 'sovereign lady and lord and guardian of the entire kingdom of Denmark'; her status was, however, ambiguous, and she never issued coins in her name. She was brought up by a daughter of St Bridget of Sweden, and was highly educated. She proved herself able, determined and skilled in diplomacy. She ruled on behalf of her young son Olaf, who died in 1387, and then on behalf of her great-nephew Erik, whom she chose as her heir at the request of her nobles. It was at his coronation in 1397 that she promulgated the Union of Kalmar, which brought the three kingdoms together and lasted until 1523.

*Margaret of Denmark*

THERE WERE TWO OTHER QUEENS on the fringes of Europe at the same time. In 1370, Hungary and Poland were both ruled by Louis the Great, a member of the French house of Anjou. The kingdoms were never united. He had two daughters: Mary became queen of Hungary, and although she was crowned 'king of Hungary' aged eleven, her mother was regent until Mary's marriage to the emperor Sigismund three years later, who then became king. Her sister Jadwiga, who became queen of Poland, was also crowned 'king' and does seem to have played a part in the chequered relations between the Poles, the Teutonic Order and the pagan Lithuanians: she married their prince Jogailo, who converted to Christianity and was crowned as her partner in kingship under the name Wladislaw. Jadwiga continued to be involved in the government of Poland, and in diplomatic negotiations, though her chief interest was the promotion of the Roman creed in her husband's territories which included both recent converts and adherents of the Orthodox faith.

Another branch of the ubiquitous house of Anjou had been established in the kingdom of Naples in 1266, when the pope offered Charles count of Anjou the old Sicilian territories – technically subject to the papacy – as part of his struggle with the successors of the emperor Friedrich II. Charles I's grandson, Robert the Wise, died without a male heir, leaving the kingdom to his four-year-old granddaughter Joanna. Joanna had an extraordinary career and reputation, with four marriages, the murder of one husband and her own eventual murder. She was praised by Boccaccio, Chaucer's contemporary, in his book *On Illustrious Women*. He called her 'more renowned than any other woman of our time for lineage, power and character', even though he was writing before she became the sole ruler of the kingdom on the death of her second husband. 'The Queen enjoys governing. She wishes to do everything, because she has waited a long time for this moment', wrote the archbishop of Naples.[7] She issued gold coins in Provence in 1372 showing herself in armour, in the style of the French king's coinage, and proclaiming herself queen of 'Provence, Forcalquier, Sicily and Jerusalem', as visible evidence of her position as a wielder of real power. If Joanna had died before the Great Schism of 1378, when two popes were elected, she might have gone down in history as a successful ruler: but the new Roman pope, who was in a position to challenge her, did not approve of her and wanted to replace her with a man, even though she had been a stalwart supporter of his predecessor. She declared allegiance to the French pope at Avignon, and named a new heir, Louis I, duke of Anjou, in place of her cousin, Charles of Durazzo. Deprived of the succession to the throne, Charles, with the support of Rome, forced Joanna to abdicate and later had her murdered.

*Joanna of Naples*

History repeated itself to some extent when Joanna II, descended from another branch of the house of Anjou, inherited Naples in 1414. She was crowned by a papal legate in 1419 and is therefore one of the very few queens who actually reigned in their own right, which she did successfully until her death in 1435. She failed, however, to settle the question of who should succeed her, and René of Anjou, grandson of Louis of Anjou, was driven out by a rival claimant, Alfonso V of Aragon. We know very little about Joanna's reign, as the archives in Naples were destroyed in 1943, a tantalising loss in that both René and Alfonso V had particularly splendid courts. It is quite possible that Joanna's state papers and accounts would have revealed a magnificent lifestyle similar to theirs and appropriate to her kingly status. The two Joannas who ruled Naples are the only figures who might have had some claim to the essentially 'male' Aristotelian virtue of magnificence, male only because independent female kingship is so rare during the fourteenth and fifteenth centuries.

*Joanna II of Naples*

QUEENS MIGHT NOT BE MONARCHS, but they were almost always ceremonially crowned. The tradition of crowning queens, either on their marriage to a king, or when their husband became king, goes back to the eighth century, before Charlemagne's time. This applied as a general rule throughout Europe. In England and France, where the line of succession was through inheritance, there were almost no exceptions between 1100 and 1500. In the Holy Roman Empire, the emperors were usually crowned first as kings of the Romans, and then again when they succeeded to the imperial title. Here the same situation applies, that simultaneous coronation was normal, whether as king and queen of the Romans or as emperor and empress. If the king or emperor remarried, then the queen might be crowned alone, as in the case of Karl IV's third wife, Anna von Schweidnitz in

*The queen's coronation*

**43.** The joint coronation of Charles V and his queen Jeanne de Bourbon in 1364 at Reims, when he became king. Miniature from an early fifteenth century copy of *Grands Chroniques de France*.

1354. The object in all cases was to establish the queen's status, and hence to ensure that the sons of the marriage were fully legitimate as heirs to the throne, and secure in their right to inherit. From the tenth century onwards, prayers for the queen's fertility and for male heirs were incorporated in the coronation service. This applied first to the Frankish kings, in an order of service drawn up in 960, and was adopted by the Anglo-Saxon kings in 973.

Soon after the ritual of crowning the queen was first introduced among the English kings, in 975, both Edward and Aethelred, half-brothers and sons of king Edgar, claimed the throne. The question of the queen's coronation at once came into play. Aethelred was the younger, but declared that he was the rightful heir because his mother Aelfthryth had been crowned two years previously, whereas Edward's had not. Edward succeeded his father but was murdered three years later, possibly at the instigation of Aelfthryth, and Aethelred came to the throne.

With the ritual of coronation came the tradition that the queen should sit at the king's right hand, which was specified in the Frankish order of service. This became the general practice, and was an essential part of the queen's usual role, as consort and companion to the king. In the Holy Roman Empire, the orders of service for joint coronation emphasised that when the queen was anointed, it had the same sacramental power as the anointing of the king. The implication was that they were not only joined in marriage, but also were paired as rulers, a theoretical equality which was very rarely invoked in practice.[9]

# The Queen as the King's Consort

... it is the king's task to show magnificence towards his own person and towards the persons close to him such as his wife and sons, finding them honourable habitations, making good marriages for them, and training them for knightly glory.

THE ROLE OF THE MEDIEVAL QUEEN, in the vast majority of cases, was as her husband's consort, reflecting his magnificence rather than being herself 'magnificent' in the way that Giles of Rome uses the term. Walther von der Vogelweide's picture of Philip of Swabia and Irene, the Byzantine princess he married in 1198, must be quoted again here, because it portrays so exactly the queen's expected attitude:

> King Philip strode out in all his splendour. ... He bore the Empire's sceptre and its crown. He walked with measured pace, followed modestly by the noble queen, rose without thorn, dove without gall.[10]

The queen or empress was expected to accompany her husband on his travels in peacetime, and particularly on great occasions. Anna von Schweidnitz was with Karl IV at Nuremberg when the new constitution for the Empire was promulgated. This was the so-called 'Golden Bull' because the seal of the charter was in gold. As prescribed in the charter, she sat at a separate table three metres lower than that of the emperor and three metres higher than those of the princes of the empire. On another occasion, she followed Karl as he journeyed to Rome for his coronation in 1354 with a retinue of a thousand attendants. However, it is likely that the majority of these were an armed escort as she travelled through potentially hostile country in Italy.[11]

THE MODESTY AND AMIABILITY of Irene corresponds to one of the most important roles of a medieval queen: that of intercessor with her husband. Petitions presented to a monarch often name his queen in this role. In the case of the emperor Heinrich II, a third of the documents granting such requests name Kunigunde, his queen, as the sponsor of the petition.

There are many instances of a queen's intervention in this way. Probably the most famous instance is that of Queen Philippa at Calais. She notably begged for mercy for the six citizens of Calais who came to surrender the town to Edward III after the long siege in 1346–7. As the chronicler Jean le Bel reports the scene, Edward's determination to execute *The queen as* them seems to have been very real. He ignored the pleas of his close friend Walter Manny, *intercessor* and as Le Bel tells it, only yielded at the last minute to the queen herself. Edward said that he wished she were elsewhere, as, contrary to his desire, he would have to spare them because of her pleas.[12] Similarly, we find Anne of Bohemia playing the ritual role of the queen as mediator between the city of London and Richard II at the end of his entry into London in August 1392, after Richard had deprived the city of its charter the previous year. She knelt before him, saying that no king had ever had such a welcome in London, and asking him to restore the city's privileges.

In these acts of mercy the queen is almost acting as a moderator on magnificence, which always tends to present the monarch as a remote if splendid personage. Normally her role was to appear as a suitably magnificent companion to her husband. Rich clothes were *Elisabeth of* a prerequisite for royal consorts, exemplified by an episode in the life of St Elisabeth of *Hungary* Hungary. She was married in 1221 to Ludwig, duke of Thuringia, one of the great magnates of the Holy Roman Empire, and after his death followed a very strict Franciscan regime.

Even during his lifetime, she would in his absence dress as a nun with a widow's veil, and spend entire nights in vigils. However, when occasion required, she would put on the rich clothes expected of a royal consort. She was once surprised by the arrival of important visitors, and Ludwig was concerned that she was wearing her habitual plain, indeed shabby, clothes. However, divine assistance was at hand, and she suddenly appeared in a blue robe encrusted with pearls – blue of course being the colour worn by the Virgin. And ordinarily, when she wore royal clothes, she would wear a coarse shift next to her skin, according to the evidence which her maid Isentrude gave before the papal officials during the proceedings for her canonisation.[13]

*Philippa of Hainault*

Elisabeth of Hungary was the exception rather than the rule, but lavish clothes were not necessarily the personal choice of the queen. This is true, despite modern criticisms of her conduct, of Philippa of Hainault, wife of Edward III, who dressed lavishly to match Edward III's truly extraordinary costumes. As queen, she had her own household and income but, even after 1330, when she took over the estates reserved for the queen from her mother-in-law Isabella, her expenditure easily outstripped her income. Edward was prepared to make good the shortfall, partly by gifts of garments for special occasions and partly by additional payments, since she had to appear in appropriately magnificent style. In 1348 a lavish suit was created for the service on the evening before her churching after the birth of William of Windsor.

> ... a suit of dark blue velvet of particular magnificence was made for her to wear. It consisted of a mantle and cape, open supertunic and tunic embroidered with gold birds, each bird surrounded by a circle of large pearls, the whole background powdered with a pattern worked in silks and small pearls and enlivened by 10,000 doublets [paste jewels]. Four hundred large pearls, thirty-eight ounces of small pearls, thirteen pounds of plate gold, eleven pounds of gold thread and seven pounds of embroidery silks were used in the decoration of this suit.[14]

If we add in 2,000 miniver furs for the lining, sixty ermine furs and about 50 metres of velvet, the weight when worn seems almost impossible to imagine, even allowing for an enormous train. And this was to be worn in July... For the churching itself, a similar suit with lions and oak trees on a ground of silk and pearls was created. The style of these suits, with heavily pictorial embroidery, is very similar to that of Edward's suits for the games at Guildford in 1337.

It was not until 1363, with the queen's accounts still showing a deficit, that her household was merged with that of the king. In Tudor times, someone wrote inside the book of her accounts for 1330 that they showed 'the great riches, lavish expenses and debts of the queene'.[15] There were certainly 'lavish expenses', but this accusation is wide of the mark. There is little evidence that it was Philippa personally who ordered these garments: as with Edward's companions in arms, the king was probably in charge of the costumes to be worn on such occasions; it is more than likely that 'Philippa was Edward's clothes horse'.[16] Contemporaries do not seem to have complained about it, and Philippa was remembered as beloved and benevolent rather than extravagant.

FIFTY YEARS LATER, THE FRENCH COURT also welcomed a foreign bride for the king, who was to be accused to her face of extravagance. Her first appearance in Paris was magnificent indeed, but this was her husband's work. Isabeau was the daughter of the duke of Bavaria, and her grandfather was Bernabò Visconti, duke of Milan. She was about fifteen when she married Charles VI, who had been king for five years. It was said that Charles had fallen in love with her portrait, and that he asked for her hand in marriage just three days after he met her in person. Isabeau of Bavaria was wedded to Charles VI and crowned in August 1389, and made her entry into Paris some days later. Word got around that the king and the city were preparing a particularly magnificent occasion to mark the event. The chronicler Jean Froissart decided that he would travel especially from Holland to be at 'the magnificent feasts that were to be given at queen Isabeau's public entry'.

*Isabeau of Bavaria*

Charles VI, who loved festivals, was anxious to make Isabeau's progress into Paris and her welcome by the city as grandiose as possible. The queen set out from the royal abbey of Saint-Denis to the north of Paris on 20 June in an open horse-litter, accompanied by her sisters-in-law and the leading noblewomen of France, also in horse-litters. Froissart notes that 'the duchess of Touraine was not in a litter, but to display herself the more, was mounted on a palfrey magnificently caparisoned'.[17] They were accompanied by the king's uncles and his brother and other nobles on horseback, and the streets were lined by twelve hundred citizens of Paris in their green and crimson uniforms. But this was not enough to hold back the crowd, for the royal officers were kept busy trying to keep the route clear: the enthusiastic mob of spectators blocked the way – 'it seemed as if all the world had come thither'.

*Her entry into Paris*

At the gate of the abbey of Saint-Denis, Charles VI waited to greet the queen under the first of the heraldic displays and theatrical tableaux. The sun, Charles VI's emblem at tournaments, was at the top, and below, the Virgin and angels under a starry firmament. The child in the Virgin's arms 'at times amused himself with a windmill, made of a large walnut'.[18] At the next tableau, the queen and her entourage halted: this was a castle with a battle between Richard Coeur de Lion and Saladin. When they arrived, the actor playing Richard asked permission from the king to fight the Saracens: a mock battle ensued, 'and was seen with much pleasure'. As they passed under the gate leading out of the town of Saint-Denis, again decked with a starry firmament with angels, the Trinity was shown seated in majesty. Here the queen was crowned by two angels. The whole street was hung with silks and cloths: Froissart was 'astonished whence such quantities of rich stuffs and ornaments could have come' for the whole way to Paris was hung with tapestries 'representing various scenes and histories'.

The procession now made its way to the Châtelet, the castle at the end of the rue Saint-Denis, on the north bank of the Seine. Here, there was another wooden castle with an elaborate allegory of justice. In front, there was realistic scenery which included a warren and thickets with hares and rabbits and birds 'that fled out and in again for fear of the populace'. Out of one end of the thicket came a white stag, and from the other end a lion and eagle appeared, 'well represented'. They threatened the stag, and twelve maidens with gold chaplets holding naked swords in their hands came forward to defend it.

It was now late in the day, because the whole body of people had come down from Saint-Denis at snail's pace, and the queen crossed the bridge to the Ile de la Cité and to Notre-Dame.

> A full month before the queen's entry to Paris, a master-engineer from Geneva had fastened a cord to the highest tower of Notre-Dame, which, passing high above the streets, was fixed to the most elevated house on the bridge of St Michel. As the queen was passing down the street of Notre-Dame, this man left the tower, and, seating himself on the cord, descended singing, with two lighted torches in his hand, for it was now dark,* to the great astonishment of all who saw him, how he could do it.

* The darkness meant that the cord was virtually invisible.

**44.** Isabeau of
Bavaria enters
Paris in 1389, an
illustration to a
copy of Froissart's
*Chronicles.*
Although this image
was created nearly
a century later in
Bruges, it has some
accurate details,
such as the red and
green colours worn
by the citizens of
Paris and the queen
being carried in a
litter.

At the door of Notre-Dame the archbishop of Paris met the queen, and led her to the high altar, where she offered the crown 'which the angels had put on her head at the gate of Paris'. She then left for the palace, lit by five hundred tapers. On her arrival, the city sent a present of gold and silver plate which was borne into her chamber on a litter by two men, one disguised as a bear, the other as a unicorn.[19]

The next day the queen was anointed and sanctified at Notre-Dame, and the festival banquet was held in the great hall of the Palais de la Cité. The king and queen and a handful of close associates sat at the marble table on the dais. Two lines of tables in the aisles held a further five hundred guests. It seems that there was a crowd of spectators, which made it very difficult to serve dinner and caused a problem when it came to the entertainment, a reenactment of the siege of Troy. A wooden castle 12 metres high and six metres square, with towers at the corners and a central tower, had been built in the middle of the hall; and there was a ship and a pavilion full of armed men who attacked the castle. The mock-assault started well, but the heat and crush was such that people started to faint, the queen and one of her ladies among them. The servants opened one of the doors, but the king decided to put an end to the feast before anything worse happened, and the tables were cleared.

Just three years later, in 1392, Charles VI had his first fit of madness while on his way to fight a campaign in Brittany. He attacked his brother Louis, killing five men before he was restrained. A regency council was proclaimed, and royal authority was given to the queen and her brother-in-law Louis, and to the king's uncles, the dukes of Orléans and Burgundy. The ordinance emphasised the queen's special role as mother of the royal children. In 1402, when the king's uncles began to quarrel about the direction of the government, Isabeau was 'especially' charged with appeasing the two dukes, and with managing 'the finances and other difficulties of the realm'. She seems to have carried out her duties with some skill. She was prepared to outface Jean the Fearless of Burgundy when he was trying to stir up trouble in Paris in 1405, by inciting the citizens to rebel at a time when Charles was incapacitated and Isabeau was absent. With the support of the other dukes and the constable of France, she returned to Paris in truly regal style, carried in a golden litter with an armed escort, and with three thousand armed men in her company.[20]

Isabeau had become accustomed, however, to lavish expenditure on dress, as consort of Charles VI. This drew sharp criticism from the supporters of the duke of Burgundy, who labelled it the folly of a foreign woman, attacking her as someone who did not respect French customs. Jean Jouvenel des Ursins, a contemporary chronicler, records an episode in 1405 when the queen went to hear a sermon on a feast day, and the preacher 'began to blame the queen in her presence, speaking of the exactions she levied on the people, and the excessive spending of her and her ladies, and of other things that people said in various ways. It was ill done, and she was very discontented by it.'[21] There was obviously genuine anger, but it was enflamed by the Burgundians for their own purposes.

It is perfectly possible to read Isabeau's use of splendour as a deliberate policy to display royal power as the king's chosen deputy. She, very probably, did import some foreign fashions, or had definite ideas of her own: she seems to have worn a splendid *houppelande* at her entry into Paris, which was at that time usually a male garment. Furthermore, she is said to have introduced the *bourrelet*, a headdress rather like a wreath, made of rolled cloth covered with a rich material. Her accounts show a high level of spending, as well as a dramatic increase in her income. From 10,000 francs in 1393, her outgoings rose to 48,000 francs in 1401, and to 53,000 francs the following year. However, nearly half of the total of this set of accounts went on jewellery. One piece alone, the famous image of the Virgin with Charles VI, his squire and his horse known as the 'Little Gold Horse' or *Goldenes Rössl*, was

La requeste con|templation z plai|sance de treshaut| et noble prince| mon trescher seigneur z maistre| Guy de chastillon conte de blois| seigneur danesnes de chymay| et de beaumont destonnehone| et de la gode. Je iehan froi|sart prebstre et chappelam a mon

treschier seigneur dessus nōme| Et pour le tampz de lore tresorier| et chanonne de chymay et de lille| en flandres me suis de nouuel| resueillie et entre dedens ma fo|rie pour ourirer et forgier en la| haulte et noble matier de la|quelle du tampz passe ie me| suis ensonne Laquelle haulte| et propose les fais et aduenues commissioned by her in 1400, and eventually given as a New Year's gift to her husband in 1404. This does not reflect her personal extravagance, but the prevailing fashion among the French royal family for giving very expensive gifts at the New Year.

*Isabeau and Christine de Pizan*

A more balanced view of Isabeau emerges from a contemporary miniature in a manuscript. Isabeau loved books, and it was at her request that Christine de Pizan, then at the height of her powers, commissioned a volume of all her own works around 1413. The frontispiece shows the queen in a brilliantly painted room, wearing a very grand *houppelande* and a dramatic *hennin* (and with her lapdog at her side) while Christine, in deliberate contrast, is plainly dressed and simply coiffed as she kneels before Isabeau. But Christine is very much a witness for the defence, for, in her allegorical book *The City of Ladies*, she says that only the most virtuous will be made citizens there: Isabeau will not only be a citizen, but the first among the citizens. By the grace of God she now rules France, and 'there is not a trace of cruelty, extortion, or any other evil vice, but only great love and good will toward her subjects'.[22] Christine also cites the case of Blanche of Castile, the mother of St Louis, who was generally admired for the way in which she ruled France in his absence.

# Weddings and Dowries

WHEN GILES OF ROME SPEAKS OF the king's duty to extend magnificence to his family, he does not mention daughters. Yet the marriage of daughters certainly involved magnificence. They were usually arranged with potential alliances in mind, or at least with a strong political element. There was also an element of prestige: a marriage which made the king father-in-law to the Holy Roman emperor was particularly sought after. Two of our examples involve such matches, where the provision of suitably lavish dowries could become a drain on the king's resources.

## *Crowns for queens and princesses*

IT WAS TRADITIONAL THAT MAGNIFICENT CROWNS in the style of their native land were provided for these marriages by the bride's family as part of the dowry. This explains why queens' crowns are often very different from those of their consorts. For instance, a crown formerly at the cathedral at Bamberg may have been that of Irene, wife of Philip, king of the Romans and uncle of Friedrich II: their wedding was in 1197. She was a Byzantine princess, and her crown is strikingly Byzantine in form. Similarly, the crown of Queen Beatrice, her daughter, who married the king of Castile in 1219, was in a style quite unknown in Spain: it too has vanished, stolen from Seville cathedral in 1873, and we have only a tantalising photograph to show how elaborate it was compared with the relatively simple jewellery of the Castilian kings.[23] Even allowing for a sixteenth-century alteration to the central panel, its sinuous foliage and wealth of pearls and small jewels is remarkable for the thirteenth century.

When Margaret and her sister Joanna, the daughters of William count of Hainault, were married in a double wedding ceremony at Köln on 26 February 1324, they wore crowns which had been specially commissioned the previous autumn. Two members of the count's household travelled to Paris to buy the girls' trousseaux, and the first item on the list of their purchases is a 'crown with great sapphires, fine rubies, fine emeralds and great fine pearls from the East' made by the French royal jeweller Simon de Lille, costing 2,000 *livres* in Paris money. This was for Margaret, the elder, who married Ludwig IV, the Holy Roman

**45.** (above) Christine de Pizan presenting a copy of a volume of her works to Isabeau of Bavaria, c.1410–14.

**46.** Crown made in the 1370s in Paris, possibly for Anne of Bohemia, and later given to Blanche, daughter of Henry IV, wife of Ludwig III of Bavaria. Now in Munich, this is an outstanding piece, in terms of its quality as well as its history. It was certainly used, as repairs were made to it in 1402 and again in 1421.

Emperor. Her younger sister, Joanna, made a more modest match; her husband was the count of Jülich, and her crown was accordingly less splendid, without the sapphires and costing only 1,000 *livres*.[24]

Queens' crowns often ended up far from their origins, while those of kings and princes became part of their state's regalia. The crown of Isabella of France, whom Richard II married in 1396, is listed in his inventory in 1399. It may have come to England with his first wife, Anne of Bohemia. Henry IV gave it to his daughter Blanche when she married Ludwig duke of Bavaria in 1402, and it is still at Munich.[25] It is a beautiful and elegant object, contrasting with the aggressively masculine grandeur of the great crowns, and is probably the work of a Parisian goldsmith in the decade after 1370. It has twelve fleurons, alternately large and small, corresponding to the panels which are linked by small plaques. The pattern of sapphires, balas rubies, diamonds and pearls is carefully repeated. This implies a stock of gems sufficient to produce enough closely matching stones, and the intricate detail of enamel and tracery is astonishing. The fleurons are hollow and can be removed, and the plates were originally pinned through hinges so that the whole object is light and portable. The skill required to create this crown is emphasised when we look at the repairs carried out in 1402 before the crown was given to Blanche: it was vulnerable to damage, and one section was replaced by a London jeweller, Thomas Lamport. He has matched the original so that the new work does not immediately stand out, but once we look more closely, the enamel is less bright, the fine beading is coarser and some detail is missing.

## Dowries

WHEN ISABELLA, THE SISTER OF Henry III of England, left England for her marriage to the emperor Friedrich II at Worms in Germany in July 1235, the chief piece of jewellery in her dowry was a magnificent crown. The chronicler Roger of Wendover describes it as 'a crown of the most delicate work (engraved with four English kings, martyrs and confessors, especially chosen by the king for the care of his sister's soul), made from the purest gold and the finest gems, as befitted the dignity of the empress'. This crown, with its images of the Anglo-Saxon royal saints, was both part of Henry III's enthusiasm for their cult, and a subtle statement of Isabella's high lineage.

Wendover goes on to describe her trousseau, and we can match this with the full list of items prepared by the royal accountant, which is a rare survival, one of the earliest documents to describe the robes worn by the royal family. It is a 'roll of particulars' rather than the summary that was entered on the pipe roll after the details had been audited. This is the entry in Wendover's chronicle:

*Isabella's trousseau*

> It was said that the treasures about to be taken out of England seemed almost priceless, and not just abundant, but excessive, what with the gold collars with precious gems, reliquaries, ornaments and other womanly apparel, as well as an abundant treasure of gold and silver, with horses and a retinue, which seized the eyes of onlookers with envy. ... Moreover, in festive garments, some silk, others wool and diverse linens, and with the most dignified colours, the empress was dressed to such a degree that she shone.[26]

The entries for Isabella's garments bear out Wendover's descriptions. They are in red, blue, dark blue, dark brown and green. Two green sets of robes were trimmed with red squirrel fur as a contrast, while blue robes were trimmed with white fur from the northern squirrel. What may well have been her wedding dress was a set of three garments made from cloth of gold, of the type which used silk encased in fine gold strands, in a subtle ribbed finish.

There are riding jackets and saddlecloths, and elsewhere the wardrobe accountant noted the purchase of forty-four horses for the princess. And there are two beds covered in gold cloth from Genoa and ribbed cloth, with the mattress base in sendal silk.[27]

The keepers of the royal plate noted gifts to her from the king: a chess set and ivory tablets for other games, both with tables, gilded and embossed silver cups, and jewelled girdles. Overall, the provision for Isabella was lavish, and even her household was supplied with better livery than that given to Henry's own servants in similar positions.[28]

In addition to all this, a dowry of £20,000 had been agreed, in return for which Friedrich promised to grant his bride extensive estates in Sicily. The match was a diplomatic coup for Henry, and this apparent extravagance was designed to impress his future brother-in-law, the emperor. There were strong political reasons for the match. Henry wanted the emperor's support in his ongoing efforts to regain the French territories lost in the reign of his father, King John. Friedrich wanted to prevent further contact between his rebellious son, Heinrich, king of the Romans, and the English court. Despite the apparent success of the marriage, the conditions in which Isabella found herself when she reached Sicily were very different from the relative freedom of the English court. Unlike earlier empresses, she played little part in the political life of the empire. The chronicler Matthew Paris claimed that her English attendants had been sent home on her arrival, and she had been 'handed over to the care of Moorish eunuchs and elderly masked women'.[29] Henry wrote to Friedrich four years later to protest that his sister had not been allowed to appear crowned and in imperial garb at Friedrich's side on ceremonial occasions.[30] In the following year, 1241, she died in childbirth at Friedrich's castle of Foggia in Puglia.

II. Crown of Irene, queen of the Romans, in the Byzantine style. Now lost: this eighteenth-century engraving is the only record of it.

## The inventory of a duchess

CONSORTS WHO WERE RULERS IN THEIR own right had a different status. Margaret, countess of Flanders, wife of Philip the Bold of Burgundy, inherited Flanders on the death of her father Louis de Mâle in 1384. Philip became count, and Margaret played a part in the day-to-day government of the county. In Philip's absences, she acted for him in formal matters, and she seems to have supported him in many of his activities. They frequently travelled together to France and the Low Countries in the 1380s. In 1395 she negotiated the tax for a planned crusade. She had extensive estates of her own, and managed the affairs of these; her manor house at Germolles occupied much of her time. Its décor was based on Jean duke of Berry's new and much admired house at Mehun-sur-Yèvre, and included a sculpture by the great Claus Sluter of Philip and Margaret, rather surprisingly seated under an elm amid a flock of sheep.

These random scraps are all that we have of Margaret's life as Philip's consort. However, we do have the inventory taken after her death, which implies that she also enjoyed playing

*Margaret countess of Flanders*

the part of the consort of a magnificent prince. It is dated 2 May 1405, at Bruges, and lists all her goods, her treasure among them. Five complete crowns are listed. Each seems to have been of one piece, and they may be older crowns from the thirteenth century. By the late fourteenth century, crowns were made as circlets into which fleurons could be slotted, and the fleurons and circlets of another six crowns are mentioned.[31] There is a great crown among them, and both the circlet and the fleurons have sapphires and pearls, though the rubies are balas rather than the true rubies, which are called 'of Alexandria'. It is at least probable that this is the crown of her grandmother, Margaret of Burgundy.

*Margaret's jewellery*

There are gold collars in profusion, thirty-three in all. Half of these are variations on the broom-plant device of Charles VI, the product of the king's almost maniac determination to mark out his family, friends and followers by their dress and ornaments.[32] Brooches, which for men were more often than not a badge denoting friendship, allegiance or service, are far more numerous in Margaret's inventory (about 150) than in those of Richard II and of the French princes, and almost entirely decorative. There is indeed one badge of Richard II's white hart device, and some broom-plant designs, otherwise there is a whole gamut of the natural world: beasts tame and wild – hares, camels, lions, lambs – and of flowers, particularly the marguerite or daisy. There are little figures, a lady hawking, a shepherd's hut with a child in the doorway, enamelled on gold. In two cases, the brooches are designed to link and make up a chaplet. Buttons are listed in sets of up to thirty, several of them 'in Venetian fashion'; a number of sets are enamelled. At the end of the list of jewellery there are loose stones, but these are not connoisseur's pieces, like those of the duke of Berry, but a practical collection for repair or for fashioning into new pieces. Margaret, on the evidence of her jewels, 'had a passion for personal adornment':[33] in addition to the pieces listed above, there are purses embroidered with pearls, and gold belts, and of course clothing to match. As duchess of Flanders and wife of one of the French royal dukes, she was both a prince and a prince's consort, and dressed with appropriate magnificence.

## The tragedy of Isabella of Aragon

A LESS HAPPY STORY IS THAT OF THE marriage of Isabella of Aragon. In early childhood, there had a been a proposal to marry her to the king of Armenia, which failed.[34] In 1311 Friedrich duke of Austria approached her father Jaime II of Aragon for the hand of his daughter. She was then six, but such youthful betrothals were considered perfectly normal; the marriage itself might take place some years later. We have a great deal of the correspondence between Jaime II and Friedrich, and later between Jaime II and his daughter after her arrival in Austria. Friedrich starts the wooing in fine style, sending ambassadors to say that he is not marrying for money, and wishes to wed 'on account of your excellent nobility, wisdom and power, and the beauty of your daughters'. They declared that there was no prince more suitable than their master Friedrich, known as 'the Handsome', who was courteous, wise and noble, and tall. Isabella was the fourth daughter, but her elder sisters were either betrothed or destined for a nunnery.

*Isabella of Aragon's dowry*

The negotiations were detailed, and took some time to settle, but in 1313 everything was agreed, and by September her dowry was being assembled. In fact, Friedrich was not particularly wealthy, and money was probably a major factor in the marriage: the provision of money from Jaime later became critical. We have a complete listing of Isabella's dowry and details of her escort, which are the fullest that survive for any medieval marriage. She was given two crowns, and a third was to be repaired. There are good quantities of jewels, and circlets, and a mass of rings. For the table there are a silver salt in the form of a ship with the arms of Aragon, a handsome gold cup and lid, and a gold eagle as a table ornament. Cutlery, including a special *brogetas* for eating mulberries and napkin rings, is also provided. A large quantity of different kinds of cloth, much of it from the Netherlands, is supplied to be made up into garments, and other materials for items to be made up, possibly on arrival in Austria. Hand towels and silver basins for handwashing, tableware in silver, Tunisian and Murcian carpets, and chests in which to pack all this are listed. The most remarkable item is a chess set with a board of green jasper and crystal: beneath the crystal are 'imaginary figures', and there are four lions embossed on the corners. The chessmen – 'two bands of soldiers' – are also in crystal and jasper with silver-gilt mounts.

The eight-year-old Isabella was accompanied by a small group of her own countrymen. She had her own chancellor and majordomo, and her own confessor: Friedrich was opposed to this, but Jaime reasonably pointed out that she did not understand German, and needed a Catalan priest.[35] There were two fools, Fros and Freoli, but the Austrians did not appreciate their performances, and they were soon sent home. And, most important of all, there were her three personal attendants: Blanca, the eldest, Bonanat Cardon and the latter's cousin, Alamanda Sapera, whose letters home tell us much of her story. Isabella herself was a lively correspondent as well.

*Isabella's journey to Austria*

The princess set out in September 1313, and journeyed by way of Carpentras, where she met the pope, through southern France to the court of Savoy, and then on to Vienne on the River Rhône. She met Friedrich's brother and sister on the Rhine in December, and at the end of January, the wedding ceremony, which had been performed by proxy, was repeated in person by the bridal couple. It is at this point that the politics behind the match between Aragon and Austria become clear. The sudden death of the Holy Roman Emperor Heinrich VII in August, a month before Isabella left for Austria, meant that her husband was now the leading candidate for election as king of the Romans, and then coronation as Heinrich VII's successor. Jaime's objective throughout the negotiations was for an alliance which would make him the father-in-law of the emperor: he could not have expected it to come so quickly to fruition.

*Isabella's marriage*

There was however one major obstacle, a rival candidate with almost equal support. In the event, a dual election took place: Friedrich was elected by five of the prince-electors, Ludwig of Wittelsbach by the other four. Rival coronations took place on the same day, 25 November 1313. Isabella became queen of the Romans as soon as she was married. Her coronation took place in Basel on Whitsunday in 1314; Alamanda Sapera wrote personally to Jaime II with her report of the occasion. Immediately after the wedding, Friedrich had to write a very different letter, explaining that the costs of the occasion and of keeping Isabella's retinue had left him very short of money. Isabella's attendants were sent home, leaving her only two of her fellow countrywomen to accompany her. Her father was reluctant to hand over her dowry, since he knew that Friedrich was likely to use it for the costs of warfare, first against the Swiss, who defeated him at Morgarten in 1315, and then against Ludwig of Wittelsbach. The campaign against Ludwig opened well, but ended in disaster at Mühldorf in 1322. Friedrich was captured, and it was three years before he was released. There was a brief hope that he would be recognised by the papal court as king of the Romans, since Ludwig had quarrelled irrevocably with the pope, but it came to nothing. Isabella fell seriously ill about the time of his return, and never properly recovered. Friedrich died in January 1330, followed by Isabella five months later. Her story was the reverse of the golden coin of magnificence, a fate repeated all too often by the daughters of ambitious princes, but rarely recorded in such vivid detail.[36]

# 7 | THE PRINCE'S ENTOURAGE

◆ *The court and court festivals* ◆ *Livery and membership of the court*
◆ *Livery badges and collars* ◆ *Orders of knighthood* ◆ *Artists and*
*craftsmen: the prince's* valets de chambre

## The Court and Court Festivals

MAGNIFICENCE IS A PHILOSOPHICAL CONCEPT, as we have seen. Magnificence, however, would be nothing without its physical aspect, the worldly show which reflects the glory of the ruler. After the person of the prince himself, that glory is chiefly seen in his immediate surroundings, in the culture of his court, in the costumes of his entourage, in the quality of the artists and musicians he employed, and the décor of his castles and palaces. (A good menagerie was an asset.) And when he was not at home, his public appearance, magnificently attired and magnificently escorted, was an essential display of his wealth and power.

Giles of Rome, our guide to magnificence, has this to say about the prince's entourage:

> Thirdly, the magnificent man should have behave properly towards some special persons, as being persons worthy of honour. For magnificence appears especially clearly, when anybody does great things to those who are particularly worthy.[1]

These 'special persons' are his courtiers, and it is in the late thirteenth century that the court as a social centre comes into its own. The French court, the wealthiest in Europe and with the riches of Paris, the greatest city of the time, at its disposal, was the leader of fashion for much of this period, and the other royal courts took it as their model. The relatively sober court of St Louis gave way to a much more relaxed and sociable environment under his grandson Philip IV. The scandal of the behaviour of three of his daughters-in-law, who were said to have met their lovers in secret in the isolated Tour de Nesle, was perhaps a reflection of this, but the discovery of their affairs led to their imprisonment. Philip's sons all died without male heirs, but under the new Valois dynasty, Philip VI, who came to the throne in 1328, continued to hold substantial festivals. The misfortunes of the French kings in the wars against England, culminating in the capture of Jean II at Poitiers in 1356, meant that the French royal court was in disarray, and it was only under Charles V in the latter part of the century that it revived.

*The scandal of the Tour de Nesle*

*The French royal family as collectors*

The reformation of the French government was Charles's great achievement; a combination of new tactics, which countered the weakening power of England and an overhaul of the administration, brought unparalleled prosperity to Paris by the time of his death in 1380. His taste was scholarly and artistic and the craftsmen and merchants of the capital were well able to supply him. The chronicler at Saint-Denis declared that the beauty of the objects he and his brothers collected lay both in the quality of the work and equally in the richness of the materials from which they were made.[2]

In the next reign this passion for collecting remained a strong element in the courts of the four royal princes, Orléans, Berry, Anjou and Burgundy, who ruled as the regency during the minority and later madness of Charles VI. In his intervals of sanity, the king showed much enthusiasm for festivals, and spent lavishly on them: disapproving chroniclers blamed his madness on his love of diversions of this kind. The development of Burgundy into a major power in the fifteenth century was marked by the apogee of the chivalric festival under Philip the Good from 1430 onwards, while his contemporary, René d'Anjou, who by contrast held resounding titles – king of Jerusalem and king of Naples – but not the lands that went with them, held similar but less lavish festivals almost as a consolation for his loss of real status. In the greatest of these festivals, all the arts were brought into play to highlight the almost regal power of the Burgundian dukes: dress and display, great feasts, jousts with elaborate symbolic and literary programmes, were on a scale which was the envy of Europe, and which outshone the French royal court itself. And chivalry in its final medieval form became the ideal of the courtier, combining warlike skills in the joust with accomplishment in music and poetry, and the refinement of manners through the particular ethic of the court itself, courtesy.

*The Burgundian court*

The English court began to hold chivalric festivals under Edward I; under his grandson Edward III the tournament became a central part of royal festivities. This, merged with the French tradition inherited from his mother Isabella, daughter of Philip IV, led to a spectacular series of festive occasions in the first two decades of Edward III's reign. This was a brief flowering: as the fortunes of war went against the English, and with Richard II's lack of interest in participating in tournaments, subsequent rulers were more concerned with political and military problems. While the Burgundian princes went from splendour to splendour, the English court was mired in the problems of the regency during the minority of Henry VI and the subsequent Wars of the Roses. Even Edward IV, consciously modelling himself on his namesake and ancestor, and with strong chivalric and artistic interests, never succeeded in mounting a major festival.

*The English court*

In eastern Europe, French influence was also strong: in Bohemia, King Jean, who had been brought up at the French court, attempted without success to introduce tournaments, and retreated to spend much of his time in France until his death at Crécy in 1346. His son, Karl IV, became Holy Roman Emperor; he too had been brought up at the French court, and used Paris as the model for his transformation of Prague into a major European centre, of prime intellectual and artistic importance, founding a university and rebuilding the city. The complex politics of the empire occupied much of his time, and he preferred serious pursuits in his leisure time. Like his nephew Charles V, his court was cultured, devout and formal: the greatest festival in which Karl IV took part was that at Paris in 1378 when he visited his nephew. Karl's second marriage was marked at the Congress of Krákow in 1364, held by Casimir III, king of Poland, uncle of the bride. He, like Karl IV, had reformed Poland on the French model, recasting the laws and creating the university at Krákow. The Congress was a spectacular gathering of the rulers of Europe, to celebrate the wedding.

*French influence in eastern Europe*

Elsewhere in Europe, the Visconti dynasty at Milan was linked to the English court by the marriage of Violante Visconti to the third son of Edward III, Lionel duke of Clarence. The Anglo-Italian links, whose most notable result was in literary terms, namely Chaucer's acquaintance with Boccaccio, did not survive the death of Lionel soon after the wedding, but the Sforza seem to have adopted something of the magnificence of Edward III's court. In Spain, the court of Aragon had inherited the culture of the troubadour courts of the south of France, as it was part of the same linguistic territory: the *langue d'oc* extended south of the Pyrenees, and under the thirteenth- and fourteenth-century kings, Barcelona, Valencia and Toulouse (then part of Aragon) were the scene of notable festivals. Peter IV, who became king in 1336, was known as 'the Ceremonious', and the handbook written for his court in Majorca in 1344 was a model for the similar instructions drawn up for the

*The courts of Italy and Spain*

papal court at Avignon. The Aragonese court was in touch with the courts of England and France, who vied for influence in Spain from the mid thirteenth century onwards, beginning with Edward I's marriage to Eleanor of Castile. The kings of Castile, occupied both with the *reconquista*, the attempt to drive the Moslems out of Spain, and with serious civil wars, seem to have started to celebrate festivals and tournaments later than Aragon: Alfonso XI, who founded one of the earliest royal orders of chivalry in 1330, held events connected with his Order of the Sash in the decade following, but the order itself did not flourish. In the early fifteenth century, under Juan II, 'a king who was to be famous only for his love of amusements, and who delegated his power to the constable of Castile', the Castilian court was once again remarkable for the scale of its entertainments.

## Livery and Membership of the Court

ONE OF GILES OF ROME'S MOST SPECIFIC injunctions is that magnificence should also extend to the appearance of his court and the officers and servants who are closest to him:

Because it is most fitting for the king's prudence that he should rule his household properly, and that he should provide them with necessaries in a fitting and orderly way: and because fitting provision seems most conducive to a state of honour, so that kings and princes are encouraged to behave honourably and prudently in such matters, we need to look at the way in which clothing is provided for their servants....

Secondly, in the matter of dress, consideration must be given to uniformity of the servants' appearance. For as the servants appear to belong to one prince or to one ruler, (leaving aside the status of each person) it seems very much to follow that they should be dressed uniformly. For there are in the dwellings of kings and princes persons of varied status; therefore all those who are seen to be at the same level, or who do not stand in much distance from one another, should be clothed in the same way, so that by the conformity of their clothing it will be known that they serve the one prince.

Thirdly, in the provision of clothing the person's status should be maintained. For not all deserve to be equal in dress. For in such dwellings there are not only lay persons, but also clerics, and among both some are superior and some inferior, because of which it is fitting that each should be dressed differently.[3]

The Burgundian historian Georges Chastellain reasserts the theme two centuries later: 'After the deeds and exploits of war, which are claims to glory, the household is the first thing that strikes the eye, and that which it is therefore most necessary to conduct and arrange well.'[4]

*The livery system*

THE EARLIEST ENGLISH EVIDENCE of the livery system, whereby retainers received regular gifts of clothes from their lord as part of the recompense for their service, comes at the end of Henry II's reign, in 1179/80, when the king gave robes to his knights and serjeants costing £113. The chronicler Roger of Wendover notes similar gifts by John, and they continue under his successors.[5] Livery was also given out by great lords, and those who wished to imitate them: when the leader of a band of robbers was tried for a variety of crimes, including invading Richmond castle and holding a Christmas feast there, he was said to have clothed his men 'as if he were a baron or an earl'.[6]

Livery in its original sense meant 'delivery', the handing over of garments or wages to members of the royal household, but by the early thirteenth century, members of the English court were entitled to the delivery of cloth twice a year to make their summer and winter wear, and a hundred years later this had developed into a system of different cloths graded according to their rank, with furs issued to the royal family, the great lords, knights and squires and the clerks who served in the household.[7] In the process 'livery' acquired an additional meaning, clothes which identified the wearer's rank and allegiance to the king, and the clothing so distributed became standardised. At first this standardisation was simply convenience: if clothing was being made for a small group of the household, a certain amount of material of the same type would be ordered for simplicity. The reason for a distribution of this kind was very much a matter of prestige: John de Droxford, keeper of the wardrobe, wrote to Ralph de Stokes, clerk of the stores, while Edward I was campaigning in Scotland:

> Because there are sixteen valets who were in the garrison of Stirling and who follow the king every day on the road, which valets are badly dressed, I order you to deliver to them, of the king's gift, four cloths of a suit [i.e. of the same colour], the price of cloth being forty shillings or four marks at most.[8]

Gifts of actual clothes could be replaced by money, and the amounts paid out reflected the hierarchy of the household: knights banneret, who had their own retinue, were given £10 13s 4d in 1289/90, while ordinary knights, wardrobe clerks and chaplains had half this, lesser officials a quarter, and the lowest ranks a mere 5s.

Mentions of robes of a specific colour occur in 1214, when King John and his close associates wore green at Christmas. Outside the court, the idea of uniform began to appear in the late thirteenth century in the footsoldiers of the medieval armies, and livery also came to mean a colour which identified a person as the follower of a particular lord or – in the cities – a member of a particular guild. Chroniclers in the early fourteenth century comment on the appearance of guilds at town parades all in the same colours. We find the same tradition in royal entries into cities, where groups of citizens ride out of the gates to greet the ruler. In Paris, this occurs in 1364 and 1380, when Charles V and Charles VI came to the city after being crowned at Reims. On these two occasions the citizens wore green and white halved. Nine years later, for the coronation of Isabeau of Bavaria, the colour changed to green and red. In London, the members of the city guilds all wore blue, with devices distinguishing the different guilds, for the entry of Henry VI in 1432.

*Liveries and colours*

The visual effect of similar clothing was used at many court festivals, but one of the most notable examples arose from a particular event. This was the making of fashionable jackets called 'aketouns' for the men who helped Edward III to overthrow Roger Mortimer in 1330. Originally an undergarment designed to give protection from the chafing of armour, made of quilted cotton, they became a fashionable item early in Edward III's reign. In November 1330, a few weeks after the conspirators had successfully seized Mortimer, the queen's supposed lover and the effective ruler of England in her name, at Nottingham, seven very luxurious aketouns were made in striking purple, green and red, of silk and velvet and linen, and adorned with silver and gold embroidery. The king and William Montagu, the leader of the plot, had already adopted the aketoun in the previous summer, and there must be some kind of link between them and the other recipients, though one or two of them do not entirely fit what we know of the conspirators. These 'aketouns' prefigure similar groups of costumes – though much more modest in number – found at royal tournaments and games of the period. Edward had had red cloth tunics made for himself and twelve fellows for 'the

*Edward III's aketouns*

**47.** Issuing livery to members of the king's household, from Walter de Milemete's treatise *De Nobilitatibus*, c.1325–30.

game of the society of Craddok' in the spring of 1328. And on such occasions, throughout his reign, more than one set of clothes is made for the king: one for him to wear, and the others to give to his close friends.

We have a very full listing of the clothing provided for the English court at Christmas 1360, which gives some idea of how the recipients of livery were divided into groups. At the head of the list are the royal family, dressed in marbryn cloth, probably a variegated pattern: we use the word 'marbled' today for paper with random colouring. Stella Newton, who studied this roll closely, believed that the clothing was dark in colour, because if it had 'been bright in colour, this certainly would have been mentioned'. Given the frequent absence of colour descriptions in the accounts, this is not really tenable, but it is fair to say that the king and queen and their children and relatives would have formed a distinctive and striking group. The fur trimmings alone, of ermine,[9] marked them out, because this was firmly reserved for them alone. Furs were graded accorded to status: miniver came next, followed by squirrel, both red and grey, and then lamb, ranging from budge, fine black lambskin originally imported from Algeria, down to native white lambskin. Budge was reserved for craftsmen, the king's tailors, masons and his armourers. The household servants were given four metres of 'shortcloth' and four metres of striped cloth, probably the broad striped cloth used for 'mi-parti', clothes with two colours divided vertically: some received budge because of their standing within the household. The ordinary servants and minstrels were given lamb. Specific clothing was given to clergy and to knights. The two household knights also had mi-parti cloth similar to that of the servants, but of better quality. In 1363 a much larger group of knights, fifteen in all, were given the same kind of cloth and furs. The king's valets, those of the king's confessor and of the duke of Brittany, were all given identical clothing. The royal gardeners and carpenters were clothed like the lower servants, while the king's bargemen did not receive any fur at all. Rank is being very carefully delineated here.

The clearest picture of the grading of liveries is in the description of the emperor Karl IV's entry into Paris in 1378. The king of France rode out with his officials:

> each rank dressed in the same robes, that is to say: chamberlains, two types of robes, one of velvet and the others in two shades of scarlet; masters of the royal household in two kinds of velvet, one dark blue and the other tawny; the knights of honour, dressed in vermilion velvet; the squires of the bodyguard and of the stables in blue camocas; the ushers at arms in two kinds of camocas, part blue and part red; the officers of the household – pantlers, butlers and squire carvers – in satin cloth of two kinds, white and tawny, as were the officers of the dauphin of Viennois, the king's eldest son; and the cooks and squires of the kitchen in houppelandes of silk with fur capes with pearl buttons on them; the valets of the chamber, fifty-two in number, all in robes of black with grey and white stripes; fifty to sixty sergeants at chambers, with brown strips on vermilion; and so with all the other ranks, each rank distinguished by its robes.[10]

Visually, this would have been most impressive, in a society where the only other uniforms to be seen were those of the clergy in religious processions.

## Livery badges and collars

ALTHOUGH THE EARLIEST REFERENCES to both badges and mottoes date from around the time of the foundation of the Order of the Garter and are from English records, it is in France that the royal court developed them as part of a much more hierarchical form of livery. The intensive use of royal livery in France began with Jean II in the 1350s. Here we find *devises* in the form of badges, whose design was a heraldic image combined with a motto. They were usually either embroidered onto clothing or woven into the fabric. The mottos were partly personal and partly political, and are similar to those found with coats of arms. These *devises* are mentioned, along with the royal livery and the idea of the king's retainers as a company, in the small section of his surviving accounts, for the years 1351 to 1355.[11] Robes were issued twice or three times a year, with different clothing for the clerics (secretaries, notaries and exchequer clerks) and for the members of the royal household. There is even less information for the reign of Charles V, and it seems that he preferred to emphasise the royal emblem of the *fleur-de-lis* which was repeatedly used on clothes and tapestries and other decorations.

*Badges and devices*

It was Charles VI who used collars, badges and livery most actively as the distinguishing mark of his court, and issued vast quantities of robes.[12] From May 1382 until the end of his reign, he and his council specified the colours of the clothing to be issued to the royal household each year, which applied to all members of the 'king's companionship' (*compaignie du roy*) and included the king and the royal princes. There were additional distributions for special occasions such as tournaments, civic entries or the great feasts of the church. Hundreds of suits of clothing in the king's colours were distributed following each edict. The mottoes of which we have a record were 'Hope', first used in 1387, 'You are there' from 1390 and 'I love her who is most beautiful' from 1394. The king's favourite motto 'Never' was introduced in 1394 and was used regularly until 1409. 'In good part'

**48-50**, p.115

appeared before 1420.[13] The pictorial elements ranged from the plants of broom, which were traditional among the Valois kings, to branches of may for May day and birds and beasts. The liveries were worn all the time by members of the household. Others who were only at court occasionally but who had been issued with livery wore them when they were in attendance on the king.

The livery was supplemented by the issue of a very small number of gold collars, averaging twenty a year, distributed as a mark of the king's favour. They were quite distinct from the collars of the new orders of secular chivalry which appeared from the mid fourteenth century onwards. Both livery and collars could be distributed to women as well as men. From the list of collars in her inventory, it would appear that Margaret duchess of Flanders was a regular recipient of the king's letter entitling her to wear a particular royal collar.[14] This system did not survive the king's death; Charles VII restricted the livery (which he himself wore) to members of his immediate household, and it was abandoned entirely in the 1470s under Louis XI.

*The king's gold collars*

Charles VI's most important badge was a crowned and winged white stag. Like some of the orders of knighthood of the period, a legend was attached to its first use. The royal accounts have an entry for 17 September 1382, a payment to Colin the smith for a branding iron of a *fleur-de-lis*, which was used to mark a stag which the king had hunted in the forest of Compiègne. It had taken refuge in a stable at the leper-house at Choisy, and the king ordered that it should be released into the forest once it had been marked. The chronicle written at Saint-Denis elaborates on this: the king had noticed that it had a very old collar of gilded copper on its neck, and ordered it to be captured in nets rather than hunted with the hounds. An inscription was found on its collar which read in Latin, 'Caesar gave this to me'.[15] The device was first used on the critical campaign against the Flemish rebels who opposed the duke of Burgundy who had claimed the county on the death of Louis de Mâle. This culminated in the French victory at Roosebeke in November 1382, and the badge of the winged and crowned stag, perhaps because it was associated with the success of the expedition, continued to be used for the next twelve years, during which time it appeared everywhere, embroidered on clothing, in the form of jewels, engraved on plate and painted on the walls.[16]

*Charles V's winged stag*

The reference to Caesar is connected with the theme of the Nine Worthies, great leaders of the heathen, the Old Testament and Christians. Caesar is the last of the trio of heathen leaders, and had ruled France. Stags were famous for their longevity, and the king's capture of the stag shows that he is Caesar's worthy successor. Fifty years later, when his cousin Philip the Good of Burgundy founded his Order of the Golden Fleece, he appealed to the classical legend of Jason and the Argonauts, and the whole passage about the stag reads like an origin legend set up for a new knightly order which never came to fruition.[17]

There was a curious episode in 1389, when Charles VI's lavish distribution of wealth to anyone who approached him – 'where his father would have given a hundred crowns, he gave a thousand', led his officials to try to limit his gifts by melting down all gold coins which came into the treasury to create a huge statue of a golden stag, thus limiting the amount of cash available. However, they were soon replaced, and only the head of this statue was finished.[18] It was doubtless converted back into coin as soon as possible.

Collars were always a mark of high status, and survived into modern times as part of the dress of members of knightly orders. Devices, when issued as jewelled badges, were still a mark of distinction, but they were used much more widely simply as a visual image identifying the followers of a prince: they were not exactly heraldic, but functioned as a kind of heraldic shorthand at a time when coats of arms were increasingly complex. After

*Ducal devices and colours*

the moment in 1392 when Charles VI became mad – he believed he was made of glass, and might shatter at the least touch – the devices reflect the varying influence over the council of the four royal dukes. These were his cousin the duke of Orléans, and his three uncles, the dukes of Anjou, Burgundy and Berry. Tigers, wolves and knotted clubs appear during the ascendance of the duke of Orléans. After his death in 1407, murdered by the henchmen of the duke of Burgundy, the emblems of Jean the Fearless replace his victim's symbols with peacocks, lions and the letter 'y'. And the colours change too: originally they were the royal green and white, but in 1408 it was a mixture of the royal green and the Burgundian red. In 1413, when Charles of Orléans regained control of Paris, his troops entered the city in the livery of Orléans (black, white and red) and of his father-in-law and ally Bernard d'Armagnac (white and violet).

Charles VI wore collars given him by the rival dukes, but avoided those with the most aggressive devices: the crossbow, the thorns, the flint and the plane (a Burgundian device which showed that the duke would plane the knots off the Orléans club). In 1400, for May day that year, the total was 352 'houppelandes' for the courtiers and 139 for the members of the household – nearly 500 in all.[19] Even the royal treasury was unable to sustain this kind of expenditure, and, not surprisingly, by the end of his reign in 1422, that treasury was virtually empty.

The royal dukes could not compete with the king, and indeed used the system to provide liveries for their own followers: hence the appearance of their devices on the king's livery. Yet they were similarly obsessed with devices and colours. In addition, the dukes created their own knightly orders, but these were as short-lived as the royal Order of the Star.[20] This riot of knightly ornaments and honours is reflected in the accounts of Louis d'Orléans between 1393 and 1397. Black, as with Philip the Good of Burgundy and Amadeus VIII of Savoy, was his favourite colour.[21] This was a fashion that survived into the fifteenth century: Alfonso V of Naples habitually wore black with a gold chain or clasp.[22] This was relieved by the use of green on occasions, and a handful of red garments. Louis's devices were the wolf, the crossbow, the porcupine, a nest, and an interlace of six colours.[23] The device of the nest is very rarely used, and seems to be a counterpoint to the swallow of Charles VI. The porcupine is exclusive to the members of Louis's personal chivalric order. The commonest devices are the wolf, used frequently by the duke and his family on embroideries or as a gold pendant to a collar, mentioned forty-five times. The crossbow marks out members of his household, and appears sixty-five times. A typical garment using devices has on the left hand side a large embroidered wolf with a gold collar, and on the right sleeve three crossbows, embroidered, outlined in pearls and made up of golden balls. On occasion, Louis had identical garments made for himself and the dukes of Burgundy and Berry, with the king's device of a swallow, his own wolf, Jean duke of Berry's bear and daisies for Margaret of Flanders, Philip's wife. Jean the Fearless of Burgundy presented 315 gold planes to his courtiers in 1406, with those for the nobles set with diamonds.[24]

The multiplicity of devices at the French court during the last two decades of the fourteenth century is a reflection of the very real power struggles between the king's brothers during the period of Charles VI's madness.[25] It was a custom that continued into the next generation: René d'Anjou used no less than fourteen devices, admittedly over a long period; the motto 'According to God's will' predominates, as it is used with four different images. René, as a poet and writer, adopted new devices according to his personal circumstances rather than as a political statement, and several of them referred to his love for his two wives. Others related to tournaments, which often had a theatrical element, in which the device played a part.[26]

*A riot of ornaments and honours*

IN ENGLAND, BY THE MIDDLE OF the fourteenth century, livery and the payment of pensions, which had previously been limited to the working members of a lord's household, including his clerks, were now being used to form groups or affinities. In war time, the indentures of retinue between military commanders and their followers were increasingly important. This followed Edward III's changes to the way the army was organised in the preparations for the campaign in 1346 that culminated in the battle of Crécy. Great lords now had both their household and a band of men retained by them, as well as occasional agreements, often with advisers or lawyers. And in peacetime, there was sufficient lawlessness for lords to feel the need for retaining followers to support them, often physically. These men, too, came to wear the lord's livery, by which they were identified. A group of men in the same livery could seem threatening to individuals or to the followers of a rival lord. Their baleful influence extended beyond lawsuits to a kind of gang mentality, which could undermine public order in times when central authority was weak.

*Livery and uniform in England*

In 1377, with the death of Edward III, the question of the abuse of liveries by lesser lords suddenly became a problem of major concern to parliament. It emerged first as a complaint that men were being given liveries to support defendants in lawsuits and other quarrels, and that the retinues formed in this way were becoming conspiracies to thwart justice.[27] Ten years later, when nothing had been done about the abuse, a new petition to parliament spoke of badges as being in use since the first year of Edward III's reign, 1327.[28] Edward III and Edward prince of Wales had used badges occasionally, either as personal presents or in connection with the Order of the Garter. Badges or devices appear in relation to tournaments, where the knights were divided into teams: in 1331, for a tournament held at Stepney in which the king took part, Sir Robert Morley's team of twenty-five knights had golden arrows as their emblem.[29] Although there is no real evidence to support the use of badges outside the royal court, it is clear that the members who presented the petition in 1377 clearly regarded badges as a particular menace.

*The misuse of livery under Richard II*

Livery was distinctive enough when a large group of retainers appeared in their lord's colours. It was used in England during the Wars of the Roses, in much the same way as the royal dukes had used theirs during the regency in France due to Charles VI's madness. In 1458, when a council was held at Westminster to establish peace after the battle of St Albans, William Worcester reported to his master Sir John Fastolf that the duke of York had arrived with a following 'only to the number of 140 horsemen', while the Earl of Salisbury was accompanied by 400 horsemen, of whom 80 were knights and squires.[30] Seen *en masse*, the livery colours were enough; but meeting any one of these men on their own, it would not be easy to recognise the livery, particularly as medieval dyes had a relatively narrow range of colours.

From the reign of Richard II onwards, badges became the shorthand form of showing allegiance to a particular lord. Badges were immediately recognisable, and made a single individual into a representative of a powerful lord, able to coerce others into doing as he wished. Indeed, no formal payment needed to be made. In 1384 Richard II, attempting to raise direct support among the gentry of East Anglia, sent out one of his sergeants to distribute silver and gilt badges to those who had pledged loyalty to him. He was arrested by one of the local lords, as parliament had recently affirmed its opposition to badges.[31] Richard introduced his famous badge of the white hart at the great tournament at Smithfield in 1390, and we find him distributing it to his followers in Cheshire a month or two later to reinforce his influence there.[32]

Alfonso V of Aragon and Naples used a wide range of badges from 1415 onwards, over a period of twenty-three years. One reflected his love of books and learning, an open book

**48.** Devices of the royal dukes of France from a treatise exculpating Jean the Fearless of Burgundy from the murder of Louis d'Orleans. The wolf, the device of Louis d'Orleans, tears at the crown hanging from a tent with the broom and may branch emblems of the king, and is driven off by the lion, the device of Jean the Fearless as count of Flanders.

**49, 50.** The devices of Charles VI: the motto on both miniatures is '*James*', '*Never*', but on the left the hangings have sprigs of broom and the king is wearing a robe with peacock feather patterns; on the right, there are plain hangings, and the king's robes have hounds with a coronet as their collar.

whose Latin inscription can be translated as *A wise man will rule over the stars*. Others represented a variety of objects: the chair in the Grail stories in which only the hero of the Grail could sit unharmed; the Mountain of Diamonds, inscribed 'The work of nature, not of art'; and the ear of millet symbolising incorruptibility.[33]

## Orders of knighthood

*The Orders of St George and of the Sash*

THE EARLIEST PRINCELY ORDERS of chivalry appear in the first half of the fourteenth century. The motives for their foundation, in the case of both the fraternal Order of St George in Hungary and the Order of the Sash in Castile, were to provide a bond between the king and his closest companions. The Hungarian order was short-lived, and we know almost nothing about its activities, though tournaments were specifically mentioned. The Order of the Sash was a combination of a royal élite corps in wartime and a tourneying society in peacetime. It was founded in 1330 by Alfonso XI and several tournaments were held. However, once he became engaged in his successful wars against the Moslem kingdoms of southern Spain, it seems to disappear as an institution. By the end of the century, the sash was a royal emblem, apparently independent of its origins.

*The Company of the Garter*

The 'company or knightly order' of the Garter, founded by Edward III in 1349, had a different background. From the start, it was associated with the college of St George at Windsor Castle, and the chapel of St George. Its main purpose was commemorative, to attend the annual service on 23 April each year, and to provide for the saying of masses on the death of any of the companions. The earliest statutes of the order that survive have only two clauses about secular matters. The problem with the early history of the order is that the records were not properly kept. In 1378 the records were said to have been 'remissly and negligently kept'. What we can say with confidence is that the Garter knights had nothing to do with tournaments as part of their statutory duties. Nor were tournaments held on the anniversary dates. The only exception, in 1358, was when Edward held a special festival for the two kings who were his captives at that point, Jean II of France and David II of Scotland.

*The Company of the Star*

The French rival to the Company of the Garter was the 'Knights of Our Lady or of the Noble House', generally called the Company of the Star, founded in 1352. This is unequivocally a knightly company, an attempt by Jean II to revive the ideals of knighthood among knights 'starved of honour and glory', centred on a mansion to be built near Paris. There was an annual gathering, on 15 August each year, the feast of the Assumption of the Virgin, to whom the order was dedicated. The statutes were concerned with the knights' conduct in warfare and their duty to give the king 'loyal counsel'. In contrast to the Garter statutes, the knights have specific, secular duties. Again, there is no mention of tournaments.

The Company of the Star suffered its first catastrophe in the year of their foundation at the battle of Mauron, when 'no fewer than eighty-nine knights of the Star were killed there' because the statutes provided that they should never retreat more than three hundred metres from a battle. They were to fight to the death, or yield as prisoners. This may be an exaggeration on the part of Jean le Bel, the chronicler who is our only source for this vow. The battle of Poitiers in 1356 certainly delivered the *coup de grace* to the Company. Jean le Bel continues: 'I think it has come to nothing and their house has been left empty'.

The Company of the Garter, by contrast, grew in reputation as a result of the English victories, though it too suffered when the tide of war turned against it. By the end of Richard II's reign it was moribund and largely forgotten, with ten vacancies and several members who were simply royal favourites. Under Henry IV, who had been a knight of the Garter since 1377, the Company was revived, the vacancies filled, and the nature of it changed. In 1408, the knights were challenged to fight as a team against a company assembled for the purpose by the seneschal of Hainault, but Henry IV turned down the offer on the grounds that the knights of the Order never fought as a group.

The real revival was to come under Henry V, with the appointment of William Bruges as Garter herald, and the widening of the scope of the order. Until 1416, the only foreign knights admitted to the order had been the relatives by marriage of the sovereign. When Henry V had the emperor Sigismund of Germany elected in that year, he opened up a new dimension: the use of membership as a diplomatic weapon. The next such election failed, because Philip the Good of Burgundy refused the honour. However, between 1422 and 1485, seventeen out of eighty elections were of foreign princes. The election of Charles the Bold of Burgundy in 1471 was regarded as one of his twelve 'magnificences' after his death.

JEAN II OF FRANCE WAS NOT the only ruler who felt that a knightly order would add lustre to his reputation. A number of attempts were made to imitate the Garter by other princes, particularly in the period up to 1364. By 1430, when Philip the Good of Burgundy founded the Order of the Golden Fleece, only one other order survived, in Savoy. This, the Order of the Collar was a purely local institution: it had only fifteen members, all from the Savoyard nobility. Philip the Good set the membership of the Golden Fleece at twenty-four, in close imitation of the Garter. Its first companions were entirely drawn from his court and he envisaged ther order as a means of uniting his very varied territories. The Burgundian 'state' was an amalgamation of numerous previously independent – and often hostile – units, and one of the important features of the order's meetings was the settlement of disputes between its members. It was also to some extent independent of the duke, as elections of new members were not subject to his veto. In effect, it was a kind of inner circle within his administration, made up of men whom he trusted or wished to win over. It was smaller than the ducal council, and its main purpose was to foster loyalty and a sense of chivalric pride. Some of his councillors were administrators rather than territorial lords, and would not therefore have qualified as companions. It was not long before Philip began to use it to secure loyalty or allegiance outside his territories: a group of four Burgundian allies among the French dukes were elected together in 1440 and, as with the Garter, kings also became companions. This was not always straightforward, as the insignia of the order were to be worn every day, and in the case of Alfonso V of Naples, this clashed with the requirements of his own newly-founded order.

*The Order of the Golden Fleece*

The prestige which the Order of the Golden Fleece rapidly acquired was due in no small measure to the sheer public exposure which the Burgundian court afforded. It rivalled and even exceeded Paris in the number of visitors who came to it, partly because of its central situation in Europe. French magnates sometimes spent long periods at court, and foreign diplomats were usually to be found there. In contrast to England, the duke's court was a far more public platform. The Order of the Golden Fleece, as its highest honour, was a key element in the ducal display of magnificence. Olivier de la Marche, the official responsible for organising the annual feast, was in charge of an occasion which was a sharp contrast to the modest Garter feasts, for which we have no records.[34]

At the age of 76, La Marche sent a letter to the emperor Maximilian, then head of the order as ruler of Burgundy, setting out the organisation and management of the 'noble feast of the Golden Fleece' as he remembered it from his service under Philip the Good and Charles the Bold.[35] The proceedings last four days, with four masses. La Marche goes into the least details, with plenty of rhetorical flourishes, but all the necessary instructions for his

*The organisation of the Order*

successor are there, including those for the procession to and from the church for the annual services. A room with a high seat for the head of the order and two rows of benches for the knights is to be provided for the annual assembly. For the actual feasts, tables need to be set out in the hall: the high table is for the knights of the order, and another for its four officers; then there is provision for the guards, and a table for any visiting ambassadors who wish to watch the proceedings. To one side there is a stand with a trellis in front, so that the ladies of the court can also be spectators; they are also to be served like everyone else. The detail is intriguing, down to the seasonal foods which are to form part of the menu, such as 'fresh butter in May', and, in more serious mode, the chivalric ritual for dealing with knights who are in some way in disgrace. On the first day, the leading citizens of the town are to be invited, and given a separate room for dining; on the second, the prelates of the region, and on the third and fourth any suitable persons who have not been invited previously. At the end of the meal, wine and sweetmeats are to be served to the high table only, and the most distinguished guest is to hand the sweetmeats to the duke, while the heir apparent, if he is present, is to pour his wine.

The carefully prescribed ritual and the length of the meeting is all calculated to make the greatest possible impression. It is a deliberate contrast with the usual Burgundian feasts, with their sideshows, musicians and elaborately decorated tables. The business of the conclave could be very serious as well; the loyalty which the order was intended to foster was not always evident, and on occasion knights made severe charges against each other. Nonetheless, these occasions were set up to project the image of the duke as a sovereign in a way that no other nobles of his rank could emulate, by creating a magnificent solemnity about his person.

## Artists and Craftsmen: The Prince's *Valets de Chambre*

NOT ALL MEMBERS OF THE COURT were employed on the same terms. In the twelfth and thirteenth century, artists were employed by the prince on an *ad hoc* basis, and there is nothing to indicate that even men who were frequently working for the court were regarded as part of the prince's entourage, or that the mere presence of the artist there added to his lustre. From the beginning of the fourteenth century we begin to find a closer link between artist and prince. The first examples come from Naples, soon after the Angevin king Robert I came to the throne. In 1310, an artist named Montano di Arezzo, evidently from the Tuscan town of that name, was given a post in the king's entourage, 'among the men of the household'. And twenty years later, the most famous Italian painter of that period, Giotto, was made a member of the household when he was on an extended visit to Robert's court. In 1313, an illuminator of manuscripts named Maciot was listed among the *valets de chambre* of the royal household.[36] The test of the closeness of the artist's connection to his patron was, in general, whether or not he held this title. The *valets de chambre* are in ways a very mixed group: they include the prince's tailor, his barber and his pharmacists, as well as those who attend to his dress and his immediate personal needs. We can only surmise as to why artists and craftsmen should be included in this group. It has been suggested that they were 'personally companionable' and entertaining, but this seems doubtful.[37] Perhaps a better way of looking at it might be that it was difficult to classify the role of an artist attached to the court. The problem was solved by including them in this class, which had no hierarchy to it.

The idea that art was a distinct and superior sphere of activity to that of the craftsman

Valets de chambre

and the decorative painter is something that is found in classical literature, but is blurred in the Middle Ages. The comment by Ovid that 'the workmanship surpassed the materials' was taken as a sign that the skill of the artist lay in his ability to transmute what he had to hand, rather than in using his inspiration to create something rich and rare.[38] Men such as Master Hugh of Bury St Edmunds, who designed the massive bronze doors of the abbey and its seal as well as illuminating one of the most splendid of all twelfth-century bibles and probably executing frescoes at Canterbury Cathedral, were valued for the multiplicity of their expertise. The same was true of the painters whom we first meet as part of princely households in the following century.

At the beginning of the fourteenth century, we find the first official royal painters in France: Evrard d'Orléans and his descendants held the title for six decades, from the reign of Philip IV until the early years of Charles V. Girard, Evrard's son, accompanied Jean II when he went as a prisoner to England in 1357, at the king's insistence, and Jean – either Evrard's son or brother – succeeded him as painter until the end of the reign. This did not preclude the appointment of other royal painters, such as Jean de Bandol, designer of the Angers tapestry, who is named as 'peintre du roi' in the entry recording the payment to him from the duke of Anjou for his designs.

*French royal painters*

In England, royal painters, although less closely linked to the king than in France, appear a little later. At the beginning of Edward III's reign, we find designers called *protractores* working with embroiderers; the word implies that they drew up the overall plan and design, and it is possible that the embroiderers had some freedom as to the details.[39] For three counterpanes for the churching ceremony for Philippa of Hainault after the birth of Edward the Black Prince in 1330, a team of 114 embroiderers was needed, and they and the two designers in charge, John de Kerdyff and John de Chidelee, spent eleven weeks on the project. It was certainly true that Edward III's painters were as much designers as actual painters. Hugh of St Albans, in charge of the murals at Edward's new chapel of St Stephen at Westminster, also worked on the great streamers on the royal ships. He may have designed the stained glass at St Stephen's, and he or other painters designed the patterns for the elaborate pictures embroidered on the king's festival costumes and for the scenery at court entertainments. He was in touch with the new art from Italy, as his will describes a 'six piece Lombard panel painting which cost me £20 while still unfinished'.[40] His successor under Richard II, Gilbert Prince, who had worked under Hugh of St Albans, was even wealthier, even though he fulfilled the same kind of role, painting the decorative stands and equipment needed for tournaments and masked balls at court. He also provided the banners for ceremonial and military use, but instead of designing embroideries, we find him commissioned to execute patterns for textiles, drawings of gold letters to be sent to the 'weaver of the cloth of gold', whom Richard II had brought from Lucca to supply him with this material.[41] Richard also had draughtsmen working exclusively for his embroiderer, instead of employing Gilbert Prince to draw out the patterns.

*English royal painters*

THE FRENCH ROYAL DUKES SIMILARLY appointed artists and illuminators, and indeed other craftsmen and artists in the broadest sense – musicians, goldsmiths, and embroiderers – as *valets de chambre*. Among them we find famous names such as Jan van Eyck and Barthelemy van Eyck, the Limbourg brothers. Another of the duke of Burgundy's *valets de chambre* was Jean de Cambrai, who rose from being a stone-cutter in 1375 to *valet de chambre* in 1397, and then recipient of a royal collar of the broom from Charles VI in 1403, who addressed him as 'esquire'.[42]

Melchior Broederlam was the official painter to Louis de Mâle by 1381, and when Philip the Good became ruler of Flanders three years later, he was kept on as his painter in Flanders, and became *valet de chambre*, like so many other artists and craftsmen. His principal work was the decorations at the ducal castle of Hesdin, from 1385 to 1388. This was in addition to his paintings, of which two triptychs for Philip's mausoleum at Champmol survive: these are important precursors of the work of artists such as Jan van Eyck later in the century.

At Dijon, Jehan de Beaumetz worked for Philip decorating the chapel of one of his castles in the 1380s, and then moved on to Champmol. On Beaumetz's death in 1397, Philip employed Jean Maelwael, who also worked for Queen Isabeau of France, and who was appointed, like Beaumetz, as his *valet de chambre*. He too worked on the decoration at the Chartreuse de Champmol. And Maelwael was the uncle of the Limbourg brothers, whose miniatures rank as some of the most resplendent of the period. Philip was the first to employ them, when they were still apprenticed to a Paris goldsmith, which suggests that Maelwael brought them to the duke's attention. The Limbourgs entered his service in 1402 with the task of creating a 'very beautiful and notable Bible', which took at least a year and probably much longer. They then disappear from sight and reemerge in the service of Jean duke of Berry, for whom they went on to create the famous *Très Riches Heures*.

*Philip the Good's artists*

THE MOST INTIMATE RELATIONSHIP of prince and artist, however, was that of Barthélemy van Eyck and René d'Anjou. Quite soon after René died, it was believed that the sumptuous pictorial element in his book on tournaments and his romance *The Book of the Heart Seized by Love* was by the king himself, and it was only in the twentieth century that the real artist was discovered. Barthélemy was a *valet de chambre* and later held the higher ranks of a *valet tranchant*, responsible for carving the king's meat at table, but he was also one of the king's closest companions. At Tarascon, René's capital in Provence, van Eyck's studio was immediately next to the king's rooms in 1457, and fourteen years later, there was similarly a room for him at the castle of Angers with direct access to his patron's apartments.[43] This very close collaboration is confirmed by looking at the magical illuminations for *The Book of the Heart Seized by Love*, where text and picture mirror each other to perfection. René was unusual enough in being a royal author who wrote fiction; he was also 'intimately involved in all aspects of his artists' productions, from the conceptual stage to the finished work'.[44] His treatise on tournaments is paralleled by the work of other princes, such as Friedrich II on falconry and Gaston Phébus count of Foix on hunting. René's book is unique in that the text and pictures combine to form the first known illustrated handbook on a technical subject. They are so closely integrated that when the work was copied, the scribes in eight out of nine cases used the same page layout and the same positioning of the pictures, whereas normally they would have invented their own design for such a copy.

*Barthélemy van Eyck and René d'Anjou*

Jan van Eyck, who may have been related to Barthélemy, was employed on the usual more general terms: in 1426, Philip the Good's writ appointing him *valet de chambre* says simply that his duty is to paint for him 'as often as it shall please the duke'. But we also find him sent on confidential missions on the duke's behalf between 1426 and 1429, possibly diplomatic; he was certainly a member of two groups sent to inspect a possible bride for the duke. In both cases, he had a specific mission, to paint the duke's intended bride. The first was in September 1427, when princess Eleanor, sister of Alfonso V was the candidate, but by the time they reached Valencia, she had already been engaged to the infante of Portugal; no portrait was therefore required.[45] He next went with a group sent to Lisbon in 1429 to negotiate the details of Philip's marriage to Isabella of Portugal. His portrait of her is lost, but if it was true to type, it would have been without flattery, in his usual candid

*Confidential missions*

but restrained style. It is not impossible that previous missions may have involved his skill as an artist, perhaps to record the appearance of castles or towns which the duke might find himself besieging, or other valuable visual information.

The sculptor André Beauneveu worked in the courts of France and Flanders from 1359 until his death around 1400, and may possibly have worked briefly in England in 1371–2.[46] The chronicler Jean Froissart wrote of him when Beauneveu was in the service of the duke of Berry in the last decade of the fourteenth century that there was no sculptor 'better than or equal to him in any land, nor anyone of whose statues so many remained anywhere'.[47] He was responsible for the effigy of Charles V at Saint-Denis, which was ordered by the king in 1364, sixteen years before his death, and went on to work for Louis de Mâle at Courtrai. The count founded a chantry chapel there in 1374, and Beauneveu was immediately engaged to create his tomb. Again, it was ten years before the count died, and this pre-ordering of a monument was to ensure that it would be suitably magnificent for posterity, made by one of the most eminent sculptors of the age, and that his executors would not skimp on the project. The timing was also because these works took a long while to complete; Louis de Mâle's tomb was still incomplete at his death. Beauneveu's next employer was Jean duke of Berry, at the Sainte-Chapelle belonging to the duke at Bourges, now completely destroyed. It was a building similar to that in Paris, and was badly damaged by lightning; Louis XV ordered the ruins to be demolished in 1757, and the duke's effigy and the glass were moved to the cathedral. All that remains of Beauneveu's work are two statues of prophets and some of the stained glass.

*André de Beauneveu*

There were other masters at work, of almost equal stature, during Beauneveu's lifetime. Jean de Liège, who was responsible for the effigy of Philippa of Hainault, wife of Edward III, in Westminster Abbey, and Guy de Dammartin and Jean de Cambrai, who also worked at Bourges. All of them moved from patron to patron, from project to project, though because of the timescale of such enterprises, they were more static than the artists who were their fellow-countrymen.

Claus Sluter first appears in the records as a member of the guild of stonecutters in Brussels in about 1379; six years later he was hired by Jean de Marville, on behalf of Philip the Bold, as an assistant in his studio at a rate of pay which indicates that he was already recognised as exceptional. Marville had been appointed as the duke's *ymagier* or sculptor of statues in 1372, and on his death in 1389, Sluter took over. He became *valet de chambre* to Philip the Bold in the year of Marville's death, but he was unusual among holders of this title in that he was employed by the duke on an exclusive basis for most of his career – admittedly only twenty years – working in the same place. He is recorded as making a special journey to one of the castles of Jean duke of Berry to study the work of André Beauneveu; likewise, his work at Dijon was evidently viewed and admired by other sculptors.

*Claus Sluter*

The men who became *valets de chambre* had attained their position because the royal and princely courts were the centres of artistic culture of all kinds, and apart from the church, were the only source of employment of this sort. The range of artistic, musical, literary and other cultural endeavours at court even extended as far as the collection of exotic animals, and it is to this wider picture of court culture that we now turn.

# 8 | MAGNIFICENCE AND THE ARTS

◆ *Patronage* ◆ *Music* ◆ *Minstrels and musicians* ◆ *Royal chapels*
◆ *Composers* ◆ *Literature* ◆ *Manuscripts and libraries* ◆ *Writers*
◆ *The Decorative Arts* ◆ *Wall paintings* ◆ *Tapestries* ◆ *Heraldry*
◆ *Menageries*

## Patronage

PATRONAGE OF THE ARTS WAS closely associated with princely magnificence. The prince's ability to use his resources to employ painters, musicians or scribes, and to reward writers, was another aspect of his 'doing of great deeds' for the public good. Until the fourteenth century, patronage of the arts was closer to simple employment of craftsmen, very much of the moment: paying a minstrel for playing at a feast, a scribe for a luxurious manuscript or a painter for decorating a room. Gradually this moves towards a more permanent arrangement, where the prince pays salaries and retains musicians and scribes in his chapel or in his scriptorium, and employs the same painter for all his important work. By the late fourteenth century this has developed into a kind of competitive patronage: princes now seek out distinguished performers or artists to add to the lustre of their courts, offering higher salaries or taking them on after the death of their employer or the dispersal of his court. This competition was particularly acute between the royal dukes in France, but also involved Flanders, England and Spain, as well as the eastern and southern European kingdoms occupied by the descendants of the duke of Anjou.

## Music
### Minstrels and musicians

MINSTRELS WERE THE UBIQUITOUS providers of music at court festivals, especially at weddings and tournaments, yet it is very hard to come by hard facts about them. There are two reasons for this. Firstly, the term 'minstrel' derives from the Latin word *ministerialis* meaning someone who holds an office. After the time of Charlemagne *ministerialis* comes to mean 'craftsman'. In the twelfth century, *troubadours*, called *trouvères* in northern France, and related to the German *minnesänger*, all of whom are sometimes described as minstrels, were poets and composers who performed their own compositions. By the beginning of the fourteenth century, the Latin word was generally used to describe a musician. Secondly, 'minstrel' applied not only to players of musical instruments, but also to singers and entertainers in general: story-tellers, poets, mimes, mimics, conjurors and even magicians, jugglers, animal trainers and acrobats. The other common word for the musicians who attended princely courts was *jongleurs*, who were performers at a humbler level, and are often called minstrels in the twelfth and thirteenth century. And it is difficult to disentangle the reality from the mixture of evidence: what minstrels themselves tell us in poems they wrote, from the dry entries of payments in the royal accounts, and from the lurid condemnations of them by the church.

All types of minstrel appeared at the great court gatherings to provide music and entertainment. They might also compose descriptions of such occasions, and perform the epics they had created, but actually playing for the king and nobility was their prime function. From the twelfth century onwards, we hear of musicians gathering at the princely courts when a festival of any kind was to take place; numbers were often exaggerated to make the event sound like a great success.

In the small courts of the nobles of southern France, the troubadours created the most literary court culture of the medieval period. The troubadours themselves varied in rank from nobles like Guilhem IX, grandfather of Eleanor of Aquitaine, who was duke of Aquitaine in the early twelfth century, to men of the humblest status who made their way in the world through their musical or poetic skills. Some troubadours may have written both words and music, but a large number of lyrics borrowed existing tunes; this was so common that there was actually a name for the process, *contrafactum*, related to our word counterfeiting. This could result in the music for a love song being used for a song which was a political satire. It does indicate that there were probably a large number of troubadours who were not composers. The image of the troubadour in surviving manuscript illuminations is generally that of a man or woman holding an instrument, and since the ability to play music was one of the major courtly accomplishments, it is fair to regard troubadours as performers who were also poets, and more rarely, composers. The court occasions at which they performed were much less formal than the great festivals of the north.

*Troubadours*

In the thirteenth century we meet our first musician-king. The troubled reign of Alfonso X, 'the Learned', of Castile, contemporary of Jaime II of Aragon, contrasts sharply with his cultural achievements. Alfonso was highly ambitious, and attempted to impose a kind of kingship which was alien to the Spanish feudal society of his day, resulting in a series of revolts by his nobles and eventually civil war with his son. Like Henry II, he had a firm idea of good government as being administered by the king, rather than a system in which royal authority derived from the general assent of his subjects. He compounded this by a series of foreign adventures in an unsuccessful pursuit of his election as king of the Romans, and thus successor to the Holy Roman Empire, during the intense competition for the imperial title after the death of Friedrich II in 1250. His lack of success in the political sphere was to some extent due to bad luck, but it is not unreasonable to say that he lacked judgement in practical affairs. His nickname, 'el Sabio', is often translated as 'the Wise'. In fact he was 'Learned' rather than 'Wise'.

*Alfonso X of Castile*

Alfonso was a polymath not unlike Friedrich II, with whom he shared an interest in astrology. His major achievement was the *Siete Partidas*, ostensibly a law code, but in fact a much more comprehensive code that covered everyday life in many aspects, with recommendations rather than enforcement of laws. Much of it is almost a philosophical discussion, and some of it surprising, such as the idea that there should be silence during mealtimes at court, during which works on chivalry should be read aloud, rather as scripture was read to certain orders of monks as they dined. As to music, his contribution was the extraordinary *Cantigas de Santa Maria*, compiled around 1280. It is a collection of 420 songs in the Galician dialect which he had used in his youth. Some of the poems are probably by Alfonso himself, and the exceptional richness of the manuscript illuminations make the manuscripts themselves an example of royal magnificence. The subject matter of many of the cantigas is the miracles of the Virgin, common to the popular religious literature of the different languages of Christian Europe, and the music which accompanies the poems

Cantigas de Santa Maria

is drawn from Gregorian chant, early French polyphony, northern French secular songs and Spanish popular song.

Soon after the Cantigas de Santa Maria were compiled, we find a distinction developing between the minstrels and the travelling players, marked by the appointment of minstrels as members of the royal household, and the establishment of a guild of minstrels in Paris. This division between the settled musicians and the wandering players became a real social distinction; membership of the guild offered a security and respectability not accorded to their predecessors.

Jaime II of Majorca formally instituted a body of musicians in his palace in the early fourteenth century, declaring in the document which set up this arrangement that

*Palace musicians*

> It is lawful, as ancient traditions tell us, that there should be mimes or *jongleurs* in
> the houses of princes, given that the performance of their duties gives rise to that joy
> which princes should above all seek, so that they avoid all sadness and anger, and show
> themselves more gracious towards their subjects.[1]

This view was shared among his fellow-princes, and as early as 1284 we have a substantial list of musicians in the household of Philip III, who commissioned Giles of Rome's treatise. By 1315, under Louis X, there are two trumpeters, one drummer and a player on the psaltery, a kind of zither; they are paid a daily wage, and two years later are given the right to eat at court. An edict of Jean II while he was duke of Normandy actually lists the instruments that minstrels play, namely 'drums (nakers or timbales), the half-flute, cornet, Latin gittern or Latin guitar, the Bohemian flute, trumpet, the Moorish gittern or guitar, the vieille'.[2]

The itinerant musician seeking to make a living from tournaments and other festive occasions was a very different figure from the player who was recognised as belonging to the royal court, even if they had no official status and no regular income from the king. Travelling musicians gathered at public events, often in huge numbers. Even if we make allowance for the inability of medieval chroniclers to estimate the numbers of a crowd, the evidence of the royal accounts shows long lists of minstrels' names. At the knighting of Pandolf Malatesta and his sons at Rimini in 1324, 150 minstrels are said to have turned up in search of business.[3] This compares with the very small numbers actually on the payroll of the English royal household, who rarely seem to amount to more than a dozen until the end of the fourteenth century; but they were supplemented on special occasions – for example the weddings of the daughters of Edward I and the king's own second wedding in 1299 – by minstrels from as far afield as Scotland, Holland, Carcassonne and southwest France.[4]

*Itinerant musicians*

One of the best-documented of all the festivals in terms of minstrels was the knighting of Edward of Caernarfon, soon to be Edward II, in 1306. This event is recorded on the only roll of accounts exclusively concerned with minstrels in the whole of the surviving medieval material from the royal exchequer. It is a single roll of parchment, with two separate sets of accounts in different languages on it, the French written on the back of the Latin. It has taken a great deal of scholarly skill on the part of the editor to decipher exactly what its contents mean, as it is very much a working document – not rough notes, but by no means a finished and formal list. We learn much about the instruments the minstrels played, and about the lords for whom they worked, but almost all of them remain faceless figures. What does emerge is that they represent a group of players who were associated with members of the court or even the king himself, and therefore the hopeful wandering musicians who also attended have no part in the payments made. Edward of Caernarfon gave 200 marks (£133.33) to 'King Robert and certain kings of heralds and to various other minstrels' and

on Affonffo re Castela

Esta e a primeira cantiga re loor re

**51.** (above) The court of Alfonso X: three vielle players and a scribe writing a music score on the left.

**52.** (below) A queen and her musicians, from the romance *Meliadus*. Northern Italy, c.1350.

**53.** (above) Arab and Christian musicians playing together.

this was distributed by the keeper of the prince's treasury. The list is not complete, as the named entries amount to £115.66, and the balance was given to other unnamed minstrels.

By tracing these names through the surviving account books of the Exchequer for the reigns of Edward I and Edward II, a surprisingly detailed picture of the minstrels can be built up, one which is broadly true not only for this period, but for the fourteenth century as well.[5] Firstly, we have 'King Robert and certain kings of heralds', who are kings in the sense of leaders and organisers, and who seem to have been responsible for both overseeing the minstrels and for providing additional minstrels as required, presumably choosing some of them from the hopeful itinerants who appeared when the feast was about to start. It is in this role, that we shall turn to them again when we look at the organisation of feasts. 'King Robert' himself was actually one of the king's squires, and by 1306 he had been in Edward I's service for nearly thirty years. He was to serve Edward II until 1320, so spent at least forty-three years in the royal service. He is called Robert *parvus*, or Robert Little, and his main duties seem to have been as a straightforward squire of the household to the king, one of the small group who attended the king on campaign and were responsible for his personal safety. In particular, he fought alongside the king in the Scottish campaigns from 1300 to 1307. He was probably a trumpeter, and may also have played the drums: the 'kings of heralds' were, as far as we can tell, always professional musicians in the first place. It is even possible that this was his specific function in warfare, as he is called the 'king's trumpeter'. Several other lords attending the feast had two trumpeters, and nineteen in all are listed in the account, second only to twenty-six harpers. We find Robert organising five specific events between 1304 and 1320: two feasts for the churching of ladies of the court, the knighting ceremony of 1306, a feast on New Year's Day, and one feast abroad, at Amiens in 1320 when Edward II did homage to the French king for his lands abroad. In each case, he is named as the distributor of the fees paid to the minstrels.

Below Robert in the household were other minstrels, some of them of equal rank as squires. A list of payments in 1284/5 distinguishes between the minstrels who are also squires, and therefore were paid 7½d a day, and those who are plain minstrels and paid three pence less. One of the squire-minstrels is William, the psaltery player. A psaltery was a kind of zither, often triangular, with a soundboard and plucked strings: there seem to have been many variations on the basic style. He was a man of sufficient standing to have his own seal, and this survives: it is tempting to think that the handsome bearded face on it portrays William himself.[6]

Of the musicians listed on the accounts, apart from trumpeters and harpers, there are nine players of the *crwth* or Welsh harp, seven drummers, two pipers, eight players of stringed instruments, one organist and a bell-player. Obviously the harp would have been the dominant sound, probably largely played solo, or as an accompaniment to a singer. Similarly the other stringed instruments would – as far as we can tell – rarely have been played as an ensemble. But harps were about to go out of fashion.

Under Edward II, influenced by the French fashions favoured by both Isabella, his wife, and his favourite Piers Gaveston, the four longstanding king's harpers of Edward I disappear. As prince of Wales, Edward had had his own establishment, and thirteen musicians are named as his. Most of them belong to the retinues of the nobility, eight of them being identified as servants of ladies. Many of the retinues simply have two trumpeters: for some reason, trumpeters appear with one exception in pairs: and interestingly, there is only one harper among them, but six players of the vielle.

In the fourteenth century, court music moved away from the popular roots of the minstrels, and much of it was provided by men like Philippe de Vitry and Guillaume de

Machaut, who were clerics and trained in church music. The vast majority of Machaut's enormous poetic and musical output is secular, despite his background, and we have more than a hundred such compositions by him, mostly ballads and rondeaus, both for soloists and for groups of singers. The singers, too, were often drawn from the royal chapel for festive occasions, and motets and songs were specially written for royal entries and for the great Burgundian feasts. Equally, the tradition that music-making was part of courtly education survived, and is clearly documented: from Jean the Fearless playing the flute and the shawm as a boy, to Charles the Bold organising a group of sixteen gentlemen who knew music to accompany him in his leisure hours.

*Church music and secular music*

However, there is very little evidence as to the pieces played, since the chroniclers rarely mention them, and even the detailed accounts of eye-witnesses do not help. For instance, Olivier de La Marche, describing a feast which he himself directed and in which he participated, gives the text of the verses sung, but no indication of who wrote the music. What we do know is that the standard of playing was exceptionally high: among the minstrels were two blind players, whose performance was so marvellous that the composers Binchois and Dufay were jealous; the two sons of one of them, also blind, were superb players of the vielle forty years later.

In the household ordinances of Edward II of England in 1318, two trumpeters and two minstrels are to be taken on as members of the household, with the right to eat with the household or in the king's chamber as well as wages and livery. The trumpeters are there partly to summon the court to dinner, while the other minstrels may have performed without them in the king's private apartments; the ordinance specifies that they shall provide quiet music if so required. It is hard to tell how many minstrels were on the payroll, and how many were brought in for special occasions. By 1344 Edward III had sixteen minstrels paid at half the rate of the musicians of his chapel, according to a summary of the members of his household: five of these were trumpeters, with five pipers, two string players and two drummers.[7]

*Royal trumpeters*

Independently of the royal court, the Parisian minstrels formed a guild in 1321 'for the reformation of their craft and for the general good', and effectively created a monopoly for themselves within the city. Among the signatories are a fair number of women, and evidence from manuscript illuminations shows that they played a wide range of instruments; but it seems that the performers at the royal court were largely male.

In fourteenth-century Spain, the terminology was different: the *joglars* were the local musicians, and the *ministrile* were foreign visitors. The latter brought with them the latest musical fashions from abroad, while the *joglars* provided the day-to-day music at court. The household ordinances of Peter IV of Aragon, 'the Ceremonious', in November 1344, provided that there should be four *joglars* at court, of whom two were to be trumpeters, one a player of the tambourine, and one a horn player. When the king dined in public, they were to play at the beginning and end of the meal, and after them any visiting *joglars* whom the king wished to hear. In that year, the visitors consisted of the *joglar* of the bishop of Pamplona, Colin, *joglar* of the king of France, and Margarita, an English *joglar*. Peter IV also employed bagpipers. By the end of the century we find the minstrels playing in small groups, typically based round a flageolet and a bagpipe. Juan I had a small group until 1378, when he appointed twelve musicians under Midach, 'king of the minstrels' (who may well have recruited them) including nine wind players and six string players. These were full-time appointments, and included leave during Lent, when they were not allowed to play in public but went to the 'schools' of minstrels which usually took place annually in France and Flanders. They were only required to return to the court at the end of May, so spent

Joglars *in Aragon*

a considerable part of the year abroad; they used this time to buy new instruments, and presumably to learn the latest musical styles and songs to perform on their return.[8]

The most sophisticated of princely courts as far as music was concerned, that of Burgundy, came into being in the late fourteenth century, and its musicians were organised in much the same way throughout the century of its existence. The lay performers were divided into the trumpets, 'high' minstrels and 'low' minstrels, according to their instruments. However, the trumpets had a fairly narrowly defined function: they played fanfares to announce the prince or to accompany a ceremonial, using straight trumpets with banners attached, familiar even today from English royal occasions. Their numbers grew from four to twelve over time. The 'high' minstrels played wind instruments which were loud enough to be used outside or in great halls, while 'low' minstrels played flutes and stringed instruments more suitable for smaller, intimate occasions in private chambers.

It is from this musical world that the glories of the Aragonese court of Alfonso V in both Barcelona and Naples were to flower. From 1413, when he first came to Barcelona from the court of Castile where he had been brought up, Alfonso maintained a musical establishment 'surprising for those times'.[9] He continued the tradition established by his predecessor Juan I of sending his minstrels from Aragon to the royal courts of Castile, Navarre and Portugal, and to the count of Foix, and later to Burgundy. In 1420 he bought his first organ, and his enthusiasm for the organ meant that he employed the most eminent organists of his day, who were also organ-builders. When in 1428 one of them wanted to leave Barcelona to exploit a newly-invented organ in France, Alfonso asked him to stay in Aragon, and ordered that his invention should not be used elsewhere.[10] After Alfonso had conquered the kingdom of Naples, his palaces there included specially designated 'music rooms', and one of these contained a Flemish organ with eighty-four pipes of up to a metre high, bought from Gerard of Holland 'to be played in the palace in his presence' in 1456.[11] There was also a checker, which seems to have been a primitive clavichord, which gave the king 'much pleasure'. Wind instruments were used on informal occasions, except for the five regular trumpeters, whose role, as at other courts, was ceremonial.

For Alfonso's great triumphal entry into Naples in 1443, the number of trumpeters was increased to twelve, to match the grandeur of the occasion.[12] And from Naples his musicians visited France, Germany, the Low Countries and England, and later Burgundy. Nor was he above luring star players from other courts, as he did in March 1444, when four of the minstrels of the king of Castile were handsomely rewarded for joining him in Naples. In 1451, Alfonso had the largest chapel choir in Europe after Henry VI, with twenty-four singers. His court poet Antonio Beccadelli claimed that 'whoever is outstanding in music is drawn by rich rewards to Naples. Every day ... splendid music is played during the services making all hearts glad and joyful'. Secular music at the court was also of the highest standard, with lute and guitar as particular specialities: the king ordered lutes specially from a *luthier* in Valencia. In the 1450s there were five players of the chirimia, three guitarists and five flautists. The secular repertoire was probably largely Spanish music, particularly the polyphonic love songs. Most unusual of all was his military band of trumpets, trombones and drums, which imitated Moorish and Turkish music.[13]

*Burgundian court music*

*Alfonso V's musicians*

**54.** Musicians from *The Luttrell Psalter*, c.1330. From top, clockwise: organ, bagpipes, hurdy-gurdy, nakers (drums).

et adozate in monte sancto eius. quo
niam sanctus dominus deus noster.

Ybilate deo omnis terra : seruite do
mino in leticia

Introite in conspectu eius : in exulta
tione

Scitote quoniam dominus ipse
est deus : ipse fecit nos ⁊ non ipsi nos.

Populus eius ⁊ oues pascue eius
introite portas eius in confessione
atria eius in ympnis confitemini illi.

Laudate nomen eius quoniam

## Royal chapels

THE ROYAL CHAPEL WAS ORIGINALLY the king's private place of worship, centred on his relics and fulfilling the need for a daily liturgy within the court, with which the chapel travelled. The earliest chapel is to be found under Charlemagne, and the idea of a chaplain, a priest who is principally concerned with that chapel, appears two centuries later. There is a fully-fledged papal chapel by 1100, and Louis VII established a static chapel in the Palais de la Cité in Paris by a charter of 1154. The Sainte-Chapelle was the first of the major royal chapels, completed by St Louis in 1248. Here, at the beginning of the fourteenth century, the regular liturgical ceremonies started to require the presence of musicians. By 1340, its complement of musicians had grown to a total of twenty-three choral staff, and when Edward came to found both St Stephen's chapel at Westminster and the Garter chapel at Windsor in 1348, he copied these numbers exactly, outdoing the French kings by having two choirs of this size.[14]

*The royal chapel of Jean II*

The fully-fledged musical chapel only emerges after 1350; the model both in France and elsewhere seems to have been the pope's chapels at Avignon.[15] Jean II had probably the largest court chapel in western Europe, with seventeen members, though not all of these were musicians, and even when he was a captive in England at Somerton castle in Lincolnshire, with a limited household, there were sufficient clergy skilled in music to perform polyphonic music, and a portative organ was transported there for the chapel's use.[16] Gace de la Buigne, who was appointed first chaplain of the royal chapel in 1351, has left us a vivid evocation of the complexities of polyphony in a poem on hunting which he wrote for Jean's youngest son, Philip, later duke of Burgundy: rather delightfully, he says of the noise of hounds in full cry that no-one heard such melody even in the king's chapel, where

> some sing the *motetus*, others make a double hocket; the tallest sing the tenor, the others the counter-tenor. The clearest voices sing treble without delay, and the smallest the quadruple, making a redoubled fifth. Some make a minor semitone, others a major semitone ...

The royal chapel was maintained by Charles V when he came to the throne; Christine de Pizan in her account of his daily life reports that he had mass celebrated every day 'gloriously, with melodious and solemn singing'.[17] The king's chapels were imitated by the French royal dukes, and music became the hallmark of a princely chapel. A treatise on music of the time says that some singers applied techniques wrongly, and when challenged, claimed that they were following the practices of the 'singers in the chapel of magnates' who 'would not do this without reason, since they are the best singers'.[18]

*The Burgundian royal chapel*

When Olivier de la Marche wrote his manual on Charles the Bold's household and its organisation in 1475, he began with the 'the service of God and his chapel, as this should be the beginning of all affairs'.[19] The chapels of the Burgundian dukes were acknowledged by contemporaries to be the best and largest of their kind. Most of the great composers of late medieval polyphonic music were to be found there. However, the musical side of the chapel seems to have existed at the whim of the duke rather than as a permanent part of his court. Philip the Bold became duke in 1364, but only established chapel musicians in January 1384, when his father-in-law Louis de Mâle, count of Flanders, died. Louis had a fine team of nine musicians and, after a brief delay, Philip employed them all, and added a further six new members by 10 July.

In 1391, after a visit to Avignon, where the papal chapel of Clement VII was famed for its quality, Philip hired six men from the pope's singers, and a further four after Clement's death in September 1394. Philip worked his singers hard: he was very devout, and required a full musical service to be performed at all eight of the canonical hours, as well as two masses, and a vigil of the dead on Sunday evenings. The duke himself only appeared at the mass and at matins. The chapel was very much an itinerant one, and accompanied the duke on all his travels. They were only excused if the duke had been hunting and they could not keep up with him.

*Philip the Bold's chapel*

The first chaplain, head of the prince's chapel, from 1400 onwards was Jean de Templeneuve, who, like the royal artists, was occasionally sent on secret diplomatic missions 'for certain necessities that our lord did not want to declare'. He was also of sufficient status to participate, albeit on a modest scale, in the ritual gift-giving, the *étrennes*,[20] on New Year's Day. The whole chapel was also provided with liveries, as might be expected, but these were lavish and colourful. In January 1388, the twelve chaplains were in green, a monk in white, four clerks in blue, and the cantor in grey. At Philip's death, the chronicler at Saint-Denis wrote that he was not unduly generous in maintaining the churches of his duchy, but that

> he was very careful to see that divine service was celebrated in royal style wherever he was staying. He maintained in his chapel, to lend more splendour to the ceremonial, a much greater number of musicians than any of his ancestors; and I would blame his excessive prodigality in this, were it not a particular mark of his devotion to God.[21]

Jean the Fearless disbanded the musicians when he succeeded his father and did not replace them until a decade later. When he did so the turbulent political situation in 1415 may have been the reason, because he had been using Parisian musicians for his chapel services. The new establishment was smaller and considerably less well paid than his father's musicians. Again, when he died in 1419, having had chapel musicians for just four years, the group were disbanded. Philip the Good once more waited for ten years after he came to power to re-establish them, though when he did so, seven of John's former chaplains returned to his service.

The princely chapel was now moved to the Sainte-Chapelle at Dijon, the official home of Philip's newly created Order of the Golden Fleece, as from January 1432. Olivier de la Marche, recording the meeting of the order at Ghent in 1445, said of the singing at vespers by members of the chapel that it was 'one of the best and most harmonious chapels, and with a greater number of chaplains than anywhere else'.[22] It was Charles the Bold who was passionate about music. The chronicler Jean Molinet tells us that he 'ordered expert musicians to come from Rome to teach those in France proper modulations', and that he 'collected the most famous singers in the world and kept his chapel full of such harmonious and delectable voices that the pleasure they gave was next only to the glories of heaven'.[23]

*The Sainte-Chapelle at Dijon*

MUSIC AT THE ENGLISH COURT could not compete with the glories of Burgundy at its height. But before the Burgundian chapel was fully established, in the 1360s and 1370s, Edward III had musicians at the Garter chapel in Windsor Castle who were the match of any group in Europe. The requirements for the celebration of large numbers of masses may have encouraged the striking development of St George's into one of the major centres of the new polyphonic music from 1360 onwards. The records of the chapel are much fuller than for most other centres, so it is not easy to find a point of comparison. What we can say is that St George's was home to John Aleyn, composer of the motet in praise of

Edward entitled *Sub Arcturo plebs vallata*,* 'one of the most complex and remarkable ... motets ... to have survived from anywhere in Europe' from this period. Aleyn was a canon from 1362 to 1373, and the implication is that, from the start, St George's was one of the major musical centres of England.[24] The Garter services were performances of a rare quality, and the polyphony which was developed there was in the forefront of the musical language of the time. Another piece, addressed to the Virgin Mary, one of the patron saints of the Garter, begs her to protect the English army and especially Edward himself, 'worthy king of battle'. The choirs of royal chapels not only enhanced the king's magnificence by the splendour of their music, but also praised the king directly. We find similar motets with topical allusions in Burgundy in the 1390s, in praise of Philip the Bold's attempts to resolve the papal schism.[25]

Leo of Rozmital, visiting England in 1466 found Edward IV's chapel very impressive: 'We never heard more joyful or suave musicians than there; there were about sixty singers in the choir.'[26] In fact the description of Edward's household in the Black Book shows that there were twenty-six chaplains, two yeomen of the chapel, who were choristers whose voices had recently broken, and eight children of the chapel, a rather smaller number.[27] The Chapel Royal, as it began to be known in the fifteenth century, fluctuated in numbers: it was increased from sixteen to twenty-four by Richard II, and enlarged by Henry V to thirty-two chaplains and twelve choristers. This was apparently a deliberate move to make the chapel appropriate in scale to his status after the treaty of Troyes as king of England and future king of France. An account of the chapel in 1441 gives the highest figure, thirty-six chaplains and ten choristers. It was highly regarded on the Continent, and English performance standards were singled out for praise.

THE ROYAL CHAPEL IN ARAGON was founded in 1345 by Peter the Ceremonious.[28] It was relatively small, with a maximum of eight singers; unusually, Queen Eleanor had six singers in her own separate chapel, and Joan, the heir to the throne, had a similar establishment. Most of these singers came from the papal court at Avignon, but when Joan became king, Catalan singers were recruited. By the time Fernando I came to the throne in 1412 there was a strong musical tradition. When Alfonso V succeeded Fernando, he drew on this musical tradition and his own enjoyment of music to create one of the finest chapels in Europe. He himself had always loved music; as prince, writing to his father in 1413 apologising for detaining some of the king's musicians, he described his 'great delight in listening to their sounds and new works'.[29] For his royal chapel, he employed French and German singers, and in 1420 was among the first princes to have musicians to accompany the choir for services in his royal chapel.

As personal attendants to the king, most of the Aragonese royal chapel came to Naples after Alfonso captured it in 1442, but they were gradually replaced by Spaniards. The chapel was extended to twenty singers soon after the establishment of the court at Naples, and then to twenty-four adults and an unknown number of choirboys by 1451.[30]

THE QUALITY OF THE MUSIC was not the only aspect of the royal chapel intended to impress visitors. The furnishing and plate which the chapel contained was as fine as anything that the king possessed for secular use, and was just as carefully valued in the royal inventories. The vestments, too, were rich, and sometimes surprisingly interchangeable with the elaborate royal costumes. The chapel of St George at Windsor, home to the

* 'Under Arthur's reign, the sheltered people ...'.

Order of the Garter, possessed 25 sets of vestments and 43 copes, with far fewer clergy than Canterbury Cathedral, which had 69 sets of vestments but only 45 copes. Those at St George's were of the highest quality. One of the vestments, of cloth of gold 'powdered with various birds', had been the wedding dress of Joan of Kent when she married the Black Prince. The furnishings, in the small space of a chapel, had far more visual effect than in a cathedral, and there were carpets and cushions with the arms of the royal family and the knights of the Garter.

For a wider overview of the potential riches of the chapels, we have the inventory made on the death of Charles V. He had a number of chapels, in the three palaces in and around Paris, and also in his castles in the countryside. Nonetheless, the total are astonishing: gold objects included 27 weighing over 35 kilos in total, 19 statues of the Virgin and saints, 29 reliquaries with precious stones, and a great chalice with rubies, sapphires and enamelled figures. As to silver, there were 27 crosses including one with cameos, sapphires and pearls weighing 25 kilos on its own. As well as sets of silver statues, there were whole scenes from the Bible as groups of figures in silver. *The furnishing of royal chapels*

In terms of vestments and furnishings, Charles possessed 63 'chapels' of differing colours and designs. These chapels were like the 'chambers' of tapestry, complete suites of all the pieces of fabric needed in a room, which we shall come to shortly. The chapel included vestments for all the participating clergy as well as the altar frontals and the cloths needed to cover the altar. Different sets were needed for the various feasts of the church, for Lent and for Advent, and any ordinary church would probably have had four or five sets. Given that the chapels were very much designed to be portable, 63 sets is vastly in excess of what was actually needed.[32] *The inventory of Charles V's chapel*

The music and the setting made the chapel services powerfully theatrical, and very much one of the elements of a ruler's court by which his reputation was made. John duke of Bedford, as regent of France, had to present the English chapel in Paris as a match for the chapel of Charles VI and that of Jean the Fearless. Again, it is the survival of his accounts which enables us to understand the scale of expenditure needed to compete. He acquired grand pieces from one of Charles VI's chapels, and from the ransom of the duke of Alençon, captured by the English in 1424. Even so, he commissioned quantities of new pieces from the Paris goldsmiths, some of them 'impressively, almost ostentatiously, large'.[33]

The motives for the recruitment of the finest singers and the creation of a magnificent setting in which they performed was not simply that of enhancing a ruler's reputation. The deep piety of the kings and princes of the late fourteenth and fifteenth century is easy to overlook: Karl IV, whose autobiography has episodes of almost mystical experience, is the foremost example. He combined this with a passionate devotion to relics, and a deep knowledge of theology. He was by no means alone: other notably pious princes were Charles V of France, Henry V and VI in England and Philip the Bold in Burgundy. For them, the royal chapel was the focal point of their spiritual life. In any of the courts of Europe, personal religion played a far greater part than all the other ceremonials that we are about to survey. *Piety and the royal chapels*

## Composers

AMONG THE PERFORMERS AT COURT, whether singers or instrumentalists, there were always some who were composers as well. They do not seem to have been paid for composing, and it was part of the life of a princely musician to produce new works, though by no means all of them did so. Indeed, many compositions have come down to us without a composer's name, which shows that no very great prestige was attached to this part of their duties. Fifteen of the Burgundian musicians who served after the reign of Philip the Bold have left their name on one or more pieces, and we also find Jean the Fearless maintaining a music school in Paris, led by Jean Tapissier, who had been *valet de chambre* to his father. Tapissier was a composer, and later composers in the Burgundian court were often given that title; but he does not seem to have been a member of the ducal chapel. Jacques Vide was appointed *valet de chambre* to Philip the Good in 1423, evidently in part for his musical skills, as he was put in charge of two young singers in the choir; he later became one of the duke's secretaries and a diplomat, and is known to have composed eight *rondeaux*. More typical is Pierre Fontaine, appointed chaplain in 1403 and a member of the chapel until 1447, particularly as his surviving works are all secular songs. These were presumably for the gentlemen of the court skilled in music, such as those recruited into a group by Charles the Bold a few years later.

Gilles de Binche, known as Binchois, is a major figure in the musical history of Europe, and it is with his appointment to the newly re-formed chapel in 1430 that the golden age of Burgundian compositions begins. We have a very large number of works from his hand, and he was with the chapel for about twenty-five years. He provided religious music in a relatively conservative style, presumably because this was to Philip the Good's taste, and his secular music is also restrained compared with his contemporaries Guillaume Dufay and John Dunstaple; even its form is largely restricted to the *rondeau*, admittedly the most popular song form of the period. Patronage might secure a composer-singer a good post, but it may also have limited his freedom to experiment.[34]

Under Charles the Bold, the new duke's enthusiasm for music led to the appointment of two musicians as *valets de chambre*. Before Charles succeeded to the title he was already very active in the music of the court and one composer, the Englishman Robert Morton, was frequently given leave of absence from the chapel to serve Charles. We find Charles personally selecting men whom he wished to bring to the court in the 1460s: Antoine Busnoys was headhunted from Poitiers, and given the unofficial title of singer to the duke. Two of Charles's composer *valets de chambre* were with him on the military campaigns at the end of his reign.

THE GREAT CONTEMPORARY OF BINCHOIS in England, John Dunstaple, did not have a ducal court to rival that of Burgundy where he could find a patron.[35] Instead he seems to have been attached to three royal and ducal patrons during his career, which lasted from the second decade of the fifteenth century until his death in 1453. The first of these was probably John, duke of Bedford, who as regent of France could rival the French royal dukes, though the links are tenuous. He then appears in connection with Queen Joan, widow of Henry IV of England, who made payments to him from 1427 to 1436. Finally he was in the household of Humphrey duke of Gloucester, where he was described as 'servant and member of the family and household of the duke'. He appears in other guises: as a country gentleman in eastern England, and as an astronomer and mathematician. This was a period when English music was highly innovative, and much prized abroad – a contemporary manuscript from the court of Ferrara contains much of his work – but the royal court during the minority of Henry VI obviously had none of the personal patronage which the Burgundian dukes could offer.

Guillaume Dufay, the third of the trinity of great composers who dominated the polyphonic music of the first half of the fifteenth century, had a long and rather chequered career in the service of the Church before finding a princely patron. He joined the papal chapel when he was about thirty, having been in minor ecclesiastical posts in the north of

France and in the service of Cardinal Aleman at Bologna until then. For the next seven years, he was dependent on the fluctuations of Church politics. In early 1434 he appears as master of the chapel to Amadeus VIII of Savoy, just in time for the celebration of the wedding of the duke's son to the daughter of Jean II, king of Cyprus. The duke of Burgundy was among the guests, as was Binchois, and the two heard and much admired a pair of blind vielle players in the duchess's service. Amadeus, supported by cardianl Aleman, became anti-pope in 1440. Rather than break with the established church, Dufay preferred the safety of a post as a canon at the cathedral of Cambrai, where he had been born and where his mother lived, under the aegis of Philip the Good of Burgundy. But he returned to Savoy between 1452 and 1458, with the formal title of master of the chapel, as a friend of Louis, the successor to Amadeus. The duke was unable to find a benefice for him so that he could retire to Savoy, and once again Dufay went back to Cambrai, writing occasional pieces for Philip the Good and Charles the Bold. What Dufay lost through the lack of a single powerful patron, he gained in musical experience: he probably had wider knowledge of the range of music being composed throughout Europe than any of his contemporaries. His reputation was overshadowed at his death by the new men of the late fifteenth century, Jean de Ockeghem and Josquin des Prés.

*Guillaume Dufay*

Court patronage was probably more important to musicians than to other artists or craftsmen, as only the princes could afford to maintain a chapel on a grand scale, and only the court could offer opportunities to perform or compose both secular and sacred music in the latest fashion. The movement of musicians between courts is an intriguing feature; was this just restlessness, or were the princes outbidding each other for the services of the stars of the day? The princely chapels of the fifteenth century saw music flourish and develop in a way unknown to earlier patrons.

# Literature
## *Manuscripts and libraries*

KINGS AND PRINCES HAD ALWAYS OWNED books: law books, books on theology, books on statecraft, and books for entertainment containing the romances of Arthur or the deeds of Charlemagne. They had been stored in the princely chamber, in chests or cupboards, but with no special place or priority. The first royal library to have a place set apart for it was that of Charles V of France, who in 1367 or 1368 had all his books gathered together and put in a separate room in the palace of the Louvre. He put Guillaume de Malet, one of his *valets de chambre*, in charge of the collection. The royal accounts show that the king saw his librarian almost every day, and Charles supervised the acquisitions and the shelving of gifts. Some books remained elsewhere, at Vincennes and Fontainebleau, but the library at the Louvre was intended by the king to be a permanent institution, housing not only his books but also many of the splendid objects and curios he had gathered. And it seems that it was open for scholars to work there. At his death there were 1,200 manuscripts in all. But under Charles VI the royal dukes borrowed books from the library and failed to return them, taking advantage of his lack of authority. When he died, the remaining 863 books were bought by the regent of France, the duke of Bedford, and when the latter died in 1435, the collection was dispersed.

*The library of Charles V*

The libraries of the royal dukes were on a similarly lavish scale. Jean duke of Berry was the most enthusiastic collector of richly illuminated manuscripts, and his library was in constant flux: a total of over three hundred manuscripts are listed in the four surviving inventories, but many other surviving examples have his signature or devices on them. He both gave away and received manuscripts throughout his life, even in his last days, and was the best customer that the Parisian booksellers had. It was not a scholar's collection; his manuscripts are listed along with his jewels and other *objets d'art* rather than as a separate library catalogue, and he does not appear to have had a librarian.[36] The books he owned included at least thirty-eight romances of chivalry.

*The library of Philip the Bold*

The Burgundian dukes began modestly.[37] Philip the Bold had only thirty manuscripts in his library, and a further forty in his chapel. Many of the library manuscripts were presentation copies or works dedicated to him, and he seems to have bought little in the way of books. Jean the Fearless added twenty-seven books to the chapel, and vastly expanded the library, to nearly two hundred manuscripts, though given his reputation as being better with the sword than the pen, it seems that many of these may have been gifts or inheritances. It is under Philip the Good that collecting as such really begins, and at his death in 1467 there were 866 books in all, according to the catalogue, which gives some details about many of them as to age, script and even the metres of the poetry. A contemporary said of him that he was 'the Christian prince, without reservation, who is best provided with an authentic and rich library'.[38] He was an active buyer of books, and many came from earlier collectors. Besides this, Philip also commissioned translations, copies, new illuminated copies and new versions of texts. For example, he not only owned a very important thirteenth-century copy of the Arthurian romances of Chrétien de Troyes, but had two of the stories reworked into prose. These commissioned manuscripts often contained a prologue dedicating the work to the duke, and a miniature showing the author presenting the work to his patron. The work of illumination was given almost exclusively to local Burgundian artists, and the script was a bold form designed for easier reading with fewer lines to the page, which resulted in impressively large volumes.

*Alfonso V: books on campaign*

Alfonso V of Aragon was another monarch who gathered a formidable library, whose history takes us into the beginnings of the renaissance of classical learning in Italy in the fifteenth century. His collection began when he came to lay claim to the kingdom of Naples on his father's death, and developed a deep interest in classical literature and civilisation. By 1430 his collection was large enough for him to have a librarian to look after it. He took books with him, not only when his household was travelling, but also when he was on campaign, and he encouraged scholars to come to his court and use the library. A recent biographer tells us that his books

> followed the king on campaign housed in a tent next to his own living quarters.
> Often in the middle of the night, it was said, he would call for a light and settle to
> reading. Nor was war allowed to bring the literary soirées to a complete standstill:
> bemused visitors to his camp would sometimes come upon the incongruous spectacle of
> Alfonso, surrounded by courtiers and soldiers, listening to Panormita read Livy
> or Caesar...[39]

**55.** (opposite) Philip the Good is presented with the *Chronicles of Hainault*, by the author Jean Wauquelin. The miniature is by Rogier van der Weyden.

Fellow rulers who wished to gain his favour sent him manuscripts; a fine manuscript came from Cosimo dei' Medici in Florence, and from as far afield as England Humfrey duke of Gloucester sent a French version of the same text. The king's ambassadors, hearing that hard up clerics at the council of Basle in 1439 were selling manuscripts, were given immediate authority to spend the vast sum of 1,000 ducats for two specific texts. His court became the nursery for the new breed of humanists, learned in Greek and theology. When Alfonso invaded southern Italy, the library was housed in the castle of Gaeta near Naples for a time in 1436, and moved to Castelcapuano when Naples itself was captured. In the 1450s

Our che que toute
creature de raison
ble entendement de
sire et appete sauoir
z oyr choses nouuelles pour la re
creation et esioyssement de son co
raige. z ossy que eus ou record des
choses aduenues anchiennement
z meismement des haultes et nobles
proesses et emprises des nobles
hommes procrees et engenres des
haultes et nobles procreations et
lignies tous preudommes ayans
lentendement esleuet en honneur
quant ilz teils fais oent record sen
esiouent z esmeuuent en plus grant

perfection de valeur z de proesche
Est il que a ceste instance moy non
digne poure de sens et menre a le
tendement debille et foible de ceste
haulte matere mettre a effect. Se
non que Il me fust comande comme
il est depar mon tresredoubte z tres
puissant seigneur monsieur phelippe
par la grasse de dieu Duc de bour
goingne de lotringhe de brabant et
de lembourt Conte de flandres dar
tois de bourgoingne palatin de hay
nau de hollande de zelande et de
namur marquis du saint empire
Seigneur de frize de salins z de ma
lines me suy determines z disposes

the ambassador in Venice was sent a list of classical authors with the request to find 'well written and authentic' copies of their works, and the librarian went from Naples to Aragon in 1455 in search of theology and humanist works.[40]

As with Charles V's library, Alfonso's was a scholarly workplace, chiefly for his secretary, Lorenzo Valla, a humanist who tried to restore late medieval Latin to its classical purity, demolished the papal forgery – the so-called 'Donation of Constantine' by which the pope claimed secular power over the Holy Roman Empire – and championed faith and deeds as the way to salvation, a century before Luther. This inevitably led to retribution from the Church authorities, but Alfonso defended him in a scholarly fistfight which continued until Valla's departure for the papal court in 1447.

## Writers

THE RELATIONSHIP BETWEEN MEDIEVAL PRINCES and writers was a tenuous one: 'the king might employ tailors, armourers, goldsmiths, tapestry-makers, and painters; he did not ... employ poets'.[41] In this context, literature has been called 'an impossible profession',[42] in that the prince did not normally commission work directly from authors.

*Literary patronage*

The poet or writer might seek the prince's patronage, usually presenting or dedicating a particular work to them; or they might take a hint from a possible patron and create a work which they hoped would earn them a reward. One of the most famous romances was apparently brought about in this way. This was the earliest known version of the story of Lancelot and Guinevere, by Chrétien de Troyes. In the prologue, the poet says that the countess of Champagne has given him the subject matter and the meaning of it, and has asked him to make it into a poem. Alternatively, an author might present a manuscript of his work to a prince, in the hope of reward or at least princely approval. Jean Froissart had begun his career at the English court, writing love poems and a verse chronicle for Philippa, wife of Edward III. Nearly half a century later a friend arranged for him to give Richard II a copy of the love poems when he visited England in 1395. Froissart describes his reaction to the gift, with its suitably magnificent binding:

> [The king] opened it and looked into it with much pleasure. He ought to have been pleased, for it was handsomely written and illuminated, and bound in crimson-velvet, with ten silver gilt studs, and roses of the same in the middle, with two large clasps of silver gilt, richly worked with roses in the center.[43]

It is only in the fourteenth century that we begin to find authors enhancing the reputation of a prince for magnificence by appearing at his court. Perhaps the first clear example of

*Petrarch and Robert of Anjou*

this is the relationship between Robert of Anjou, king of Naples, and Petrarch, the Italian poet whose reputation and connections were truly international.[44] Petrarch, famous both for his Latin poetry and for his Italian lyrics, was offered the title of poet laureate, a revival of the Greek tradition of crowning a poet with a laurel wreath at great festivals, by both the University of Paris and the Roman senate. Philip IV of France had naturally wanted Petrarch to be crowned in Paris, but the poet chose the offer of the Roman senate. Even so, he was anxious that the choice should be seen to be a matter of judgement and not a mere whim on the part of the Senate. Declaring that Robert of Anjou 'is the one man among mortals whom I freely accept as judge of my talents', he travelled to Naples in March 1341 for a formal public examination, on the lines of those required before a university degree was conferred. Robert opened the proceedings by asking Petrarch for a definition of the benefits that poets could bring to society at large, to which Petrarch replied in a speech lasting for the rest of the day. On the second day he was examined on broad questions of philosophy, natural history, biography and Greek and Latin historians, as well as on his extensive travels. The proceedings concluded on the third day with Petrarch reading from his Latin epic *Africa*, which had first brought him fame. Robert then issued a decree proclaiming Petrarch worthy of his laurels, and asked that he should be crowned at Naples, but Petrarch pointed out that the invitation had originated with Rome. Robert, unable for political reasons to go to Rome, lent Petrarch his coronation mantle for the ceremony which took place on the Capitol on Easter Sunday, 8 April 1341.

Other rulers were also keen to attract Petrarch to their court, and when Petrarch went to visit a friend in Milan in 1353 the lord of the city, Giovanni Visconti, offered him a house in the city if he would settle there. The Viscontis had a problematic reputation, and Petrarch's friends tried to dissuade him from accepting their patronage. He accepted the offer nonetheless, and wrote many of his major works at Milan and later at Pavia, where Galeazzo Visconti built a new castle and gave Petrarch a house nearby. Milan remained their capital. It was at Milan that the feast for the wedding of Edward III's son Lionel, duke of Clarence, to Violante Visconti took place, at which Petrarch sat at the high table with the princes and great nobles who attended the ceremony. He remained at the Visconti court until his death in 1374.

Guillaume Machaut was both poet and composer, and was a generation older than Chaucer; by the time he was thirty he was well established in the household of Jean king of Bohemia, who had been brought up at the French court, and served Jean as secretary from 1330 onwards. What little we know of Machaut's career is a series of grants of the post of canon, when it became available, at different cathedrals in eastern France: Verdun, Arras and finally Reims, where he was installed in 1338. Thereafter, he combined his relatively light duties at Reims with his peripatetic employment in Jean of Bohemia's household. This seems to have lasted until the king's death at the battle of Crécy, but he does not seem to have had a formal post at the court of his son, the emperor Karl IV. Apart from his clerical post, his very high reputation was sufficient for him to rely on the kind of occasional *largesse* that musicians and poets received. One gift in particular is interesting: Machaut received three hundred gold francs for a romance – presumably a manuscript – which he gave to Amadeus of Savoy, the 'Green Count', at Paris in 1368. Amadeus was there for the visit of Lionel duke of Clarence on his way to Milan, at which point Chaucer may have been in the latter's company. The majority of his poems are courtly lyrics, yet the popularity of his work was such that he did not need the direct connection to a single court, usually with the duties (however nominal) of an official post attached. Instead, he names many patrons in his poems.These include Jean II and Charles V of France, the dukes of Berry and Burgundy, and the king of Cyprus, as well as a number of other French nobles.[45]

Patronage was central to the career of Geoffrey Chaucer. He was probably about eighteen when he is first recorded as a member of the court, in the household of Edward III's daughter-in-law, Elizabeth, the first wife of Prince Lionel, later duke of Clarence. Payments were made to him by Elizabeth until 1359, when Lionel came of age, and he then appears in Lionel's accounts. In 1360 Chaucer was in France with the royal army, and was captured and ransomed before the beginning of March. We then have no record of him until 1366, when he went to Navarre, with a passport from the king of Navarre empowering him to ask the royal officials about anything he wished to know; and the following year he was on the payroll of the royal household as a *valet*. This seems to correspond with the appointment of artists connected with the French princely households as *valets de chambre* who later went on confidential diplomatic missions. After Chaucer's last mission abroad in

*Guillaume Machaut*

*Geoffrey Chaucer*

1373, we find him as a *valet de chambre* to Edward III, and he remained in this post after the accession of Richard II. His first surviving poetry probably dates from around 1370, the elegy for the death of Blanche of Lancaster, and the appointment is perhaps related both to his diplomatic service and his new status as poet.

Unlike the artists at the Burgundian court, Chaucer had a full-time career in royal service. At the point when this began, he ceased to be a *valet de chambre*, but remained a member of the court. The famous frontispiece to a manuscript of his *Troilus and Criseyde*, from the early fifteenth century, showing him reading to the court, is probably a genuine testimony to the way in which he was remembered in the decades after his death. In his poem, *The House of Fame,* he portrays himself as an official 'making all his reckonings' and going home to read with such concentration that he is 'dumb as any stone' and until he is in a daze.[46]

*Jean Froissart*

Jean Froissart, Chaucer's contemporary, came, by his own account, from Hainault to the English court because of Queen Philippa. She was also from Hainault and was still very much in touch with her homeland. Froissart presented her with a verse chronicle on the events since the battle of Poitiers. He claimed that she was so pleased with it that he became a clerk of the queen's chamber. During his time in England, he certainly moved in court circles and met many of the most important figures of the English court as well as the aristocratic French captives who had fought at Poitiers. He travelled to Bordeaux to see the Black Prince in 1367 and a year later accompanied Lionel, duke of Clarence, to Milan, and when news of Philippa's death reached him on the way home, at Brussels in 1369, he did not return to England. His position there was perhaps not secure enough without her, and the fact that he quickly found a new patron abroad, the duchess of Brabant, seems to confirm that it was the personal link to Philippa rather than any formal appointment that had kept him in England for nearly a decade.

For the next fifteen years Froissart was attached to the court of Brabant, and was given a benefice at Cambrai in 1372 by Duke Wenceslas as a means of providing him with an income while he worked on his new project. This was a prose chronicle commissioned by Robert de Namur recording events that led up to the wars between England and France. From this point on, his patrons were French, and the second book of the chronicles was commissioned by Gui, count of Blois. The change of patronage meant that his standpoint moved from favouring the English and Hainaulters to a more pro-French stance, an attitude which hardened over time. Patronage and impartiality did not always mix, and at moments he incorporates French propaganda wholesale. The most extreme instance is the supposed massacre at Limoges perpetrated by the Black Prince in 1370. But this was of course what Froissart's patrons wanted to hear. In 1393, he was rewarded by the duke of Orléans for a copy of his collected poems, and in 1395 he presented another copy of this book to Richard II at Eltham. He found England uncongenial, and at odds with his memory of the court thirty years earlier. After this, he seems to have retired to Cambrai, not far from Chimay, the place where he had been a canon since 1384. The various versions of his *Chronicles* which appeared during his lifetime were to some extent rewritten to match the interests of his current patron. Here he revised the chronicle yet again, and that final version aims at a more balanced view.

Chaucer and Froissart both had lucrative posts, more than adequate for their livelihood. Christine de Pizan, by contrast, was left a widow with three children at the age of twenty-five, and wrote to live. She had good connections to the court, because her husband was one of the royal secretaries. Many of her numerous works were dedicated to or commissioned by the French royal dukes. Philip the Bold was the dedicatee of one manuscript, and another was dedicated to Charles VI and a copy given to Philip. This gift resulted in a commission for a biography of Charles V; but when Philip died in 1404, it had not been completed. She therefore presented it to Jean duke of Berry as a New Year's gift a few months later. She was a favourite of Queen Isabeau, as we have seen, but after the French defeat at Agincourt, the French court was no longer able to provide the kind of patronage she needed, and she retired to a convent. Her last work was a poem in praise of Joan of Arc, addressed to Charles VII. If her biography of Charles V contains flattering references to the members of his family, the portrait she draws of him seems to be perfectly genuine, and is a valuable source for the day-to-day life of a late medieval prince.

# The Decorative Arts
## Wall paintings

I N THE TWELFTH CENTURY, PRINCES WOULD have required painters for decorative rather than artistic work in the modern sense of painting; the latter was to be found in miniatures in manuscripts, a particular craft which rarely interacted with murals or sculptures.* Both painters and sculptors were itinerant workers; sculptors often worked in teams, particularly on churches, where the distinctive style of a particular team sometimes allows us to trace their movements. Painters of this period would have worked on an *ad hoc* basis, as far as we can tell from the very few surviving frescoes. There are a handful of entries in the English exchequer records which mention payments for wall painting in the twelfth century. We know that Henry II, for example, had murals in his chamber at Winchester, 'very beautifully drawn and coloured': Gerald of Wales tells us that after his sons rebelled against him in 1172, he filled a space in the decoration with a picture of an eagle preyed on by its nestlings, one of which was perched on the eagle's neck ready to peck out its eyes. This, the king explained to Gerald, represented the tragedy of his life.[47]

*Frescoes in royal residences*

We do have some idea of what these early wall paintings were like from an illustration in the early thirteenth-century chronicle by Peter of Eboli in praise of the emperor Heinrich VI. This has a page showing the – admittedly imaginary – decoration of one of his palaces. There are five scenes from the Old Testament at the top, and then a monumental portrait of Friedrich Barbarossa as emperor, flanked by Heinrich VI, his successor, and Philip, his second son. At the bottom, Friedrich Barbarossa is shown on crusade, fighting his way through the forests of Bulgaria.

The finest secular wall paintings to survive from this period are those at Schloss Rodenegg in South Tirol, dating from not later than 1250 on the basis of the style of the armour. These depict scenes from the Arthurian romance of Yvain (Ywein in German) and are much more sophisticated than the scenes in the Sicilian manuscript. This is probably what we should imagine as typical of the early thirteenth-century pictorial cycles in castles and palaces, such as those commissioned under Henry III in mid thirteenth-century England. Here the relatively extensive royal records tell us the names of the painters for the first time: Master William, a monk of Westminster, and Master Walter of London. William is called the king's painter in 1267 and Walter, who came originally from Durham, seems to have been his successor.[48]

Henry III commissioned wall paintings for many of his palaces, castles and houses, though very little survives. We do have watercolours of some paintings at the palace of

* Master Hugh at Bury St Edmunds is something of an exception; see p. 119.

Westminster before the devastating fire of 1834, which engulfed St Stephen's chapel and other buildings. These record the king's great chamber, known as the Painted Chamber, which was probably the most remarkable of the rooms for which Henry ordered murals. These were started in the 1230s, and damaged by fire in 1263; repairs and further work continued until 1297, when it was stopped to defray the cost of Edward I's Scottish wars. The resulting splendour was one of the sights of London, and Brother Simon 'the illuminator'* and his companion Simeon, en route from Dublin to the Holy Land in 1323, duly came to see

*The Painted Chamber at Westminster*

> the celebrated palace of the kings of England, in which is that famous chamber on whose walls all the warlike stories of the whole Bible are painted with wonderful skill, and explained by a complete series of texts accurately written in French to the great admiration of the beholder and with the greatest royal magnificence.[49]

'All the warlike stories of the Bible' would hardly have fitted into the walls of the Painted Chamber, and the scenes recorded in the watercolours were largely centred on the Jewish military hero Judas Maccabeus, with other scenes drawn from the story of Elisha and of the fall of Jerusalem. The most striking image to have come down to us is one of the pairs of Vices and Virtues in combat, *Generosity and Covetousness* and *Courtesy conquering Anger*. These monumental figures flanked the windows, and portray a favourite theme of the period. The early nineteenth-century watercolours which record them are probably too pallid, though these were frescoes, which were not as intense as the colouring in the more familiar world of medieval manuscripts. The Old Testament scenes, for which we have only the fragmentary images which survived at the end of the eighteenth century, were largely battle images, with elaborate captions in the bands between the sequences of frescoes. As Paul Binski says in his detailed study of the room,

> When new and fresh, the effect of the Old Testament scenes in the Painted Chamber must have been astonishing. Brilliantly coloured and gilded, the stories ran around the room in registers, completely draping the walls above the dado as far as the ceiling, and amounting to several hundred feet of narrative ... Their extent and quality made them one of the wonders of the metropolis...

The design and effect of the paintings was carefully controlled by Henry. Early in the enterprise, he told Odo the Goldsmith, who seems to have been in charge, to abandon a proposed series of illustrations of stories from the bestiary, because it would clash with the other scenes. And on the wall above his bed the coronation of Edward the Confessor was painted, echoing the veneration of the saint in the abbey next door. In the Painted Chamber at Westminster, besides the history of the Maccabees – one of the obscurer parts of the Old Testament nowadays – there were secular scenes. Around the fireplace were the labours of the months, familiar from prayerbooks, where they illustrated the calendar of saints' days. Here the artist could be realistic: one order for such a painting in the queen's chamber specifies 'the figure of Winter which by its sad look and other miserable portrayals of the body may be justly likened to Winter itself'. Elsewhere, Henry specified scenes from histories and romances, including the romantic version of the story of Alexander, and the epic accounts of the Crusades. The siege of Antioch was the subject of one of the latter poems, and there were 'Antioch chambers' at Westminster and the Tower, and at Clarendon, the palace near Salisbury which had been transformed by Henry II from a

---

* i.e. illuminator of manuscripts.

Norman hunting lodge into 'a noble and famous house belonging to the king himself' in the 1170s.[51] Also at Clarendon was an 'Alexander chamber', decorated with the exploits of Alexander as related in thirteenth-century romances, on the orders of Henry III, and a fresco of the famous duel between Richard I and Saladin, a subject also found on tiles from royal houses.

When there was no pictorial decoration, the walls were often painted with flowers or imitations of drapery; in thirteenth-century England this was invariably green. Patterns of stars on a green ground were Henry III's favourite, and in the fourteenth century the *fleur-de-lis* on its dark blue ground is an obvious design for the French royal palaces. The famous miniature of Christine de Pizan reading to Queen Isabeau of France around 1400 shows a variety of wall paintings of this kind, which the artist renders in such a way that they cannot be mistaken for real drapery.

*Patterned wall painting*

The wall paintings at Philip the Bold's castle of Hesdin, which he inherited from Louis de Mâle in 1384, were done to the duke's own plan, by his painter Melchior Broederlam. They have long since vanished, but William Caxton saw them, and has left us this description:

> But I know well that the noble duke Philip, first founder of this said order* had a room made in the castle of Hesdin, in which the conquest of the Golden Fleece by Jason was skilfully and curiously depicted; I have been in that room, and seen the painting of that story.[52]

In other rooms there were paintings on the Trojan War, and Broederlam spent in all three years working there. He took charge of the famous 'machines', and designed tiles and textiles as well.[53]

IN THE ABSENCE OF WALL PAINTINGS in a princely context, we have to turn to the papal palace at Avignon to get an idea of what such work might have looked like. Only one room survives with its décor largely intact, the so-called 'Room of the Stag', in the Wardrobe Tower, built in 1342, and decorated by November 1343.[54] The wardrobe was of course the financial centre of a medieval court, and the pope had a *studium* there, an office which also doubled as a room, in that it contained a bed. The images here are entirely secular, almost designed to distract the occupant from the business he had to undertake. Here the pope is surrounding himself with the trappings of a noble of the period: his arms appear in the frieze, and hunting was of course the noble sport *par excellence*. The painting on the west wall from which the room gets its name, the stag hunt, is the most damaged area, because a chimney was installed here in the eighteenth century; the scenes of the return from hawking (east wall), fishing in a pool (north wall) and the ferret hunt (south wall) are those which give the greatest impression of the depth and richness of the unknown artist's work. There may well have been more than one artist, and the figures are clearly Italianate in style rather than French. The background is a landscape which manages to be both naturalistic and stylised at the same time; the trees in the hawking scene are given foliage which might come off a tapestry. The overall effect is indeed that of a room hung with tapestries, particularly as the wall below the dado is painted to represent a hanging textile; we know that the rest of the palace was filled with tapestries bought in the decade before the decoration of the *studium*. But the detail and the expressions on the faces of the people who populate this world are of course much finer, and the depth of colour more intense. It is a panorama of the different kinds of hunting and fishing, reminiscent of those borders in books of hours where a hunt is in progress to amuse the lord as he fidgets at his

*The papal palace at Avignon*

* The Order of the Golden Fleece.

devotions. If this were a prince's palace, we would accept these scenes as entirely normal; here, they serve to remind us of the pope as prince of the Church, claiming superiority over all the princes of this world and outdoing them in magnificence. The frieze above the paintings indicates his status: his arms are placed between the crossed keys of St Peter, the shield of the church, and the *fleurs-de-lis* of the king of France.

The Italianate nature of the Avignon paintings leads us on to another major artist working in an Italian court, Pisanello, who first came to Mantua in 1439 with an established reputation. He was highly regarded by Lodovico III Gonzaga, the marquis of Mantua, and the decoration of the hall at the entrance to the palace in Mantua was entrusted to him soon after his arrival.[55] He worked on the project for two years, before going to Naples and the court of Alfonso V. Lodovico was a *condottiere*, somewhere between a professional soldier and a mercenary. The scenes he commissioned depicted a tournament described at length in the Arthurian romance known as the *Prose Lancelot*. Although Pisanello selects just one episode to illustrate, his narrative scene is as complex as the account in his source. He abandons the traditional visual frames of individual episodes, and creates an extraordinarily fluid sequence of images. The fresco is badly damaged, and was left incomplete, but what remains conjures up the violence and vigour of the tournament, which continues uninterrupted from one wall to the next. The figures are often seen from strange foreshortened perspectives, head on or from the rear, with fallen knights in agonised postures. It was intended as a dramatic room which immediately proclaimed Lodovico's ambition to be a successful commander.

## Tapestries

THE ALTERNATIVE TO WALL PAINTINGS was hangings, normally tapestries. These had the great advantage that they could be moved with the prince as he travelled from place to place, but very little survives in the way of secular tapestry until the late fourteenth century, and we have to rely on literary sources and account books for descriptions and details. The accounts record many tapestries as part of a *chambre*, meaning the complete furnishing of a room, particularly a bedroom. The *chambre* set was usually named either for the subject of the main tapestries or for the occasion for which it was used. Furthermore, they could be changed according to the season, and according to the prince's whim. Jean II had sets for Easter, All Saints (1 November) and Christmas.[56] Typically, the set consisted of the bed hangings – a tester above and curtains around it, with a bedcover and cushions – and tapestries, and other cushions for elsewhere in the room, all in the same pattern.

*Tapestry sets or chambres*

The inventory of Charles V lists a total of fifty-five such *chambres* belonging to the king stored in the palace of the Louvre.[57] It opens with three heraldic *chambres*, the first entirely decorated with the royal *fleur-de-lis*, the next with the arms of France and Navarre, and the third with the arms of France and Bohemia. This last set, in blue satin, had probably belonged to his mother, Bonne of Luxembourg, sister of the emperor Karl IV; it had an elaborate set of hangings for the bed, and ten tapestries, with a total length of 52 metres, 2.5 metres high, which would have decorated the most spacious of bedrooms. This was not the largest such set: the city of Paris gave the king a *chambre* in red silk, the bed hangings embroidered with brooches, roses and pearls, and with eighteen tapestries 130 metres overall by four metres high, which must have been intended for a hall rather than a bedchamber.

A number of the sets seem to be simply of rich material, such as that in green samite, a satin with a particular sheen. Those with motifs are generally of heraldic or floral designs. One set is singled out as a 'very beautiful green *chambre*, worked as tapestry in silk, with an overall pattern of leaves of different kinds, and with buildings, in the midst which is a lion which two kings are crowning, and a fountain in which swans are at play'.

Charles V was evidently more austere in his tastes than his brothers, for whom tapestries with grand scenes, of the kind that are familiar from later centuries, were the latest fashion. The first sign of this is in the accounts of Louis d'Anjou: by 1364, Louis already owned sixty-six tapestries, many of them with narrative scenes.[58] There are a large number whose subjects are taken from the epic poems about the crusades, referring to his family's claim to the kingdom of Jerusalem, or biblical scenes. Other scenes from old French epics are frequent, and there are two episodes from the romance of Lancelot. The others are light-hearted images of the god of love, girls hunting in the woods, and a knight proposing to a townswoman. Charles V was followed in his enthusiasm for tapestry by Philip the Bold. In 1369, Philip married Margaret, heiress to Flanders and Artois, and in 1371 he visited Arras; we know this because he gave money to 'several men making tapestry'. It was after the death of his father-in-law, Louis de Mâle, that he started to buy tapestries in quantity to give as gifts and for his own use.

*Louis d'Anjou's tapestries*

The exceptional set of Apocalypse tapestries for the cathedral at Angers, designed by Jean Bandol, court painter to Charles V, show us what tapestry should really be like.[59] Too often, we see time-worn examples, whose colours have faded badly, and which retain only their monumental quality. The Angers tapestries have been preserved in the cathedral treasury, away from the light, and are not only in excellent bright condition, but are also the largest recorded set of their kind. Because they were not intended to be moved, they could be made larger than the practical requirements of the king's household would allow. It is these tapestries that allow us to get some idea of the startling effect that tapestry must have had in the new spacious rooms of royal palaces lit by windows with slender Gothic tracery.

In 1422, the English took over the government of Paris in the name of Henry VI, on the death of Charles VI, and the collection of royal tapestries was sold off or passed to the duke of Bedford, regent of France in Henry's name. Here we find not just figurative tapestries, but tapestries which depict recent events; these are listed among the pieces taken by the duke's agent, Jehan Brigge, in 1432.[60] The finest piece seems to have been the *chambre* depicting the jousts at the abbey of Saint-Denis when the princes of the house of Anjou were knighted in 1389.* At the head of the bed there was an armed knight on horseback, with a lady leading him by the bridle and two queens looking on; his standard was displayed between two men holding lances, and lances were spread on the foreground. Other items were obviously chosen for their historic interest: the tapestry of Duke William who conquered England is described as 'old, ragged and worn', as is that of the encounter in 1351 known as the Battle of the Thirty, a tournament fought in Brittany between knights from the French and English armies. Likewise, the 'great tapestry of the jousts at St Inglevert' held in 1390 is noted as 'ragged'. It looks as if these were pieces which the king liked to take with him on his travels, and although special wrappings were often made to protect them, frequent moves were destructive. We have a record of how many carts were needed to move Philip the Good's tapestry for a ceremonial occasion: when he held the wedding feast for his marriage to Isabel of Portugal at Bruges in 1430, a cortège of fifteen carts was needed.

*John of Bedford acquires Charles VI's tapestries*

Philip the Bold's purchases at the end of the fourteenth century also reflect the change to pictorial tapestries. Two massive orders placed by him in 1395, said to amount to a kilometre of tapestry,[61] specify a wide range of subjects: the deeds of Charlemagne, and of

* See the account of this occasion on p. 210.

Godfrey de Bouillon, leader of the First Crusade, the romance of Perceval, and the Nine Worthies. In 1404, he owned pieces showing Bertrand du Guesclin's defeat of the English at Pontvallain and Cocherel in 1364. The most grandiose of his chambres was that of the 'History of Fame', ordered in 1400 for 3,000 crowns; next came a set depicting Charlemagne for 2,500 crowns in 1394. His successors as dukes were equally prodigal in their spending. In 1449, eight large tapestries depicting the history of Gideon and the Golden Fleece were ordered by Philip the Good, to be completed within four years, at a cost of 8,960 crowns. These were in connection with the Order of the Golden Fleece which he had founded twenty years earlier. When Philip went to Paris for the ceremonies to celebrate Louis XI's coronation in September 1461, the tapestry was hung in the great hall of his Paris mansion, the hôtel d'Artois, 'and every day people flocked to see him there'.[62]

*The dais of Charles VII*

The most truly 'magnificent' of all surviving medieval tapestries comes from the court of Charles VII. This 'dais' shown opposite would have been suspended in a wooden frame above his throne, and dates from 1430–1440. The designer was probably the court painter Jacob de Littemont. It is not impossible that it was made for his coronation at Reims in July 1429, in the presence of Joan of Arc. However, it is an object without a history. It was unknown until 2008, when it was bought by the Louvre from a specialist in tapestry. The previous owner had been a private collector, who had acquired it as a nineteenth century piece, and its extraordinary state of preservation would certainly have concealed its true age. In terms of magnificence, it ranks with the Goldenes Rössl and the chapel of the Holy Cross at Karlstejn.[63]

# Heraldry

HERALDIC ART, ON THE FACE OF IT, appears to be the simple repetition of patterns or symbols which are determined by the traditions developed in the early stages of heraldry in the twelfth century. These symbols become more complex with the introduction of differences, the same shield with an additional element to indicate, for instance, that the bearer is the eldest son of the lord whose shield it is. Yet by and large heraldic shields or devices are, in artistic terms, balanced and in proportion. Even when the repertoire of heraldic objects extends to crests and seals, the same sense of composition and order applies. This must to some extent be the result of conscious design, and the presence, however anonymous, of an artist or designer who is creating the image.[64]

Heraldic design is one of the most constant elements of the display of magnificence, and such a display would become meaningless without designs which were regular and easily recognisable. To some extent, towards the end of the Middle Ages, we find the combination of multiple designs which have to be read carefully as a means of expressing magnificence, such as the shields of sixty-four quarters of the German nobility. These are shields which prove that the bearers come from a family all of whose members have been noble for five generations, and each 'quarter' shows the relevant arms. But most heraldic decoration uses much simpler and easily recognisable symbols.

Appropriate personal heraldry appeared on clothing as early as 1128. Geoffrey Plantagenet's arms were little golden lions, and he is described as having these embroidered on his boots at his marriage to Henry I's daughter Matilda. His memorial plaque in the 1150s shows him wearing a cap with a golden lion on it, and holding his lion shield.[65] Devices were to be found on horse armour and on the royal saddle cloths and horse caparisons from the 1140s onwards, and little armorial plaques were attached to the harness: stirrups were

**56.** The royal canopy of Charles VII, designed by Jacob de Littemont, probably around 1450. This astonishing textile was only discovered in 2008, and is the sole surviving example of the type of canopy under which the king sat when he was formally enthroned.

marked with the owner's arms. In a sense, this was an extension of the device on the knight's shield to his armour and trappings. In the thirteenth century we find the first evidence for heraldic painting in a secular context, when Henry III gave orders for his royal arms to be painted on the shutters of his great chamber in the Tower of London in 1240.[66] And the later painting of heraldic shields in halls and chambers is foreshadowed by the great display of such shields at the meeting of Henry III and Louis IX in Paris in 1254. The two kings dined in the great hall of the Knights Templars, and the chronicler Matthew Paris noted that, according to the custom in France, 'as many shields as possible were hung on the four walls'. Chests were frequently painted with arms, as in the case of the Calais chest still in the National Archives. This was made to hold the Treaty of Calais, a peace treaty between England and France ratified in October 1360, and has ten shields painted on it, including those of the kingdoms, of the prince of Wales and the dauphin of France, and of two of the chief negotiators. Towards the end of the fourteenth century, the custom of going on crusade with the order of Teutonic knights, who were fighting the heathen in the Baltic territories, led to a tradition whereby the arms of the crusaders, who came from all over Europe, were commemorated in the great hall of the order at Marienburg. These were eagerly scanned by newly arrived knights, to see if they could find members of their family recorded there.

Heraldic designs recur again and again in the inventories of tapestry, and heraldry was everywhere in the interiors of princely palaces and castles. We have the verbatim records of a case in the English court of chivalry in 1385–6, when Sir Richard Scrope and Sir Robert Grosvenor disputed the right to the arms *Azure, a bend or*. These eyewitness accounts paint a vivid picture of a world where heraldry was everywhere. Sir John Warde

> said that he had a chamber in a manor house called Gynendale, where the arms
> of Scrope are set up and depicted on the wall, in which chamber were also the
> arms of the Lord Neville, of the Lord Percy, of the Lord Clifford, and others,
> which had been in the said chamber for one hundred and sixty years, as the
> Deponent's father told him.[67]

Sir Bertram Montboucher remembered how

> Sir Henry Scrope, elder brother of the said Sir Geoffrey, who was father of the said
> Sir Richard that now is, used the same arms entire, and placed them in his halls,
> on his beds, vessels, and burial places, as appears to this day.[68]

If this was the usage at the modest level of Yorkshire country gentlemen, the ubiquitous presence of arms in princely surroundings was much more nuanced and intentional. Porches or gateways, doorways inside the building, stained glass windows, keystones of vaulted ceilings, as well as wall paintings and tapestries, could all bear their owner's mark.

One of the earliest commissions for the decoration of the interior of a castle which has come down to us specifies heraldic decoration. A contract between Mahaut countess of Artois and a painter named Pierre de Bruxelles in 1320 for the decoration of her residence just outside Paris specifies very closely what the pictures should be. They are scenes of warfare in which knights are prominent, and the heraldry is clearly the most decorative element. The figures are specified as follows:

> ... the image of the count of Artois everywhere depicted with the arms of the said
> count, and other images of knights bearing several colours with their arms wherever
> they appear; and it will be discovered what arms they bore when they were alive. [69]

Military magnificence involved vast quantities of heraldic painting, far greater than the modest quantities needed in the world of tournaments. The main requirements here were for banners, tents and standards. In 1350, Edward III was preparing a fleet to challenge the Castilian fleet returning from its annual voyage to Flanders, which was rumoured to be planning an attack on the English wine convoy from Bordeaux. As part of the preparations, twelve streamers and sixteen banners were ordered, including a massive streamer for the king's ship, *La Seinte Marie*, a cog of about 240 tons; it was the second largest ship in the fleet.[70] Even among these huge flags which hung at the stern with the arms of the king, this example was exceptional: it measured 37 metres long and 7 metres deep, with a figure of the Virgin Mary at the head quartered with the king's arms. Edward had a particular devotion to the Virgin as *stella maris*, 'the star of the sea', since he had once invoked her in a violent Atlantic storm in 1343 on his way back from Brittany, and had survived, founding the monastery of St Mary Graces near the Tower in gratitude.[71] Other ships had streamers with images which identified them: a figure of St Thomas for the *Cog Thomas*, which the king had also used as a flagship, St Edmund for *La Edmond*, and an 'E' for *La Edward*. As well as these capital ships, the smaller ships had banners: for *La Faucon*, this was simply the king's arms. The streamer for *La Seinte Marie* was painted, but for the *Cog Thomas* a woven image was bought in. There were a multitude of methods, and a multitude of smaller standards: many of the items were made by cutting and sewing coloured worsted to make the heraldic patterns, while the figures such as leopards were embroidered. There are bulk orders for a thousand pennons with St George's cross, 250 standards with leopards embroidered on them, eighty standards with leopards and lilies.

*Military heraldry*

The workers involved included painters, draughtsmen and stainers; in earlier years, Hugh of St Albans, the king's official painter, had been brought in to paint 'cloths' for the king's ships, which may have been a simpler kind of flag. The labour required was considerable: the streamers and banners required a total of 2,064 days' work, for which forty-eight people were involved. The overall effect would have been dramatic, a naval spectacle to match anything in the context of court or city. Perhaps the emphasis on display here is to underline an unusual aspect of Edward's magnificence: very few kings ever led their fleet into battle. The encounter with the Spanish off Winchelsea was inconclusive; the Spanish escaped largely unharmed, but were balked of their prey.

In 1385, Philip the Bold had similar banners and streamers made for his galley by Melchior Broederlam, his painter in Flanders. These were evidently for a special occasion when a full range of his arms was to be shown, as duke of Burgundy, count of Flanders and Artois, and of Rethel. In 1386 for the ducal ship he ordered sixty banners with his arms, and thirty pennons with his device. Pennons with the various separate arms for each of his titles and four large pennants with his device were also made, and there was an additional charge for gold letters on the white tails of these. The sail was painted with his device and the background was covered in blue letters and daisies.[72] Broederlam also painted caparisons for tournament horses, banners, standards and pennons, and made decorations for the wedding of Philip's son in 1401. Jean de Beaumetz, based in Dijon, was required to produce four hundred ducal ensigns in 1391–2, This familiarity with heraldry influenced other work by Philip's artists; when the Limbourg brothers came to illuminate the *Très riches heures*, they included in the miniature for January a tapestry with scrupulously correct heraldic details. At the highest level, heraldry and the world of fine art were interlinked.

*Philip the Bold's heraldic banners*

**Frontispiece**

# Menageries

THE OWNERSHIP OF RARE AND EXOTIC animals was a mark of princely status, and the prestige of having a menagerie goes back to the emperor Augustus at the beginning of the Christian era. For him, it was not simply a matter of display, but a genuine interest in natural history. He is said to have had 420 tigers and 260 lions, a large collection of African animals such as panthers and leopards, a rhinoceros, the first hippopotamus to be seen in Rome, and elephants. Crocodiles, bears, eagles and seals were also included.[73] Subsequent emperors continued the tradition, and their menageries sometimes supplied exotic beasts for the gladiators in the public arena. The tradition of combats between men and wild animals continued in Byzantium after the division of the Roman empire. In the West Charlemagne reinforced his image as heir of ancient Rome by asking Haroun al Raschid, emperor of Baghdad, to send him an elephant and some monkeys, which duly arrived in 797. The elephant, named Abul-Abbas, was shipped to Pisa, and then taken over the Alps. It followed Charlemagne's court for thirteen years, dying at his palace at Lippeham on the Rhine. Otto I, emperor in the second half of the tenth century, had the first recorded menagerie in western Christendom. It was in Saxony, and included gifts from embassies from Rome, the Saracen world, and Byzantium, consisting of lions and camels, monkeys and ostriches.[74]

*The menagerie of Henry I*

We first meet the famous menagerie of Henry I at Caen in Normandy. Ralph Tortaire, a monk from Fleury on the Loire, sent a poem to a friend which described his excitement at seeing the wealth of the town at some time between 1110 and 1115. He arrived there on market day, and he was amazed by a procession which appeared soon afterwards. The king and his soldiers rode at the head of a cavalcade whose purpose was to show off the exotic creatures he kept in the castle. First came an Ethiopian with a young lion, which he beat to make it roar, terrifying the onlookers. A fine leopard on horseback (presumably with its keeper) followed, and then a lynx. A troop of men led a camel, whose harness was covered with medallions, and finally an ostrich.[75] The description is obviously tinged with learned images: the Ethiopian and the leopard riding on horseback sound like poetic tradition rather than reality.

The scene at Caen presumably took place before Henry moved the menagerie to England and added a building to his hunting lodge at Woodstock in Oxfordshire to house it. The historian William of Malmesbury records lions, leopards, lynxes and camels there, which correspond to Ralph's description, and adds a porcupine, the only one on record in a medieval menagerie, sent to him by the lord of Montpellier in southern France. He also mentions an ostrich which he saw in the days of Henry I, describing it as very large, feathered and unable to fly.[76]

*Friedrich II's elephant*

There was a kind of hierarchy attached to the animals found in princely menageries. Elephants were a gift between emperors, or kings of high status. Friedrich II, for whom natural history and the newly emerging sciences were a matter of fascination, was given an elephant by the sultan of Egypt when he succeeded in negotiating the return of Jerusalem to the Christians in 1229.[77] In 1234 the elephant and several camels and dromedaries were sent to Cremona to be cared for there. This was evidently the base for the imperial menagerie. In the following year, the elephant was sent on its travels. It went to Florence and Lucca,[78] and it was on its return that the chronicler Salimbene saw the menagerie, including the elephant, passing through Parma on its way to Cremona.[79] From Cremona, Friedrich took it into Germany in the same year; he was at Colmar in March with 'a multitude of camels'.[80] The emperor then appeared at an imperial council at Ratisbon where, faced

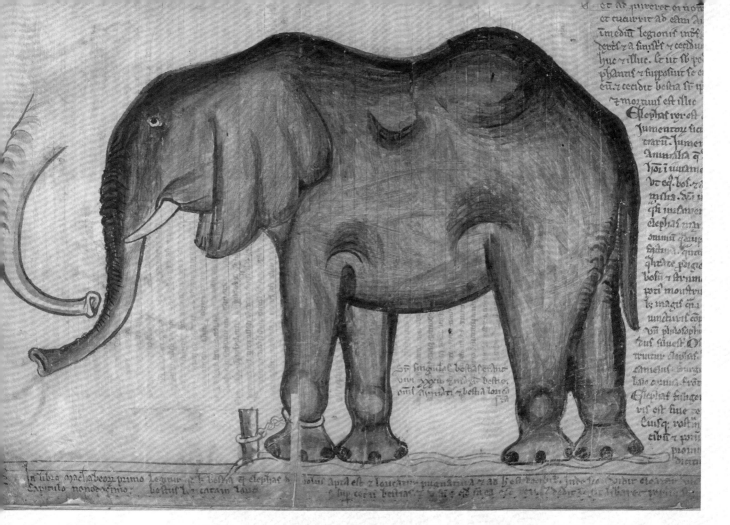

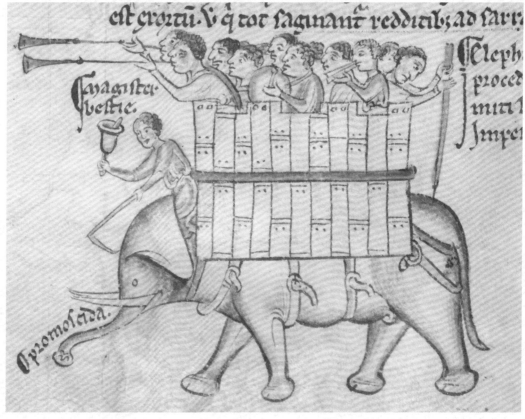

**57.** (above) Matthew Paris travelled to London to draw Henry III's elephant from the life. His account of the episode tells us that the elephant 'assisted him in exemplary fashion'.

**58.** Friedrich II's elephant at Cremona, with a castle full of musicians on its back. The 'master of the beast' rings a bell to advertise its coming; he and his assistant at the back both have goads.

with a rebellion on the part of his son, he put on a show of splendour. His wagon train was adorned with gold and silver, with purple satin coverings, and it was accompanied by Saracens and Ethiopians leading camels and dromedaries, monkeys and leopards from his menagerie.[81] The elephant was shown at Cremona in 1241 to Richard of Cornwall, brother of Henry III, who was deeply involved in the politics of the empire and later became king of the Romans.[82] In 1245 the monks at Verona had to provide hospitality for the emperor, one elephant, five leopards and twenty-four camels as he passed through the city.[83] The elephant died at Cremona seven years later.[84]

*Henry III's elephant*

Towards the end of Louis IX's disastrous crusade in Egypt, in the course of which he was captured and had to be ransomed, Louis was negotiating with his erstwhile captors to form a new alliance against the sultan of Damascus. In the course of these negotiations, the emirs of Egypt gave the French king an elephant, which he had shipped to France.[85] It seems to have been this elephant that Louis IX gave to Henry III in 1254, when Henry was in Paris on his way back from Gascony in December.

Just why Louis should have given Henry the elephant is unknown, but Henry evidently accepted it with some enthusiasm. On 13 December he appointed one of his clerks to be the senior keeper of the elephant, and to make sure that John Gouche, its handler, had everything he needed to get the beast to England. It was at Wissant in February, when the sheriff of Kent arranged for it to be shipped across the Channel, probably direct to London. Its arrival was evidently imminent at the end of February, when the sheriffs of London were ordered to have an elephant cage 15 metres by 30 metres constructed within the Tower of London.[86] Writs for the expenses of keeping the elephant are recorded in October 1256, and the cost from December 1255 to September 1256 was almost £25. It was the first elephant ever to be seen in England, and it attracted much attention, and crowds came to inspect this extraordinary creature. The greatest artist of the day, Matthew Paris of St Albans, seems to have gone specially to draw the elephant and its keeper, Henry de Flor. There are two versions of the drawing, one of which looks to be the original sketch from life, in which the elephant 'assisted him in exemplary fashion' as he says in his notes.[87] It is one of the earliest known drawings from life in English medieval art. Alas, the elephant did not survive for long as a visible symbol of Henry's magnificence. Just two annual payments for its upkeep were made to the sheriffs of London, and it died on 14 February 1257 in the depths of the English winter.

Leopards and lions, more or less the same in heraldry, were of course symbols of kingship. Friedrich's gift of three leopards to Henry, as a thank you present after his marriage to Isabella of England, were specifically sent as a reference to Henry's royal arms.[88] They

*Leopards and their symbolism*

were of course different animals in the real world, and the heraldic leopard is technically a lion *passant guardant*, walking and looking outwards, because leopards were definitely kept in the English royal menagerie for centuries. Leopards could evidently be tamed: in the 1390s, there was a leopard in the park of Philip the Bold's castle of Conflans which was a special pet, apparently tame enough for his children to ride. One of the duke's messengers was paid for procuring 'a carpet for riding on the leopard', and when the leopard fell ill, it was carefully nursed, wrapped in winding-sheets and padded with carpets and coarse sackcloth. It was dosed with a spiced medicine containing among other things nutmeg, cloves, sugar, cinnamon and two pints of olive oil.[89] Perhaps there was a certain frisson about the Burgundian dukes-to-be riding the symbol of English power, in a world where symbols were very important.

THE RANGE AND DIVERSITY OF the creatures paraded before the public was another way of declaring magnificence. Friedrich II's menagerie was the most extensive in medieval Europe: the only record of a camel in medieval England is one given to Henry III by his son-in-law. The exchange of gifts between Friedrich and the sultan of Egypt, al-Kamil, brought the emperor pelicans and exotic animals from India in return for peacocks and polar bears. On another occasion, the sultan produced a giraffe for him, the first to be seen in Europe.[90] Polar bears were also owned by Philip IV of France and Henry III, who was given one by the king of Norway in 1252.[91] Its keeper used to fasten it with a long rope and allow it to catch fish swimming in the Thames; this was obviously a popular show, as the king granted him the right to charge the onlookers whatever he wished. Similar permission was given to Jakemyn de St Pierre when he brought two leopards back from Guyenne for Edward I.

The French kings had a menagerie in the Louvre, and in the case of Charles V there was also one at his former town house, the hôtel de St Pol, but the inhabitants were largely lions and leopards, and camels. Charles V did have pools at St Pol for both seals and porpoises, but there seems to have been nothing more exotic than this.[92] Jean duke of Berry had menageries at two of his châteaux, at Mehun-sur-Yèvre and at Bourges, where the main inhabitants were bears. The bear was his favourite emblem, to be found on the richest of his manuscripts and on monuments, inscriptions and heraldry for over fifty years of his life. He even seems to have had a small troop of travelling bears, his favourites among those cared for by his bear-keeper Colin de Bléron, named Maillard, Brunelle, Chapelain and Valentin. Medieval writers placed particular emphasis on the bear's similarity to man: its upright stance, the use of its paws to catch fish or gather leaves, and its ability to throw objects.[93] Menageries of some kind seem to have been very common among princely households; René d'Anjou had assorted beasts at Angers, and we learn quite incidentally that Alfonso of Aragon had 'ten camels, two lions, two lionesses, a leopard, ten ostriches and four lynxes' which appeared in a parade to greet the emperor Friedrich III in 1452.[94]

*Jean duke of Berry's bears*

# 9 | MAGNIFICENT ARCHITECTURE

*◆ Capital cities ◆ Paris: The Louvre ◆ London: St Stephen's chapel ◆ Prague: Karl IV and Prague ◆ Naples ◆ Castles for kings and emperors ◆ Castle residences ◆ Windsor ◆ Bellver ◆ Vincennes ◆ Karlstejn ◆ Churches, shrines and relics ◆ Collecting relics ◆ Relics as an aspect of magnificence*

## Capital Cities

THE PRINCE'S CAPITAL CITY WAS IN many ways the focal point of his magnificence. It was here that he most often appeared in public, whether in day-to-day life or when he was receiving embassies and entertaining guests of equal standing. The capital was also the backdrop to his most splendid ceremonies, feasts and entries, and in many cases it was physically dominated by his palace, set at the highest point of the city or distinguished by the height of its towers. It was here too that the prince's particular church was usually to be found, the church most important to his dynasty. This was rarely the same as the centre of the Church's own activities in the city, and was often integrated in or very close to his palace. And from the twelfth century onwards, the city was deliberately provided with streets which were designed for processions and triumphs, as a setting for the ceremonial rites which were part of the prince's formal entry into his capital, or of the arrival of another sovereign as visitor. In the most extreme case, we shall see how the emperor Karl IV remodelled Prague with magnificence in mind.

### Paris

THE FOREMOST CITY IN EUROPE (and the city in which the emperor Karl grew up) was Paris. It was the richest city in Europe for much of the Middle Ages, reflecting the wealth of France, and in turn displaying the magnificence of the French kings, who adorned it with three palaces in and around the city. Within them there was a display of architecture whose scale and splendour were unmatched elsewhere. Paris was a great commercial centre, and its university, the Sorbonne, was the acknowledged centre of European intellectual activity from the twelfth century onwards.

THE LOUVRE
The Palais de la Cité, described earlier, was hardly altered by subsequent kings of France. However, they ceased to use it as their principal residence from the reign of Charles V. The château of the Louvre was originally built as a part of the defences of Paris by Philip Augustus, as a castle just outside his new city walls, which enclosed a large area of the right bank. Philip was concerned with the threat from the Anglo-Norman realm, and the border with Normandy was only 130 kilometres away. The Louvre was both a fortress and a prison, and was frequently used for high-ranking prisoners in Jean II's reign. Like the Tower of London, it

contained the royal menagerie.[1] And like the Tower, it had its uses as a means of controlling the city if the citizens rebelled. In 1357, however, when Étienne Marcel, the provost of Paris, rose against the regency which Jean II's capture at Poitiers had made necessary, he and his followers gained control of the Louvre. When Charles V came to the throne in 1360, he ordered a new set of fortifications to be raised, which brought the castle within the city walls. Five years later, he began – at vast cost – to convert it into a royal residence. He had not felt safe in his town house during the Parisian revolt, and it would have been difficult to strengthen the fortifications of the Palais de la Cité. At the Louvre, there was space to do this. Within its new fortifications, the circular keep and the old outer walls were almost untouched. The interior was remodelled, with new buildings against the outer walls, which consisted initially of apartments for the king and queen. It was not designed as a grand meeting place: the hall, which would have been the focal point of any major state occasion held there, was about a tenth of the size of the Great Hall of the Palais de la Cité. Indeed, the largest room in the king's apartments was about the same size as the hall of the Louvre, showing that it was very much a place where the king's most important visitors, whether French administrators or nobles or foreign dignitaries, came to confer with him. There was a study off the king's great chamber and, towards the end of Charles's reign, his library as well. There was a ceremonial staircase – a spectacular double spiral in the courtyard in a hexagonal tower – ornamented with figures of the royal family, clearly designed to impress visitors in the same way as those in the Grand'Salle of the Palais de la Cité.

## London

UNUSUALLY, EARLY RECORDS of a royal residence in the city of London are shadowy: the later Anglo-Saxon kings seem to have had a palace not far from St Paul's Cathedral. Towards the end of his reign, Edward the Confessor built a new palace at Westminster, 2.5 kilometres outside the walls, alongside the very spacious Romanesque church which was the main focus of his plans. The creation of the cluster of palace and abbey church was therefore the work of one man, at one specific time; the palace chapel was insignificant until it was rebuilt by Edward III. To the east of the city, the Normans created the Tower, again outside the walls, which William Fitzstephen in his description of London written in the 1170s called 'the fortress palace', and the Tower did include the necessary spaces for a royal residence. It was used as such throughout the medieval period, as a secondary alternative to Westminster. But it remained primarily a fortress, guarding the city, and guarding against that city when the citizens were in a rebellious mood. For all practical purposes, the royal presence was not within London, but at Westminster and outside the city's boundaries.

ST STEPHEN'S CHAPEL

Westminster Abbey was a major royal church, but St Stephen's chapel, within the palace of Westminster was specifically redecorated to reflect Edward III's reputation and wealth in the years following his victories over the French. The chapel had been in existence since the end of the twelfth century. It was in a parlous state by 1292, and was largely rebuilt between then and 1297. Work was suspended until 1315, and as late as 1348 it was still only an empty shell, awaiting its furniture, glass and decoration.

At this point, Edward was involved in setting up the Order of the Garter which he intended to base at Windsor. Here the problems with the chapel were very similar. Although Edward himself had been baptised in the castle chapel, dedicated to Edward the Confessor, it had been in disrepair since the beginning of his reign, following storm damage.

He decided to issue letters patent re-establishing both chapels on the same lines, and these were issued on the same day. These documents give no hint of the fact that the chapels in the king's two noblest residences were both in need of work. Rather, the text lays emphasis on the king's personal involvement with them. Both had been begun by his ancestors, and he had completed the building at St Stephen's, while he recalled that he had been 'washed in the holy water of baptism' at the chapel at Windsor.

*The interior of St Stephen's*

We know a good deal about the decoration, furnishing and layout of St Stephen's chapel, which survived, much altered but with fragments of the original still in place, until the palace of Westminster was destroyed by fire in 1834.[2] It was on two storeys, with the lower chapel dedicated to the Virgin and the upper chapel as the private royal family chapel, to which distinguished visitors might also be admitted on state occasions such as baptisms or weddings. There are also references to pilgrims, probably visiting the golden statue of the Virgin in the lower chapel, who were only to be admitted as far as the threshold; but a charter of the canons recorded that they should have access 'without let or hindrance of the King's ministers of the palace'. The upper chapel may possibly have been visible as well.[3] Its décor was certainly such as to imply that it was intended for some degree of public display: it was a carefully planned and elaborate programme laid out in such a way that it portrayed the royal family in parallel with the Holy Family, interweaving other themes of their personal devotion. The east end had two tiers of paintings. The upper tier showed the Three Kings presenting their offerings to the Christ child to the left. In the centre Mary presented Christ to the high priest in the Temple, while to the right the shepherds worshipped the new-born child. Linked to these scenes, on the left of the lower tier, were the figures of Edward and his sons, with St George drawing their attention to the scenes above them, while the right hand side showed the queen and her daughters. Between these two sets of portraits stood the high altar.

*A personal chapel for Edward III*

The emphasis on the Virgin is explained by the dedication of the chapel, but St George seems to be present as Edward's personal patron. The figure of the saint in the fresco, whose gestures indicate that he is presenting the king to the Virgin and Child in the tier above, is unparalleled in contemporary art. Donors often appear in paintings, but their patron saint is usually portrayed as standing over them protectively rather than actively promoting their cause. The Magi or Three Kings, who figure prominently in the upper tier above Edward and his sons, were also the object of the king's personal devotion. He made offerings at their shrine in Köln in 1338, and continued to give gifts of gold, frankincense and myrrh on the Feast of the Epiphany.

The king's best painters and craftsmen worked at St Stephen's for at least a decade. As many as forty painters were at work there in 1350, and a substantial team of stained glass makers was also on the site. The glass for the Windsor chapel was made here as well. The importance attached to the work is underlined by the problems encountered when the stalls were being designed. The original seating was a two-tiered Purbeck marble bench running round the outer wall,[4] and changing this to the stalls required by a collegiate church proved difficult. In July 1351, after work had been going on for two years, the stalls were removed, and the carpenters were ordered to work on 'raising various panels for the reredos of the said stalls in order to show and exhibit the form and design of the said stalls to the treasurer and other members of the king's council'.[5] As well as the thirty-eight stalls, the private 'closets' for the king and queen and their children were built at the eastern end of the nave: the royal family 'would have had an exceptionally good view of the altar murals which, in characteristically medieval illusionistic play, depicted themselves similarly "closeted" in perpetual prayer'.[6]

**59.** (above) Edward III and his sons, from a drawing of the frescoes in St Stephen's chapel, destroyed in the fire of 1834. It illustrates superbly the idea that magnificence should extend to the king's family. Philippa of Hainault and their daughters were depicted on the other wall.

**60.** The heart of the Angevin kingdom of Naples: Castelnuovo, as rebuilt by Alfonso V in the 1440s.

The murals were hidden behind panelling and forgotten for many centuries. In 1800 the act of union with Ireland was passed, which meant that an additional hundred MPs would join the House. Extra space was urgently needed, and a major refurbishment of St Stephen's chapel was put in hand which led to the destruction of what remained of Edward III's chapel. John Topham, introducing a series of engravings which recorded the paintings in 1795, described the effect of the chapel from the fragments which were still visible:

*St Stephen's in 1795*

> It is necessary to observe that the whole of the architecture, and its enrichments, on the inside, are in gilding and colours, appearing extremely fresh; and what is remarkable and singular, the columns are decorated with a sort of patera, and several of the mouldings are filled with ornaments so minute, that those on the spandrels and grand entablature, could hardly be perceived by the eye from the pavement of the chapel; but the artist designed that the whole of the work should have the same attention paid it, and that one universal blaze of magnificence and splendour should shine around, making this chapel the ne *plus ultra* of the art ...[7]

To understand the motive behind Edward's magnificent refurbishment of St Stephen's, we have to look to the Sainte-Chapelle in Paris.[8] There was a tradition of establishing *Saintes Chapelles* in France which could only be built by direct descendants of St Louis. If we count Edward as part of that family (as he indeed was) his is a relatively early example: the bulk of such foundations in France date from later in the fourteenth century.[9]

*St Stephen's and the Sainte-Chapelle*

The provision for clergy at St Stephen's in the letters patent of 8 December 1355 is identical with that at the Sainte-Chapelle, and the architecture of St Stephen's echoed that common to the French royal private chapels, which were similarly buildings on two levels. However, Edward was working with an existing structure, and did not attempt to rival the soaring architecture and dazzling windows of the upper chapel of the Sainte-Chapelle. Nor did he have a relic to match the Crown of Thorns. The result was splendour of a very different kind, and with a different focus.

*A dynastic chapel*

The prime purpose of St Stephen's was introspective: it was a dynastic chapel where prayers were to be said for past, present and future members of the royal family, and which was designed to reinforce the idea of kingship as a divine calling, setting them apart from their subjects. Many of the objects within the chapel were emblazoned with the royal arms, and the arms of the great baronial families were also worked into the decoration. The commemoration of family connections on tombs was becoming a commonplace at this period, with arms and figures of important relatives or colleagues incorporated in the design. At St Stephen's, however, Edward is celebrating members of his living family, looking at themselves as if in a mirror. The paintings were completed during a decade when Edward was consciously creating an elaborate family settlement involving marriage alliances which could have led to English princes ruling in Flanders and Brittany. And by the end of the decade, all but one of his sons had taken part in the campaigns in France.[10] There is nothing of the past here, no ancestral portraits: it is a bold statement of the power and wealth of the present generation, of their recent military triumph and their hoped-for dynastic success in France.

## Prague

### KARL IV AND PRAGUE

The Holy Roman Empire never had a fixed capital, and its centre was always the city of the principality or kingdom of the current emperor. Whether imperial status made much difference to that city depended entirely on the personality of the incumbent. When Karl IV was elected, he set about a deliberate transformation of Prague to create the magnificence appropriate to his new status. In the process, he changed it from a modest regional city into a setting with multiple traces of a grand propaganda programme. His upbringing at the French court meant that he used Paris as his distant model, and the result also had considerable similarities with the English royal complex at Westminster.

However, Karl had to work with a very different topography, with two royal castles set on hills framing the city. His father had become king of Bohemia by marriage, and spent little time in his kingdom, preferring travels abroad and his own home, the duchy of Luxembourg. The Přemyslid kings of Bohemia had built a castle on Hradčany, the hill which dominates the west bank of the city in the late ninth century, including the church of the Virgin Mary, which may have been a royal burial place. In 930 Wenceslas I created another church to house a relic of St Vitus, who became the patron saint of Bohemia. This was in turn replaced around 1060 when Prague became a bishopric. Wenceslas had been hailed as a saint and martyr after his murder in 935, and his tomb was in the rotunda; this part of the earlier church became a chapel within the new building. A bishop's palace was added and, at some point, not later than the reign of Ottokar II, a royal palace was also part of the site. Ottokar, who created a short-lived empire that included Austria and lands as far as the head of the Adriatic, considerably enlarged the castle precinct and either built or enlarged the palace.

*The origins of Prague*

When Karl IV came to Prague in 1333 as heir to the Bohemian throne, Bohemia was relatively wealthy, thanks to the silver mines at Kutna Hora, discovered in 1298. In the 1340s the mines were producing at least 20 tons of silver a year, and were the major source of silver in Europe at this time. Karl took up residence in the city, but the palace was a ruin, having burnt down in 1301, and his first task was to renew it. He had spent seven formative years at the court of France, followed by several years in Italy, and was familiar with the Palais de la Cité and the Sainte-Chapelle, as well as Italian painting and architecture. Over the next forty years he transformed the city in the light of this upbringing. His agenda included not only the work on the palace but also the rebuilding of the cathedral of St Vitus and the shaping of the most personal of his edifices, the new castle at Karlstejn. In 1356 he was crowned as Holy Roman Emperor, and Prague became an imperial city. Karl refashioned it accordingly, extending the defensive walls around the palace and cathedral and adjacent buildings until it was one of the largest such sites in the world.

*Prague in 1333*

Karl wrote his autobiography around 1350, when he was in his thirties – unusually early, and perhaps an indication of his sense of destiny. In it he remembers that when he came to Bohemia,

> I found the kingdom desolate. Not a castle free that was not pledged, so that I had nowhere to lodge except in houses in cities like any other citizen. Prague had been desolated and destroyed since the days of king Ottakar. So I decided to build a new palace, which should be large and handsome. It was built at great cost as is evident today to whomever looks at it.[11]

Most of Karl's palace was rebuilt from 1490 onwards, and it has to be reconstructed from a variety of evidence. One of the main features was a great hall on the first storey. This is not the current great hall, a monumental space of the early fifteenth century, but it was a substantial enlargement of the previous Romanesque hall which stood in the same place, and which Karl widened, supporting the extension on the piers of a new loggia below. The entry copied the sequence of that to the Palais de la Cité, with a wide staircase set at right angles to the courtyard leading to an imposing landing with large traceried windows which opened into the newly enlarged hall. If the comparison with Paris is correct, this would have been used on ceremonial occasions to highlight the emperor and his entourage, who would have been clearly visible and isolated in splendour as they made their way into the palace.[12] After 1355 a series of 120 panel paintings – at this point a relative novelty – of his forebears hung in the landing. And in 1370, the two towers which stood on the front overlooking the city were covered in lead and gilded, 'so that they shone splendidly in fair weather, and could be seen from far off'.[13]

*The creation of Prague New Town*

Work on the palace was complete when Karl made his next move in his ambitious plans for Prague as a truly imperial capital. This was the creation on the east bank of the river Vltava of a vast extension to the original settlement there, a 'new town'. This was to contain from the beginning churches, monasteries and a new university, as well as a huge cattle market, a horse market and a hay market for the practical needs of the city. It used, as far as possible, a grid plan, and was enclosed by a wall with tall watchtowers, visible boundary markers on the level land. Karl had already bought most of the land which at the southern end reached as far as the castle of Vyšehrad.[14] Beyond this lay the gate by which Karl entered Prague when he made a formal imperial entry, and it seems that one of the purposes of the layout of the new town was to provide a ready-made triumphal way for such processions. In Paris and London such processional routes were already well established; the old town at Prague was much smaller than either of these, and the new town, which linked the old palace at Vyšehrad with that on Hradčany, offered the opportunity to create an impressive way through the city. The starting point was the Vyšehrad; from there the procession descended the hill to the Emmaus monastery, one of the first buildings in the New Town. Karl linked this with the origins of Christianity in Bohemia by bringing in Benedictine monks from Croatia who used the old Slavonic liturgy. A short distance away was the largest town square in medieval Europe, the massive cattle market, now called Charles Square. From there the route led into the old town. The west bank and the palace were reached across a newly built bridge, which was likewise rechristened after Karl in the nineteenth century. This was only begun in 1357, and was not finished until 1402, so Karl must always have crossed on a temporary structure. The processional route ended at the courtyard in front of the palace on the Hradčany, whose role in ceremonial events we have just noted.

*Relics, processions and town planning*

Karl's prestige as emperor and his enthusiasm for relics made the moment when the imperial treasure was handed over to his envoys in Munich, on 12 March 1350, a particular moment for celebration. The relics associated with the imperial regalia included the lance used at the Crucifixion and one of the nails from the Cross. When Karl brought the treasure to Prague two weeks later, work on the new town had been in progress for less than two years. The Vyšehrad was remembered and revered as the palace of the Přemyslid kings before the new palace was built, and Karl seems to have deliberately extended his plans to incorporate it into the city. The idea of a processional route from the southern gate to the cathedral may owe as much to his acute sense of the historical past as to any traditional ceremonial routines. However, when the pope had agreed to Karl's request for a feast day (on the Friday after Easter Sunday) in honour of the relics, with indulgences for those who attended it, a chronicler noted that 'such a multitude of men gathered from all parts of the world that no-one would believe it unless they had seen it with their own eyes',[16] and this was one of the reasons for the huge space of the cattle market. For the purposes of showing of the relics, Karl set up a wooden platform, on which they could easily be seen by a crowd.[17] Along the way, he created holy sites associated with the relics, rededicating a church to St Longinus who had pierced Christ's side with the Holy Lance. Where Louis had simply inserted a marvellous chapel into his palace for the Crown of Thorns, Karl made his relics a central theme running through his entire new city. Above all, it was spacious: its huge squares were larger than almost all the examples further west in Europe, and its streets were as much as three times the width of similar streets elsewhere.

Many of the numerous churches in the New Town were founded by Karl with reference to particular events in his own life, or in the context of the imperial past. We will take just three examples. To mark his coronation as king of Bohemia in 1347, he founded a huge Carmelite church, Our Lady of the Snows. The monastery of St Ambrose housed monks from San Ambrogio in Milan, the place where Karl had been crowned king of Lombardy. And he built a monastery dedicated to Charlemagne, whom he regarded as a saint, known as the Karlshof or Karlov. The groundplan of the latter was octagonal, like Charlemagne's palace chapel at Aachen, then the imperial capital.[18] The creation of the New Town was in effect a single operation in a limited timespan, without parallel for size and splendour in the medieval world. Aristotle had named building as one of the means to magnificence, and this was a project which amply qualified for that accolade.

*The New Town as autobiography*

Karl was a scholar, whose tutor had been Pierre Roger, then newly licensed to teach theology and canon law at Paris, and one of the most distinguished lecturers of the time: he later became pope as Clement VI. Few princes of the time had such a grounding in philosophical thought, and quite apart from Giles of Rome's treatise, which Karl could have read in either French or Latin, he may have read Aristotle in the Latin version which had been in circulation since the mid-thirteenth century. His actions follow Aristotle's prescription for magnificence closely:

> Magnificence is an attribute of expenditures of the kind which we call honourable, e.g. those connected with the gods – votive offerings, buildings, and sacrifices – and similarly with any form of religious worship, and all those that are proper objects of public-spirited ambition ...[19]

There were indeed elements which corresponded to Aristotle's original, secular definition of magnificence: at one extreme, new market halls and spaces for the public at large, and at the other the founding of the University of Prague. It was the first full university west of the Rhine, in the German-speaking lands, and the first of a series of such foundations in eastern Europe: Cracow followed in 1364, Vienna in 1365, and Pécs in Hungary in 1367. Karl had obtained papal permission for his new institution in 1347, and it was natural that it should be included in his 'new town'.[20]

*Magnificence and church-building*

When Karl's procession with the imperial treasure in 1350 reached its destination on the Hradčany, the religious rites were performed in the cathedral of St Vitus. This was dedicated to the patron saint of Bohemia and next to the royal palace, and was in the process of being rebuilt. The church had been founded by St Wenceslas himself, and was unfinished when he was murdered in 935. The site was therefore doubly sacred, particularly since Wenceslas's body was transferred there about thirty years later, and the cathedral was rebuilt in the 1070s. Karl's first donation to the old cathedral had been in 1333, when he first arrived

*St Vitus*

in Prague; he presented twelve silver statues of the apostles for the tomb of St Wenceslas. These were pawned by his father Jean in a moment of financial difficulty three years later. However, when matters improved, perhaps in atonement for the earlier sacrilege, Jean made a very generous donation to the cathedral specifically for the eventual rebuilding of it. This took the form of 10 per cent of his annual revenues from all the silver mines in the kingdom of Bohemia, including those at Kutna Hora, and would have worked out at over two tons of silver a year.[21] It was Karl who took the matter forward. Turning again to his old tutor, he persuaded the pope to make Prague an archbishopric, and when this was done, he set about raising a building to match his aspirations for the city.

*The choir of St Vitus and royal burials*
Karl was involved in the work from the beginning, and chose a typical late Gothic plan, with a choir surrounded by radial chapels. It was this choir which became the mausoleum, and the whole of it forms a monument to the dynasty, with Karl's ancestors and patron saints represented by statues, busts and tombs. At the highest level, in the clerestory, Christ and the Virgin were flanked by Wenceslas and Vitus, the patron saint of Bohemia. Below that, statues of the royal family, consisting of Karl and his four wives, and his son Wenceslaus and his wife, were placed at the level of the triforium, so that they appeared immediately above the altar.[22] The chronicler Beneš Krabice of Weitmile, who was one of the directors of the building work, records that in 1373, 'the bodies of the former Bohemian dukes and kings were brought from their old graves' and reburied in the new chancel, which became the mausoleum of the rulers of Bohemia.[23] Karl himself was buried there in 1378.

St Vitus was a very personal project, and it is appropriate that Karl himself, with his almost obsessive love of portraits of himself, was the subject of five statues and paintings here. Two of his other passions, the devotion to St Vitus and to St Wenceslas, were the driving forces behind his involvement. He had acquired the body of St Vitus at Pavia in 1355, something which he regarded as one of his greatest achievements, and wrote from Pisa on 22 January 1355 to the clergy in Prague to announce the event, instructing that his letter was to be read out in all the city's churches.[24]

It was after the arrival of these relics that Peter Parler, a German aged only twenty-three, was appointed architect. He became famous as a sculptor, and he and his family were responsible for many of the multitude of portraits of Karl IV. Karl's ancestors and relatives were celebrated in a series of statues in the apse of the cathedral; the apse itself was modelled on that of Charlemagne's imperial church at Aachen.

The overall result of the rebuilding is very much characteristic of the changing tastes of its imperial patron. What began as traditional French architecture at the beginning of the work ends as a new style original to Bohemia, which was to influence later German cathedral-building. The architects had to include the most sacred parts of the old church to start with, and the chapel to St Wenceslas was in a totally different mode which related to Karl's new palace-castle at Karlstejn rather than anything on the Hradčany.

*St Wenceslas and his crown*
The presence of St Wenceslas, who had joined St Vitus as one of Bohemia's national saints, was critical to the glory of the cathedral, and Karl was particularly devoted to his worship. When in 1347 he was crowned king of Bohemia, he had the lavish crown which had been used in the ceremony placed on the skull of St Wenceslas, and ordered that future kings should only remove it for the day of their coronation. Otherwise it was to be kept in the sacristy, and placed on the skull on certain feast days.[25] The chapel of St Wenceslas was the crowning point of pilgrimages to the cathedral, and the layout of the apse was designed as the prelude to this extraordinary space, in the angle of the nave and south transept, carefully sited on the exact spot where the saint had been buried in the original rotunda church.

Apart from its soaring Gothic roof, the chapel is in the highly individual Romanesque style which Karl favoured for his special and personal chapels at Karlstejn, the castle where his private collection of relics was kept. As at Karlstejn, this is a closed space, with two narrow entry portals, and windows much smaller than the space within the framing Gothic arches. Its décor is an echo of the description of the New Jerusalem in the Book of Revelation, where the foundation of the walls of the heavenly city are described as 'garnished with all manner of precious stones': jasper, sapphire, chalcedony, emerald, sardonyx, sardius, chrysolyte, beryl, topaz, chrysoprasus, jacinth and amethyst. The result is a kind of rough-hewn magnificence, with many of the stones named in the Bible present, but set in a manner which resembles a kind of primitive masonry. There are equally primitive crosses which form the only patterns among the irregular pieces, and frescoes on a gold ground in the lower tier of walls, depicting the Crucifixion, with Karl and his fourth wife Elizabeth kneeling like donors on either side on the east wall, and figures of saints elsewhere. The tomb of Wenceslas is likewise patterned with precious stones. It has been suggested that these stones are an echo of the riches of the churches of Rome, but they lack the regularity of Roman marble panelling while seeking to outshine them in terms of the materials used. It is a highly individual style, complemented by the equally unusual style of the frescoes.

*The Wenceslas chapel*

Prague is the most remarkable of the royal capitals of late medieval Europe, the concept of one man, Karl IV himself. Karl was notable for both his ability to change his plans, and for his decisiveness in carrrying them out. The plan which reshaped the palace and cathedral and added a huge area to the city was not preconceived; rather, it was a series of positive responses to changing circumstances. Yet by the time of Karl's death the city had been rebuilt as a whole, its various magnificent buildings linked into a unity, to the glory of the emperor and the empire. It is only because his successors failed to make the Holy Roman Empire their own, but were replaced by the Habsburg dynasty, that his grandiose concept, magnificently executed, was to become a relatively obscure backwater within a century of his death.

## Naples

WHEN ALFONSO V CONQUERED NAPLES in 1442, Castelnuovo, the main fortress and palace of his Angevin rival, René d'Anjou, was almost a ruin. He began to rebuild it the following year, and work was still in progress at his death in 1458. Only the chapel of the earlier castle, standing on the seaward side, was incorporated into the new work, which drew on both medieval tradition and the new ideas of the Renaissance. The bombards which Alfonso himself had used successfully against this very castle had not entirely replaced the old siege engines, as the fall of Constantinople in 1453 was to show. The architecture of Castelnuovo attempted to deal with both threats, besides incorporating the features of magnificence, spacious halls and apartments which were vulnerable by their very size. A new raised walkway was placed at the base of the massive round towers, which themselves rose from a huge sloping base designed to counter the impact of cannon balls. Rising straight from the sea, the design impressed contemporaries: Aeneas Silvius Piccolomini, the humanist who became Pope Pius II, said that nothing since the days of the Medes and Persians had rivalled the castle at Naples, and another writer called it 'more beautiful than anyone could believe'.[26]

*The Castelnuovo at Naples*

**60**, p.157

On the landward side, a huge space was enclosed by an outer wall and ditch, leading to the triumphal arch which formed the palatial Renaissance entrance. This is the best preserved part of the fifteenth-century castle. The design of the arch draws on the latest Renaissance ideas; behind these is a shadow – perhaps more than a shadow – of the Roman imperial ideas of an earlier ruler of Sicily and Naples, Friedrich II.

## Castles for Kings and Emperors

*Ingelheim*

THE MEMORY OF THE PALACES OF the Roman emperors survived in the Holy Roman Empire, though the future of royal residences outside the capital was to become the castle rather than the palace. It says much that Charlemagne built his palace at Aachen in the imperial tradition, unfortified and within a fortified town. Ingelheim on the Rhine, where Charlemagne built one of his major palaces, is an example of such a conversion. The original design was deliberately classical, as a reminder that since his coronation at Rome in 800 he was the successor to the palace-building emperors of Rome. The complex included a throne room, which was excavated at the end of the twentieth century. In 1160, a little more than a century after its completion, the palace was converted into a fortress, and the great courtyard with its arcades was given battlements by Friedrich Barbarossa, becoming part of the defences of the town. The palace entrance became the main town gate.

*Later imperial palaces*

The use of imperial palaces as bases for the emperors' travels declined in the tenth century, however, as they increasingly demanded hospitality from local lords and abbots. Such palaces as there were, belonged to the ruling dynasty; they served various purposes, from modest buildings like that of Friedrich Barbarossa at Gelnhausen near Frankfurt, to true palaces such as that at Goslar in Saxony. Goslar was built on the site of a hunting lodge by Heinrich II in 1005; the architect of the main buildings was Benno, later bishop of Osnabrück, renowned for his skill, who was summoned by Heinrich III in 1048 to extend the palace. It was he who designed the so-called 'Emperor's House', a two-storey structure containing two large halls, 47 metres long and 15 metres wide, with a single line of columns down the centre. The imperial throne was at the west end of the upper hall; it was a bronze chair on a plinth within an enclosure, perhaps created for the last imperial visit to the palace in 1253. The hall had an open arcade onto the courtyard, giving a view over the other palace buildings and the cathedral, but, more importantly, allowing the crowd outside to see the ceremonies taking place within. This was a deliberate display of imperial ritual which would have otherwise been visible only to the aristocratic audience. After 1253, there was a dispute over the imperial title which lasted for twenty-five years until the first of the Habsburg emperors was elected. The palace at Goslar, now no longer in the emperor's own domain, was abandoned, having been a major imperial centre for two centuries,.

## Castle Residences

CASTLE RESIDENCES, BUILT PARTLY FOR military and political purposes, were a different kind of display of magnificence. They were designed to be shown to fellow-princes and to important visitors, rather than the prince's subjects at large. Indeed, their very inaccessibility was in itself impressive, a demonstration of hidden wealth and power in addition to what was familiar and known. It was here that the almost legendary collections of jewels, relics and manuscripts were kept; the reaction of Leo of Rozmital's secretary to the sight of Charles the Bold's private treasure is typical of the kind of impression they made on the privileged few who saw these objects,[27] and the special case of Karlstejn, Karl IV's retreat, is even more remarkable.

## Windsor

HENRY III REBUILT THE PALACE OF Westminster in the mid thirteenth century at vast cost. The project which most nearly matches it in terms of royal expenditure came a century later, at Windsor under Edward III. Windsor, 40 kilometres from London, had been the site of a major royal residence under Edward the Confessor, and had been granted to Westminster Abbey by him. William I brought it back into royal ownership, and in the charter said that it seemed 'suitable and convenient for a royal retirement on account of the river and its nearness to the forest for hunting and many other things'. This royal house seems to have been at what is now Old Windsor, just over 3 kilometres from the site of a motte-and-bailey castle which William built soon after the conquest. Crown-wearing ceremonies were held here until Henry I's time: at Whitsun 1110 the king moved the feast to 'New Windsor, which he himself had built'. In fact the building work seems to have continued until almost the end of his reign, creating a castle standing on the cliff above the Thames, with a rampart and ditch to the east and south. Within the walls was the new royal residence.[28] This is roughly the present Upper Ward of the castle.

*The origins of Windsor*

Between 1165 and 1185, Henry II extended the accommodation, and built a curtain wall round the whole site. He included an area to the west, which became the Lower Ward, and added a new great hall whose outer wall was the curtain wall of the castle, 30 metres long and 9 metres wide. The overall plan of the outer walls of the castle changed little in subsequent rebuilding. This would have been a very substantial space for an ordinary royal castle, and underlines the dual nature of Windsor as both palace and castle. However, it was twice besieged in the turbulent years following Henry's death, in 1193 and 1216, and substantial repairs were needed.

During the minority of Henry III, from 1216 to 1227, most of the work on the castle was defensive, including the building of the 'Great Tower'. When the king came of age, he indulged his passion for building here as well as at Westminster. After Henry married Eleanor of Provence in 1236, expenditure of over £10,000 during the next two decades produced a splendid set of new chambers, halls, and a cloister for the queen's apartments, which were put to frequent use by the queen and the royal children.[29] A new chapel was dedicated to Edward the Confessor; its magnificence can be judged from the surviving doorway with its elaborate ironwork and expensive Purbeck marble columns.

*Henry III and Windsor*

By this time, Windsor was 'both a very strongly fortified castle and a very large royal palace'. It lay within a day's journey of London, and offered greater safety and comfort than either Westminster, with no defences, or the Tower, with its much more limited living space. In the difficult early years of Edward II's reign, it was again used by the royal family as a secure place. Queen Isabella came to Windsor when she was expecting her first child, and it was here that Edward III was born in 1312.

*The birthplace of Edward III*

Windsor was one of Edward III's favourite places. There are records of 235 visits to Windsor, as compared with 273 occasions when he was at Westminster, and a mere 67 at the Tower of London. Given that it was not part of the machinery of government, it is an exceptional figure. Towards the end of his reign, it was his chief residence, with an average of nine visits a year.[30] The castle was surveyed in 1327, and many defects noted, but no major work was done until 1344, when Edward ordered the construction of the 'house of the Round Table'. It was intended as the home for his projected knightly order of chivalry of the same name, to be modelled on that of King Arthur, and marks a remarkable attempt to harness magnificence and the ideals of chivalric romance to the entirely practical question of knightly morale in the field. Edward was attempting to claim the throne of France, and after a disastrous attempt to create and finance an alliance with continental princes, he knew that he had to rely on his own resources. Creating an *esprit de corps* by means of a knightly order had been tried by the kings of Hungary and Castile in 1325 and 1330 respectively, but the English project was much grander.

*The house of the Round Table*

When the 'house of the Round Table' was excavated in 2006 by Channel 4's *Time Team* programme, the finds gave some idea of how magnificent the building was intended to be. When the initial research was being done for the television programme, in which I was involved, we looked at Thomas Walsingham's contemporary chronicle. Walsingham was well informed about court matters, and tells us that the diameter of the round table building was 200 feet, that is, twice the length of the great hall at Windsor. I said firmly that this was clearly a misreading of Roman numerals, something not unknown in medieval texts, and that it would be much smaller: recent writers on Windsor had said the concept of such a large structure 'might seem improbable, even fantastic'.[31] A month or two later, I was shown the ground radar survey results. A huge circle had been drawn on the plan inside the buildings in the Upper Ward. I asked what its diameter was: 'A hundred and ninety-nine feet', was the answer. Walsingham was extraordinarily accurate.

After the crown-wearing at which Edward announced his intention to institute an order of three hundred knights, work on the house of the Round Table was begun in February 1344, after the bridges into the castle had been strengthened. By March, 720 men were working on the site, but after the end of that month, the workforce rapidly diminished, and during the summer it dropped from thirty men to fifteen or so by the autumn. There were other demands on the treasury, and work was not resumed in 1345, though the walls had been covered in straw to protect them during the winter. It was demolished in the early 1360s.[32]

In 1348, Edward issued two charters, one for the re-foundation of St Stephen's at Westminster, and the other for the creation of the College of St George at Windsor, to be the home of the new company of the Garter, which was not initially a knightly order but a foundation to commemorate the victory at Crécy in 1346. Two years later, the initial work began: the existing, partly ruined chapel was renovated and quarters for the warden and twenty-four canons of the college were built beside it.[33] Work on the castle itself included the installation of the first known clock in England in the Round Tower on the motte (and candles provided to guard it at night), and temporary lodgings for the king and queen.

*William of Wykeham's rebuilding*

The rest of the castle was transformed by William of Wykeham, who as clerk of the works 'caused many excellent buildings in the castle of Windsor to be thrown down, and others more beautiful and sumptuous to be set up'.[34] He began work in 1356, and the results were so successful that he eventually became bishop of Winchester. The cost – we have the detailed accounts – was £50,772 over twenty-seven years, a hundred times that of the ambitious but abortive Round Table building.

Wykeham oversaw what has been called 'among the most important building projects of the late Middle Ages ... It cost more than any other structure erected for a medieval English king, and it enabled the royal household and the court to reside magnificently in the castle where Edward had been born.'[35] It was an immense labour: one chronicler claimed that 'almost all the masons and carpenters throughout the whole of England were brought to that building', and it was impossible to get good workmen for any other projects because the king had forbidden anyone else to hire them.[36]

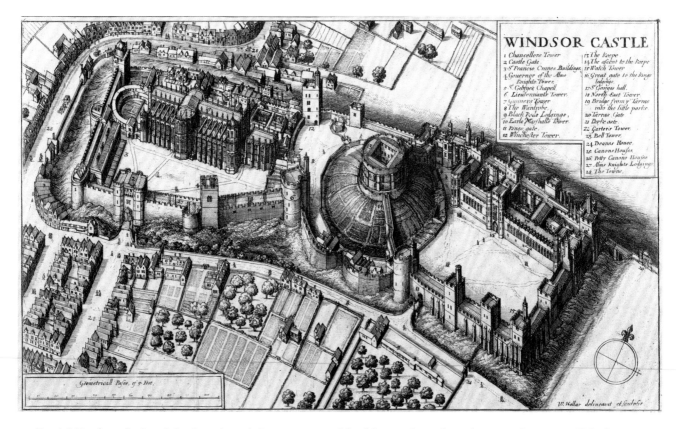

WINDSOR CASTLE

1 Chancellors Tower
2 Castle Gate
3 S.r Frances Crines Buildings
4 Gouernor of the Alms
   Knights Tower.
5 S.r Georges Chapell
6 Lieutennants Tower.
7 Gunners Tower
8 The Wardrobe
9 Black Rods Lodgings
10 Earle Marshalls Tower
11 Kings gate
12 Winchester Tower.

13 The Keepe
14 The ascent to the keepe
15 Watch Tower
16 Great gate to the kings
   lodgings
17 S.t Georges hall.
18 North-East Tower.
19 Bridge from y.e Tarras
   into the little parke.
20 Tarras Gate
21 Darke gate
22 Garters Tower.
23 Bell Tower.
24 Deanes House.
25 Canons House.
26 Petty Canons House.
27 Alms knights Lodgings
28 The Towne.

Geometricall Pase, of 5 Feet.

W. Hollar delineavit et sculpsit

By 1368, the whole of the interior of the upper ward had been cleared, and a complex series of palatial apartments created. The king's apartments, grouped round a cloister at the west end of the new buildings, consisted of eight rooms, ranging in size from his great chamber, where he received visitors and transacted public business; he also dined there, and there was a 'bed of estate' on which he sat or lay. Stairs in one corner led to the Rose Tower, which appears to have been a viewing platform over the surrounding park. His audience chamber, for private conversations, was next to the great chamber. Beyond that was a private dining chamber and his actual sleeping quarters, closet, and private chapel.

The queen's rooms adjoined the king's bedchamber, and she had a suite of great chamber, dining chamber and second chamber beyond. Her dancing chamber was on the ground floor below the great chamber, looking out onto the larger of the two cloisters. These had wooden galleries on the first floor, which probably looked similar to the interior of Bellver. On the south-eastern end of the new range was the room now known as St George's Hall, lit entirely from the south, by a single row of tall windows. Its complex roof is almost as ambitious as the famous reconstruction of Westminster Hall at the end of the century.

The new range of buildings was next to the unfinished house of the Round Table, which had been intended to impress visitors with its magnificence. The latter was probably demolished fairly soon after the new work had begun, as it would have impeded access to the construction site. This first attempt at magnificence was replaced by something equally impressive. Anyone entering the upper ward through the postern gate was presented with a façade of exceptional length – 118 metres – occupying the entire north side of a very large open court. Twenty-six traceried windows[37] were divided into two groups by a three-storey crenellated gatehouse immediately facing the entrance. It was an unexpected vista at a time when the interiors of many castles were a mass of practical buildings in stone or timber, or had developed in a way which precluded the creation of such spaces.

III. Windsor Castle: Wenceslas Hollar's 'birds' eye view' engraving, c.1658.

*The layout of the castle*

It was at Windsor in 1358 that Edward III held one of his most impressive feasts, using the spacious new court he had created. Two of the guests were there against their will: David king of Scotland and Jean II king of France, both in captivity in England. The most recent biographer of Edward III, Mark Ormrod, calls this event the climax of 'one of the most sustained and purposeful demonstrations of royal magnificence witnessed in medieval England'. By a careful mixture of rigorous insistence on the reality that they were prisoners and a series of feasts and festivals offered as gracious gestures towards their royal status, Edward conveyed to the world the power of his position. Jean II, who had been under house arrest at the Savoy palace in London, was moved to Windsor during the winter. The tournament held at the castle on St George's day was designed to evoke the king's new status as sovereign of the Order of the Garter, whose knights had been in the forefront of his armies, and the links which he had made between the castle and King Arthur in his plans for a Round Table, which lay unfinished and gigantic in the Upper Ward. We know little about the actual event, but Jean II is said to have commented wryly on the way in which the king dined off gold and silver and paid for it with wood – the wooden tallies which the exchequer used for accounting, in other words credit. As always, magnificence could be seen as extravagance and as a symbol of power at the same time.

## Bellver

BELLVER, BUILT BY THE ARCHITECT Pere Salvatge for Jaime II of Majorca in the first decade of the fourteenth century, is unique in its style and purpose.[38] It is clearly a summer residence, designed as such, and at the same time a perfectly serious fortress. It sits on the hillside above Palma, the capital, and is circular in shape, with a donjon attached on the outside of the circle. Much of the structure is timber, so only the donjon would have been really defensible, though the whole castle is surrounded by a formidable ditch. Its function as a fortress was never tested. Majorca had been part of the kingdom of Aragon from its conquest from the Moslems in 1232 until 1295, when it became a separate Christian kingdom. When Peter IV of Aragon reconquered the island in 1343, it does not appear to have been besieged.

Between its completion in 1310 and the reconquest, it was indeed used as a palace by the kings. It belongs to a very small group of three circular or polygonal buildings on a similar scale, whose relationship to each other is not clear, but all of which have this dual palace/fortress role. The other two are Castel del Monte and Queenborough, the lost castle of Edward III on the Isle of Sheppey in Kent. The interior has a courtyard open to the sky, surrounded by a wooden gallery on the ground floor. The royal apartments are on the first floor, with spacious chambers, possibly a hall, and a chapel and kitchen. The ground floor rooms are practical, store rooms, offices, and even a forge. The first floor rooms have airy vaults and a stone gallery facing onto the courtyard, though defensive requirements mean that the outer windows are small. The towers in the wall are circular, and from the air its profile recalls that of Castel del Monte, with the octagons transformed into circles.

Jaime II was also responsible for continuing work on the palace and cathedral within the city of Palma. La Almudiana is on the site of the alcazar of the Muslim rulers of the islands, and rebuilding had been begun in his father's reign. It has always been a fortified building, but it has inherited a good deal from the original Moorish palace, and has two courtyards linked by a bath house, with fine balconies and colonnades. At the very large Gothic cathedral of Santa Maria in Palma, he was also responsible for the building of the burial place of the kings of Majorca, the *capilla real*, between 1314 and 1327. The nave is within

**61.** Castle or palace? The remarkable inner courtyard of Bellver Castle, Palma de Mallorca. There are parallels with circular castles and the 'house of the Round Table' in England.

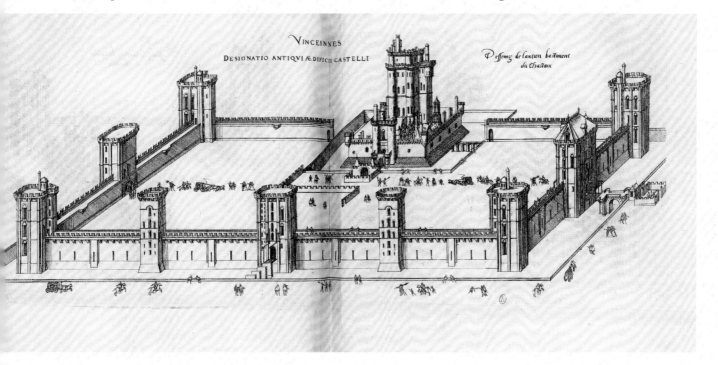

**62.** Vincennes, a sixteenth century view by the architect Androuet du Cerceau.

a metre of the height of the largest French cathedrals of the period and has exceptionally slender pillars. Jaime was evidently trying to develop the usual pair of royal palace and cathedral to match other European capitals. His buildings, modest in scale but essentially magnificent in conception, remain as a memorial to his frustrated ambition of creating a kingdom based on Majorca.

## Vincennes

*The tower as residence*

VINCENNES, THE GREAT CASTLE TO THE EAST of Paris which was the favourite residence of Charles V, is an unusual site which demonstrates how the distinctions between royal residence, castle and palace can be very blurred. It began in the twelfth century as a hunting lodge conveniently close to the capital, and was extended by St Louis as an unfortified residence on a grander scale. A new building, intended for the king's personal apartments, was begun under Philip VI, but the onset of the Hundred Years' War brought the realisation that the king was not safe there, outside the walls of Paris. A keep was therefore constructed, which remains the dominant feature of the castle today; it was completed with a perimeter wall 50 metres square in 1369. Charles V then created a new precinct a kilometre in each direction, to include a chapel, the royal residence of Philip VI and the buildings needed for his household It was to be, in effect, a walled royal town.[39] The chapel was a princely Sainte-Chapelle, despite the proximity of that in the Palais de la Cité, with its own relic, but with a single storey only. The building was interrupted by the troubled times after the end of Charles's reign, and was finally completed in 1552; the projected foundation of a college of canons was never fulfilled.

*Public and private spaces*

The keep, the tallest in Europe at its completion, was not purely defensive. On the second floor, Charles had his study and his library, and the interior of the keep was designed to be a comfortable residence adapted to his lifestyle, despite its outward warlike appearance. An inventory of the contents taken on his death in 1380 lists them room by room, so that we have a clear idea of the layout of the royal suite, with a great chamber, a study and an oratory, containing an extraordinary richnesss of artworks and manuscripts.[40] His living quarters were in the courtyard below, three grand rooms with large east windows: in 1378, when the emperor Karl IV came to visit him, he vacated his own room, and moved to an adjacent one. There was also a smaller study and oratory adjacent to these.

There are similarities between Vincennes and Windsor, such as the enthusiasm for installing clocks, but two important differences.[41] Charles V did not rebuild the old royal residence, but surrounded it with new work. First, the magnificence of the castle consisted more in its massive enclosed space, the length of its tower-studded walls, than anything within. Secondly, the tradition that anyone could have access to the king to present petitions meant that French royal palaces had to be divided into public and private spaces, whereas in England admission to the palace was only open to those on royal business or invited by the king. This very often meant that the spaciousness of Windsor or Westminster was not possible. For instance, the French kings dined publicly in the great halls of Vincennes, the Louvre and the Palais de la Cité, and therefore there had to be a viewing gallery for spectators, and arrangements for access. Similarly, petitions were traditionally presented after the king had attended mass, and so access to the outside of the chapels was needed. The king himself moved in formal procession from one private part of the castle to another, and appropriate spaces for ceremonial and onlookers had to be provided.[42]

The evolution of Vincennes is reflected in the references to the castle in royal documents, which always give the place where they were issued. Until 1369 Vincennes is always called a manor, house or hostel; but once the keep was complete, it becomes a tower and then usually a castle. This reverse of the usual sequence is also apparent from the workmanship of the keep, which is to a much higher standard than that of the earlier buildings. Charles V, forced to build defensively, maintained the style of a palace in terms of the quality of the decoration and the design, where usually the keep would be of purely practical and less finished construction.

It was the king's pride and joy: during the emperor's stay, Charles showed his cousin, the king of the Romans, and his retinue 'the tower, each floor, its furniture and furnishings, right up to the top; and they thought it was the most beautiful and marvellous sight they had ever seen'.[43]

## *Karlstejn*

KARLSTEJN IS THE THIRD ELEMENT in the emperor Karl IV's programme of building in and around Prague. It was begun in 1348 on a site hidden in the hills 25 kilometres west of the city. Its original purpose seems to have been as a summer retreat for the emperor; it is difficult to see any great strategic value in its position in the valley of a tributary of the Vltava. The final form and purpose of the castle evolved over the seventeen years which it took to construct it. Karl was known for his habit of reacting skilfully and decisively to new situations, and two factors appear to have been important in the end result. Two years after it was started, Karl brought the imperial treasure to Prague, and decided to keep it at Karlstejn. The upper part of the castle, the great tower and lesser tower, echo the layout at the former imperial treasury at Trifels in the Rhineland, a place which Karl may have known.[44] The layout of the castle is defensive, with multiple enclosures and narrow wooden bridges between the towers which make access difficult, particularly as the lesser tower can only be reached from the second floor of the castle. Karlstejn was besieged in 1422 during the Hussite wars, when stone-throwing machines and bombards were placed on the surrounding hills, and the royalists had to raise a very large army to drive off the enemy and raise the siege.[45]

*The purpose of Karlstejn*

The castle as a fortified treasure house for the imperial regalia was therefore the first stage. The chronicler Beneš Krabice records the dedication of the main chapel in the tower of the castle at Karlstejn in 1365, saying that

> The emperor built this castle with wonderful workmanship and the strongest of walls, and made in the upper tower a spacious chapel, which he surrounded with walls of pure gold and precious stones and adorned it with both relics of the saints and fine vestments for the dean and the chapter or college which he established there, and ornamented it with very precious pictures. There is no castle or chapel in the whole world with such priceless workmanship and status, for in it he kept the imperial insignia and the whole treasure of his kingdom.[46]

From 1354 to 1356, Karl added to his collection of relics, which was his 'sacred obsession', a remarkable group of items connected with the Passion, followed by the gift of two thorns from the Crown of Thorns from his nephew the dauphin Charles of France at the end of the year. These items were to be housed at Karlstejn, not as subsidiary items to the imperial treasure, but as the focal point of the castle.

What had once been a secure place for earthly treasure now became a private inner sanctum in which to store up treasure in heaven. The two chambers of the Trifels treasury may have been the models for the emperor's private inner sanctum at Karlstejn, a place

**63.** (right) Karlstejn castle, built by Karl IV between 1348 and 1365, during which time it evolved from a summer residence into the fortress in which the imperial regalia and the emperor's collection of relics were kept.

**64.** (below right) Karlstejn: interior of St Catherine's chapel, the private oratory of Karl IV, where the relics of the Passion which he had gathered were originally kept. Above the door the emperor and his wife Anna hold the cross which contained several of these relics.

**65.** (above) Karlstejn: the narrow passage outside the chapel of the Holy Cross deliberately restricts access to the religious heart of the castle.

where he could retreat to meditate or to fast and pray. The foundation charter of the college of priests who were to serve the two chapels in the castle, issued on 27 March 1357, outlines the spiritual framework which Karl envisaged as the rationale for this enterprise. The castle and its chapels were to be devoted to the commemoration of the relics, which represented the divine choice by which he had been raised to the imperial dignity. Incidentally, Karlstejn thus fulfils the Aristotelian requirements of magnificence perfectly, as both a great public building and as a temple, its prestige enhanced by the hidden treasure at its heart.

To underscore the message of his 'castle of spiritual pleasures (*geistliches Lustschloss*)',[47] Karl set out a very elaborate architectural and pictorial programme for himself and the highly privileged visitors who were admitted to the chapel which housed the relics. There is no contemporary evidence of any pilgrimage to Karlstejn,[48] and it is almost designed to defy rather than invite admission. Today, it is possible to visit it privately with a guide, and to do this is to relive something of the original atmosphere. It is very much a place for the emperor's personal worship, in keeping with his request, when he visited Paris in 1378, to be left alone to meditate on the relics in the Sainte-Chapelle. To be permitted by the emperor to enter the chapel of the Holy Cross was clearly a mark of high esteem.

*'a castle of spiritual pleasures'*

The path begins in the courtyard of the castle, and leads through the emperor's apartments upwards to the narrow passages and wooden bridge to the Lesser or Marian Tower. These are not the grandiose public stairways of the palace at the Hradčany, but are deliberately difficult of access. The lesser tower housed the college of canons and the chapel of St Mary and oratory of St Catherine, where the Passion relics were originally placed before the Great Tower was completed. This was the private oratory of Karl IV where he would spend entire days, the most personal space in the complex. A small opening between the chapel and the oratory was the only means of communication when the door was closed; food and important despatches were placed in it when necessary. Above the door the emperor and his third wife Anna are shown elevating the massive gold cross which held the Passion relics, now in the treasury at St Vitus. Above the altar, they are shown again, apparently touching the hands of the Virgin and of the Christ Child who reach out to them. The cross motif is repeated in the figures of the apostles in the frieze at the top of the walls. Apart from the frieze, the walls of the chapel are set with semi-precious stones, in a series of geometric shapes, and the roof bosses are studded with gemstones, including a gem carved with the head of the Medusa, reused from elsewhere. The restrained light heightens the intensity and richness of the interior, and if the chapel indeed once held the gold cross of the Passion relics, it would have shone out in the semi-darkness.

*A journey to the Holy Cross chapel*

In the chapel of St Mary, where the canons performed the daily round of services, Karl is shown being presented with two thorns from the Crown of Thorns by his nephew Charles, dauphin of France, and receiving another relic from a fellow sovereign, either the king of Cyprus or the king of Hungary. A third scene shows him putting them into the reliquary cross similar to that commissioned by him in 1357, now in the treasury at St Vitus' Cathedral. The remainder of the frescoes are a sequence of scenes from the Apocalypse with a detailed commentary, probably completed before 1362. The Apocalypse is often found as a separate text in manuscripts of the period. M.R. James lists nearly a hundred examples, including wall paintings and stained glass, from the thirteenth to fifteenth century.[49] The reason for the choice of this subject is not clear, but it is only part of the original décor. Most of the rest was destroyed in the sixteenth century, when the castle was partially rebuilt.

The rooms in the Lower Tower are the prelude to a journey which takes you physically and spiritually upwards, through purgatory to paradise. The staircase leading to the bridge to the Great Tower records the stories of Karl's saintly and royal ancestral martyrs,

Wenceslas and Wenceslas's grandmother Ludmilla. The murals use the novel technique of linear perspective, and have much in common with Italian painting. They would have been startling to Karl's privileged visitors. As you mount the stairs, the ceiling colour changes first from red to blue, and then from blue to the starry deep blue vault of heaven, before we come to the narrow passage leading to the Chapel of the Holy Cross itself. This is a space which has to be experienced; it is almost impossible to provide an adequate two-dimensional image of it.

The entrance to the chapel of the Holy Cross is deliberately very small, and archaic in style, as if to indicate a holy of holies which is difficult to enter, a paradigm for paradise. The first impression is of a vast gold space, focussed on the altar. Above it is a small Madonna and Child. The centre of the altar is empty: the Holy Cross itself is absent. Master Theodoricus, of whose origins nothing is known, and for whose highly dramatic style there are no parallels, is the presiding genius. He is called the 'emperor's painter' in a document from 1359, and was later master of the painters' guild in Prague. There are 129 portraits on the walls. These are the main decorative element, a Christian army rallied round the precious spiritual treasure on the altar. Their hierarchy is not clear, though we can recognise groups of saints, patriarchs and prophets, holy virgins and holy widows, and certain saints. Most of the hierarchies are orthodox, as prescribed by the Fathers of the Church, but Karl, as always, has added his own ideas. The Virgin in the centre of the altarpiece is flanked by the patron saints of his kingdoms of Bohemia and Lombardy, Saints Wenceslas and Palmasius. And hierarchies unknown to spiritual authorities are included: holy rulers, beginning with Charlemagne, and holy knights, reflecting Karl's own views on this subject. Each figure is a vivid portrait, highly coloured and remarkably alive. The walls are an apparently random pattern of coloured marble and semi-precious stones up to the dado, from which the shapes of crosses slowly emerge. The gold work too comes into focus: there is immensely varied detail in the patterning. Around the chapel runs a railing of *fleurs-de-lis* and thorns, reminding us of the relic at the heart of the chapel. It is a space which defies all attempts to photograph it as a whole; yet if a single interior had to be chosen to represent magnificence, it would have to be this chapel. It was a holy of holies, open only to a very few privileged visitors, who could also claim the generous papal indulgence prescribed for those who came there. Such remission of sins were usually reserved for places which attracted mass pilgrimages: this further enhanced the special aura attached to Karl's most dramatic creation.

*The Great Tower and the Holy Cross chapel*

**66.** Karlstejn: interior of the chapel of the Holy Cross. The walls are encrusted with roughly cut precious stones, while above the gilded ceiling seems like a lightweight fretwork. 127 portraits – male and female saints, kings, princes, emperors, queens, princesses, empresses – are arrayed around the walls. Many are by master Theodoric.

## Churches, Shrines and Relics

RELICS ARE AN IMPORTANT ASPECT OF princely magnificence, and in order to understand them we need to go back to the first centuries of Christendom. Relics had been an integral part of the worship of the Christian Church since the days of the first martyrs in Rome, when their fellow-worshippers sometimes literally gathered up their remains for burial. By the early fourth century, the theologian Basil of Caeserea could declare that 'those who touch the bones of martyrs participate in their sanctity'. Objects associated with saints or which had been in contact with their relics were also regarded as having the same power. There is evidence, even at this early date, of a trade in relics among elite Christian families. In AD 326 St Helena, the mother of the emperor Constantine, was supposed to have discovered the True Cross when she went to Jerusalem. The announcement of this event seems to have triggered a wave of enthusiasm for the collection of relics for private use.[50] By the sixth century there was a regular pilgrimage to

the Holy Land, and relics brought back by those who went there were especially valued. Furthermore, in the first years of the toleration of Christianity, many churches were built either to mark the site of a martyrdom or to house the relics of a specific saint at the place where he or she had been buried.

*Relics, reliquaries and ownership*

Technically, under ecclesiastical law, relics could not be bought or sold, and this applied until the practice of enclosing the relics in magnificent gold and jewel casings developed. Such reliquaries were first used in Byzantium in the seventh century, and as these containers grew in size and splendour, it was impossible to prevent money from changing hands. The pretext was that it was the container which held the relic, the reliquary, which was being sold, and that the custody of the relic was transferred at the same time: there was nothing to prevent such a transfer. Relics were not supposed to be visible except on special occasions, and in 1215 the Fourth Lateran council, summoned by the pope, declared against the display of 'old honourable relics'.[51]

*St Louis buys the Crown of Thorns*

In reality, princes were highly aggressive purchasers of relics, the most notorious example being that of the purchase by St Louis of France of the great relic of the crucifixion, Christ's Crown of Thorns, from the Frankish emperor of Byzantium. The long history of the Crown of Thorns reaches back into that of the Byzantine empire, and to the imperial palace chapel of the Virgin of the Pharos. This contained the exceptional collection of relics of the Passion amassed by the rulers of Byzantium over many centuries. The Crown of Thorns probably arrived at some time between 614 and 629.[52] In 1204 a crusade set out for Palestine with the object of recapturing Jerusalem from the Muslims. The crusaders reached Venice, where they were unable to pay the Venetians for the cost of transport to their destination. After some months, the Doge offered to lend them ships free of charge if they agreed to go first to Byzantium and take the city, which the Venetians saw as a prime commercial rival. This extraordinary proposal was accepted, despite the fact that Byzantium was a friendly Christian power. The city was taken, and a Frankish ruler, Baldwin, installed.

Thirty years later, his successor of the same name left Byzantium to seek aid from the rulers of the Christian West. He met with little response, but, according to the bishop of Sens, who was deeply involved in what followed, he mentioned to St Louis and his mother that he would have either to sell or pawn the Crown of Thorns to raise money. It seems that Baldwin offered to give it to St Louis, on the understanding that a gift would be forthcoming in return. However, in the emperor's absence, the leaders of Constantinople had already pawned it to the Venetian merchants in the city for 13,134 gold pieces. The loan they had obtained had to be repaid by 19 June 1239, and the leaders of the Franks saw no hope of raising it.[53]

The Crown had to be taken to Venice, but there was a danger that the Greek enemies of Baldwin would try to intercept it at sea. Friedrich II, hearing of the situation, offered an escort, and a certain Brother Andrew took charge of the relic: when the party arrived in Venice, the Crown was taken to St Mark's amid general rejoicing. Two Dominican friars were therefore sent to Venice with the necessary papers and money, and with the help of French merchants trading there were able to negotiate the redemption of the loan. St Louis had in effect bought the relic for France. When the friars and their prize were near Sens, about 110 kilometres from Paris, they were met by the king and his family and the bishop of Sens. On 10 August the silver case containing the Crown was opened, and the multiple seals which had been attached in Constantinople and Venice were broken. The Crown in its golden covering was shown to those present, 'an inestimable pearl'. The container was then sealed again and taken into Sens, in procession. The king, his brother and the guards went barefoot, while the people celebrated. The same scenes were repeated the next

**67.** (above) Karlstejn: in the chapel below that of the Holy Cross, Karl IV is shown with his most treasured relics. From left: Charles V of France gives him two thorns from the Crown of Thorns; a king, either of Cyprus or Hungary gives him an unidentified relic; and Karl puts relics into the cross depicted in plate 66 above.

**68.** Karlstejn: St George: Master Theodoric's style is unmistakeable, emphasising the face and eyes, and partly open mouth to give his figures an air of amazement – which the onlooker may well share.

day, when the Crown was deposited in the royal oratory of St Nicholas. Soon after it was transferred to Saint-Denis, when building work began on the chapel which was to house it began. Further relics were bought from the Venetians in 1241, including another piece of the True Cross discovered by St Helena, and the Holy Lance.

## Collecting relics

THE EMPEROR KARL IV WAS PROBABLY the most enthusiastic collector of relics in the medieval period. We have seen how, on his state visit to Paris in 1378, he spent a very long time meditating on the Crown of Thorns, and a French chronicler called him 'very curious and careful about relics'. His acute consciousness of his place in history was not simply that of a prince in the timeline of the political world, but included the sacred role of kingship and hence his place in a history which was intimately linked with God's purposes as revealed in scripture. Relics were an essential link between the two worlds in which he moved. A full catalogue of all the relics that he is known to have possessed has recently been published, and runs to no less than 605 separate items, relating to about three hundred saints or sacred objects such as the True Cross.[54]

*Prague cathedral treasury*

The treasury next to the cathedral in Prague reflects this enthusiasm, even though it holds only a very small proportion of his acquisitions. Central to his collection was of course the imperial treasure, which came to Prague early in 1350. This was followed by a steady flow of such items as he travelled through Italy from 1353 to 1355; and he acquired relics of the Passion from his nephew Charles in 1356, while the latter was still heir to the French throne. The high point of the acquisitions was when he suceeded in obtaining the body of St Vitus, the patron saint of Bohemia, in Pavia in 1355; we have seen how this was central to his rebuilding of Prague Cathedral. The treasury of St Vitus' Cathedral contains a substantial number of items associated with Karl IV, including the Holy Cross from Karlstejn, with the wooden panels on the back which enable the pieces of the True Cross to be extracted for veneration, or new fragments to be added. There is also a cross enclosing a relic of Christ's loincloth which Pope Urban V presented to Karl; the engraved plates show the gift being made.

## Relics as an aspect of magnificence

THE FRENCH KINGS GAVE THORNS from the Crown of Thorns relic to foreign royalty and to the descendants of St Louis, who built ten of their own Saintes Chapelles between 1315 and 1505, each of which contained such a thorn. Edward III, as a descendant of St Louis, built St Stephen's chapel at Westminster as his own version of a Sainte-Chapelle, but without the thorn which would have given it the correct status. Jean duke of Berry founded two such chapels, and that at Bourges was particularly celebrated for the extensive collection of relics which he assembled there. These were dynastic buildings, commemorating and celebrating the princes who created them by the extensive use of heraldry and portraiture. At the Sainte-Chapelle itself, each Easter, the king presided in his coronation robes over the display of the Crown of Thorns, acting in his role as priest-king in mediating between the divine object and his people.[55]

Relic-hunting expeditions were launched: in 1400, Philip the Bold of Burgundy sent his chamberlain to Rhodes and the Byzantine territories in search of the head of St George, paying him 300 francs for his travel expenses alone.[56] And princes could put pressure on the custodians of relics in their own territories to allow them to take a part of them for 'custody' in their collections: thus in 1412 Jean duke of Berry had the tomb of St Radegonde in the cathedral at Poitiers opened. He proposed to remove parts of the relics for his chapel at Bourges, a request to which the bishop, prior and canons acceded 'more from fear than for any other reason'. They later claimed that a miracle had restored to them the missing parts, and that the duke's trophies were false.[57]

Among the extravagances of the late fourteenth century in France, the collection of relics came high on the list. Charles V and his brothers were avid acquirers of relics, which they housed in remarkable casings and which formed an important part of their treasure. Existing relics were newly adorned: in 1392 Charles VI gave a golden casket weighing 100 kilos to the abbey of Saint-Denis to house the body of the patron saint of France. These massive pieces of gold and jewels have largely disappeared. What remains are the detailed inventories which tell us so much about the secular magnificence of these princes, and thanks to these documents we can gain some idea of their collections, destined, according to Christine de Pizan, to be shown to foreign visitors so that 'they can give an account of them in their own country' and spread the prince's fame.[58] This was particularly important at the beginning of the reign of Charles VI when the royal dukes were jockeying for power and influence. The reliquaries were treated as part of the prince's treasure: as with secular pieces, they might be used as security for loans or even melted down or sold in dire emergency. The inventories describe the reliquaries in minute detail for valuation purposes, but rarely mention the name of the saint or the nature of the relic which the jewelled case contains. Indeed, the reliquary was sometimes sold and the relic itself put aside until such time as a new case could be made. They were often used as gifts, particularly during the period when the competition over New Year gifts was at its most intense.[59] The inventories were usually drawn up on the death of the owner: Jean duke of Berry was an exception, as his inventories form a narrative of the acquisitions and disposals of items over a period of time, from 1401 to his death in 1416.[60] In terms of numbers, Jean owned 111 relics in 1401, and Charles VI in 1400 more than 180. The inventory of Philip the Bold at his death is incomplete, yet still lists sixty-one relics.

These vast quantities of relics were not for public display.[61] Christine de Pizan has in mind only privileged dignitaries when she says they are to be shown to foreign visitors. The act of limiting access to them and secluding them in private chapels served to increase their magnificence, by making the sight of them an exclusive experience. Their fame was enhanced by the fact that, unlike relics in religious foundations, they were not intended to attract crowds of pilgrims. Ownership of treasures which were out of sight but whose fame was spread by those fortunate enough to glimpse them was another strategy for proclaiming the prince's magnificence. They might also appear at specific festivals, notably the relevant saint's day, to return to their seclusion for the rest of the year. In some cases, the relics had a deep personal meaning for their owners: Karl IV and Karlstejn is the extreme example of this.

*Charles VI and the royal dukes as collectors of relics*

# 10 | MAGNIFICENCE ON DISPLAY

*◆ Civic entries ◆ London ◆ Paris ◆ Entries in the French provinces,
Spain and the empire ◆ State visits ◆ Karl IV and Charles V,
Paris 1378 ◆ Charles the Bold and Friedrich III, Trier 1473
◆ Towards the Renaissance: Naples*

## Civic Entries

THE ENTRY OF A RULER INTO A CITY was a moment of political tension, when the superiority of king or emperor had to be acknowledged on the one hand and the freedom – limited though it was – of the city had to be recognised. In the Holy Roman Empire, there was a further element, that of the recognition of the emperor as legitimately elected: during the eleventh and twelfth centuries and on rare occasions later, this election could be contested. It therefore became the custom for the new emperor to undertake a journey round the major centres of power in his new domains, to confirm the allegiance of the princes and identify himself as the new ruler.

*Civic entries in classical times*

The origins of this imperial reception by a city go back to classical times, starting with the successors of Alexander the Great in Greece, who were formally welcomed by a procession of citizens led by the priests. We find a church ritual in place at the great abbeys of the Holy Roman Empire in the twelfth century, which were also regularly used by the emperors on their travels, and these rituals were later adapted by the towns.[1] From the thirteenth century onwards this was gradually superseded by a parade, increasingly a staged event whose object was the glorification of the monarchy and the celebration of its power, as well as a demonstration of the city's wealth and power.

*Isabella of England enters Köln*

The first detailed description of such an entry is that of the English princess Isabella's reception at Antwerp in the summer of 1235, on her way to marry the emperor Friedrich II. Friedrich had been married twice before, but this was the first time that the wedding had taken place within his domains. Isabella landed at Antwerp, and the clergy of the town and surrounding region came out to meet her 'in solemn procession, in precious vestments, with lighted candles, in an orderly fashion, ringing bells and singing joyous songs, with masters of every kind of musical art and their instruments'. She was then escorted to Köln, en route for the actual wedding at Worms, by a large group of armed nobles, since there were fears of a French plot to ambush her and prevent the marriage. At Köln, ten thousand citizens, or so the chronicler guesses, emerged from the town, with flowers and festive ornaments. Riders gave a traditional display of horsemanship, mounted on Spanish horses, 'spurring on their fine horses to a gallop, they broke canes and spears on each other, as if in a tournament'.[2] There were ingenious boats which seemed to row on dry land, which were in fact pulled by horses concealed under silken covers: in them sat clergy who sang melodies never heard before, to the accompaniment of an organ. The princess was then led through the streets of Köln by the town officers; when she saw the townswomen sitting in the windows and standing at the corners of the streets, wanting to catch a glimpse of her, she removed her hat and veil so that everyone could see her. This won the hearts of the people, particularly as she was very beautiful. She was lodged in the archbishop's palace, where a choir of girls sang and played various instruments all night, while a strong guard was mounted on the walls.

## London

THE FIRST ENGLISH ROYAL ENTRIES WITH decorations and ceremonial seem to be based on Continental models. The earliest surviving record of such an occasion is the visit of the emperor Otto IV to his uncle King John in 1207 in London, when 'on the king's orders the city was made resplendent with flowers, hangings and wax torches and certain lavish devices, with peals of bells and processions'.[3] In 1223, Jean of Brienne, king of Jerusalem, came to England seeking support for a new crusade, and a chronicler from Palestine records that 'at all the cities, castles and boroughs where he came and went, people came out to him in procession and made great feasts for him', as if this was the norm.[4] Thirteen years later, the marriage of the emperor Friedrich II and Isabella at Antwerp and Köln is reflected in the entry of her brother Henry III and Eleanor of Provence into London after their marriage, and before Eleanor's coronation, in 1236. Once again it is the chronicler Matthew Paris who describes the entry:

> Summoned to this nuptial feast, a multitude of nobles of both sexes, as great a number of clergy, a populous crowd of ordinary people, and a huge variety of minstrels came together, so many that the city of London could scarcely contain them in its capacious bosom. The whole city was bedecked with flags and banners, garlands and hangings, candles and lamps and certain prodigious inventions and representations, and the smallest blemishes of all the buildings were mended with clay, plaster and wood. The citizens of London went out to meet the king and queen on swift horses, with showy harness and ornaments. And that day they went to Westminster, to fulfil the office of butler which belonged to them by ancient right, at the royal coronation, dressed in silk, with mantles worked with gold, and with changes of clothes, mounted on expensive horses, sparkling with new bits and saddles, riding in close order. They carried with them three hundred and sixty gold and silver cups; the king's trumpeters went before them, and horns sounded, so that such a marvellous novelty left everyone astonished.[5]

*Eleanor of Provence enters London*

It was traditional to hang the city streets with cloths and tapestries, even for routine royal entries. Coronation entries were naturally marked by extensive celebrations.[6] Edward II and Isabella of France were married at Boulogne in 1308, and Isabella's coronation as queen took place on their arrival in London. They were met by a great crowd of citizens, and entered the city, which 'appeared like a new Jerusalem with its highways adorned with jewels'.[7] At Isabella's coronation, the Londoners wore the arms of France and England on their clothing as they went about their traditional duties. There was such a crush of people that one man was killed when a wall in the church collapsed. Another chronicler declares that the feast was badly organised and mismanaged, with no-one in charge of the serving of the food. Because of the crowd the king had to come into the abbey by a side-entrance, screened by an awning.

The English royal entry does not reappear until 1377, possibly because the coronation of Edward III took place at a time of political uncertainty due to the deposition of his father. The event was hastily arranged for 1 February 1327. Although he spent nearly two months at Westminster at that time, there is no record of him being in London, or indeed at the Tower just outside its eastern boundary. The only entry of the period was more in the nature of a triumph, that of Edward prince of Wales with his captive Jean II of

muint an butte feite. com e
le eftoit. ge ne uos enconi
neus. Car ge men uoul reto
ner fo: un grant conte.

nur missite yuayn qui ame
noit auce soi le chr de loeno
ys. quant les dames vurent
vrent missite yuayn. qui a

**69.** (above) Entry into a city. Arthur enters Camelot, from the romance *Meliadus*, c.1350. The entry is in the German imperial style, which would have been familiar to the artist, who was working in imperial territory in northern Italy.

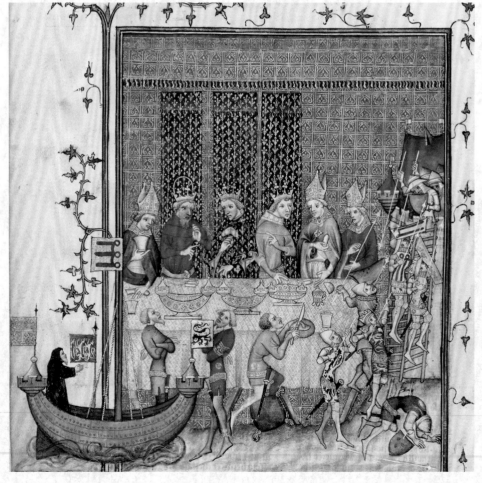

**70.** The feast given by Charles V in honour of Karl IV at Saint-Denis in 1378, with the *entremets* of the siege of Jerusalem in 1099 being played in the foreground and to the right.

France in 1357. There was an interesting theatrical moment on the way from Plymouth to London, when 'one day, near a forest, five hundred men in green coats and mantles were set in ambush, and when the said king of France passed through the said forest, the men in question appeared before the king of France and his company as robbers or evildoers with bows and arrows and spears and wooden shields'. John asked the prince who they were, and was told they were foresters who chose to live in the wild, and it was their custom to assemble every day in this fashion.[8] When they reached London, they were welcomed by Henry Picard, the mayor of London, accompanied by citizens and aldermen, and

> a multitude of people on horseback came from each craft guild of the said city of London, variously decked out in costumes newly made for the occasion, in great numbers. And the people of each London guild in turn preceded the said king of France, making good cheer; and as the procession passed through London wine was offered in abundance to all who wanted to drink, on account of the amazing spectacle. And in the middle of London's Cheapside, near to the goldsmiths' quarter and at their instigation, two very beautiful girls were set up on a kind of platform cunningly rigged up with some ropes leading from the goldsmiths' quarters to that of the saddlers, and these girls sprinkled gold and silver leaf on the heads of the riders below, while the king of France and the prince of Wales and the others who were riding there looked on; on account of which, many people applauded this amazing scene ... And as the king of France rode through the city of London he was dressed in a robe of black motley lined with miniver in the manner of an archdeacon or other secular clerk.[9]

This was the precursor of a series of formal royal entries into the city of London which ran from the last quarter of the fourteenth century until the middle of the fifteenth century, when they were interrupted by the Wars of the Roses. The single spectacle in Cheapside multiplied into a whole series of dumb shows of increasing splendour and elaboration, until the inspection of these tableaux made the entry into a lengthy perambulation through the city for the royal party.

The scripts for these occasions were written by clerics. The underlying scenarios reflected their expertise in Christian theology and symbolism, particularly as applied to the king as God's representative on earth. The detailed message of each scene was explained in placards, which were later supplemented by a custodian who declared the meaning to the king in a formal speech. Songs and religious music were woven into the action, and literary accounts of the whole proceedings, which may have also served as the original programme for the tableaux, were provided; the most distinguished contributor to this genre was John Lydgate, generally regarded as the heir to Chaucer's poetic eminence.[10]

A basic ritual developed at London, containing a number of themes repeated on each occasion. When the king arrived at London Bridge, he was greeted by the statue of a giant. This later became a moving figure, and the giant was accompanied by a giantess, representing Gog and Magog, the traditional guardians of the city.[11] The placing of the tableaux was gradually formalised, and an accepted route for the procession was established, passing the landmarks of the city, the crosses and the public fountains or conduits that dominated the streets. Cheapside, with both cross and conduit, was the main thoroughfare of the city, and it was here that the most impressive spectacles were generally placed. The procession left the city by the gate leading to Westminster, marked today by Temple Bar.

When Richard II came to the throne at the age of ten, following the deaths of his father in 1376 and his grandfather the following year, all the anxieties over the rule of a king who was still a minor came to the fore. It is in this context that we can best understand the decision to renew the traditional procession from the Tower to Westminster, through the city of London. The king needed to be shown to the people to reassure them, with a display of unity among the great lords and the citizens to allay any fears of discord. Accordingly, on 15 July, the day before the coronation itself, the magnates of England and the Lord Mayor and aldermen of the city were at the gate of the Tower at 9 a.m. to take their place in the procession. Ahead of them went the representatives of the different wards and their musicians. The mayor and aldermen rode immediately before the magnates, who surrounded the king: Richard rode alone on a great warhorse in a large space in their midst. As they set out, the trumpeters positioned on an aqueduct and a nearby tower 'made a marvellous sound'. Most of the participants were dressed in white, perhaps as the symbolic colour representing the king's youth and innocence. The aqueduct was made to flow with wine, and the fountains which it fed spouted wine for three or more hours while the procession passed. In the middle of Cheapside there was a painted canvas tower with four turrets, occupied by four very beautiful girls, the same age as the king, who tossed gold coins in front of him, as for his father the Black Prince in 1357. On the tower was a spire, and above it an angel stood holding a golden crown in its hands: 'it was so cleverly made that on the arrival of the king, it bowed to him and offered him the crown'.[12]

*Richard II's coronation entry*

The greatest show in Richard's reign came about from rather different circumstances.[13] The city of London had refused the king's request for a loan in 1391, and Richard had taken his revenge by withdrawing the city's charter and putting it under a warden whom he appointed, while the mayor and city officials were imprisoned. The Londoners settled their quarrel and repurchased their charter the following year, at a cost of £10,000, and the expense of a very elaborate entry for the king's formal restoration of their rights at St Paul's in August 1392. The occasion was recorded in five hundred lines of florid Latin verse by John of Gaunt's confessor, the theologian Richard Maidstone.[14] This was appropriate, since the theme of the entry was that of the Second Coming: Richard had entered his kingdom in the pageant of 1377, and he was now coming again, a Christlike analogy which can be found elsewhere in paintings he commissioned about this time. There seems little doubt that the king or one of his close associates dictated the scenario of the pageant – it is tempting to suspect Maidstone of being responsible – and the citizens simply organised its staging. He is represented as Christ the bridegroom taking back his errant spouse.

*Richard II and the rebellious city*

The king and queen were met in the traditional manner outside the city and escorted by a huge procession of the guilds in their liveries and musicians down Cheapside, where the first fountain ran with wine, and an angelic choir and musicians sang as the king passed. In the middle of Cheapside there was a 'marvellous tower', on which a crowned angel stood. Here, an element from the 1377 entry was repeated. As the king and queen stood and admired it, the angel descended 'without steps or stairs', floating in the air, holding a crown in each hand, which were given to the royal couple, followed by wine in golden cups. The angel then rose up in a cloud to the top of the tower. At the fountain before St Paul's, the three orders of angels stood around a throne, singing and playing all kinds of musical instruments – the poet lists seventeen – as Richard and Anne passed into the cathedral. The last pageant was at Temple Bar, the way out of the city towards Westminster. Here John the Baptist, a saint to whom Richard was particularly devoted, stood in a 'desert', where all kinds of trees grew, and seventeen kinds of wild beast ran wild, attacking each other and leaping and running here and there. St John greeted Richard, and an angel came down from the roof to present two golden tables depicting the crucifixion. The procession made its way to Westminster, where a throne had been prepared for the king. Here the queen came forward, as the traditional intercessor who persuaded the king to right wrongs. She begged Richard to have mercy on the city: 'My king, my sweet love, no king since Brutus, even Arthur himself, has had such a welcome.' At this the king addressed the citizens, and restored their liberties.

It may be the survival of Maidstone's description that makes this appear one of the most elaborate and splendid of all royal entries, with a very complex programme. But it does differ from most court rituals of this kind, in that it is very much designed round a specific occasion and circumstances, the quarrel of Richard II with the city and its resolution, rather than a pageant of the usual sort, for an entry, a coronation or a wedding, where the imagery is more general. There are obvious common factors. Advent, which is particularly emphasised in the 1392 pageant, could always be made to apply to the coming of the sovereign or his consort into a city for the first time. The analogy with the new Jerusalem is found in Paris and in the Low Countries. And the bridal element in 1392 would have been familiar from wedding entries. All this is worked skilfully into a single coherent programme, reflected in the individual themes of the tableaux.

The same programme was repeated with variations under Henry V and Henry VI. The length of the ceremony extended to a full day when Henry V returned to England after his victory at Agincourt in 1415.[15] Most of this time was taken up by walking through the city, looking at the displays and listening to at least four choirs and other musicians. The day culminated at the far end of Cheapside leading to St Paul's. Here the tower of the conduit had been transformed into a representation of the throne of heaven itself under a sky-blue canopy and clouds, with 'a figure of majesty in the form of a sun … emitting dazzling rays' in the place of God, surrounded by archangels singing and playing instruments. This and the preceding tableaux were described by the chronicler as 'tributes of praise to the honour and glory, not of men but of God'. Henry's own demeanour reinforced this: he rode 'with an impassive countenance and at a dignified pace' in a simple purple gown, as if 'pondering the matter in his heart, rendering thanks and glory to God alone, not to man'. Once again, while the city had organised and constructed the marvels of the pageant, the king and the court had undoubtedly dictated the themes and tenor of the occasion.

Later entries always provided variations on the original scheme, some of them for the sake of novelty, others to mark the particular occasion. When Catherine of Valois came to London for her coronation as queen of England in 1420, Gog and Magog were moving figures, accompanied by lions which rolled their eyes and moved their limbs, eight pairs of singing angels, and an image of St Petronilla, patron saint of the French royal family.[16] The amount of money spent varies widely: Henry VI's coronation entry in 1429, which only gets the briefest of mentions in the chronicles, cost a mere £8, compared with about £80 for Catherine of Valois's welcome.

However, when Henry VI returned from France, and his resplendent coronation festivities and entry in Paris, the Londoners put on one of their grandest shows, on 21 February 1432. Even the weather was favourable, a beautiful spring day after heavy winter rains. The theme of the pageant was declared at London Bridge, where the king entered the city. Here there was a tower in which a giant stood – evidently not the traditional Gog and Magog – sword upraised, with a motto from the Psalms, 'His enemies I will cover in confusion',[17] with two antelopes supporting the arms of England and France. This and the subsequent tableaux all had large placards with quotations from Scripture, and the programme of the pageant used these verses to celebrate the entry as the coming of a new king who would unite England and France and bring prosperity to the city. And they also offered advice to the young king on how a monarch should rule his people.[18] Henry is cast as a royal Messiah in the scenes which followed.

*London entries from Henry IV to Henry VI*

At the tower by the drawbridge in the middle of London Bridge were Nature, Grace and Fortune, presenting him with science, cunning, prosperity and riches. They were flanked by seven girls in white dresses powdered with gold suns, who gave him seven white doves representing the seven gifts of the Holy Ghost, and seven in white with gold stars, who presented him with pieces of 'the whole armour of God' from St Paul's description of it.[19] At the entry to Cornhill stood Lady Wisdom and the Seven Liberal Arts, each showing their attribute, 'wonderly i-wrought'. At the conduit in Cornhill was a tableau of a king 'on a certain lofty and exceedingly beautiful Throne of Justice' with Mercy, Grace and Pity, the inscription reminding him to 'love equity and right'. Henry rode 'at an easy pace' to the Great Conduit, where an earthly Paradise was represented. The culmination was at the Cross in Cheapside. Here a genealogy showing the king's descent from St Edward the Confessor and St Louis was displayed on a royal castle of jasper green with two green trees growing on it. One had a placard declaring the king's right to rule England and France, with all the king's royal forebears in full armour and surcoats of leopards or lilies. The other was the Tree of Jesse, showing Christ's ancestors from David onwards. Finally, before Henry reached St Paul's, he passed the Little Conduit, where the Trinity sat in majesty, surrounded by angels whose songs invoked blessings on the king.

A rather more modest welcome awaited Margaret of Anjou in 1445, fresh from the festival devised for her wedding by proxy to Henry VI at Nancy by her father René. When she arrived in London for her coronation as queen, the same chronicler merely comments that there were 'many notable devices' in the city. He focusses instead on the queen herself, who made a great impression:

> The queen came from the Tower in a horse-litter, with two steeds with trappers of white damask powdered with gold, matching her clothes, and the pillows and the hangings of the litter. Her hair was combed down to her shoulders, with a gold coronal with rich pearls and precious stones. There were lords on horseback and ladies in chariots, nineteen in all, with their gentlewomen.[20]

These rituals stem from a particular political situation: the tension between the king's power and the independence of London as a city where that power was delegated by charter to the mayor and corporation. The theme of the parade is the king's magnificence and his God-given status, which the city acknowledges and praises, while at the same time emphasising its wealth and splendour and its own special place in the glory of the kingdom.

## Paris

THE FRENCH KINGS WERE ALWAYS CROWNED at Reims, and on their return to the capital from their coronation a formal entry into the city seems to have been the general rule from the thirteenth century onwards. Jean II, in the autumn of 1350, was welcomed on his return from his 'joyful accession' to the throne by the citizens.[21] The 'great bridge' and the streets were draped with rich cloths, and the guilds of Paris paraded in uniform. The Lombards living in Paris, the bankers of the day, wore robes half and half of different colours of tartarin silk, and tall hats in the same style. The citizens all formed a procession, and led the king into the city, accompanied by a variety of musicians. The description of Charles V's entry after his accession in 1364 reveals that the Parisian citizens had costumes halved white and green. These were evidently the royal colours,[22] and were used again in 1381 at Charles VI's accession.

Entries of this sort were not confined to Paris. Traditionally, whenever a new king visited a particular city for the first time during his reign, a solemn entry would be staged, at which the king would promise to respect its rights and liberties. The citizens would respond with an oath of loyalty. By the mid fourteenth century, this had evolved into a kind of modest festival with a dinner and festivities to follow. At Tournai in 1355, Jean II was greeted by a procession of 120 citizens on horseback and jousting was part of the occasion. There were simple decorations, and a dumb show at which gifts were presented to him.[23] By 1389, when Charles V undertook a kind of grand tour of the towns of the southern part of France, the imperial custom of using a canopy beneath which the king rode as he entered a town appears at Montpellier. It was also used at Béziers and Lyon, and in the fifteenth century becomes a regular part of the ceremonial. This custom, and the hanging of the streets with tapestries, seems to derive from the religious processions for the feast of Corpus Christi, when the sacrament was paraded through the streets under a canopy. The tapestries were evidently regarded as a particularly important feature, with religious overtones. The chronicler of the abbey of Saint-Denis refers to streets hung with tapestries for a Paris entry in 1380 as 'like a temple' and in Spain in 1420, at Lérida, the town council restricted the hanging of tapestries to 'the marriage of the queen' and the Corpus Christi procession.

*Civic entries in the French provinces*

After the entry of Queen Isabeau in 1389, there was a long pause in the custom of French royal entries. This was due both to the madness of Charles VI and to the political situation. In 1422 the infant Henry VI of England became king of France by the terms of the treaty of Troyes. He was opposed by the dauphin Charles, Charles VI's son, who made a formal entry into Limoges in the same year, as a symbol of his claim to be the true king of France. Despite Charles's coronation at Reims in 1429 as Charles VII, it was his rival Henry VI who formally entered Paris as king on 5 November 1431.

*Henry VI enters Paris as king of France*

The ceremonies were reported to the mayor of London by an eye-witness; his letter was duly copied into the city archives, and reveals a programme based on the entry of Queen Isabeau forty years earlier. Henry was just short of ten years old at the time, and rode a white hackney more suited to his age than a courser. After he and his companions had robed at the chapel of Saint-Denis, the festival began with the appearance of the goddess Fame and her companions. A herald rode with Fame and led this 'mystery' to the king: the herald bowed and explained who the personages were. At the drawbridge of Saint-Denis there was a tableau of a shield with a silver ship in full sail on it, the arms of the city of Paris. The ship was manned by twelve sailors, who presented three hearts. Out of one there appeared two white doves, from the next birds flew out, and the third contained scented violets: this symbolised the love of the citizens for their king. It was clearly a scenario written by the English administration, since it was exactly the citizens' loyalty that was in doubt.

As the king came into Paris itself, four citizens came forward and held a canopy above him, with the French *fleur-de-lis* on an azure background, and with sun, moon and stars on the fringes. At the Saint-Denis gate, ' [the king] looked at the mermaids for a long time. There were three mermaids there very ingeniously done, and in the middle of them there was a lily, whose buds and flowers spouted out milk and wine for everyone to drink who wished or who could. Above, there was a little wood where wild men frolicked about and did very pretty tricks with shields; everyone liked watching this.'[24] The next tableau was of the Nativity; the actors were living statues, and did not move, even though there were at least 160 people in the scene. The same technique of living statues was repeated at the great scaffold at the Saint-Denis gate, where there were three scenes from the life of St Denis, the patron saint of France, with placards proclaiming what the actors represented.

The clergy of all the churches along the rue Saint-Denis stood outside the church doors in full vestments, each holding a reliquary. One of the churches had the arms of St George in a reliquary: this was brought before Henry as he passed, and he kissed it devoutly. Near the next fountain, another wood was planted, with hunters and dogs in it: as the king passed, a stag ran out across the road, in front of the king, and turned back into the wood, where it was captured.

The procession now reached the Châtelet, the fortress guarding the Ile de la Cité. At this key point, the union of France and England was the theme, with figures with the heraldic emblems of the leading members of the French and English courts, and crowned shields of the arms of France and England. Below this the provost of Paris stood, his hand stretched out holding a petition to the king (played by 'a boy of the King's age and build, royally dressed ... with two crowns ... hanging above his head'),[25] with his colleagues around him, and a mass of people below representing the different ranks of citizens. Again, this was all in dumb show, with motionless actors, and another long inscription in verse explaining the scene. Further on, as he passed the hôtel Saint-Pol, one of the French royal mansions, Henry's grandmother Queen Isabeau, widow of Charles VI's widow, stood at the window. Henry doffed his hood to her. Isabeau bowed to him, and turned away in tears, torn between loyalty to her son and love for her grandson, rival claimants for the throne.

*Charles VII enters Paris as king of France*

Seven years later, in 1438, Charles VII entered Paris for the first time since his coronation. For this occasion, a number of the items from Henry's entry appear to have been recycled. The main procession, however, was very different. Unlike his father, Charles VII disliked these occasions and was nervous and unprepossessing in appearance. However, he played his part to the best of his ability.[26] The king rode in full armour, on a horse with the arms of France on the housings preceded by three knights and a squire on horses whose housings were adorned with flying stags. The four carried the royal armour and surcoat, and another squire his great sword. The archers of his bodyguard followed, and there were two groups of eight hundred archers under their captains, as well as eight hundred lancers, many of whom were lords, knights and squires. This was a military parade, in contrast to the ten-year-old English king mounted on a hackney. The tableaux were religious, depicting the life of Christ; 'there were several fine mysteries ... angels singing at the outer gate, and at the fountain at the Saint-Denis Gate many beautiful things that would take a long time to describe; in front of the Trinity a representation of the Passion, as it was done for the little King Henry when he was consecrated in Paris.'[27] When Henry had come to Paris, a tableau was needed to reassure him of the city's loyalty. When Charles appeared before the gates, the city officials offered him the keys of the city,[28] apparently the first time this had been part of an entry ceremony. As for the citizens at large, the onlookers cried 'Noel, noel!' and wept openly at the return of the man whom they regarded as the true king.

THE ENTRIES OF HENRY VI AND CHARLES VII show how important such occasions could be in terms of reinforcing their respective claims to the French throne. The contrast is not only between their different characters. Henry VI plays the role of peacemaker, bringing harmony to the kingdoms of France and England. Charles VII proclaims his right to the throne, and the fact that he has the power to enforce that right. In 1438, the final victory over the English was fifteen years off, and the Parisians had been fickle in their allegiance to the Valois kings in the past. Charles needed their support, and they rewarded him by displaying their loyalty.

## Entries in the French provinces, Spain and the empire

IN 1449 CHARLES VII ENTERED ROUEN FOR the first time, as the Hundred Years' War neared its end.[29] Here the king was asserting not only his personal right to rule, but the independence and integrity of France itself. Rouen, as the capital of the duchy of Normandy, had been in French hands since 1204, and was one of the greatest cities of France; and it had been – long ago – a centre of English rule. The entry was led by his chancellor, Guillaume Jouvenel des Ursins, with a white hackney at the head of the whole procession. The king's great seal was displayed for all to see on a special high saddle, as the sign of royal authority. The royal archers, in embroidered jackets striped in red, white and green followed, with the archers of the other great lords. The heralds of the princes and of the king were next, all in their tabards of arms, and then the musicians, the trumpeters resplendent in crimson.

> Then came the king, in complete armour, on a stately charger with housings, reaching to the ground, of blue velvet, covered with *fleurs-de-lis* in embroidery. On his head was a beaver hat lined with crimson velvet, having on the crown a tuft of gold thread. He was followed by his pages dressed in crimson, – their sleeves covered with silver plates, the armour of their horses' heads was of fine gold, variously ornamented, and with plumes of ostrich feathers of divers colours.[30]

*Charles VII enters Rouen in 1445*

Outside Rouen, Charles was met by his lieutenant in Normandy, the count of Dunois, and other officials, who had brought with them the archbishop of Rouen and other Norman bishops and the chief inhabitants of Rouen. They gave him the keys of the town, and the clergy came out to meet him, singing the *Te Deum*. Enguerrand de Monstrelet, the chronicler who recorded the day, wrote: 'It is certain, that in the memory of man, never was king seen with such a handsome body of chivalry, so finely dressed, nor so great a number of men at arms as the king of France had with him on his regaining his good city of Rouen'. Within the town, the pageants were largely secular: a fountain with a lamb, the arms of Rouen, 'who spouted out liquors from his horns', and a flying stag with a crown on its neck (one of the badges of Charles VI, his father), which kneeled as the king passed. When the royal ceremonies had ended, the popular rejoicing was such that great bonfires were made in all the streets, and the next three days were declared holidays. Tables were set out in the street 'with meats and wines for all comers, at the expense of the inhabitants'.[31]

BY THE FIFTEENTH CENTURY, the rituals for a royal entry were to some extent prescribed and formalised. Customs varied considerably: the entries of the kings of England, France and the French princes, and of the Spanish peninsula were consistent in their use of tableaux and scenery, while the entries of the emperors of Germany continued to be in the nature of a parade. In Spain, the displays were full of action, often involving mock battles mounted by the guilds. In Valencia both the furriers and the bridle-makers built dragons. When prince Joan entered the city in 1373, the bridle-makers' dragon was far larger, with a polecat on its head. It moved its tongue and cheeks and breathed fire and smoke. It was accompanied by twenty or more wild men, with crude weapons such as branches, long clubs and wooden axes, followed by the bridle-makers, dancing and in fine costumes. When they encountered the men accompanying the duchess, the latter pretended to kill or drown or hang the dragon, and the wild men rushed to its defence. Galleys mounted on wheels were also used for mock battles.[32] This seems to have been a traditional performance in Valencia, as it was repeated ten years later for Joan's father Peire IV, and again the following year.

*The kings of Aragon enter Valencia*

In 1392 it was once more repeated for Joan when he had become king, though there were problems getting the galleys through the streets because they were too large.

In 1399 Martí of Aragon's entry into Valencia culminated at the Aljafería palace with a tableau representing a starry heaven divided into various stages, on which God the Father was at the top, surrounded by seraphim, and which was populated by saints bearing palms.[33] From this a cloud came down from which an angel descended, singing wonderfully, and strewed letters on coloured paper describing the ceremonial. In the years following, the kings of Aragon were received at the gates of any city they visited by angels and saints who offered them the keys of the city in sign of submission. The king had become the vicar of God. In 1459 the gate by which Joan II entered Valencia again depicted Paradise, with God presiding over it: two fiery comets were sent by him to mark the beginning of the ceremonial.

*German civic entries in the fifteenth century*

The German imperial entries often involved impressive numbers of men. These events were a political act, rather than a festival, and there was little in the way of special displays and scenery in the streets. At Bern in 1414 Sigismund, as king of the Romans and therefore heir to the imperial title, was accompanied by Amadeus VIII, count of Savoy, and 1,400 men. The men of Bern sent five hundred young men in uniform out to greet him, while at the gates of the city the clergy waited for his appearance bearing the most precious relics from their churches. The mayor offered him the keys of the city, and a gold canopy was raised over the king. The procession then made its way through the city, while the population lined the streets.[34] In 1442, after his coronation at Aachen, Friedrich III visited a number of imperial cities and towns, and the arrangements for each of these were relatively standardised. His arrival at the Swiss town of Sankt Gallen in that year is a good example. The imperial escort numbered eight hundred men on horseback and many more on foot. The first encounter between Friedrich III and the people of Sankt Gallen took place outside the town. As the imperial party approached, the rulers of the town came out to meet him in the countryside, with an escort of the young men of the town, in heraldic uniform, either of the imperial arms or those of the town, and a band of musicians. When the two groups met the townsmen knelt before the emperor, and speeches of welcome were made on both sides. A joint festival procession then formed up, and escorted the emperor into the town. As he approached, all the bells in the town were rung, and trumpeters, pipers and drummers played. Then the clergy sang psalms appropriate to the arrival of a ruler, and four townsmen carried the canopy beneath which the emperor rode. The procession halted at the abbey church, where a *Te Deum* was sung followed by a royal mass. The emperor was then escorted to his lodgings, in the abbot's quarters. The next day, the townsmen offered the emperor gifts of money and provisions; and on some occasions this was followed by dancing in the evening.

These imperial entries were modest affairs, following the original ritual which can be traced back to Roman times. The relations between the emperor and the imperial cities were on a different footing to those between the European kings and their capitals. For a start, there was never an imperial capital as such. The city at the centre of the personal domains of the emperor was the nearest equivalent. Even the imposing religious entries of Karl IV at Prague in the second half of the fourteenth century lack the theatrical element found outside the empire.

# State Visits

A FORMAL STATE VISIT BY ONE RULER to another was a relatively rare event. We have looked at Henry III's journey to Paris, and the cumulative effect of the development of court culture, and the way in which it echoed the magnificence of the ruler, can be seen in another such journey over a century later. In both these cases, and that of the journey of Friedrich III to Naples in 1452, there was no urgent political purpose in view. However, the question of magnificence and its effect in diplomatic negotiations comes very much to the fore in the meeting of Charles the Bold of Burgundy with Friedrich III at Trier in 1473.

## Karl IV and Charles V, Paris 1378

THE PURPOSE OF THE VISIT OF THE EMPEROR Karl IV to his nephew Charles V in Paris in 1378 is not entirely clear. There were both political and personal reasons behind it. The emperor had been brought up at the French court for seven years, and his sister Bonne had married Jean II. It seems, however, that he had not been back to the French capital for nearly fifty years.[35] The emperor announced his intentions by a letter in the summer of 1377, in which he mentioned a desire to go on pilgrimage to several shrines and a wish to speak to the king. Politically, the emperor's main concern was affairs in Italy, where Pope Gregory XI had just returned to Rome, ending the papal exile in Avignon which had lasted since 1309. There was also the issue of the succession to the throne in Hungary and Poland. In both countries there was no male heir, and the kings were both foreign, members of the ubiquitous house of Anjou. Karl IV was to be accompanied by his chief counsellors and officials to discuss these matters.

*Karl IV's motives for visiting Paris*

In the event, Karl IV seems to have been motivated first and foremost by piety, wishing to see the relics in Paris. One of the reasons he gave for his journey was to add new relics to his own treasury. The tone of the visit was foreshadowed at the outset, when a religious problem arose. The emperor reached Cambrai on the borders of the Empire shortly before Christmas, and announced that he wanted to enter France and celebrate the church services in full imperial state. This would have been seen as an infringement of French sovereignty

> since the emperor was used to reading the seventh lection of the matins in ceremonial vestments and the insignia of his magnificence. He was warned in advance by the king's people that he could not do so in France and that it would not even be allowed. He then agreed in good will to remain in Cambrai to perform his service...[36]

When Karl IV reached Compiègne on 31 December, he was suffering from gout and his ill-health was a continuing problem throughout the visit. The king, who also suffered from ill-health, heard of this and sent one of his personal carriages and a litter so that the emperor could travel in greater comfort. When the emperor reached Saint-Denis, the great royal abbey just outside Paris, he had to be carried into the church on a litter so that he could pray there. Later in the day he asked to be taken to the treasury to see the relics; he was carried there in a chair, 'and stayed there for a long while, finding great pleasure in it'.

There is an eye-witness narrative of the next twelve days in the official French chronicle, written at Saint-Denis. It is the first detailed portrayal of a medieval state occasion that we have. In the manuscript of the chronicle the text runs to twenty-six double-column pages with superb miniatures. There are detailed descriptions of the activities of each day, its ceremonials, the gifts exchanged, and the feasts which were held. The emperor was evidently seriously unwell for much of the time, and this restricted the entertainments somewhat. He had to be carried everywhere in a litter, though he insisted on riding a mile or two into Paris on the splendid warhorse which his nephew had presented to him. The courtiers were present throughout, in varying numbers, and court rituals for the feasts and processions were carefully observed. Other protocols came into play as well. The king carefully chose for the emperor and his son, Wenceslas, king of the Romans, two black horses, 'because according to imperial custom, the emperors made their entry into the cities in their domains on a white horse. The king did not want that to happen also in his kingdom, so he ensured that no sign of the emperor's dominion could be seen.'

*Constraints on the visit*

On Monday 4 January, the emperor made his formal entry into Paris. The large numbers of the royal escort and of the emperor's people meant that special measures had to be taken to control the crowds. Sergeants had cleared the Grande Rue of people and carts, and guarded it to prevent any access. They acted as escorts to the procession, and the king's bodyguard, armed with staves, offered additional protection. Only forty or so horsemen accompanied the royal party into the Palais de la Cité. The emperor was given a room overlooking the gardens on one side, and the Sainte-Chapelle. Here he rested, as he had a fever as well as being tired from the journey. The king dined in his chamber in the emperor's absence. The following day, the king did not visit the emperor, who received a delegation from the city of Paris in his room, until the emperor sent for him and asked for a private conversation. Only the Chancellor of France was present, and they talked for three hours. This was the first of a series of such conversations. On the Tuesday evening, the great feast that had been planned was held without the emperor.

*Karl's entry into Paris*

**71**, p.195

On the Wednesday morning, the emperor only reappeared to hear mass at the Sainte-Chapelle and to see the relics there with a guard in place to prevent visitors. There had been crowds in the palace the previous day, contrary to the king's instructions to limit access. Karl IV's devotion to relics was such that he wanted to see the great reliquary with the crown of thorns at close quarters. His chair could not be taken up the narrow staircase, and he had to be manhandled, in considerable pain, up and down the stairs. He prayed before the reliquary for a long time, and then had himself lifted in order to kiss the relics. He was well enough to attend the great feast prepared in his honour at lunchtime. The only concession was that the meal was reduced from four courses, amounting to forty pairs of dishes, to three courses and thirty pairs of dishes. There were two interludes enacting the siege of Jerusalem in 1099. The day ended with the king and emperor dining in their chambers, and holding a private conversation afterwards.

*Karl at the Sainte-Chapelle*

The next part of the visit was across the river, at the king's newly built palace of the Louvre, which had until his reign been a medieval fortress. It now had spacious apartments as well as the king's study and his library. A specially equipped boat had been prepared for the emperor, with rooms containing beds and even a fireplace. It was at the Louvre that the emperor received a delegation from the University of Paris, replying to their speech in Latin. At the same time, the king held a meeting of his council, and something of the agenda behind his long talks with the emperor emerged. Charles V was anxious to secure the support of the emperor in the continuing struggle between England and France, particularly since Edward III had died the previous summer, and the council approved his approach. The following day, a great assembly was held in the hall in the Louvre, with all the imperial dignitaries and the royal council, at which Charles V set out his case. The emperor assured him that he would support him against the English, 'who ask for and want to have peace when they are at a disadvantage; however, as soon as they are at an advantage, they do not maintain the peace at all'. On the Saturday, the emperor reconvened the meeting to say

*Karl at the Louvre*

that he had not expressed himself strongly enough, and would ensure that his son Wencelas, king of the Romans, and his allies all offered the same support.

The remaining days were spent at royal castles around Paris, firstly up river at the queen's residence, the hôtel Saint-Pol, where he met members of the royal family, including the queen's mother Isabella. Karl IV had been married to Isabella's sister, and they reminisced, with tears in their eyes, about those they had lost. They met again in private after lunch, and the queen and her sons also came to see him. The day ended by torchlight at Charles V's favourite residence, Vincennes, both fortified palace and castle. Here, on the following day, the emperor reinforced his commitment to supporting the French king by making his son Wenceslas swear that he would honour and serve Charles V as long as he lived. In return, the emperor named the dauphin Charles imperial vicar-general for the kingdom of Arles, on the border between France and Germany. On Tuesday 12 January the emperor went on pilgrimage again to Saint-Maur and thence to the château of Beauté, a manor house within the enclave of Vincennes, where his attack of gout and fever seems to have run its course, as he was able to walk round the whole of it with only slight assistance. He stayed until the following Saturday; the king was at Vincennes, but came to Beauté every afternoon to talk with him. These discussions seem to have centred on the problems of the succession to Hungary and Poland. Before Karl IV left, he was presented with 'great and honourable gifts' which the chronicler does not list because they have been recorded on a roll of parchment, 'completely and individually described'. When king and emperor parted, they both 'wept so much that people noticed it', all too aware that they were unlikely to meet again.

*Political negotiations and departure*

## Charles the Bold and Friedrich III, Trier 1473

A CENTURY LATER, AT THE HEIGHT OF the power of the duchy of Burgundy, there was another spectacular encounter between a Holy Roman Emperor and his French neighbours. Burgundy was under the leadership of Charles the Bold, a man for whom the word magnificence might have been coined, hailed by some as the new Alexander the Great. The rich lands that he ruled lay partly in France and partly in the Empire; he was the great-grandson of Philip of Valois, who had acquired Flanders in 1369 by marrying the countess Margaret. His court was the apogee of Burgundian splendour, as John Paston, sent on an embassy there in 1468, discovered. His awed description to his mother is typical of the response of visitors:

> As for the duke's court, I never heard of one like it for lords, ladies and gentlewomen, knights, squires and gentlemen, except for King Arthur's court. Indeed, I have not the wit or memory to write to you of half the noble events here...[37]

It was particularly the throng of nobility accompanying the duke that impressed him. This was part of a deliberate policy on Charles's part, which he deployed to good effect on diplomatic occasions.

The Burgundian dukes were as rich and powerful as most of the monarchs of western Europe, and the idea that they should become kings had been among their more hopeful ambitions. Charles's father, Philip the Good, had toyed with the idea in 1447, when Friedrich III's envoys suggested that his duchy of Brabant might become a kingdom within the Holy Roman Empire. Philip was not happy with this, he wanted to be an ally of the German ruler but independent of him. The scheme was briefly revived in 1459, and again abandoned.[38]

*From duchy to kingdom*

Charles had a different and more ambitious scheme. He had only one child, Mary, and a marriage between her and Maximilian, the emperor's eldest son, was the bait he offered the emperor, in return for making him king of the Romans. He would then become emperor on Friedrich's death, and Maximilian would become king of the Romans and succeed both to the imperial title and to the Burgundian lands. Duke and emperor met at Trier on 30 September 1473, Friedrich having made plain his objection to handing the empire to Charles, even if his son would in due course succeed him. Charles set out to dazzle the emperor, and indeed the whole of Europe. He arrived with a retinue of over one thousand, in the most luxurious livery: we have the exact account, and the total cost was £38,830.[39] Seven days after his arrival, he gave a feast on an equally lavish scale, which even in an age of extravagant entertainment, made a huge impression on those who took part in it. It was written up by an anonymous eye-witness, and manuscript copies circulated under the title *A Small Book on the Magnificence of Burgundy*.[40] It made such an impression that it was translated from Latin into German and Dutch.

On 7 October the duke of Burgundy invited his imperial majesty and all his great lords and princes to come and dine with him. The abbey church of St Maximin and the great hall, where they were going to eat, were made ready and decorated with cloths and tapestries at indescribable cost. And so the Emperor came with all his lords and princes in great pomp and magnificence to St Maximin's with some fine good fellows preceding him, well-skilled and armed according to knightly custom and exercises. The Emperor was dressed in an extremely costly cloth of gold robe, with a very fine and precious cross on his breast. The duke went out to the abbey gates to meet him wearing an exceptionally fine tabard of cloth of gold and silver. He also wore many fine precious stones that stood out and twinkled like stars, valued at 100,000 ducats. His tabard was open on either side to show off the beauty and richness of his hose, on which he was wearing the [Garter of the] Order of King Edward of England.

After this they went into the church to hear mass. There stood all the lords of the [two] princes, each in his correct place, dressed in new clothes. The knights wore red, black and sanguine velvet, but the principal lords of the chamber were dressed in blue robes of cloth of gold. The lords of the Order of the Golden Fleece wore costly sanguine. There were eight of the princes' heralds and six Kings-of-Arms clothed in damask down to their feet. Accompanied by all these lords, the duke led the Emperor into the church with wonderful pomp and splendour. One side of the church was hung with rich gold and silver tapestries embroidered with the Passion of our Lord Christ Jesus; the other with the story of how Jason got the Golden Fleece in the land of Colchis.

When mass was over the duke led his imperial majesty by the hand into the hall where they were going to eat, which had been so superbly and expensively adorned and prepared that it seemed like King Ahasuerus' splendid feast. This room was hung with rich cloth of gold tapestries with the history of Gideon the regent of Israel and many precious and costly stones were sewn into them, which stood out and twinkled like stars.

At one end of the hall stood a treasury,* ten stages high, on which stood firstly, thirty-three gold and silver vessels of many kinds. Item, seventy jugs, large and small. Item, a hundred dishes and cups decorated with pearls and precious stones. Item, six large silver ladles and twelve gold and silver basins for washing hands. Item, six unicorns' horns, two of which were the length of an arm. Item, six silver jugs, each of twelve quarts. Item, a large silver basket, to hold the reliquaries on the princes' table.

* A buffet – see p. 245 below.

**71.** The feast given by Charles the Bold for the emperor Friedrich III in 1473. The illustration is in the much cruder style of German manuscripts of the period, and conveys little of the magnificence which Charles was trying to present.

**72.** Al fresco dining from Gaston Phébus, *Livre de chasse*, in the style which Alfonso V might have used when he entertained Friedrich III at Naples in 1452.

There were three tables, and everything on them, by way of jugs, cups, dishes and related things, was of gold and of silver. His imperial majesty sat in the middle of the first table and, on his right, the archbishop of Mainz, the archbishop of Trier, the bishop of Liège and the bishop of Utrecht. On the other side sat the high-born prince Duke Charles of Burgundy, Maximilian, archduke of Austria, the Emperor's son, Duke Stephen of Bavaria, Duke Albert of Bavaria-Munich and Duke Ludwig of Bavaria ...

In the first place thirteen dishes were presented and served, ushered in by sixteen trumpeters and twelve princes dressed in cloth of gold ... Besides these twelve princes were another hundred princes, lords, knights and noblemen, all clad in cloth of gold and silver, each according to his rank. Next time twelve dishes were brought, and the third time ten.

When the meal was over thirty bowls, cups and dishes of gold and silver were brought, decorated with precious pearls and costly stones, containing all kinds of confections and spices. One of them, standing before the Emperor, was valued at 60,000 gulden. After grace had been said all these lords went again into the church to hear vespers; after which the prince with all the lords accompanied the Emperor back to his palace by torchlight with much splendour and festivity.

*Failure of Charles's plan*

Charles had assembled all the great nobles of his territories to serve the emperor, and was using the sheer numbers of such 'princes', as the chronicler calls them, to impress on Friedrich III that he was worthy of the status of a king, and indeed of a future emperor. The household of the Burgundian dukes was famous for its scale, and travellers reported with amazement on the numbers of people who lived at the court as retainers of the duke. The negotiations dragged on throughout October, and Charles realised that he could not obtain his first objective, the succession to the empire. So on 23 October he lowered his sights, and demanded merely important concessions from the emperor. This was in public. In private, the scheme offered to Philip the Good in 1447 was revived, with the difference that surviving documents dated early November show that the emperor was preparing to 'restore and create the kingdom of Burgundy' – which had not existed under that name since the tenth century.[41] Preparations were made for the emperor to crown Charles at Trier itself before the end of November, but either the emperor changed his mind or the negotiations broke down. Friedrich III announced on 24 November that he was leaving immediately, and boarded his galley on the Moselle at dawn. One of Charles's councillors tried to delay him until the duke could take his leave of him; the emperor waited for half an hour for him to appear, and then ordered his rowers to start.[42] According to the chronicler Philippe de Commynes, this diplomatic insult, 'to the great shame and humiliation of the duke' caused a deep rift between the two countries. 'The Germans were offended by the pompous and ceremonious language of the duke, which they took for pride; the Burgundians were offended by the Emperor's entourage and poor clothes.'[43] Nonetheless, the majesty of Empire had trumped ducal magnificence.

IV. Frieze of Alfonso V's triumph in 1443, above the entrance to Castelnuovo in Naples.

# Towards the Renaissance: Naples

ALFONSO V OF ARAGON AND NAPLES WAS responsible for two remarkable entries in the mid fifteenth century which draw on the medieval tradition, but which, in their use of themes from the triumphs of the Caesars, point the way forward to the entries of the Renaissance. The first of these was in February 1443, to celebrate his capture of Naples itself the previous June. Here all the panoply of the princely and imperial entries of the preceding centuries was combined with a procession in the antique classical style.

The opening moment was theatrical in the extreme: Alfonso rode into the city through a breach which had been made in the walls for the occasion, alone. Inside, a triumphal car awaited him, drawn by four white horses with golden bridles, on which there was a gold and purple throne, and the king's chosen device, the Siege Perilous of the romances of the Holy Grail. This was the seat at Arthur's round table at which only the hero who would achieve the Grail quest could sit without being consumed by heavenly fire. The procession which followed was closely modelled on that accorded to a victorious general returning to Rome. The chariot drawn by four white horses was a reference to that of the sun god Apollo. The king was bare-headed under a canopy borne by eight men, which cost 1,400 ducats and was of gold brocade. At his feet were six crowns on a large cushion, representing the kingdoms over which he ruled.

*Alfonso V's victorious entry into Naples, 1443*

He was greeted by two allegorical scenes presented by merchants from Florence and Catalonia; the first offered a vision of a world-changing Caesar, and hailed him as king of peace, bringer of prosperity. The Catalans' tableau was a tower with the Siege Perilous on it, surrounded by virtues – clemency, constancy, magnanimity and liberality – and inscribed with the motto 'The Lord is my helper and I shall look in triumph on my enemies'. A mock fight between knights and Turks followed, and when it ended the actor playing one of the virtues proclaimed that the king had achieved the adventure of the Siege Perilous by his conquest of the city.

When the play-acting was finished, the procession formed up. We can see the procession in the memorial of the occasion commissioned by Alfonso, an intensely classical frieze carved on the Castelnuovo gate. Trumpeters preceded the king's chariot, and his officials followed, with ambassadors from foreign princes, and then Alfonso's son, Ferrante, the newly-created duke of Calabria. At the cathedral, Alfonso stopped to pray and then mounted his chariot once more and went to Castelcapuano, which had been the palace of René d'Anjou, the defeated Angevin claimant to the throne. There the procession ended. Not since the days of Friedrich II had an entry with such emphatic echoes of ancient Rome been seen in Italy. It was celebrated by chroniclers, poets and artists, all eager to praise such magnificence.[44] There are a number of paintings and a medal by Pisanello all created within thirty years of the event, at a time when works of art representing recent events are rare, which underline the extraordinary impact of Alfonso's echo of past glories.

The second of Alfonso's ritual entries was, admittedly, a more personal visit. Nonetheless, it elicited the kind of awed response which was to become familiar at the courts of Renaissance princes, and was treated by Alfonso as an excuse to demonstrate his magnificence.[45] The wedding of the emperor Friedrich III to Alfonso V's niece Eleanor took place in Rome at the time of his coronation there in March 1452. At the beginning of April the bridal pair came to Naples to visit Alfonso. When the royal party entered the city and processed through the streets, they were accompanied by trumpeters and the great nobles of Alfonso's court. Tableaux of the various guilds and corporations were on display, but equally impressive was a different kind of display, not encountered elsewhere. The shops set out their finest wares, to show the riches that Naples had to offer, and bankers heaped gold and silver coins outside their premises. Towards nightfall, torches were lit as the king and his guests made their way to their lodgings. The following day a banquet, repeated during the visit, was set out in the great hall at Castelnuovo. The buffet on which the royal gold and silver plate was set out was so high that spiral staircases were built on either side for the butlers to access it. Another towering structure was at the end of the hall, three storeys high, for the musicians so beloved of Alfonso V – wind, brass and strings who played during the banquet and for the dancing afterwards. Prodigious waste was also a feature: the Germans in Friedrich's retinue fed their horses on surplus sweetmeats, and the Portuguese ambassador said that as much food was wasted as was eaten.

*Alfonso V welcomes Friedrich III to Naples, 1452*

Next day, Alfonso invited the emperor's retinue to take anything they wanted from the shops in Naples at his expense, though Friedrich ordered them to limit themselves to just one item. The royal cavalry paraded through the streets, the Captain General at the head of four hundred superb horses ridden by the king's guard, each in gold surcoats over armour and carrying a pennant of the royal arms, with a page at their side. Four hundred more horses of equal splendour followed, ridden by young men in plumed helmets with a lance, perhaps a nod to the new fashion for classical dress. The king and his guests were stationed on a dais in front of the Incoronata chapel near the Castelnuovo, where they reviewed the next and somewhat surprising parade.

*An exotic parade*

The royal menagerie, led in chains by their keepers, now appeared. Behind them were drums and trumpets, and then two groups of exotic warriors. The first were mounted on light Arab horses with Moorish harnesses, and dressed in rich Moorish clothing. Behind them came a group dressed as Balkan light cavalry, on horses bred from the Spanish stallions at the royal stud. When the procession came to a halt with the royal standard before the dais, four gigantic Catherine wheels organised by merchants from Florence and other fireworks were set off. These lit up the allegorical figures and heraldry on the huge arches on which the Catherine wheels were mounted for an hour or more:

one onlooker said that 'it seemed like hell, and it took twenty hours for the smoke to clear'.

The traditional three days of jousting ensued, and at the end of the week Easter intervened. After this pause, Friedrich III was presented with further magnificence, beginning with a tour of the city and its shipyards, including the arsenal with its great storehouses and the reserve galleys held on dry land. Thirty galleys lay at anchor, and a resounding salute was fired from their guns. The massive lighthouse, visible from thirty miles and fuelled for twenty hours' continuous burning, and the spacious quayside were next, and another salute from the guns marked the end of the sightseeing. The grand finale was a hunt on an almost unimaginable scale. A hundred falconers were employed on the first day, and the royal party watched the hawking from a building specially reconstructed for the purpose, which overlooked the plain behind Naples. On the second day the hunters rode across the foothills of Vesuvius, where Alfonso explained to the northerners the wonders of the extraordinary landscape in which they found themselves. When they arrived at the royal park at Astroni, an *al fresco* banquet lasted for three hours before the hunt took place on the plain below. It culminated with the killing of a massive boar by the king's son Ferdinando and Friedrich himself. 'The authors who were present at this time wrote that no tongue, not even that of the most eloquent and famous orator could worthily describe the many ways in which the magnanimity of Alfonso was demonstrated on that celebrated occasion.'

*Military power and a spectacular hunt*

# 11 | MAGNIFICENT CEREMONIES AND FESTIVALS

*◆ The Feast of the Pheasant: taking the crusader vow ◆ The stages of a prince's life ◆ Knighting ◆ Three royal knighting ceremonies ◆ Coronation feasts ◆ Wedding feasts ◆ Seasonal festivals ◆ New Year ◆ Maying ◆ Tournaments*

## The Feast of the Pheasant: Taking the Crusader Vow

THE MOST MAGNIFICENT AND ECCENTRIC festival of the medieval period was, as might be expected, held by one of the dukes of Burgundy. The reason for it was highly unusual. The Feast of the Pheasant was to do with a planned crusade. Philip the Good had determined to lead an army against the infidel from the time in 1451 when he first heard of the threat posed to Constantinople, the beleaguered capital of the remnants of the Byzantine empire, by Sultan Mohammed II. Internal politics, and notably the open revolt of Ghent, one of the most important towns in his duchy of Flanders, had prevented him from acting. In the late summer of 1453 the city fell to Mohammed. It was only at the end of the year that the political situation was stable enough to allow him to revive his plans. What he had in mind, like crusading princes for the past four hundred years, was a great alliance of western rulers which would raise a crusading army. Its objective would be to retake Constantinople as a first step towards Jerusalem.

Philip chose to hold a great banquet to mark the formal start of the recruitment process on 17 February 1454. At the centre of the feast, a ceremony was planned in which he would take the crusading vow. His lords and knights were expected to follow his example. His major domo, Olivier de la Marche, described the proceedings at great length in an official record of the banquet. A rather shorter and livelier account is given in a letter from one of the duke's minor officials to a friend:

> Last Sunday my lord the duke gave a banquet in the hôtel de la Salle in this town [Lille] ... The dishes were such that they had to be served with trolleys, and seemed infinite in number. There were so many side-dishes, and they were so curious, that it's difficult to describe them. There was even a chapel on the table, with a choir in it, a pasty full of flute-players, and a turret from which came the sound of an organ and other music. The figure of a girl, quite naked, stood against a pillar. Hippocras sprayed from her right breast and she was guarded by a live lion who sat near her on a round table in front of my lord the duke. The story of Jason was represented on a raised stage by actors who did not speak. My lord the duke was served at table by a two-headed horse ridden by two men sitting back to back, each holding a trumpet and sounding it as loud as he could, and then by a monster, consisting of a man riding on an elephant, with another man, whose feet were hidden, on his shoulders. Next came a white stag ridden by a boy who sang marvellously, while the stag accompanied him with the tenor part. Next came an elephant ... carrying a castle, in which sat Holy Church, who made piteous complaint on behalf of the Christians persecuted by the Turks, and begged for help. Then, two

knights of the Order of the Golden Fleece brought in two damsels, together with a pheasant, which had a gold collar round its neck decorated with rubies and fine large pearls. These ladies asked my lord the duke to make his vow, which he handed in writing to Golden Fleece King-of-Arms to read out ... Holy Church was overjoyed, and invited the other princes and knights to vow ... And it was announced that everyone who had sworn, or who wanted to swear, should hand in their vows in writing to Golden Fleece ...

All this I saw. I took the trouble to stay till nearly 4 a.m., and I believe that nothing so sublime and splendid has ever been done before. The knights wore robes of damask, half grey, half black; the squires wore satin in the same colours... My lord the duke had so many diamonds, rubies and fine large pearls in his hat that there was no room for any more, and he was wearing a very fine necklace. It was said that his jewels were worth 100,000 nobles, more or less.[1]

The writer gives a wonderful impression of the impact of the festival and its images on the bystanders. A slightly different view comes from Olivier de la Marche, who probably organised it. He reveals that there were three tables only in the hall and a mere handful of diners. There was a space set aside for those who wished to see the ceremony, and it was quickly filled by men and women, most of them in disguise, perhaps because they did not wish to be identified as not having been invited as guests. The onlookers included knights and ladies of noble birth, among them the writer of the letter we have just quoted. Some had come long distances by sea and by land because the duke's widespread announcement of the event had aroused such interest.

*Spectators at the feast*

Each table had different *entremets*. The duke's table had the chapel and the girl mentioned in the letter, followed by an extremely realistic ship complete with crew and complicated rigging and a fountain in glass and lead, with glass trees and flowers, and a meadow with rocks formed of sapphires and other rare jewels: the mechanism of the fountain was completely hidden. The second table had nine *entremets*, beginning with a pie in which twenty-eight musicians played in turn. The other eight all appear to have been models of figures, landscapes or buildings. Three similar scenes were on the third table, described as follows:

Entremets *of every kind*

There was a sort of forest in India, in which various strange beasts were to be seen, which moved of their own accord. The second *entremets* was a moving lion attached to a tree, in the middle of a meadow, and there was the figure of a man who beat the dog in front of the lion. The third and last ... was a merchant who passed through a village, with a tray round his neck full of all sorts of knicknacks.[2]

These were the sophisticated automata, provided by Colard le Voleur, the master of the automata at Hesdin.[3] In addition to these mechanical amusements, there were 'living *entremets*'. These formed a kind of continuous narrative throughout the proceedings, beginning with a horse which entered the hall backwards with two trumpeters mounted on it back to back. This and all the following *entremets* were accompanied by sixteen knights in the duke's black and grey livery. The second was a goblin in the form of a man with a gryphon's lower body and feet: an acrobat had his feet on its head and his hands on its shoulders. The goblin rode on a boar, and both were covered in rich green silk. As he moved round the hall, the musicians in the pie played a strange tune on a German cornet.

Several of the *entremets* referred to the Greek legend behind the duke's Order of the Golden Fleece. The Golden Fleece was the treasure seized by Jason and the Argonauts.

One of Jason's adventures was to overcome fire-breathing bulls and this was acted in dumb show. Two more episodes from the history of Jason followed, separated by the appearance of a fiery dragon which flew high up through the hall and vanished, and then by a heron which rose from one end of the hall and was killed by two hawks; it was dressed according to the rules of hunting, and presented to the duke.

*The entry of Holy Church*

The climax of the feast, and the point at which the crusading agenda was revealed, was the entry of Holy Church. A huge giant appeared with a halberd in one hand, leading an elephant with the other. On the elephant was a castle, in which sat a lady dressed in religious clothing, like a nun or anchorite. A modern historian claims that this was Olivier de la Marche in disguise.[4] They approached the duke's table, where La Marche sang a complaint in a high falsetto voice identifying the character he was playing as 'Holy Church, your mother', and described her journey to the emperor and to the king of France in search of help against the enemy who had chased her out of the Holy Land. She addressed an eloquent plea to the duke in person, and a motet entitled 'The Lamentation of the Holy Mother of the Church of Constantinople', set by Gilles Binchois, one of the greatest composers of the age, was sung. Meanwhile, the pheasant, after which the feast was named, was brought in by two knights of the Order of the Golden Fleece.

*The crusading vow*

At this point, Philip, swearing by the Virgin, and the ladies present, and the 'noble bird' before him, took a vow to go on crusade against the 'Great Turk'. His son Charles and other nobles took the oath, and other knights were invited to hand in their vows in writing the next day. All these pledges were recorded in the official account of the banquet. But the banquet was not yet at an end. Once the vows had been taken, a lady in religious habit with 'God's Grace' embroidered on her shoulder in gold letters, appeared, accompanied by torchbearers and musicians, and she was followed by others representing the twelve virtues. 'God's Grace' declared that they had been sent from heaven as a sign of divine approval of Philip's vows. With this the 'ceremonies and mysteries' ended, and the courtiers – probably with some relief – turned to the traditional end of a feast, the dancing, which lasted until almost three o'clock.

Philip's public declaration of his crusading intentions had been made in high style. Two years later, a detailed plan of action, entitled 'Advice concerning what is necessary for my lord the duke's crusade' was drawn up, but the second sentence admits that the 'duke does not know when he will set out'.[5] Over the following decade he made serious attempts to assemble an alliance of the rulers of Christendom to undertake such a crusade. In the end, the reluctance of both the emperor and Charles VII of France to have anything to do with it eventually led to the abandonment of the idea: Philip's illegitimate son Anthony, who rejoiced in the title of Grand Bastard of Burgundy, attempted to fulfil his father's ambitions in 1464. The death of Pope Pius II, whose ardent enthusiasm had kept the idea alive, while the crusaders waited to embark at Marseilles, brought the great design initiated at the Feast of the Pheasant to an end.

# The Stages of a Prince's Life

CRUSADING VOWS WERE RARE OCCASIONS, and were usually made in religious surroundings. Other great ceremonies marked the stages of the prince's life. Traditional moments for festivities were co-opted in the cause of magnificent display. Likewise, the chivalric rite of knighting, originally purely secular, was first adopted by the Church, and then became a festive occasion from the twelfth century onwards. And the coronation of a king, the moment when he could first appear in the magnificent style required of him, was also established as an occasion for secular ceremony and feasting at about the same time.

## Knighting

KNIGHTING WAS OFTEN THE FIRST PUBLIC ceremony at which a prince appeared, and was often regarded as a requirement before a king was crowned. Although almost all nobles were knighted with some celebration, the knighting of the heir to the throne was sufficiently special for the king to be able to levy a special tax for the occasion.

The knighting of Henry II's father, Geoffrey of Anjou, at Rouen in 1128 is said to have been accompanied by a feast and jousting. But Jean of Marmoutier, the chronicler who tells us this, was writing in the 1180s, and is likely to reflect what was happening in the late twelfth century. A page of his chronicle is devoted to the ceremony, in a wonderful attempt at a high-flown rhetorical style. Jean begins by describing the ritual bath which preceded the actual knighting. He depicts the rich dress of the newly knighted count, followed by his first appearance armed and mounted:

*A twelfth century knighting ceremony*

> They brought for the heir of Anjou a Spanish horse, wonderfully caparisoned, which was, they said, so swift that many birds in flight were slower. They put on him an incomparable mail-shirt, woven with double rings, so that no lance or javelin could pierce it; his foot armour was also made of double rings, and golden spurs were put on his feet; his shield, with the images of golden lions, was hung around his neck; and on his head was placed a helm shining with many precious stones, so well-tempered that no sword could cut into it or dent it; he was given an ash spear, with an iron point from Poitou, and finally he was girded with a sword from the king's treasury, placed there long ago, to the fabrication of which Weland, the most superlative of smiths, had devoted much labour and care.[6]

Alas, the effort of composing this seems to have exhausted Jean's inspiration, and all he manages to add is that the celebrations lasted for seven days after the knighting.

Curiously, the first account of a festival associated with knighting comes from outside western Europe, from the Frankish kingdom of Cyprus in 1223. The Frankish conquerors of Cyprus and of the kingdom of Jerusalem had brought western feudalism to both countries, and with it the whole paraphernalia of knighthood and chivalry. This is what a local chronicler has to say:

> It happened that the lord of Beirut made his two elder sons knights, in Cyprus; one was sir Balian, who was later constable of Cyprus and lord of Beirut; the other was sir Baldwin, who was steward of Cyprus. And this knighting was the greatest festival and the longest that was held beyond the seas of which anyone knows; much was given and spent, and there was much holding of mock-tournaments

and imitation of the adventures of Britain [i.e. king Arthur] and the Round Table and many kinds of games.[7]

Knighting often took place in conjunction with another event. In 1254 Albert I of Brunswick was knighted in connection with a marriage, and at once 'made many counts and squires knights, beyond measure'; the feast is said to have lasted for a week.[8] The scale of such an occasion can be judged from the expenditure at the triple knighting of the sons of Meinhard II of Görz-Tyrol at St Veit in Carinthia in 1299, following the defeat of their rivals, when they held a tournament attended by five hundred knights. Once knighted, they created new knights in turn in the traditional fashion, and 'distributed gifts, showing the glory of their wealth and their goodwill towards the nobles of the land', making their enemies blush to emulate them and their loyal friends more loyal. 'They incurred expenses beyond all measure, buying purple cloths and silks as well as clothing of different colours from the Venetians on credit, who have not been paid to this day', causing problems for the Carinthian nobles and citizens in trying to do business with Venice.[9] The surviving acccounts of the dukes of Tyrol confirm this, showing luxuries brought from Venice, and also from Florence: the latter included furs, spices and linen for forty-eight table-cloths.

*The development of knighting festivals*

THE REQUIREMENT THAT A KING should be a knight before his coronation could present problems. When Alfonso IV of Aragon was crowned in 1328, the church service was immediately preceded by Alfonso dubbing himself knight, on the principle that he could only be knighted by someone of equal or higher rank. The previous evening, he and the knights who were to be dubbed by himself and his two sons went in procession to the church of San Salvador:

*Knighting at a coronation*

> First of all came, on horseback, all the sons of knights who were carrying the swords of the noble knights, and then came the swords of the nobles who were to be new knights; and after the swords of the said nobles came the sword of the Lord King ... and after the sword of the Lord King came two carriages of the Lord King with two wax tapers; in each wax taper there were over ten quintals of wax. They were lighted, though they were hardly wanted, for the other lights were so numerous that one could see as well as if it were bright daylight. And behind the two wax candles, came the Lord King, riding on his horse, with the most beautiful harness ever made by the hands of masters, and the sword was carried before him ... the richest and most beautifully ornamented that Emperor or King ever carried; and behind the said Lord King came his arms, which a noble was carrying ...[10]

The king and the knights kept vigil that night, and at the opening of the service in the cathedral the next day, the king put on clerical vestments of the utmost opulence, 'as if he were going to say mass', and placed the sword and his crown on the altar. During the mass, the king had his spurs put on by his sons, and then took the sword from the altar, prayed, kissed the cross of the sword, and girded it on himself. He then drew it from its scabbard three times, defying all the enemies of the Catholic faith, then undertaking to defend widows and orphans, and finally promising to maintain justice. Once mass had finished, he took the crown from the altar and crowned himself, and sat in state on the royal throne, where he dubbed the knights. It was a highly unusual ceremony, perhaps unique among both knightings and coronations in the combination of self-knighting and self-crowning.

## Three royal knighting ceremonies

THE KNIGHTING OF EDWARD II WHILE HE was still prince of Wales was the most remarkable ever seen in England.[11] Very often the knighting ceremony took place during warfare, as in the case of his son Edward III, and, while Edward I had military motives for creating a great event centred on the dubbing of his son, this was a rare peacetime knighting. In the spring of 1306 Edward was faced with the rebellion of Robert Bruce in Scotland. In February, Bruce had murdered his rival for the kingship, John Comyn, at the high altar of Greyfriars church in Dumfries. Edward needed urgently to raise an army, but was short of the knights who would lead it. Men preferred to pay a fine rather than take up the onerous military duties that knighthood might involve. However, there were many potential knights who might be lured into serving by the prospect of being knighted with due pomp and ceremony by the prince, immediately after he himself had been dubbed. In addition, the expenses of buying the equipment for war were normally at the new knight's expense. Instead, Edward added the incentive of offering to provide this at the expense of the royal exchequer.

*Knighting as a means of recruiting an army*

A month after the rebellion in Scotland had taken place, on 6 April 1306, Edward issued a letter to the sheriffs of the English counties. He announced that he intended to confer knighthood on the prince of Wales. He therefore ordered them to proclaim that anyone qualified to be a knight and who wished to be knighted should come to London before Whitsun 'to receive the necessary equipment from the king's wardrobe and at his gift, so that they might receive knighthood from him on the same day'.[12] The king's other motive, almost equally important, was to collect the traditional 'feudal aid' payable when his eldest son was knighted. But his main objective, as Elias Ashmole, Windsor Herald in 1672, said, was 'to adorn the splendour of his Court and augment the glory of his intended Expedition into Scotland'.[13]

*Edward I sends out a summons*

The sheriffs seem to have sought out the sons of men who would normally have taken up knighthood because their fathers held that rank, though a few were men who had made their own way in the world, such as John le Blound, mayor of London. The total number who responded was around three hundred; we have the names of 282 knights, but only partial lists survive.[14] This was a very satisfactory response, and the extensive preparations, which had been under way since the beginning of April, were justified. When the candidates for knighthood arrived in London, they were issued with purple cloth, fine linen, silk and cloaks woven with gold thread. Although the palace at Westminster was spacious, there was not enough room for such a throng. The gardens near the Templar headquarters (now the Temple) were levelled. The apple trees were cut down and walls demolished, so that the would-be knights could pitch their tents there. They dressed in cloth of gold, and it was at the Temple that they kept the traditional all-night vigil on the eve of knighthood. The prince of Wales and the most distinguished of the candidates, however, performed their vigils in Westminster Abbey. They expected to do so in some comfort, as the exchequer records show that beds were provided for them. Edward's clothing for the vigil, a blood-red velvet tunic with a red cape, is listed with the red velvet covers for a bed also for the vigil. But the trumpets and tubas and joyful shouting were such that the monks could hardly hear each other across the choir.

*A mass ceremony at London*

The next day the king girded his son with the sword of knighthood in the palace, and granted him the duchy of Aquitaine. The prince, now he had been made a knight, entered the abbey church to raise his fellows to the same status of military glory. There was such a crush of people around the high altar that two knights were crushed to death and others fainted even though at least three knights were escorting them for their safety. The prince had to mount the high altar, and perform the ceremony among the war-horses which his companions had brought into the church.

The feast which followed has gone down in history as the 'feast of the swans'. Two swans adorned with gold nets and gilded piping and covered by a piece of pure green silk were placed before the king. The king swore by God and the swans that, dead or alive, he would set out for Scotland and avenge the death of John Comyn, the treachery of the Scots and the harm done to the Church there. His son vowed likewise, adding that he would not sleep for two nights in the same place until he had helped his father to achieve this. The rest of the magnates took the same oath, declaring themselves ready to follow him while he lived, and after his death to set out for Scotland to fulfil it.

*The Feast of the Swans*

But why the swan, and why the vow? The prince's curious promise goes back to pagan vows in Celtic literature, and many Celtic stories were used as sources for the Arthurian romances. At the end of the twelfth century the poet Chrétien de Troyes used elements from these tales in his romance *Perceval*, about the hero of the original Grail quest. Among them is the idea of a vow at a feast. Perceval is at a feast when a hideous girl rides in and denounces him because he has failed to ask the question which will heal the mysterious Fisher King. In response, Perceval vows not to sleep for two nights in the same place until he has asked the question and obtained the answer. Fifty knights follow him in vowing that they will seek out any marvel that they can find. It is on this story that Prince Edward modelled his vow.

The most puzzling part of the ceremony is the swan on which the general vow was taken. However, most manuscripts of *Perceval* contain another episode which provides a convincing explanation for its presence. Arthur is at Caerleon when he is told that a boat has appeared, drawn by a swan, in which the body of a handsome knight lies, transfixed by a lance. A letter is in his purse, asking the king to avenge his death with the same lance that killed him. Since in 1306 Edward's vow was to carry out an almost exact copy of such a vengeance, it seems very likely that this lies behind the otherwise baffling ritual.[17]

SEVEN YEARS LATER, PHILIP THE FAIR of France knighted his three sons, also at Whitsun, a traditional time for royal knighting. The celebrations in 1313 were described by a chronicler who probably witnessed the event as unequalled in all French history, rivalling the biblical feast of Ahasuerus, which was the yardstick by which such occasions were measured.[18] As with the knighting of Prince Edward, we have a mass of documentation which enables us to reconstruct the details of the occasion. Even more remarkably, five illustrations of the event survive in a book completed – so the scribe claims – on the very day of the feast itself, and presented to Philip the Fair's wife Jeanne.

*The knighting of Philip IV's sons*

Edward II came to Paris for the occasion at Philip's special request.[19] His wife Isabella was Philip's daughter, and this was therefore a family affair, the knighting of her brothers. It was also the occasion when Philip and Edward took the cross, vowing to go on crusade; unusually, Isabella and Jeanne also took the crusading vow. The arrival of Edward and Isabella marked the beginning of the ceremonies. They encamped outside the walls of the city on 1 June and made their formal entry on the following day, when the citizens marched out to meet them and to escort them in.

The festivities were centred on the Palais de la Cité, where work on reconstruction had begun in 1298, and was still in progress. It was probably in the immense Grand' Salle that the feast on the evening of 2 June was held. The feast was followed by the vigil which preceded the knighting ceremony. For this vigil, the princes and almost two hundred other

73. (above) An encampment, showing fourteenth-century tents. From an Italian copy of the romance of *Meliadus*, c.1350.

74. Philip IV and his family, from a manuscript dated 1313. The picture is remarkable because it shows four kings (Philip and his three sons) and two queens (Jeanne of Navarre and Isabella, queen consort of England).

knights went across to Notre-Dame. After a night spent in prayer, the assembled company heard mass before the ritual of knighting. The upper miniature on the manuscript page shows Louis, Philip's eldest son, being girded with the sword by Edward II, while his father gives him the ritual slap, telling him that this was done so that he would remember the occasion.[20] This was followed by the same ritual for Philip's two younger sons, and then the mass knighting of the other candidates, shown in the middle miniature. Their departure for the banquet given by Philip is in the final picture: musicians head the procession, followed by the two kings and the rest of the company.

The next six days were occupied by feasting and entertainments. The feast given by Edward II, in tents at Saint-Germain-des-Prés, was a very public affair, and we have an eye-witness account of it. The tent flaps were opened, so that the guests were in full view, and the rich hangings of the interior were on display. The food was served by squires on horseback, and even though it was full daylight, torches were lit in a show of pure extravagance. A castle of love, built by the armourer of Prince Louis, was set up as the scenery for the entertainment at the feast. The traditional game played here was the defence of the castle by ladies, who pelted the besieging lovers with oranges.[21] Other feasts were given by Philip the Fair at his palace of the Louvre, and by Philip's brother and half-brother. But there was also more serious business afoot: on 6 June Philip, Edward and Louis and many of the French nobles and clergy took the crusading vow. A large open space was needed for this mass ceremony, so a bridge of boats was constructed to connect the Ile de la Cité with the Ile Notre-Dame upstream. Here, after sermons from the pope's commissioner for the crusade and other clergy, Philip, Edward II and many nobles, as well as a vast number of clerics and laymen, took the crusading oath. This was Philip's fulfilment of a vow made the previous year during a meeting with the pope at Vienne, in return for the pope's unwilling agreement that the Knights Templars should be suppressed. The nobles were followed by the ladies of the court the next day. Their vows specified that they would only set out if their husbands did so, and there were later complaints of coercion.

On Thursday 7 June, Edward II and Isabella overslept, missing a planned conference with Philip and the ladies' crusading ceremony. Isabella later took the vow, after obtaining special concessions from the cardinal, on the last day of the festive period, Saturday 9 June. That afternoon, however, they witnessed an extraordinary parade, said to be that of all the people of Paris. Certainly a crowd such as this had never been seen before. They gathered once more on the Ile Notre-Dame, and led by mounted trumpeters, crossed to the Ile de la Cité, where they paraded in front of the royal palace, watched by the two kings and Prince Louis. The procession probably included the men of the Great Watch of the city, clad in livery, and the guilds of Paris, likewise in their individual liveries, to the sound of drums and trumpets. Edward returned to his lodgings at Saint-Germain-des-Prés, and that evening, as he and Isabella returned from yet another feast, the royal couple watched the parade march past from a little tower: Edward declared his astonishment that 'so many wealthy and such noble persons could come forth from a single city'.[22]

Within all these feasts and parades, entertainments – which the chroniclers call 'many enchantments' – were presented. These were partly scenarios acted out by members of the court, though the chronicler does not expand on these. The French chronicler does, however, tell us at length of the tableaux which lined the streets of Paris in the style of a royal entry into the city. These were evidently designed to impress Edward II and the attendant nobles, as well as the chroniclers who reported it to the wider world.

Edward II made his way homeward from Poissy, just outside Paris, on 6 July. He had had to raise loans to keep pace with the expenditure of the French king. 'The magnificence

**75.** The coronation of Henry the young king, son of Henry II, from a manuscript of the life of Thomas Becket written fifty years later. Henry II is serving his son in the right hand panel.

**76.** The knighting of the sons of Philip IV in 1313. Left, one of the princes is knighted; below, men of lesser rank rejoice at their admission to knighthood. The bottom right picture shows a joyful procession after the ceremony. The figure in scarlet with three lions on his surcoat is Edward II, godfather to the eldest son of Philip.

of the *feste* of 1313 witnessed Philip's grandeur and authority ... It outshone the Feast of the Swans of 1306', write the editors of the detailed account of the occasion.[23] Edward struggled to repay his loans, but he did benefit in other ways, since during the weeks following the knighting, the two kings held lengthy diplomatic negotiations, and Philip was generous in his answers. Magnanimity was another aspect of magnificence.

*The knighting of the princes of Anjou*

WHEN CHARLES VI OF FRANCE knighted the young princes of Anjou on Sunday 2 May 1389 at the royal abbey of Saint-Denis north of Paris, the chronicler of the abbey was an eyewitness of the proceedings, which were on the grandest scale. He notes that knights from England and Germany were among those present.[24] When the princes rode up to the abbey on the evening before the knighting, they wore deliberately simple costumes, in an antique style: long flowing dark grey gowns trimmed with fur, without a trace of gold. Behind their saddles was a roll of cloth of the same kind, because, says the chronicler, this was the way that squires used to set out on a journey. They then changed into the costumes in which they were to be knighted, and went to observe their vigil after supper. Because they were so young – Louis, the elder, was only twelve – the princes' vigil was a token only, and they were sent to bed to rest for the next day's ceremony of knighting. On the Monday, a tournament began with a procession of twenty-two knights in gilded armour with green shields bearing the king's emblem who rode into the first court of the abbey. From there each knight was escorted by a lady also in green, her dress covered in gold and jewels, mounted on a palfrey. The ladies tied silk ribbons from their dresses on the knights' arms and the whole procession was accompanied by minstrels. The lists were outside the abbey walls: an enclosure with stands and barrier about 200 metres long had been specially built for the purpose. The jousters were some of the most distinguished knights in France. The king himself jousted, as did members of his family. Among the knights were Regnault de Roye, who had fought a famous chivalric duel in Portugal, and one of the squires was the future Jean the Fearless of Burgundy. The countess of St Pol, half-sister of Richard II of England, was escorted by the king.

The monk of St Denis, so enthusiastic in his descriptions of the ceremonies and the tournament, adds a disappointed postscript:

> The fourth night saw the end of the dances and the excesses which followed them.
> I would have abandoned the recital of these events ... if it had not been for the advice of many wise men, who told me not to pass over them in silence, as they would serve for an example for the future, for good or ill. I insist that posterity should avoid such disorder; for it must be said that the lords, in making day of night, gave themselves up to every kind of gluttony and were urged by drunkenness to such debauchery that, regardless of the king's presence, several of them stained the sanctity of the house of God and abandoned themselves to lasciviousness and adultery.[25]

It was not a new complaint, for preachers for two centuries had linked the aftermath of tournaments with the sins of the flesh: the real scandal was that it should happen in one of the holiest royal churches in France.

## Coronation feasts

CORONATIONS WERE IN THEMSELVES festivals, celebrating the inauguration of a new ruler. From the eighth century onwards, as kingship became an increasingly distinctive and powerful office, feasts were probably held on such occasions. Although the English coronation rites for the actual religious ceremony can be traced back to the time of King Edgar at the end of the century, the earliest clear mention of a feast is at the controversial coronation of Henry II's eldest son, Henry 'the young king', in 1170. We only know about this because the latter showed his true character, proud and quarrelsome, when his father served him at table after the ceremony. The archbishop of York commented that no other prince in the world had such a distinguished servant, whereupon the fifteen-year-old young king replied, 'Why are you astonished? Shouldn't my father do this? He is of lower rank than me, as son of a queen and a duke, while I come from royal blood on both sides!'[26]

*The coronation feast of Henry the young king*

We have a detailed description of the coronation of his brother Richard I in 1189, which lists all the clergy and magnates present, and describes the rites and the oaths sworn by the king in detail. Afterwards

> the king took off his crown and royal robes and put on a lighter crown and lighter clothes; and so he came to dinner crowned. And the archbishops and bishops and abbots and other clergy sat with him at his table, each in order according to his rank. The earls, barons and knights sat at other tables, and they feasted splendidly.[27]

The scale of the feast can be glimpsed from entries in the royal accounts, which show that at least 1,770 cups, 900 pitchers and 5,050 dishes had been bought for the occasion.[28]

IT IS ONLY WITH THE EMERGENCE of historians who come from an educated but secular background that we begin to hear of the details of the coronation feasts. Ramon Muntaner, a soldier by profession, who had fought with the powerful Catalan forces throughout the Mediterranean, turned chronicler at the end of his life, and produced a vivid and detailed account of his own times. Muntaner was an eyewitness at the coronation of Alfonso IV of Aragon at Saragossa in 1328, which sounds as if it was a moderately disorderly and very enthusiastic affair. When the nobles assembled for the festival

*Aragon: the coronation of Alfonso IV*

> they went to the Aljaferia, which is a palace of the Lord King, and no one rode by their side, but each noble, riding on a valuable horse, was placed at the head of the new knights he had made. He who would see good horses, handsome and well arrayed, here could he see them. And sons of knights carried before them on horseback, each the sword of his lord, or of his brother, or of his relation who was a new knight; and, behind, came the other sons of knights, carrying their arms on horseback, and so no one else dared ride with them; rather, each went thus with trumpets and kettledrums and flutes and cymbals and many other instruments. Indeed, I tell you that there were over three hundred pairs of trumpets; and there were other jongleurs, wild knights[29] and others, more than a thousand, so that the shouts and the noise were such than it seemed as if heaven and earth were crumbling.[30]

Muntaner also describes a very unusual musical performance by a prince. At the feast following the coronation on Easter Day, the Infante Pedro insisted on acting as major-domo and, with his brother Ramon Berenguer and twelve nobles, he approached the king to serve him:

> And the Lord Infante En Pedro, with two nobles – all three hand in hand and he in the middle – came first singing a new dance he had composed; and all those who were bringing the dishes responded. And when he came to the table of the Lord King he took the bowl and tasted the contents and set it before the said Lord King, and then set down the carving board. And when he had thus placed the first dish before the Lord King, and

had finished the dance, he took off the cloak and tunic of cloth of gold trimmed with ermine and many pearls which he was wearing and gave them to a jongleur, and at once, other very rich garments were ready for him, which he put on. and he kept the same order with all the dishes served; at each dish which he carried, he sang a new dance he, himself, had composed, and gave away the garments he was wearing, all very splendid.[31]

After the feast, the king held a solemn crown-wearing, in which the Infante Pedro also played a part:

[A] very rich and splendid seat was erected for the Lord King and for the Archbishops to sit in the same order in which they had sat at table. And the Lord King, with the crown on his head as he had sat at the table, and with the orb in his right hand and the sceptre in his left, rose from the table and came to sit on the aforementioned seat in the palace. And around him, at his feet, sat nobles and knights and we citizens. And when all were seated, En Romaset, the jongleur, sang in a loud voice a new song ... which the Lord Infante En Pedro had composed in honour of the said Lord King.[32]

This was followed by another composition of the prince's which he gave to the jongleur En Comi, 'because he sings better than any other Catalan', to sing; and finally another jongleur recited a long poem, also by the prince, on how the royal government should be managed.

Two years later, when Alfonso XI of Castile was to be crowned at Burgos,

*Castile: the coronation of Alfonso XI*

he put on his royal clothes embroidered in gold and silver with symbols of lions and castles, on which were mounted many large and small pearls, and many stones – rubies, sapphires and emeralds – among them. And he mounted a horse of great price, and the harness of this horse, on which he rode that day, was of high value; for the cantle and pommel of the saddle were covered with gold and silver on which there were many stones; and the saddlecloth and the girth and parts of the harness were of gold and silver thread, embroidered so subtly and so well that until then no saddle had been so well made in Castile.[33]

The procession from the archbishop's palace to the church was more orderly than that for the king of Aragon, and a large crowd of squires accompanied Alfonso. These were all to be knighted the following day, to mark the occasion. When the procession came into the cathedral, the king and queen took up seats on each side of the altar, on high daises, from which they came down when the crowns had been blessed during mass. Alfonso was anointed by the archbishop and taking up the crowns, first crowned himself and then the queen, following the Spanish tradition of self-coronation. The knighting ceremony which followed the next day was on a massive scale, and included members of many of the most noble families in Spain; it ended with a banquet at which the king declared that two things about this festival had greatly pleased him: that all the knights had kept a vigil in their armour the night before the coronation, and that they had all come to dine with him in his palace.

*England: the coronations of Edward II and Edward III*

FOR THE ENGLISH KINGS AFTER Richard I, the first coronation feast for which a description survives is that of Edward I, where there is a strange story about the great lords who came 'to do him honour and reverence as he sat at table'.[34] Alexander, king of Scotland, Edward's brother Edmund, and four earls all appeared in succession with a hundred knights. Each group in turn dismounted, presumably outside the hall, and let their horses loose. Anyone who caught one of the palfreys could keep it as his own. This may well be true, as the account of it was written down within living memory.[35] It could well reflect the spirit of Edward's court and its youthful lords.

The relations between Edward I and his lords were not always so cheerful, while for Edward II the first months of his reign and his coronation were marred by the extreme dislike of the English lords for the earl of Cornwall, Piers Gaveston, the son of a minor Gascon lord who had first entered Edward's household as a squire seven years earlier, and whose close friendship with the king and meteoric rise to fortune had aroused their hatred. Gaveston played a major part in the coronation ritual itself, alongside the earls who were the traditional attendants of the king, and at the coronation banquet appeared in a purple robe trimmed with exceedingly expensive pearls. The tapestries commissioned for the occasion were of the arms of Edward II and Gaveston, not those of the queen as might have been expected. It was an omen of a troubled future which was to lead to the violent deaths of both men. Yet the occasion itself was a magnificent one, including many of Queen Isabella's relatives, the future Holy Roman Emperor Heinrich VII and the count of Savoy, and seems to have passed off peaceably.

Matters were very different in 1327, when Edward III was crowned, just two months after his father had abdicated. Perhaps in order to emphasise the legitimacy of the succession and the absence of opposition, his coronation celebrations were exceptionally lavish. The clothes prepared for the king were of outstanding quality, and the account entries describe them in somewhat awestruck detail as to material and patterns. They nearly bankrupted the exchequer, already in a parlous state because of his father's mismanagement:

> The coronation feast that followed in Westminster Hall was an event of breathtaking scale and grandeur. The king's throne, adorned with samite cushions, was placed under a canopy of canvas cloth of gold, with a red and yellow silk valance. The surviving financial accounts indicate expenditure of well over £1,000 on other soft furnishings for the abbey and palace. Details of the expenditure on the provision of jewels and plate are lacking, but the cost is likely to have run to several thousand pounds. And the expenses of the royal household on food and other provisions for the occasion ran to over £1,300, by far the largest recorded amount for a single feast in the whole of Edward III's reign. This very deliberate extravagance was intended to create the appropriate impression of political stability and royal magnificence.[36]

## Wedding feasts

WEDDING FEASTS AS SUCH were a well-established tradition. There was a strong secular element in wedding feasts; for the medieval Church, marriage was as much a worldly contract as a sacrament. It was only in the eleventh and twelfth centuries that the list of sacraments, around which the central ceremonies of the Church revolved, was clearly defined. This was the moment when marriage was firmly established as a religious rite.[37] An anecdote about the emperor Heinrich III, whose wedding in 1043 was celebrated 'in royal style, as is befitting', reveals that this royal style included a feast.[38] However, the chroniclers noted that the 'king' of the minstrels who attended the feast left unrewarded, and was not even offered food and drink. This was obviously a remarkable breach of custom, and it has been persuasively argued that Heinrich's piety led him to despise the minstrels and players whose presence was traditional on such occasions. His predecessor two centuries earlier, Louis the Pious, Charlemagne's son, was said never to have smiled at their songs or displays.

By contrast, the wedding of the emperor Heinrich V and Matilda, daughter of Henry I

*The wedding of Heinrich V and Matilda*

of England, in 1114, has been called one of 'the greatest triumphal feasts that has ever taken place in Germany'.[39] No-one then living could recall a time when so many princes of the highest rank had gathered in one place: five archbishops, thirty bishops, five dukes and an innumerable crowd of counts and abbots. The generosity of the emperor was such that no historian could describe the gifts given to the guests, and no chamberlain could judge their value. The emperor evidently subscribed to the traditional view of a wedding feast, and the chroniclers noted that the presence of a vast number of jugglers and players added to the splendour of the occasion.[40]

WEDDINGS WERE ALSO THE MOST public of court festivals; it is clear that in addition to the minstrels and players there was a strong public participation, both as spectators of the procession of the bride and as part of the general festivities. The procession was important in terms of introducing the new countess, queen or empress to the population, in an age when public appearances were the only way of identifying the ruler and his spouse. The addition of tournaments as a regular part of wedding celebrations further encouraged the presence of spectators. Detailed accounts of wedding festivals are rare in the thirteenth century, but there is an extraordinary tale of a wedding in Bratislava in 1264, at the expense of the king of Hungary, Bela IV, whose son married the daughter of the margrave of Brandenburg. It is half real, half fictional: the names of Conrad, master of the cooks, and Gozo, the chamberlain, are mentioned, and we can believe in the bridles and saddles decorated with gold and silver. Rich textiles are listed: 'scarlet'[41] and 'brunat', both kinds of cloth, silk of different sorts, as well as ermine and other furs, but they are said to have cost 20,000 pounds. Messengers were sent to Breslau, Prague, Saxony, Meissen and Thuringia to invite their lords and, to enable the crowds of guests to cross the Danube, a bridge broad enough for ten horsemen to ride abreast was built – again, a little bit of poetic licence. Wine was bought in huge quantities so that there was no danger of running out, and so much feed for horses that it made five piles 'higher than the church in Solenau'. The meadows were filled with cows and pigs which would last the guests for four weeks, and when after the event the king's clerks added up the amount of wheat used to make bread, it amounted to 1,000 bushels.[42]

From the early fourteenth century we have a series of accounts of the weddings of the Bohemian royal house, beginning with that of Elizabeth, heiress of the kingdom of Bohemia, whose brother-in-law had attempted to seize the throne. Heinrich VII, the ruling Holy Roman Emperor, arranged for her to marry his son Jean of Luxemburg, and the marriage was therefore a major political event. The ceremony was held at Speyer in September 1310, and we have an eye-witness account couched in enthusiastic terms by the court chronicler. There were huge crowds in the streets and the windows were filled with people eager to see the event. The houses were hung with purple cloth. After the emperor and his entourage, including the bride, had entered the city, Jean arrived in a separate procession, accompanied by a company of fifty knights with banners of a white lion on a red ground, and went to the cathedral, where his father crowned him as king of Bohemia. This was followed by the wedding, which seems to have been a relatively brief service; bride and groom slept apart that night. The following morning, there was a magnificent mass, for which the new queen was dressed in the French style. Her husband accompanied her to the church to the sound of trumpets and all kinds of instruments for the blessing of their union.

The wedding feast which followed was somewhat marred by an altercation between the archbishops of Köln and Mainz as to who should have precedence in the seating, a quarrel which was perhaps typical of such occasions. The chronicler describes how Jean succeeded in calming them, and then waxes lyrical about the splendour of the king's appearance and indeed about everything concerned with the feast. His enthusiasm was shared by the crowds in the street who watched the jousts held immediately afterwards; he claims that 'there was hardly a street or a square in the town where the jousters did not ride in glorious array'.[43] The Bohemian knights aroused the admiration of the spectators by jousting with spears thicker and longer than those to which the knights of the Rhineland were accustomed. Whenever a Bohemian appeared in the lists, the onlookers shouted 'Here's a Bohemian! Here's a Bohemian!' as they splintered their lances on their challengers with devastating results. That evening, after further feasting, the bride and groom were led to their chamber, where the traditional blessing of the bed was carried out before the doors were closed. The chronicler adds that no-one slept much that night because of the continuing celebrations in the town.

FROM THE MID FOURTEENTH CENTURY onwards wedding festivals also become an important conduit for international cultural contacts, bringing together members of widely-separated courts who would not meet in other circumstances. The best example of this is probably the journey of Lionel, duke of Clarence, Edward III's third son, to Milan, for his marriage to Violante, daughter of Galeazzo II Visconti, in 1362.[44] Lionel left England in early April. When he reached Paris on 9 April he was a guest at the royal palace of the Louvre. Here he was welcomed by the dukes of Berry and Burgundy, the king's brothers, and dined with the king. The following day there was a feast in his honour, attended by the king and queen. He then dined alternately with the dukes and the royal couple until his departure on 13 April. We next hear of him at the court of Amadeus VI of Savoy, known as the 'Green Count' from his favourite clothing. Lionel reached Chambéry around 11 May, where the count laid on two days of feasting, dancing and singing in his sumptuous castle.[45]

*Lionel duke of Clarence travels to his wedding in Milan*

As Lionel approached Milan on 27 May, Galeazzo came out of the city to greet him, accompanied by his wife and eighty ladies in embroidered scarlet gowns with white sleeves and gilded belts, and with a troop of thirty knights and thirty squires on great warhorses with jousting saddles. They escorted the duke into the city; with him came Amadeus of Savoy, the English lords who had travelled with him, and two thousand soldiers. A week later, the marriage took place in the porch of the cathedral, with Galeazzo's brother Bernabò and Amadeus as the bride's sponsors, followed by a pontifical mass. The feast which followed is one of the first for which we have the full menu, running to eighteen courses. With each course, magnificent gifts for the bridegroom were presented: liveries, weapons, hunting dogs, sparrowhawks and peregrines, followed by armour for the joust, armour for war, bolts of cloth of gold and silk, horses with saddles, helmets, shields and lances, coursers, destriers for jousting with gilded bridles and tabards of red and crimson velvet decorated with gold. For the last three courses the gifts were a magnificent hat with a great flower of pearls and a cloak covered in pearls trimmed with ermine, twelve fat (and rather incongruous) oxen, and two coursers called 'the Lion' and 'the Abbot' for the duke and seventy-seven horses for his escort.[46]

Among those present, after the list of nobles, we find Petrarch, the most famous poet of his day. This leads us to the intriguing possibility that it was here that Geoffrey Chaucer, who was certainly abroad during 1368, met his Italian counterpart. Furthermore, Guillaume Machaut gave a copy of one of his works to Amadeus of Savoy while the latter was in Paris. Jean Froissart travelled with the count and wrote songs for the festival at Chambéry. It is often difficult to trace the movements of poets and writers, whose status at court was relatively lowly, and even if we cannot show that Chaucer did indeed meet these luminaries, the presence of such men shows how such a journey as Lionel's could link the different cultures in each court, with potentially remarkable literary results.

*Philippa of Lancaster marries the king of Portugal*

EDWARD III'S GRANDCHILDREN married into continental families on several occasions, and we have accounts of the wedding festivals of three of them. Philippa, the daughter of John of Gaunt, married the king of Portugal, João I, in 1387, as part of a treaty by which João was to assist Gaunt in his efforts to gain the throne of Castile, which he claimed by right of his wife Constanza. João committed himself to raising a Portuguese army by the beginning of the year, but had not yet done so, and was hesitating about the date for the marriage. Philippa had arrived in Oporto in December, and Gaunt pointed out that if the marriage did not take place before the beginning of the preparations for Lent on 3 February, it could not take place until after Easter, because marriages were not performed during Lent. It was therefore a hurried affair, and the king had to apologise to those of his council who were unable to attend because of the short notice given. The betrothal ceremony was held on 2 February, after the king had ridden all night to reach the city, and he then announced that the actual wedding would be celebrated on 12 February. A space for tournaments was cleared by using gardens near the centre of Oporto, and hard-pressed officials struggled to organise the processions, games and nightly entertainments in time. On the day itself, the king and queen rode side by side out of the palace dressed in cloth of gold, wearing jewelled crowns, preceded by musicians; 'as is customary at weddings, noblewomen and citizens' daughters came along at the back, singing. So great was the crush and so small the space between palace and church that it was impossible to control and marshal the huge crowds.'[47]

The couple were duly married at the church door, and then went in to mass. Once the service was over, they returned to the palace, where the feast had been set out; the tables included some reserved for local merchants and ladies and girls from the city. The entertainments during the meal were those traditional in Spain and Portugal, particularly tightrope walking and acrobatics. Dances and singing followed, and 'in the evening, the archbishop and other prelates with many burning torches blessed the king's bed with those benedictions that the Church has ordained for such occasions',[48] before withdrawing and leaving the couple together. Fernão Lopes, the official royal chronicler, writing fifty years later, assures us that for the weeks before and after the wedding, feasting and tournaments took place not only in Oporto, but 'in all the towns and cities of the realm, as was normal at that period'.[49]

*Richard II of England marries Isabella, daughter of Charles VI of France*

The wedding of Richard II and Isabella of France in 1396 was a much grander and more formal occasion. His first wife, Anne of Bohemia, daughter of the emperor Karl IV, had died in 1394. In March 1396 his envoys in France signed a truce with Charles VI, as a condition of which Richard and Isabella, Charles's daughter, were to be married. The two kings met in person for the first time at Ardres near St Omer in October 1396, where the preliminaries to the ceremony were celebrated with great pomp, on a scale rivalled only by the much more famous encounter between Henry VIII and Francis I of France at the 'Field of the Cloth of Gold' in 1520, on the same site. Both kings were accompanied by a bodyguard of four hundred gentlemen, and Charles VI had sixty-four nobles with him. Richard II is estimated to have spent over £10,000 on the meeting at Ardres. As soon as the treaty had been signed, Charles VI summoned the most skilful jewellers of Paris, and ordered from them 'the costliest gold chains, bracelets, collars, rings, chokers and crowns, dresses of all colours and kinds, cloths of gold and silk, all decorated with various paintings and precious stones, carriages, saddles and harness of gold and silver for the horses'.[50] Among these treasures were special collars of Charles's personal emblem, seed pods of broom, set among green branches and flowers. Richard for his part used his badge of the white hart, with a gold collar and chain. The two kings exchanged these jewels, wearing each other's emblems as a sign of amity and alliance, as part of a massive exchange of gifts designed to underline the importance that the two sides attached to the treaty and to the marriage.

The ten-year-old princess set out for Calais with a train 'of a magnificence that outdid anything that had been seen before then, and, if we may say so, exceeded even the king's resources'.[51] A gentleman rode before her carriage bearing her golden crown. She arrived at Ardres to find a massive encampment in place: 120 tents for each of the kings, grouped into two facing camps. In front of the main body of tents were two royal pavilions: one in the form of a great square hall for Charles, and a vast tower for Richard. Halfway between the halls a great stake had been driven into the ground: this was where the kings were to meet. Elaborate regulations for security forbade the carrying of arms in the neighbouring towns and banned anyone from following the kings and their companies, particularly any food-sellers or merchants. No games or sports which might lead to disputes were allowed and musicians were only to play with official permission.

*Isabella's procession to Calais*

The two kings left the town of Ardres on 27 October with four hundred knights each, in battle order, and halted at their respective encampments. Nobles from both sides visited the other camp, inquiring what dress should be worn during the ceremonies. Richard is said to have replied – perhaps uncharacteristically – that the treaties already signed were a signal of the warm affection between both parties, and 'luxurious clothes would in no way improve the existing relations'.[52] The two parties then went to the king of France's tent, where two thrones stood under a canopy of cloth of gold: here a secret council was held, and gifts exchanged again, this time a little solid gold vessel and a jewelled collar.

*The meeting of the kings at Ardres*

The deep attachment of the royal courts to the symbolism of badges was reflected in what we would see as a very unexpected way. On the first day, Richard's entourage wore the 'livery of the queen of England who died lately',[53] namely the red gowns with white diagonals which had been used by Anne of Bohemia. And at the end of the second day, Richard gave a collar of the queen's livery to Charles VI, who fastened it around his own neck. A possible explanation of this is that Richard, who was known to have been passionately devoted to Anne, was implying that he would be equally devoted to Isabella.

*Symbolic gifts*

Isabella arrived on the Monday, with a brilliant cortège: 'Beholding such magnificence, you would have thought you were seeing that gathering of goddesses which poets describe in their fictions.'[54] It was, the chronicler claims, the most dazzling escort of its kind anyone could remember. A final banquet took place, at which the kings were served by the highest nobles of both countries, and after which gifts were once more exchanged. Finally, Richard went to Calais, where, on 4 November, the nuptial mass was held. The actual formalities of the marriage had been carried out at the signature of the truce in March, by proxy; so the chronicler describes Isabella as 'the young queen' throughout his account of the October meeting. Once again, this underlines the distinction between the marriage as a contract between individuals and the Church's blessing of such a contract.

THE WEDDINGS OF THE DUKES of Burgundy are as spectacular as the other great Burgundian festivals. They culminate in the wedding of Charles the Bold in 1468, minutely described by Olivier de la Marche, who was responsible for organising it. On the morning of Saturday 25 June, the fourteen ships carrying his bride, Margaret of York, daughter of Edward IV, arrived off Sluys and anchored to wait for the tide before entering port. That evening, after dark, Margaret came ashore to the sound of eight trumpets, and was escorted by torchlight through the streets by the courtiers sent by the duke to meet her and a procession of the townspeople. Two days later, the duke paid a private visit, and on the Thursday, he returned with a larger escort and the dancing went on until late at night. A week after she had landed, Margaret was taken by water to Damme, a mile from Bruges, and once again torchlight processions accompanied her to her lodgings. On the Sunday morning, the duke joined her for mass, said in her rooms by the bishop of Salisbury, and the marriage ceremony was performed. Margaret was then taken in a horse-litter with a company of English knights and Burgundian knights of the Order of the Golden Fleece; she was dressed in cloth of gold and wore her crown, but there was a downpour during the short journey.

*The wedding of Charles the Bold and Margaret of York at Bruges, 1468*

At Bruges she was welcomed by a parade of the townspeople drawn up in formal array, the clergy and religious communities and the town officials. They were followed by the archers and members of the duke's household and family, and a splendid turnout of musicians and heralds in magnificent tabards, with great war trumpets and other instruments: six of the heralds were kings of arms. Margaret joined this procession in her litter, and her ladies rode alongside her on horses draped with crimson cloth and in five gilded chariots. Behind her came the foreign merchants of Bruges, from Italy, Spain and north Germany. As she came into the town there were ten tableaux, all on the theme of marriage, beginning with that of Adam and Eve, and largely drawn from the Bible, the exceptions being the marriage of Cleopatra and Ptolemy and a heraldic display alluding to the union of England and Burgundy. The streets were hung with tapestries, and enterprising citizens with houses along the route charged a crown for a window seat. The gateway to the duke's lodgings was decorated with his arms and mottoes, flanked by an archer and a crossbowman who dispensed red and white wine to all and sundry. In the courtyard hippocras flowed from the breast of a pelican.

That evening, the duke and duchess dined in the great hall which had been refurbished for the wedding with a very rich gold and silk tapestry of Gideon and a huge dresser displaying the duke's plate, with a great gold cup at the top. Two of the chandeliers were in the form of castles, with hunters and men with camels coming and going; both had seven mirrors, each 40 cm across, underneath, so that it seemed as if there were ten thousand people in the room. The meal itself was served in dramatic fashion: on the high table there were six ships with three masts, with full rigging and everything shipshape and Bristol fashion, in which the roast was served. Some of these astonishing silver models of ships, known as nefs, complete with rigging and miniature crew, which were the standard centrepieces of such occasions, still survive.

*Olivier de la Marche describes the wedding feast*

Around them were caravels and dinghies with sweetmeats, and towers which represented the duke's countries and towns, with the appropriate banners and labels identifying them – La Marche carefully copies out the entire list. At the end of the first night a great unicorn, made in a lifelike fashion, entered the hall; on it a leopard sat, holding in one paw a banner with the duke's arms, and in the other a daisy, symbol of the bride, which it presented to the duke. Next was a lion as large as the greatest of warhorses, ridden by a dwarf dressed as a shepherdess. The lion opened and closed its mouth, and sang a song welcoming the bride as the 'beautiful shepherdess'. Finally, there was a dromedary, so well made that it seemed 'more alive than otherwise'; its rider opened two great baskets on its back and threw out strangely painted birds which might have come from India. These flew around the room, 'which was most pleasing'. With this the banquet ended, and wine and spices were served. 'And nothing more was done that day, and there were no lengthy dances after supper; because it was three in the morning before the tables were cleared. And the bride was led to her chamber; and as for the rest of the secrets of that night, I leave them to the understanding of the noble pair ...'[55]

This was followed by ten days of jousting and banqueting, which La Marche records in detail, together with the plot which was obligatory on such occasions: the Burgundian tournaments both drew on literature and were part of the court literature, in that the descriptions of them are a kind of distinctive literary form – the sports pages of the day.[56] As to the displays at the banquets on other nights, there were also a gryphon which walked round the hall, a model of Charles the Bold's latest castle, at Gorcum, inhabited by animals who played musical instruments, and as a grand finale, two giants and an enormous whale, 18 metres long and higher than a man on horseback, which moved its fins, body and tail. It went round the room, and ended at the duke's table, where it opened its mouth and two mermaids emerged, with combs and mirrors in their hands, and sang a strange song. Twelve knights of the sea, half human and half sea horse, came out of the whale, and danced with the mermaids to the sound of a tambourine in the whale's belly. But the knights grew jealous of each other, and started to fight, at which the giants rounded them up and sent them back inside the whale.

# Seasonal Festivals

IT IS ALWAYS DIFFICULT TO DISTINGUISH between a courtly festival which may be based on a folk tradition and something which originates in courtly circles and then later becomes a popular celebration. There may have been a number of minor celebrations with a popular origin at court, such as the curious custom that the English kings, certainly under Edward I and Edward II, were surprised in their bedchamber on Easter Monday by the queen's ladies and fined by them for a breach of the king's peace: they received the handsome sum of £14 for this in 1290.[57] Two popular traditions, however, the celebrations of New Year and May, stand out as part of court ritual, and are particularly prominent under Charles VI of France.

## New Year

THE TRADITION OF GIVING GIFTS AT the New Year was a ritual that developed in Rome, with the establishment of a proper calendar. Originally spring gifts or *strenae* were exchanged on 15 March, and this ritual was transferred to 1 January after this became the official start of the year. We hear of *strenae* in Sicily in 1160, when Maio of Bari, the powerful admiral of Sicily, was accused of embezzling a diadem which should have been given to the king on New Year's Day.[58] The word is recorded in French in 1165, but the formal custom only reappears in France in the fourteenth century, becoming a ceremony in both France and England by the end of the century.

The first actual list we have is that for Queen Philippa's New Year gifts in 1330, where personal gifts were given to members of Edward III's household.[59] These are graded by rank: five of the household knights have belts worth 20s and wallets or scrips worth 26s 8d, three others have the same belts, but wallets worth 20s; the squires' belts are 8s and their wallets 9s, down to the musicians who seem to have had standard issue wallets from the stores and belts worth 3s. The queen's attendants were given brooches worth between 12s and 13s 4d, and 30 gold florins. In 1364 we find a personal gift from Edward to Philippa on New Year's Day[60] of two corsets, one blood-red, embroidered with the motto '*Myn*

**77.** The 'Little
Golden Horse
of Altötting',
c.1400. The
greatest surviving
masterpiece
from the Parisian
jewellers of the
period, this was
a New Year's
gift from queen
Isabeau to Charles
VI. The king
kneels before the
Virgin, attended
by two squires:
one proffers his
helmet, while the
other, fashionably
dressed, holds the
king's horse below.

*biddenye*', perhaps a term of endearment, and a black one with '*Ich wyndemuth*' inscribed in pearls, silks and gold.

A rather confused list of gifts from Edward prince of Wales and Aquitaine over a period of several years contains a list of New Year gifts, though not all the items are specifically identified as such. On 1 January 1348, the prince gave the king an enamelled gold cup he had bought the previous June. The queen was given a brooch with three balas rubies and an emerald, and his old tutor, Bartholomew Burghersh the elder, received a similar jewel. His sisters Isabella and Joan received elaborate brooches, and his household knights were given 'ouches' or clasps set with pearls or diamond rings. His physician, John Gaddesden, received a golden rose.[61] Our knowledge of New Year gifts in England is hampered by a lack of records. There are four surviving rolls dating from 1391 to 1397 which describe the gifts given by Henry, earl of Derby, before he came to the throne as Henry IV. These give a glimpse of what was happening.[62] There are gifts to the king and queen, to high-ranking ladies and to close relatives, but only two or three gifts to his fellow magnates, unlike the French exchanges described below. The most expensive item is a gold tablet valued at £12 given to the countess of Norfolk. When Henry became king, over thirteen New Years in his reign he spent an average of around £500 a year. This represents about one third of his total recorded purchases from goldsmiths.[63] Fragmentary records fill in some details, and show gifts to the great magnates and to particular members of his household. After that we have no information about such gifts under Henry V and Henry VI, though there is a ballad written by John Lydgate to accompany the gift of an eagle on New Year's Day to Henry VI by Queen Catherine at her castle at Hertford at some time between 1422 and 1429.

Frontispiece

FROM 1380 ONWARDS, the French royal accounts reveal an astonishing series of New Year gifts, on a much grander scale than those in England. The kind of ceremony at which they were exchanged is commemorated in one of the most luxurious of all the miniatures of the period, the opening page for January in the *Très Riches Heures* of Jean, duke of Berry. Jean sits in splendid attire as the visitors arrive for a feast, while the court fool says, 'Come nearer, come nearer', as if to encourage them. Recent writers have read the picture as a portrayal of the New Year gift exchange. The duke's inventories record a huge number of items received on such occasions between 1401 and 1416, including 177 jewels or pieces of jewellery and twenty-four manuscripts.[64] What the royal accounts reveal are nearly seven thousand gifts, valued at 520,000 *livres tournois*, rather more than the annual income of Jean the Fearless as duke of Burgundy, relating to such gifts during the reign of Charles VI, between 1380 and 1422. The exchange is chiefly between Charles VI and his uncles, the dukes of Burgundy,[65] Berry and Anjou, and their families. There are occasional entries for Sigismund, emperor of Germany, and Richard II. Gifts were also given to members of their households. In all, there are 373 names in the lists, a relatively tight-knit group.[66] Furthermore, the giving of gifts seems unaffected by the violent political rivalries among the French dukes during this period. Even the gift-giving relationship between Louis of Orléans and Jean the Fearless of Burgundy, who was to have his cousin murdered in Paris in 1407, only to be killed in turn by the victim's son at the bridge of Montereau twelve years later, was still in place as late at 1404. 'At the court, on a festival day, one did not advertise one's hatred, greed or rancour. It was good manners to put on a smile.'[67]

Most of these gifts were exchanged by messenger. Only in 1413 do we hear of two participants in this custom meeting on New Year's Day, Jean the Fearless and Jean duke of Berry.[68] The vast majority of the objects listed are personal jewellery, such as brooches and rings; goblets and pieces of plate are frequently mentioned, and at the top end of the

**77**, p.221

scale, there are reliquaries and crosses. The most famous piece of goldsmith's work of this period is a New Year's gift. It is the so-called 'Little Golden Horse' or *Goldenes Rössl*, an image of the Virgin and Child in front of which Charles VI is kneeling, with an attendant knight holding his golden helmet, and below the platform on which the king appears, his groom holding the horse from which the piece takes its name. It was given to Charles VI by the queen, Isabeau of Bavaria, on 1 January 1404, and was carefully described in every detail in the entry recording its receipt. The creators of this remarkable piece had used the latest techniques, which allowed enamel to be used on three-dimensional objects, so that the figures of the king and his two attendants have enamel cloaks which are as rich as the clothes themselves must have been. The whole process is shot through with the ambivalent relations – competitive, hostile, intimate – between the French royal family. The gifts also reflect an extraordinary development in the skill of the Parisian goldsmiths and their counterparts in the Netherlands. With the death of Charles VI and the brief reign of Henry VI in Paris, the troubled politics of the next decade seem to have put an end to the practice, which was not revived in France until the age of Louis XIV. It looks suspiciously as if the enthusiasm of one or more of the participants made a traditional and casual custom into a short-lived cultural fashion. Gifts as rewards were part of court life, given freely on any suitable occasion, to a minstrel at a feast or to a member of a retinue at a tournament. The gifts at the French New Year festival function differently. They are an exchange, as acknowledgement of status, blood-relationship or simply as a display of wealth.

## *Maying*

**78.** (opposite) The month of May, from the calendar in *Les Très Riches Heures du duc de Berry*. This corresponds very closely with the poem by Eustache Deschamps describing the maying ceremony at the king's chateau of Beauté.

THE MONTH OF MAY AS HARBINGER of spring appears in troubadour literature in the twelfth century, almost as a poetic commonplace. A famous poem, 'The First of May', by the troubadour Raimbaut de Vaqueyras, declares that the day brings him no rejoicing in the absence of his lady.[69] So the Maying poems which figure prominently in the work of the French poet Eustache Deschamps, in Geoffrey Chaucer's 'The Knight's Tale', and in the lyrics of Charles d'Orléans, captured at Agincourt in 1415 and a prisoner in England until 1440, belong to an earlier but relatively obscure tradition, with its roots in folk practices.

There is good evidence from the thirteenth century for some kind of springtime folk ritual on the first of May with a strongly sexual element. At La Fère in north-eastern France in 1207, the men and women were allowed to take branches from the lord's woods on May Day, while the practice was forbidden by St Louis in 1257 in the woods of an unidentified convent. Similarly, it was banned in 1270 in the woods belonging to the Parisian abbey of Saint-Germain-des-Prés.[70] The gathering of May boughs is recorded as a custom on the first of the month by Heinrich Suso in Germany, writing in about 1330.[71] Bishop Grosseteste, in thirteenth-century England, condemns the games which are said to bring in the summer and the autumn.[72] If the basis of courtly maying is indeed folk custom rather than a literary theme, the courtly tradition transforms it into a ceremony which replaces sexual licence with a very formal courtly restraint.[73]

Eustache Deschamps describes the court maying of Charles VI at the château of Beauté-sur-Marne in 1385. Watching from a bank overlooking the castle, he saw

a most noble company of young people clothed in green, and other people of rank who carried billhooks for their task and began to cut leaves ... In the woods ladies and squires sang new songs because the weather was so sweet and beautiful, gathered flowers, grasses and little branches from which they made belts and hats...[74]

Then the king appears, dressed in green, with his escort, and jousting follows; after which the participants kneel before the king and declare that they have 'sacrificed to May' and they all retire to Beauté, where the rooms are hung with rich green silk. Beauté-sur-Marne was part of the enclave centred on the royal palace at Vincennes and was a manor house rather than a fortified building, one of two retreats from court life created by Charles V, who restored it in 1373 and died there in 1380. Its name – which preceded any poems about it – and its purpose made it an ideal setting for a poetic evocation of May Day, but Deschamps is writing about a real event. The image for May in Jean duke of Berry's book of hours (the *Très Riches Heures*) is equally poised between the realistic and the fantastic.

Two years later, Charles VI commissioned a total of twenty-eight 'houppelandes', a newly fashionable overgarment, so that he and his companions 'could all be dressed alike on the first day of May'.[75] By 1400, he ordered a livery, that is, an issue of clothes to a large number of his courtiers entitled to winter and summer clothing, so that they might 'wear the livery that the said lord has made on the first day of May'; 352 houppelandes were made, embroidered with intertwined broom and 'mai' (the latter probably being simply green branches, not the English hawthorn).

# Tournaments

THE TOURNAMENT WAS AN ADJUNCT to royal festivals in the fourteenth and fifteeenth centuries. It replaced the games which Geoffrey of Monmouth had imagined in the twelfth century, but it was a less suitable event. Its place in court ritual and the display of magnificence is equivocal at best, partly because of its origins, and partly because it plays no particular role in the actual festival. It is as if the gathering of so many knights at festivals and ceremonies was too good an opportunity to hold a tournament that jousting became a kind of automatic coda to the event. It also vastly prolonged the proceedings. In extreme cases, such as that of the wedding of Charles the Bold and Mary of York, the jousts lasted as long as the wedding festivities. Furthermore, there was always the danger that the king might not appear in the most favourable light. Some were expert jousters, such as Edward III, who was known to appear incognito, as one of the ordinary knights. Others, like Richard II, apart from an occasional joust in his youth, chose not to take the risk. He was one of the few monarchs to use a tournament as a way of promoting his magnificence, at Smithfield in October 1390.[76] A chronicler at Westminster described it as providing 'the nobles and gallant knights of many place with a reason for visiting London', highlighting its unusual nature. It was here that Richard introduced his famous badge of the White Hart. There was a distinct agenda here, as he had only recently declared himself of age and assumed his personal rule in May of that year. The king was seeking to find common ground after the dissensions during his minority, and the tournament was one element in a wider campaign of rallying support, perhaps echoing his grandfather's tournament at Cheapside in 1331, which was held in similar circumstances.

TOURNAMENTS HAD ONCE HAD a dubious reputation. They had been denounced by the Church and banned in most of western Europe in the twelfth century. Their military origins and violent reputation meant that it was mainly in north-west France, on the borders of France and Flanders where French royal control was weak, that the sport – if it could be called a sport – survived.

It is only with the appearance of a ruler who participated enthusiastically in such events that the tournament becomes respectable and a regular part of court life. It is an important moment, because it shows the potentially civilising aspect of the court. For the tournament to become acceptable, it needed to be formalised, and the enthusiasm – and aggression – of the participants controlled. This had been happening during the thirteenth century, and the reign of Edward I marks the beginning of the transition. While heir to the throne, he had been a famous tourneyer, travelling in northern France to take part in illicit tournaments in 1262. When he came to power in the civil war at the end of his father's reign, one of his actions was to issue a public edict in 1267 allowing tournaments to be held throughout the kingdom, on his own authority and that of his brother, Edmund, and cousin, Henry of Almain. After Edward became king, he stopped in France again in 1272 to take up a challenge to a tournament from the count of Châlons as he returned from the Holy Land on his way to his coronation. The resulting encounter, the so-called 'Little Battle of Châlons', was indeed more like a battle than a sporting occasion, and illustrated exactly the dangers which had so far prevented royal participation in tournaments. The English, outnumbered by two to one, were attacked by infantry and cavalry in battle order, bent on taking captives and spoils. The chronicler Walter of Guisborough claims that the infantry cut the girths of the English knights.[77] The count himself engaged Edward in a duel, and when he found he could make no impression with his swordplay, seized Edward round the neck and attempted to drag him from his horse. Edward was the stronger, and it was the count who fell, at which the Burgundians assaulted the English in earnest. Edward forced the count to surrender to an ordinary knight because of his disgraceful behaviour, and the English drove off their opponents. If a tournament could degenerate into this kind of brawl, it was no place for a king to be.

*Edward I and tournaments*

Edward, however, was undeterred, and on his return to England held a number of tournaments, combining them on occasion with court festivals. In his hands, the tournament became a kind of political instrument, a means of celebrating the military power of the king. This comes to the fore in the Welsh wars, and is linked to Edward's interest in the Arthurian legends: the Arthurian romances often include lengthy descriptions of tournaments, and Edward was anxious to demonstrate to the Welsh that he had inherited Arthur's mantle. The first royal festival to include a tournament was the 'round table' held at Nefyn in 1284, to celebrate his victory over the Welsh leader Llywelyn ap Gruffudd. The exact nature of a 'round table' is not clear, but there was certainly jousting and probably some Arthurian play-acting in furtherance of his claim to be the true heir of Arthur. The following year, at an assembly of his magnates at Winchester, at which forty-four squires were knighted, he held a tournament which celebrated not only the knighting ceremony but also the conquest of Wales. It is very probably for this occasion in 1285, designed to publicise his achievement in a way that a festival in the remoter parts of Wales could not, that the celebrated round table which still hangs in the great hall of Winchester castle was made.[78] Familiar through frequent reproductions, this massive piece of furniture is one of the very few physical survivals of the artefacts made for medieval court festivals.[79] One further round table gathering, again in the context of conquest, was that at Falkirk in 1302, during the war against Scotland, possibly commemorating his victory over Wallace there in 1298. The connection with Arthur, and hence the use of the round table, was that Edward, in setting out his claim to Scotland to the pope, had cited Arthur's supposed overlordship of the Scottish kingdom.

*Tournaments as celebrations of victory*

Even if tournaments could be used to celebrate victories, they remained unpredictable events, particularly in circumstances where there was any degree of hostility between the participants. Soon after the accession of Edward II, his favourite Piers Gaveston, in whose company Edward had fought in the lists and to whom he had given lavish armour for the lists, held a tournament at Wallingford against the leading magnates of England. Gaveston, newly returned from an exile imposed by Edward I because of his undue influence over his son, raised as large a force of the younger knights of the kingdom as he could, and roundly defeated the earls of Arundel, Hertford and Surrey and their retinues. Much the same happened at a tournament at Faversham in honour of Edward's marriage to Isabella of France; Gaveston himself requested the cancellation of a tournament at Stepney which was intended as part of the coronation festivities, and another event at Kennington organised by Edward was boycotted by the barons. Edward responded by banning tournaments in a series of edicts in the following years, as the tensions between him and the magnates erupted into civil war.

*Tournaments as means of recruiting support*

If tournaments and the enthusiasm for jousting could be turned against a king, it could equally be enlisted to help him. This idea seems to have occurred at much the same time to two kings whose hold on their lands was far from secure. In 1326, Károly I of Hungary, who had finally secured his claim to the throne some five years earlier after a long drawn-out struggle with the rebellious nobility, founded the Fraternal Society of St George, the earliest known knightly order headed by a monarch. Politically, this group of fifty knights was intended to form a powerbase for the king, but it included a strong social element, and one clause of its statutes decreed that the knights were to follow the king in all his knightly pursuits and tournaments. In similar fashion, the Order of the Sash in Castile, founded by Alfonso XI in 1330, had tournaments as a central element in its activities. Alfonso, like Károly, had fought hard to establish his authority: he came to the throne aged three, and the resulting regency was a period of turbulence. The Order was intended to create a bond of personal loyalty between the king and his knights. Every meeting of the Order was to include a tournament, and the king could summon the companions of the Order to any tournament he chose to proclaim in the intervals. There are records of only two tournaments, one to celebrate Alfonso's coronation in 1332, and another at Valladolid in 1334. Alfonso himself was an enthusiast for the sport, and the knights of the Banda were expected to fight as a team against the same number picked from the knights who came to challenge them. The fighting at Valladolid was fierce, and the four judges had to intervene to halt the tournament. Enrique II, Alfonso's son, revived the custom at Seville in 1375 in his father's memory, but this was the last we hear of the Order in action.

*Edward III: the tournament as royal sport*

It is in England under Edward III that the tournament is first successfully integrated into court life. Ironically, Edward learnt his tourneying skills from Roger Mortimer, the favourite and possibly lover of his mother, Isabella of France, during her regency. No less than eighteen tournaments can be traced in the years 1328–9, the most intense period of such events in the whole of Edward's reign. Mortimer may have been using them in an attempt to distract Edward from any interest in affairs of government; but in 1330 Edward and his companions from the lists successfully overthrew the regency, and Mortimer was executed.

For the moment, things continued as before: one chronicler said that Edward, aided and abetted by his closest companion, William de Montagu, proceeded to lead 'a jolly young life'.[80] Now tournaments became an integral part of the activities of the royal court. The Woodstock event marked the birth of Edward's eldest son, Edward, in 1330 and his daughter Isabella's birth was similarly celebrated in 1332. The group of knights consistently present at these occasions has at its core the conspirators who had so recently helped Edward overthrow Mortimer, and among them are many of the major military leaders who served Edward in his subsequent victories. It was a tight-knit group, and Edward seems to have been on familiar terms with them, not standing on his dignity as king. On two occasions he jousted under the leadership of other knights, as a *miles simplex*, as if to imply that he was a knight among knights on the tournament field.

But these were also occasions with a political end in view, which varied with circumstances. And two great spectacles were mounted to impress the citizens of London and show them their new king and his companions. English kings rarely came to the city; the Tower of London to the east and Westminster to the west lay outside the city walls, and they travelled between the two without passing through the city, by using the river. So the king was less visible in London than his counterpart in Paris. The great tournament at Cheapside in September 1331 lasted for four days, and began with a parade the like of which had not been seen in the city before:

> At the time for which the tournament was arranged, the king, earls and barons and all the knights in the kingdom gathered in London, and on the Sunday, the eve of St Matthew the apostle, William, who was captain of this solemn occasion, appeared with the king and other chosen knights in splendid clothing, with masks like Tartars. There came with them the same number of the most noble and beautiful ladies of the kingdom, all wearing red velvet tunics and caps of white camel's hair cloth; and each knight had on his right hand side a lady whom he led with a silver chain. The king had at his side the lady Eleanor his sister, a most beautiful girl. All of them, both knights and ladies, came at the hour of vespers, riding in pairs down the middle of Cheapside, preceded by more than sixty squires all dressed in the same uniform; and they were followed by their jousting horses covered with fine horsecloths; and thus, to the sound of trumpets and a variety of other instruments, they rode to their lodgings.[81]

The citizens were duly impressed: 'never were such solemn jousts seen in England', noted one of them.[82] This of course was part of the agenda; and when the court travelled,* tournaments were often a way of showing the court to the local populace. They may also have been part of Edward's contact with local magnates, occasions where he could talk informally to them or celebrate his latest victory with them. In 1341–4, the relatively difficult period after the failure of his first campaigns against France, there was a continuing series of jousts, as far afield as York, Hereford, Norwich and Canterbury. The eight jousts recorded in 1348 marked the triumphant conclusion of the campaign in Normandy, the victory at Crécy and the capture of Calais.

For the knights of the court, particularly the younger group around Edward prince of Wales, the frequency of jousting in these years meant that they came to regard the tournament as a normal part of court life. Edward had made the tournament almost a royal monopoly, and it undoubtedly played its part in the remarkable *esprit de corps* of his closest associates which in turn enabled the later victories at Poitiers in 1356 and Najéra in 1367. Furthermore, the ambience of the tournaments became more theatrical and more akin to play-acting: the skill of the jousters was highlighted by increasingly elaborate armour and trappings, and sometimes by masks and disguises – the Cheapside procession is one of the earliest examples. Later in Edward's reign there were further political costumes: in 1343 at Smithfield, Edward and his team dressed as the pope and twelve cardinals, a reference to a dispute with the pope over the taxes levied by the papacy, and in 1359, at the same place, the royal team were robed as the mayor and aldermen of London, as a compliment to their hosts. There are two examples of tournaments at night. In 1327 at Clipstone, the king wore

---

* Edward rarely spent more than two or three weeks in the same place until the very end of his reign.

armour with a covering of purple velvet with gold embroidery, presumably designed to glitter in the torchlight, while at Bristol in 1358 the event seems to have been held indoors.

ALTHOUGH JOUSTS WERE HELD after the wedding of Philip VI in 1328 and after the coronation of Charles V in 1364, there were few tournaments in France itself, royal or otherwise, until the accession of his son. Charles VI was an avid jouster in the early years of his reign. The greatest of these events was the festival for the knighting of his sons at Saint-Denis in 1389 which we have already described; these were followed by jousts in March 1390 at which the prizes and gifts to the ladies cost 2,054 francs.

Even after his madness began, Charles remained an enthusiast. His fondness for all kinds of festivities was held to have brought on his feeble-minded condition, but his physical skills were evidently unimpaired. In 1411 clothing was given to thirty members of the king's household for jousts at Whitsun in Paris; we find him taking part in jousts for the marriage of his brother-in-law, Ludwig of Bavaria, in 1413, and in 1415 he entered the lists when jousts were held in honour of the duke of York, sent to arrange Henry V's marriage to Charles's daughter Catherine. However, the English occupation of Paris marked the end of such court festivals. The tone was set by Henry V's remark after his marriage to Catherine in 1420: when jousting was suggested, he replied that they ought to go out and do some real fighting. In 1431 the jousts after Henry VI's coronation at Paris were remarked on for their modest scale: the coronation and jousts were reputed to have cost no more than a citizen's family would spend on a marriage. Charles VII and Louis XI were equally averse to such events; it is as if the joust became associated in the minds of the French kings and their court with the disasters of Charles VI's reign and with the lavish life-style of their great rivals, the Burgundian dukes.

IT IS THE KINGS OF CASTILE who take up the fashion for court festivals involving tournaments in the early fifteenth century. Despite Alfonso XI's enthusiasm for such matters when he founded his Order of the Sash, records of tournaments in Castile are sparse through the troubled years of the later fourteenth century, and it is only when Juan II came of age in 1423 that they were revived. The king's 'natural condition was to hold jousts and do things which he enjoyed' and he largely delegated the government of Castile to his constable, Alvaro de Luna, 'the greatest man uncrowned'; de Luna also jousted and held resplendent festivals on his own account, particularly in the decade between Juan's coronation in 1414 and his majority. It may be that, as with Edward III and Mortimer, the regent was also the king's tutor in such matters.

The most spectacular festival of the period was the *Passaje Peligroso de la Fuerte Ventura* (The Perilous Passage of Great Adventure) held at Valladolid in June 1428 and the other challenges which followed it. Both setting and scenario were very complicated. In the main square a fortress was built, with a high central tower and four surrounding towers. At its foot was a belfry and a pillar, on which a gilded gryphon stood, holding a great standard. Two outer fences with sixteen towers completed the 'fortifications'. In each of these towers stood a lady dressed in finery. A tilt made of cane ran from the fortress across the square to two more towers and an arch inscribed 'This is the arch of the perilous passage of great adventure'; on one of the towers was fixed a great golden wheel, called the 'wheel of fortune'. When the challengers arrived, they were greeted by fanfares and a lady who warned them that they could go no further without jousting; they replied that they were ready. The king, on a horse caparisoned in silver and gold, took up the challenge, and broke two spears; he was followed by the king of Navarre, with twelve knights 'all like windmills', who also broke a spear. The jousting was fierce: Enrique was stunned by his opponent, and one of his squires was so badly wounded that he died two hours later.

Six days later, the king of Navarre gave his festival; he and five other knights were the defenders, dressed in tasselled gorgets. He broke a number of spears on the first challengers; then Juan appeared, his lance on his shoulder, with twelve knights riding in similar fashion. In two courses, he carried off his opponent's crest, a highly skilled feat, and broke a lance; many other lances were broken before the proceedings ended with a magnificent dinner, during which many knights jousted in war armour by torchlight.

Next, on Sunday 6 June, Juan gave his own festival, in honour of his daughter's forthcoming marriage to Duarte, the heir of Portugal. A tent was pitched at the top of a flight of steps covered in cloth of gold, and the king appeared in the lists dressed as God the Father, each of his accompanying knights as an apostle with a scroll bearing his name and carrying one of the instruments of the Passion. Six of the prince's men appeared in surcoats decorated with smoke and flame, and six with mulberry leaves on theirs. Juan broke three spears and the prince five; 'and the jousts lasted until there were stars in the sky'.

The decline of jousting in Spain after Juan II's death again illustrates how much such matters depended on the monarch's enthusiasm and support for the sport. Furthermore, the fighting techniques of the tournament were beginning to change. In 1430, at the wedding of Isabel, daughter of the king of Portugal, to Philip the Good, duke of Burgundy, Jean Le Fèvre, the duke's herald, wrote a very detailed account of the actual wedding and notes carefully a new style of jousting that he saw in Portugal for the first time. On the Saturday, four days after the ceremony

> a joust was held in the Portuguese fashion . All the lists that had been erected were taken down; they made a single list across, of strong wood, as high as the horse's shoulders, which was hung with blue cloth ... And they jousted along the list, one on one side and the other on the other, with shields of the best steel and helmets of the same kind, in war saddles.[83]

Although jousting separated by a central barrier is the accepted image of a medieval tournament, historically speaking, it only applies to individual combats, and then only from the 1430s onwards.

BURGUNDY'S REPUTATION AS THE HOME of chivalry and jousting made a great impression on members of Charles VII's much more austere court. Georges Chastellain, in his biography of Jacques de Lalaing, one of the stars of the tournament in the mid fifteenth century, describes the French courtiers comparing the two courts:

> Among other things, they started to talk about the court of Philip of Burgundy, the grand style in which he lived, and the jousts, tournaments and contests which were held there every day, and some of the French said: 'There is no prince like the duke of Burgundy of France, and no-one as courtly as him: he is of good spirits, wise and generous, more than anyone else.' As they spoke, the count of Maine and the count of St Pol moved to one side and said to each other: 'We need to do something which will make people talk about us. You have heard the ladies being told that every day there are feasts, jousts, tournaments, dances and songs at the court of the duke of Burgundy, and you see a vast number of us at the king's court just sleeping, drinking and eating, without exercising ourselves in arms, and it is not right for us all to pass our time in idleness.'[84]

The count of Maine was brother to René, duke of Anjou, who almost certainly ruined himself while trying to remedy the situation presented by Chastellain. René's fortunes were additionally depleted by his unsuccessful attempts to claim his complicated inheritance, which extended to Sicily and the kingdom of Jerusalem, the former securely in the hands of Alfonso V of Aragon. René had inherited the duchy of Lorraine through his wife, but was defeated in 1432 and captured by the nearest claimant in the male line with Burgundian help, and had to pay a heavy ransom to his cousin Philip the Good of Burgundy. In Naples, he was defeated by the Aragonese who took the city in 1441. He turned from his misfortunes in the political and military world to courtly amusements, besides writing romances and a treatise on tournaments which is the standard work on the subject. In the years following his return from Naples, he gave four of the most dramatic jousts and festivals of the day, rivalling even those of his enemy Philip the Good. The first of these was for the wedding of Margaret, his daughter, to Henry VI of England, which took place by proxy at Nancy in 1445, and could have been a riposte to the mutterings about the idleness of the French court. A long description of the jousts survives, written by an eye-witness who had obviously carefully kept the score.

René and his cousin Charles VII of France vied for the attention of the crowds. Charles VII chose as his colours green and gold. He rode into the lists on a horse with a caparison of green cloth of gold, in a short mantle of green velvet with gold brocade. His pages' horses had caparisons of green velvet sewed with golden suns, and even his lances were covered in green velvet. René was judged to be the more splendid of the two, on a horse whose caparison was of purple velvet with embroidery of estocs or short thrusting swords, and the golden cross of the kingdom of Jerusalem, to which he had laid claim. His short mantle was of the same material. His followers wore yellow velvet, with turquoise hats with ostrich feathers or with long scarves with golden estocs. One of the horses led by the pages had a covering of yellow velvet with Turks' heads on it, perhaps a reminder of the struggles of the kings of Jerusalem against the infidels.

Visual effect was all-important. As an extreme example, there are the extraordinary contrivances which enlivened the jousts at Châlons-sur-Marne held in 1445. This occasion was not strictly a court festival, but a private challenge between six nobles from the entourages of the duke of Burgundy and the count of Anjou. They were all dressed in cloth of gold, save one who was in cloth of silver. Most of the pages and gentlemen were in velvet, dripping with gold, in exotic patterns. And the count of Charny had a veil of silk mounted on an iron frame on his helmet which extended to cover both him and his charger, down to the ground.[85]

René was as successful at dreaming up these performances as he was inept and unfortunate in the real world. The 'Enterprise of the Dragon's Maw' at Chinon in 1446 actually took as its theme the very real misfortunes that had befallen René in the previous few years. Four knights were defending a place marked by a raging dragon on a pillar, where they jousted with any passing knights accompanied by a lady. Ladies who rode alone had to promise to return with a suitable challenger. René decided to challenge them; his own chosen device for the occasion was a black shield sown with golden tears, and he carried a black lance: he jousted so well that he was awarded the overall prize.

René's next plot for a challenge was based on Arthurian romance. It centred on a wooden castle built near Saumur, which he named *Joyeuse Garde*, the legendary Arthurian castle of lovers in Cornwall, to which Tristan brought Iseult, and Lancelot brought Guinevere. He and his fellow defendants undertook to hold it for forty days. René's entry into the lists began with a procession led by two Turkish attendants with scarlet and white turbans

*René d'Anjou: his tournaments*

**79, 80, 81.** Three pictures from René d'Anjou's *Livre de tournois*, the manual in which he outlined the protocol for holding a tournament. Left: To begin proceedings, heralds are sent to negotiate the details of the tournament with the challenger. Above: The knights assembled in the lists before the tournament starts. Right: The prizes are awarded at the end of the three days' event.

leading live lions on silver chains, followed by musicians and trumpeters on horseback and two kings of arms carrying their books 'of honour and nobility', and the four judges. A dwarf in Turkish costume bore the device chosen by the king for the occasion, a golden shield sown with pansies. Behind him came René, led by a very beautiful lady who held his horse by a scarf attached to its bridle. A copy of the shield stood on a marble pillar nearby, which challengers touched with their lances to indicate that they wanted to joust.

*René d'Anjou: his manual on tournaments*

An exquisite illuminated manuscript was drawn up soon after the end of the tournament to record the results of the jousts; it is now lost, but we do have what is probably an even more magnificent text, the book on tournaments and jousting written by René d'Anjou and illuminated by an artist who worked for him on two other texts, Barthélemy van Eyck. Barthélemy had evolved a distinctive style of his own by the time he came to create the *Treatise of Tournaments of King René*[86] in the 1460s. It is lavishly laid out, with numerous full-page and double-page pictures, many of which are masterpieces in their own right. René begins his account with the preliminary announcements of the challenge to a tournament carried by heralds to neighbouring lords and princes, and goes on to describe the tournament armour to be used, all carefully delineated. The next stage is the construction of the lists, which are drawn empty to show how they are laid out, and the reception of the knights in the town: here there are streets with the houses lined with shields above the doors and banners from the upper windows. We watch the judges and squires ride into the town, and then see the ladies inspecting the banners and helms of the participants in a nearby cloister. The stages of the tournament are spread across three double pages, and the last image is of the prize about to be awarded by the ladies in the candle-lit room where the evening's dance is to be held. It is as near as we can come to actually taking part in a court festival; the artist not only brings to life the events of the tournament, but peoples it with wonderfully realistic individual figures and faces.

Tournaments undoubtedly contributed to magnificence. The king or duke who held the grandest tournaments gained reflected glory, even if he did not joust himself – which relatively few princes did. Full scale tournaments were generally associated with other events, and if knights organised jousting, it was usually in the more modest form of the *pas d'armes*, where only a small number of knights participated. However, from Friedrich I's festival at Mainz in 1184 (where the tournament was planned but cancelled) onwards, almost every formal gathering where a large number of knights are present seems to have a tournament attached. The tournament does not necessarily have anything to do with the main event. It may well be no more than a very practical use of such a gathering – coronation, wedding, festival or whatever – to indulge in a favourite sport.

# PART THREE

---

# THE
# MANAGEMENT OF
# MAGNIFICENCE

---

# 12 | MAGNIFICENT EXTRAVAGANCES

◆ *Medieval cookery* ◆ *Cookery books and the* Viandier Taillevent
◆ *Subtleties and* entremets ◆ *Master Chiquart* ◆ *The feast* ◆ *The buffet:*
*displaying wealth* ◆ *The reception of guests* ◆ *The serving of the meal*

*On Feasts* Firstly, the time must be right. For it is fitting that a feast should be held at the right time, neither stormy nor too late. Secondly, the place must be suitable, spacious, pleasant and safe. Third, the guests should be good company, with smiling faces. For a feast is worthless if the guest's face is troubled. Fourth, there should be a multitude of dishes, so that if someone does not like a dish, he may relish another. Fifth, a variety of wines and drinks is needed. Sixth, the servants should be well-mannered and honest. Seventh, the company of friends as dinner guests is welcome. Eighth, there should be a cheerful sound of singers and musical instruments. For it is not the custom of nobles to celebrate a feast without a harpist or other musicians. Ninth, there should be copious numbers of lights and candles. For it is indecorous to feast in the dark, and even dangerous because of flies. And the candles should be fixed in candelabra, the lights in lamps, and the necessary candles should be lit. Tenth, everything that is served should be a delicacy. For it is not the custom to offer coarse and common foods at a feast, as would be done at a supper, but rather special and light and delicious things should be placed in front of the diners, particularly in a lord's house. Eleventh, the feast should be by day. For when men go out to work, they bring forward their supper. For food eaten too close to night time is harmful, and to dine then is displeasing. The twelfth is that there should be no charge, because invitations to supper should not involve the diners in expense. It is dishonorable to compel anyone who has come of their own accord to pay his share after the dinner. Thirteenth, there should be quiet and pleasant sleep, for one should rest after supper, because it is sweet to sleep then.

Bartholomew the Englishman, *Encyclopedia*, c.1235

## Medieval Cookery

IT IS ONLY IN THE LAST THIRTY OR forty years that medieval cookery has been studied carefully by both scholars and practising cooks, and we now have a much clearer idea of the medieval kitchen and what it produced. Where the recipes came from, and many of the methods and ingredients, are still very much matters of debate. On the one hand, there was evidently some kind of survival of classical Roman practices, summed up in the excerpts from a book attributed to Apicius, who was probably Marcus Gavius Apicius, famous as a gourmet in the first century. Seneca says that his elevation of cookery to a science had corrupted his contemporaries, and Pliny said he was 'born to enjoy every extravagant luxury that could be contrived'.[1] The book which was later simply known as 'Apicius' was copied in the fifth or sixth century, and was known at the time of Charlemagne, when a shortened version, but with some items added, was produced.[2] At that point it was ignored until the great rediscovery of classical texts from the late fourteenth century onwards.

We know that fine food continued to be appreciated after the collapse of the Roman empire in the west from a story told by Gregory of Tours in the late sixth century. He tells how the nephew of the bishop of Langres was captured and enslaved, and how the bishop's cook Leo set out to rescue him. Leo arranged for himself to be sold as a slave to the man who owned the bishop's nephew, and his new master asked him what he could do:

> 'I am highly skilled in preparing all dishes which are fit to be eaten at a rich man's table', replied Leo, 'and I am prepared to assert that no-one can find my equal in the culinary science. Indeed, I tell you this: if you want to prepare a banquet for a king, I can cook such royal dishes for you, and none can do it better than I can.' 'Well,' said the Frank, 'tomorrow is Sunday, and on that day I shall invite my neighbours and relations to my house. I want you to prepare a meal at which they will marvel and exclaim: "Why, we have not seen better food in the King's palace!"' 'My master has only to order a good supply of chickens', answered Leo, 'and I will do what you command.' Everything which he had asked for was made ready. Sunday dawned, and he cooked a magnificent meal, with every imaginable delicacy. When they had all eaten their fill, the Frank's relations said how much they had enjoyed their meal and went off home.[3]

Leo gains his master's trust, and waits for a year before successfully escaping to freedom with the bishop's nephew. It is reasonable to assume that Leo had some knowledge of recipes like those in Apicius, given the strong survival of late Roman culture in Gaul at this time, but we have no positive evidence of what he did to the chickens. Nonetheless, this little episode sums up neatly the objective of any medieval prince in giving a great feast: to present something which will reflect his power and wealth, so that his guests return home impressed by what they have seen and eaten. And the trusted position earned by the cook underlines his importance.

Leo is something of an isolated figure. Before the fourteenth century, we have very few records of cooks and cookery, and only literary sources such as the medieval romances. The authors of these are maddeningly inclined to assume that their listeners would be entirely familiar with the menus of the magnificent feasts offered by legendary figures such as Arthur or Alexander to their courts. Even Wolfram von Eschenbach, in his great romance about the Grail, which he envisages as a source of wondrous food, is tantalisingly brief. He can name the fifty-eight different jewels that adorn the bed of the Grail's king, but all he says of the feast that follows is that 'they took from the Grail dishes wild and tame, this man his mead, that man his wine'.[4] The chroniclers who describe Friedrich Barbarossa's feast at Mainz in 1184 are equally reticent on the subject – the supply of food 'was inestimable, and could not be told by any man's tongue'.

The cook's secrets, like those of the masons, were handed down by word of mouth; we do not possess any twelfth- or thirteenth-century cookery books. On the other hand, we do know something about the food and feasts of the period. King John's household accounts at the beginning of the thirteenth century show that he bought enormous quantities of food for his Christmas feast, but that the fare was not particularly spectacular: pork, chicken, a small number of pheasants and other game, much fish, salt eels and herrings, and a selection of spices – pepper, cloves, cinnamon, nutmegs, ginger and saffron for colouring. A hundred pounds of almonds went into the sauces. Although the range of herbs and spices was nothing like as wide as that of Roman cookery, it was a considerable advance on what would have been used a hundred years earlier.

One of the earliest detailed menus for a feast which we have comes from an unexpected source. *The Treatise of Walter of Bibbesworth* dates from around 1234–5, and is a fascinating document in that it is for teaching the children of land-owning families Anglo-Norman (showing that their native tongue was already English). It is a wonderful source of information about all kinds of ordinary day-to-day affairs. At the end of the book, the author says 'Now the French for arranging a feast':

> A young man of fashion came here from a dinner
> And told us about the feast, how the service was arranged.
> Without bread, wine and beer no feast will be comfortable,
> But they had as much as they wanted of all three, the boy told us.
> He talked about another feast and the courses they had to eat.
> First the boar's head well armed and the snout fully garlanded,
> Then venison with frumenty and many other varied things:
> Cranes, peacocks and swans, kids, sucking-pigs and hens;
> Then they had rabbits in gravy, all coated in sugar,
> Mace, cubebs and cloves and plenty of other spicery,
> 'Food of cyprus',* maumeny, red and white wine in plenty;
> Then plenty of other roasts, each alongside another,
> Pheasants, woodcock and partridges, fieldfares, larks and plovers roasted,
> Brawne, crisps and fritters or rose-sugar as corrective;
> And when the table was cleared, blanch powder as whole sweetmeat,
> And other noble things in plenty ...[5]

*English feasts in the thirteenth century*

The bishop of Hereford's accounts for Christmas 1289 show us a much wider variety of spices. The spice cupboard was replenished in anticipation of his feast with the cloves, cubebs (a kind of black pepper), and mace listed by Bibbesworth. In addition, however, there are saffron, galingale, cinnamon, ginger, pepper, cumin, liquorice, aniseed, coriander and gromwell. Some of the items among the bishop's spices came from distant lands. The spice trade, which had continued on a small scale since Roman times, now flourished once again. The Crusades had led to a ban by the pope on trading with the Arabs, but nevertheless the Italians established a regular commerce with them. The Arabs in turn obtained cinnamon from the East Indies; pepper, nutmeg and mace also came from there, brought either overland or in dhows round the coast to the Persian Gulf. Ginger, also for medicinal use, had continued to reach Europe in small quantities since Roman times, but was now brought from the Far East in considerable shipments. Aniseed, cumin and coriander were obtainable in the Mediterranean, while the saffron crocus, gromwell and liquorice root were native plants.

*Florence: spendthrift gourments around 1285*

All this points to some knowledge of how to concoct complex spiced dishes; but we have no definite evidence of what the results were like until we turn to thirteenth-century Italy. And here we meet our first medieval gourmets. In about 1285 a group of twelve young noblemen of Siena, lovers of good living and high spending, decided to pool all their resources and to lead as luxurious an existence as possible until their combined wealth was exhausted. Among their number was one Niccolò de' Salimbeni, who, as Dante tells us, first discovered how to use cloves, 'a costly cult and passion'.[6]

Early commentators on Dante's poem suggested a number of explanations for this

---

* Food of Cyprus: a dish of almond milk flavoured with ginger. Maumeny is minced beef and chicken with almonds and spices, coloured red or blue.

remark. One writer claimed that Niccolò used to grow cloves and basil in the same piece of ground because this gave a better flavour to the cloves. Others say that he was the first to roast pheasants and partridges with cloves, or simply the first to introduce cloves to Siena (though this seems unlikely, as they were already known as far afield as England). A more thoughtful commentator offers various opinions:

> Some say that this Niccolò made his servants clean cloves for him, but this is easier said than done. Others say that he put cloves into roast meats, but this was neither a new invention nor any great extravagance. Others say that he had pheasants and chickens roasted over a fire made of cloves. And this I do believe, because it was the vainest, most extravagant habit, an entirely new invention; and there are stories about him to the effect that he had gold florins cooked in sauce, which he would suck and throw away.[7]

But the most interesting detail comes from Francesco da Buti, writing in about 1380:

> This Niccolò de' Salimbeni was one of the Spendthrift Brigade, and because they all tried to discover sumptuous and gluttonous dishes, it is said that blancmanges and Ubaldine fritters were invented then, and other similar things, about which their cook wrote a book.

The idea of recipes or receipts was familiar from classical times onwards, but they almost always occur in a medical context. It is important to remember that diet was an important part of medieval medicine, and that such items as the recipes for sauces which can be found in the twelfth century are potentially part of the treatment for an illness rather than simply the notes left by a cook.[8]

Given that the cooks were much less likely to be literate than the doctors, and as modern cooks know all too well, the environment of a kitchen is anathema to books of any sort, it is no surprise that the first manuscripts which contains cookery recipes separate from medical ones appear as late as the end of the thirteenth century. One such book is English, written in Anglo-Norman, and is a collection of legal documents in various hands, the only exceptions being two items on precious stones and the list of recipes, headed 'How to make food and spiced wine'.[9] The style of the recipes is not that for an ordinary kitchen, and indeed not even for everyday menus at court. Thirteen of the dishes contain sugar, which was a rare and luxurious item at the time, first encountered by the crusaders from western Europe in Palestine, and largely imported through Venice. Other dishes show an Arab influence. This is confirmed by another collection of very brief recipes, also in Anglo-Norman, dating from the early fourteenth century. There are entries for white, green and yellow Syrian food, as well as Spanish food, all of which are variations on almond milk, rice – both imported foods – and chicken. The Spanish dish also contains pistachios, very much a rarity. Both collections are obviously from a noble household or from the royal court itself, for feasts of the grandest sort. It is tempting to think, with the 'Spanish food' and the possible connections to Palestine, that both books may stem from the kitchen of Edward I, famous as a crusader and married to Eleanor of Castile.

Another unusual ingredient is pasta, which appears in the recipe for 'cressee', best translated as criss-cross, where noodles are made from best white flour and eggs, flavoured with ginger and sugar, and half the mixture is coloured with saffron. It is then laid out in a lattice with the two colours woven at right angles, boiled, and served with grated cheese and butter or oil. Ravioli, too, makes an appearance. These two recipes seem again to come from Arab sources, where pasta was used in medicine as an element of diet; they could have come by way of Sicily, but English connections with the Anglo-Norman kings of Sicily had

*An Anglo-Norman cookery book*

ended with the death of the last of the dynasty at the beginning of the thirteenth century. It is more likely that they came from the same source as the Syrian and Spanish dishes.[10]

## Cookery books and the Viandier Taillevent

THE MOST INFLUENTIAL OF ALL MEDIEVAL cookery books was that known as the *Viandier Taillevent*, the collection of recipes attributed to Guillaume Tirel, known as Taillevent, cook to Charles V of France, whose career began as a kitchen boy to the French queen in 1326. He was cook to Philip VI of France in the late 1340s and then to Philip's grandson, Charles V, both before and after he succeeded to the throne in 1364. Finally, he held the same office under Charles VI until 1392, dying in 1395 at around the age of eighty. The book that bears his name may well be his own compilation, but its basis is an earlier thirteenth-century collection by an anonymous author. Essentially, it is a list of dishes, with very little about technique, and nothing about menus, organising feasts or even the occasions on which certain dishes should be served. However, there is a section on the special dishes to be served to the prince between courses at great feasts. These were not part of the everyday cookery for the court. It is a text which enjoyed a great reputation, particularly after the introduction of the printing press: it first appeared in print in 1490, and in the following century no less than fifteen editions were produced. Jean duke of Berry, the leading collector of illuminated manuscripts in the fifteenth century, had a de luxe copy which he bought from a Paris bookseller in 1404. It is the rather improbable last item in a volume of romances.

We have a similar collection to that of Taillevent in the *Forme of Cury*, the headnote to which declares that it was 'compiled by the chief master cooks of King Richard the second' and was held to be 'the best and most royal book' on the subject belonging to any Christian king. There are several versions of it, which between them contain over two hundred recipes, beginning with 'common pottages and meats' for the household, and then offering 'curious pottages and meats and subtleties for all manner of estates both high and low'.[11] The recipes are brief and to the point, simply the procedures to be carried out as each ingredient is added. Even though the book is said to have been compiled with the approval of the masters of physic and philosophy at court, this is a very simple practical outline with no literary pretensions. It is not even clear at which point the break between ordinary household recipes and the grander items actually occurs.

*The menu for the wedding feast at Milan in 1361*

The wedding feast for Lionel, duke of Clarence, and Violante Visconti in 1361 was lavish enough for several accounts of the menu to be recorded, including one extremely detailed listing. The actual cooking was mainly a combination of roasted or boiled meat and grilled or boiled fish. The cook's art depended largely on his skills in the presentation of 'false' dishes. All the courses offered both meat and fish, and the first five courses were all gilded. The first was gilded piglets with fire in their mouths, and gilded fish called 'little pigs', a punning combination. This was followed by gilded hares, with gilded pike, and then a large gilded calf with gilded trout. Quail and gilded partridges were again accompanied by gilded trout, and the next course combined gilded duck with herons and carp. Beef and fat capons with garlic sauce were matched with sturgeons. The capons were repeated in the next course, with meat and fish in a lemon sauce. Patés and beef followed, accompanied by eel patés. The ninth course, marking the mid point of the banquet, consisted of jellies of meat and fish. Salted meat and lampreys were served next, before the first roast dishes, roasted goat and shad, appeared. More elaborate dishes followed: hares, kids, and fish cooked in their own juices followed by venison and beef cooked in pastry cases. Capons and hens coloured red and green, with apples and cedrons (a large sweet lemon), were the prelude to the main display piece, peacocks, which would have been presented with their tails and heads attached to the roast; these were served with vegetables, beans, greens and salted tongue, and the fish to match was carp, also highly esteemed. A final course of roast meat consisted of rabbits, swans, peacocks and ducks, accompanied by eels. The last two courses were dessert: junket and cheese, and finally fruit, including cherries.[12]

Presentation and colouring are all-important here. Gilding, used in the first courses, was done by glazing the finished dish with egg yolk at the last minute, just before the dish was served. A modern version of a gilding recipe suggests mixing egg yolks, saffron and honey, and painting this onto the meat, returning it to the oven for five minutes to let it set. In the most luxurious cases, gold leaf was laid on over a layer of wheat starch. As well as saffron, a whole palette of colourings was available from the spice cupboard, such as sugar and spice balls 'of all sorts and colours', alkanet and turnsole for red and blue dye respectively; green of course appeared naturally, and the green sauces would probably have been composed to ensure a strong colour, but a mixture of parsley, white wine and flour was also used.

*Presentation and decoration*

Another visual feature was the roast dishes in the form of the birds and beasts from which they came. The most famous of these was the boar's head, reconstituted with brawn, and with an apple in its mouth, which survived as a Christmas dish well into the twentieth century. Peacocks were an obvious display item: a roast goose was actually the base for this, adorned with the peacock's head and feathers. Swans, too, would be similarly treated; real swans of this kind may have been the centrepiece at the feast of the swans at the knighting of Edward II.

If real birds could be reconstituted, fabulous beasts could also appear before the diners. The cockatrice, born of a cock's egg hatched by a toad, winged and with a stare which could kill a man, figured in the recipe books: it was made by roasting a suckling pig and a chicken together, so that it had the forequarters of a pig and the wings of a chicken. The result was then painted and gilded according to the cook's imagination.

## Subtleties and entremets

A GREAT FEATURE OF MEDIEVAL FEASTS from the fourteenth century onwards were the *entremets*, dishes served at the end of a section of the feast. Initially, there were usually two parts to the menu, but by the mid fourteenth century there could be as many as ten divisions, as at the wedding of Lionel and Violante Visconti in 1361 At first, the *entremets* were simply extra items between courses, or the 'false' dishes we have already discussed. They then became special dishes of delicacies, and seem to have been served to the lord's table only, or to a group of tables with noble guests. A Latin *Book of Cookery* early in the next century has a 'monk's head', made of fruits and pastry and with a crenellation round it 'like a castle'. The same book also describes figures sculptured in pastry, giving as an example a jongleur with musical instruments, which must be very carefully handled when putting them in the oven. The *Viandier* gives fourteen examples of *entremets*, including detailed instructions for presenting a roast swan at table, since it could not have been carved in the usual way. The bird, roasted and gilded with pastry mixed with egg yolks is then encased in a wire framework, over which the skin and feathers are stretched, and the head and neck are reattached. The framework can evidently be lifted off before the dish is carved and served.

Similarly, there are decorated dishes, such as the gilded dishes with 'helmeted cocks' who are made to ride on the back of roast pigs: the cocks are roasted, and given a helmet of glued paper and a lance attached to their breast. And there are tarts cut with crenellated edges and filled with pieces of chicken spiked with the banners of France and of great lords. For some dishes, gold and silver leaf is used, as well as special effects which make flames come out of the nostrils of the animals which the dishes model.

By the end of the century, the *entremet* had been either supplanted or supplemented by the subtlety proper.[13] A version of Taillevent's *Viandier* from this period lists five 'recipes' or rather sets of instructions for such creations, which do not involve the cook at all, but are the work of artisans: carpenters, smiths and painters. The writer calls them 'painted *entremets*', and the materials used, beside wood, iron and paint, include parchment and even wool for balls to be thrown when attacking a castle held by Saracens. The distinction between this type of *entremet* and the subtlety is very difficult to establish, as the whole range of items from 'false' dishes to full-scale dramatic episodes enacted at the banquet can be called by either term. It is clear that in the ordinances of Humbert II of Vienne, who ruled from 1333 to 1349, *entremet* refers to a specially cooked dish reserved for the high table. The prince was to be served a sufficient quantity to send it to others, according to his pleasure, so that such a helping became a mark of princely favour.[14] Some set-pieces could involve both cookery and drama. The 'four and twenty blackbirds' of the English nursery rhyme is a distant memory of a real recipe found in two medieval cookery books. The pie was indeed baked, but with a separate crust. The birds were put in the pie, and the crust was put on top. The crust was then removed before the guests, and the birds were released, giving the illusion that the pie had been baked with them inside.

These special dishes for *entremet* seem to have evolved from a choice delicacy into a display of the cook's art in pastry or in other means which allowed the creation of models and figures. As these became more and more realistic, they were often not intended to be eaten. The next step, as the cook's ambitions grew, was to introduce stage scenery and props. These stage-set pieces soon gave way to actual dumb shows in the late fourteenth century, and even to spoken interludes in the next century. The *entremets* of the late Middle Ages belong to the world of the civic entries and the king's games, with their dramatic tableaux and cleverly staged effects.[15]

The *entremets* took many forms. In 1399, when Martí was crowned king of Aragon, there were two *entremets* in which armed men fought with wild creatures. The first was a serpent-dragon, breathing great flames at the attackers, 'which it did very well'. For the second, a large and very realistic rock appeared, with a huge leopard with a great wound on its left shoulder standing at the summit, and rabbits, pigs, partridges, doves and other birds on it which flew around the room while the armed men tried to kill the leopard: but wild men appeared and counter-attacked, driving them back. When they were victorious, a small crowned child emerged from the wound, dressed in the royal arms and carrying a naked sword.[16] In 1414, at the coronation of Fernando I of Aragon, 'a very fine Gryphon, all gilded and as large as a horse entered, with a golden crown round its neck and, breathing fire the whole time, it cleared the way through the people so that the dinner could be served'. Similarly, Olivier de la Marche, describing Philip the Good's Feast of the Pheasant in 1454, talks of 'living *entremets*, moving and being led', the participants being a procession of grotesque figures who moved around the guests in the hall.

# Master Chiquart

I T IS VERY FORTUNATE THAT IN 1420 Amadeus VIII of Savoy asked his cook, Master Chiquart, to write down his experiences as a key member of the *domus providencie*, the provisioning of the household. The dukes of Savoy had had a reputation for magnificence and stylish living since the mid fourteenth century, when Amadeus VIII's grandfather, 'the Green Count', had cut a splendid figure among his fellow-princes. Chiquart had been employed by Amadeus VIII since the late 1390s. Somewhat reluctantly – he claimed to 'have many times refused and spoken against it' because of his little learning and understanding, and because 'I have no book nor writings made concerning this nor memoirs' – he set down what he had learnt in the course of his service, and did so stylishly and with eloquence.

*On Cookery* is an unusual book, as it is actually organised around the structure of a festival to be held over two days, with a dinner on the first day, and dinner and supper on the second. There are two menus given, one for an occasion when meat may be eaten, and a second in case the festival falls on a fish day: these were normally Friday and Saturday, but also the whole of Lent and other specific dates in the Church calendar. Next there are dishes for guests who are unwell or have specific dietary needs. What is striking is that we are in the presence of a creative chef. Chiquart goes beyond the common stock of recipes which form the basic repertoire of the cook and either elaborates on these or gives recipes which have no parallel elsewhere.

Furthermore, his instructions are closer to those we would expect to find in a modern cookery book (save only the absence of quantities for many of the ingredients). Many medieval cookery books read like notes or an aide-memoire: Chiquart is instructing his readers in what he has learnt of his art. Part of that art is to know the amounts to use: early in the book, he specifies in one recipe that the cook should put in 'just the proper amount, so that there is neither too little nor too much'.[17]

Menus were arranged according to certain basic principles, and the order of service generally conformed to an accepted pattern. At a great feast, the dishes would also be colour-coordinated to demonstrate the cook's skill. In Chiquart's first menu, the predominant colours for the first course are gold and green, produced by saffron, yolk of egg and the gold serving dishes, and the green vegetables and herbs. The second course, of 'bruets', almond milk stews, was white, while the third course was red, lampreys in beef gravy. This was followed by a yellow course, German broths cooked with onions or fish in batter in a green sauce, which had to be carefully judged to come out as a bright and festive green, not a sombre dark green. The final course consisted of decorative pies.[18]

Meat and fish, if served roast or boiled, were always accompanied by a sauce, and Chiquart gives fifteen recipes for them. Since these were the most important dishes on the menu, everything depended on the cook's skill in this area. The value placed on sauces is indicated by the name given to a cinnamon sauce in a German cookery book, which is specified as a 'sauce for lords'. Interestingly, cinnamon seems to have been very rare in Germany, but was used quite widely elsewhere in Europe.[19]

*Master Chiquart's menus*

The soups and stews, which might also be based on almond milk or eggs, formed the majority of dishes, and were the most complex, requiring a careful balance of meats, colours and spices. The list of ingredients for Chiquart's German broth is as follows:

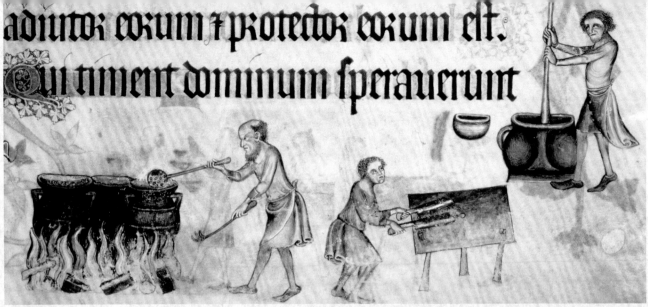

adintor eorum ⁊ protector eorum est.
Qui timent dominum sperauerunt

dedit filiis hominum

**82, 83.** (above) Cooking a feast:
pictures from *The Luttrell Psalter*,
c.1320–40.
Top: cooking pots being tended
on a fire; a chopping board;
pounding food in a mortar.
Above: cutting up poultry; spicing
the dishes; carrying the dishes
into the hall.

**84.** A late example of a ship-salt:
the Burghley nef from 1527.
No intact medieval nefs of
quality survive.

Capons, pork or lamb, kid or veal; onions; bacon fat; almonds; beef stock; good white wine, verjuice; white ginger, grains of paradise, a little pepper, nutmeg, cloves and mace, saffron for colouring, a lot of sugar; salt.[20]

Chiquart includes a full and detailed account of how to make a 'raised *entremet*' of a castle of love, a precursor of the *entremets* of the Burgundian court in the following decades. Some of the technicalities remain unexplained: sadly, Chiquart does not tell us the exact secret of how the castle is constructed or how the effects of piglets and swans spitting fire and the fountains might work. All he gives are the recipes for cooking the food which decorates it and instructions for creating the peacock.

> For a raised *entremets*, that is a castle. For its base you need a good big four man litter, and on that litter you need four towers ... In every tower there must be archers and crossbowmen to defend that fortress. Furthermore in every tower there will be a candle or torch to give light. The towers will show branches bearing flowers and fruits of every sort of tree, and upon those branches will be birds of every variety. In the courtyard at the foot of each tower there will be what follows: At one of the towers, a boar's head emblazoned and glazed breathing fire. At another tower, a large pike; that pike will be cooked in three ways – the one-third at the tail, fried, the one-third at the middle, boiled, and the one-third at the head, roasted on the grill. That pike will be placed at the foot of the next tower looking out, its mouth breathing fire ... At the foot of the next tower a glazed piglet looking out and breathing fire. And at the foot of the last tower a skinned and redressed swan, likewise breathing fire. In the centre of the courtyard below the four towers there should be a fountain of Love. Through a spout there should gush rosewater and mulled wine. Over that fountain should be set cages holding doves and every sort of flying bird ... Alongside the fountain should be a peacock which has been skinned and redressed ... with its wings stretched out; and make its tail spread open, and hold its neck up high, as if it were alive, by fixing a wooden stick in the neck and supporting it.
>
> At the crenels around that courtyard should be hens, skinned, redressed and glazed, and glazed hedgehogs, and glazed meatballs and Spanish pots made of meat and all glazed. The moulded work of paste, that is to say: hares, brachet hounds, stags, wild boars, the huntsmen with their horns, partridge, crayfish, dolphins, all that moulded work is of pea and bean muellery. Of moulded paste make all the castle's curtain walls which will go around the castle, and they should be hanging down long enough that the bearers of the said castle cannot be seen. Those curtain walls, up to height of two feet above the ground should be painted with waves and great tossing billows; in those waves should be painted all sorts of fish, and on the billows and waves should be painted galleys and ships full of all sorts of armed men in such a way that it would seem that the ships are coming to assail that castle of Love, looking as if it were on a great rock in the sea.[21]

*Master Chiquart's* entremets

The four beasts at the foot of the towers may refer to the crests of high ranking members of the court, all members of the Savoyard knightly Order of the Collar.[22] What we have here is a complicated confection from the kitchen, in which heraldry and theatre were as important as the skills of the cook. The result was designed to be carried in with music and appropriate pomp so that everyone could see it.

---

* A west African spice somewhere between cardamom and pepper.

THE IMPORTANCE OF *entremets* or subtleties and the way in which they were explained to the onlookers is shown by the verses which John Lydgate wrote to accompany the three subtleties at the coronation feast of Henry VI. After the first course, which included 'viande royal planted with lozenges of gold, boars' heads in castles armed with gold, a red jelly with white lions in it, a royal custard with a leopard of gold sitting in it, a fritter like a sun with a *fleur-de-lis*, there was a subtlety of St Edward the Confessor and St Louis dressed in their heraldic arms leading the king, also dressed in his arms. Lydgate's verses were either on a placard placed beside the subtlety or were declaimed by a herald:

> Behold two kings right perfect and right good,
> Holy Saint Edward and St Louis:
> And see the branch born of their blessed blood;
> Live, among Christian sovereigns most of prize,
> Inheritor of the fleur de lys!
> God grant he may through help of Christ Jesu
> This sixth Henry, both reign and be as wise
> Resembling them in knighthood and virtue.

The second and third courses had similarly gilded and heraldic dishes, including a pie ornamented with pointed pieces of pastry decorated with golden leopards and *fleurs-de-lis*: the two subtleties showed Henry VI with the emperor Sigismund, an ally of England following the victory at Agincourt, and Henry VI presented to the Virgin and child by St George and St Denis as patron saints of England and France, also accompanied by Lydgate's verses.

Two centuries later, Ben Jonson described what could easily have been Chiquart's creations:

> A master cook! why, he is the man of men,
> He's a professor; he designs, he draws,
> He paints, he carves, he builds, he fortifies,
> Makes citadels of curious fowl and fish.
> Some he dry-ditches, some motes round with broths,
> Mounts marrow-bone, cuts fifty angled custards,
> Rears bulwark pies; and for his outer works,
> He raiseth ramparts of immortal crust,
> And teacheth all the tactics at one dinner ...[23]

Court festivals of all kinds required a massive degree of organisation and huge financial resources. By the end of the Middle Ages, all departments of the king's household would be involved, from the king's armourer and the royal stables to the pavilioners and the king's painters, and finally to the cooks required to produce banquets which were spectacles in themselves, with numerous courses and dishes which were designed as much to be paraded before the diners as to be eaten. Friedrich Barbarossa's gathering at Mainz may have been vaster than anything that followed, but he would have been astonished by the scale of fifteenth-century festivals in terms of lavish display and consumption, and the sheer personnel and finance required – quite apart from the drama and machinery involved.

# The Feast
## *The buffet: displaying wealth*

O N THE TABLES, AND IN LATER CENTURIES also on a buffet at the end of the hall, there would have been a spectacular display of plate. The buffet or cupboard was a tall set of open shelves designed to accommodate the varied pieces, which ranged through containers for the precious salt, highly valuable in the medieval world, which were sometimes nefs in the shape of fully-rigged ships, but always elaborate or carefully fashioned in silver or gold; table fountains which ran with wine and water, and, as the dishes were served, vast gold chargers laden with delicacies. An inventory of the plate belonging to Louis d'Anjou, son of Jean II of France, drawn up in 1365, runs to over a thousand items, among them many which were made specifically for display.[24] This was admittedly one of the largest collections of plate among the French royal princes. The buffet was a focus of much attention, to the extent that when Charles V entertained his uncle the Holy Roman Emperor in 1378, the display had to be guarded, according to Christine de Pizan: 'The two great displays and the dressers had barriers around them, so that people could only enter at certain points which were guarded by knights charged with that duty.'[25]

Cups were of silver or gold; a superb enamelled standing cup or hanap, known as the Royal Gold Cup, and dating from the 1380s, survives in the British Museum.[26] The grandest pieces would be placed in front of the host on the high table, or even on a separate table. At the feast given by Gian Galeazzo of Milan in 1395, following his inauguration as duke, the display of plate dominated the space in which the feast was held: Gian Galeazzo and his guests went in procession

*The king's gold and silver plate*

> to the court called the Arenga, at the head of which was placed a spacious, enormous table under a canopy of drapes woven with purest gold, in the midst of which was placed the ducal plate, the sight of which was truly most grand. And on one and the other side were two other buffets of silverware, of lesser pieces.[27]

Georges Chastellain, a member of the household of Philip the Good of Burgundy and official chronicler to the knights of the Order of the Golden Fleece, was at the feast of the Order held at The Hague in May 1456. The centrepiece of the hall where the feast was held was dominated by three massive buffets:

> draped and far apart from one another, one of which was a buffet of state entirely garnished with vessels of gold set with precious stones, of five or six stages in height, intended for men to admire. The second buffet was for the use of the Knights of the Order, and was full of gilt plate and also laden with rich furnishings on a multitude of shelves; nothing could have been richer. The third buffet, from which those seated at the other tables were served was entirely set out with silver vessels, of which there were so many, and the height [of the buffet] was so great that the like has scarcely been seen.[28]

*Buffets of state*

Elsewhere we read of buffets so high that there were staircases on either side so that the shelves could be accessed and others, as at the Feast of the Pheasant in 1454, with wooden barriers to protect it. Olivier de la Marche was evidently proud of the buffet for which he was responsible at the wedding of Charles the Bold and Margaret of York in 1468:

> In the middle of the hall was a high and rich buffet, in the shape of a lozenge. The base of the buffet was enclosed like the lists in a tournament, and the whole of it was covered in tapestry with the duke's arms. From the base upwards there were steps loaded with

plate, with the largest pieces at the bottom, and the richest and most delicate at the top. So at the bottom were the great silver-gilt pieces, and at the top were the gold pieces set with jewels, of which there were a great many. And at the very top of the buffet there was a rich jewelled cup, and on the corners there were large unicorns' horns, very large and beautiful. And none of the plate on the buffet was used to serve food that day.[29]

The kind of pieces that might have been on display are to be found in the French and English royal inventories. They represented the prince's visible wealth, but the value of the objects displayed seems to vary considerably. We have a specific list of the 'plate to be placed on a buffet when the duke dines in state' belonging to John, duke of Bedford, in 1432. As regent of France, his reputation for magnificence should have been particularly important in terms of proclaiming that he represented Henry VI as the true king of France and England. The list runs to 128 items, beginning with four gold cups. The range of objects is very wide. The covers on some of the cups had elaborate jewellers' work, knobs which represented fruits and foliage, or a castle. At the other extreme, many pieces were practical silver plate for use at table.[30] The items were valued in 1443 at the relatively modest sum of £848, about 15 per cent of the total value of the goods delivered to his executor. Olivier de la Marche's description of the buffet at the wedding of Charles the Bold in 1468 implies that the duke owned far more fine pieces than Bedford, but the only figure he gives is that for the ordinary serving plate that Philip the Good had left to Charles, which he estimates at a wildly exaggerated £40,000. The Bedford inventory does however tell us much about the type of objects which would have made up the display.

*The nef*

The outstanding piece on most princely tables was very striking, and almost totally impractical. This is the nef, an ornamental ship-model made in silver, silver-gilt or gold. Nefs appear from 1381 onwards in the ducal accounts in Burgundy, and they are classed with *drageoirs* or sweetmeat dishes. These nefs were put on the prince's table as a mark of honour, in front of his place. In 1382, one of the duke's nefs needed repair, so it may have been acquired a few years earlier.[31] At the same time a nef 'with two sirens' is recorded, a design which reappears in the famous Burghley nef a century later, which again confirms that this is the princely version of the nef. In 1387 the duke has a nef made for his wife, perhaps the nef 'with the sheep' in the newly fashionable pastoral mode that is in the inventory in 1397.

We can trace the history of one of these superlative creations in the French and English royal accounts. This was a nef called the 'Tiger', given by Jean duke of Berry to Charles VI of France as a New Year present in 1395. Charles's clerks recorded it as follows:

> A gold nef borne on the back of a bear; the said bear is lying on a table of gold spangled with *fleur-de-lis*, and has a collar and muzzle set with fifteen balas rubies and seventeen fine pearls. On the castles[32] of the said nef there is a terrace on which two tigers crouch, each looking in a mirror and each having a collar set with three small balas rubies and eight little pearls.[33] And it was given to the king by my lord the duke of Berry, and weighs 34 marks and half an ounce of gold.[34]

On 27 October of the following year, during the meeting at Ardres near Calais when Richard II's marriage to Isabella of France was negotiated, Charles gave this piece to Richard; an English clerk who wrote about the occasion described the gift as 'a gold nef on a bear, and at each end a tiger looking in a glass'. It passed into the English royal treasury, but disappears during the reign of Henry VI, when it was pawned to Richard, duke of York. It was valued at only a little less than the total of Richard II's plate listed above. In style, it must have

**85.** The Royal Gold Cup. This was made in Paris in the late fourteenth century and given by Jean duke of Berry to Charles VI in 1391. It passed to John duke of Bedford, regent of France at some time before 1434, and then to the English royal collection until 1604. Made of solid gold, it is enamelled with scenes from the life of St Agnes in brilliant colours, including the much prized 'clear red' which is technically very challenging.

**86.** The Huntsman Salt. The crystal bowl on the huntsman's head would contain salt, and the figure would be placed symbolically before the lord of the feast at the high table. English, c.1450.

**87.** A silver-gilt ewer from Paris, c.1330. Guests would wash their hands before the meal, and ewers and basins figure prominently in the inventories of royal plate.

**88.** A beaker decorated in grisaille enamel, probably for the Burgundian court, made in the Netherlands c.1425–50. The images at the foot are of a peddler who has fallen asleep being robbed by apes.

been not unlike the *Goldenes Rössl*, where there is indeed a tiger, which was one of Charles VI's emblems.

The duke of Berry owned a total of sixteen nefs. As one might expect, the finest were grandiose in the extreme. Only a few details are given in the accounts: one, which relates to the 'Tiger' nef, has four tigers as the support for the nef itself, although this had been taken apart by 1413.[35] There were two metal nefs: one mounted on a castle with the enamelled arms of the duke and a Greek inscription, with lions on the two castles, valued at much the same price as the Tiger nef, and another on a bear, the duke's badge, with figures holding his shield on deck.[36] Two nefs were made of other materials: one of amethyst, the other of cut crystal with silver-gilt mounts, with two flying serpents. Serpents reappear on another silver-gilt nef with Samson on the deck.[37] The masterpiece of the collection was a nef used as a salt cellar. It was in the form of a ship made from a sea-shell, and had a wounded swan on one castle and an armed bear on the other. Encrusted with precious stones, it rested on a four-wheeled chariot, and had a cover with a *fleur-de-lis* set in jewels on it.[38] The most impressive piece of all had been destroyed by 1413: a nef which must have been huge, with figures of St Louis and the legendary 'twelve peers of France'. It had a crew of angels sailing it, one at the helm, and angels in the crow's nest with the saint's shield and banner.[39]

Nefs were to be found outside France and Flanders. The emperor Karl IV was presented with a large nef, weighing 190 marks, by the provost and merchants of Paris when he visited the city in 1379; again, this emphasises the high symbolic status attached to such objects, as an appropriate gift for the highest rank of all.[40]

VERY LITTLE ACTUALLY SURVIVES OF THE pieces which would have been on display on princely tables. Cups and practical objects were obviously less liable to go out of fashion, while objects such as the hugely elaborate table-fountain from the fourteenth century now in the Cleveland Museum, a Gothic fantasy of crockets and pinnacles, would have been out of place a century later. It lacks the basin in which it was mounted, and the actual working of the mechanism is a mystery, but we can imagine the wine spouting upward from the mouths of the dragons on the upper platform to drive four waterwheeels. Below, another set of waterwheels are driven by the pipes in the mouths of the naked figures below, and on the lowest level more wine spouts from the animal and human heads on the eight towers.[41]

## The reception of guests

FROM THE SETTING OF THE FEAST, let us turn to the proceedings at the feast itself. Bartholomew the Englishman, whose description of when and how a feast should be held has already been quoted, gives this account of the guests:

> [A]t feasts, first meat is prepared and made ready, guests are invited, benches and stools are set out in the hall, and tables, cloths, and towels are ordered, issued and prepared. Guests are seated with the lord at the head of the table, and no-one sits down until the guests have washed their hands. Children are seated in their place, and servants at a table by themselves. First knives, spoons and salts, are put on the tables, and then bread and drink, and many different dishes; household servants busily help each other to do every thing diligently and talk merrily together. The guests are entertained with lutes and harps. Now wine and now dishes of meat are brought out and served in portions. At the end come fruit and spices, and when the guests have eaten, tablecloths and the last course are cleared, and guests wash and wipe their hands again. Grace is said, and guests

*A Gothic table-fountain*

**94**, p.269

thank the Lord. Then for gladness and comfort, drink is brought yet again. When all this is done, men take their leave ...[42]

Behind even this relatively homely feast lay a wealth of ceremonial, ritual and social etiquette. For a great feast, the space would have to be cleared, as the great hall of a castle or palace was used for many other purposes. In some cases there would be a permanent high table, usually on a dais, placed across the width of the hall, as in the Grand' Salle of the palace of the French kings on the Ile de la Cité in Paris.

Before the feast began, the guests had to be seated. Rank and status was paramount in the placing. This was the duty of the marshal of the hall, who was responsible to the marshal of the household, and who was specifically required to keep order in the hall itself. Seating at the high table, at which the prince or lord sat with the most distinguished of the visitors and courtiers, was crucial. We can illustrate the deep attachment to rank and precedence with two twelfth-century scenes. One is at the feast at Mainz in 1184, when a quarrel over precedence between the abbot of Fulda and the archbishop of Köln over the right to sit on the emperor's left hand was settled in favour of the archbishop. The result was an enmity which lasted for two generations and had serious political consequences for the emperors.[43] It was echoed in 1298, when at a court day feast in Nuremberg, the archbishop of Köln asserted that he should be seated on the right of the emperor; the archbishop of Mainz argued with him and took the seat from him by force, at which his rival left the hall, declaring that the matter should be settled by a duel. And given that there were more than forty princes of the empire at Mainz in 1184, a very large proportion of the total, it is perhaps surprising that this seems to have been the only dispute.

*Seating the guests*

The second example comes from literature. It has been argued with some conviction that the round table of King Arthur is a kind of wish-fulfilment on the part of the barons of the Angevin empire, who chafed under the powerful and unifying rule of Henry II after their dominance of the political scene under King Stephen. Arthur is not a king on a dais, but a member on the same footing as the others of the round table, a layout which minimises the question of precedence.[44] Round tables are very rare in the Middle Ages, and are usually found in a domestic setting: the great round table at Winchester was probably made for a tournament there, and was certainly not Edward I's normal mode of dining.

In the later Middle Ages, there was a trend towards an extremely opulent feast with a very select group of guests, which focussed closely on the figure of the ruler. These are quite often illustrated in manuscripts, but are less often described by chroniclers, who prefer the grandiose, crowded festivals which display power as well as wealth in their sheer numbers. In 1395, after his investiture as duke of Milan, Gian Galeazzo Visconti dined with twelve guests of honour on an extensive and luxurious menu, in a room where a wealth of silver plate was displayed on buffets along three sides, with the huge ducal table covered with a cloth woven with gold thread along the fourth.[45] It was an increasingly common formula in the fifteenth century, and even the great Feast of the Pheasant in 1454 had only three tables for the diners.[46] This arrangement allowed much more room for the onlookers and the participants, and indeed the roles of spectator and participant were interchangeable, as had been the case ever since the time of the tournament at Le Hem in 1278. Furthermore, access to such festivals was carefully controlled, with guards at the doorways and viewing platforms provided for selected guests.[47]

*Feasts for the few*

89. (above) The Winchester Round Table. Recent research has suggested that this was made for a knighting ceremony and tournament held by Edward I at Winchester in 1285. The painting is Tudor, and the table was probably plain when it was first used.

90. Feast from *The Romance of Alexander*, a de luxe manuscript illuminated at Tournai in 1344. There are four attendant squires; the two standing at the ends of the table may be carvers, while two cupbearers kneel before the king.

## The serving of the meal

THE RULES FOR SERVING OF THE FOOD were very strict. There were books which recorded how this should be done, the so-called 'courtesy' books which were a commonplace from the twelfth century onwards, and which go back to the courts of the bishops of late Carolingian times in Germany, where the idea of good manners was part of their culture. As time went on, the books attempted to codify the general idea of good behaviour and to make it a guide to the minutiae of everyday life at court as much as an overriding ideal. The result is that, by the fifteenth century, the books prescribe in an almost ritual fashion exactly how a meal should be served; and carving – a very necessary skill, given the number of animals and particularly of birds which had to be dismembered at a feast – acquired a vocabulary only a little less complex than that of the huntsmen who had provided the game on the carver's dish.

Up to the fourteenth century, the chief offices of the household were often the hereditary duty of the greatest lords in the land; originally these were real appointments in the royal service. As the administration grew more complex, the titles became honorific, but the duty of serving the prince himself personally at great feasts remained. Enforcement of these duties could cause resentment; when Albert I, king of the Romans and heir to the empire, held court at Nuremberg in 1298, the princes who elected the emperor served him at table, except for the hereditary cupbearer, Wenceslaus II of Bohemia. Albert insisted that he be served, whereupon Wenceslaus had his own full regalia brought, mounted his horse, and rode into the hall followed by his chamberlain bearing the golden cup and by his retinue, also on horseback, causing chaos. Only then did he take the cup and offer it to the king, having made the point about his real status. This personal service was clearly a touchy subject: at the wedding of the earl of Cornwall to the daughter of the count of Provence in 1243, royal letters patent were issued, confirming that the barons who served the king at the feast on that occasion 'did so voluntarily, at the king's request, and not out of duty', in case it was cited as a precedent on future occasions.[48]

*The officers of the household*

Before the prince could eat, the food had to be checked for poison by his personal squire, and one of the commonest methods of doing this was by the test of the 'serpent's tongue'. These were in fact fossilised sharks' teeth, and the thirteenth-century medical treatise *Breviarium* practice claimed that 'if any poison is set before it on the table, it at once begins to sweat'. Special pieces of table silver sometimes had these 'serpent's tongues' set into them. Louis d'Anjou had a special tongue-tree or *languier* from whose branches hung fifteen such teeth on silver chains, alternating with precious stones. The trunk fitted into a basin, and the food was probably laid in this for testing.[49] Such items would only appear on the tables of the greatest princes; the pope was particularly careful in this respect, and Philip V of France gave Pope John XXII a *languier* with six serpent's tongues in 1318.

*Testing for poison*

The English regulations for serving a meal are clearly laid out in John Russell's *Book of Nurture*,[50] in which a would-be household officer learns the duties of being a butler, including the skill of carving, a sewer or server, who set out the dishes on the table, the chamberlain who was in effect the lord's valet, and finally the marshal. Most of the guests would eat out of a shared dish, a mess, typically divided between four people. The list begins with popes, emperors, kings, princes, cardinals and archbishops, who would ordinarily dine in private – 'all these of dignity ought not to be in the hall' – but would be at the high table at a feast, and would have a dish to themselves. The next rank, bishops, marquises, viscounts and earls, abbots, the mayor of London, the chief justices and barons, can share a dish between two or

*The marshal*

three. Below them come those of knightly rank, and clergy such as abbots and archdeacons, doctors of law and divinity, for whom one dish between three or four is appropriate. The rest are given one dish between four, but they must be seated at tables according to a more general status, squires and their equivalents being the lowest. Each 'estate' must be seated in such a way that they do not mingle with the others. And there are particular rules – *pace* the episode at Mainz in 1184 – for precedence of the archbishop of Canterbury over the archbishop of York. Canterbury and York must sit apart, and York is not to be served before Canterbury. These particularities cover all kinds of situations such as the status of a lady of royal blood who has married a knight (both are seated as royalty) down to the precedence of the abbots: Westminster is the first, the abbot of Tintern the last.

Given the huge numbers of people at a great feast, the possibilities of chaos must have been endless, and the marshal's job was not an enviable one. Robert Grosseteste, bishop of Lincoln, drew up instructions for his household some time before 1240, and later wrote them out for the countess of Lincoln. They are a remarkably detailed picture of the workings of a court, and show how the marshal functioned. The lord himself was positioned at the centre of the high table, so that everyone could see him; but he could also see everything that was going on, and had two officials standing by to sort out problems. As to the marshal,

*Instructions for the marshal*

> [he shall] take care to supervise your household in person and especially in the hall, to see that your household conduct themselves indoors and out of doors respectably, without dispute or noise or bad words. At each meal he ought to name the servers who are to go to the kitchen; he himself ought to go all the way before your steward as far as your place until your meal is served to you, and then he ought to go and be at the far end of the hall in the middle aisle and see that the servants go orderly without noise with the dishes to all parts of the hall, to the officers who have been appointed to divide out the food so that this is not – because of favouritism – placed or served out of order. Concerning this you yourself ought to keep an eye on the serving until the dishes are placed in the hall and then attend to your own meal.[51]

This would work in the relatively small-scale court of a bishop like Grosseteste, but at a great royal feast, there would be almost total reliance on the marshal and his staff.

A further complication was the number of dishes to be served to each guest. The household ordinance of Edward IV in 1471 spends a great deal of time specifying the exact rations for each member of court, from the king downwards,[52] and the same principle was applied more broadly at feasts. Two English feast menus from the second quarter of the fifteenth century divide the guests into those in the upper hall and those in the lower hall: at the wedding of the earl of Devon, the 'upper' guests were served thirty-two dishes, and the 'lower' guests fourteen. The contrast was even sharper at the investiture of the bishop of Wells, with forty-five dishes for the first group and seventeen for the second. This did not mean that the more distinguished guests were expected to eat more: Grosseteste explains that the lord's dishes must be well filled so that he could distribute choice morsels to the guests around him. The prince would be served roasted poultry, including birds such as cranes or herons, as well as roasted pork or mutton, as the meats of choice, since the ability to roast in quantity was restricted to the grander households until the late Middle Ages. Huge separate kitchens, such as that found at Glastonbury Abbey, were required for this purpose.

# DEVISING THE FESTIVAL

# 13

◆ *The prince's household and the court* ◆ *Programmes for great events*
◆ *The master of ceremonies: Olivier de la Marche* ◆ *Housing the festival*
◆ *'Kings' of minstrels and heralds: gangmasters for great occasions*
◆ *Food for the feast: the cook* ◆ *Master Chiquart* ◆ *Entertainments and*
*players* ◆ *Masks, disguises and scenery* ◆ *Acrobats, buffoons and tregetours*
◆ *Mechanical marvels* ◆ *Dances*

## The Prince's Household and the Court

IN THE EARLY MIDDLE AGES, the responsibility for the ruler's personal welfare, his lodgings, food and clothing and the maintenance of his family was in the hands of an informal group of servants within the court. Their status depended on their personal appointment by that ruler. In the thirteenth century, as the administration becomes more formal, the royal household emerges as an administrative entity. It was to become one of the largest organisations in the prince's realms. In England, the chancery dealt with the transaction of government business and the exchequer with government finance. The household of the king becomes the third element, dealing with his personal affairs, his private estates and expenditure, as well as the purely mundane aspects of his well-being. The household becomes a kind of parallel to the public institutions of government, with its own finance department within the king's wardrobe, its own clerks in the department of the privy seal. The 'privy' seal was so called because the letters issued by them carried the king's private seal, and were closed, unlike the letters patent issued by the chancery, where the seal was appended to an open document.

Court festivals and feasts were part of the king's private life, and were therefore dealt with by the officials of the household. From the days of Charlemagne onwards, we can trace chamberlains who look after the king in his private chamber, so to speak, rather than his public persona as ruler. By 1135, a document describing the constitution of the royal household of Henry I of England speaks of a master chamberlain. This became a hereditary office by the end of the twelfth century, while the other chamberlains continued as working administrators. Likewise, there was a hereditary steward who was in nominal charge of the wardrobe, and working stewards who ran the department. In France and elsewhere, there was little distinction between chamber and wardrobe, and the French 'master of the king's hostel' or majordomo, dealt with all aspects of the king's affairs.

*The chamberlain*

By the fourteenth century, personal service at the king's table had become a way of advancement for young squires or nobles anxious to make a career at court. The French court had a system whereby officers of the household served for between one to three months, on a fixed rotation, and several men could hold the same title. The most sought after office was that of butler, because serving the king's wine did not involve any menial contact with food. There were four butlers, three head officers in the pantry, and two in the kitchen. These men only carried out the ceremonial functions of serving the king at table. They were not responsible for buying and organising the wine or food, and were known

*Service at the king's table*

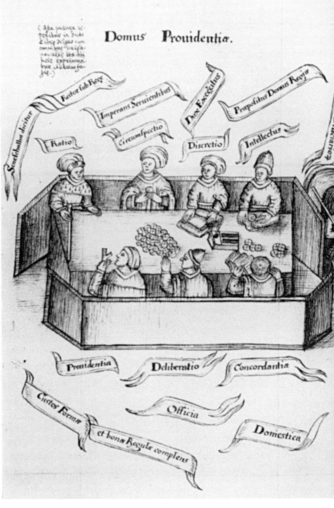

*Ordinances of the household*

as officers 'of the mouth'. Familiarity with court rituals and procedures was an essential part of an ambitious courtier's knowledge, and there were as many as 150 of them in the French court by 1400, as the practice of appointing alternates spread to the subordinate officers.[1] The chamberlain or his delegate was ultimately responsible for the organisation of the prince's festivals, often according to a prescribed ceremonial. This was true for festivals which recurred regularly, such as the feast days of the Christian church, or occasionally, such as weddings and baptisms, or once in a prince's lifetime, such as coronations. Here, however, we are not concerned with the regular ceremonials of the prince's life, such as those recorded for Charles V's daily routines by Christine de Pizan.[2] It is the occasional, and often much more dramatic, occasions of magnificence that concern us.

The complexities of the household were such that they needed to be recorded in writing. Ordinances for the prince's household can be found in many states. The English and French royal ordinances have survived better than those for ducal or lesser households. The most comprehensive is the 'Black Book' which describes the household of Edward IV. This divides the household into two parts: the *Domus Magnificencie* and the *Domus Providencie*. The original has not survived, but one of the copies contains two drawings which define the two elements of the household. The 'magnificent' part of the household is represented by the king at table, with his attendants, while the 'provident' part shows the king's wardrobe which provides the money to fund the magnificence. The division was a real one: the 'provident' steward reigned over the departments which fed the king and his court, kitchen, buttery, bakehouse and pantry, and the marshalsea, which dealt with the horses – numbering some hundreds – required for household purposes. The 'magnificent' chamberlain was in charge of the personnel who staffed the king's residences, both the public area of the hall and the private region of his chambers. He was also responsible for the royal chapel and the physical wardrobe and personal valuables belonging to the king.

## Programmes for Great Events

MANY OF THE COURT FESTIVALS, particularly the royal entries and the weddings with their political overtones, have a strong programmatic element. The question of how these programmes were created has received little attention, because of a lack of evidence. The scenarios themselves do not survive, so we have to work back from descriptions of the event. Nor do we have evidence of payments to the men who created the scenarios, and do not know whether they were written on the orders of the ruler or of the city fathers.

Even where there is no programmatic element, the symbolic element must have been considered and the appropriate costumes or pageantry ordered. There is often a ritual element, which, even if traditional, had to be followed and the necessary instructions given. For example, the emperor might visit a particular town only once in many decades, possibly well beyond the memory of anyone in the town. Yet the prescribed ritual of welcoming him outside the walls of the town and escorting him through the gates, as well as the rituals of homage and of recognition of the town's rights, appear to follow a well-established pattern. A plausible explanation would be that there were officials in the emperor's entourage who sent the necessary instructions – not necessarily very elaborate – to the town authorities beforehand.

*Traditional rituals*

In the case of festivals within the court, particularly in the fairly private festivals of the French and English royal courts in the fourteenth century, it seems likely that the king himself gave the necessary instructions. Did Edward III brief his supplier John of Cologne on the embroidery to be used for the next celebration? From the way in which personal mottoes and emblematic designs were used, it seems quite likely. Charles VI likewise took a personal interest in the costumes for festivals. At the wedding of one of Isabeau of Bavaria's ladies in waiting, the king and a group of nobles dressed as wodewoses or wild men. The Saint-Denis chronicler claimed that 'the king, who allowed himself too easily to indulge his taste for such pleasures, wanted to give himself this diversion; he enlisted six of the young lords of the court, and this is what they did'.[3] When they danced in this disguise, an inquisitive onlooker (said by Froissart to be the duke of Orléans, the king's brother) wanted to see who they were, and put a torch too close to their costumes. The disguises contained pitch, and several of them were burnt to death. The king himself was not with the dancers at the time, and this stroke of luck saved his life. The monk of Saint-Denis who recorded this tragedy waxed eloquent on the iniquities of such wanton revelries.

The royal entries, particularly those into Paris and London, are the most elaborate examples of programmatic pageantry. Here, there must have been collusion between court and city to maximise the propaganda element of proceedings, and to avoid any tactless scenes. We have already described the extraordinarily complicated theological and political background of Richard II's entry into London in 1392; the intellectual resources needed for such programmes were readily to hand in the court itself, and did not require outside

*Planning a festival*

intervention. Any princely court was home to many officials who were clerics of some standing, and men like the probable author of the 1392 programme, Richard Maidstone, were by no means uncommon. Knowledge of classical literature, necessary for such episodes as the labours of Hercules or the adventures of Jason and the Argonauts, could have come either from the clerics or through courtiers who had read one of the many French versions of the classical stories. And the same courtiers could also have been familiar with the Arthurian romances.

*Explaining the tableaux*

However, many of the entries and festivals were too complicated for the presenters to be able to rely on the audience's ability to interpret them. It is clear that placards were very often displayed next to tableaux, as at the royal entries into London. These are only rarely mentioned in descriptions of such occasions, probably because they were taken for granted. There were also summaries of the whole occasion: we have seen how at Martí of Aragon's entry into Valencia in 1399, an 'angel' descended from a cloud to scatter coloured papers with an account of what was about to be presented.

*The* Bestiary *as a source of images*

The *entremets* at feasts and the pageant tableaux in the royal entries borrow much of their symbolism from *The Book of Beasts or Bestiary*. This work, current from the twelfth century onwards, is best described as natural history (taken from Pliny) with a moral or theological interpretation. It is founded on the medieval belief that everything God created existed both physically and as a sign of divine purpose. The animals were described to the best of the author's ability, given that he had never seen many of them. Some of them were purely fabulous, such as the gryphon, popular at feasts simply because it was something exotic: a feathered lion, with an eagle's head and wings, known for its terrible ferocity. A typical example of the moral fables which are the other element in the book is the panther. The panther is said to sleep for three days after it feeds. When it awakes, it emits a great roar, and its breath is such a sweet odour that all the animals follow it, except the dragon, which flees. In theological terms, it is seen as the image of Christ's descent into hell after the crucifixion, his release of the souls there who follow him to freedom, and his defeat of the devil. So when we read of one of these beasts in the pageantry of a festival, it is not just a curiosity, but part of the message that the occasion is presenting.

## *The master of ceremonies: Olivier de la Marche*

IT IS IN BURGUNDY, FAMOUS FOR ITS lavish entertainments, that we can see most clearly the majordomo at work as master of ceremonies for festivals. Olivier de la Marche held this post under Charles the Bold from 1461, when Charles was still heir to the throne, to his death in 1477. He was one of four men with this title, of whom the grand majordomo was the chief. In ordinary times, they were responsible for the duke's meals and for his wardrobe, but even this was immensely complex, and La Marche wrote a detailed account of their duties, which runs to thirty-eight pages. It took 'three officials, several knives, at least three serviettes and a mass of detailed rules'[4] to bring the duke some bread. If this was everyday life, the organisation of a great feast was unbelievably complicated. He was responsible on a regular basis for the feasts of the ducal Order of the Golden Fleece, and wrote another treatise on this, a hundred pages in length: a modern historian has called him 'the greatest authority of the age on court ceremonial and rituals'.[5]

La Marche naturally played a key part in the organisation of the Feast of the Pheasant in 1454, the greatest of all the Burgundian festivals, and he records in his *Mémoires* how a committee was set up to manage it, consisting of

**91.** At the wedding of one of queen Isabeau's ladies in waiting in 1393, Charles VI and a group of nobles disguised as wild men danced in a masquerade. An onlooker trying to identify who they were held a torch close to them, and the costumes, which contained pitch, caught fire. Charles himself escaped, but several dancers were burnt to death.

**92.** A princely marriage feast, from a mid fifteenth-century miniature from Flanders illustrating a historical romance. The married couple are at the table on the left.

**93.** The siege of the Castle of Love, from a fourteenth-century ivory mirror back. The ladies, having defended themselves by throwing flowers, welcome the victorious knights as they storm the ramparts.

Jean lord of Lannoy, knight of the Order of the Fleece, a knowledgeable and inventive man, and a squire named Jean Bourdault, a very notable and discreet man. And the good duke did me such honour as to want me to be summoned to it: we held several meetings, to which the chancellor and the chamberlain were summoned ... as well as the greatest men and those closest to the duke; and after deliberating on our opinions it was agreed as to how the ceremonies and mysteries should be carried out.[6]

Similarly, in April 1468 he worked for several days at a time on the forthcoming wedding of Charles the Bold to Margaret of York. His account of the occasion is in the form of a letter addressed to Gilles du Mas, majordomo of the duke of Brittany:

And because in such a high and triumphal house as that where you are in a position to arrange the feasts and receptions of princes and princesses when they come to you, and because I am not sure whether there might be anything in this noble festival of the wedding of milord of Burgundy which you might wish to remember for the right time and place, I have collected as best I can what I saw of this feast to send to you.[7]

He proceeds to write about twenty thousand words, describing every detail from the moment he first saw Margaret at Sluys to the end of the six days' jousting which concluded the proceedings. In the course of this, we learn that, among other things, he agreed the details of the work to be done on the furnishings and items for the table with the painters of the royal household, as well as preparing props and a stage for the interludes on the labours of Hercules.

## Housing the festival

A temporary hall at Westminster in 1308

WHEN EDWARD II WAS CROWNED at Westminster in 1308, the palace itself was in disrepair, and partly for this reason, and partly because the king wished to make a splendid display which would attract a great crowd of spectators, a 'strong and solemn hall was raised along the whole length of the wall of the palace on the bank of the Thames'. This must have been at least 150 metres long, and was built to seat the king's counsellors and the barons. Orders were given to cover it with beech boards 'because of the crush of the people'. Fourteen smaller halls were also erected parallel to it, towards the great gate of the palace, leaving enough room for pedestrians and knights on horseback to move in and out.[8] In addition, forty ovens were to be provided in the palace, and the doorways of both the abbey and the palace were to be protected by palisades and hurdles. Temporary breaches were made in the walls of the palace to allow for goods needed for the occasion to be brought in. Some of these measures were probably attempts to avoid the scenes of chaos at the knighting of Edward II in the abbey two years earlier.

Medieval court festivals were complex, costly and competitive. To mount a great event of this kind required lavish finance and a well-organised administration, and only a handful of rulers could aspire to do this. When the French knights compared their king's efforts in this sphere with those of the dukes of Burgundy, they were ashamed to acknowledge the inferiority of the French court. They were not merely lamenting the lack of entertainment, but the loss of face that resulted. We have a report on the cost of the wedding of Charles the Bold and Margaret of York at Bruges in 1468, and the attendant ceremonies and feasts. It was prepared by one of the duke's officials, possibly La Marche himself. It begins with the building work required, and the construction of a great wooden hall at Brussels, which was brought to Bruges in pieces, 40 metres long by 20 metres wide and 18 metres to the roof pitch. It was lined with tapestries and placed on the tennis court in the duke's mansion there. There were thirteen small rooms for the serving and preparation of the feasts. The high table, on a removeable dais, was 15 metres long and 1.5 metres wide; at the other end was a viewing gallery and a gallery for the musicians. At each side, there were two tables 7.5 metres long. The furniture was completed by a huge buffet in the middle of the room, made up of three 5 metre squares, each with six shelves, on which the duke's gold and silver vessels could be displayed for the main feast. The pantry and the kitchen of the mansion were refurbished. Even so, the road alongside the duke's mansion had to be blocked off and a temporary structure added. The neighbouring house was partly taken over to provide more room for the kitchens.

*The temporary hall at Bruges in 1468*

The lengthiest and most intriguing part of the list is the itemisation of all the details of the construction of the scenery for the *entremets* and other table items, such as the thirty covers made of wood representing the duke's chief cities – castles, cupolas, belfries, towers – to cover the pies. One of the main subjects of the *entremets* was the twelve labours of Hercules, performed on some kind of stage, as there is an item for a curtain which can be raised and lowered.[9] The costumes and scenery needed for these are summarised as follows:

*Building scenery for the* Labours of Hercules

> Item, the twelve stories of the twelve labours of Hercules, richly ornamented, the playing of which lasted three days, namely the Monday, Thursday and Sunday, the last day of the feast. Several models were made for these stories, richly trimmed and decorated with paintings, such as two gold cradles, in which were the young Hercules and his brother; and the serpents came which wanted to devour them, but Hercules took them by the neck and held them so fast that he killed them. There were also several other beasts: dragons, lions, oxen, sheep, beasts with three heads and some with seven heads, devils and hell mouth, women riding horses armed and dressed, fighting Hercules; seven giants also fighting Hercules, great rocks, deserts, boats which were needed for the stories, and several other fabrications, which would take too long to list, all made of rich material, painted, with gold and silver, silk and buckram, to be as lifelike as possible.[10]

The master painter was Jacques Daret from Tournai, who brought several other painters with him. He worked for fourteen days, and was paid 21 *livres* for his salary and maintenance. Jean Hennekart was paid for hiring two messengers to go in search of painters because the duke's wedding feast was to last much longer than expected; they visited Ghent, Brussels, Louvain, Valenciennes, Lille, Cambrai and eight other towns in a desperate effort to get the necessary workmen. And Jean Scalkin's chandeliers are described in loving detail, as well as the great fountain of rose-water he created for the table of the duke and duchess, with a mirror upside down reflecting both the fish swimming in the fountain and joyful little people dancing the morisco.[11]

La Marche, however, continued to worry about the expense of all this and the competition that resulted. When Jean I of Cleves married the daughter of the comte d'Étampes in 1455 he wrote that he feared that nobles trying to imitate the prince 'made such great celebrations and festivities and set about holding meals called banquets, which started by not being expensive, but were raised and grew into great gatherings and costs for meat and other dishes, and from lords to princes; and the expenses multiplied, and each one wanted to show himself greater than his predecessor'.[12]

## 'Kings' of minstrels and heralds: gangmasters for great occasions

*Heralds as public announcers*

THE ORGANISATION OF THE MUSIC and announcements was in the hands of kings of minstrels or kings of heralds from the late thirteenth century onwards. It is fair to say that before the fifteenth century there is very little evidence of a permanent official role for heralds, and the evolution of the 'king at arms' is even more obscure. What the early records reveal is that 'herald' in the thirteenth and fourteenth century means little more than a man who is a public announcer and a messenger. Now the place above all where we find minstrels and heralds from the twelfth century onwards is at tournaments. One of the necessary skills for the success of such an occasion was the ability to identify knights by their arms, and it is from this that their expertise in heraldry arises. In the biography of William Marshal, who rose to fame in the late twelfth century through his prowess in tournaments, the waiting crowd at a tournament was entertained by 'a singer who was a new herald of arms', implying that there was some kind of recognition of his expertise in identifying the participants. Minstrels saw them as ignorant rivals. The minstrel Jacques Bretel, describing a tournament in northern France in 1285, writes with admiration about the knowledge of a herald who actually knows what he is talking about.

*'Kings' as gangmasters*

However, these men were freelances with no actual formal status. They were, if you like, travelling players who turned up and found employment when a tournament was announced, and were valued for their skills. They were organised by 'kings', and we find both 'kings of heralds' and 'kings of minstrels'. These men played a vital role in both paying the minstrels and recruiting them as and when required. It is important to remember that tournaments in the twelfth and thirteenth centuries were by no means regular events; they occurred sporadically and at widely scattered sites. The so-called 'kings' of this period, whether of minstrels or heralds, who begin to appear regularly in royal accounts, have been mistaken as forerunners of the modern kings of arms, who first acquire responsibility for the rules and administration of heraldry in the early fifteenth century. These twelfth and thirteenth century kings are festive kings, responsible for controlling an unruly group of people. They are like the king of the ribalds, in charge of gaming and prostitutes, found in Gascony in 1314; or the perhaps more familiar *rex fabe*, king of the bean, at a medieval Christmas (hence our bean-feast); or the similar king of fools. They are more serious than these, but they are kings, as we have said, for a particular occasion, or, if they are good at their job, for repeated but separate occasions given the sporadic nature of tournaments.

*A worthless king at arms*

A satirical poem by Bertran de Born describes Eleanor of Aquitaine as sending a tax receipt on the torn-up tabard of a 'king of arms'. This has been taken as evidence for such an official in her household. In fact, it is a reference to the worthlessness of the receipt, written on the equivalent of a piece of scrap paper, left over after a tournament by a gangmaster. Bertran himself points out that it did not save the taxpayer from the knives of his creditors.

Like other medieval tradesmen the men who specialised in providing services for tournaments may have formed themselves into loose organisations by the thirteenth century, when we find a legal document in 1276 in which 'Peter king of the heralds beyond the Trent on the northern side' undertakes to settle his debts. It is a curious document, as it includes an unusual clause specifying that he is paying his creditor for his debts 'owed to him from the beginning of the world down to 18 March 1276'.

The poet known as Adenes le Roi was a prominent figure in Flanders and France from the 1260s until his death around 1300, and his title is due to his position as king of minstrels. At the English court between 1272 and 1307, we have the names of at least fifteen possible kings of this sort. Typically, they appear to be in charge of a group of minstrels, or of all the minstrels at a particular occasion; 'king Baisescu' and 'king Caupeny' share out royal gifts between the minstrels at the great feast for the knighting of Edward II when prince of Wales in 1306. Such men are also called heralds, yet there is no question that they are minstrels, because in the same year 'king Caupenny' is paid with other minstrels 'for performing plays and making their minstrelsies in the presence of the Queen'. 'Caupenny' was from Scotland, and is given the title 'king Caupenny of Scotland'. He had first attended a court ceremony in 1290, the wedding of Edward's daughter Joan to Gilbert of Clare. The last mention of him is in 1307, and he very probably played for Edward I in his last illness. He seems to have been regularly employed, but never as a member of the royal staff. We also hear of the 'king of Champagne', the leader of the minstrels from that county. A king of heralds is paid for making a proclamation about the prohibition of tournaments in England at Northampton on Christmas Day 1300, in his role as a public crier.

*Sharing out the spoils*

There is also the problem of heralds' nicknames. Prominent heralds had nicknames, which have in the past been identified as possible titles of office: a certain Bruiant appears as a herald in William Marshal's biography, at the end of the twelfth century, and the herald whom Jacques Bretel admires is also called Bruiant: he appears in a poem about the tournament at Chauvency in 1285. There is yet another in the accounts of Edward II. 'Bruyant' means loud or noisy: in modern French, 'un homme bruyant' is a loud talker. This, and the comment – again from the Marshal's biography – that knights have to have three or four heralds in tow to lend vocal support, simply means that these men were loudmouthed cheerleaders. Equally, two or three heralds named 'Norrois' or 'Norroy' are simply from the north, and there is no real evidence that this was any kind of title.

A figure akin to the herald appears in Spanish festivities, the 'savage knight' (*caballero salvatge*) who is recorded from 1234 onwards, and seems to be an announcer and spokesman for the minstrels, who was able to cry out the name, arms, country and lineage of participants in tournaments, and festivities: a *jongleur* named Pere Salvatge (Peter Savage) was given the job of distributing money among the minstrels at the coronation of Alfonso of Aragon in 1286,[13] fulfilling the same function as the kings of heralds.

*'Savage' or 'wild' knights*

# Food for the Feast: The Cook

IT WAS ON THE STEWARD OF THE HOUSEHOLD or his equivalent that the physical burden of organising a festive occasion fell. This involved, beside the kitchen itself, all the departments of the *domus providencie*. The pantry is so called from the French *pain*, bread, and is responsible for supplying this: slices (*tranches* in French) were used as 'trenchers', onto which food was served, and the trencher was then eaten afterwards. The pantry also provided cheese and *patisserie*, as well as table linen. The buttery, headed by the butler, was responsible for wine and other beverages, while the bulk of the work was carried out by the kitchen. The last of the four 'services of the mouth' was the fruitery, which was also responsible for the candles.

The king's cook was an important individual, responsible for the running of the kitchen and the menus as well as the actual production of the food. By the end of the thirteenth century, royal cooks appear in the records as important figures. St Louis' French royal household in 1261 had three cooks: Nicholas of Soisy, Isembart and William Guillore.[14] Isembart is known to have served into the reign of Louis's son Philip the Fair until at least 1286.[15] In 1264, we are told that Conrad was master of the cooks when the son of Bela IV of Hungary was married at Bratislava.[16] In 1279, the household ordinance of Edward I lists two king's cooks, master Thomas and William de Werewelle, the dinner cook. They were helped by two buyers, three named kitchen staff and master Ralph the saucer, who evidently enjoyed a status similar to master Thomas.

## Master Chiquart

*Staffing a prince's kitchen*

WE HAVE QUOTED MASTER CHIQUART from the court of Savoy earlier, and his book gives us real insight into the medieval kitchen in operation. The recipe for 'broet tyolli' says that the cook is to take 'as much meat as the master cook shall indicate'. He was clearly on the spot and very much working hands on. The kitchen staff on the ducal payroll at the court of Savoy was twenty strong, compared with the thirty-four at the much larger and grander Burgundian court, and Chiquart had a kitchen clerk who instructed the actual cooks as to the number of portions to be prepared. Throughout his book, he refers to directing 'your companions', and a high degree of organisation and teamwork was essential. The individual cooks were usually specialists in a particular area with their own assistants, the most skilled being the pastry-maker and sauce cook, while others butchered and roasted the meat.[17]

Chiquart was also in charge of the planning of feasts. In 1400, Philip the Bold of Burgundy visited Amadeus VIII, and a suitable feast was prepared by Master Chiquart. As the celebrations were held on a Friday and Saturday, meat was not included, as these were fast days, when eating meat was proscribed by the Church. He has left a record of the feast in his book, which gives both the menu and some general instructions as to its preparation:

I, Chiquart, prepared and ordered to be prepared several notable dishes for the dinners and suppers for that banquet ... to wit:

Get big salt fish such as salt mullets along with big pieces of fillet of salt pike along with several other salt fish; set these out in fine dishes. Then, with that, get herrings and set them out in another fine dish by themselves. For all that has just been mentioned no other sauce is needed but mustard. And peas and the purée and a purée of greens will be the pottage for that serving, with a White Almond Broth, a Brown Sorengue of eels and the pies, and fish tripe carefully cleaned and prepared to make an Arbaleste. For the *entremets* of the first serving, pike cooked in three ways, that is, fried in the middle; the third at the head, boiled; and the tail third, roasted: other ones boiled in the middle, roasted at the head and fried at the tail. Because the above fish are called Glazed Pilgrim Pike, they should have over them a good roast lamprey, which will be staffs of those pilgrims; anyone who does not have any lamprey can use eel– and if you do not have any lamprey, use eel. The staff, that is the lamprey, should be eaten with lamprey sauce, and the eel with garlic green verjuice sauce; of the pike the boiled part should be eaten with green sauce, the fried and roasted parts with green verjuice or with oranges.

At the second serving, first get all sorts of sea-fish set out by themselves in great gold dishes; fresh-water fish – big pike fillets, big carp fillets, big trout, fresh pollack,[18] dace, big fillets of bleak, big perch and other fish. Lamprey in lamprey sauce; a Salamine; a yellow Larded and Boiled dish of tench, with sops; rice with the Venison of Dolphin; and crayfish in vinegar. Of the sauces appropriate for the above-mentioned fish no mention is made. For the *Entremets*, Parmesan Pies, each one gilded and embanded with the arms of the lord to whom it is served.

For the supper: first, roasts of pickerel and pollack and all sorts of suitable roast fish – they are served with green sorrel verjuice; and White Sops of almonds, with fish jelly; white sea-fish and white freshwater fish; Norse pasties, fried squid and fried fish in saupiquet [piquant sauce].[19]

Chiquart actually begins his treatise on cookery with notes on how to organise a 'most honourable feast'. These notes at once open a window on the mundane matters on which the success or failure of such an event depended. Cattle, sheep and pigs are to be bought from the butcher, 'and for this the butcher will be wise and well-advised if he is well supplied, so that if it happens that the feast lasts longer than expected, one has promptly what is necessary; and also, if there are extras, do not butcher them so that nothing is wasted'. In other words, the butcher is buying in animals and keeping them in his fields until he needs them. The quantities are massive, though as we have no figures for the number of guests we cannot assess them in terms of individual consumption. For each day of the feast he recommends 200 kids and lambs, 100 calves and 2,000 head of poultry. For a major feast lasting a full week, these figures would be multiplied by five, and fish would also be needed for the two fast days.

*Provisions for the feast*

We can compare Chiquart's figures with English royal feasts from the thirteenth and fourteenth centuries, and these show that they are indeed realistic. At Christmas 1251, Henry III and his guests ate 830 red, fallow and roe deer, 200 wild boar, 1,300 hares, 385 young pigeons (squabs) and 115 cranes; and that was merely the wild game. Supplying this would have been difficult: while the deer might come from the king's deer parks, and the squabs from his dovecotes, the other game would have to be hunted and probably preserved in some way, in brine or salt. For the knighting of Edward II in 1306, the figures for meat required were 400 oxen, 800 sheep, 400 pigs and 40 boars.

Preparations had to start early. The 'purveyors of game', 'clever, diligent and skilled' should have forty horsemen at their disposal to get

deer, hares, rabbits, partridges, pheasants, small birds – whatever number of those they can get of them – whatever waterfowl they can find, doves, cranes, herons, any wildfowl – whatever sort of game they can obtain. They should set about it two months or six weeks before the banquet; and all of them should bring or send whatever they have been able to get at least three or four days before the banquet so that that game can be hung and properly prepared in each case.[20]

*Ordering the game*

This again implies some means of preserving the bag, as there would otherwise be no point in starting so early.

As to spices, Chiquart divides these into 'major spices' – white and Mecca gingers, cinnamon, grains of paradise and pepper itself. The 'minor spices' include both spices such as nutmeg and cloves, and colouring agents and decorative items. Also under this heading came practical items, such as wheat starch and over 100 metres of fine tissue for straining, as well as almonds, rice and candied fruits, pine nuts and dates. However, so that the cook could work faster, 'one should grind to powder the aforesaid spices and put each separately into large and good leather bags'.

*Buying spices*

In order to do this banquet as well as possible and without blame or fault, the household stewards, the kitchen squires and the chief cook should meet to locate, inspect and organise good, adequate places in which to carry out the cooking activities. That space should be large enough that great double dressing tables can be set up in such a way that the kitchen squires can move comfortably between the dressing tables and the worktables, in order to deliver the prepared dishes and to receive them.'[21]

The stewards are evidently in charge of the guest list, and the numbers to be invited to the feast, as they only reappear in Chiquart's book to tell the cook how many partridges in *tremollete* sauce, evidently regarded as a special delicacy, should be put in front of each important guest, ranging apparently from six for a king downwards. These were not necessarily for his personal consumption: Grosseteste explains to the lord that his plate must be piled high so that 'you can share your plate courteously to right and to left along the whole high table, so that if you so wish, everyone can have the same food as you'.[22]

*Kitchen equipment*

The kitchen equipment is obviously vital for the cook, and Chiquart has a detailed list, with practical comments such as 'check the space for making sauces', and 'do not trust wooden spits because they will rot and you could lose all your meat'. Equally there must be enough fuel: 'one thousand cartloads of good dry firewood, a great storehouse full of coal'; and of course you need to be sure that you can get more if necessary. If the feast is held in winter, the kitchen will need sixty torches, 10 kilos of wax candles, and 30 kilos of tallow candles to be used as lights when visiting all the various parts of the kitchen, including the separate building which houses the pastrycooks. Finally, 'if it happens that you are not provided with enough cooks and workers, you should send a summons to places where one can find them', perhaps the cookshops which were to be found in all major towns, or one of the local guilds of cooks which begin to appear about this time, to make sure the feast can be handled efficiently.

*Catering for special diets*

But there could be complications: 'there may be some very high, mighty, noble, venerable and honourable lords and ladies who will not eat meat,' for these there must be fish. And, he might have added, this would also apply if the feast fell on a fast day; he is vague as to how the fish are to be got, unlike his instructions about game. Furthermore, some of the guests will come with their own cooks who will prepare certain dishes, and space and provisions must be found for them so that they do not hold up the service of the feast as a whole. Another problem is invalids: 'It would be a miracle if there were no ailing or sick people, nor any afflicted with infirmities or maladies'. So, having talked to the doctors, he offers recipes for sixteen restoratives and special fortifying dishes, including stuffed crayfish and a purée of spinach and parsley.

## Entertainments and Players

*Ludi: courtly games*

THE ROYAL ENTERTAINMENTS CALLED *ludi* or games which are part of the more intimate court festivals, Christmas or family occasions, such as baptisms or weddings often had an element of play-acting. We have an account for the expenses of the festivities held by Mahaut, countess of Artois in about 1306[23] which clearly involved some kind of game, since there are entries for the harness of 'six knights and six ladies who jousted together'. There was obviously some kind of plot, as there is also a bill for a fish and for 'the three-headed serpent from which Robert of Artois and William de Vyane emerged'. The ladies were dressed in chemises with furred mantles instead of armour, and had 'heads' instead of helms. As so often, such games are best illustrated by events at the court of Edward III, where we have the details of expenditure on what the exchequer clerks called simply '*ludi*', the king's games. Such games were pure entertainment, overlaid only by a deliberate display of splendour and an often elaborate use of images and mottoes. They included music, dancing and the use of masks and disguises, possibly with some dramatic theme or simple play-acting, though this has left no positive traces. The word *ludi* covered a wide range of activities, from gambling through entertainments to actual plays.

The only traces of the content of a royal entertainments of this sort are pieces by John Lydgate, who was a member of the chapel royal at Windsor in the 1420s, written for Henry VI's Christmas feasts.[24] These are called 'mummings' by the scribe who wrote the manuscript in which they survive, and were evidently acted by members of the royal household, though it is possible that travelling players were involved. The scenario of the show presented at Hertford around 1427 involved the appearance of six 'rustics' who complained about the tyranny of their wives, who replied in kind; the king allowed them to continue to rule over their husbands for another year while the matter was investigated. It is a theme common in folk tradition, and is also found in fifteenth-century poetry; the whole performance might have lasted half an hour.

A rather different theme was used for an entertainment at Eltham, either the year before or after the Hertford occasion, where gifts were presented to the king and his mother by Bacchus, Juno and Ceres, and good wishes offered for their future peace and prosperity; a rather more conventional and very brief poem.

In contrast, jousts, which are public occasions, do sometimes have a political or topical theme. Here masks were used to disguise the participants, and were often satirical.[25] The costumes were used on these occasions for the preliminary parade, not in the jousting itself: the account of the 1331 tournament at Cheapside gives a very clear picture of the proceedings, and specifies that in this case the participants were *ad similitudinem Tartarorum larvati*, 'masked like Tartars'. *Larvati* is a word generally associated with hideous or devilish masks; the Tartars were obviously represented as nightmarish figures of pagans. The Tartars were a powerful and menacing force on the borders of Christendom at this period, raiding the Byzantine Empire and controlling Russian affairs. Twelve years later at Smithfield, Edward's team appeared dressed as the pope and twelve cardinals, an allusion to the dispute over the use of papal taxes raised in England to help the French cause, about which Edward was protesting at the time.[26] In 1359, again at Smithfield, both teams, including the king and four of his sons, dressed as the mayor of London and the twenty-four aldermen of the City; in this case, it was probably a compliment to their hosts.

*Jousts in disguise*

In April 1362, a tournament was planned in Cheapside to mark the wedding of Edward, prince of Wales. Two days before the event, one of the greatest storms ever to occur in England in recorded times struck, cutting a devastating swathe across the country. The unfinished choir of Vale Royal Abbey in Cheshire was blown down, and London was a scene of havoc and devastation. The tournament did not take place, but monks at Reading and Canterbury recorded that the prince and his knights had planned to dress as the seven deadly sins, and the hurricane was a divine judgement on this blasphemy. Reading between the lines, it seems more likely that the extreme violence of the storm demanded an exceptional act of impiety to explain it, and that the idea of this disguise was a figment of the imagination on the part of one or other of the monks.[27] Tournaments with religious disguises were not unknown elsewhere, and in Spain in 1428 the king of Castile and his knights dressed as God and the twelve apostles: no dire consequences are reported on this occasion.[28]

Games could also be mock-fights, as in the kingdom of Aragon at the end of the thirteenth century. When Jaime I of Aragon was visited in 1274 by Alfonso X at Valencia, the chronicler Ramon Muntaner watched the festival for his arrival:

And from the time they entered the territory of the Lord King of Aragon twelve days passed before they came to the city of Valencia; and when they were in that city no man could describe the decorations of the houses and the games and diversions, the round tables and joined platforms for jousts between wild knights, tourneys, knightly exercises, galleys and armed *lenys* which seamen dragged along the rambla in carts, and battles of oranges ... What shall I tell you? Fifteen whole days the feast in Valencia lasted, and no artisan nor other workman did any work, but rather, every day, the games and dance and balls were renewed.[29]

*Fighting with oranges at Valencia*

The fight with oranges may have been an established tradition, as eighty years later we find the same event repeated. We have the accounts for the festivities held when Peter IV of Aragon visited Tortosa in 1358 with his brother, the infante Fernando, who was marquis of the city. Here the details of the battle emerge more clearly. The oranges were bought and delivered to a vessel moored on a quay on the river Ebro which runs through the city. Sailors who manned this vessel and others were paid for three days, during which the lords fought each other with oranges from the boats. Over 1,600 oranges were purchased in all, and musicians from the neighbourhood were recruited for the event.[30] A similar battle was repeated when Martí I and his queen, Blanche of Navarre, entered the town in 1401: apparently 11,500 oranges were used.

A different kind of battle was the siege of a 'castle of love', in which a stage set of a castle was manned and defended by ladies, while the knights attempted to take it by storm. The best description of such an occasion comes from an Italian source:

*The castle of love*

> This was how the game was played: a mock castle was built, in which there were ladies with their maids or attendants and servants, who defended the castle very wisely without the help of a single man. The castle was equipped with the following defences: white and grey squirrel fur, sendal silk, purple cloth, samite and scarlet and painted fabrics and ermine. What can one say about the golden crowns set with chrysolites, sapphires, topazes and emeralds with pearls, with which the ladies protected their heads against the attack of their opponents? This castle had to be captured, and it was captured with the following missiles and siege engines: apples, dates, muscat, little cakes, pears, figs, roses, lilies and violets, flasks of balsam, perfume and rosewater, ambergris, camphor, cardamom, cinnamon, cloves, honey mixed with wine, as well as all kinds of flowers and spices, sweet-smelling and glorious to behold.[31]

This is the only written description of such an occasion, and we cannot point to a court festival where it took place. It almost certainly did so, for it is a theme which is popular in medieval art and literature. We find it illustrated in manuscripts such as the famous *Luttrell Psalter* and the book of advice which Walter Milemete presented to Edward III, on ivory mirrorbacks, and tapestries. Louis II of Anjou had a table fountain representing the siege, with the castle defended by ladies with staves and shields, one of the largest pieces of plate in his collection.[32]

**93**, p.257

## Masks, disguises and scenery

MASKS AND DISGUISES WERE AN essential part of Edward III's Christmas entertainments, but it is only the erratic survival of royal accounts that makes them seem unusual. Masks have far older origins, in such mysterious customs as the 'Little Stag' who is recorded as a good luck figure dressed as a stag as far back as the fourth century AD.[33] More specifically, there are references to larvae, originally meaning 'spectres' but now describing masks, in Oxford around 1250, and what seems to have been a kind of Hallowe'en trick or treat is recorded on the Welsh border in 1284, involving 'monstrous masks'.[34] The first recorded use of masks in the carnival at Venice also dates to this period. In Edward III's reign there are numerous records of expenditure on 'vizors' and on 'heads', and for two occasions we have detailed descriptions of what was ordered. For the king's revels at Guildford at Christmas in 1347, the original bill from John of Cologne, maker of armour and costumes, and supplier of embroidery, survives, giving more detail than the summary on the annual account roll. This battered sheet of parchment lists a series of different disguises: fourteen heads and busts of girls, fourteen heads of bearded men, fourteen silver angels with curly hair, fourteen silver-plated dragons' heads with a black mane, fourteen heads of swans. To go with these there are tunics decorated with the eyes of peacocks and gleaming with stars. The following year, forty-four masks were made for a tournament at Canterbury, followed by 280 'vizors' provided for a tournament at Lichfield, for 'dukes, ladies and girls', who were allowed to keep them. These were made up from moulded leather, *cuir bouilli*, from which tournament armour and helmet crests were also made, a lightweight and highly malleable material. At Otford eleven years later, there are twelve heads each of lion cubs, elephants, men with bats' wings and wild men and twenty-seven heads of virgins.

*Masks for Christmas*

*Vizors and heads*

The inclusion of busts and bats' wings imply that the 'heads' covered the upper part of the body, and were not simply masks, but something nearer to headpieces, which came down over the shoulders. This is supported by evidence from contemporary illustrations. Similar 'heads' were evidently worn by the tourneying ladies at the court of Artois in 1306. In some cases, there are tunics associated with the heads. Usually the disguises are decorative or fabulous, and no theme emerges. For Christmas games at Merton in 1349, there were simply masks of dragons' heads and crowned heads of men. At Windsor in 1352, however, we find thirteen devils and thirteen friars in black with white scapulars, a clear reference to the Dominicans. This must refer to some contemporary event or dispute; but whether the Dominicans drove off the devils, or the Dominicans themselves were demonised, we cannot tell. Sadly, no actual costumes or even fragments of costumes survive, but we do have manuscript illuminations which show what they were like. A miniature in *The Romance of Alexander* written in the 1340s has men wearing 'vizors' and dancing; their richly decorated tunics indicate that these are courtiers rather than minstrels.

ROYAL GAMES AND TOURNAMENTS frequently involved a certain amount of scenery, usually painted backcloths or simple objects, which required the services of an artist. There are large numbers of entries referring to the work of painters on such occasions, but very few give any details of the work carried out. One exception is Edward III's Christmas feast in 1337, at Guildford, for which timber and canvas were provided and painted to resemble 'a wood with various trees', seemingly inhabited by the fifteen baboons for whom heads, tunics, hose and gloves were made. Timber, canvas, wood and plaster could all be swiftly transformed into decoration by the use of techniques such as stencilling. Hugh of St Albans, who painted not only murals but such heraldic items as banners for the king's ships, probably provided decorative material for tournaments and festivals, as did his assistant (and later successor) Gilbert Prince for Richard II. Prince's assistant Thomas Litlyngton followed him; there seems to have been an informal understanding that their workshop was a kind of royal studio. Similarly, we can trace court painters in the French and Flemish accounts who did work of this kind.

*Scenery at court revels*

But the painters did far more than simply paint: their role was that of a kind of general factotum. A typical figure is Edward Fitz Odo, painter and goldsmith and evidently a skilled artist in his own right, who worked for Henry III in the 1240s, and who also did everything from building a new porch at the palace to buying candles for church feasts.[35]

There was of course no government works department; everything created for the king came from independent workshops, very often in the city of London; and the same applied in the capital cities of all medieval rulers.

The scenery required for royal festivals did not evolve greatly over the centuries, and certainly the *mise en scène* for the *Pas de la joyeuse garde* and the *Pas du perron* held by René d'Anjou in the 1440s was not all that different from the fairly minimal needs of the tournament at Le Hem in the thirteenth century. The appearance of this scenery is very rarely recorded in the manuscripts, though we do have good images for the *Pas du perron* in the unique manuscript of the poem about it. The 'perron' itself, literally 'a big stone', turns out to be a fairly simple square classical column with a shield attached to it, which the challenger has to strike in order to attract the defender's attention. There is also a picture of the procession, including the two real lions which defended the perron led by dwarves in oriental costume.[36] As with Edward III, this simple scenery would have been carried out by the king's painter and his assistants, who would be skilled craftsmen rather than artists in our modern sense. The nearest we can get to some idea of the imaginative work which could arise out of such events is the extraordinary romance written by René and superbly illustrated by one of the van Eyck family, Barthélemy, who worked for some years in his service. *The Book of the Heart Seized by Love* is a kind of allegorical tale, dreamt by René himself, which begins with a vision in which Love takes his heart from him, and gives it to Desire. The adventures concern the journey of Heart and Desire to free Sweet Grace, the Heart's lady, from the enemies of Love. In one of the finest pictures, we see Desire asleep while Heart reads the inscription on a marble slab above a spring, about which he had dreamt the night before. The slab is a kind of perron, and inscriptions played a part in the *pas d'armes*.

## Acrobats, buffoons and tregetours

WE HAVE ALREADY LOOKED AT the knighting of Edward II in 1306 and the minstrels who were there. They were not the only entertainers. Matilda Makejoy first appears in the royal accounts at the Christmas feast held by Edward I at Ipswich in 1297,[37] and is listed on the minstrels' account, but with no further note as to what she did. However, other evidence shows that she was a *saltatrix* or acrobat, and she reappears as a minstrel in 1312, entertaining Edward's younger half-brothers at Framlingham.

This type of entertainment was a long-established profession, going back to classical times, and involved a huge repertory of special movements: a poem about an acrobat who became a monk, and had no other skills that he could use to honour the Virgin Mary, describes his pirouettes, somersaults and jumps, the French, Spanish, Breton and Roman turns, walking on his hands, and 'the vault of Metz', which he performed in her honour. There is a splendid illustration of a girl like Matilda balancing on the points of two swords, while a piper and a drummer provide a circus-like accompaniment.[38]

When Richard, earl of Cornwall, returned from crusade in 1241, he landed at Trapani in Sicily, and went in search of his brother-in-law, the emperor Friedrich II. He spent four months with him, and was shown the emperor's elephant at Cremona; it may have been there that another entertainment was presented in his honour.

> And on the emperor's orders, he saw and examined with delight many and diverse unfamiliar games and musical instruments, which had been prepared to entertain the empress. Among these amazing novelties, he praised and admired one in particular.

**94.** This table fountain from 1320–1340 would have been used for water and wine, and the liquid would have flowed down from the top and out through the gargoyles at the lowest levels. On the way, it drove water-wheels with bells attached. The machinery is similar to that used in water-clocks of the period.

**95.** René d'Anjou's allegorical romance *The Book of the Heart seized by Love* tells of his dream of the adventures of his Heart in search of love. The illuminations are by Barthélemy van Eyck: here, at dawn Heart comes to the black slab which marks the Spring of Chance, while his page Desire sleeps under a tree.

Two elegant Saracen girls stepped onto four round balls on the smooth floor, one onto two balls, the other onto the remaining pair; and on these balls they moved to and fro, clapping their hands – wherever they wanted to go, they were carried there by the rolling balls, twisting their arms and singing and playing, moving their bodies in time to the music, clashing cymbals or wooden clappers with their hands, cheerfully and with extraordinary movements. And they offered a marvellous spectacle to all who watched, as did other jugglers.[39]

*A tribe of hangers-on* John of Salisbury in the late twelfth century described the tribe of hangers-on who followed the musicians, the actors, mimics and jugglers whom he contrasts with those who had once presented the classical tragedies and comedies. Today's lot, he says, have none of their nobility, and are a disgrace to the courts who welcome them because they have too much time on their hands:

> Hence the procession of mimics, jumping or leaping priests, gladiators, wrestlers, sorcerers, jugglers, magicians, and a whole army of jesters. They are in such vogue that even they whose exposures are so indecent that they make a cynic blush are not barred from distinguished houses. Then too, a surprising fact, they are not turned out when with more hellish tumult they defile the air and more shamelessly disclose that which in shame they had concealed.[40]

The existence of such acts is confirmed by a reference to a play a century before John was writing, which involved an actor's penis, a tame bear, and honey.[41] This also ties up with a payment to 'Bernard the Fool, and 54 of his companions coming naked before the King, and dancing' when Edward II was at Pontoise in northern France in 1312.[42] Edward was fond of such fooleries: in 1326, he rewarded his court painter, Jack of St Albans, 'who danced on a table and made him laugh exceedingly'.[43]

As to sorcerers, John calls them 'praestigiatores', performers of conjuring tricks. Magicians, literally 'evil doers', are described at length by John, but the ones most likely to have been at a feast are the fortune-tellers, palmists and users of crystal balls. He also describes trained horses, puppet shows and illusionists, and these reappear in a description of entertainments *Tregetours* at the court of Lippe in north-east Germany around 1220, where a performer 'produces different figures by magic and deceives the eyes with the dexterity of his hands'.[44] Magicians who create major illusions are twice invoked by Chaucer. In 'The Franklin's Tale' the squire Aurelius is dying of love for Dorigen, who refuses to be unfaithful to her husband unless Aurelius can clear the coast outside her castle of the rocks which wreck so many ships. The squire's case is hopeless, as Dorigen intends it to be, but Aurelius' brother recollects that he has heard of men called *tregetours*, who at feasts

> ... within an hall large
> Have made come in a water and a barge,
> And in the hall do row up and down.
> Sometimes hath seemed to come a grim lion;
> And sometimes flowers spring as in a mead;
> Sometimes a vine, and grapes both white and red;
> Sometimes a castle, all of lime and stone.
> And when they wished, voided it anon.
> So seemed it to every man's sight.

96. Men wearing visors, from *Romance of Alexander*, c.1344. The visors were mounted on shoulder frames, and were used as disguises in entertainments at court. There are records of the purchase of large numbers of visors for Edward III's feasts in the 1330s and 1340s.

97. (left) Saracen dancing girls entertained Richard earl of Cornwall at the court of Friedrich II at Trapani in Sicily in 1241. This is Matthew Paris's marginal picture of them, perhaps from the description of one of Richard's entourage.

98. (right) The poet Hiltbold von Schwangau, rather improbably in armour, shown dancing with two girls, while a musician plays a *vielle*. It comes from the great collection of *minnesang* (love-song) poets called the *Manessische Liederhandschrift* written beween 1304 and 1340.

He goes to Orléans, where he was a student, to search for such a man; when he finds what he is seeking, the magician

> showed him, before he went to supper,
> Forests, parks full of wild deer;
> There saw he harts with their horns so high,
> The greatest that were ever seen by eye.
> He saw a hundred of them slain by hounds
> And some with arrows bled from bitter wounds.
> He saw, when these wild deer had gone,
> These falconers on a fair river bank
> Who with their hawks had the heron slain.
> Then saw he knights jousting on a plain;
> And after this he did him such a pleasing thing
> That he showed to him his lady in a dance
> And made him think that he danced with her.[45]

In a twelfth-century romance version of the siege of Troy, we hear of similar marvels produced by a woman who is a jongleur. She produces gryphons, lions and tigers, serpents and falcons, as well as ships sailing over a sea in which fish are swimming.[46] In the thirteenth century, the bishop of Paris, William of Auvergne, had a considerable knowledge of the occult literature of the time, but was at the same time very interested in scientific learning or 'natural philosophy'. He regards magic as chiefly concerned with working marvels, among which there may be some things that employ 'natural magic' inherent in certain objects. Most magical apparitions, however, are the work of demons. He describes delusions which are 'mockeries of men or of demons', beginning with '*traiectationes*' (sleights of hand) which are the root of the word *tregetour*. Then he turns to magic candles, such as that made of wax and sulphurated snakeskin, which when burnt gives the illusion that the house is full of writhing serpents, like the modern 'pharoah's serpent' firework. More to our purpose is the castle complete with gates, towers and walls, which some magicians can produce: but William ascribes this purely to black magic, requiring sacrifices and prayers to infernal deities, and says that it is only effective when shown to simple folk.[47]

Tregetours are also invoked by Chaucer in *The House of Fame*, along with jugglers and magicians, 'pythonesses', charmeresses, old witches, sorceresses, though the example he quotes presents a fairly homely illusion:

> There saw I Colle the tregetour
> Upon a table of sycamore
> Play an uncouth thing to tell:
> I saw him carry a windmill
> Under a walnut shell.[48]

And Chaucer's successor John Lydgate talks of 'Master John Rykell, sometime tregitour' of Henry V, and his 'sleights and turnings' of his hand.[49] Tregetours appear in England from the early thirteenth century, and literary references make it clear that they are regarded as similar to minstrels: 'there were many minstrels, enough that many kinds of entertainment were pursued that day, tregetours in the halls and pavilions, and storytellers with various tales'. It is found as a surname: there is a Simon le Tregettour in Cambridgeshire in the 1270s. And it has overtones of nigromancy or black magic at one extreme, and sleight of hand, 'guile under a hat' at the other. Tregetours were probably skilled practitioners of party magic, and they may have used automata. Their performances, interestingly, are described as 'minstrelsy' by the royal clerks: we meet Janius the tregetour performing his minstrelsy before Edward II in 1311,[50] and being paid the handsome sum of 20 shillings for doing so.

OTHER VIGNETTES OF PERFORMERS come from an unlikely source, a book of specimen letters by Boncompagni da Signa, who wrote it in Florence around the year 1200. He gives samples of letters recommending musicians and performers to princes or lords who might want to employ them, and gives these curious customers fictitious names: Saltarellus is commended for jumping like a stag and running up ropes like a mouse, Falandrellus can imitate the birdsong appropriate to the hour of the day or, even more amazing, bray so convincingly that you would think there was a real ass in the room. Then there are the showmen like 'Pasaioculare' – 'Lack-eyes' – who although he is blind, can show things by images and iron instruments better than sighted people can.[51] Next come the players or jesters, who select names which they use as part of their acts or which in themselves make people laugh. Boncompagni heard about these from Guidoguerra, a courtier of the count of Tuscany. One of them was called Magpie, and he used to climb up trees as if to fly off. Another pair were called 'Bad Night' and 'Bad Health': the first used to lie naked on the roof while it snowed and the north wind blew, the other would also lie naked but between two fires having rubbed himself with pork fat until he cried, 'My wages have been well paid!', meaning that he had been given a roast pig for his work.[52]

*Circus acts*

## Mechanical marvels

WE KNOW THAT PHILIP THE GOOD was very interested in mechanical devices, as he had inherited an extraordinary collection of these at his castle at Hesdin, 95 kilometres south of Calais. These had been installed by Robert II, count of Artois, in 1298, and were made for him by Master Guissin, who continued to service them for the next ten years. They were described by a clerk from Philip the Good's chancery when Philip had them refurbished in 1432. There was a particular fondness for practical jokes, notably for devices which soaked the unsuspecting visitor with water, covered them in flour or soot, or even dropped them through the floor into a sack full of feathers. One room contained a variety of tricks, some mere schoolboy humour and others relatively sophisticated:

> In the entrance, there are eight conduits for wetting women from below and three conduits which, when people stop in front of them, cover them all over with flour. When someone tries to open a certain window, a figure appears, sprays the person with water, and shuts the window. A book of ballads lies on a desk but, when you try to read it, you are squirted with soot, and if you look inside it, you can be sprayed with water. Then there is a mirror which people are invited to look at, to see themselves all white with flour; but, when they do so, they are covered with more flour. A wooden figure, which appears above a bench in the middle of the gallery announces, at the sound of a trumpet, that everyone must leave the gallery. Those who do so are beaten by large figures holding sticks ... and those who don't want to leave get so wet that they don't know what to do to avoid the water. In one window a box is suspended, and above the box is a figure which makes faces at people and replies to their questions, and one can both see and hear the voice in this box.[53]

The mechanisms available to Master Guissin when he created the machines would have been miniaturised versions of military siege-engines and other such equipment. Later accounts show that he used hoists and pulleys, counterweighted levers and of course plumbing systems. Clockwork had also been used since at least the mid fourteenth century. Bellows were used in a table fountain at about the same time, and waterwheels were incorporated into them.[54] And models used either as table decorations or in *entremets* in the feasts of the Burgundian dukes, often of ducal castles or towns, were enlivened in a different way, by the use of automata. Such machinery may have been relatively widespread at feasts, but the only full account is at the Feast of the Pheasant in 1454.[55]

*Automata at Byzantium*

Automata had been known in the west since the tenth century. There is a spectacular description of such a machine by Liudprand of Cremona, who was sent on an embassy to Byzantium in 949, and met the emperor Constantine Porphyrogenitus. He was shown into the imperial presence to find that

> In front of the emperor's throne there stood a certain tree of gilt bronze, whose branches, similarly gilt bronze, were filled with birds of different sizes, which emitted the songs of the different birds corresponding to their species. The throne of the emperor was built with skill in such a way that at one instant it was low, then higher, and quickly it appeared most lofty; and lions of immense size (though it was unclear if they were of wood or brass, they were certainly coated with gold) seemed to guard him, and striking the ground with their tails, they emitted a roar with mouths open and tongues flickering. Leaning on the shoulders of two eunuchs, I was led into this space, before the emperor's presence. And when, upon my entry, the lions emitted their roar, and the birds called out, each according to its species, I was not filled with special fear or admiration, since I had been told about all these things by one of those who knew them well. Thus, prostrated for a third time in adoration before the emperor, I lifted my head, and the person whom earlier I had seen sitting elevated to a modest degree above the ground, I suddenly spied wearing different clothes and sitting almost level with the ceiling of the mansion. I could not understand how he did this, unless perchance he was lifted up there by a pulley of the kind by which tree trunks are lifted.[56]

These extraordinary Byzantine automata hark back to the inventiveness of the ancient Greek craftsmen a thousand years earlier, particularly Hero of Alexandria. The memory of such devices was preserved in the medieval romances. These offer numerous fantastic descriptions of copper warriors defending magic castles, and lifelike musicians playing instruments. There were even birds whose song was so convincing that, like the nightingale recorded accompanying the cellist Beatrice Harrison in 1924, real birds came down and sang with them. And the techniques for making automata survived in the work of Arab scientists such as Al-Jazari. Though his work was only translated into Latin in the sixteenth century, travellers to the east reported seeing automata, and we can identify these as being based on the principles which Al-Jazari set out.[56]

There is a painted *entremet* of Lohengrin described in the fifteenth-century version of the *Viandier*. This is a wheeled cart with four men pushing it concealed under a floor-length drape. The 'little boat' is presumably in the shape of a swan, and the whole thing is effectively a carnival float. A simpler *entremet* from the same source involves a damsel with

*Making a fire-breathing lion*

a lion, the lion being made so that it can breathe fire by giving it 'a brass-lined mouth and a thin brass tongue, and with paper teeth glued in the mouth; and put camphor and a little cotton in the mouth and, when it is about to be served before the lords, set fire to this.'

The Burgundian *entremets* were much more complicated and theatrical. Some of the techniques of Hero of Alexandria used in Byzantium were known in the medieval West, though his most advanced work, on air and pneumatic machines, was not among these. The notebook of Villard de Honnecourt, an artist from north-east France in the late thirteenth century, shows clockwork mechanisms. Edward III had a clock at Windsor around 1350, and by the end of the fourteenth century, we have the clock at Wells, where jousting knights pursue each other round the top, and the 'Jack' at the foot of the clock bangs his heels on the quarter hour. At Strasburg in 1343, the cathedral clock had a cock which flapped its wings, opened its beak, thrust out its tongue, and crowed each noon.[57] It is still in the Strasburg Museum, and a diagram of its mechanism shows an ingenious but relatively simple series of rods and levers driven by a rotating spindle. And we have already seen how mechanical angels were used in London pageants as early as 1377, among other theatrical devices. Given the resources of the dukes of Burgundy, it would have been perfectly possible to create a set of automata for the *entremets*, particularly as Colard le Voleur, who was responsible for maintaining the 'engines' at Hesdin, was summoned to Lille to work on the *entremets* for the famous Feast of the Pheasant in 1454.[58] Colard was described as a painter, and it seems that because the automata involved creating models with a hidden mechanism, the painters were responsible not only for the figures, but also for their workings.

*Clockwork and clocks*

The *entremets* in 1454 also included a series of scenes from the classical story of Jason. This is a good example of the kind of background references which have to be spelled out today, but would have been obvious to contemporary Burgundian courtiers. The Order of the Golden Fleece had been founded by Philip the Good in 1430, and took the Argonauts, the company of heroes who accompanied Jason on his quest for the fabled Golden Fleece at Colchis, as its model. Jason had therefore been adopted by the Burgundian dukes as a kind of dynastic legend, which accounts for its appearance at the greatest feast of Philip the Good's reign. This was a performance by an actor giving a dumb show on a stage with a curtain, and may possibly have involved puppeteers manipulating such monsters as the dragon which he slew, and the armed men who sprang up when he sowed the dragon's teeth. This scenario implies that models must have been made and painted, and that there could also have been a painted backcloth or scenery, so that carpenters and painters were involved. A similar installation was used for the presentation of the labours of Hercules at the wedding of Charles the Bold in 1468.

## Dances

WE KNOW ALMOST NOTHING about the actual forms of medieval dance, one of the most regular elements of court celebrations, and *de rigueur* at weddings and at major tournaments. Dancing always took place after supper, and there are frequent references to dancing continuing until late at night. In 1430, at the wedding of Philip the Good of Burgundy and Isabella of Portugal, the dancing lasted almost until dawn, and 'both ladies and knights changed their dress two or three times'. Special costumes for dancing are recorded in 1389, for the knighting of the young princes of Anjou, when dancing suits were made for Charles VI and his brother Louis duke of Orléans of scarlet satin, with borders embroidered with gold thread 'of Cyprus'.[59] Otherwise we merely get glimpses of the dances: at the court of Savoy in 1362, 'when the minstrels ceased playing, the ladies did not stop, but danced and sang hand in hand all the evening and into the next day. And when one stopped singing, as soon as she finished, another lady or girl took up the song.'[60] And on occasion the emperor himself took to the dance floor: at Konstanz in 1442 Friedrich III[61] danced in the house of one of the patricians of the town; he is recorded as enjoying himself, dancing six times, with different partners. Somewhat surprisingly, we hear of prizes being given for the dancing after a tournament: Richard II, after the Smithfield tournament, offered a prize for the lady or girl 'who shall dance best or who shall be the most joyful'.[62]

*Dancing chambers*

Purpose-built 'dancing chambers' are found in English royal castles in the fourteenth century. One was built for Philippa of Hainault at Windsor, and Henry of Grosmont had one at Leicester,[63] while Richard II and Anne had one at Eltham Palace. In general, aristocratic dances took place indoors, and this supports the argument that the court dances developed a style quite distinct from that of traditional 'folk' dances such as the *carole*, danced holding hands in a circle. The popular dances were often energetic and springing, while court dancers typically kept their feet on the floor, the movements sliding and measured. The *estampie* is recorded frequently, and we have examples of it in musical manuscripts; it has an opening and closing section, with a repetitive middle section. The formations were in rows rather than circles, and sometimes in pairs or threes.

*The 'morisque' and its dancers*

The other specific dance that recurs a number of times is the 'morisque'. This is basically a style of dance from the Moslem world, introduced to the West by way of Sicily; we have met the dancing girls whom Friedrich II employed to entertain Richard, earl of Cornwall. 'Moorish' dancers were also known in Valencia, and it is claimed that they were employed at the court of Aragon from the beginning of the fourteenth century:[64] at the beginning of the fifteenth century, both Fernando and Alfonso V when he was still heir to the throne engaged them for entertainments.[65] After he became king, in 1418, Alfonso V summoned such dancers to come to his court immediately, to enliven his festivals.[66] And there is some evidence that a company of such dancers, male and female, existed in Játiva near Valencia, as a large number of dancers were brought to Barcelona in a group in 1425. In Savoy in 1352, we meet the word 'morisco' for the dance itself for the first time when 'dances, morisques, and mummeries'[67] conclude a feast.

**99.** Dancers performing a *carole*, to words and music which appear on the same manuscript page below the left hand miniature. At the foot of the page, the men wearing visors (see plate 96) are dancing with the file of courtly ladies on the right.

As with most minstrels and players, they travelled in small groups. We also find women working alone, commanding high fees. Alfonso V paid 'Nutza the dancer', a Moorish *joglar* from Valencia, 25 gold florins in 1417.[68] Some had an international reputation: a dancer named Graciosa was paid by Isabeau of Bavaria at the French court in 1409, and is described as belonging to the household of Alfonso V of Aragon in 1417; she also travelled to Navarre and Castile by 1429. Occasionally they met with a hostile reception: Alfonso had to intervene on behalf of Catherina, who danced and sang in Moorish robes which were not to the taste of some of his officials. At the end of René d'Anjou's reign, at the little court he had established at Tarascon in Provence, we find these 'morisques' again, staged in a form that is the forerunner of our modern ballet, but danced by members of the court, including René's son-in-law. The 'Morisque of the Sirens' is self-explanatory, and both this and the morisque of 'King Adrastus' involved costumes.

At the court of Philip the Good of Burgundy, the stately *basse-dance* was popular, but the morisque was increasingly in demand. Olivier de la Marche records that Philip's son Charles, although not naturally drawn to such 'lazy behaviour', was nonetheless very ready to take part, and danced very well.[69] The morisco involved more than dancing: lavish costumes were needed, and we have an account of 1428 submitted by Hue de Boulogne, the duke's painter, for seven dresses 'in several colours in a strange fashion, suitable for dancing the morisque, enriched with furs, gold and silver, Saracen letters and ... gold fringes'; these were evidently intended as oriental costume. In addition there were headdresses, rather like the masks of the previous century, with long-necked serpents as crests, decorated with gold bangles which shook as the dancers moved. Each costume had a pair of hose with gold serpents biting the wearer's knees, from which drops of blood fell. Beards and strange wigs and little bells completed the deliberately weird appearance of the performers.[70]

A un ostel endroient / sen ont une trouuee
li sergant le roi / lont errant aportee
et i coroune dor / li ont elchief posee
Des menestreus huchier / fist li rois grat maree
Tout entour le pays / adroite auirounee
Cascuns aporte trompe / ou vielle atempree
Tacaires et tabors / de grande renomee
Uers la feste sen vont / chantant de randource
Laigle fu deuant yaus / qui bien fu empenee

Comment elios et enemidus et autres
seruit graint feste et reuel.

Edens sa feste entra
li rois et li suuant
A uent pozestendu
uont le liu comprendant
A force et uiertu
uont la feste fendent
La charole souuri / si les vont ataignant
Elyos par accort / aloit pardedeuant
Laigle en haut paraument / portoit desor i gant
Emenidus laloit / de molt pres costiant
Dautre part martiens / quon apele persant
Qui affaitiement / laloient adestrant
et por li alegier / le keute susportant
Les trompes font taisir / si vont en haut cantar

Ensi ua qui amours / demaine a son commant

A qui que soit dolours / ensi ua qui amours
As mauuais est langours nos bus mais no porquat
Ensi va qui amours / demaine a son commant

En ce point quelyos / aloit la pietiant
et cascuns a son chant / hautement respondant
Griu et macedonois / saloient meruellant
A quoi ciex fais seruoit / quiert en aparant
et ciex quile sauoit / loz aloit denonchant
et disoit en basset / et loz aloit nonchant
As dames as pucelles / qui amors vont siuant
et en qui amors maint / et sont tout sen gmant
Cest li pris des ueus / qui tant furent parant
et Elyos laloit / as plusors portendent
q ozmettre et rasachier / et puis repourostiant
et de pluseurs autour / saproche en dariant
Pardeuant fezonas va souuent ampassant
et deuers edea / se trait en sousploiant
puis vers ydorus / sen va ratrauersant
Pardedeuant pozus / ydore et floridant
Caulus et ariste / et gadifer lenfant
Perdicas le baudrain / qui le vis ot luisant
Tout ensemble en va / deuant tous remoustrant
et que plus fort sera / sdz aus abandonnant

All these dances were constrained by the limits imposed by an indoor space. Philippa's 'dancing chamber' at Windsor would seem to have been a room of between 20 and 30 metres in length and 10 metres in width, furnished with six tables, six benches, five sets of steps and seven pairs of trestles.[71] If it had been filled, like the 'daunsynge chamberes' of Queen Dido in Chaucer's *The Legend of Good Women*, 'ful of parementes, Of riche beddes, and of ornementes', there would not have been all that much for dancers.[72]

*Preaching against the dance*

WE HAVE TO DEDUCE MOST OF what we know about dance from manuscript illustrations, as there are very few verbal descriptions. The most vivid and certainly biased accounts that do survive come from preachers attacking the erotic element in dancing, as well as the lewd displays by entertainers. The latter would have danced in an energetic and much more balletic style, often as soloists. 'The dance is a circle whose centre is the devil', wrote Jacques de Vitry in the mid thirteenth century,[73] and many medieval sermons start from this viewpoint. The circle refers to the one dance for which there is some evidence of its form, the *carole*, from which our word carol derives, as the dancers often sang as they danced. A preacher in fifteenth-century Germany devoted an entire sermon to the evils of dancing and its diabolical temptations:

> There are above all three things with which the devil seduced men by using women: looking, talking and touching. All three occur in dancing. They look at each other and wink with their eyes, there is indecent talk, gestures and songs. The hands and the entire body are touched, which kindles and increases the fire of unchastity, to which many a virtuous child falls victim.[74]

The monastic chroniclers took a dim view of dancing as they did of extravagances of fashion. At a tournament in Caernarvon to celebrate the birth of the future Edward II, the chronicler at Wigmore Abbey recorded that when many of the courtiers were dancing in a room on the first floor 'in a shameless fashion', the floor collapsed, and there were a number of casualties.[75] And we have noted the attack on the debauchery which followed the dancing by the chronicler at Saint-Denis describing the festival there in 1389.

Turning to the evidence of illustrations, those in the Manesse Codex collection of German courtly songs show nobles dancing. Their posture indicates a sedate swaying movement, certainly nothing vigorous or unseemly. Hiltbolt von Schwangau has a lady in either hand, and is dressed in chain mail, surcoat and helmet, as if he had just come from a tournament, while a musician plays the *vielle*. Our best examples of collective dancing come from the richly illuminated manuscript of the *Romance of Alexander* completed at Tournai in 1344, showing what seem to be *caroles*. These delicate, decorous figures are as near as we can get to the much more energetic and vibrant reality of a medieval court dance.

# FINANCING, ORGANISING AND CREATING MAGNIFICENCE | 14

◆ *The cost of magnificence*   *Royal resources*   *The bankers*
◆ *Organising and creating magnificence*   *Buying and making clothes*
  *Buying gold and jewels*

## The Cost of Magnificence
### *Royal resources*

MAGNIFICENCE WAS COSTLY: HOW WERE the jewels, the costumes and the feasts financed? From the early twelfth century onwards, certain occasions when a prince might be expected to spend in order to maintain his status were recognised as moments when his subjects should contribute. The princes of medieval Europe ruled through what was essentially a system of personal loyalties. Homage, the bond between the lord and his vassal, relied on an act of fealty in which the vassal, in return for the lord's protection and maintenance, swore to aid him in all his enterprises. Originally this aid was purely military, but by the early twelfth century it began to be extended to other aspects of the lord's life, such as occasions when he might have exceptional expenses. In a society where money payments were becoming the norm, there were moments when the vassal's physical aid was less useful than financial support, and this requirement for aid became a cash payment, and eventually a straightforward tax. In 1111, a charter between lord and vassal over lands in the county of Anjou specifies that the lord was entitled to payments for four reasons: if he had to pay a ransom, if his eldest son was being knighted, if his eldest daughter was being married, and if he wished to buy land. The second and third of these 'feudal aids' relate directly to our present subject. Effectively, they replaced an informal and unreliable expectation of gifts on such occasions, and they were applied with varying consistency across Europe.

It was only in England, in Magna Carta, that the feudal aids were actually enshrined in law rather than custom, and even there they were not directly linked to the feudal duties of a vassal. It was more a question of money that the king took 'when they could and when they could get nothing better';[1] Henry I had simply taxed his subjects for the marriage of his daughter Matilda to the German emperor in 1110; sadly, we have no record of what was raised and how it was spent. Henry II followed his grandfather's example in 1168, but this was in fact a feudal levy on his tenants, based on the number of knights' fees they held. As to the aid due on the knighting of his eldest son, this ceremony was, on the balance of probability, carried out by William Marshal while Henry the young king was in revolt against his father.[2]

*Feudal aids in England*

What we do have on record is Edward III's financing of his sister Eleanor's wedding.[3] She was betrothed to the count of Guelders, which lay between Holland and Germany, in 1331. Edward was clearly fond of his sister, who was famed for her beauty, and wanted to do his best for her. However, his treasury was almost empty, because his mother had spent most of Edward II's accumulated wealth in the previous three years. He started by raising money from an Italian banker, the Bardi of Florence, to pay £1,000 as a dowry to the count. His next step was less orthodox. Feudal aids were due on the marriage of the king's daughter, but not on the marriage of his sister. So he sent what were almost literally begging letters to the clergy, who were taxed separately from the laymen, and who had not been taxed for some years. These requested 'a subsidy in aid' of the costs of the marriage, with a promise that if they paid up, it would not be 'drawn into a precedent'.[4] It was circulated to the clergy by sixteen special envoys, each given a specific area, and was obviously delivered as a personal message from the king. Even so, the initial response was poor; only eight answers were positive, and there were endless excuses of poverty and general inability to pay. The king was not deterred, and another round of persuasion brought the total of payments to forty-one. The following year, those who had not answered were asked to do so, and those who had made excuses were told that their excuses were insufficient, and unless they paid, the king would be highly displeased. In the end, two-thirds of the clergy paid, partly because there had been an exceptional harvest; so by persistence and good luck, the king raised enough to pay for the wedding expenses, but not for the dowry.[5]

Edward III finances his sister's wedding

In France, the feudal aid was never enshrined in law, though St Louis claimed aid on several occasions: for going on crusade, for his ransom and, in 1267, for the knighting of his son and the marriage of his daughter, aids which he claimed were 'legally his, and due to him by common law'. There was resistance to this demand, and a case came before the French Parlement in 1270: the verdict was that unless a community could actually prove that it was exempt, it was bound by the common custom of the land. This left the issue open to flexibility on the king's part, though it was subsequently held that exemption from taxes, which some communities enjoyed by charter, did not apply to feudal aids, which were not taxes. Another way of avoiding the issue was for the community to offer a gift of the same amount as the aid, as this did not prejudice any future claim of exemption. Philip III levied an aid for his son's knighting, with some difficulty. The issue of aids still rankled, nonetheless, and when Philip IV announced the double aid for his sons' knighting and the marriage of Isabella in 1308, a major conflict between the king and the local communities ensued. The aid was not fully collected, and attempts to do so ended in 1312. If the exercise had been costly, the principle of the royal right to aids had been upheld. Even though the sums were not enough to pay for the events in question, the aids still provided enough money for it to be worth the trouble of collecting it.

## The bankers

THE EXPANSION OF TRADE FROM THE twelfth century onwards meant that payments had to be made across long distances, particularly to and from the Italian trading cities and the fairs of northern Europe where international goods were actually sold. The difficulties of moving coin in bulk, and of finding sufficient coin in the first place, led to the development of bills of exchange: in plain terms, a firm from the Netherlands who had bought cloth from an Italian merchant would find someone local who had a debtor in Italy, and pay them at home. In exchange the debtor in Italy would be instructed to pay the Italian merchant, and no actual money needed to be moved across Europe.

Bills of exchange

The bills of exchange were the forerunners of the first actual banks, which took deposits of money, and paid interest on deposit accounts. The banker would then trade with this money, either lending it out at a higher rate of interest or investing in trading ventures. In trading towns, it was common for individuals to have personal accounts: in Venice in 1300 over ten per cent of the population used banks. Kings started to borrow from banks for extraordinary events, such as the need to pay an army for a campaign: in the absence of a standing army, there was no obvious mechanism for dealing with these large and often unexpected demands on royal finances. And if money could be borrowed for warfare, it could also be found for peacetime requirements.

It was the Italian bankers, by and large, who met this demand, with well-established offices in key cities. Dino Rapondi, originally from Lucca, established three branches of his firm in Paris, Montpellier and Bruges, and he himself became a citizen of Paris. He was a merchant dealing in the silk for which Lucca was famous, and he also acted as banker, chiefly to Philip the Bold of Burgundy, to whom he lent large sums for the building of the Charterhouse at Champmol and the Sainte-Chapelle at Dijon. On one occasion towards the end of the reign of Charles V, royal officials seized 18,000 francs in cash which he was transporting to Bruges; this did not apparently affect his trading. In 1384 he was given royal letters of safeguard, allowing him and his brothers to live in France and trade freely there. His relationship with the dukes of Burgundy was so close that a writer in Lucca recorded in his chronicle that Rapondi was implicated in the murder of Louis d'Orléans in 1407. His brother Giacomo supplied both Philip the Bold and Jean duke of Berry with illuminated manuscripts.[6] When he died in 1415, his trading and banking had made him one of the wealthiest merchants in Europe.[7]

*Dino Rapondi*

It was probably Rapondi who helped to fund the state visit by the emperor Karl IV to Charles V in Paris in 1377–8, which cost the French king a great deal. The author of the *Grandes Chroniques* ends his account of the visit as follows:

> It should be known that the entire expenditure which the emperor and his people had in the lodgings in Paris, was paid and defrayed by the king, as was the case also with all the gifts that needed to be defrayed from the time he entered the kingdom until he left it, even though it was given in the name of the cities, was at the cost and expense of the king.[8]

An estimate of the total involved can be recovered from the royal records, which are reasonably complete at this point. It was at least 51,000 francs, and may have been over 57,000 francs; even then, there are probably items for which we no longer have the relevant entries. Of this, 35,000 francs was for housing and feeding the emperor and his court, including payments to the emperor's officials and servants. The remaining 22,000 francs went on presents, chiefly for the emperor and his son Wenceslas. This represented about 14 per cent of the king's annual expenditure. However, the marriage of Charles's brother, Philip the Bold, duke of Burgundy, in the same year, was considerably more expensive at 70,000 francs.[9] The two events together seem to come to over 30 per cent of the king's entire revenue for the year.

An earlier princely visitor to Paris was not as fortunate as Karl IV. Edward II was the son-in-law of Philip IV, but when, as we have seen, he attended the knighting of Philip IV's sons in 1311, he left the city in serious debt. He had had to borrow the equivalent of £15,000 from the French chancellor, Enguerrand de Marigny, and £33,000 from Philip himself, to cover his expenses. This was in addition to sums he had raised through Antonio Pessagno of Genoa, who acted as his financial agent, and was actually with him in France. Pessagno had started modestly as a supplier of spices, and expanded his business to the point where in 1312 he was addressed as 'the king's merchant' in royal writs. Just before Pessagno went to France, a rival merchant wrote that Pessagno 'is now in such a condition that he fears nobody … and is so generous in the court … that everybody likes him'.[10] The money advanced by Philip IV was paid through him, and he also handled at least part of an enormous loan from Pope Clement V negotiated at the end of 1313. In 1315 Pessagno was

*An expensive visit*

knighted by Edward, and the scale of his transactions can be gauged by a statement a little before this that he had been repaid £104,900 out of a total of £111,505 borrowed by the king. The Paris expenses were more than half of this, which gives some idea of how costly magnificence could be. Pessagno was later employed as an administrator by Edward, and although he had to resign as seneschal of Gascony because he had alienated the notoriously touchy local nobles, he seems to have played a part in Edward III's accession to the throne in 1330, since in the Christmas list of the king's household, he appears as a banneret.

*Tommaso Portinari*

FLORENTINE BANKERS WERE CENTRAL to the finances of Charles the Bold, and the manager of the Medici bank at Bruges from 1465 onwards, Tommaso Portinari, played a major role in the Burgundian court. Portinari's appproach was unusual: he both lent money to the duke and supplied him with the luxuries for which the Italian merchants in the Netherlands were famous. A member of the bank, Carlo Cavalcanti, had started to sell silks and brocades to Philip the Good shortly before his death in 1467, and the involvement of the bank with the duke's administration rapidly became so close that Portinari became a ducal councillor before the accession of Charles. He came to manage directly some of the duke's revenues, as well as acting as banker when money was required for troops. This was in its way remarkable in itself, and the importance of his position was emphasised when Charles met with Friedrich III at Trier. Among the list of clothing distributed on that occasion, designed to impress Charles's magnificence on the emperor, is an entry for Portinari. He is one of nine men, almost an inner council of the duke's officials, who are dressed in crimson-violet satin with a pourpoint of crimson satin. He also handled loans to the Burgundian nobles at Bruges, and when the prince of Mantua, Rodolfo Gonzaga, ran short of cash due to the expensive culture of the Burgundian court in 1470, it was to Portinari that he turned for funds.[11]

Portinari was basically an entrepreneur rather than simply a banker, and was looking at the possibilities for increasing Florentine trade through Bruges, particularly at the expense of the rival silk merchants from Lucca. When it came to the vast amounts of splendid materials needed for the duke's wedding to Margaret of York in 1468, the bill for silk, wool and cloth of gold came to 53,773 *livres*; five years later, for the Trier meeting, the total was 27,300 *livres* (probably including the material for Portinari's own costume). As the duke's banker, Portinari also collected Margaret of York's dowry from her brother, Edward IV, and paid it over to the ducal treasury.

Of Charles the Bold, a modern historian, says that 'few medieval rulers wasted a great inheritance as quickly as he did'.[12] When he met his unexpected death in battle at Nancy in 1477, there was a very considerable debt outstanding to the Medici bank, though how much of this was loans and how much purchases is not known. Portinari was criticised for his readiness to lend to Charles, who was known to be a capricious customer, but he was impressed by the duke: in a letter in 1475 to the duke of Milan, Portinari described his master as 'glorious', 'unconquered' and 'magnificent'. Magnificence might be expensive, but magnificent customers were what bankers liked. Indeed, Portinari had provided the duke with money, merchandise and magnificence in equal measure.

NONE OF THESE LOANS, AS FAR as we can tell, involved the pawning or sale of treasure, the prince's stock of gold and jewels. Just as jewellery was often broken up to reuse the stones and melt down the gold to make new pieces, so it was also treated as ready specie, to be pawned or sold for ready money. Crowns were quite often pawned. There is the spectacular example of Edward III's pawning and redemption of his great crown.

He had used it, together with his second crown and Queen Philippa's crown, in 1339 for a loan of £16,666, when he was desperate for money to pay his allies in Flanders. Such transactions were not uncommon, as jewellery was a form of ready cash or security, but to pawn the great crown as well as two others indicates the seriousness of his situation. In 1343 negotiations had begun for its redemption from the archbishop of Treves and the duke of Guelders, although the principal finance had actually been provided by Vivelin Rufus, a Jew from Strasbourg. It seems to have cost around £8,000 to redeem them. At the end of 1343 the great crown was still in pawn, but by 16 January of the new year, Edward had his second crown back, just in time to wear it at the festivities at Windsor, and he paid the negotiators handsomely for their efforts. Richard II was to pawn it again 1382–4.

*Pawning jewels and crowns*

Pawning was by no means uncommon. One of the earliest royal inventories of jewels that we have was created after Louis X's death in 1316 to decide which jewels were to be sold to pay for his funeral.[13] Pawning of jewels is recorded in Charles VI's inventory of 1400, where it is noted that items which had been pawned to Olivier de Clisson in 1391, one of his chief commanders, were redeemed in 1395.[14] And in the disastrous years after the English victory at Agincourt, Charles VI sent his father's gold and his wife's jewels to the mint, as well as precious gold dishes given by the duc de Berry, to be melted down for ready money.[15]

Flanders provides similar examples. In 1306, Robert, count of Flanders, pawned various small items to Denis d'Albe for 200 gold pennies; there is no record of repayment. Again, he pawned a crown and other pieces valued at 1732 Parisian florins in 1308.[16] In 1319 he pawned the furnishings of his chapel to the *echevins* of Ypres, for an unknown sum. In 1342 the crowns of Louis I, count of Flanders, pawned to Rasse le Foriez, are pledged by Rasse to Jehan de Rez 'merchant and moneychanger, living in Paris'. In 1361, Louis de Mâle pawned a number of items, ranging from five crowns to two small silver bottles, to Jean Moyse of Valenciennes for 6,000 gold florins. Louis was known for his lavish lifestyle, but this was evidently a temporary problem, as the letters recording the loan were endorsed on 13 July 1362 to say that the count had repaid the sum in full.[17]

## Organising and Creating Magnificence

MAGNIFICENCE COVERED ALMOST ALL the visual aspects of the prince's life. So far we have looked at what was produced, and for what purposes and occasions. It is time to look at the craftsmen and merchants whose skills and knowledge provided the wherewithal to create magnificence. The majority of the records which relate specifically to 'magnificence' are those for making clothes and for buying jewellery, so our focus will be on these.

### Buying and making clothes

WE BEGAN WITH ALFONSO X'S DECLARATION that the ruler should be magnificent in his person and clothing, so we will look first at the ruler's buyers of cloth and his tailors. With the expansion of trade in the twelfth century, silks began to be available through merchants trading through the great fairs of northern Europe. Beginning in the mid twelfth century, fairs were established in the towns in Champagne on the road to Paris from northern Italy, at Provins and Troyes, which were also only a week's journey from the great trading towns of Flanders.[18] Here the Italian merchants could sell the luxuries that they imported from the Mediterranean and buy the cloth for which Flanders was famous, and which in its finest weaves was itself a luxury. By the end of the thirteenth century, the Italian merchants had a formidable international sales network. In 1299, for the knighting of Otto III, duke of Carinthia, and his two brothers, merchants from Florence supplied green cloth from Douai, black cloth from Ypres, blue cloth from Paris and red material, probably silk, from Milan, quite apart from the 'purple cloths of different colours bought from the Venetians on credit', which had not been paid for some years later. As a result of this the Carinthians were blacklisted by the merchants and their orders refused.[19]

*The fairs of northern Europe*

These fairs, based on an annual meeting at a place which was not necessarily a major centre of commerce for the rest of the year, declined as the Italian merchants, and later French and Flemish merchants, established branches in the major trading towns of Bruges, London and Paris. In the Mediterranean, there were colonies of merchants from north Italy at most of the capital cities such as Barcelona, Naples and Palermo. The fair now became an annual event in towns with these settlements of foreign merchants, and the fairs of the Low Countries were important down to the fifteenth century. Pero Tafur, a Spanish traveller in 1438–9, recorded his visits to fairs, and when he came to Antwerp wrote: 'I have seen other fairs, at Genoa in Savoy, at Frankfurt in Germany, and at Medina[20] in Spain, but all these together are not to be compared with Antwerp.' What impressed him was the sheer range of products available: for a start,

> Here was all Italy, with its brocades, silks and armour and everything which is made there, and indeed, there is no part of the world whose products are not found here at their best.

This was no longer a specialist marketplace, and he noted at random pictures, cloths of arras, goldsmith's work, and outside the gates, every kind of horse. Tafur also comments that 'the Duke of Burgundy comes always to the fair, which is the reason why there is so much splendour at his court'.[21]

AMONG THE FEW FOURTEENTH-CENTURY royal French accounts which survive is that for the coronation expenses of Philip V in January 1317.[22] The French kings were crowned at Rheims, and we have few details of any festivals connected with such occasions; but the sheer scale of the expenditure is remarkable. The clerk in charge, Geoffroi de Fleury, carefully totalled the costs, and arrived at a sum of 8,548 *livres*. For comparison, the monthly expenditure of the entire royal household seventy years later was approximately 10,000 *livres*. Half of this was spent on items for the king and queen, chiefly furs and cloth, but two items stand out: a gold belt and *fleur-de-lis* set with rubies and emeralds for the queen priced at 800 *livres*, and a remarkable bed and hangings which was even more expensive at 900 *livres*. On the hangings, embroidered parrots and butterflies were sewn. The wings of the butterflies were decorated with the arms of the king and his brother, the duke of Burgundy, and the bill for making nearly 2,000 of these individual pieces was 600 *livres*.

*The cost of a coronation*

The range of different materials available is shown in a remarkable list of the cloth bought for Edward III's coronation in 1327. We have a summary of the expenses for the coronation made by John de Feriby, controller of the wardrobe. This is incomplete, but nonetheless amounts to £786 10s 7d. It is particularly interesting as the first part details the purchasing of the cloth. The orders were lavish, with much use of cloth of gold and other silks. Some of the items seem to have come from as far afield as China and the Mongol empire, silk brocades called 'nak', some of which had gold patterns. Twenty-nine of these accounted for £98 of the cost. No size is given for these, but 250 metres of the next category, figured silks, were bought for £68. The largest expenditure was on 'diaspers', again a figured silk, woven in a single colour and then brocaded with highlights of gold and silver thread, so that ground and pattern caught the light in different ways, giving a very rich effect. 'Diaspers' accounted for a third of the total bill. Not all the cloth was used: it was common practice to buy more than was needed, and then sell it back to the suppliers. Twelve of the 'naks' were returned in this way.[23]

IN ENGLAND THE ROYAL TAILORS and the royal armourers worked in the offices of the great wardrobe, in houses rented for them in the City, and in the Tower of London; it was an operation on a large scale, an industry which depended on the court and the government for most of its business. In both England and France, the highly expensive operation of embroidering costumes was part of the armourer's work. This unlikely combination is difficult to explain: it may be because so much embroidery of the mid fourteenth century involved gold and silver metallic thread, or because a good deal of embroidered work was for military use on banners and pennants for ships.

*Royal tailors in England*

We do however get a glimpse of the frantic preparations for royal occasions in the workshops which supplied the royal clothing. John Marreys, the king's tailor, was put under considerable pressure when he had to provide robes for the feast held by Edward III at Windsor for the establishment of his proposed Order of the Round Table in January 1344. Edward wanted new robes in the grandest style, and he wanted them quickly. Marreys made robes of red velvet, and had to employ eight furriers for three days and two others for a day, working 'in the greatest haste' to complete the order. His bill also included 28 kilos of candles 'to give light for the making of the said garments'.[24]

This was not the first time that Edward had put in an order which tested the capacity of his suppliers: at Worcester in 1329, Francolin de Murkirk, his painter, had to make twelve tunics which required 400 peacock feathers and four tunics for the king's squires decorated with eagles' heads. Francolin had to buy large quantities of candles, like John Marreys, so that the work could be completed in time.[25] And in France in 1352, we find Nicholas Vaquier, the king's armourer, making three great embroidered stars for the king's chamber for the first assembly of the new Order of the Star 'in great haste, working night and day'. The same year, he was given an order for a horse caparison and a hanging for a chamber on 8 September, to be worked with 8,544 *fleurs-de-lis* and to be ready by 1 November. This time the embroiderers not only had candles for working day and night, but they were also supplied with wine.

THE ABILITY OF THE WORKSHOPS to produce these garments at all depended in turn on the cloth merchants. The timetable for the clothing for Edward III's coronation was a real test of their ability to meet a sudden demand. Edward II had been captured in Wales on 16 November the previous year, and the decision as to what to do next seems to have been formally taken around Christmas, so there were only four weeks in which to make the arrangements. Fifteen merchants were involved, the regular suppliers to the court in the previous reign. Seven are Londoners, two are from York, and one is a member of the Florentine company of the Bardi based in London. Between them, they were clearly able to supply relatively large quantities of expensive materials from stock, and it is interesting that the merchants were prepared to send materials on an approval basis. A later entry on the receipt roll notes that sixty out of the 146 pieces of tapestry on his list were returned to the London and York merchants who had supplied them.[27]

*Cloth merchants*

Antoniono Bachino, the Genoese merchant, sold cloth to Edward III over a period of thirty years, from 1327 to 1358, and was referred to as the 'king's merchant' in 1335; at the same time, he was paid a stipend of 100 marks. James Nicolas – who may have been Italian – was a member of the company of the Bardi in Florence, who not only sold the fine cloths made in Florence but also silks from other Italian cities and from the Middle East, possibly even from China. The Bardi company was a family-owned firm of an entirely new type, which held its working capital in the form of shares: in 1310, they renewed these shares for twenty-one years, and there were fifty-six in all, which could be held by family members, employees or outsiders.[28]

*John of Cologne*

One merchant in particular recurs in Edward III's accounts for nearly thirty years. This was John of Cologne, Edward III's armourer, who came to London by 1329. He was a craftsman in his own right, and a skilled embroiderer. He operated on a large scale, and must have held quite extensive amounts of material; as early as 1331 he was paid the huge sum of £356 3s 7d for his work on costumes, saddles and suits of armour for the jousts held at Cheapside in September that year. By 1337 he was wealthy enough to have a large house in Clerkenwell and by 1342 he was in royal service as king's serjeant. He succeeded to the post of king's armourer in 1345. He is sometimes described as working in the Tower, but the armourers in the Tower actually date from the beginning of Richard II's reign.[29] Rather, he would have been an independent merchant with a large establishment, possibly in the Steelyard, which was the home of the German merchants from the towns of the Hanseatic league, with a team of smiths and embroiderers, in what amounted to a highly organised factory.[30] He supplied masks for the king's entertainments, streamers for his ships, and robes and garters for Edward III's new order of that name.

Apart from the stock belonging to the merchants, the English 'great wardrobe' itself and its French equivalent, the *argenterie*, were another possible reserve supply of cloth, though most of their stock must have been the standard issue of liveries for the court and for other practical purposes, rather than the luxury silks and velvets. It seems most likely that these were special purchases for each occasion.

## Buying gold and jewels

THE JEWELS AND GOLD WHICH WERE vital to princely magnificence were usually supplied directly by the craftsmen who made them. William of Gloucester, goldsmith to Henry III of England, is a good example. He first appears making a chalice and repairing crystal candlesticks, a modest enough task, in 1251. He then provided over £100 worth of jewels and gold for the marriage of the king's daughter Margaret to Alexander III of Scotland at York the same year, and quickly became a major purveyor to the king. He must have had a fair-sized workshop: he produced 141 rings in 1253 alone, along with both secular and religious items, from plate for the royal table to a bishop's mitre and crozier.[31]

*Simon de Lille, jeweller*

Simon de Lille was probably from Hainault, but his career seems to have been entirely in Paris, from at latest 1305 until 1348.[32] He was the favourite goldsmith of the counts of Hainault. The dowager countess bought a crown and a brooch from him for 600 *livres* in 1310, and he then made the crowns for her granddaughters' weddings in 1323. By this time he was officially goldsmith to Charles IV of France, and stayed on in that position under Philip VI until his death, paid a stipend of 60 *livres* per year. It was for Charles IV that he made a reliquary for the head of St Martin of Tours at the cost of 3000 *livres* in 1323, given to the cathedral at Tours in December of that year. He also lent 200 gold 'royals' in coin to Louis de Mâle, count of Flanders, in 1335. His son Jean de Lille became a goldsmith, as did other members of his family.

It is with Charles V, his brothers and his son, that the work of the French goldsmiths reaches its apogee. Jean Duvivier was active in Paris from 1364 to 1404, and like other artists and craftsmen, was appointed valet de chambre to the king. In 1378, he made jewels to be presented to Wenceslas, son of the emperor Karl IV. He was probably responsible for making the great crown of Charles V, which was only rivalled by Edward III's great crown in its wealth of stones and sheer massive splendour. This was among a series of pieces which were reviewed by Charles VI's officials in March 1401, and Duvivier had to use thirty-eight rubies to mend it. At the same time, he took apart another crown for its jewels, as well as two or three brooches, for a small crown to be made for Philip the Bold.[33] Charles VI also used Guillaume Arrode of Paris for repairs to existing jewels, and there are occasional records of purchases from him. By and large the most impressive pieces do not appear in the surviving accounts.

*Jean Duvivier, royal jeweller in Paris*

In 1396, before Charles VI met Richard II at Ardres to negotiate the marriage of his daughter Isabella, the Saint-Denis chronicler tells us that the king ordered a mass of material – crowns, collars, gold chains, headdresses, gold cloths and patterned silks embroidered with precious stones – all of which had to be ready in the shortest possible time, and that the skill and readiness of the workers were able to meet his demands.[34]

JEAN, DUKE OF BERRY, PROBABLY the most active buyer in the market for gold and jewels, had dealings with at least forty men involved in the trade as goldsmiths, money changers or jewel merchants. He also dealt directly with foreign merchants: in his inventory of 1402, five from Genoa, five from Florence and one from Venice. This last was Louis Gradenigo, who sold him two particularly fine stones, the 'dimpled ruby' and 'the ear of wheat' ruby, for 3000 gold ecus each, in September and November 1412. The previous January he had given the duke a ring with a little cabochon ruby as a New Year gift, which seems to have paid off. Gradenigo is described as a 'Venice merchant staying in Paris', so he may have travelled to and fro to replenish his stock. As a book collector the duke obviously dealt with booksellers, his favourite being Reginald Montet. Among the manuscripts he bought were the Arthurian *Lancelot du Lac*, almost certainly illuminated, for 300 ecus, and the de luxe edition of Taillevent's *Viandier* for 200 ecus.

*Jean duke of Berry*

Philip the Bold had a favoured merchant, the Genoese known as Pierre Labourebien, who was one of his regular suppliers; he bought 720 gold francs' worth of rings from him between July and November 1386. The next year Philip returned an 11 carat diamond for which 4,000 francs were credited to his account. In a list of payments on 18 June 1388, his three bills totalling 2,350 francs are substantially the largest total.[35] This figure is dwarfed by the price for a statue of St Christopher set with precious stones, sold to the duke for 6,400 francs in 1389, and paid for in instalments.[36] The following year, a ring with a great cut diamond, three pearls and a ruby cost 4,600 francs: a note says enigmatically that 'the duke put it in his box'.[37]

*Philip the Bold*

Alfonso of Aragon was another great connoisseur of jewellery. He bought from merchants who made the journey to Naples, and from his own Catalan subjects, and Castelnuovo, his Naples palace, had a tower called 'Torre d'Oro', where his treasures filled 430 caskets. He once bought a jewel from a merchant called Lucchese Spinoli and declared after he had paid for it that he felt that it was 'a gift rather than a purchase'. A silver and crystal fountain brought by Venetian merchants cost him 4,000 ducats in 1443, though this was modest compared with his purchases from a later visitor. Guillaume le Mason came from Paris in 1455 with a large selection of stock, which Alfonso inspected at leisure; in the course of a fortnight he spent 12,000 ducats. His best acquisition was a piece which would have been

*Alfonso V of Aragon*

placed on his table at feastdays. This was an octagonal gold salt, which was supported by eight figures. The lid was surmounted by a queen with a banner in one hand and a diamond in the other. Two more salts were among his purchases, one set with diamonds, pearls and rubies, the other mounted on an elephant decorated in enamel.[38]

There were intermediaries as well. A good example is Nicolas Bataille, who was instrumental in organising the huge Apocalypse tapestry for Louis, duke of Anjou. He was collector of the taxes payable on tapestries produced in Paris, and obviously well placed to contract out the work to the right studios. He appears twice in the duke's account as having the tapestry made for the duke, and once as paying out money for wine for the workmen of Robert Poisson who were doing the actual weaving.[39] Philip the Bold also went to Bataille when he wanted a tapestry of Tristan and Iseult in 1395.[40]

Friedrich II's<br>Australian<br>cockatoo

THE RAREST AND MOST EXOTIC items came from far afield. The long chain of trade contacts that ended in medieval Europe began as far afield as Australia. This was demonstrated by the recent discovery of an illustration of an Australian cockatoo in a manuscript of Friedrich II's treatise on falconry, written in the mid thirteenth century from the materials surviving after the emperor's own copy was destroyed.[41] The cockatoo was given to Friedrich by the sultan of Egypt, al-Kamil, and would have probably come by the Silk Road from China, having been brought from Australasia by traders from that area who are recorded in Canton at this period. Alternatively, it could have come by sea to the head of the Persian Gulf where Arab ships made the two-year round trip to China, then overland to Egypt, where large Arab ships regularly traded in the Mediterranean as far as Andalusia, and Venetian merchants came constantly to Alexandria.

Long distance trade<br>from the Far East

The same extensive network of non-European traders brought other costly products for the luxury trade to the Muslim traders, with whom the Venetians regularly dealt. These included spices from Java, silks from China – hence the presence of a piece of Chinese silk dated to about 1325 in an excavation in London[42] – and of course the precious stones of India, Ceylon and Burma. Perhaps strangest of all was the lapis lazuli beloved of the artists who illuminated manuscripts, the pure blue of heaven, which even today is found only in the same mines that operated in the medieval period, in the remote mountains of Afghanistan and Baluchistan.[43] The value of silk was such that it was worth the expense of bringing it overland from China – hence of course the Silk Road – rather than by sea, the usual route for the bulkier spices.

Pearls suitable for jewellery and clothing were only found in the Persian Gulf and Indian ocean; the pearls in European oysters are small and of little use. The great clearing point for these was Hormuz, an island on the north side of the entrance to the Persian gulf, a wealthy port which was part of the Persian empire from 1262 onwards. They were then exported to Baghdad, and thence east to China and west to Europe. Diamonds came from the vast mines at Golconda, but were only highly valued once the northern European jewellers discovered how to cut them as facetted stones.[44] Even bringing rare materials from places within Europe was fraught with difficulties. Abbot Suger, writing about his efforts to rebuild the royal abbey of Saint-Denis outside Paris in an appropriately rich style, pondered in the early twelfth century on how he might get porphyry from Rome to adorn his new church. He imagined how the transportation of such material would have to be handled: his friends' fleet would protect the convoy in the Mediterranean against attacks by Saracen pirates and would accompany it into the *Mare Anglicum*, where the precious cargo would be unloaded at the mouth of the Seine, thence to be conveyed upstream to Saint-Denis.[45]

# EPILOGUE

# 15 | THE SPIRIT OF MAGNIFICENCE

◆ *The Twelve Magnificences of Charles the Bold* ◆ *Power* ◆ *Display*
◆ *Did magnificence work?* ◆ *The audience* ◆ *Magnificence and extravagance* ◆ *Magnificence and reality*

THE COURT OF THE RULERS OF BURGUNDY has been a major theme in our analysis so far, and the dramatic demise of the Burgundian state marks in many ways the end of medieval magnificence. In December 1475, Charles the Bold of Burgundy, who was as ambitious in his wars as in his pursuit of magnificence, conquered the neighbouring duchy of Lorraine. It was part of his plan to make Burgundy an unassailable power in the heart of Europe. His military successes had shown his skill, and when he addressed the nobles of his newly conquered territory, a chronicler recorded that he 'preached to them as if he had become God'.[1] His expansionist aims were next directed southwards, ostensibly in support of the dukes of Savoy, who were at war with the Swiss city of Bern. Bern had constructed an extensive but ramshackle alliance of German and Swiss towns and cities who felt threatened by Charles's aggression. In the course of the next two years, they inflicted two massive defeats on him. At Grandson, fifty miles southwest of Bern, they surprised him when he was in process of moving camp, and took enormous booty because Charles maintained his splendour while in the field. Charles then moved against Bern itself, but when he attempted to seize the roads leading into the city as a preliminary to a siege, he was driven off, and the result was that all Bern's allies raised troops in its support. This hastily assembled force surprised Charles and his army as they were moving camp near the town of Murten, which was under siege. Again, the Burgundians were overwhelmed, and the Swiss helped the young duke of Lorraine to regain his lands. Charles reacted by moving to besiege Nancy with a relatively small force, and without securing the hinterland. Once again, the Swiss allies reassembled, and the odds at the battle of Nancy were in the region of 20,000 Swiss against 5,000 Burgundians. The latter were annihilated, and Charles was killed, apparently when his horse failed to clear a stream. His body was only identified two days later.

CHARLES HAD BEEN THE MOST PROMINENT figure in the politics of Europe for the previous decade, and even before his dramatic death, Georges Chastellain had drafted two lists of his achievements and adventures. Chastellain, who died in March 1475, had been employed for twenty years as the duke's official chronicler, and was a member of his council. The first list recorded the duke's military exploits. The second, Chastellain's account of the actions and appearances which constituted 'magnificence', is a wonderful insight into the concept of magnificence at the moment before it was invaded by the 'high inventions' and 'removed mysteries' of the Renaissance praised by the English purveyor of theatrical magnificence to James I, Ben Jonson.[2]

# The Twelve Magnificences of Charles the Bold

THE FIRST magnificence of Duke Charles, may God have mercy on his soul, was at Brussels where he was enthroned, with his naked sword held by the esquire of his body, and made the inhabitants of Ghent come before him crawling on their elbows and knees with all their deeds of privilege, and in their presence had this cut up and torn to pieces as he wished, which should always be remembered as nothing like it has ever been seen.

*January 1469*

THE SECOND was at Bruges, in the church of Our Lady, where he held the first festival of the Golden Fleece, in the presence of the pope's ambassadors, the duke of Guyenne, the king of Sicily, the king of Naples, the king of Scotland, the duke of Calabria and the duke of Brittany.

*May 1468*

THE THIRD was immediately after the celebration of his wedding, again in Bruges, both for the rich and sumptuous jousts which were held there, and for the various excessive luxurious displays of pomp in the hall during the festival.

*July 1468*

THE FOURTH magnificence was the audience which he held after he had come to power, which he held in the various towns as he came and went, presenting himself publicly in front of everyone to hear all lawsuits.

*1468 onwards*

THE FIFTH magnificence was shown by the great fleet which he maintained at sea for a very long time against the French and the earl of Warwick.

*May–October 1470*

THE SIXTH was at St Omer, when he received the French ambassadors, and his throne was covered with cloth of gold from top to bottom and on all sides to a height of five feet, such as had never been seen.

*July 1470*

THE SEVENTH was at Trier before the emperor Friedrich, shown in many superb ways.

*October– November 1473*

THE EIGHTH, at Valenciennes, [was] at the festival of the Golden Fleece, where he changed the cloaks from scarlet to crimson velvet, and his entry was marvellously full of pomp, as were the jousts and tournament.

*May 1473*

THE NINTH was shown in the translation of the body of his father, Duke Philip, with remarkable and most appropriate ceremonies and by which he gained praise and glory.

*December 1473– February 1474*

THE TENTH was at Ghent, when he received the Order of the Garter.

*February 1470*

THE ELEVENTH was at Malines, where he came to sit in state in his parliament in his ducal robes, and entered the town wearing a hat which a multitude of people thought was a crown.

*July 1474*

THE TWELFTH and last magnificence was at the siege of Neuss, where all sorts of things, both goods and spices, were for sale just as at Bruges or Ghent, and where, while keeping up the siege, he attacked the emperor and all the power of Germany.

*July 1464– June 1475*

**100.** Tommaso Portinari, by Hans Memling, c.1470. He was manager of the Medici Bank in Bruges, and supplied not only money to Charles the Bold, duke of Burgundy, but also luxury goods. With Charles the Bold's sudden death in 1477, Portinari's loans were not honoured, and the firm went bankrupt.

**101.** Charles the Bold distributes copies of his ordinance for the discipline and equipment of his military levies to his commanders, c.1475. The magnificent cloth of gold robe that he is wearing is typical of his style of dress on state occasions.

The magnificences, which Chastellain simply writes down in roughly chronological order, fall into two main groups: magnificence as the exercise of power, and magnificence through display.

# Power

THE FIRST AND FOURTH MAGNIFICENCES are unlike anything that we have so far discussed. Chastellain considers the exercise of ducal power as a form of magnificence, perhaps thinking of Aristotle's original characterisation of it as 'doing great deeds'. The humiliation of the rebellious city of Ghent, his great fleet raised against the English, and his siege of the city of Neuss in defiance of the imperial army are magnificence demonstrated by deeds which show the might of Burgundy. At Ghent in 1469, Chastellain shows us a very different side of Charles. Two years earlier Charles had made his solemn entry into Ghent as the new duke in July 1467, but the event ended in violent disturbances raising old grievances from twenty-five years earlier in the wake of his father's suppression of a rebellion in the city. Charles had to make his escape, with his treasure and his wife Mary. Negotiations over this very personal affront to the duke were protracted. By January 1469 he had forced the city authorities to surrender all their privileges to him, in return for a new grant, and it is this surrender ceremony that Chastellain has in mind. In the presence of numerous envoys invited for the occasion – seventeen are named in one account – Charles, seated on a high throne and surrounded by knights of the Golden Fleece and other dignitaries, received the banners of Ghent from the officials of the city's guilds, who begged for mercy. The privileges which allowed Ghent to elect its own rulers were read out and Charles at once annulled them. The document was cut to pieces on the spot. The city's humiliation was complete, and Charles, after reciting their treachery against his father, and his own narrow escape, declared them guilty of the 'most enormous crime of lèse majesté'. Nonetheless, he continued, if they would be in future 'his good people and children', he in turn would be their 'good prince'.

*Charles the Bold and Ghent*

Similarly, in the public audiences held by Charles from the beginning of the reign, he appears as the austere, self-righteous despot, whose word is sufficient to settle lawsuits and impose his will on his subjects. The petitions were simply read out, and Charles would reply 'Let it be done', 'Null', 'Set aside', while the assembled dignitaries sat in silence for hours on end. The same procedure was followed at his weekly audiences throughout his reign, to the intense irritation of his courtiers. It demonstrates Charles's control over the operation of law. The fifth magnificence concerns a different kind of power, that of raising a huge fleet when he was at war with the English. Both of these are an extension of the idea of magnificence which is peculiar to Chastellain.

*Charles the Bold and justice*

The eleventh magnificence is also concerned with power. At Malines, in July 1474, Chastellain tells us that Charles wore a hat that many people thought was a crown. It could be a coded description of the proceedings; in reality it was a ducal hat with an archduke's coronet.[3] This was at a session of the ducal parliament, at which Charles created a kind of supreme court for the extensive lands held by the Burgundian dukes in the Low Countries. He held these as a vassal of either Louis XI or of Friedrich III, to whose courts appeals could be made. This new court, from which there was no appeal, cut directly across his feudal obligations, and was a declaration of independence. It may have been planned before the failure of his ambition to become king was known; the effect was to make him sovereign in his own lands, even if he lacked the title to go with it. The Flemish were not impressed; the chronicler of the small state of Guelders, newly purchased by Charles, was openly scornful:

> Exalting himself and extolling his name over all the Emperors, kings and princes who have existed in the Roman Empire since the incarnation of the Lord, having entered Malines in pompous state, he had the effrontery to institute and establish ... a certain supreme court, called a *Parlement*, after the example of the kings of France; like some strange and abominable idol to be worshipped by his subjects in all his lands.[4]

Instead of 'king', Charles had to be content with the self-proclaimed title of 'sovereign lord', which he used in all his documents from 1474 onwards.

## Display

CHARLES'S BURNING AMBITION TO BE independent of France and a king in his own right also lies behind the sixth and seventh magnificences, which involve display rather than the exercise of power. The French king, Louis XI, was equally determined to resist this, and sent an embassy which in effect demanded Charles's obedience. The French envoys came to Saint-Omer to deliver their message, and found the duke seated on a royal throne with five steps. Normally, Charles's ducal status would have been symbolised by three steps. This defiance of the accepted norms was compounded by the heraldic colours of the throne, which was draped in cloth of gold, but set on a podium covered in black silk. Burgundy was technically a French duchy, and Charles's colours should therefore have been the blue and gold of France. Charles received the envoys in the coldest possible fashion, and having read their message, declared that Louis was the friend of all his enemies, and had spurred them on to insult him and quarrel with him. He then followed this up by quoting a saying from his mother's native Portugal that 'those who are friendly with one's enemies are condemned to the devil in perpetuity'. Even his own courtiers were shocked at this language, Chastellain tells us, which he puts it down to Charles's lack of self-restraint. Six months later Burgundy and France were at war. Charles had used magnificence as a means of defiance; the message was plain to both the French and his own men.

*A declaration of independence*

In 1473, the event celebrated in the seventh magnificence, the meeting with Friedrich III at Trier took place. Here the duke's 'superb' display failed to impress the emperor, and Charles was unable to persuade him to grant the long-desired royal title. Here again the audience for magnificence was a fellow-ruler, and Charles was evidently unable to appreciate that the emperor would not be impressed. Louis XI certainly had no truck with magnificence, and Friedrich III was not inclined to indulge in such behaviour. If they took notice, they probably thought that Charles was foolish to spend his money in that way.

*An imperial rebuff*

The twelfth magnificence is more complicated to explain. Charles's tortuous relations with the Holy Roman Empire and the states within it had led him to an alliance with the archbishop of Köln. The latter was involved in a minor quarrel with the local towns which had escalated into open rebellion. Charles set up a siege of the most important of these towns, Neuss, on the west bank of the Rhine opposite Düsseldorf at the beginning of August. It is doubtful if Charles expected a long siege, but the resistance was fierce, and the camp, like that of Edward III at Calais, grew into a veritable town. Chastellain was not present at the siege, and died shortly afterwards, but Jean Molinet, his pupil, was with the army and sent him long and vivid letters about it. When Molinet came to write his continuation of Chastellain's history, he underlined Chastellain's definition of it as a

*The siege of Neuss*

'magnificence' with a full description of the town, where anything that could be purchased at Ghent or Bruges was to be found or could be made by craftsmen. There was a church, and Charles, as was his custom, sang every day, sometimes with his musicians. As for the display of clothing and the crowds of visitors, they were the same as at feasts in peacetime. A treaty with Savoy and Milan was to be announced in the church in the camp on 3 April 1475, and the duke appeared in his habitual cloth of gold, with a sable lining sewn with silver thread. He wore an extraordinary hat of black velvet with a plume so heavily encrusted with rubies, diamonds and pearls that the plume itself was invisible. Panigarola, the Milanese ambassador, who had helped to arrange the treaty, was seated next to him, and it is his description that gives these details. Charles publicly congratulated him at the end of the ceremony. Panigarola returned the compliment by ending his letter home 'I particularly wanted to inform your lordship about this solemnity because every act of this prince is done with majesty and much ceremony.' All this took place eight months into a siege, during which he had defied the power of the Holy Roman Empire and the cities, as well as holding off Louis XI by means of a six month long truce.

Throughout the siege, foreign envoys came and went, and the king of Denmark appeared in person. Molinet could only plead that his poor pen 'did not suffice to describe the magnificence in its gleaming splendour'. And when at the end of May a truce with the emperor was finally agreed, the citizens of Neuss came to see the Burgundian camp. Many were admitted to Charles's tent, and the rabble was such that an extra entrance had to be cut. Charles, unable to turn them away because of the truce, spoke with the nobles and wealthy merchants, who were offered refreshments. Others venerated him as if he were a saint, throwing themselves on the ground before him. Panigarola watched this remarkable performance for four or five hours at a time.

The second and eighth magnificences are concerned with the chapters or assemblies of the knights of the Order of Golden Fleece which were another occasion for display. The first such meeting in Charles's rule was exceptionally lavish because of its proximity to his wedding. In effect, the second and third magnificences in Chastellain's list are concerned with only one event, the celebration of Charles's wedding to Margaret of York, described in chapter 11, and undoubtedly the most spectacular of all his magnificences.

*The Order of the Golden Fleece*

The eighth magnificence, at Valenciennes in May 1473, was a relatively routine occasion. Once again, Charles invited ambassadors: the pope's emissary, and the envoys of Naples, Venice, Metz and England. The statutes of the Order permitted the knights to scrutinise the duke's behaviour and offer suggestions for amendment. In 1468, the criticism had been quite mild and general. At Valenciennes it was another matter, with seven detailed criticisms.[5] The duke's speech in reply is preserved in the minute book of the Order. It is a lengthy self-justification, but its tone is moderate, and very unlike his undiplomatic outburst at Saint-Omer. There were splendid jousts to round off the meeting. The Metz envoys were duly impressed, but all in all it is puzzling as to why Chastellain thought it a magnificence.

Chastellain evidently revered the orders of chivalry, since he also includes as the tenth magnificence Charles's receipt of the Order of the Garter in the list.* Edward IV's envoys invested Charles with the insignia at Ghent on 4 February 1470, but we know nothing about the proceedings. Charles wore the insignia on St George's Day in 1471 and 1472, and probably each year thereafter; St George was already his personal patron saint. He also wore it at Trier in 1473. It marked a personal honour, given to close relatives of the

* Charles was Edward's brother-in-law.

English king, and also a definite marker of his break with the French king, who, hearing of the investiture, told the duke of Brittany that Charles 'had declared himself the mortal and longstanding enemy of the realm, in taking the Order of the Garter of England'.[6]

IT IS A LITTLE SURPRISING TO FIND the reburial of his parents in the list of Charles's magnificences. However, once we look closely at what this involved, it soon appears that in terms of publicity, it was one of his greatest achievements.

*Magnificence and mortality: Charles the Bold reburies his parents*

Charles's father Philip the Good, in his first will, dated 1426, had expressly forbidden the traditional splendour of a chivalric funeral in his first will dated 1426 with a catafalque (or 'burning chapel') of hundreds of candles around the coffin, and solemn parades of heraldry, warhorses and knightly accoutrements. This ban was removed in his second will, dated 1441 and he was buried at Bruges in 1467 with some chivalric honours. His embalmed body was clothed in the simple white Carthusian habit, in accordance with his instructions. He had planned a tomb in the abbey of Champmol at Dijon, the mausoleum of the Burgundian dukes, which Charles's grandfather Philip the Bold had founded and where he was buried. When his father's tomb was ready, Charles the Bold gave instructions for his father's body to be disinterred and taken there for reburial. It was to be accompanied by a cortège which he deemed suitable for a prince of Philip's reputation. He also ordered that his mother's body should be brought from the abbey at Gosnay north of Lille by a second cortège.

Jean de Haynin was summoned to join this procession, and has left a detailed account of the journey.[7] They set out from Gosnay on 31 December, taking the coffin to a nearby church each night. The bells were rung at each village they passed through. On 2 January at Valenciennes, the first city on the route, the first ceremony was held, with a catafalque of a hundred candles, and a mass attended by the local abbots and nobles. They reached Gembloux on 7 January, where they met the other cortège who had come from Bruges. That night, a simple service was held in the church, and the bells were rung for most of the night. The joint company consisted of 250 men on foot.

On 8 January, they reached Namur, where the full ceremonies which Charles had specified were carried out. These were set out in careful detail and hark back to the burial of the last count of Flanders, Louis de Mâle, in 1384. There is even a horse with the armorial of the late duke, although the ritual of offering horse and rider at the altar at the funeral in 1384 was not followed.[8] Strikingly, the heraldry employed is that of the Flemish provinces, and not that of Burgundy itself.

The procession was headed by two heralds wearing the duke's arms, in mourning, followed by four kings-at-arms, wearing crowns, and carrying the banners of Brabant, Flanders, Artois and Hainault, accompanying two horses in the caparison of the duke. Next came two knights, one carrying his tournament helm and crest, the other a shield, accompanied by a squire with the duke's pennon and a knight with his banner. These preceded the coffins on two hearses covered in red velvet, each drawn by six horses. Beside the duke's hearse were twelve friars; on his coffin lay a sword with a black velvet scabbard and a golden hilt, and one of the duke's gold coronets set with jewels. Both coffins lay under a cloth of gold with a gold and black pattern. Eight knights carried the corners of the drapes on each hearse. As the cortège made its way through the streets, 'the windows were full of people who had come to see the stately honours; and some of them wept copiously, and others not'. In the church, the burning chapel was twice the size of that at Valenciennes, 'but the candles were small' The four banners carried by the kings-at-arms were placed at the corners of the scaffold.

La Chapelle ardante

**102.** (right) The booty seized by the Swiss from Charles the Bold's tent at Grandson; the miniature gives only the vaguest impression of the luxury of the objects, as the rather dull goblet on the table is actually a spectacular and very highly valued crystal and gold piece, and the jewels are sketched in light colours.

**103, 104.** (above) Catafalques (*chapelles ardentes*) were the most spectacular element of magnificent funerals. A relatively simple catafalque at the funeral of Anne of Brittany in 1514 is shown with mourners. The catafalque of Charles the Bold's great grandson the emperor Karl V at Brussels in 1555 is probably one of the largest ever constructed, and is closer to that created for Philip the Good and Isabella in 1474.

The entry of the cortège into Dijon on 6 February used the same prescribed ritual. Charles had arrived in the city on 25 January, and the Dijon ceremonies therefore included his guard, who marched in companies, two by two, behind the hearses. The knights of the Order of the Golden Fleece were also present, and six of them carried the duke's hearse-cloth.[9] Three masses were said in the chapel next to the ducal castle which was the home of the Order. The catafalque was built as a model of a church, hung with velvet and black silk, its size (12 metres long and 3.5 metres wide) only limited by the space available: it was the work of the duke's master-carpenter. On 10 February, a similar procession formed up to accompany the hearses to the abbey of Champmol. Here the final services were held, followed by the requiem mass the next day.

The reburial of Charles's parents was probably seen and remembered by more people than any other event during the existence of the medieval duchy of Burgundy. The two cortèges covered a total of 870 kilometres, with torches blazing, and with bells rung in every city, town and village through which they passed. Namur, Valenciennes and Dijon were all substantial places.[10] And such a procession would have been the most striking event in most of their lives. Philip the Good, as his posthumous nickname suggests, had been a generally beloved figure, and this was an excellent way for Charles to remind his subjects that he was Philip's heir. It is an unexpected form of magnificence, and almost certainly the most effective of the 'magnificences of Charles the Bold'. This remarkable operation, held at the most inclement time of year, was part of a wider plan which failed to materialise. Why should the reburial, which was postponed several times, have to be carried out in the depths of winter? The procession struggled through torrential rain and floods which actually halted its progress before the entry into Dijon and again at the final stage from Dijon to Champmol. The costs of the reburial were huge, and a vast number of people were involved. At each stop, hundreds of candles were used, on occasion perhaps as many as a thousand.[11] Elaborate heraldic displays were erected in each church, as part of the catafalque, and were echoed in the formal entries into the major towns. And the reception of the procession in these towns involved equally rich responses in terms of personnel and settings: rich tapestries were hung in the streets (and had to be dried out afterwards because of the weather).

The clue to the timing of the reburial lies in a series of letters about the timing of the start of the journey for the reburial cortèges. The first date set was November 20, two days after the coronation of Charles as king of Burgundy, which he was hoping to arrange with Friedrich III at Trier. It was postponed when negotiations proved difficult. As soon as it was known that there would be no such event, the reburial was delayed further to 10 December. Further complications meant that the two processions finally set out on 2 January.[12]

The combination of an inauspicious planned date for the reburial, followed by delays which seem to tie in with the failure of the interview at Trier, seem to be a strong indication that this was a display of dynastic magnificence intended to be Charles' first royal act. Unexpected as the form of this 'magnificence' seems, it was actually the most effective in terms of propaganda of all of them. If it had been combined with his coronation, as seems to have been intended, it would have been a truly dramatic opening to his reign.

# Did Magnificence Work?
## *The audience*

BEFORE WE CAN BEGIN TO ASSESS whether magnificence produced the desired effect, we have to look at the audience for the various elements which go to make the prince magnificent. Different occasions were aimed at different audiences, and some of these audiences could be very small. Equally, events involving hundreds or, very rarely, thousands of people might be watched by fewer spectators than participants. Gauging audiences is very difficult, as there are literally no records, and very few chroniclers give any idea of the number of onlookers.

We can safely point to displays of magnificence which were addressed to a select group of individuals. These usually involved the rarest and most precious of princely possessions. Privileged visitors, usually fellow-rulers and always of high status, were admitted to the prince's private rooms or treasury, and the riches of his personal apartments would be revealed. Particular collections – jewels, say, or books – would be opened up, and shown to fellow-connoisseurs for close examination or displayed en masse to impress by quantity rather than quality. A good example is Leo von Rozmital's visit to Charles the Bold of Burgundy in 1466, when he and his companions saw treasures 'so abundant that we never thought to see the like', arranged in many cabinets, guided by their keeper, who claimed it would take him three days to show them all. Charles V's library in Paris was one of the first great secular collections since classical times. The king granted access to it to the writers and scholars whom he wished to encourage, and to his brothers and fellow bibliophiles, the French royal dukes. Their appreciation of it is ironically confirmed by their depredations after Charles's death, during the minority of his son Charles VI, when the dukes helped themselves to a large portion of the library, which had lost 188 volumes out of a total of about eight hundred by 1411.[14]

*The audience: individuals*

Relics were perhaps a special category. In 1254, on Henry III's sightseeing visit to Paris, his interest was in the people, fashions and architecture of the French, and especially in seeing the Sainte-Chapelle and 'the incomparable relics which were in it'. Likewise, the emperor Karl IV in 1378 had the same objective. Karl, as a passionate seeker of relics himself, spent a morning inspecting the treasures there, and praying before the Crown of Thorns, despite having to be carried bodily up the stairs and lifted in order to kiss the relics. The possession of the Crown of Thorns gave great prestige to the French kings, particularly because it emphasised their status as direct descendants of St Louis. Even Karl himself could not compete at this level. The Crown of Thorns was also displayed to the congregation on Good Friday; the Sainte-Chapelle is relatively small, and this too was a select occasion, for the French court and perhaps a few visitors.

Karl IV owned the greatest collection of relics of his day, and access to the Karlstejn, where the most spectacular items were housed, was again restricted to a small and privileged audience. There were, in any event, relatively few visitors to Prague compared with Paris or London, as it lay far to the east of the other capitals. It was only the focal point of the Holy Roman Empire until Karl IV's death. Karl's relics, including the dazzling imperial relics, were displayed to a largely local audience when they were paraded through the city on the processional route that the emperor had created.

Religious displays were appreciated and recorded by a different audience, the contemporary chroniclers. Because history was largely written by the clergy and by monks until the fourteenth century, this element of magnificence gets a disproportionate amount of coverage. Princes were well aware that the arrival of a new relic and its installation in a royal

*The audience: contemporary chroniclers*

church would have an eager reception. Furthermore, the element of pilgrimage to relics meant that the churches that housed them were anxious to publicise their new acquisitions. From the prince's point of view, such occasions often combined personal devotion with the opportunity to impress both their devout subjects and the church hierarchy. When Karl IV acquired the body of St Vitus, the patron saint of Bohemia, at Pavia in 1355, he sent an announcement about its imminent arrival to Prague, ordering that it should be read out in every church in the city, where the cathedral dedicated to the saint was being spectacularly rebuilt.

*The audience: cities and citizens*

PRAGUE OWED EVERYTHING TO KARL, and was never a rebellious or hostile city. This was not the case with the wealthy cities to the west, whose economic power was sufficient for them to chafe under royal authority. Paris notoriously rebelled against the king after the disastrous defeat at Crécy; Ghent and Rome both declared a form of civic independence in the 1340s. The formal entry of the sovereign into a city, recorded in detail from the thirteenth century onwards, was carefully designed to recognise the delicate relationship between the prince and the citizens. The ritual of sending out a body of clergy and officials to escort the prince through the city gates was carefully observed, implying that the ruler was seeking the assent of the city for his visit. The streets were refurbished and hung with rich materials and carpets. The development of this formal parade into a festival that might stretch over two days both declared the prince's magnificence to the citizens, and allowed them to demonstrate their own wealth at the same time. Without an audience the astonishing tableaux and theatre of royal symbolism and angelic visitations that resulted would have had no point.

The programme of these events was evidently negotiated between the city and the king, and the court might provide the libretto, as with Richard II's entry into London in 1392. The audience included both the citizens and the courtiers, and indeed the prince himself. Civic entries are the most public arena for magnificence, and the easiest to understand today, when it is difficult to appreciate that displays limited to a small number of people might be an effective means of propaganda. There are instances where it seems that a large part of the population was involved. The eyewitness account of the knighting of Philip IV's sons at Paris in 1313 claimed that a parade on the afternoon of 7 June included 'all the people of Paris'.[15] And there was certainly much enthusiasm for such spectacles. Sometimes the crowds were disruptive. At Karl IV's visit to the Sainte-Chapelle, Charles V had to give orders for the guards at the palace of the Louvre that day to admit only nobles, knights and squires, as there had been too many people the day before. This incident indicates that an audience was expected and usually welcomed. The courtyard and grand staircase at the Louvre were indeed designed for royal occasions to be visible, with large windows onto the internal corridors. This had always been the case at palaces, the earliest medieval example being that at Goslar, where the imperial residence had a similar arrangement.

*The audience: congregations*

Church ceremonies were also intended as public spectacles, and duly attracted crowds. On at least one occasion at Westminster Abbey, the knighting of Edward II in 1306, the royal party was in serious danger from the crowd. It was a recognised hazard, in 1308, for Edward II's coronation, the temporary hall erected for the feast was specifically covered with beech boards 'because of the crush of the people'.

Coronations and crown-wearings were intended as public presentations of the king and queen. It is possible that a balcony at Winchester Castle was specially built for a crown-wearing by Henry II and Eleanor in the 1150s. Less obviously, royal feasts were attended by spectators. Spacious halls are a feature of royal buildings from the eleventh century onwards. Westminster Hall remained the most extensive of palace halls until the sixteenth century, with the Grande Salle at the Louvre a close rival, followed by that at Prague and the spectacularly arched Grand Tinel at Barcelona. The Grande Salle was the scene of a dramatic episode due to overcrowding by onlookers at the wedding feast of Charles VI and Isabeau of Bavaria. During one of the entremets, the heat became such that the queen and one of her ladies fainted. As a result, the king decided that the feast would have to be brought to an immediate close.

*Managing the audience*

If audience management was not a skill in thirteenth-century Paris, the Burgundian dukes had acquired it by the fifteenth century. A 'feast' might be served to a mere handful of people, perhaps as few as four or five, and there would be provision for guests who merely watched the ceremonial service of the duke and his companions. Privileged visitors, including ambassadors – who might be included as diners if they were in favour – would be admitted to a section of the hall. The onlookers never appear in the manuscript miniatures of the feasts. Olivier de la Marche describes a feast at Lille in February 1453, with the duke and a number of his family, as well as many knights and ladies. The duke and his party looked for some time at the twelve *entremets* set up for the dinner. Meanwhile

> the room was full of nobles, and very few others. There were five stands, well arranged, for those who did not wish to sit at table, which were quickly full of men and women, most of them disguised, and I know that there were knights and ladies from grand families, who had come a long way, both by sea and land, to see the feast, which was much talked of.[16]

Tournaments attracted very enthusiastic audiences, and were also eagerly sought after by knights. It is difficult to establish exactly why they were so regularly the conclusion of any magnificent event. In part, as we have suggested already, it may simply be that the number of knights present meant that it was easy to organise a tournament. There is also clear evidence from the list of Charles the Bold's magnificences that holding a lavish tournament enhanced a prince's reputation. Chastellain praises the celebrations for Charles's wedding firstly for 'the rich and sumptuous jousts which were held there', and only after that for 'the various excessive luxurious displays of pomp in the hall'.[17] The sheer space given in La Marche's account of the same wedding says a great deal about the attitudes and enthusiasms of the courtiers. His essay on the entire proceedings runs to about 15,000 words, of which one third are on the wedding, and one-third are a blow-by-blow account of the tournament.[18] Or rather a blow-by-blow account combined with a fashion parade: La Marche's coda deserves to be quoted:

> As far as the aforesaid jousts and tournament are concerned, the affair we have described was honourably carried out in all harmony and in greater richness than I can possibly put down in writing without being over-long about it. There was not a single day that on the seats, in the jousts and at the banquets many people were clothed in rich bejewelled and embroidered dresses with rich drapes, caparisons and harness changing each day; and similarly at the banquets and dances. Even my lord duke and my lord the bastard* and their pages wore different liveries each day, and the other princes and lords likewise.

---

* Anthony, Grand Bastard of Burgundy was Philip's son, and in the absence of a legitimate heir, second only to the duke himself.

For the most part, these magnificences were for immediate consumption, for the nobles and courtiers and foreign participants in the foreground. In the background are their followers and the citizens, and the common people of the locality. There was then a remoter audience, who would have heard about the magnificences by report. The merchants of the Low Countries and of the Italian cities maintained a news service second to none in Europe, and had done so for a long time. Some of the best reports of the battle of Crécy in 1346 are to be found in Italian newsletters. News was vital to their business: they had large loans outstanding to most of the kings and princes of Europe, and victory or defeat in war meant prosperity or disaster to them. In peacetime, they would watch for the waxing or waning prestige of the different rulers, and their levels of expenditure. Tommaso Portinari, the manager of the Bruges branch of the bank of the Medici of Florence, sent letters back about most of Charles' magnificences, and he was just one of a number of such agents.

*Reports of magnificence, from merchants*

There were also the official envoys of other European states. Although permanent ambassadors were still in the future, the position of Burgundy in the centre of Europe and the complexities of its relations with its neighbours meant that it was a hive of diplomatic activity on specific issues. Only a handful of the despatches sent home by envoys survive, but these visitors must have been one of the prime targets for magnificence. The first assembly of the Order of the Golden Fleece in 1468 demonstrates this neatly. Tommaso Portinari reports on the extraordinary purchases by Charles the Bold, such as a payment of 1,000 gold marks for 1,200 small gold bells for twelve sets of harness.* He adds that 'this will be something that will be talked about for a long time'. According to the chronicler Georges Chastellain, who was present, the envoys of the duke of Brittany, who had never been at an assembly of the Order before, 'praised it very highly and held it in great esteem'.[19] The list of eight groups of envoys is surprising until we remember that the meeting of the Order was intended to precede the wedding of Charles the Bold to Margaret of York, to which their rulers would have been invited. In fact, due to delays by the papal chancery, the wedding took place two months later.

*Reports of magnificence, from envoys*

We have already discussed this wedding, the third of the magnificences. Olivier de la Marche wrote about it as its organiser. There are other historical accounts, and Portinari's letters. Much the most interesting version is a description of it written by someone who went to watch 'as my pastime'. Jean de Haynin, an officer from Hainault in Charles the Bold's army, belongs to a section of the audience for magnificences who have very rarely left any record of their reactions to the ducal festivities. He wrote his account as soon as he reached home after the end of the tournaments. He admits that he was not privy to the innermost ceremonies, and could only present what he had seen as a simple spectator. He gleaned information by asking *gens de bien*, well connected people, and notes when he forgot to do so. He had gone expecting to see something quite out of the ordinary, and his memorandum shows that it more than satisfied him. He too is impressed by the gold bells on the harness of the duke's horses. He is dazzled by the tapestries, walks through the rooms assigned to the duchess, Charles's sister and Anthony, the Grand Bastard. And he tells us what it cost to rent a window overlooking the market place where the jousting took place.[20] He takes it for granted that princes should live like this, and thinks himself very fortunate to have seen it all: there is no comment about extravagance, only a feeling of admiration and loyalty.

---

* Bells on tournament horses are recorded as early as 1288 (in Venice), as a means of warning passers-by.

FINALLY, THE PRINCES' PALACES ARE IN some cases the most durable and most frequently seen aspect of their magnificence. In cities where the prince had a palace within the walls, the ordinary citizens would be reminded of his wealth and power directly in the course of their daily lives. The palaces of the Louvre and the Ile de la Cité in Paris are the foremost examples of this. At Prague and in Palermo the palaces dominate the city, whereas in London the king lived outside the walls, two miles away at Westminster, and for better or worse, was less visible to the Londoners. The castle-palaces outside the cities, such as Windsor, Karlstejn and Vincennes were seen only by nobles and foreign envoys, but were nonetheless built on magnificent principles. Everything the king did had to be appropriate to his status.

## Magnificence and Extravagance

WHAT WAS MAGNIFICENT TO A KING often looked like extravagance to preachers or monks writing chronicles. Richard II was accused by the author of the chronicle of Evesham Abbey of spending £20,000 on a single robe embroidered with precious stones. Sometimes chroniclers have access to royal accounts, and can be very accurate, but there is no reason to think that the Evesham chronicler was in possession of inside information. In the inventory of Richard's possessions after his death, the most valuable item, the great crown, is valued at £33,584. Even the most elaborate dress is unlikely to have been valued at even a quarter of that amount.

Much more to the point is that Richard II and his circle were clearly using a version of Giles of Rome's work. Nigel Saul, his most recent biographer, writes that 'The body of ideas which Richard had gleaned from Giles ..., sharpened and refined by the humiliations of the 1380s, lay at the heart of the policies which he pursued from 1389.[21] When Roger Dymock, a leading Dominican friar, presented the king with a diatribe against the puritanism of the Lollards, he addressed Richard as one of the 'magnificent rulers', and the ideas he attributes to Aristotle may well in fact have beeen those from *On the Governance of Princes*. Dymock invokes the biblical story of Solomon and Sheba to show that the Lollards were wrong in demanding the abolition of all trades dealing in luxury items. His argument is curious, to say the least, and is probably his own invention. He claims that it was the sight of the 'sumptuous and beautiful buildings, excellent meals and ornate clothing' that led the queen of Sheba to praise Solomon's wisdom.[22] His conclusion is that the queen's reaction demonstrates that it is fitting for a king to have just such buildings, meals and clothing as part of his magnificence.

However, kings were also concerned about excessive luxury on the part of their subjects. The so-called 'sumptuary laws' which appear from 1279 onwards deal with excessive display on the part of the king's subjects, from the great barons downwards, and set out a scale of grandeur dependent on income and status. The laws create a formal structure *Sumptuary laws* of society where rank is demonstrated by the way a person dresses, and restrict the use of certain rich materials accordingly. The use of furs, and of gold cloth and other exotic materials, are carefully limited, particularly for the lords whose power could challenge the king. Furthermore, this sliding scale of grandeur helps to preserve the king's display of unique magnificence.

The first major sumptuary law of this kind was issued by none other than Philip IV shortly after he came to the throne, in 1294, building on an ordinance issued by his father in 1281.[23] It is tempting, though there is no direct evidence, to regard the sumptuary law as a way of reinforcing the distinctive position of the king as prescribed by Giles of Rome. There are two strands of thought involved here.[24] On the one hand there is a strong economic element, which attempts to limit expenditure on luxury goods imported from abroad, at a time when these were increasingly available. On the other, there is a reaction against the increasing richness of dress as something which could subvert the medieval ideal of a hierarchic society. Preachers fulminated against the lower class for aping the dress of their betters, and even nobles could step out of line. Piers Gaveston's purple robe at Edward II's coronation in 1308 was seen as a way of declaring himself the king's equal.

It was exactly at this kind of imitation that the French decree of 1294 had been directed. The detailed restrictions effectively prevented the great lords and indeed the wealthy merchants of the cities from rivalling Philip's kingly appearance. Citizens, including the merchants, are forbidden to wear ermine, *gris*, (the winter fur of the northern red squirrel), or *vair*, which was *gris* alternated with the white belly fur to form a striped pattern, and were to hand over any of these furs by the following Easter. They were not to wear gold or precious stones, or gold or silver crowns. All except the most senior clergy were similarly forbidden to wear fur. And changes of clothing were carefully restricted by rank: the highest nobles, with an income of over six million *livres*, could have four robes a year. Knights and the higher clergy could have two robes, but wealthier knights and bannerets were allowed an additional robe for summer. The cost of the robes for different ranks of society was carefully specified by the cost of the cloth, ranging from 25 *sols* for half a metre down to 10 *sols* for ordinary citizens. In effect, just as royal liveries were graded according to the recipient's status within the household, ordinary dress was similarly controlled. Only the royal family was exempt from these restrictions.

Similar laws were in force in Spain, the earliest evidence being in the thirteenth-century *Siete Partidas* lawcode of Alfonso X, which prescribed that only members of the royal family might be buried with gold ornaments. Restrictions were in place for the living as well, and in 1348 Alfonso XI summarised the early laws into a definitive code.[25] *Ricosommes*, the great lords of Castile, are the highest of the three categories; below them come knights and squires, and then the population at large. No-one except the royal family may wear gold, pearls, amber or enamel, or cloth embroidered with gold, silver or pearls. Ribbons or cords are allowed on mantles, and the knights of the Order of the Sash may decorate their sashes with anything except gold or precious stones. It is not clear how effectively these ordinances were enforced, although similar laws were enacted in England and elsewhere. The Spanish code prescribes severe penalties; however, we have no actual evidence of any cases brought against offenders.

In the context of magnificence, these laws are part of an increasing desire to see society as an ordered and structured institution, on whose stability the prosperity of the state depends. The king is the ultimate source of this security, and at the highest level, the sumptuary laws restrain his great lords from imitating his presence and personage too closely. Likewise, for the great lords, the laws prevent rich merchants from imitating the great nobles. The church, with its strictly hierarchical organisation was a model for this idea of clothing by rank.[26] Sermons might be preached against lesser mortals for extravagance in dress, and trying to falsify their position in society. Magnificence, however, was admired by the church, and was seen as a guarantee of the social order. Prelates, after all, could compete with princes in magnificence of dress and surroundings.

# Magnificence and Reality

THE PANOPLY OF MAGNIFICENCE presented in these pages has an air of unreality about it. This is 'show', a world away from the harsh realities of medieval life, from warfare, plague and poverty. Yet it is more than just escapism or self-indulgence. Chastellain's list of Charles's magnificences is set alongside his exploits of war, as if these were the prince's exploits of peace.

Magnificence was part of the complex way in which a medieval ruler was judged. There were princes such as René d'Anjou, with his string of titles – king of Naples, titular king of Jerusalem, duke of Anjou, Lorraine and Bar, and count of Provence – who would seem to be a candidate for magnificence. Of these, Naples was a reality of sorts for seven years, until in 1442 he was driven out by Alfonso V of Aragon. The duchy of Anjou and the county of Provence were the only places where he was genuinely the ruler, and it was in these territories that he indulged his taste for display, particularly in the form of the tournaments for which he was renowned. His success or failure as a monarch did not depend on his magnificence, but on his luck and skill on the battlefield and in diplomacy. He was, in short, a magnificent failure.

MAGNIFICENCE IS PROPAGANDA, sometimes blatant, sometimes subtle. It is driven by the desire of kings to present themselves as set apart from ordinary mortals, and more specifically as deriving their authority from no other worldly power. The way in which medieval rulers laid claim to that special status in the world at large, away from the theories of philosophers, the decrees of popes, and the arguments of lawyers, depended on showing the world that appearance is the reality, and that the epigraph of this book is their best guarantee of success: that 'who seems most kingly, is the king'.

# ✳ APPENDIX I

## Giles of Rome and *On the Government of Princes*

Giles of Rome was born around 1245. Nothing definite is known of his family, and the idea that he was a member of the aristocratic Colonna family is a late tradition. The Colonnas were very active both in secular politics in Rome, and in the politics of the papacy. He entered the Augustinian order, who sent him at a young age to their convent at Paris for his education. Here he seems to have been a pupil of Thomas Aquinas when the great philosopher was in the city between 1269 and 1272. Giles's earliest works date from around 1270. This was the period when the controversy over the relationship of Aristotle's philosophy and the teachings of the church was at its most acute. Giles became one of the leading interpreters of Aristotle, and most of his commentaries on the latter were written in the following decade, including those on physics and metaphysics, on procreation and on the soul. Later, he worked on the books on rhetoric, which influenced (not necessarily for the better) his own style. These studies led him into dangerous subjects, where the conflict between Aristotle's views and the doctrine of the church was at its most marked. In 1277, the bishop of Paris, Étienne Tempier. condemned the heretical views held by other scholars at the university, and separately condemned 51 articles in Giles' commentary on the four books of *Sentences* of Peter Lombard, which had become a kind of standard textbook on theology at that period. Giles claimed that this condemnation was not on the advices of the masters, but of a few zealots. He wrote a counterblast to their arguments and left the university.

We do not know where Giles went after his work was condemned at Paris. He is next heard of at Padua in 1281, and the composition of *On the Government of Princes* is usually placed in this period, between 1278 and 1281. There is a tradition that he was the tutor of Philip III's son, but this is probably based on the dedication of the book, and his friendship with Philip IV after he succeeded to the throne in 1285. Giles probably remained in Italy until the accession of Philip IV, and he can be traced at the assemblies of the Augustinian order during these years.

When Giles returned to Paris, the pope, Martin IV, died, and the new pope, Honorius IV, ordered that the articles condemned in 1277 should be re-examined. By 1287, Giles was not only free to teach the forbidden ideas, but had become a master of theology. He played an increasing part in the affairs of the Augustinian order, and was named its official Doctor, in the academic sense, just as Thomas Aquinas was the official Doctor of the Dominicans. He became prior general in 1292, but in 1295 he was appointed archbishop of Bourges. He was close to the next pope, Boniface VIII, and spent long periods at the papal court. He now wrote his most famous work, *On the Power of the Church*, which affirms papal superiority over kings, and which is at odds with much of what he had written in *On the Government of Princes*. This change of heart was not well received in France, and Giles spent some time at the papal court between 1303 and 1305, when a French pope, Bertrand de Got, was elected, taking the name of Clement V. The two men had quarrelled over Bertrand's declaration that Bordeaux would no longer be subject to the see of Bourges soon after he became archbishop of Bordeaux. Giles spent the next ten years largely at Bourges, but was at the papal court when he died in 1316.

## *Extracts from* On the Government of Princes

*References are to the edition published in Rome in 1556*

*f.59v*
### BOOK II, PART I, CHAPTER XVII

But concerning what is good and useful (as is dealt with in *Ethics* book four) there are two virtues, liberality and magnificence. These two virtues are both concerned with expenditure and money; but not in the same way. For liberality (also called generosity) is said to be concerned with moderate expenditure, whereas magnificence is said to be concerned with great expenditure.

*f.64v*
### BOOK II, PART I, CHAPTER XIX

So magnificence will be the mean between parsimony and consumption; just as liberality is the mean between avarice *[f.65]* and prodigality. Thus it appears that magnificence is as follows. For just as liberality means checking acts of greed and the restraining wastefulness, so magnificence means checking small bounties and restraining acts of consumption. And just as liberality means making acts of expenditure and gifts proportionate to one's means, so magnificence means making acts of expenditure suitable for great works. Having seen what magnificence is, it remains to look at the objects with which it is concerned. For a man (for now) can be related to four things: to God himself, to the whole community, to certain other persons, and to himself. For that man of magnificence ought to have proper relations with all of these, but above all he should not be positioned equally with respect to all of them.

First and foremost, a man should be magnificent towards the gods, establishing (if means allow) magnificent temples, honourable sacrifices, worthy preparations. *Ethics* book four tells of the honourable expenses which the magnificent man should make for the gods.

Secondly, we look to the magnificent man (if the opportunity occurs) to contribute reasonable sums towards the whole community. For such good things for the community are in a certain way divine. Consequently the Philosopher, i.e Aristotle, says that gifts for the community have a similarity to gifts consecrated to the gods. For the divine good is very imperfectly represented in just one person alone, but shines out beautifully in the whole community.

Thirdly, the magnificent man should have behave properly towards some special persons, as being persons worthy of honour. For magnificence appears especially clearly, when anybody does great things to those who are particularly *[f.65v]* worthy.

Fourthly, the magnificent man ought to behave properly towards his own person; for anyone ought to behave magnificently concerning great works in respect of his own person. Now those can be called great works which last through his whole life, such as homes and buildings, or things which happen only rarely in a man's whole life such as marriages and military service. For, as is said in *Ethics* book four, it is fitting for the magnificent man to prepare a dwelling decently, and he ought to strive the more to make his dwellings admirable and long-lasting, that he may make them as it were sophisticated and handsome. So it also befits the magnificent man to make magnificently his marriages and periods of military service and such things as occur rarely. So it is clear concerning what sort of thing magnificence is; because it concerns expenditure appropriate for great works. But principally it is concerning great sums of money spent on things divine and on the whole community. So therefore it is concerned with great sums of money spent on worthy persons and on the giver himself.

Having shown what magnificence is, and how it relates to others* we can now show how we can make ourselves men of magnificence. For just as liberality is more the opposite of greed than of prodigality, so magnificence is more the opposite of parsimony than of consumption. So, if the opportunity occurs, we shall make our own selves magnificent, by inclining to consumption, so that even in great works expenditure may rather be superabundant than deficient.

## f.66

## BOOK II, PART I, CHAPTER XX

THAT IT IS GREATLY TO BE DETESTED THAT KINGS AND PRINCES
SHOULD BE SMALL ACHIEVERS, AND THAT IT IS APPROPRIATE FOR
THEM TO BE MAGNIFICENT.

The Philosopher in *Ethics* book four touches on the six characteristics of the small achiever himself.

## f. 66v

So if it is detestable for the king's majesty to fail in everything, to lose great and good things through little effort, to be always slow and to do nothing promptly, and never to seek how he might achieve great works of virtue but how he might spend modestly, always spending money with sadness and gloom, and when he does nothing, to believe that he is achieving great works: how much more all these things mar the king's majesty, and it is completely abhorrent for a king to be a small achiever.

But that it would be fitting for the king himself to be a magnificent man is sufficiently proved by my previous words, in which we showed the things of which magnificence consists.

For we said that magnificence is principally concerned with works for God and for the common good – and therefore with worthy persons and with oneself.

Since therefore the king is head of the kingdom and a person of honour, revered and a public figure, and it is his task to distribute the goods of the kingdom, it is absolutely fitting for the king himself to be a magnificent man.

For because the king is head of the kingdom, and in this treads in the footsteps of God who is head and chief of the universe, it is absolutely necessary for the king to show himself to be a person of magnificence in respect of holy temples and in preparations of the things of God.

Because the king is a public person under whom the whole community and the whole kingdom is ordered, it is crucial for him to show magnificence in works for the common good which affect the whole kingdom. Further, because he has the chief responsibility for distributing the kingdoms' goods, it is completely fitting for him to show magnificence

*esset de leui – Latin corrupt.

towards worthy persons, to whom good things worthily belong. Moreover (as we said above), the king's person should be revered and worthy of honour, and it is the king's task to show magnificence towards his own person and towards the persons close to him such as his wife and sons, finding them honourable dwellings, making good marriages for them, and training them for the top army posts.

*f.67v*

BOOK II, PART I, CHAPTER XX

### WHAT THE MARKS OF THE MAGNIFICENT MAN ARE; AND THAT KINGS AND PRINCES SHOULD HAVE THOSE MARKS.

The Philosopher in the third chapter of the *Ethics* entitled 'On magnificence' touches on the six qualities of the magnificent man which kings and princes should have. The first quality is that the magnificent man should be like a man of knowledge. For it was said that one looks to the magnificent man to provide proper funding for great works. But one cannot know for what fundings are fitting for what great works without the possession of knowledge and intelligence.

The second quality of the magnificent man is the amassing of great sums not for self-display but for the general good. For this is common to all virtues: that we act not for favour or glory from men but for the sake of the good. But this is said to be a special feature of magnificence. For since in works of magnificence, as when one shows oneself to be magnificent towards worship of the gods and towards the state and towards persons of worth, one appears particularly glorious and particularly praised by man, it is difficult in such circumstances not to seek men's praise. And because virtue is concerned with the good and the difficult, it especially behoves the magnificent man in his magnificent works and largesses to aim fundamentally for the good and not for men's praise or favour.

The third quality of the magnificent man is to make his expenditures and largesses gladly and promptly. For the man who thinks long and hard before he makes his expenditures, and who reins them in even if they are modest and of little worth, behaves wrongly even when he spends much money. And so the generous or magnificent man, starting with an equal outlay or even sometimes from a lesser, does the work more acceptably than the small-achiever and the greedy. It is not difficult to see that these characteristics should be in kings and princes, for these especially should be men of knowledge and intelligence, who know what outlays are suitable for what works. It is to these especially that we look to make large gifts and very generous outlays for the sake of the good. For those especially ought to aim at the good who ought to direct their kingdom at the good. So also we look upon them to make their outlays gladly and promptly. For (as was said above) because our natures are content with modest amounts, actual riches are worthless, unless fitting outlays and reasonable expenses stem from them.

Therefore the more that kings and princes abound in means and riches, so much the more is it fitting for them to make larger returns and to repay them more gladly and promptly. For it is also better for kings and princes to seek more ways of showing the outstanding results of their virtues, than to save their money and expenditures. And they should be outstandingly generous, and always doing works of magnificence. Therefore it is right for kings themselves to be outstandingly generous and to be always doing magnificent works. Therefore it is right for kings themselves to have all the qualities of the magnificent man but more fully and more perfectly. And so the Philosopher in *Ethics* book 4 wants to say that not everybody is able to be magnificent, because not everybody is capable of great expenditure. But, as is said in the same place, such people have to be noble and famous. Therefore the nobler a man is than others, the more it behoves him to exhibit magnificent things and to have the qualities of the magnificent man.

*f.230v*

## BOOK III PART II CH. XVII

### IN WHAT WAY KINGS AND PRINCES SHOULD PROVIDE CLOTHING FOR THEIR SERVANTS.

Because it is most fitting for the king's prudence that he should rule his household properly, and that he should provide them with necessaries in a fitting and orderly way: and because fitting provision seems most conducive to a state of honour, so that kings and princes are encouraged to behave honorably and prudently in such matters, we need to look at the way in which clothing is provided for their servants.

*[f.231]* Secondly, in the matter of dress, consideration must be given to uniformity of the servants' appearance. For as the servants appear to belong to one prince or to one ruler, (leaving aside the status of each person) it seems very much to follow that they should be dressed uniformly. For there are in the dwellings of kings and princes persons of varied status; therefore all those who are seen to be at the same level, or who do not stand in much distance from one another, should be clothed in the same way, so that by the conformity of their clothing it will be known that they serve the one prince.

Thirdly, in the provision of clothing the person's status should be maintained. For not all deserve to be equal in dress. For in such dwellings there are not only lay persons, but also clerics, and among both some are superior and some inferior, because of which it is fitting that each should be dressed differently.

# ✤ APPENDIX II

## Magnificence before Giles of Rome

For students at the twelfth century cathedral schools, Cicero's definition of magnificence as an aspect of fortitude survived in a very popular late Latin commentary on one of his other works, *The Dream of Scipio*, written by Macrobius in the fifth century AD. According to this, fortitude manifests itself as magnanimity, trustworthiness, security, magnificence, constancy, faithfulness, and patience.[1] It is a minor element in Ciceronian thought, but one which was familiar to the handful of early medieval scholars who read the classics. One of these was a pupil at the cathedral school at Chartres, William of Conches, who wrote a treatise on the teachings of the classical philosophers on morals, and used Macrobius' definition. He was tutor to the young Henry II, later renowned for the learned atmosphere at his court.[2] By a curious twist of fate, William's definition was picked up by a man who became one of Henry's deadly enemies. This was Gerald of Wales, whose career began in the service of Henry II. Highly ambitious, a vivid writer and eventually a vitriolic propagandist, he never forgave Henry's sons for their refusal to appoint him as bishop of St David's. His ambition extended beyond this, since he hoped to persuade the pope to make St David's an archbishopric. On his retirement from the court, he wrote a manual entitled *Instruction for a Ruler*, which begins as a fairly orthodox tract on the virtues of a good king. He follows William of Conches in his ordering of the virtues, and the first fifteen chapters of Book One are mainly theoretical. It is when he moves to the topic of tyrants that he gets into his stride; stories of tyrants and their fates are grist to his mill, and this eventually leads him, in the final version of the book, written at least a decade later, to the much more exciting subject of the Plantagenets and their iniquities.

Magnificence does occur in the Bible. It is relatively rare. It is, perhaps unsurprisingly, absent from the New Testament,[3] mentioned seven times in the historical books of the Old Testament, and mostly to be found in the Psalms. Here it is used to translate the Greek μεγαλοπρεπής, and in almost all cases it refers to the splendour of God or of a king. Similarly, a search of one of the major collections of Latin medieval religious literature, the *Patrologia Latina*, shows that the majority of mentions relate to theological debates on the psalms.

It does show up, however, in a handful of secular works which are included in the *Patrologia*. The chronicler William of Tyre uses it with moderate frequency, and English historians of the early twelfth century are also familiar with magnificence. There is no easy way of searching a corpus of this material, but it seems safe to assume that they use it in the 'Ciceronian' sense outlined above. The context is always that of kingly magnificence. Magnificence appears in saints' lives as well, but the source of most citations is from the formal language of regal and imperial legal acts and official letters. We are back with the late Byzantine use of the word 'magnificence' as in 'Your Highness' or 'Your magnificence'. It was still in use in Germany in the twentieth century as the correct way of addressing the rector of a university on formal occasions.[4]

# ❋ ENDNOTES

## 1. Splendour and Magnificence

1. Conrad Leyser in the introduction to Kantorowicz, *The King's Two Bodies*, x.
2. Geoffrey of Monmouth, *History of the Kings of Britain*, 212–14.
3. Otto of St Blaise, *Ottonis de Sancto Blasio Chronica*, 37.
4. Arnold of Lübeck, *Arnoldi Chronica Slavorum*, 87.
5. *The Life and Death of Thomas Becket*, 46–7.
6. Robert de Torigni, *Chronique*, i. 312.

## 2. Dynasties, Kings and Courts

1. Einhard in *Two Lives of Charlemagne*, 6.
2. The phrase is from Nelson, *Politics and Ritual*, 292.
3. Gregory of Tours, *The History of the Franks*, Bk III ch.30, 187.
4. Gregory of Tours, *The History of the Franks*, Bk.VII, ch.14, 398.
5. Barlow, 'The King's Evil', 17.
6. Barlow, 'The King's Evil', 19.
7. Saul, *Richard II*, 418–21, discusses the three cases mentioned here.
8. Tractate 24a 'On the Consecration of Prelates and Kings', *English Historical Documents*, ii. 676.
9. Hincmar of Rheims, *De ordine palatii*, ch.25, 78.
10. Paden, *The Poems of the Troubadour Bertran de Born*, 164–5.
11. Jaeger, *The Origins of Courtliness*, 82.
12. Peter of Blois, Epistle 14, *Opera Omnia*, 5.
13. Nelson, 'The Rites of the Conqueror', 131.
14. Biddle, 'Seasonal Festivals', 62–3.
15. Schramm, *History of English Coronation*, 58.
16. Armstrong, 'Inauguration Ceremonies of the Yorkist Kings', 71–2. For Richard II, see p.90 below.
17. Klewitz, 'Festkrönungen' 65.
18. *Ibid.*, 74.
19. Schmidt, 'Königsumritt', 230.
20. Rösener, Hoftage.
21. von der Vogelweide, *Gedichte*, 130; author's translation.
22. See Buccellati, *The Iron Crown of Monza*.
23. Now in the Imperial Treasury at the Hofburg Palace in Vienna. There is an extensive literature on it: the most recent works are Mentzel-Reuters, 'Die goldene Kröne' and *Die Wiener Reichskrone*, Vienna 1995.

## 3. The Culture of Kingship

1. Spufford, *Power and Profit*, 60-64
2. Amatus of Montecassino, *History of the Normans*, 156.
3. Jaubert, *Géographie d'Édrisi*, ii. 77.
4. *The Travels of Ibn Jubayr*, 346–7.
5. Borsook, *Messages in Mosaic*, xxiii, n.5.
6. The contemporary accounts of this episode vary considerably; the best summary is in Weir, *Eleanor of Aquitaine*, 73.
7. Borsook, *Messages in Mosaic*,17.
8. Borsook, *Messages in Mosaic*, 38.
9. Guy de Maupassant, *Sicily*, 4.
10. *Puglia, terra dei Normanni*, 63.
11. Mitchell, 'The Arch at Capua', 124 n.
12. Andrew of Hungary, *Descriptio Victoriae*, 571.
13. Piero della Vigna, 'Encyclica ad fideles imperii', in Huillard-Bréholles, *Historia diplomatica*, VI, 137–9.
14. Van Cleve, *The Emperor Frederick II*, 407–9 quoting inscription (my translation); Esch, 'Friedrich II und die Antike', 212–13; Piero della Vigna in Huillard-Bréholles, *Historia diplomatica*, VI, 137–9.
15. Esch, 'Friedrich II und die Antike', 202.
16. See below, p.59 for coinage; for sarcophagus, pp. 45 and 47.
17. See Radke, 'Palaces of Frederick II' for a general overview and analysis of the overlap between palace and castle.
18. *Puglia, terra dei Normanni*, 55.
19. For a detailed analysis of the structure see Götze, *Castel del Monte*, 89–104; for the mathematical analysis, *ibid.*, 183–205.
20. Van Cleve, *The Emperor Frederick II*, 306.
21. Chronicle of S. Giustina in Padua, quoted in Radke, 'Palaces of Frederick II', 179.
22. Matthew Paris, *Chronica Majora*, v.475.
23. Matthew Paris, *Chronica Majora*, v.475–83.
24. Quoted in Delhumeau, *Le Palais de la Cité*, 50.
25. Rollason, *The Power of Place*, 20.
26. Binski, *Painters*, 42–3.
27. Inglis, 'Gothic Architecture', 67.
28. Brown, *History of the King's Works*, i.16–17.
29. For a full discussion of Henry III's motives, see Binski, *Westminster Abbey*, 1–9.
30. Binski, *Westminster Abbey*, 43.
31. Wright, *Political Songs*, 67.
32. For Henry III and the relic of the Holy Blood, see Vincent, *The Holy Blood*, 7–14, 23; Binski, *Westminster Abbey*, 143.
33. *Flores Historiarum*, ii.190.
34. Tout, *Chapters*, i.96.

35. Brown, *History of the King's Works*, i.529–33.

36. Williams, 'San Isidoro in Léon', 179.

37. Krüger, 'Fürstengrablegen in Nordspanien', 34.

38. Viñaya González, *Léon Roman*, 38–40, 85–6.

39. Viñaya González, *Léon Roman*, 89.

40. Viñaya González, *Léon Roman*, 106.

41. http://www.dom-speyer.de/daten/domspeyer/seiten/bauwerkgrablege.html#, accessed 17 September 2018.

42. Erlande-Brandenburg, *Le roi est mort*, 70–4.

43. Brown, 'Burying and Unburying', 242.

44. Brown, 'Burying and Unburying', 246–7.

45. *Westminster Chronicle*, 8–9.

46. Deér, *Dynastic Porphyry Tombs*, 80.

47. Deér, *Dynastic Porphyry Tombs*, 40–1.

## 4. Defining Magnificence

1. Ullmann, 'Development of Medieval Idea of Sovereignty', 5.

2. Kantorowicz, 'Mysteries of State', 87.

3. Kantorowicz, 'Mysteries of State', 14.

4. Spufford, *Power and Profit*, 66–67.

5. 'doctor fundatissimus'. On Giles of Rome's career, see Appendix I.

6. Aristotle's *Nicomachaean Ethics*, bk. 4 ch. 3, 72–4.

7. Cicero, *De inventione*, 332.

8. Pharr, *Codex Theodosianus*, 4.22.3.

9. Knowles, *Evolution of Medieval Thought*, 256.

10. Kempshall, 'The Rhetoric of Giles of Rome', 162; Briggs, *Giles of Rome's 'De regimine principum'*, 11–19.

11. See Briggs, *Giles of Rome's 'De regimine principum'*, 108.

12. Giles of Rome, Bk III, Part II, Ch.XVII; 1556, 230v.

13. Kelly, *The New Solomon*, 63.

14. Jones, *The Royal Policy of Richard II*, 157n.

15. Myers, *The Household of Edward IV*, 86.

16. Kempshall, 'The Rhetoric of Giles of Rome', 189.

17. Nomore, *A Feast for the Eyes*, 115-20.

## 5. The Image and Person of the Prince

1. See Prou, 'L'art monétaire', III.i 439; Alexander and Binski, *The Age of Chivalry*, 476–8, 490–2; items 615, 617, 619 (Aquitaine); 660, 664 (England); Grierson, *Monnaies du moyen âge*, items 302, 304 (Sicily); 376, 387, 389 (France); 450 (England); 411 (Aquitaine).

2. Spufford, *Power and Profit*, 14.

3. Paris, Archives Nationales, J.358, no. 12.

4. Alfonso X, *Las Siete Partidas: Volume 2: Medieval Government*, 288 (Part II, Law V).

5. Estow, 'Gold in Castile', 136.

6. Schramm, *Herrschaftszeichen und Staatsymbolik*, I, 84.

7. Ganz, 'Pictorial Textiles'.

8. Bauer, 'Il mantello di Ruggero II', 279; for the subsequent history of the mantle, *ibid.*, 286–7.

9. Cited in Bauer, 'Il mantello di Ruggero II', 280, from K. Schauenburg, 'Die Kameliden in Altertum', *Bonner Jahrbücher*, CLVI–CLVII, 1955–7, 82.

10. Coatsworth and Owen-Crocker, *Clothing the Past*, 94–7. It is now in the Herzog Anton-Ulrich Museum, Brunswick.

11. See https://trc-leiden.nl/trc-needles/individual-textiles-and-textile-types/secular-ceremonies-and-rituals/imperial-mantle-of-otto-iv-1175-1218, accessed 5 November 2018.

12. Jasperse, 'Matilda, Leónor and Joanna', 523–47.

13. Monnas, *Merchants, Princes and Painters*, 4–5.

14. Monnas, *Merchants, Princes and Painters*, 15.

15. Douët d'Arcq, *Comptes de l'argenterie*, xxvii; Monnas, 'Textiles for Coronation', 3, 8, 29.

16. Nicolas, 'Observations on the Garter', 9–17; for the price of warhorses, see Ayton, *Knights and Warhorses*, 237, 240.

17. As a measure of relative values, the annual wage for William Fitzwarin as knight of the queen's chamber in 1333 was £6 13s 4d: London, Society of Antiquaries, MS 208, f. 9.

18. Nicolas, 'Observations on the Garter', 52.

19. *Calendar of Close Rolls, Henry III*. VII,.

20. See p.206 below.

21. Pannier, *La noble-maison de St Ouen*, 88.

22. Barber, *Edward III and the Triumph of England*, 87.

23. Eadmer, *History of Recent Events*, 114.

24. Matthew Paris, *Chronica majora*, iv.547. A note in the margin reads, 'A manifest example of the greed of the Roman court'.

25. See the list of the major surviving pieces in Michael, *The Age of Opus Anglicanum*, 20–1. Two vestments have pieces of secular embroidery incorporated in them, but there are no entries for purely secular garments.

26. Browne et al., *English Medieval Embroidery*, 42.

27. Kew, The National Archives, E101/388/8 m.6, an account for 1337–8.

28. *Ibid.*

29. Staniland, *Embroiderers*, 13–14.

30. Staniland, *Embroiderers*, 30.

31. Douet de l'Arcq, *Comptes de l'argenterie*, 145–6.

32. Barrigón, 'An Exceptional Outfit for an Exceptional King'. This supersedes the descriptions of these textiles in Gómez-Moreno, *El Panteon real de las Huelgas de Burgos*, which is still the most detailed account of the tombs and their contents.

33. Alfonso X, *Siete Partidas*, I, xiii, law xiii.

34. Barrigón, 'An Exceptional Outfit for an

Exceptional King', 168.

35. Newton, *Fashion in the Age of the Black Prince*, 15, quoting The National Archives, E101/388/8.

36. Even odder, the style was believed to have been borrowed from Poland, and the shoes were therefore called 'cracows'.

37. Delachenal, *Histoire de Charles V*, i.44.

38. See p.210 above.

39. Douet de l' Arcq, *Comptes de l' argenterie*, 298.

40. Barroux, *Fêtes de Saint-Denis*, 29.

41. Coatsworth and Owen-Crocker, *Clothing the Past*, 258–61.

42. See David, *Philippe le Hardi*, 74–7, for the detailed description of Burgundian clothing of this period.

43. Gay, *Glossaire*, s.v. 'bourrelet' and 'hennin'.

44. Gay, *Glossaire*, s.v. hennin.

45. Evans, *Dress in Medieval France*, 55.

46. See note 1 at the beginning of this chapter.

47. Munby, *Edward III's Round Table*, 184–5.

48. A monstrance is a large standing case of precious metal with a glass or crystal window displaying a relic.

49. Gaborit-Chopin, *Inventaire des meubles de monsieur le duc de Normandie*, 31.

50. Stratford, *Richard II and the Royal Treasure*, 145–7, 149–54.

51. Labarthe, *Inventaire de Charles V*, items 1–10, 12–17.

52. Stratford, *Richard II and the Royal Treasure*, 3–4.

53. Stratford, *Richard II and the Royal Treasure*, 263.

54. See p.76 below.

55. Richardson, *The Tower Armoury*, 190.

56. Dehaisnes, *Documents*, i.124-5.

57. Dehaisnes, *Documents*, i.385.

58. Spufford, *Power and Profit*, 358–61; Estow, 'Gold in Castile', 132–3.

59. *Cronica de don Alfonso el Onceno*, in Rosell, *Crónicas* 330.

60. Wolfram, *Parzival*, stanza 791, 252–3.

61. Falk, 'Cutting and Setting of Gems', 20–1; see also Falk, *Edelsteinschliff im späten Mittelalter*.

62. Stratford, *Richard II and the Royal Treasure*, 13.

63. We have inventories for all four of the brothers: see Labarte, *Inventaire du Mobilier de Charles V* (Charles V); Guiffrey, *Inventaires de Jean duc de Berry* (Jean de Berry, 1410–1416); Dehaisnes, *Documents ii.* 825-855 (Philip of Burgundy, 1404); Moranvillé, *L'inventaire de l'orfèvrerie et des joyaux de Louis Ier* (Louis of Anjou).

64. Guiffrey, *Inventaires de Jean duc de Berry*, i. 99–136

65. Riedmann, *Die Beziehungen der Grafen*, i, 582; Bumke, *Courtly Culture*, 136.

66. Evans, *Dress in France*, 33.

67. Nangis, *Chronique* 237.

68. Planche, *Charles d'Orléans*, 683–7.

69. Pannier, *La noble maison*, 71.

70. Barroux, *Les fêtes royales*, 32.

71. Prost, *Inventaires*, ii.527.

72. Newton, *Fashion in the Age of the Black Prince*, 37.

73. Stratford, *Richard II and the Royal Treasure*, 23.

74. Labarte, *Inventaire du mobilier de Charles V*, 25.

75. Delachenal, *Charles V*, i.64.

76. Letts, *Travels of Leo of Rozmital*, 28.

77. Schramm, *Herrschaftszeichen und Staatssymbolik*, III, 986–9, plate 108.

78. Laking, *A Record of European Armour*, i.232; Gay, *Glossaire*, s.v. harnais.

79. Stratford, *Richard II and the Royal Treasure*, 260.

80. Froissart, *Oeuvres*, v.419.

81. Jones, *Bloodied Banners*, 26.

82. Taburet-Delhaye, *Paris 1400*, 81.

83. Olivier de la Marche, *Mémoires*, ii. 11–12; translation from Vaughan, *Philip the Good*, 279.

84. Martindale, *Heroes, Ancestors, Relatives and the Birth of the Portrait*, 6, 8, 23–5.

85. Martindale, *Heroes, Ancestors, Relatives and the Birth of the Portrait*, 32; see also *Les fastes du Gothique*, item 323, for a detailed discussion of the painting.

86. Labarte, *Inventaire du mobilier de Charles V*, 242.

87. Legner, 'Ikon und Porträt', 222.

88. Petrarca, *Letters on Familiar Matters*, 9.

89. Sherman, *Portraits of Charles V*, 10.

90. See Sauerlander, 'Die Naumburger Stifterfiguren', 191–7.

91. Dynter, *Chronique*, III, 76.

92. Rosario, *Art and Propaganda*, 28, plate 7.

93. Given-Wilson, *Chronicles of the Revolution*, 68.

94. Gardner, 'Seated Kings', 124–6.

## 6. Queens and Princesses

1. Chibnall, *The Empress Matilda*, 1.

2. For a listing of queens regnant in medieval Europe, see Wolf, 'Reigning Queens in Medieval Europe', 170, 180–8.

3. Chibnall, *The Empress Matilda*, 1.

4. See Taylor, 'Valois Succession and Salic Law'.

5. Reilly, *Kingdom of León-Castilla under Queen Urraca*, 354.

6. See Hay, *The Military Leadership of Matilda of Canossa*.

7. Boccaccio, *Famous Women*, 467, 471, 473; Leónard, *Angevins of Naples*, 401–2.

8. Fössel, *Die Königin im mittelalterlichen Reich*, 27–42 for details.

9. Fössel, *Die Königin im mittelalterlichen Reich*, 49.

10. See p.20 above.

11. Fössel, *Die Königin im mittelalterlichen Reich*, 87.

12. Le Bel, *Chronique*, ii.167.

13. Elliott, 'Dress as Mediator', 299.
14. Newton, *Fashion in the Age of the Black Prince*, 34.
15. Quoted by Ormrod, *Edward III*, 127.
16. Pers. comm, August 2019.
17. Froissart, *Oeuvres*, xiv.100, for the description that follows.
18. For an example of this as an illusionist's trick, see p.273.
19. Lightbown, *Secular Goldsmiths*, 39.
20. Duong, *Isabeau*, 40.
21.Juvenal des Ursins, *Histoire de Charles VI*.
22. Christine de Pizan, *City of Ladies*, 212.
23. Schramm, *Herrschaftszeichen*, 75.
24. Dehaisnes, *Documents*, i.250.
25. Stratford, *Richard II and the Royal Treasure*, 258.
26. Roger of Wendover and Matthew Paris, *Flores historiarum*, quoted in Wild, 'The Empress's New Clothes', 1.
27. Wilkinson, 'The Imperial Marriage', 30–1.
28. Wild, 'The Empress's New Clothes', 15.
29. Matthew Paris, *Chronica majora*, iii.325.
30. Matthew Paris, *Chronica majora*, iv.19.
31. Dehaisnes, *Documents*, ii.857–8.
32. See pp.111–13 below.
33. Vaughan, *Philip the Bold*, 192.
34. Finke, *Acta Aragonensia*, i.344.
35. Finke, *Acta Aragonensia*, i.348.
36. Schrader, *Isabella von Aragonien*.

## 7. The Prince's Entourage

1. Giles of Rome, Bk II, Part I, Ch.XIX; 1556, 65v.
2. Bernard Guenée, cited in Taburet-Delhaye, *Paris 1400*, 19.
3. Giles of Rome, Bk III, Part II, Ch.XVII; 1556, 230v.
4. Quoted in Nash, *No Equal in any Land*, 19 (Oeuvres V p.364).
5. Lachaud, 'Liveries of Robes in England', 282.
6. Lachaud, 'Liveries of Robes in England', 280.
7. Vale, *The Princely Court*, 99 ff.
8. Quoted in Lachaud, 'Liveries of Robes in England', 286.
9. Miniver and ermine are made from the white winter coat of the stoat; ermine has the black tails included to give a patterned effect.
10. Delachenal, *Chronique des regnes de Jean II et Charles V*, ii. 213-5.
11. For what follows, see Beaune, 'Costume et pouvoir', 141–4.
12. Paviot, 'Ordres, devises, sociétés chevaleresques et la cour', 274 ff.
13. Taburet-Delhaye, *Paris 1400*, 398.
14. Boulton, *Knights of the Crown*, 427–9; Beaune, 'Costume et pouvoir'.
15. The story of the hunt at Compiègne fails to account for the wings and the colour of the stag. Froissart, as was sometimes his habit, gave free reign to his imagination, and explained these by a dream in which the king was transported to Flanders in pursuit of a falcon given to him by the count of that country.
16. Beaune, 'Costume et pouvoir', 138.
17. The nine worthies were a frequent theme in court entertainments and later in popular poetry.
18. [Dionysius] *Chronique du Réligieux de Saint Denys*, i. 608–9.
19. Beaune, 'Costume et pouvoir', 144.
20. Paviot, 'Ordres, devises, sociétés', 275; Boulton, *Knights of the Crown*, 271–8, 547; Chattaway, *The Order of the Golden Tree*.
21. *Vetir le prince*, 62.
22. Ryder, *Alfonso the Magnanimous*, 310.
23. Vassilieva-Codognet, 'L'Étoffe de ses rêves', 64.
24. Vaughan, *John the Fearless*, 234.
25. Paviot in *La cour et la ville*, 275; for the bear device (and live bear) of Jean duke of Berry, see Guiffrey, *Inventaires de Jean duc de Berry*, cxxviii–cxxx.
26. Mérindol, *Le roi René et la seconde maison d'Anjou*, 170–7.
27. *Parliament Rolls*, vi. 50; Saul, 'The Commons and the Abolition of Badges', 305 ff.
28. *Westminster Chronicle* s.a. 1388, quoted in Saul, 'The Commons and the Abolition of Badges', 308.
29. Edward prince of Wales issued eagle brooches, which had a particular resonance as a mark of high honour, to nine of his knights around 1350. The entry is in a list of issues covering 1346 to 1352; dated 20 December, but no year given. *Register of Edward the Black Prince*, iv.73. Siddons, *Heraldic Badges*, i. 66 identifies them as badges, but see above for eagle brooches as an existing tradition, p.285. The following entry is probably unrelated, and may refer to the Windsor tournament of 1349.
30. Davis, *Paston Letters*, ii. 532.
31. One of Richard's badges is illustrated in Alexander and Binski, *Age of Chivalry*, item 725; *Westminster Chronicle*, 186–7 for parliamentary opposition to check.
32. Bean, *From Lord to Patron*, 204.
33. Ryder, *Alfonso the Magnanimous*, 317–18.
34. The exception is 1358, which was not one of the ordinary annual feasts but a festival in itself.
35. 'Épitre pour tenir et célébrer la noble fête de la Toison d'or' in La Marche, *Mémoires*, iv.158–89.
36. See Martindale, *Rise of the Artist*, 35–7, for what follows.
37. Martindale, *Rise of the Artist*, 38–41.
38. Binski, *Painters*, 19.
39. Staniland, *Embroiderers*, 23.
40. Binski, *Painters*, 14–15.
41. Monnas, *Merchants, Princes and Painters*, 44.

42. Martindale, *Rise of the Artist*, 48.
43. Sturgeon, 'Text and Image in René d'Anjou's *Livre des tournois*', 74.
44. Sturgeon, 'Text and Image in René d'Anjou's *Livre des tournois*', 1.
45. Ryder, *Alfonso the Magnanimous*, 340.
46. For an overview of his life and work see Nash, *No Equal in any Land*.
47. Froissart, *Oeuvres*, XIV, 196-7.

## 8. Magnificence and the Arts

1. Bernhard, 'Recherches sur la corporation des menetriers', i.380.
2. Du Cange, *Glossarium*, s.v. *Minstrelli*.
3. Barber and Barker, *Tournaments*, 79.
4. Vale, *The Princely Court*, 292–3.
5. Bullock-Davies, *Menestrallorum Multitudo*: for Robert Little, see *ibid.*, 159–62.
6. The National Archives, E101/684/62/3.
7. Society of Antiquaries, *A Collection of Ordinances … for the Government of the Royal Household*, 11 (recte 9).
8. Gomez Muntané, *La música espanola*, 220–3.
9. Anglès, *Scripta Musicologia*, II, 970.
10. Anglès, *Scripta Musicologia*, II, 996.
11. Ryder, *Alfonso the Magnanimous*, 337, 339.
12. Gomez Muntané, *La música espanola*, 292.
13. Ryder, *Alfonso the Magnanimous*, 338.
14. Bowers, 'Music and Musical Establishment', 174–5.
15. Anheim, 'La chapelle du roi de France', *passim*.
16. Wright, *Music at the Court of Burgundy*, 12–15.
17. Christine de Pizan, *Livre des faits*, i.44.
18. Poindexter, 'Chapel'.
19. Printed in La Marche, *Mémoires*, iv.1-94. The quotation is on p.2.
20. See p.220 below.
21. Bellaguet, *Réligieux de St-Denys*, iii.346.
22. La Marche, *Mémoires*, ii.87; for a full list of personnel from 1456 to 1467, see Marix, *Histoire de la musique de la Cour de Bourgogne*, 242–74.
23. Quoted in Fiala, 'La cour de Bourgogne', 384.
24. Bowers, 'Music and Musical Establishment', 178–9. *Sub Arcturo* is recorded on Herald HAVPCD 236 (1999).
25. Wright, *Music at the Court of Burgundy*, 131.
26. Letts, *The Travels of Leo of Rozmital*, 54.
27. Myers, *The Household of Edward IV*, 135–7.
28. Gomez Muntané, *La música espanola*, 231–5.
29. Gomez Muntané, *La música espanola*, 171 n.139.
30. Ryder, *Alfonso the Magnanimous*, 336–8.
31. Barber, *Triumph of England*, 289–90.
32. Labarthe, *Inventaire du mobilier de Charles V*, xi-xiii.
33. Stratford, *The Bedford Inventories*, 67–71.
34. Fallows, 'Binchois'.
35. Bent, 'Dunstaple, John'.
36. Guiffrey, *Inventaires de Jean duc de Berry*, cxli–clxxxii, discusses all aspects of the collection.
37. For a brief history of the Burgundian library see Dogaer and Debae, *La librairie de Philippe le Bon*.
38. David Aubert, quoted in Dogaer and Debae, *La librairie de Philippe le Bon*, 3.
39. Ryder, *Alfonso the Magnanimous*, 319.
40. Ryder, *Alfonso the Magnanimous*, 320.
41. Firth Green, *Poets and Princepleasers*, 11.
42. Tout, 'Literature and Learning', 381.
43. Froissart, tr. Thomas Johnes, IV.426.
44. I have used the account of Petrarch's examination in Léonard, *Les Angevins de Naples*, 285–6.
45. See Leach, *Guillaume de Machaut*, ch.1, 7–33, for an outline of his life and patrons.
46. *Works*, 288, ll.652-8.
47. Gerald of Wales, *De principis instructione*, 295–6.
48. Martindale, *Rise of the Artist*, 35.
49. Binski, *The Painted Chamber*, 1.
50. Binski, *The Painted Chamber*, 71.
51. Brown, *History of the King's Works*, i.129.
52. Quoted in Van Buren-Hagopian, 'Images monumentales', 226; my version of original English.
53. Binski, *Painters*, 19.
54. See Vingtain, *Avignon*, 225–84, pls. 39–55.
55. This is disputed: I follow Syson and Gordon, *Pisanello*, 48–9 rather than Woods-Marsden, *Gonzaga of Mantua*, 38–46.
56. Douet d'Arcq, *Comptes de l'Argenterie*, li.
57. Labarthe, 'Inventaire de Charles V', 362–71.
58. Ledos, 'Fragment de l'inventaire', 171–6.
59. See Joubert, 'Le Saint Christophe de Semur-en-Auxois' for the identification of Hennequin of Bruges as Jean Bandol.
60. Guiffrey, 'Inventaire des tapisseries de Charles VI', ii. 407–14.
61. David, *Philippe le Hardi*, 92.
62. Jean Maupont, quoted in Vaughan, *Philip the Good*, 126.
63. Rykner, 'Charles VII's canopy'.
64. Hablot, 'Art, ésthetique et productions héraldiques', 26–31.
65. For this and the following examples, see Cherry, 'Heraldry as Decoration', 123ff.
66. Cherry, 'Heraldry as Decoration', 128.
67. Nicolas, *Scrope versus Grosvenor*, 385.
68. Nicolas, *Scrope versus Grosvenor*, 312.
69. Richard, *Mahaut comtesse d'Artois*, 270.
70. For the preparations, see Staniland, 'Court Style', 239–42; Cushway, *Edward III and the War at Sea*, 144; The National Archives, E/101/392 m. 2.
71. Barber, *Edward III and the Triumph of England*, 261.
72. Dehaisnes, *Documents*, ii.636.

73. Loisel, *Histoire des ménageries*, i.163.

74. Widukind of Corvey cited in William of Malmesbury, *Gesta Regum*, ii.372.

75. Bouet, 'Raoul Tortaire', 9.

76. William of Malmesbury, *Gesta regum*, i.409, ii.371–2.

77. Paris, *Chronica Majora*, iii.179.

78. Sommerlechner, *Stupor Mundi*, 175.

79. Salimbene, *Cronica*, i.131.

80. *Annales Colmarienses, Monumenta Germaniae Historica Scriptores*, XVII, 189.

81. Continuation Eberbacensis in *Monumenta Germaniae Historica Scriptores*, XVI, 348.

82. Matthew Paris, *Chronica majora*, iv.167.

83. Scheffer-Boichorst, *Zur Geschichte des XII und XIII Jahrhunderts*, 286–7.

84. Sommerlechner, *Stupor Mundi*, 175.

85. Joinville, *Life of Saint Louis*, 296.

86. Cassidy and Clasby, 'Matthew Paris and Henry III's Elephant', 2–4, and references there.

87. Lewis, *The Art of Matthew Paris in the* Chronica Majora, 213–16.

88. Paris, *Chronica Majora*, iii.324.

89. David, *Philippe le Hardi*, 94.

90. Stefano, *La cultura*, 86.

91. Sands, 'Extracts from Documentary Records in the Tower', 166.

92. Loisel, *Histoire des ménageries*, i.168–75.

93. Pastoureau, 'Les ménageries princières', 19–21.

94. See p.198 below.

# 9. Magnificent Architecture

1. Delachenal, *Charles V*, ii.2788.

2. See Howe, 'Divine Kingship and Dynastic Display'.

3. *Calendar of Charter Rolls*, 1341–1417, 134.

4. Howe, 'Divine Kingship and Dynastic Display', 262.

5. Tracy, *English Gothic Choir-stalls*, 50.

6. Howe, 'Divine Kingship and Dynastic Display', 264.

7. Topham, *Some Account of the Chapel of St Stephen*, 8 (note to plate VIII).

8. See Billot, *Les saintes chapelles*.

9. Edward I had begun to rebuild the chapel in 1297 in the style of the Sainte-Chapelle, but at that point there was no re-foundation of the chapel, and no claim to the kingdom of France, but simply a princely rivalry. See Alexander and Binski, *Age of Chivalry*, cat. no. 324.

10. Ormrod, 'Edward III and His Family', 408, 413.

11. Nagy and Schaer, *Karoli IV Imperatoris Romanorum Vita*, 31--34.

12. Crossley, 'The Politics of Presentation', 113–15.

13. Beneš z Weitmile, *Kronika*, 541.

14. Fiala, *Nové Město Pražské 1348–1784*, 15.

15. Crossley, 'The Politics of Presentation', 129–31.

16. Beneš z Weitmile, *Kronika*, 519.

17. Bauch, *Divina favente clemencia*, 366.

18. Crossley, 'The Politics of Presentation', 126.

19. La Marche, *Mémoires*, iv.2.

20. Rashdall, *Universities of Europe*, ii. 214–15.

21. Erben, *Regesta diplomatica Bohemiae*, IV, 411–13; Spufford, *Power and Profit*, 358.

22. Hausherr, 'Zu Auftrag, Programm und Büstenzyklus des Prager Domchores'; Crossley, 'Politics of Presentation', 162–4.

23. Beneš z Weitmile, *Kronika*, 547–8.

24. Printed in Pešina, *Phosphorus*, 460–1.

25. Beneš z Weitmile, *Kronika*, 514–15.

26. Filangieri, *Castelnuovo*, 45.

27. See p.82 above.

28. Tatton Brown, 'Windsor Castle before 1344', 17–20.

29. Tatton Brown, 'Windsor Castle before 1344', 24–6.

30. See itinerary in Ormrod, *Edward III*, 609–31.

31. Brindle and Priestley, 'Edward III's Building Campaigns', 204.

32. Munby, *Edward III's Round Table*, 445–2.

33. Brown, *History of the King's Works*, ii. 876–7.

34. Ranulph Higden, *Polychronicon* in Hope, *Windsor Castle*, i.182.

35. Wilson, 'The Royal Lodgings of Edward III', 15.

36. Ranulph Higden, *Polychronicon* in Hope, *Windsor Castle*, i.184.

37. Wilson, 'The Royal Lodgings of Edward III', 57.

38. Munby, 'Reconstructing the Round Table', 131–3.

39. Billot, *Les saintes chapelles*, 46.

40. Labarte, *Inventaire du mobilier de Charles V*, 263–8.

41. Whiteley, 'The Courts of Edward III and Charles V', 155.

42. Whiteley, 'The Courts of Edward III and Charles V', 161–3.

43. *Grandes Chroniques*, ii.265.

44. Crossley, 'Politics of Presentation', 134–6, with comparative plans.

45. Purton, *The Medieval Siege*, ii.236.

46. Beneš z Weitmile, *Kronika*, 533.

47. Seibt, *Karl IV*, 392.

48. Rosario, *Art and Propaganda*, 21 n.12.

49. James, *The Apocalypse in Latin*, 10–21.

50. Bowes, *Private Worship*, 84.

51. Angenendt, 'Relics and Their Veneration', 26.

52. Krueger, 'Religion of Relics', 13.

53. Cornut, *De susceptione coronae spinae*, 29–31.

54. Bauch, *Divina favente clemencia*, 599–684.

55. Billot, *Les saintes chapelles*, 24.

56. Gaude-Ferragu, 'Le prince et les restes saints', 382.

57. Gaude-Ferragu, 'Le prince et les restes saints', 384.

58. Gaude-Ferragu, 'Le prince et les restes saints', 379n.

59. See p.220 above.

60. Gaude-Ferragu, 'Le prince et les restes saints', 381.

61. Gaude-Ferragu, 'Le prince et les restes saints', 393.

## 10. Magnificence on Display

1. Drabek, *Reisen und Reisezeremoniell*, 74 ff.

2. Paris, *Chronica Majora*, iii.322.

3. Paris, *Historia Anglorum*, ii.109.

4. Perry, 'A King of Jerusalem in England', 625.

5. Paris, *Chronica majora*, iii.336–7.

6. Lancashire, *London Civic Theatre*, 44.

7. 'Annales Londonienses', in Stubbs, *Chronicles of the Reigns of Edward I*, i.152.

8. Galbraith, *Anonimalle Chronicle 1333–1381*, 41.

9. Scott-Stokes, *Chronicon Anonymi Cantvariensis*, 34–7.

10. Sponsler, *The Queen's Dumbshows*, 121–3.

11. According to the legendary history of Britain as recounted by Geoffrey of Monmouth in the twelfth century, Goemagog was a Cornish giant, one of the last of the original inhabitants of Britain: the name comes from the Old Testament, but exactly how they became associated with London is unclear.

12. Thompson, *Chronicon Anglie*, 155.

13. Kipling, *Enter the King*.

14. Wright, *Political Poems and Songs*, i.282–300.

15. Coldstream, 'Pavilion'd in Splendour', *passim*. The article includes a reconstruction of the Cheapside tower in this pageant (159).

16. Barron, 'Pageantry on London Bridge', 94, 96.

17. Psalms 131.18. The description of the entries of Henry VI and Margaret of Anjou are in Gairdner, *Historical Collections*, 173–5 and 186.

18. Kipling, *Enter the King*, 147.

19. Ephesians 6.11–17.

20. Brie, *The Brut* i.489.

21. Guenée and Lehoux, *Les entrées royales*, 47 ff.

22. Beaune, 'Les devises royales', 141.

23. Guenée and Lehoux, *Les entrées royales*, introduction.

24. *Journal d'un bourgeois de Paris*, 269.

25. *Journal d'un bourgeois de Paris*, 270.

26. Vale, *The Princely Court*, 11, 198.

27. *Journal d'un bourgeois de Paris*, 319.

28. Vale, *The Princely Court*, 199.

29. BN, MS fr. 2679, f. 322v.

30. Monstrelet, *Chronicles*, ix.75–84,

31. Monstrelet, *Chronicles*, ix.75–84,

32. Bonet, *Monarquia en escena*, 202.

33. The Spanish descriptions of royal entries confusingly use the word 'entremès' for the dumb shows or tableaux presented on these occasions. For *entremets* at feasts, see chapter 12 below.

34. Drabek, *Reisen und Reisezeremoniell*, 15.

35. I have been unable to find a record of him visiting Paris since he left the city, aged fourteen, in 1330.

36. Paris, *Les grandes chroniques*, vi.411.

37. Author's translation; see Davis, *Paston Letters*, i.235.

38. Vaughan, *Philip the Good*, 288–9, 378.

39. The figure is from Vaughan, *Charles the Bold*, 140; he does not explain which currency is intended.

40. Bernoulli, *Libellus de magnificentia ducis Burgundiae*, 361–4.

41. The territory of the ancient kingdom had been divided into upper and lower Burgundy. These were merged in the tenth century to form the kingdom of Arles. The kingdom of Burgundy envisaged by the emperor seems to consisted of the personal domains of Charles the Bold within the empire.

42. Vaughan, *Charles the Bold*, 149–51.

43. Commynes, *Mémoires*, i.139.

44. Helas, 'Herrscherlicher Einzüge', 134–9.

45. For what follows, see Ryder, *Alfonso V*, 349–57.

## 11. Magnificent Ceremonies and Festivals

1. Vaughan, *Philip the Bold*, 144–5.

2. La Marche, *Mémoires*, ii.353.

3. See below, p.273.

4. Cartellieri, *The Court of Burgundy*, 147; no source for this information is given.

5. Vaughan, *Philip the Bold*, 360.

6. Halphen, *Chroniques des comtes d'Anjou*, 180.

7. Raynaud, *Les gestes des Chiprois*, 31.

8. Weiland, *Braunschweigische Reimchronik*, 557.

9. Viktring, *Liber certarum historiarum*, i.324.

10. Muntaner, *Chronicle* ii.723.

11. Bullock-Davies, *Menestrellorum Multitudo*, ix–xli. She believed that there was no evidence for an Arthurian background to the feast: for a possible Arthurian link see p.206 below.

12. Rymer, *Foedera*, I.ii 983.

13. Ashmole, *The Institution ... of the Garter*, 37.

14. Bullock-Davies, *Menestrellorum Multitudo*, xx.

15. The National Archives, C47/3/30.

16. Chrétien, *Complete Story of the Grail*, 42.

17. Chrétien, *Complete Story of the Grail*, 225. See also the vow of the pheasant above; in literature, a romance about Alexander the Great was entitled *The Vows of the Peacock*.

18. Paris, *La chronique métrique*, line 4921. The reference to Ahasuerus is from the beginning of the Book of Esther, 1.5–7. Descriptions of the knighting

of Friedrich Barbarossa's sons in 1184 and that of Philip the Fair's father in 1267 are among the occasions when this passage was cited by chroniclers.

19. Brown and Regalado, *'La grant feste'*, 59 and note.

20. This was a survival of the Roman ceremony for freeing slaves, called manumission, and was incorporated into other medieval rituals such as the apprentice's initiation as a journeyman.

21. See p.265.

22. Paris, *Chronique métrique*, lines 5070–4.

23. Brown and Regalado, *'La grant feste'*, 73.

24. Bellaguet, *Chronique du Religieux de Saint-Denys*, i.587.

25. Bellaguet, *Chronique du Religieux de Saint-Denys*, i.599.

26. Vergil, *Polydori Vergilii Anglicae Historiae*, 215–16.

27. 'Benedict of Peterborough', ii.83.

28. Gillingham, *Richard I*, 107. For the tournament at the coronation of Joan of Navarre in 1403, see Beauchamp Pageant.

29. See p.265 below for the 'savage' or wild knight in Spanish festivals.

30. Muntaner, *Chronicle*, ii.719.

31. Muntaner, *Chronicle*, ii.730.

32. Muntaner, *Chronicle*, ii.731.

33. Rosell, *Cronicas de los Reyes de Castilla*, i.235.

34. Brie, *The Brut*, i.179–80.

35. The original is in the Anglo-Norman Brut continuation to 1307, Cambridge University Library, MS Ee 1, f. 136.

36. Ormrod, *Edward III*, 57; I have amended the description in the light of Monnas, 'Some Medieval Colour Terms for Textiles', 27–8.

37. Brooke, *Medieval Idea of Marriage*, 274.

38. Altenburg, *Feste und Feiern im Mittelalter*, 403.

39. Altenburg, *Feste und Feiern im Mittelalter*, 413.

40. Altenburg, *Feste und Feiern im Mittelalter*, 412.

41. Scarlet is a type of cloth at this period, not necessarily red: we find 'green scarlet', for instance, in English royal accounts.

42. Ottokar, *Reimchronik*, 7552–7783; author's translation.

43. Loserth, *Die Königsaaler Geschichts-quellen*, 275.

44. Cook, 'The Last Days of Chaucer's Earliest Patron', 30–85.

45. Froissart, *Poésies*, ed. Scheler, i.223.

46. *Annales mediolanenses*, 738–40.

47. Lopes, *The English in Portugal 1367–87*, 233.

48. Lopes, *The English in Portugal 1367–87*, 233.

49. Lopes, *The English in Portugal 1367–87*, 235.

50. Bellaguet, *Chronique du Religieux de Saint-Denys*, ii.50–1.

51. Bellaguet, *Chronique du Religieux de Saint-Denys*, ii.50–1.

52. Bellaguet, *Chronique du Religieux de Saint-Denys*, ii. 458–9.

53. Meyer, 'L'entrevue d'Ardres', 212.

54. Bellaguet, *Chronique du Religieux de Saint-Denys*, ii.467.

55. La Marche, *Mémoires*, iii.138.

56. See p.229 ff. below.

57. Vale, *Princely Court*, 239 and references there.

58. Hugo Falcandus, *The History of the Tyrants of Sicily*, 101–2.

59. The National Archives, E 101/384/18.

60. The National Archives, E101/394/16 m. 6.

61. *Register of Edward the Black Prince*, iv.69.

62. Lutkin, 'Luxury and Display', 157, 173–8.

63. Lutkin, 'Luxury and Display', 162, 167.

64. Guiffrey, *Inventaires de Jean duc de Berry*, i.ix.

65. Hirschbiegel, *Étrennes*, 133.

66. Vaughan, *John the Fearless*, 106–7.

67. Autrand, *Jean de Berry: l'art et le pouvoir*, 48.

68. Boettner, *Past Presents*, 602.

69. The tune *Kalenda maya* which is associated with it is probably the most celebrated of all the troubadour melodies.

70. du Cange, *Glossarium*, iv.198 s.v. maium.

71. *Life of Henry Suso* (ch.14), 39.

72. Crane, *The Performance of Self*, 40 and n.

73. Crane, *The Performance of Self*, 46–7.

74. Deschamps, *Oeuvres completes*, ii.206–7.

75. Douët d'Arcq, *Nouveau recueil de Comptes de l'Argenterie des rois de France*, 129–31.

76. Lindenbaum, 'The Smithfield Tournament of 1390', 1, 3.

77. Guisborough, *Chronicle* 210–12.

78. Morris, 'Edward I and the Knights of the Round Table'.

79. Morris, *A Great and Terrible King*, 202.

80. Gray, *Scalacronica*, 106–7.

81. Annales Paulini, in Stubbs, *Chronicles of the Reigns of Edward I*, 354–5.

82. Aungier, *Croniques de London*, 62.

83. Le Fèvre, *Chronique*, ii.170.

84. Chastellain, *Oeuvres*, viii.40–1.

85. Piponnier, *Costume et vie sociale*, 68; Leseur, *Histoire de Gaston de Foix*, 179–83.

86. This is the title given at the end of the original manuscript.

## 12. Magnificent Extravagance

1. Pliny, *Natural History*, Book 9, ch. 30.

2. The most recent edition of 'Apicius' is that of Grocock and Grainger, 2006.

3. Gregory of Tours, *History of the Franks*, 176.

4. Wolfram, *Parzival*, stanza 809, 259.

5. *The Treatise of Walter of Bibbesworth*, tr. Dalby, 152–5, lines 1107–34.

6. Dante, *Inferno*, xxix.127–9.

7. For the original of this and the following quotation see https://dante.dartmouth.edu for a searchable online copy of the commentaries.

8. *Petits propos culinaires*, unsigned, 98, 2013 7–10.

9. Hieatt and Jones, *Two Anglo-Norman Culinary Collections*, 874.

10. Laurioux, *Histoire culinaire*, 220–30.

11. Hieatt and Butler, *Curye on Inglysch, (including the Forme of Cury)*, 20.

12. *Annales Mediolanenses* in *Rerum Italicarum Scriptores*, xvi. cols 739–740.

13. See Quéruel, 'Des entremets aux intermèdes', 146 ff.

14. Lambert, *Du manuscrit à table*, 91.

15. Scully, *Art of Cookery*, 109.

16. Bonet, *La monarquia en escena*, 212.

17. Chiquart, *Chiquart's On Cookery*, 121.

18. Salvatico, *Il principe e il cuoco*, 30 ff.

19. Laurioux, *Histoire culinaire*, 27.

20. Chiquart, *Chiquart's On Cookery*, 176.

21. *Ibid.*, 136–44.

22. Salvatico, *Il principe e il cuoco*, 112.

23. Jonson, *Neptune's Triumph* in *The Works of Ben Jonson*, 639.

24. Lightbown, *Secular Goldsmiths*, 10–11; Laborde, *Notice des émaux, bijoux… du musée du Louvre*, ii.

25. Christine de Pizan, *Le livre de Charles V*, ii.112.

26. Lightbown, *Secular Goldsmiths*, 75–82.

27. Benporat, *Feste e Banchetti*, 141–2.

28. Chastellain, *Oeuvres*, iii.253, author's translation.

29. La Marche, *Mémoires*, iii.120.

30. Stratford, *The Bedford Inventories*, 56–57, 341–48.

31. Dehaisnes, *Documents*. i. 590, 591; 634, 749 – repairs in 1386 and 1397; 649, 749 – duchess; 853.

32. The raised fore and aft decks of the ship.

33. In the medieval moral tales in the Bestiary, the tigress was supposed to abandon her cubs if she saw her reflection in a mirror; this allowed hunters to capture them.

34. Stratford, *Richard II and the English Royal Treasure*, 286.

35. Guiffrey, *Inventaires*, i.110, 114.

36. Guiffrey, *Inventaires*, items 613 and 615, i.164–5.

37. Guiffrey, *Inventaires*, item 622, i. 166, 653, 172, item 633, i. 168.

38. Guiffrey, *Inventaires*, item 649, i. 171.

39. Guiffrey, *Inventaires*, i. cxix and item 784, ii.103–4.

40. *Chroniques des règnes de Jean II et Charles V*, ii.227.

41. Lightbown, *Secular Goldsmiths*, 45–6, pls. XLVII–LI.

42. Bartholomaeus Anglicus, *De Proprietatibus rerum*, book VI, chapter XXIII, 265.

43. Rösener, 'Die Hoftage Kaiser Friedrichs I', 373.

44. Schmolke-Hasselmann, 'The Round Table: Ideal, Fiction, Reality'.

45. Benporat, *Feste e Banchetti*, 13.

46. See Epilogue, p.201 below.

47. La Marche, *Mémoires*, ii.354.

48. *Calendar of Patent Rolls, Henry III, III 1232–47*, 408 (1243).

49. Lightbown, *Secular Goldsmiths*, 29–30.

50. Russell, 'Book of Nurture'.

51. 'The Rules of Robert Grosseteste' in Oschinsky, *Walter of Henley*, 387–409, 405.

52. Myers, *The Household of Edward IV*, 90 ff.

## 13. Devising the Festival

1. Morez in *La cour et la ville*, 249.

2. Christine de Pizan, *Le livre de Charles V*, 42–8.

3. Bellaguet, *Chronique du Religieux de Saint-Denys*, ii.64–71; Froissart, *Oeuvres*, 84–92.

4. Millar, 'Olivier de la Marche', 57.

5. Myers, *The Household of Edward IV*, 4.

6. La Marche, *Mémoires*, ii.339–40.

7. La Marche, *Mémoires*, iii.101–201.

8. Brown, *History of the King's Works*, Appendix D, Schedule of Works at Westminster 1307–1311, 1043–4.

9. See p.239 for discussion of *entremets*.

10. Laborde, *Les ducs de Bourgogne*, ii.324–5, item 4422.

11. Régnier-Bohler, *Splendeurs*, 1106.

12. La Marche, *Mémoires*, ii.335.

13. Bonet, *La monarquia en escena*, 36.

14. Douët d'Arcq, *Comptes de l'Hôtel des Rois de France*, iv.

15. Lalou, 'Fragments d'un journal', 148.

16. See p.214 above.

17. Scully, *The Art of Cookery*, 27, 32.

18. *Coreginus hyemalis*, found in the Swiss lakes.

19. Chiquart, *Chiquart's On Cookery*, 283–85.

20. Chiquart, *Chiquart's On Cookery*, 100.

21. Chiquart, *Chiquart's On Cookery*, 105.

22. Oschinsky, *Walter of Henley*, 404.

23. Vale, *Princely Court*, 364–5.

24. Sponsler, *The Queen's Dumbshows*.

25. For masks, see p.265 below.

26. Adam of Murimuth, *Chronicon*, 173–5.

27. John of Reading, *Chronicon*, 151; *Chronicon Anonymi Cantuariensis*, 118–9.

28. Barber and Barker, *Tournaments*, 98.

29. Muntaner, *Chronicle* ii. ch.23.

30. Bonet, *La monarquia en escena*, 40.

31. Rolandinus of Padua, *Cronica*, 45–6.

32. Laborde, *Notice des émaux*, ii.36.

33. Twycross, *Masks and Masking*, 28 ff.

34. *Dictionary of Latin from British Medieval Sources*, *sv* larva.

35. Vale, *Princely Court*, 263.

36. Russian National Library, Saltykov-Chichedrine, MS Fr.F.p.XIV, 4, f. 22, f. 6.

37. British Library, MS Royal 10 E iv, f. 58.

38. British Library, MS Royal 10 E iv, f. 58.

39. Matthew Paris, *Chronica Majora*, iv.147.

40. John of Salisbury, *Frivolities of Courtiers*, 38.

41. Southworth, *The English Medieval Minstrel*, 6.

42. Bullock-Davies, *Menestrallorum Multitudo*, 67.

43. Binski, *Painters*, 10–11.

44. Althof, *Das Lippiflorium*, 28–9.

45. Chaucer, 'The Franklin's Tale' in Robinson, Chaucer, lines 1142–51, 1189–1201.

46. Luengo, 'Magic and Illusion', 8.

47. Thorndike, *A History of Magic*, ii.346.

48. See the description of Isabeau's entry into Paris in 1389 for this as a child's toy.

49. Lydgate, *Dance of Death*, 64, 513–16.

50. Janio the juggler: 'Janio le tregettor, facienti ministralsiam suam coram rege ... 20s.' (Lib. Comput. Garderobæ, an. (4 Edw. II. fol. 86), MS. Cott. Nero C VIII, f. 86.).

51. 'ferrea instrumenta' in Latin; perhaps an iron frame with spheres filled with water to act as lenses?

52. Boncompagno da Signa in Rockinger, *Briefsteller und formelbücher*, 164–5.

53. Vaughan, *Philip the Bold*, 138–9.

54. *Fastes du Gothique*, 191.

55. See p.241 above.

56. Liudprand of Cremona, *Complete Works*, 197–8.

57. Truitt, *Medieval Robots*, 122.

58. See Epilogue, p.201 below.

59. Barroux, *Les fêtes royales*, 29.

60. Froissart, *Oeuvres*, i.223.

61. Altenburg, *Feste und Feiern*, 491–9.

62. Barker, *The Tournament in England*, 110, quoting British Library, MS Lansdowne 285, p. 109.

63. Fowler, *The King's Lieutenant*, 215.

64. Anglès, *Scripta Musicologica*, ii.984.

65. Gomez Muntané, *La musica espanola*, 285, and for what follows.

66. Anglès, *Scripta Musicologica*, ii.971.

67. Servion, Jean, *Gestez et croniques*, ii.

68. Anglès, *Scripta Musicologica*, ii,973.

69. La Marche, *Mémoires*, ii.334.

70. Account quoted in Marix, *Histoire de la Musique de la Cour de Bourgogne*, 48.

71. Hope, *Windsor Castle*, i.190.

72. Chaucer, 'Legend of Good Women', in Robinson, *Works*, 501, lines 1106–7.

73. Quoted in Lecoy de la Marche, *La chaire français*, 413; this is based on St Augustine, sermon CCCXI, and ultimately goes back to Matthew 11.17, but the image is de Vitry's own, and not Augustine's.

74. Quoted by Bumke, *Courtly Culture*, 227.

75. *Annales Monastici*, iv.489.

## 14. Financing, Organising and Creating Magnificence

1. Reynolds, *Fiefs and Vassals*, 365–7.

2. Strickland, *Henry the Young King*, 82–4.

3. For what follows, see McHardy, 'Paying for the Wedding'.

4. McHardy, 'Paying for the Wedding', 45.

5. Unusually, Eleanor's accounts, including the wedding expenses, survive: see Safford, 'An Account of the Expenses of Eleanor'.

6. Monnas, *Merchants, Princes and Painters*, 12.

7. http://corpus.enc.sorbonne.fr/testaments/testament_149, accessed 22 November 2018.

8. Paris, *Grandes chroniques*, vi.411.

9. Šmahel, *Parisian Summit*, 415.

10. Kaeuper, 'The Frescobaldi', 82–3.

11. For what follows, see Walsh, *Charles the Bold and Italy*, 120–36, who refutes earlier assessments of Portinari as a 'financial condottiere' who lent recklessly to the duke.

12. Fryde, 'Public Credit', 505.

13. Henwood, *Les collections du trésor royal*, 15.

14. Henwood, *Les collections du trésor royal*, 37.

15. Dehaisnes, *Documents*, i.174 (1306), i.186 (1308).

16. Deshaisnes, *Documents*, i, 434-6.

17. Spufford, *Power and Profit*, 144–6.

18. Johannes von Viktring, *Liber certarum historiarum*, i.324.

19. Medina is possibly Medinaceli, on the old border between Castile and Muslim territory.

20. Pero Tafur, *Travels*, 203–4.

21. Douët d'Arcq, *Comptes de l'Argenterie*, 45 ff; 52, 62, 72, for totals.

22. Monnas, 'Textiles for the Coronation', 3–7.

23. Nicolas, 'Observations on the Institution of the Most Noble Order of the Garter', 7.

24. The National Archives, E 101/384/6, rot. 2, m.1.

25. Staniland, *Embroiderers*, 30.

26. Monnas, 'Textiles for the Coronation', 20.

27. Spufford, *Power and Profits*, 22.

28. Tout, *Chapters*, iv.390.

29. Richardson, *Tower Armouries*.

30. Cherry, *Medieval Goldsmith*, 22ff.

31. Rouse, 'The Goldsmith and the Peacocks', 283.

32. Labarte, *Inventaire de Charles V*, 12.

33. Labarte, *Inventaire de Charles V*, 23-25.

34. Guenée, *Paris 1400*, 19.

35. Prost, *Inventaires*, ii.204, 283, 416; ii. 217.

36. Prost, *Inventaires*, ii.479.

37. Prost, *Inventaires*, ii.579.

38. Ryder, *Alfonso V*, 347.

39. *La tenture de l'Apocalypse*, 33–4.

40. Prost, *Inventaires*, i.170; David, *Philippe le Hardi*, 93 n.

41. Dalton, 'Frederick II of Hohenstaufen's Australasian Cockatoo'.

42. Crowfoot, *Textiles and Clothing*, 88.

43. Small quantities are found in Chile and Russia, but in a less pure form.

44. Spufford, *Power and Profit*, 316–18.

45. Deér, 'The Dynastic Porphyry Tombs', 119.

## 15. The Spirit of Magnificence

1. Vaughan, *Charles the Bold*, 357.

2. See Strong, *Art and Power*, 20.

3. Paravicini, 'Die zwölf "Magnificences"', 369.

4. Vaughan, *Charles the Bold*, 187.

5. Vaughan, *Charles the Bold*, 172–9. The texts are printed in Dünnebeil, *Die Protokollbücher des Ordens von Goldenen Vlies*, 2, 120–21 and 3, 97-104.

6. Vaughan, *Charles the Bold*, 59–61.

7. Haynin, *Mémoires*, ii. 91.

8. This strange custom, where the knight is sometimes held to represent the king in person, is at its most frequent in the late fourteenth century, and can be found at the funerals of Károly I of Naples in 1342, where, uniquely, three knights on destriers are said to 'represent the spirit and person of the king', and that of the emperor Karl IV in 1378.

9. Chabeuf, 'Charles le Téméraire', 292-313; guards 301, knights of Golden Fleece 300, 304; burning chapel 303.

10. *Librairie de Charles V*, 46. See also Kopp, *Der König und die Bücher*, 52.

11. Paravicini, 'Theatre of Death', 44.

12. The use of light in Burgundian ceremonials is discussed by Lecuppre-Desjardin, 'Les lumières de la ville'.

13. Paravicini, 'Theatre of Death', 55-57

14. Jean de Roye, *Journal ou Chronique scandaleuse*, ii 42. https://archive.org/details/journaldejeande01royegoog/page/n12 Accessed 22 December 2019.

15. Brown, 'Le grant feste', 60.

16. La Marche, *Mémoires*, ii.254.

17. Chastellain also highlights the jousts and tournaments at the assembly of the Order of the Golden Fleece at Valenciennes in 1473. These were in fact held by one of the knights of the order, Jean de Luxembourg.

18. La Marche, *Mémoires*, iv. 95–144; quote from 141–2.

19. Paravicini, 'Die zwölf "Magnificences"', 329–30.

20. Haynin, *Mémoires*, ii.17–62.

21. Saul, *Richard II*, 250.

22. Eberle, 'The Politics of Courtly Style', 175.

23. Heller, 'Sumptuary Legislation'; Jourdan et al., *Recueil général des anciennes lois françaises*, ii. 697–99.

24. For an overview of the reasons behind the sumptuary laws, see Lachaud, 'Dress and social status in England', 113–22.

25. Estow, 'The Politics of Gold', 136–7.

26. Lachaud, 'Dress and Social Status in England', 108–11.

## Appendix II

1. Macrobius, *In somnium Scipionis* i 8, 7 quoted in Holmberg, *Moralium*, 188.

2. Holmberg, *Moralium*, 7.

3. There is one mention, in the obscure book of *Jude*.

4. This paragraph uses database searches on *Patrologia Latina* and *Monumenta Germaniae Historica*. There is no easy equivalent source for thirteenth century material. I have not been able to access the Brepols *Library of Latin Texts*.

# ✳ BIBLIOGRAPHY

Adam of Murimuth. *Chronicon Adae Murimuth et Roberti de Avesbury*. Ed. E.M. Thompson. Rolls Series 93. London, 1889.

Adams, Tracy. 'Isabeau de Bavière: la Création d'une Reine Scandaleuse'. *Cahiers de Recherches Médiévales et Humanistes* 25 (2013): 223–35.

Alexander, Jonathan, and Paul Binski, eds. *The Age of Chivalry: Art in Plantagenet England 1200–1400*. London, 1987.

Alexandre-Bidon, Danièle. 'Tentures d'extérieur et de lieux publics'. *Mélanges de l'École Française de Rome. Moyen-Âge* 111, no. 1 (1999): 463–77.

Alfonso X. *Las Siete Partidas*. Ed. Robert I. Burns. Tr. Samuel Parsons Scott. Volume 1: The Medieval Church. Philadelphia, 2001.

———. *Las Siete Partidas*. Ed. Robert I. Burns. Tr. Samuel Parsons Scott. Volume 2: Medieval Government. Philadelphia, 2001.

Altenburg, Detlef, Jörg Jarnut, and Hans-Hugo Steinhoff, eds. *Feste und Feiern im Mittelalter*. Paderborner Symposion des Mediävistenverbandes. Sigmaringen, 1991.

Althof, Hermann. *Das Lippiflorium: Ein Westfalisches Heldengedicht aus dem dreizehnten Jahrhundert*. Leipzig, 1900.

Althoff, Gerd, ed. *Formen und Funktion Öffentlicher Kommunikation im Mittelalters*. Vorträge und Forschungen 51. Stuttgart, 2001.

Andrew of Hungary. *Descriptio Victorìae per Carolum Regem Siciliae Contra Manfred in Siciliae Regem*. Monumenta Germaniae Historica, Scriptores 26. Leipzig, 1925.

Angenendt, Arnold. 'Relics and Their Veneration', in *Treasures of Heaven*, 19–28.

Anglès, Hygini. *Scripta Musicologia*. Storia e Letteratura 132. Rome, 1975.

Anheim, Étienne. 'La Chapelle du Roi de France du milieu du XIIe à la fin du XIVe Siècle', in *La Cour du Prince*, 399–415,

Aquinas, St Thomas. *The Summa Theologica*. Tr. Fathers of the English Dominican Province. http://www.documentacatholicaomnia. eu/03d/1225–1274,_Thomas_Aquinas,_Summa_ Theologiae_%5B1%5D,_EN.pdf. Accessed 31 July 2018.

Aristotle. *Aristotle's Nicomachean Ethics*. Tr. Robert C. Bartlett and Susan D. Collins. Chicago, 2011.

Armstrong, C. A. J. 'The Inauguration Ceremonies of the Yorkist Kings and their Title to the Throne'. *Transactions of the Royal Historical Society* 30 (1948): 51–73.

Ashdowne, Richard. *Dictionary of Medieval Latin from British Sources*. Oxford, 2018.

Ashmole, Elias. *The Institution, Laws & Ceremonies of the Most Noble Order of the Garter*. London: ?1673, .

Aungier, George J. *Croniques de London Depuis l'an 44 Hen. III...* Camden Society. London, 1844.

Autrand, Françoise. *Jean de Berry: L'art et le Pouvoir*. Paris, 2000.

Autrand, Françoise. [et al.]. *La France et les Arts en 1400*. Paris, 2004.

Auzepy, M.-F., and J. Cornette. *Palais et Pouvoir, de Constantinople à Versailles, Saint-Denis*. Paris, 2003.

Ayton, Andrew. *Knights and Warhorses: Military Service and the English Aristocracy under Edward III*. Woodbridge, 1994.

Bagnoli, Marina, Holger A. Klein, and Mann, C. Griffith, eds. *Treasures of Heaven: Saints, Relics, and Devotion in Medieval Europe*. London, 2011.

Barber, Richard. *Edward III and the Triumph of England: The Battle of Crécy and the Order of the Garter*. London, 2013.

Barber, Richard., and Juliet Barker. *Tournaments: Jousts, Chivalry and Pageants in the Middle Ages*. Woodbridge, 1989.

Barker, Juliet. *The Tournament in England, 1100–1400*. Woodbridge, 1986.

Barrigón, Maria. 'An Exceptional Outfit for an Exceptional King: the Blue Funerary Garments of Alfonso VIII of Castile at Las Huelgas'. *Viator* 46, no. 3 (2015): 155–72.

———. 'Textiles and Farewells: Revisiting the Grave Goods of King Alfonso VIII of Castile and Queen Eleanor Plantagenet'. *Textile History* 46, no. 2 (2015): 235–57.

Barron, Caroline M. 'Pageantry on London Bridge in the Early Fifteenth Century' in Klausner, '*Bring Furth the Pagants*': 91–104.

Barroux, Marius 1862–1939. *Les Fêtes Royales de Saint-Denis en Mai 1389*. Paris, 1936.

Barthélemy, Dominique. 'Les Origines du Tournoi Chevalereseque', in Bougard, *Agôn: la Compétition Ve–XIIe Siècle*, 111–29.

Bartholomaeus Anglicus. *De Proprietatibus Rerum*. Frankfurt, 1605.

Bauch, Martin. *Divina Favente Clemencia: Auserwahlung, Frömmigkeit und Heilsvermittlung in der Herrschaftspraxis Kaiser Karls IV*. Forschungen zur Kaiser- und Papstgeschichte des Mittelalters 36, Köln 2015.

Bauer, Rotraud. 'Il Mantello di Ruggero II', in Onofrio, *I Normanni*, 279–87.

Beaune, Colette. 'Costume et Pouvoir en France à la Fin du Moyen Age: les Devises Royales vers 1400'. *Revue des Sciences Humaines* 183 (1981–3): 125–46.

Beck, Patrice. 'Fontaines et Fontainiers des Ducs de

Bourgogne'. *Mélanges de l'École Française de Rome. Moyen-Âge* 104 (1992): 495–506.

Bejczy, István P. and Cary J. Nederman eds *Princely virtues in the Middle Ages, 1200-1500*. Disputatio 9. Turnhout 2007 Bellaguet, Louis François. *Chronique du Religieux de Saint-Denys, contenant le Règne de Charles VI, de 1380 à 1422*. Paris 1839.

Benedict of Peterborough. *The Chronicle of the Reigns of Henry II and Richard I, A.D. 1169–1192*. Ed. William Stubbs. Rolls Series 49. London, 1867.

Benporat, Claudio et al. *Feste e banchetti: convivialità italiana fra Tre e Quattrocento*. Firenze, 2001.

Berges, Wilhelm. *Die Fürstenspiegel des Hohen und Späten Mittelalters*. Leipzig, 1938.

Berland, Florence. 'Du Commerce à la Cour: les Marchands Parisiens et la Cour de Bourgogne, 1363–1422'. *Hypothèses* 12, no. 1 (2009): 27–37.

Bernoulli, C.C. 'Libellus de Magnificentia Ducis Burgundiae', 332–64. *Basler Chroniken*, III. Leipzig, 1887.

Bibbesworh, Walter. *The Treatise of Walter of Bibbesworth*. Tr. Andrew Dalby. Blackawton, 2012.

Biddle, Martin. 'Seasonal Festivals and Residence: Winchester, Westminster and Gloucester in the Tenth to Twelfth Centuries'. *Anglo-Norman Studies* VIII (1986): 51–72.

Billot, Claudine. *Les Saintes Chapelles: Royales et Princières*. Paris, 1998.

Binski, Paul. *Painters*. London, 1991.

———. *Westminster Abbey and the Planatagenets*. London, 1995.

Blancard, Louis. 'Une page inédite de l'histoire de Charles d'Anjou'. *Bibliothèque de l'École des Chartes* 30 (1869): 559–67.

Bloch, Marc. *Les Rois Thaumaturges. Étude sur le Caractère Surnaturel attribué à la Puissance Royale particulièrement en France et en Angleterre*. Paris, 1983.

Blockmans, Willem Pieter and Anne van Oosterwijk. *Staging the Court of Burgundy: Proceedings of the Conference 'The Splendour of Burgundy'*. London: Harvey Miller, 2013.

Blois, Peter of. *Petri Blesensis Opera Omnia*. Patrologia Latina 207. Paris, 1855.

Boccaccio, Giovanni. *Famous Women*. Tr. Virginia Brown. Cambridge, MA, 2003.

Bonet, Francesc Massip. *La Monarquía en Escena: Teatro, Fiesta y Espectáculo de Poder en los Reinos Ibéricos de Jaume el Conquistador al Príncipe Carlos*. Madrid, 2003.

Borngässer, Barbara, and Bruno Klein, eds. *Grabkunst und Sepulkralkultur in Spanien und Portugal*. Ars Iberica et Americana 11. Frankfurt am Main. 2006

Borsook, Eve. *Messages in Mosaic: The Royal Programmes of Norman Sicily (1130–1187)*. Clarendon Studies in the History of Art. Woodbridge, 1998.

Bouet, Pierre. 'Raoul Tortaire: Mon Voyage en Normandie'. *Tabularia*, 2017. http://journals.openedition.org/tabularia/2813. Accessed 19 December 2019.

Bougard, Francois, Regine le Jan, and Thomas Lienhard, eds. *Agon: la Competition, Ve -XIe Siècle*. Collection Haut Moyen Âge 17. Turnhout, 2012.

Boulton, D'Arcy Jonathan Dacre. *The Knights of the Crown: The Monarchical Orders of Knighthood in Later Medieval Europe, 1325–1520*. 2nd edition. Woodbridge, 2000.

Bournazel, Eric. 'La Familia Regis Francorum', in Marchandisse, *À l'Ombre d Pouvoir*, 115–33.

Bove, Boris. 'Les Palais Royaux à Paris au Moyen Âge (XIe-XVe Siècles)', in *Palais et Pouvoir, de Constantinople à Versailles, Saint-Denis*, 45–79. Paris, 2003.

Bowers, Roger. 'The Music and Musical Establishment of St George's Chapel in the 15th Century', in *St George's Chapel, Windsor in the Late Middle Ages*, 171–85.

Bowes, Kim. *Private Worship, Public Values, and Religious Change in Late Antiquity*. Cambridge, 2008.

Bozóky, Eduna. *La Politique des Reliques de Constantin à Saint Louis*. Paris, 2006.

Brand, Paul, and Sean Cunningham, eds. *Foundations of Medieval Scholarship: Records Edited in Honour of David Crook*. York, 2008.

Braunfels, Wolfgang. *Charlemagne: Oeuvre Rayonnement et Survivances*. Aix-la-Chapelle, 1965.

Bray, Nicolas. 'Faites et Gestes de Louis VIII, Roi des Francais', in *Collection des Mémoires relatifs à l'histoire de France*, 389–450. Paris, 1825.

Brenk, Beate. 'Rhetoric, Aspiration and Function of the Cappella Palatina in Palermo', in Dittelsback, *Die Cappella Palatina in Palermo*, 592–603, 247–71.

Brie, Friedrich W. *The Brut or Chronicles of England*. London, 1906.

Briggs, Charles. *Giles of Rome's De Regimine Principum: Reading and Writing Politics at Court and University, c.1275–c.1525*. Cambridge, 1999.

Brindle, Steven, and Stephen Priestley. 'Edward III's Building Campaigns at Windsor and the Employment of Masons, 1346–1377', in *St George's Chapel Windsor in the Fourteenth Century*, 203–24.

Broadhurst, R.J.C., trans. *The Travels of Ibn Jubayr*. London, 1952.

Brooke, Christopher Nugent Lawrence. *The Medieval Idea of Marriage*. Oxford, 1989.

Brown, Elizabeth A.R. 'Burying and Unburying the Kings of France', in Trexler, *Persons and Groups: Social Formation in Medieval and Renaissance Europe*, 241–66.

———. *Customary Aids and Royal Finance in Capetian France: The Marriage Aid of Philip the Fair*. Cambridge, MA, 1992.

——— and Nancy Freeman Regalado. 'La Grant Feste:

Philip the Fair's Celebration of the Knighting of his Sons at Pentecost of 1313', in Hanawalt, *City and Spectacle in Medieval Europe*.

Brown, R. Allen, Howard Colvin, and A.J. Taylor. *The History of the King's Works*. Vols. i–ii. London, 1963.

Browne, Clare, Glyn Davies, and M. A. Michael. *English Medieval Embroidery*. London, 2016.

Brückner, Wolfgang. 'Ross und Reiter in Leichenzeremoniell, Deutungsversuch eines historischen Rechtsbrauches'. *Rheinisches Jahrbuch für Volkskunde* 15–16 (1964–5): 144–209.

Bryant, Lawrence M. 'La Cérémonie de l'entrée à Paris au Moyen Âge'. *Annales. Economies, Sociétés, Civilisations* 41, no. 3 (1986): 513–42.

Buccellati, Graziella. *The Iron Crown of Monza*. 2 vols. Monza, 1995.

Buchon, Jean Alexandre C. *Choix de chroniques et mémoires sur l'histoire de France*. Paris, 1838.

Bueno de Mesquita, D. M. *Giangaleazzo Visconti Duke of Milan 1351–1402*. Cambridge, 1941.

Buettner, Brigitte. 'Jacques Raponde « marchand de Manuscrits Enluminés »'. *Médiévales* 14 (1988): 23–32.

———. 'Past Presents: New Year's Gifts at the Valois Courts, ca. 1400'. *The Art Bulletin* 83, no. 4 (2001): 598–625.

Bullock-Davies, Constance. *A Register of Royal and Baronial Domestic Minstrels 1272–1327*. Woodbridge, 1986.

———. *Menestrallorum Multitudo: Minstrels at a Royal Feast*. Cardiff, 1978.

Bumke, Joachim. *Courtly Culture: Literature and Society in the High Middle Ages*. Tr. Thomas Dunlap. Woodstock, NY, 2000.

Buren-Hagopian, Anne van. 'Images monumentales de la Toison d'or: aux murs de Château de Hesdin et en tapisserie', in *L'Ordre de la Toison d'or, de Philippe le Bon à Philippe le Beau (1430–1505): Idéal ou Reflet d'une Société?*, 226–33.

Burgess, Glyn S., and Robert A. Taylor, eds. *The Spirit of the Court: Select Proceedings of the Fourth Congress of the International Courtly Literature Society (Toronto 1983)*. Woodbridge, 1985.

Burns, E. Jane, ed. *Medieval Fabrications: Dress, Textiles, Clothwork, and other Cultural imaginings*. New Middle Ages. London, 2004.

*Calendar of Close Rolls: Henry III, VII 1251–53*. London, 1927.

*Calendar of Patent Rolls, Henry III, III 1232–47*. London, 1906.

Cange, Charles Dufresne du, sire. *Glossarium Mediæ at Infimæ Latinitatis*. 7 vols. Paris, 1840.

Carqué, Bernd. 'Paris 1377–78. Un Lieu de Pouvoir et sa Visibilité entre Moyen Âge et Temps présent'. *Médiévales* 53 (2007): 123–42.

Carrard, H. 'À Propos du Tombeau du Chevalier de Grandson'. *Mémoires et Documents publiés par la Société d'histoire de la Suisse Romande*, 2nd series, 2 (1890): 151–223.

Cassidy, Richard, and Richard Clasby. 'Matthew Paris and Henry III's Elephant', https://finerollshenry3.org.uk/ redist/pdf/fm-06-2012.pdf. Accessed via Google search on title, 17/12/2019.

Catalogue. *Alfonso X El Sabio [Exhibition at Murcia 2009]*. Murcia, 2009.

———. *Federico II: immagine e Potere [Exhibition, Bari 1995]*, Bari,1995.

———. *La Librairie de Charles V*. Paris, 1968.

———. *Les Fastes du Gothique: le Siècle de Charles V*. Paris, 1981.

———. *L'état Angevin: Pouvoir, Culture et Société entre XIIIe et XIVe Siècle: Actes du Colloque organisé par l'American Academy in Rome: (Rome-Naples, 7–11 Novembre 1995)*. Istituto Storico Italiano per Il Medio Evo 45. Rome, 1998.

———. *Paris 1400. Les Arts sous Charles VI*. Paris, 2004

———. *Princely Magnificence: Court Jewels of the Renaissance [Victoria and Albert Museum]*. London1980.

———. *Rarer Gifts than Gold: Fourteenth-Century Art in Scottish Collections*. Glasgow, 1988.

Centre d'Études et de Recherches Médiévales d'Aix. *Banquets et Manières de Table au Moyen Âge*. Sénéfiance 38. Aix, 1996.

Chancel-Bardelot, Beatrice de. *La Sainte-Chapelle de Bourges: Une Fondation disparue de Jean de France, Duc de Berry*. Paris, 2004.

Chapelot, Jean and Elisabeth Lalou. *Vincennes, aux origines de l'État moderne: Actes du Colloque scientifique sur 'Les Capétiens et Vincennes au Moyen âge'*. Paris, 1996.

Chastellain, Georges. *Oeuvres de Georges Chastellain*. Ed. Kervyn de Lettenhove. 4 vols. Brussels, 1863.

Chatenet, Monique, and Mary Whiteley. 'Le Louvre de Charles V:Dispositions et Fonctions d'une Résidence Royale'. *Revue de l'Art* 97 (1992): 60–71.

Chattaway, Carol M. 'Looking a Medieval Gift Horse in the Mouth. The Role of the Giving of Gift Objects in the Definition and Maintenance of the Power Networks of Philip the Bold'. *Bijdragen en Mededelingen betreffende de Geschiedenis der Nederlanden* 114 (1999): 112–16.

———. *The Order of the Golden Tree: The Gift-Giving Objectives of Duke Philip the Bold of Burgundy*. Burgundica 12. Turnhout, 2006.

Chaucer, Geoffrey. *The Works of Geoffrey Chaucer*. Ed. F.N. Robinson. London, 1957.

Cherry, John. 'Heraldry as Decoration', in Ormrod, *England in the Thirteenth Century*, 123–134. Stamford, 1991.

———. *Medieval Goldsmiths*. 2nd ed. London, 2011.

Chibnall, Marjorie. *The Empress Matilda: Queen Consort,*

*Queen Mother and Lady of the English*. Oxford, 1991.

Chiquart, Master. *'Du fait de cuisine/On Cookery' of Master Chiquart (1420)* Transcribed and Tr. Terence Scully. Medieval and Renaissance Texts and Studies 354. Tempe, AZ, 2010.

Chrétien de Troyes. *The Complete Story of the Grail*. Tr. Nigel Bryant. Woodbridge, 2015.

Cleve, Thomas Curtis van. *The Emperor Frederick II of Hohenstaufen: immutator Mundi*. Oxford, 1972.

Clouzot, Martine, 'La Musique, un Art de Gouverner. Jongleurs, Ménestrels et Fous dans les Cours Royales et Princières du XIIIe au XVe Siècle (France, Bourgogne, Angleterre, Empire)'. *Bulletin du Centre d'études Médiévales d'Auxerre* 11 (2007).

Coatsworth, Elizabeth, and Gale R. Owen-Crocker. *Clothing the Past: Surviving Garments from Early Medieval to Early Modern Western Europe*. Leiden, 2018.

Coldstream, Nicola. '"Pavilion'd in Splendour": Henry V's Agincourt Pageants'. *Journal of the British Archaeological Association* 165, no. 1 (2012): 153–71.

———. 'The Roles of Women in Late Medieval Civic Pageantry', in Martin, *Reassessing the Roles of Women as 'Makers' of Medieval Art and Architecture*, 175–94.

Commynes, Philippe de. *Mémoires de Philippe de Commynes*. Ed. Mlle Dupont. 4 vols. Paris: 1840, n.d.

Contamine, Philippe. 'Le Sang, l'hôtel, le Conseil, le Peuple: L'entourage de Charles VII selon les Récits et les Comptes de ses Obsèques en 1461', in Marchandisse, *À l'Ombre du Pouvoir*, 149–67, n.d.

Cook, Albert Stanborough. 'The Last Months of Chaucer's Earliest Patron'. *Transactions of the Connecticut Academy of Arts and Sciences* 21 (1916): 1–144.

Cornut, Gautier. 'De Susceptione Coronae Spinae', in *Recueil des Historiens de Gaule et de la France*, XXII:27–32. Paris, c.1865

Coss, Peter, and Maurice Keen, eds. *Heraldry, Pageantry and Social Display in Medieval England*. Woodbridge, 2002.

Cox, Eugene Lionel. *The Green Count of Savoy. Amadeus VI and Transalpine Savoy in the Fourteenth Century*. Princeton, NJ, 1967.

Crane, Susan. *The Performance of Self: Ritual, Clothing and Identity during the Hundred Years War*. Philadelphia, 2002.

Crossley, Paul. 'The Politics of Presentation: The Architecture of Charles IV of Bohemia', in Rees-Jones, *Courts and Regions in Medieval Europe*, 99–172.

Crowfoot, Elisabeth, Pritchard, Frances, and Staniland, Kay. *Textiles and Clothing c.1150–c.1450*, new edition, Woodbridge 2001

Cushway, Graham. *Edward III and the War at Sea*. Woodbridge, 2011.

Cutolo, Alessandro. *Giovanna II*. Novara, 1968.

Dalton et al., Heather. 'Frederick II of Hohenstaufen's Australasian Cockatoo: Symbol of Detente between East and West and Evidence of the Ayyubids' Global Reach'. *Parergon* 35, no. 1 (2018): 35–60.

David, Henri. *Philippe le Hardi: le Train Somptuaire d'un Grand Valois*. Dijon, 1947.

Davies, Glyn. 'Embroiderers and the Embroidery Trade', in Michael, *English Medieval Embroidery*, 41–59.

Davis, Norman. *Paston Letters and Papers of the Fifteenth Century*. 3 vols. Oxford, 1971–76

Déer, Josef. *The Dynastic Porphyry Tombs of the Norman Period in Sicily*. Dumbarton Oaks Studies V. Cambridge, MA, 1959.

Dehaisnes, M. le Chanoine. *Documents et Extraits divers concernant l'Histoire de l'Art dans la Flandre, l'Artois et le Hainaut avant le XVe Siècle*. 2 vols. Lille, 1886.

Delachenal, Roland., ed. *Chroniques des Règnes de Jean II et Charles V*. Vol. II. Société de l'histoire de France. Paris, 1916.

———. *Histoire de Charles V*. 5 vols. Paris, 1927.

Delhumeau, Herveline. *Le Palais de la Cité: du Palais des Rois de France au Palais de Justice*. Paris, 2011.

Delogu, Daisy. 'Christine de Pizan Lectrice de Gilles de Rome: le De Regimine Principum et le Livre des Fais et Bonnes Meurs du Sage Roy Charles V'. *Cahiers de Recherches Médiévales et Humanistes* 16 (2001): 213–24.

Demotz, Bernard. 'L'État et le Château au Moyen Âge: l'exemple Savoyard'. *Journal des Savants*, 1987, 27–64.

Des Ursins, Juvénal. 'Chronique de Charles VI', in Buchon, *Choix de Chroniques*.

Deschamps, Eustache. *Oeuvres Completes de Eustache Deschamps*. Ed. Marquis de Queux de Saint Hilaire. 2 vols. Paris, 1880.

Deuchler, Florenz. *Die Burgunderbeute: Inventar der Beutestücke aus den Schlachten von Granson, Murten und Nancy 1476/1477*. Bern, 1963.

Dimitrova, Karen, and Margaret Goehring, eds. *Dressing the Part: Textiles as Propaganda in the Middle Ages*. Turnhout, 2014.

Dittelsback, Thomas. *Die Cappella Palatina in Palermo: Geschichte, Kunst, Funktion: Forschungsergebnisse der Restaurierung*. Künzelsau, 2011.

Diverrès, Armel, ed. *La Chronique Métrique attribuéee a Godeffroy de Paris*. Publications de la Faculté des Lettres de l'Université de Strasbourg 129. Strasbourg, 1956.

Długosz, Jan. *The Annals of Jan Długosz: Annales seu Cronicae Incliti Regni Poloniae*. Ed. Maurice Michael. Chichester, 1997.

Dogaer, Georges, and Marguerite Debae, eds. *La Librairie de Philippe le Bon: Exposition organisée à l'occasion du 500e anniversaire de la mort du Duc*, Bruxelles, 1967.

Douët d'Arcq, Louis. *Nouveau Recueil de Comptes de l'Argenterie des Rois de France*. Société de l'histoire de

France. Paris, 1874.

⸻. 'Inventaire des Meubles de la Reine Jeanne de Boulogne, seconde femme du Roi Jean (1360)'. *Bibliothèque de l'École des Chartes* 40 (1879): 545–62.

⸻. *Comptes de l'Argenterie des Rois de France au XIV Siècle*. Société de l'histoire de France. 1851.

⸻. *Comptes de l'Hôtel des Rois de France...* Société de l'histoire de France. 1865.

Douglas, David C., and George W. Greenaway, eds. *English Historical Documents 1042–1189*. Vol. II. London, 1953.

Drabek, Anna Maria. *Reisen und Reisezeremoniell der römischdeutschen Herrscher im Spätmittelalter*. Wien, 1964.

Duggan, Anne J., ed. *Kings and Kingship in Medieval Europe*. King's College London Medieval Studies. London, 1993.

Duong, Yen M. '"Désirant tout, envahissant tout, ne connaissant le prix de rien": Materiality in the Queenship of Isabeau of Bavaria'. MA thesis, University of Guelph, 2014.

Duplès-Agier, Henri. 'Ordonnance Somptuaire inédite de Philippe le Hardi'. *Bibliothèque de l'École des Chartes* 15 (1854): 176–81.

Durliat, Marcel. *L'art dans le Royaume de Majorque*. Toulouse, 1962.

Dynter, Edmundus de. *Chronique des Ducs de Brabant*. Bruxelles, 1857.

Eadmer. *Eadmer's History of Recent Events in England*. Tr. Geoffrey Bosanquet. London, 1964.

Eames, Penelope. *Medieval Furniture*. London, 1977.

Eberle, Patricia J. 'The Politics of Courtly Style at the Court of Richard II', in Burgess, The *Spirit of the Court*, 168–78.

Eboli, Petrus de. *Liber ad Honorem Augusti sive de Rebus Siculis*. Ed. Theo Kölzer and Marlis Stähli. Sigmaringen, 1994.

Ehlers, Joachim. 'Entourage du Roi – Entourage des Princes. L'aube d'une Société de Cour en Allemagne Au XIIe Siècle', in Marchandisse, *À l'Ombre de Pouvoir*, 98–105.

Eichberger, D. H. 'The Tableau Vivant - an ephemeral art form in Burgundian Civic Festivities'. *Parergon* 6 (1991): 37–64.

Einhard, and Notker the Stammerer. *Two Lives of Charlemagne*. Tr. Lewis Thorpe. Harmondsworth, 1979.

Elliott, Dyan. 'Dress as Mediator between Inner and Outer Self: The Pious Matron of the Hihg and Later Middle Ages'. *Medieval Studies* 53 (1991): 279–308.

Erben et al., Karel, ed. *Regesta Diplomatica nec non Epistolaria Bohemiae et Moraviae*. 7 vols. Prague, 1855.

Erlande-Brandenburg, Alain. *La Tenture de l'Apocalypse d'Angers*. Nantes, 1993.

⸻. 'Le Palais des Rois de France à Paris Par Philippe le Bel'. *Comptes Rendus des Séances de l'Académie des Inscriptions et Belles-Lettres* 151 (2007): 183–94.

⸻. *Le Roi est Mort: Etude sur les Funerailles, les Sepultures et les Tombeaux des Rois de France jusqu'à la Fin du XIIIe Siècle*. Bibliothèque de la Société Francaise d'Archéologie 7. Geneva, 1975.

Esch, Arnold. 'Friedrich II und Die Antike', in Esch, *Friedrich II*, 201–34.

Esch, Arnold, and Kamp, Norbert, eds. *Friedrich II. Tagung des Deutschen Historischen Instituts in Rom im Gedenkjahr 1994*.

Eschenbach, Wolfram von. *Parzival*. Tr. Cyril Edwards. Arthurian Studies 56. Woodbridge, 2004.

Estow, Clara. 'The Politics of Gold in Fourteenth-Century Castile'. *Mediterranean Studies* 8 (1999): 129–42.

Evans, James. *The History & Practice of Ancient Astronomy*. Oxford, 1998.

Evans, Joan. *Dress in Medieval France*. Oxford, 1952.

Fajt, Jiri. 'Karlstein Revisited: Überlegungen zu den Patrozinien der Karlsteiner Sakralräume', in Fajt, *Kunst als Herrschaftsinstrument*, 250–88.

Fajt, Jiri, and Langer, Andrea, eds. *Kunst als Herrschaftsinstrument: Böhmen und das Heilige Römische Reich unter den Luxemburgern im Europäischen Kontext*. Munich, 2009.

Falk, Fritz. *Edelsteinschliff und Fassungsformen im späten Mittelalter und im 16. Jahrhundert*. Ulm, 1975.

Falk, Fritz. 'The Cutting and Setting of Gems in the 15th and 16th Centuries', in *Princely Magnificence*, 20–26.

Fiala, David. 'La Musique à la Cour de Bourgogne'. *Annales de l'Est* 2 (2015): 45–60.

Fiala et al., Michal. *Nové Město Pražské 1348–1784*. Prague, 1998.

Filangieri, Riccardo. *Castel Nuovo: Reggia Angioina ed Aragonese di Napoli*. Naples, 1964.

Finke, Heinrich. *Acta Aragonensia: Quellen zur Deutschen, Italienischen, Französischen, Spanischen, zur Kirchen- und Kulturgeschichte aus der Diplomatischen Korrespondenz Jaymes II (1291–1327)*. 3 vols. Berlin, 1908.

Firth Green, *Richard. Poets and Princepleasers: Literature and the English Court in the Late Middle Ages*. Toronto, 1980.

Fleckenstein, Josef. *Curialitas: Studien zu Grundfragen der höfisch-ritterlichen Kultur*. Göttingen, 1990.

Fössel, Amalie. *Die Königin im Mittelalterlichen Reich: Herrschaftsausübung, Herrschaftsrechte, Handlungsspielräume*. Stuttgart, 2000.

Fowler, Kenneth. *The King's Lieutenant: Henry of Grosmont, first Duke of Lancaster 1310–61*. London, 1969.

Freudenthaler, Ilse Maria. 'Tarascon als Residenz Renes von Anjou'. *Mitteilungen der Residenzen-Kommission der Akademie der Wissenschaften zu Gottingen* 9, no. 2 (1999).

Froissart, Jean. *Oeuvres*. Ed. Kervyn de Lettenhove. 26 vols. Brussels, 1867.

Froissart, Jean. *Oeuvres*. Ed. August. Scheler. Bruxelles: Devaux, 1870.

Fryde, E.B., and M.M. Fryde. 'Public Credit, with special reference to North-Western Europe', in *Economic Organisation and Politics in the Middle Ages*, 430–553.

Furnivall, Frederick James. *The Babees Book [Early English Meals and Manners]*. Early English Text Society Original Series 32. London, 1868.

Gabelt, Stefan, and Lutz, Gerhard. 'Die Stifterfiguren des Naumburger Westchores', in Krohm, *Meisterwerke mittelalterlicher Skulptur*, 271–95.

Gaborit-Chopin, D. *L'inventaire du Trésor du Dauphin futur Charles V, 1363: les Débuts d'un grand Collectioneur*. Société de l'histoire d'art Français, Archives d'art Français, n.s., xxxii. Nogent-le Rotrou, 1996.

Gaier, Claude. *L'Industrie et le Commerce des Armes dans les Anciennes Principautés Belges du XIIeme à la Fin du XVeme Siècle*. Bibliothèque de la Faculté de Philosophie et Lettres de l'Université de Liège, CCII. Paris, 1975.

Gairdner, James. *The Historical Collections of a Citizen of London*. London: 1876.

Galbraith, V. V., ed. *The Anonimalle Chronicle 1333–1381*. Manchester, 1927.

Ganz, David. 'Pictorial Textiles and Their Performance: The Star Mantle of Henry II', in Dimitrova, *Dressing the Part: Propaganda in the Middle Ages*, 13–29.

———. *Two Lives of Charlemagne: Einhard and Notker the Stammerer*. Harmondsworth, 2008.

Gaude-Ferragu, Murielle. *D'or et de Cendres. La Mort et les Funérailles des Princes dans le Royaume de France Au Bas Moyen Âge*. Médiévales 50. Villeneuve d'Ascq, 2006.

———. 'Le Prince et les Restes Saints: le Culte des Reliques à la Cour (1369–1416)', in *La Cour du Prince*, 377–98.

Gaude-Ferragu, Murielle, Bruno Laurioux, and Jacques Paviot. *La Cour du Prince: Cour de France, Cours d'Europe, XIIe-XVe Siècle*. Etudes d'histoire médiévale 13. Paris, 2011.

Gay, Victor. *Glossaire Archeologique du Moyen Âge et de la Renaissance*. 2 vols. Paris, 1887.

Gerald of Wales. *Instruction for a Ruler* (De Principis Instructione). Ed. and tr. Robert Bartlett. Oxford Medieval Texts. Oxford 2018.

Gillingham, John. *Richard I*. London, 1999.

Given-Wilson, Chris, ed. & tr. *Chronicles of the Revolution, 1397–1400: The Reign of Richard II*. Manchester, 1993.

Given-Wilson, Chris. 'The Exequies of Edward III and the Royal Funeral Ceremony in Late Medieval England'. *English Historical Review* 124, no. 507 (2009): 257–82.

Gómez-Moreno, Manuel. *El Panteon Real de Las Huelgas de Burgos*. Madrid, 1946.

Gordon, Dillian, Lisa Monnas, and Caroline Elam, eds. *The Regal Image of Richard II and the Wilton Diptych*. London, 1997.

Götze, Heinz. *Castel del Monte: Geometric Marvel of the Middle Ages*. Munich & New York, 1998.

Gray, Sir Thomas. *Scalacronica, 1272–1363*. Ed. Andy King. Surtees Society. Woodbridge, 2005.

Gregory of Tours. *History of the Franks*. Tr. Lewis Thorpe. Harmondsworth, 1974.

Grierson, Philip. *Monnaies du Moyen Age*. Fribourg, 1976.

Grocock, Christopher, and Grainger, Sally, eds. *Apicius: A Critical Edition with an Introduction and an English Translation of the Latin Recipe Text*. Totnes, 2006.

Guenée, Bernard. 'Le Voeu de Charles VI. Essai sur la Dévotion des Rois de France aux XIIIe et XIVe Siècles'. *Journal des Savants*, 1996, 67–135.

Guenée, Bernard. 'Le Portrait de Charles VI dans la Chronique du Religieux de Saint-Denis'. *Journal des Savants*, 1997, 125–65.

———. 'Le Prince en Sa Cour: des Vertus aux Usages (Guillaume de Tyr, Gilles de Rome, Michel Pintoin)'. *Comptes Rendus des Séances de l'Académie des Inscriptions et Belles-Lettres* 142, no. 3 (1998): 633–46.

Guenée, Bernard. and Françoise Lehoux. *Les Entrées royales françaises de 1328 à 1515*. Paris: Editions du Centre national de la recherche scientifique, 1968.

Guiffrey, Jules. 'Inventaire des Tapisseries du Roi Charles VI vendues par les Anglais en 1422'. *Bibliothèque de l'École des Chartes* 48 (1887): 59–110, 396–444.

———, *Inventaires de Jean Duc de Berry (1401–1416)*. 2 vols. Paris, 1894.

———. 'La Tapisserie aux XIVe et XVe Siècles', in Michel, *Histoire de l'Art*, 343–73.

Guisborough, Walter of. *The Chronicle of Walter of Guisborough*. Ed. Harry Rothwell. Camden Series LXXXIX. London, 1957.

Guizot, Francois. *Collection des Mémoires Relatifs à l'histoire de France depuis la Fondation de la Monarchie Françoise jusqu'au 13e Siècle*. Paris, 1825.

Hablot, Laurent. 'Art, Ésthetique et Productions Héraldiques au Moyen Âge', in *Heraldic Artists and Painters*.

———. 'Le Décor Emblématique chez les Princes de la Fin du Moyen Âge: un Outil pour construire et qualifier l'espace', in *Actes des Congrès de la Société des Historiens Médiévistes de l'enseignement Supérieur Public, 37e Congrès, Mulhouse, 2006. Construction de l'espace Au Moyen Age: Pratiques et Représentations*, 147–65. Mulhouse, 2006.

Halphen, Louis, and René Poupardin, eds. *Chroniques des Comtes d'Anjou et des Seigneurs d'Ambois*. Paris, 1913.

Hanawalt, Barbara, and Kathryn L. Reyerson, eds. *City and Spectacle in Medieval Europe*. Medieval Studies at Minnesota. Minneapolis, 1994.

Haskins, Charles H. 'Michael Scot and Frederick II'. *Isis* 4, no. 2 (1920) 250–75.

Hausherr, Reiner. *Die Zeit der Staufer: Katalog der Ausstellung V. Supplement: Vorträge und Forschungen,*. Köln, 1977.

———. 'Zu Auftrag, Programm und Büstenzyklus des Prager Domchores', *Zeitschrift für Kunstgeschichte*, 34 (1971), 21–46.

Hay, David. *The Military Leadership of Matilda of Canossa, 1046–1115*. Manchester, 2008.

Haynin, Jean de. *Mémoires*. Ed. Dieudonné Brouwers. Société des Bibliophiles Liégeois. Liége, 1905.

Helas, Philine. 'Der Triumph von Alfonso d'Aragona 1443 in Neapel. Zu den Darstellungen Herrscherlicher Einzüge zwischen Mittelalter und Renaissance', in Johanek, *Adventus. Studien zum Herrscherlichen Einzug in die Stadt*, 133–228.

Heller, Sarah-Grace. *Fashion in Medieval France*. Gallica 3. Cambridge, 2007.

———. 'Limiting Yardage and Changes of Clothes: Sumptuary Legislation in Thirteenth-Century France, Languedoc and Italy', in *Medieval Fabrications*, 121–36.

Henwood, Philippe. *Les Collections du Trésor Royal sous le Règne de Charles VI (1380–1422)*. Paris: 2004.

———. 'Administration et Vie des Collections d'orfèvrerie Royales sous le Règne de Charles VI (1380–1422)'. *Bibliothèque de l'École des Chartes* 138, no. 2 (1980): 179–215.

Herzogenberg, Johanna von. 'Die Bildnisse Karls IV.' In *Kaiser Karl IV. Staatsmann und Mäzen*, 324–26.

Hieatt, Constance B., and Butler, Sharon, eds. *Curye on Inglysch*, (including *The Forme of Cury*), Early English Text Society. London, 1985.

Hieatt, Constance B., and Robin F. Jones. 'Two Anglo-Norman Culinary Collections edited from British Library Manuscripts Additional 32085 and Royal 12.C.XII'. *Speculum* 61 (1986): 859–82.

Hiltmann, Torsten, and Laurent Hablot, eds. *Heraldic Artists and Painters in the Middle Ages and Early Modern Times*. Heraldic Studies 1. Ostfildern, 2018.

Hirschbiegel, Jan. *Étrennes: Untersuchungen zum höfischen Geschenkverkehr im spätmittelalterlichen Frankreich der Zeit König Karls VI. (1380–1422)*. München: Oldenbourg.

Hocquet, Adolphe. *Croniques de Franche, d'Engleterre, de Flandres, de Lile et espécialment de Tournay*. Mons, 1938.

Hofmann-Randall, Christina. 'Die Herkunft und Tradierung des Burgundischen Hofzeremoniells', 150–56.

Hope, St John. *Windsor Castle: An Architectural History*. 2 vols. London, 1913.

Howe, Emily. 'Divine Kingship and Dynastic Display: The Altar Wall Murals of St Stephen's Chapel, Westminster'. *The Antiquaries Journal* 81 (2001): 259–303.

Hugo Falcandus. *The History of the Tyrants of Sicily*. Ed. Graham Loud and Thomas Wiedemann. Manchester, 1998.

Huillard-Bréholles, J.-L.-A. *Historia Diplomatica Friderici Secundi*. 6 vols. Paris, 1852.

Inglis, Erik. 'Gothic Architecture and a Scholastic: Jean de Jandun's "Tractatus de Laudibus Parisius"(1323)'. *Gesta* 42, no. 1 (2003): 63–85.

Jacoby, David. 'Silk Economics and Cross-Cultural Artistic Interaction: Byzantium, the Muslim World, and the Christian West'. *Dumbarton Oaks Papers* 58 (2004): 197–240.

Jaeger, C. Stephen. *The Origins of Courtliness: Civilizing Trends and the Formation of Courtly Ideals, 923–1210*. Philadelphia, 1985.

James, M. R. *The Apocalyse in Latin: MS. 10 in the Collection of Dyson Perrins, F.S.A.* Oxford, 1927.

Jasperse, Jitske. 'Matilda, Leonor and Joanna: The Plantagenet Sisters and the Display of Dynastic Connections through Material Culture'. *Journal of Medieval History* 43, no. 5 (2017): 523–47.

Jaubert, P. Amédée. *Géographie d'Édrisi*. Vol. II. Paris, 1840.

Johanek, Peter, and Angelika Lampen, eds. *Adventus: Studien zum Herrscherlichen Einzug in die Stadt*. Städteforschung. Reihe A, Darstellungen 75. Köln, 2009.

John of Reading. *Chronica Johannis de Reading et Anonymi Cantuariensis 1346–1367*. Ed. James Tait. Manchester, 1914.

John of Salisbury. *Frivolities of Courtiers and Footprints of Philosophers*. Minneapolis, 1938.

Joinville, Jean de. *Joinville & Villehardouin: Chronicles of the Crusades*. Tr. M. E. B. Shaw. Harmondsworth, 1973.

Jones, Michael. 'Servir le Duc: Remarques sur le Rôle des Hérauts à la Cour de Bretagne à la fin du Moyen Âge', in Marchandisse, *À l'Ombre de Pouvoir*, 245–65.

Jones, Richard H. *The Royal Policy of Richard II: Absolutism in the Middle Ages*. Studies in Medieval History X. Oxford, 1968.

Jones, Robert W. *Bloodied Banners: Martial Display on the Medieval Battlefield*. Woodbridge, 2010.

Jonson, Ben. *The Works of Ben Jonson*. Ed. Barry Cornwell. London, 1838.

Joubert, Fabienne. 'Création à deux mains: l'élaboration de la Tenture de l'Apocalypse d'Angers'. *Revue de l'Art*, no. 114 (1996): 48–56.

———. 'Le Saint Christophe de Semur-En-Auxois: Jean de Bruges en Bourgogne?' *Bulletin Monumental* 150 (1992): 165–77.

Kaeuper, R.W. 'The Frescobaldi of Florence and the

English Crown'. *Studies in Medieval and Renaissance History* 10 (1973): 41–95.

Kantorowicz, Ernst H. 'Mysteries of State: An Absolutist Concept and Its Late Mediaeval Origins'. *Harvard Theological Review* 48, no. 1 (1955): 65–91.

———. *The King's Two Bodies: A Study in Medieval Political Thought*. Princeton Classics. Princeton, NJ, 2016.

Keen, Laurence, and Eileen Scarff, eds. *Windsor: Medieval Archaeology, Art and Architecture of the Thames Valley*. The British Archaeological Association Conference Transactions XXV. Leeds, 2002.

Kelly, Samantha. *The New Solomon: Robert of Naples (1309–1343) and Fourteenth Century Kingship*. Leiden, 2003.

Kempshall, M. S. *The Common Good in Late Medieval Political Thought*. Oxford, 1999.

Kempshall, Matthew. 'The Rhetoric of Giles of Rome', in Lachaud, *Le Prince Au Miroir de la Littérature de l'Antiquité aux Lumières*, 161–90.

Killerby, Catherine Kovesi. *Sumptuary Law in Italy 1200–1500*. Oxford Historical Monographs. Oxford, 2002.

Kintzinger, Martin. 'De la Région à l'Europe. Recrutement et Fonction de l'entourage de l'empereur Sigismond', in Marchandisse, *À l'Ombre de Pouvoir*, 107–15.

Klausner, D., and Marsalek, K., eds. *'Bring Furth the Pagants': Essays in Early English Drama Presented to Alexandra F. Johnston*. Toronto, 2007.

Klein, Holger A. 'Sacred Things and Holy Bodies: Collecting Relics from Late Antiquity to the Early Renaissance', in Bagnoli, *Treasures of Heaven*, 55–68.

Klewitz, Hans-Walter. 'Die Festkrönungen der Deutschen Könige'. *Zeitschrift Für Rechtsgeschichte* 28 (1939): 48–96.

Knowles, David. *The Evolution of Medieval Thought*. London, 1962.

Krohm, Hartmut. *Meisterwerke de Mittelalterlicher Skulptur*. Berlin 1996.

Krönig, Wolfgang. 'Castel del Monte. Der Bau Friedrichs II', in Tronzo, *Intellectual Life at the Court of Frederick II Hohenstaufen*, 91–106, 1994.

Krueger, Derek. 'The Religion of Relics in Late Antiquity and Byzantium', in *Treasures of Heaven*, 5–18.

Krüger, Kristina. 'Fürstengrablegen in Nordspanien: Die Panteones Früh- und Hochmittelalterlichen KIrchen', in *Grabkunst und Sepulkralkultur in Spanien und Portugal*, 33–64.

Kurthan, Jiri, and Jan Royt. *The Cathedral of St. Vitus at Prague Castle*. Prague, 2016.

La Marche, Olivier de. *Mémoires d'Olivier de la Marche, Maître d'hôtel et Capitaine des Gardes de Charles le Téméraire*. Ed. Henri Beaune and J. d'Arbaumont. 4

vols. Société de l'histoire de France, 213, 219, 220, 240. Paris, 1883.

Labarte, Jules, *Inventaire du Mobilier de Charles V*. Collection des document inédits sur l'histoire de France: Troisième Série, Archéologie. Paris, 1879.

Laborde, Leon de. *Les Ducs de Bourgogne: 2. Preuves*. 3 vols. Paris, 1849.

Laborde, M. de. *Notice des Émaux, Bijoux et Objets Divers, exposés dans les Galeries du Musée du Louvre*. Vol. II. Paris, 1853.

Lachaud, Frédérique. 'Documents Financiers et Histoire de la Culture Matérielle: les Textiles dans les Comptes des Hôtels Royaux et Nobiliaires (France et Angleterre, XIIe - XVe Siècle'. *Bibliothèque de l'École des Chartes* 164 (2006): 71–96.

———. 'Dress and Social Status in England before the Sumptuary Laws', in Coss, *Heraldry, Pageantry and Social Status in England*, 105–24.

Lachaud, Frederique. 'Embroidery for the Court of Edward I (1272–1307)'. *Nottingham Medieval Studies* XXXVII (1993): 33–52.

Lachaud, Frédérique. 'Liveries of Robes in England c.1200–c.1330'. *English Historical Review* 111 (1996): 279–98.

Lachaud, Frédérique, and Lydwine Scordia, eds. *Le Prince Au Miroir de la Littérature de l'Antiquité aux Lumières*. Mont Saint Aignan, 2007.

Laking, Sir Guy. *A Record of European Armour and Arms through Seven Centuries*. 4 vols. London, 1920.

Lalou, Elisabeth. 'Fragments du Journal du Trésor de l'année 1352 retrouvés dans une Reliure'. *Bibliothèque de l'École des Chartes* 144, no. 1 (1986): 145–50.

Lambert, Carole. *Du Manuscrit à la Table: Essais sur la Cuisine au Moyen Âge et Répertoire des Manuscrits Médiévaux contenant des Recettes Culinaires*. Montréal, 1992.

Lancashire, Anne. *London Civic Theatre*. Cambridge, 2002.

Laurioux, Bruno. *Une histoire culinaire du moyen âge*. Paris, 2005.

Le Bel, Jean. *Chronique de Jean le Bel*. Ed. Jules Viard and Eugène Déprez. Société de l'histoire de France. Paris, 1904.

Le Fèvre, Jean seigneur de Saint-Remy. Ed. François Morand. *Chronique de Jean le Fèvre, seigneur de Saint-Remy*. Paris, 1881.

Le Goff, Jacques. 'Le Roi dans l'Occident Médiéval: Caractères Originaux', in Duggan, *Kings and Kingship in Medieval Europe*, 1–40.

Le Roux de Lincy, Antoine. 'Inventaires des Biens Meubles et immeubles de la Comtesse Mahaut d'Artois, Pillés Par l'armée de Son Neveu, en 1313'. *Bibliothèque de l'École des Chartes* 13, no. 1852 (n.d.): 53–79.

Leach, Elizabeth Eva. *Guillaume de Machaut: Secretary, Poet, Musician*. Ithaca, N Y, 2011.

Lecoy de la Marche. *La Chaire Française Au Moyen Age.* Paris, 1886.

Ledos, M. 'Fragment de l'inventaire des Joyaux de Louis Ier'. *Bibliothèque de l'École des Chartes* L (1889): 168–79.

Legner, Anton. *Die Parler und der schöne Stil 1350–1400: Europäischen Kunst unter den Luxemburgern: Ein Handbuch zur Ausstellung des Schnütgen-Museums in der Kunsthalle Köln. Köln,* 1978.

———. 'Ikon und Porträt', in Legner, *Die Parler,* 224–235.

———. 'Karolinische Edelsteinwände', in *Kaiser Karl IV. Staatsmann und Mäzen,* 356–61.

Leonard, Emile. 'Comptes de l'hôtel de Jeanne I de Navarre de 1352 à 1369'. *Mélanges d'archéologie et d'histoire* 38 (1920).

Léonard, Émile G. *Les Angevins de Naples.* Paris, 1954.

Leroy, Béatrice. 'L'animation de la Cour de Navarre (vers 1350–vers 1430)', in Marchandisse, *À l'Ombre de Pouvoir,* 235–44.

Leseur, Guillaume. *Histoire de Gaston IV, Comte de Foix.* Ed. Henri Courteault. Société de l'histoire de France. Paris, 1893.

Letts, Malcolm, trans. *The Travels of Leo of Rozmital.* Hakluyt Society: Second Series CVIII. Cambridge, 1957.

Lewis, Suzanne. *The Art of Matthew Paris in the Chronica Majora.* California Studies in the History of Art, XXI. Aldershot, 1987.

Lightbown, Ronald W. *Medieval European Jewellery with a Catalogue of the Collection at the Victoria and Albert Museum.* London, 1992.

———. *Secular Goldsmiths' Work in Medieval France: A History.* Reports of the Research Committee of the Society of Antiquaries, XXXVI. London, 1978.

Lindenbaum, Sheila. 'The Smithfield Tournament of 1390'. *Journal of Medieval and Renaissance Studies* 20 (1990): 1–20.

Linehan, Peter. *Spain 1157–1300; A Partible Inheritance.* Oxford, 2008.

Liudprand, ed. Paolo Squatriti. *The Complete Works of Liudprand of Cremona.* Washington, DC, 2007.

Loisel, Gustave. *Histoire des Ménageries de l'antiquité à nos Jours.* Paris, 1912.

Longnon, Jean. 'Charles d'Anjou et la Croisade de Tunis'. *Journal des Savants,* 1974, 44–61.

Loomis, Laura Hibbard. 'The Holy Relics of Charlemagne and King Athelstan: The Lances of Longinus and St.Mauricius'. *Speculum* 24, no. 4 (1950).

Lopes, Fernão. *The English in Portugal 1367–87.* Warminnster, 1988.

López de Meneses, Amada. 'Documentos Culturales de Pedro El Ceremonioso'. *Estudios de Edad Media de la Corona de Aragon,* Publicaciones de la Seccion de Zaragoza, V (1952).

Loserth, Johann, ed. *Die Königsaaler Geschichts-Quellen.* Wien, 1875.

Losito, Maria. *Castel del Monte e la Cultura Arabo-Normanna Federico II.* Istituto Internazionale di Studi Federiciani: Acta e Monumenta 2. Bari, 2003.

Luard, H.R., ed. *Annales Monastici.* 5 vols. Rolls Series 36. London: 1864–69.

———. *Flores Historiarum.* Rolls Series 95. London:1890.

Lübeck, Arnold of. *Arnoldi Chronica Slavorum.* Ed. J.M. Lippenberg. Hanover, 1868.

Luengo, Anthony E. 'Magic and Illusion in "The Franklin's Tale"'. *The Journal of English and Germanic Philology* 77 (1978): 1–16.

Lutkin, Jessica. 'Luxury and Display in Silver and Gold at the Court of Henry IV'. *The Fifteenth Century* IX (2010): 155–78.

Lydgate, John. *Minor Poems.* Ed. H.N. McCracken. London, 1961.

———. *The Dance of Death.* Ed. Florence Warren. Early English Text Society Original Series 181. London, 1931.

Macconi, Massimiliano. *Federico II: Sacralità e Potere.* Genoa, 1996.

Mackay, Angus. 'Signs Deciphered - the Language of Court Displays in Medieval Spain', in Duggan, *Kings and Kingship in Medieval Europe,* 287–304.

Maillard, François. *Comptes Royaux (1285–1314).* Recueil des Historiens de France, Documents Financiers. Vol. III. Paris, 1956.

———. *Comptes Royaux (1314–1328).* Recueil des Historiens de France, Documents Financiers. Vol. IV.2. Paris, 1961.

Malmesbury, William of. *Gesta Regum Anglorum = The History of the English Kings.* Ed. R. A. B. Mynors. 2 vols. Oxford Medieval Texts. Oxford, 1998.

Mane, Perrine. 'Le Lit et ses Tentures d'après l'iconographie du XIIIe au XVe Siècle'. *Mélanges de l'École Française de Rome.* Moyen-Âge 111, no. 1 (1999): 393–418.

Map, Walter *De Nugis Curialium = Courtiers' Trifles.* Ed. M. R. James, C. N. L. Brooke, and R. A. B. Mynors. Oxford, 1983.

Marchandisse, Alain. *À l'Ombre de Pouvoir: les Entourages Princiers Au Moyen Age,* Liège, 2013.

Marix, Jeanne. *Histoire de la Musique et des Musiciens de la Cour de Bourgogne sous la Règne de Philippe le Bon.* Sammlung Musik-Wissenschaftlicher Abhandlungen 28. Strasbourg, 1939.

Marks, Richard, and Paul Williamson, eds. *Gothic: Art for England 1400–1547 [Exhibition Catalogue].* London, 2003.

Martin, Therese, ed. *Reassessing the Roles of Women as 'Makers' of Medieval Art and Architecture.* 2 vols. Visualising the Middle Ages 7. Leiden, 2012.

Martindale, Andrew. *Heroes, Ancestors, Relatives and the*

*Birth of the Portrait*. The Hague, 1988.

———. *The Rise of the Artist: In the Middle Ages and Early Renaissance*. London, 1972.

Mathew, Gervase 1905–1976. *The Court of Richard II*. London, 1968.

Maupassant, Guy de. *Sicily*. Tr. Robert W. Berger. New York, 2007.

May, Florence Lewis. *Silk Textiles of Spain: Eighth to Fifteenth Century*. New York, 1957.

McHardy, A.K. 'Paying for the Wedding: Edward III as Fundraiser 1332–3'. *Fourteenth Century England* IV (2006): 43–60.

Mentzel-Reuters, Arno. 'Die Goldene Krone. Entwicklungslinien Mittelalterlicher Herrschaftssymbolik'. *Deutsches Archiv für Erforschung des Mittelalters* 50 (1994): 135–81.

Mercuri, Chiara. 'Stat Inter Spinas Lilium: le Lys de France et la Couronne d'Épines'. *Le Moyen Âge* CX, no. 3 (2004): 497–512.

Meredith, Jill. 'The Arch at Capua: the Strategic Use of Spolia and References to the Antique'. *Studies in the History of Art*, Symposium Papers XXIV, 44 (1994): 108–26.

Mérindol, Christian de. 'Le Prince et Son Cortège. La Théâtralisation des Signes du Pouvoir à la Fin du Moyen Age', in *Actes des Congrès de la Société des Historiens Médiévistes de l'enseignement Supérieur Public, 23e Congrès: les Princes et le Pouvoir Au Moyen Age*, 303–23. Brest, 1992.

———. *Le Roi René et la Seconde Maison d'Anjou: Emblématique Art Histoire*. Paris, 1987.

Meyer, Paul. 'L'entrevue d'Ardres'. *Annuaire-Bulletin de la Société de l'histoire de France* xviii, no. 2 (1881): 209–24.

Meyer, Rudolf J. *Königs- und Kaiserbegräbnisse im Spätmittelalter: Von Rudolf von Habsburg bis zu Friedrich III*. Forschungen zur Kaiser- und Papstgeschichte des Mittelalters: Beihefte zu J.F. Böhmer, Regesta imperii 19. Köln, 2000.

Michael, M. A. *The Age of Opus Anglicanum*. Studies in English Medieval Embroidery. London, 2016.

Michel, André. *Histoire de l'Art*. Vol. III.i. Paris, 1907.

Milemete, Walter de. *The Treatise of Walter de Milemete: De Nobilitatibus, Sapientiis et Prudentiis Regum*. Ed. M. R. James. London, 1913.

Militello, Fabio, and Rodo Santoro. *Castelli di Sicilia: Città e Fortificazioni*. Palermo, 2006.

Millar, Alistair. *'Olivier de la Marche and the Court of Burgundy, c.1425–1502.'* PhD thesis, University of Edinburgh, 1996. http://hdl.handle.net/1842/1540 accessed 17 December 2019.

Mirot, Léon. 'Les Cadeaux offerts à Charles VI par les Villes du Royaume'. *Bibliothèque de l'École des Chartes* 101 (1940): 220–24.

Moliez, Pauline. 'Comment expliquer l'attrait des Offices de Bouche à la Cour de France au XIVe

Siècle?', in Gaude-Ferragu, *La Cour du Prince*, 243–50.

Molinet, Jean. *Chroniques de Jean Molinet*. Ed. J.A.C. Buchon. 5 vols. Paris, 1827.

Monmouth, Geoffrey of. *History of the Kings of Britain*. Ed. Michael Reeve, Tr. Neil Wright. Cambridge, 2007.

Monnas, Lisa. *Merchants, Princes and Painters: Silk Fabrics in Italian and Northern Paintings 1300–1550*. New Haven ; London, 2008.

———. 'Some Medieval Colour Terms for Textiles'. *Clothing and Textiles* 10 (2014): 25–57.

———. 'Textiles for the Coronation of Edward III'. *Textile History* 32 (2001): 2–35.

Monstrelet, Enguerrand de. *The Chronicles of Enguerrand de Monstrelet*. Tr. Thomas Johnes. London: 1810.

Montalto, Lina. *La Corte di Alfonso I di Aragona: Vesti e Gale*. Naples, 1922.

Montecassino, Amatus of. *The History of the Normans*. Ed. Graham Loud. Tr. Prescott N. Dunbar. Woodbridge, 2004.

Monter, William. *The Rise of Female Kings in Europe, 1300–1800*. New Haven ; London, 2012.

Moranvillé, Henri. 'L'inventaire de l'orfèvrerie et des joyaux de Louis Ier Duc d'Anjou'. *Bibliothèque de l'École des Chartes* 62 (1901): 181–222.

Moraw, Peter. *Deutscher Königshof, Hoftag und Reichstag im späteren Mittelalter*. Stuttgart, 2002.

Morpurgo, Piero. 'Philosophia Naturalis at the Court of Frederick II: From the Theological Method to the Ratio Secundum Physicam in Michael Scot's De Anima', in Tronzo, *Intellectual Life at the Court of Frederick II Hohenstaufen*, 241–48, 1994.

Morris, Marc. *A Great and Terrible King: Edward I and the Forging of Britain*. London, 2008.

———. 'Edward I and the Knights of the Round Table', in Brand, *Foundations of Medieval Scholarship: Records Edited in Honour of David Crook*, 57–76.

Munby, Julian. 'Reconstructing the Round Table: Windsor and Beyond', in Munby, *Edward III's Round Table at Windsor*, 119–37. Woodbridge, 2007.

Munby, Julian, Richard. Barber, and Richard Brown. *Edward III's Round Table at Windsor: The House of the Round Table and the Windsor Festival of 1344*. Woodbridge, 2007.

Muntaner, Ramon. *The Chronicle of Muntaner*. Tr. Lady Goodenough. 2 vols. Hakluyt Society Second Series. Vols. 47, 50. London, 1920.

Muratori, L. A. *Annales Mediolanenses ab Anno 1230 usque ad Annum 1402 ab Anonymo Auctore*, etc. Rerum Italicarum Scriptores, 16. Milan, 1730.

Myers, A. R. *The Household of Edward IV. The Black Book and the Ordinance of 1478*. Manchester, 1959.

Nagy, Balás, and Frank Schaer, eds. *Karoli IV imperatoris Romanorum Vita ab Eo Ipso Conscripta:*

*Autobiography of Emperor Charles IV.* Budapest, 2001.

Nangis, Guillaume de. *Chronique Latine de Guillaume de Nangis de 1113 à 1300, avec les Continuations ... de 1300 à 1368.* Ed. H. Géraud. Société de l'histoire de France. Paris, 1843.

Nash, Susie. *"No Equal in Any Land": André Beauneveu.* London, 2007.

Nelson, Janet L. *Politics and Ritual in Early Medieval Europe.* London, 1986.

———. 'The Rites of the Conqueror'. *Proceedings of the Battle Conference* IV (1982): 117–32.

Netherton, Robin, and Gale R. Owen-Crocker, eds. Medieval *Clothing and Textiles,* 7. Woodbridge, 2011.

Newton, Stella. *Fashion in the Age of the Black Prince.* Woodbridge, 1980.

Nicolas, Sir Nicolas Harris. 'Observations on the Foundation of the Most Noble Order of the Garter'. *Archaeologia* 31 (1846): 1–163.

———. *Testamenta Vetusta: Being Illustrations from Wills...* London, 1826.

———. *The Controversy between Sir Richard Scrope and Sir Robert Grosvenor, in the Court of Chivalry.* London: 1832.

Normore, Christina. *A Feast for the Eyes: Art, Performance, and the Late Medieval Banquet.* Chicago, 2015.

Nys, Ludovic. '"Alant de Valenciennes ... a Paris as Juiaulx". Le Hainault et la France sous les derniers Capétiens et Philippe VI de Valois. Cadeaux, Trousseaux et Cassettes.' In *La Cour du Prince,* 433–48.

Oakley-Brown, Liz, and Louise J. Wilkinson, eds. *The Rituals and Rhetoric of Queenship Medieval to Modern.* Dublin, 2009.

Onofrio, Mario d'. *I Normanni: Popolo d'Europa 1030–1200.* Venice, 1994.

Opačic, Zoe. 'Architecture and Religious Experience in 14th-Century Prague', in Fajt, *Kunst als Herrschaftszeichen,* 136–50.

Ormrod, W. M. Edward III. London, 2011.

———. 'Edward III and His Family'. *Journal of British Studies* 26 (1987): 398–442.

———. *England in the Thirteenth Century.* Harlaxton Medieval Studies, I. Stamford, 1991.

———. *England in the Fourteenth Century: Proceedings of the 1985 Harlaxton Symposium,* Woodbridge 1986.

Oschinsky, Dorothea, ed. *Walter of Henley and other Treatises.* Oxford, 1971.

Ottokar von Steiermark. *Ottokars Österreichische Reimchronik.* Hanover, 1890.

Paden Jr., William D., Tilde Sankovitch, and Patricia Stäblein, eds. *The Poems of the Troubadour Bertran de Born.* Berkeley CA, 1986.

Page, Agnès. *Vêtir le Prince: Tissus et Couleurs à la Cour de Savoie (1427–1447).* Cahiers Lausannois d'histoire Médiévale 8. Lausanne, 1993.

Palmieri, Stefano, ed. *L'Europe des Anjou: Aventure des Princes Angevins du Xiiie Au Xve Siécle [Exhibition at Fontévraud, 2001].* Paris, 2001.

Pannier, Léopold. *La Noble-Maison de Saint-Ouen: la Villa Clippiacum et l'ordre de l'Étoile d'après les Documents Originaux.* Paris, 1872.

Paravicini, Werner. 'Die Zwölf "Magnificences" Karls des Kühnen', in Althoff, *Formen und Funktion Öffentlicher Kommunikation im Mittelalters,* 319-95.

———. *La Cour de Bourgogne et L'Europe: le Rayonnement et les Limites d'un Modèle Culturel: Actes du Colloque Internationale Tenu à Paris les 9, 10 et 11 Octobre 2007.* Beihefte Der Francia 73. Sigmaringen, 2013.

Paresys, Isabelle, and Natalie Coquery, eds. *Se Vêtir à la Cour en Europe (1400–1815).* Lille, 2011.

Paris, Geffroy de. *La Chronique Métrique Attribuée à Geffroy de Paris.* Ed. Armel Diverres. Publications de la Faculté des Lettres de l'Université de Strasbourg 129. Paris, 1956.

Paris, Matthew. *Historia Minor, 1067–1253.* Ed. Sir Frederic Madden. Rolls Series 44. London, 1866.

———. *Matthaei Parisiensis Chronica Majora.* Ed. Rev. H. R. Luard. 7 vols. Rolls Series 57. London: 1872–1884.

Paris, Paulin, ed. *Les Grandes Chroniques de France* Vol. 6. Paris, 1838.

*Parliament Rolls of Medieval England.* 16 vols. Woodbridge, 2005.

Parsons, John Carmi, ed. *Medieval Queenship.* Stroud, 1994.

Pastoureau, Michel. 'Les Ménageries Princières: du Pouvoir Au Savoir? (XIIe -XVIe Siècle)'. *Micrologus* XVI (2008): 3–30.

Paterson, Linda M. (Linda Mary) 'Great Court Festivals in the South of France and Catalonia in the Twelfth and Thirteenth Centuries'. *Medium Aevum* 51, no. 2 (1982): 213–24.

Paviot, Jacques. 'Ordres, Devises, Sociétés Chevaleresques et la Cour', in Gaude-Ferragu et al., *La Cour du Prince,* 271–80.

Perry, Guy. 'A King of Jerusalem in England: The Visit of John of Brienne in 1223'. *History* 100 (2015): 625–39.

Pešina z Čechorodu, Tomáš. *Phosphorus Septicornis i.e. Metropol. S. Viti Eccles. Pragensis Maiestas.* Prague, 1673.

Petrarca, Francesco. *Letters on Familiar Matters: Rerum Familiarum Libri XVII-XIV.* Tr. Aldo S.Bernardo. Baltimore, 1985.

Pharr, Clyde. *The Theodosian Code and Novels, and the Sirmondian Constitutions.* Vol. 1. Corpus of Roman Law. Princeton, NJ, 1952.

Pietzsch, Gerhard 1904–1979. *Fürsten und fürstliche Musiker im mittelalterlichen Köln: Quellen und Studien.* Köln, 1966.

Piponnier, Françoise. *Costume et vie sociale: la cour d'Anjou XIVe-XVe siècle*. Paris, 1970.

Pizan, Christine de. *Le Livre des Faits et Bonnes Meurs du Sage Roy Charles V*, Paris, 1936

Plancher, Urbain. *Histoire General et Particulière de Bourgogne*, Dijon, 1739–81

Pliny the Elder. *Natural History*. Tr. H Rackham. Vol. 3. The Loeb Classical Library 353. Cambridge, MA, 1953.

Poindexter, Adele. 'Chapel'. Grove Music Online, 20 January 2001. https://doi-org.ezproxy2.londonlibrary.co.uk/10.1093/gmo/9781561592630.article.05431.

Pollini, Nadia. *La Mort du Prince: Rituels Funéraires de la Maison de Savoie (1343–1451)*. Fondation Humbert II et Marie José de Savoie: Cahiers Lausannois d'Histoire Médiévale 9. Lausanne, 1994.

Postan, M. M., E. E. Rich, and E. Miller, eds. *Economic Organisation and Politics in the Middle Ages*. The Cambridge Economic History of Europe III. Cambridge, 1963.

Postan, M.M. *Feudal Society (1) The Growth of Ties of Dependence*. Tr. L.A. Manyon. London, 1965.

Potter, W. J. W. 'The Gold Coinages of Edward III; Part I The Early and Pre-Treaty Coinages'. *The Numismatic Chronicle and Journal of the Royal Numismatic Society* Seventh Series, 3 (1963): 107–28.

———. 'The Gold Coinages of Edward III; Part II. (A) The Treaty Period (1361–9)'. *The Numismatic Chronicle and Journal of the Royal Numismatic Society* Seventh Series, 4 (1964): 305–18.

Pradel, Pierre. 'Froissart et Beauneveu'. *Journal des Savants*, 1960, 6–11.

Prestwich, Michael. 'The "Wonderful Life" of the Thirteenth Century', in *Thirteenth Century England*, VII. Woodbridge, 1999.

Prost, Bernard., and Henri Prost, *Inventaires Mobiliers et Extraits des Comptes des Ducs de Bourgogne de la Maison de Valois (1363–1477)*. 2 vols. Paris 1902–1913.

Prou, Maurice. 'L'Art Monétaire pendant la Période Gothique', in Michel, *Histoire de l'Art*, 431–51.

Purton, Peter. *A History of the Medieval Siege, 1200–1500*. Woodbridge, 2010.

Queruel, Danielle. 'Des Entremets aux Intermèdes dans les Banquets Bourguignons', in Centre d'Études d'Aix, *Banquets et Manières de Table*, 141–58.

Quicherat, J. *Histoire de Costume en France*. Paris, 1877.

Radke, Gary M. 'The Palaces of Frederick II', in Tronzo, *Intellectual Life at the Court of Frederick II*, 179–86, 1994.

Rashdall, Hastings. *The Universities of Europe in the Middle Ages*. Ed. F. M. Powicke and A. B. Emden. New Edition. Oxford, 1936.

Raynaud, G. *Les Gestes des Chiprois*. Société de l'Orient Latin, V. Paris, 1887.

Rees-Jones, Sarah, Richard Marks, and A. J. (Alastair J.) Minnis, eds. *Courts and Regions in Medieval Europe*. Woodbridge, 2000.

*Register of Edward the Black Prince*. 4 vols. London, 1930–33. [Public Record Office].

Régnier-Bohler, Danielle, ed. *Splendeurs de la Cour de Bourgogne: Récits et Chroniques*. Paris, 1995.

Reilly, Bernard F. *The Kingdom of León-Castilla under Queen Urraca, 1109–1126*. Princeton, 1982. https://libro.uca.edu/urraca/urraca.htm , accessed 18 December 2019.

Reynolds, Susan. *Fiefs and Vassals: The Medieval Evidence Reinterpreted*. Oxford, 1994.

Ricci, Camillo Minieri. *Saggio di Codice Diplomatici Formato sulle Antiche Scritture dell'archivio di Stato di Napoli*. 2 vols. Napoli, 1882–3.

Richard, Jules-Marie. *Mahaut, Comtesse d'Artois et de Bourgogne (1302–1329)*. Cressé, 2010.

Richardson, Thom. *The Tower Armoury in the Fourteenth Century*. Leeds, 2016.

Richmond, Colin, and Eileen Scarff. *St George's Chapel, Windsor, in the Late Middle Ages*. Historical Monographs Related to St George's Chapel, Windsor Castle, 17. Windsor, 2001.

Riedmann, Josef. *Die Beziehungen der Grafen und Landesfürsten von Tirol zu Italien bis zum Jahre 1335*. Wien, 1977.

Rigby, Stephen H. 'Aristotle for Aristocrats and Poets: Giles of Rome's De Regimine Principum as Theodicy of Privilege'. *The Chaucer Review* 46 (2012): 259–313.

Rockinger, Ludwig. *Briefsteller und Formelbücher des Elften bis Vierzehnten Jahrhunderts*. Munich, 1863.

Rolandinus de Padua. 'Rolandini Patavini Cronica', in *Annales Aevi Suevici*, Ed. Philipp Jaffé. Monumenta Germaniae Historica Scriptores 19, 32–147. Hanover, 1866.

Rollason, David. *The Power of Place: Rulers and Their Palaces, Landscapes, Cities and Holy Places*. Princeton, 2016.

Roman, M. J, *Inventaires et Documents relatifs aux Joyaux et Tapisseries des Princes d'Orléans-Valois, 1389–1481*. Paris, 1894.

Rome, Giles of. *The Governance of Kings and Princes: John Trevisa's Middle English Translation of the De Regimine Principum of Aegidius Romanus*. Ed. David C. Fowler, et al. New York, 1997.

Rosario, Iva. *Art and Propaganda: Charles IV of Bohemia, 1346–78*. Woodbridge, 2000.

Rosell, Cayetano. *Crónicas de Los Reyes de Castilla, desde Don Alfonso El Sabio, hasta Los Católicos Don Fernando y Doña Isabel*. Madrid, 1875.

Rösener, Werner. 'Die Hoftage Kaiser Friedrichs I. Barbarossa im Regnum Teutonicum', in Moraw, *Deutscher Königshof, Hoftag und Reichstag im Späteren Mittelalter*, 359–86.

Rosie, Alison. 'Ritual, Chivalry and Pageantry: The Courts of Anjou, Orleans and Savoy in the Later Middle Ages'. PhD, Edinburgh University, 1989.

Rouse, Mary R., and Richard H. Rouse. 'The Goldsmith and the Peacocks'. *Viator* 28 (1997): 281–384.

Russell, John. 'On Nurture', in Furnivall, *The Babees Book*, 117–200.

Ryder, Alan. *Alfonso the Magnanimous: King of Aragon, Naples, and Sicily, 1396–1458*. Oxford, 1990.

———. *The Kingdom of Naples under Alfonso the Magnanimous: The Making of a Modern State*. Oxford, 1976.

Rykner, Didier. 'Charles VII's Canopy: A Major Acquisition for the Louvre', 26 September 2010. http://www.thearttribune.com/Charles-VII-s-canopy-a-major.html. accessed 18 December 2019.

Rymer, Thomas. *Foedera, Conventiones…* 4 vols. London, 1816.

Safford, E. W. 'An Account of the Expenses of Eleanor, Sister of Edward III, on the occasion of her marriage to Reynald, Count of Guelders'. *Archaeologia* 77 (1927): 111–40.

Salimbene, Cronica. Ed. Giuseppe Scalia, Bari, 1966.

Salvatico, Antonella. *Il principe e il cuoco: costume e gastronomia alla corte sabauda nel Quattrocento*. Torino, 1999.

Sands, Harold. 'Extracts from the Documentary History of the Tower of London'. *The Antiquaries Journal* 69 (1912): 161–72.

Sauerländer, Willibald. 'Die Naumburger Stifterfiguren: Rückblick und Fragen', in Hausherr, Die Zeit der Staufer, 169–245.

Sauerländer, Willibald, and Wollasch, Joachim. 'Stiftergedenken und Stifterfiguren in Naumburg', in Schmid, *"Memoria"*, 354-383.

Saul, Nigel. Richard II. London, 1997.

———. 'The Commons and the Abolition of Badges'. *Parliamentary History* 9, no. pt. 2 (1990): 302–15.

———. 'Richard II's Ideas of Kingship', in Dillian, *The Regal Image of Richard II*, 27–32.

Saul, Nigel, ed. *St George's Chapel, Windsor, in the Fourteenth Century*. Woodbridge, 2005.

Scheffer-Boichorst, Paul. *Zur Geschichte des XII. und XIII. Jahrhunderts*. Berlin, 1897

Schmid, Karl, and Joachim Wollasch. *"Memoria". Der geschichtliche Zeugniswert des liturgischen Gedenkens im Mittelalter*. München, 1984.

Schmidt, Roderick. *Weltordnung - Herrschaftsordnung im Europäischen Mittelalter: Darstellung und Deutung durch Rechtsakt, Wort und Bild*. Bibliotheca Eruditorum, 14. Goldbach, 2004.

Schmidt, Roderick. 'Königsumritt und Huldigung in Ottonisch-Salischer Zeit', in *Weltordnung - Herrschaftsordnung*, 53–190.

Schmolke-Hasselmann, Beate. 'The Round Table: Ideal, Fiction, Reality'. *Arthurian Literature* II (1982): 41–75.

Schnerb, Bertrand. 'La Piété et les Dévotions de Philippe le Bon, Duc de Bourgogne (1419–1467)'. *Comptes Rendus des Séances de l'Académie des Inscriptions et Belles-Lettres* 148, no. 4 (2005): 1319–44.

Schrader, Johanna. *Isabella von Aragonien: Gemahlin Friedrichs des Schönen [Dissertation]*. Leipzig, 1915.

Schramm, Percy Ernst. *A History of the English Coronation*. Oxford: 1937.

———. *Herrschaftszeihen und Staatssymbolik: Beiträge zu ihrer Geschichte vom Dritten bis zum Sechszehnten Jahrhundert*. 3 vols. Schriften der Monumenta Germaniae Historica. Vol. 13. Stuttgart, 1954.

———. *Kaiser Friedrichs II, Herrschaftszeichen*. Abhandlungen der Akademie der Wissenschaften in Göttingen, Dritte Folge, 36. Göttingen, 1955.

Schubert, Ernst. *Dies Diem Docet: Ausgewählte Aufsätze zur Mittelalterlichen Kunst und Geschichte in Mitteldeutschland*. Ed. Hans-Joachim Krause. Quellen und Forschungen zur Geschichte Sachsen-Anhalts 3. Wien, 2003.

———. 'Memorialdenkmäler für Fundatoren in Drei Naumburger Kirchen des Hochmittlealters', in *Dies Diem Docet*, 378–421`.

Schupp, Volker, and Hans Szklenar. *Ywain auf Schloss Rodenegg: Eine Bildergeschichte nach dem 'Iwein' Hartmanns von Aue*. Sigmaringen, 1996.

Schwarz, Karl. *Aragonische Hofordnungen im 13 und 14 Jahrhundert: Studien zur Geschichte Der Hofamter und Zentralbehörden des Königreichs Aragon*. Abhandlungen zur Mittleren und Neueren Geschichte. 54. Berlin and Leipzig, 1914.

Scott-Stokes, Charity, and Chris. Given-Wilson, eds. *Chronicon Anonymi Cantvariensis*. Oxford, 2008.

Scully, Terence 1935– *The Art of Cookery in the Middle Ages*. Woodbridge, 1995.

Seibt, Ferdinand, ed. *Kaiser Karl IV. Staatsmann und Mäzen [Exhibition Catalogue, Nürnberg und Köln 1978/9]*. Munich, 1978.

———. *Karl IV. Ein Kaiser in Europa 1346 bis 1378*. Munich, 1985.

Servion, Jean., and Federigo Emmanuele. Bollato di Saint-Pierre. *Gestez et Croniques de la Mayson de Savoye*. Turin, 1879.

Sharpe, R. R. *Calendar of Letter-Books Preserved among the Archives of the Corporation of the City of London at the Guildhall*. London, 1899.

Sherman, Claire Richter. *The Portraits of Charles V of France*. New York, 1969.

Shirley, Janet. A Parisian Journal 1405–1449. Oxford, 1968.

Sibyllle, Eva, and Gerhard Rösch. *Kaiser Friedrich II und sein Königreich Sizilien*. Sigmaringen: 1996.

Siddons, Michael Powell. *Heraldic Badges in England and Wales*. Woodbridge, 2009.

Šmahel, František. *The Parisian Summit, 1377–78: Emperor Charles IV and King Charles V of France*. Prague, 2014.

Small, Graeme. *George Chastelain and the Shaping of Valois Burgundy: Political and Historical Culture at Court in the Fifteenth Century*. Royal Historical Society Studies in History, New Series. Woodbridge, 1997.

Society of Antiquaries of London, *A Collection of Ordinances and Regulations for the Government of the Royal Household, Made in Divers Reigns: From King Edward III. to King William and Queen Mary. Also Receipts in Ancient Cookery*. London, 1790.

Sommerlechner, Andrea. *Stupor Mundi? Kaiser Friedrich II und die Mittelalterliche Geschichtsschreibung*. Publikationen des Historischen Instituts Beim Osterreichischen Kulturinstitut in Rom 11. Vienna, 1999.

Southworth, John. *The English Medieval Minstrel*. Woodbridge, 1989.

Sponsler, Claire. *The Queen's Dumbshows: John Lydgate and the Making of Early Theater*. Philadelphia, 2014.

Spufford, Peter. *Power and Profit: The Merchant in Medieval Europe*. London, 2002.

St Blaise, Otto of. *Ottonis de Sancto Blasio Chronica*. Ed. Adolf Hofmeister. Hanover, 1912.

Stafford, Pauline. *Queens, Concubines, and Dowagers: The King's Wife in the Early Middle Ages*. London: Leicester University Press, 1998.

Staniland, Kay. 'Court Style, Painters and the Great Wardrobe', in Ormrod, *England in the Fourteenth Century*, 236–46

———. *Embroiderers*. Medieval Craftsmen. London, 1991.

———. 'Extravagance or Regal Necessity? The Clothing of Richard II', in Dillian, *The Regal Image of Richard II and the Wilton Diptych*, 85–94.

———. 'Medieval Courtly Splendour'. *Costume* 14 (1980): 7–23.

Stefano, Antonio de. *La cultura alla corte di Federico II imperatore*. Bologna, 1950.

Stratford, Jenny. *Richard II and the English Royal Treasure*. Woodbridge, 2012.

———. *The Bedford Inventories: The Worldly Goods of John, Duke of Bedford, Regent of France*. Reports of the Research Committee of the Society of Antiquaries XLIX. London, 1993.

Strickland, Matthew. *Henry the Young King*. London, 2016.

Stubbs, William, ed. *Chronicles of the Reigns of Edward I and Edward II*. 2 vols. Rolls Series 76. London, 1882.

Sturgeon, Justin. 'Text and image in René d'Anjou's Livre des Tournois, c.1460: Constructing Authority and Identity in Fifteenth Century Court Culture, Presented with a Critical Edition of BnF, Ms. Français 2695'. University of York, 2015.

Stürner, Wolfgang. *Friedrich II*. 2 vols. Darmstadt, 1992.

Suggett, Helen. 'A Letter describing Richard II's Reconciliation with the City of London, 1392'. *English Historical Review* 62 (n.d.): 209–13.

Suso, Henry. *The Life of the Blessed Henry Suso*. Tr. Thomas Francis Knox. London, 1913.

Sylvester, Louise M., Mark C. Chambers, and Gale R. Owen-Crocker, eds. *Medieval Dress and Textiles in Britain: A Mulitilingual Sourcebook*. Medieval and Renaissance *Clothing and Textiles* 1. Woodbridge, 2014.

Syson, Luke, and Dillian Gordon. *Pisanello: Painter to the Renaissance Court*. London, 2002.

Szabó, Thomas. 'Der Mittelalterliche Hof zwischen Kritik und Idealisierung', in *Curialitas*, 350–91.

Tafur, Pero. *Travels and Adventures, 1435–1439*. Tr. Malcolm Letts. London, 1926.

Tatton Brown, Tim. 'Windsor Castle before 1344', in Munby, *Edward III's Round Table at Windsor*, 13–28.

Taylor, Craig. 'The Salic Law and the Valois Succession to the French Crown'. *French History* 15 (2001): 358–77.

Thompson, E.M. *Chronicon Anglie*. London, 1974.

Thorndike, Lynn. *A History of Magic and Experimental Science*. 8 vols. London, 1923.

Thurocz, Johannes de. *Chronica Hungarorum*. Ed. Elizabeth Galantái and Julius Kristó. Bibliotheca Scriptorum Medii Recentisque Aevorum Series Nova. VII.Budapest, 1985.

Tonnerre, Noël-Yves, and Elisabeth Verry, eds. *Les Princes Angevins du XIIIe Au XVe Siècle: Un Destin Européen. Actes des Journées d'étude organisée par l'université d'Angers et les Archives Départementales de Maine-et-Loire*. Rennes, 2003.

Topham, John. *Some Account of the Chapel of St Stephen*. London, 1795.

Tours, Gregory of. *The History of the Franks*. Tr. Lewis Thorpe. Harmondsworth, 1974.

Tout, T.F. *Chapters in the Administrative History of Mediaeval England*. 6 vols. Manchester, 1920.

———. 'Literature and Learning in the English Civil Service in the Fourteenth Century'. *Speculum* 4 (1929): 365–89.

Tracy, Charles. *English Gothic Choir-stalls*. Woodbridge, 1987.

Trexler, Richard C., ed. *Persons in Groups: Social Behavior as Identity Formation in Medieval and Renaissance Europe*. Medieval and Renaissance Texts and Studies 36. Binghamton, 1985.

Tronzo, William, *Intellectual Life at the Court of Frederick II Hohenstaufen*. Studies in the History of Art 44. Washington, DC, 1994.

Truitt, E, R. *Medieval Robots: Mechanism, Magic, Nature, and Art* Philadelphia, PA, 2015.

Twycross, Meg, and Carpenter, Sarah. *Masks and Masking in Early Tudor England*. Aldershot, 2002.

Ullmann, Walter. 'The Development of the Medieval Idea of Sovereignty'. *English Historical Review* 64 (1949): 1–33.

Vale, M. G. A. *The Princely Court: Medieval Courts and Culture in North-West Europe, 1270–1380*. Oxford: Oxford University Press, 2001.

Van den Bergen-Pantens, Christiane. *L'ordre de la Toison d'or, de Philippe le Bon à Philippe le Beau (1430–1505): Idéal ou Reflet d'une Société?* Brussels, 1996.

Vassilieva-Codognet, Olga. 'L'Étoffe de Ses Rêves: le Vêtement du Prince et ses Parures Emblématiques à la Fin du Moyen Âge', in Paresys, *Se Vêtir à la Cour en Europe (1400–1815)*, 44–66.

Vaughan, Richard. *Charles the Bold: The Last Valois Duke of Burgundy*. Woodbridge, 2002

———. *John the Fearless: The Growth of the Burgundian Power*. [3rd ed.]. Woodbridge: Boydell, 2002.

———. *Philip the Bold: The Formation of the Burgundian State*. Woodbridge, 2002.

———. *Philip the Good: The Apogee of Burgundy*. Woodbridge, 2002.

Venette, Jean de. *The Chronicle of Jean de Venette*. Ed. Richard A. Newhall. Tr. Jean Birdsall. Records of Civilization, Sources and Studies, 50. New York, 1953.

Vernier, J.-J. 'Philippe le Hardi Duc de Bourgogne: son Mariage avec Marguerite de Flandre en 1369'. *Bulletin de la Commission Historique du Département du Nord* 22 (1900): 97–143.

Viktring, Johannes von. *Liber Certarum Historiarum*. Ed. Viktor Schneider. 2 vols. Hanover, 1909.

Viñayo González, Antonio. *L'ancien Royaume de León Roman*, La Pierre-Qui-Vire, 1972.

Vincent, Nicholas. *The Holy Blood*. Cambridge, 2001.

Vingtain, Dominique. *Avignon: le Palais des Papes*. Vol. 2. Le ciel et la pierre. Saint-Léger-Vauban, 1998.

Viriville, Vallet de. *La Bibliothèque d'Isabeau de Bavière, Femme de Charles VI, Roi de France*. Paris, 1858.

Vogelweide, Walther von der. *Gedichte: mittelhochdeutscher Text und Übertragung*. Ed. Peter. Wapnewski. Frankfurt am Main, 1984.

Wahlgren, Lena. *The Letter Collections of Peter of Blois: Studies in the Manuscript Tradition*. Göteborg, 1993

Walsh, R. J. *Charles the Bold and Italy (1467–1477): Politics and Personnel*. Liverpool, n.d.

Wammetsberger, Helga. 'Individuum und Typ in den Porträts Kaiser Karls IV', in Legner, *Die Parler und Der Schöne Stil*, 79–93.

Weiland, Ludwig, ed. *Braunschweigische Reimchronik*. Hanover, 1877.

Weir, Alison. *Eleanor of Aquitaine: By the Wrath of God, Queen of England*. London, 2000.

Weitmile, Benes z. 'Chronicon', in *Fontes Rerum Bohemicarum*, IV. Prague, 1884.

Wendover, Roger of. *Liber Qui Dicitur Flores Historiarum Ab Anno Domini MCLIV*. Ed. H.G. Hewlett. 3 vols. Rolls Series 84. London, 1886.

Wetter, Evelin. 'Material Evidence, Theological Requirements and Medial Transformation: "Textile Strategies" in the Court in the Court Art of Charles IV', in Dimitrova, *Dressing the Part: Textiles as Propaganda in the Middle Ages*, 125–50, n.d.

Whiteley, Mary. 'The Courts of Edward III of England and Charles V of France: A Comparison of Their Architectural Setting and Ceremonial Functions'. *Fourteenth Century England* I (2000): 153–66.

Wild, Benjamin Linley. 'The Empress's New Clothes: A Rotulus Pannorum of Isabella, Sister of King Henry III, Bride of Emperor Frederick II', in Netherton, *Medieval Textiles and Clothing*, 3–31

———. The Wardrobe Accounts of Henry III. Publications of the Pipe Roll Society, New series LVIII. London, 2012.

Wilkinson, Louise J. 'The imperial marriage of Isabella of England, Henry III's sister', in Oakley-Brown, *The Rituals and Rhetoric of Medieval Queenship*, 20–36.

William of Malmesbury. *Gesta Regum Anglorum*. Ed. R. A. B. Mynors, R.M. Thomson, and M. Winterbottom. 2 vols. Oxford, 1998–9.

Williams, John. 'San Isidoro in León: Evidence for a New History'. *The Art Bulletin* 55, no. 2 (1973): 170–84.

Wilson, Christopher. 'The Royal Lodgings of Edward II at Windsor Castle: Form, Function, Representation', in Keen, *Windsor: Medieval Archaeology, Art and Architecture in the Thames Valley*, 15–94.

Wilson, Peter H. *The Holy Roman Empire: A Thousand Years of Europe's History*. London, 2016.

Wolf, Arnim. 'Reigning Queens in Medieval Europe: When, Where and Why', in Parsons, *Medieval Queenship*, 170–88.

Woods-Marsden, Joanna. *The Gonzaga of Mantua and Pisanello's Arthurian Frescoes*. Princeton, NJ, 1987.

Woolgar, C.M. *The Culture of Food in England 1200–1500*. New Haven ; London, 2016.

Wright, Craig. *Music at the Court of Burgundy 1364–1419: A Documentary History*. Musicological Studies 38. Henryville, IN, 1979.

Wright, T. *Political Poems and Songs Relating to English History*. Rolls Series 14. London, 1859.

Wright, Thomas. *The Political Songs of England*. Camden Society. London, 1839.

# ✣ ACKNOWLEDGEMENTS

It is always hard to know where to begin with acknowledgements. The first of these is in the dedication, to my colleagues at Boydell and Brewer. On this particular project, they have been very forbearing with an author who has probably managed to break every prescribed routine that they have so carefully established.

Next, my debts to fellow-scholars go far beyond the use of their published works, without which this book would not exist. I was surprised and pleased to find how much I owe to my teachers in Cambridge more years ago than I care to admit. Richard Vaughan's four very readable volumes on the fifteenth century dukes of Burgundy are the most immediate reference point in this book; it was an honour to be able to reissue them at Boydell Press twenty years ago, and they remain in print as the standard work on the subject. I have described in chapter four how David Knowles made medieval philosophy, which is at the heart of this book, an exciting subject.

Two readers in particular considered the text from a scholarly point of view. They not only identified items I had overlooked or misinterpreted, but also led me to a radical rearrangement of the content of the book. Professor Werner Paravicini was kind enough to encourage me when I produced previous versions of this text. His expertise in matters French, German and Burgundian has been much appreciated, and the last chapter is heavily indebted to his work. Professor Mark Ormrod challenged me to look at the audience for magnificence, a central topic which I had failed to recognise, and made many other helpful suggestions.

A particular debt is owed to the scholars whom it has also been Boydell's pleasure to publish, and my privilege to meet in person. To take just one example among many, Stella Newton was the author of *Fashion in the Age of the Black Prince*. This invaluable source is still in print after forty years. She had a remarkable career, starting as a Bond Street couturier, designing costumes for the première of T.S. Eliot's *Murder in the Cathedral*, and thence to lectures on costume in paintings at the National Gallery, and to study at the Courtauld Institute. She is one of over thirty Boydell authors whose works I have used in writing this book.

I am most grateful to those who took part in the three sessions on Magnificence at the International Medieval Congress at Leeds in 2019. Adrian Ailes, Paul Binski, Christopher de Hamel, Lisa Monnas, Jenny Stratford, and Justin Sturgeon all responded warmly to the proposal that this would be a good topic, and presented six excellent papers. Lisa Monnas, Jenny Stratford and Adrian Ailes also read the first draft of the book, and suggested areas I had overlooked as well as necessary alterations to some of the technical descriptions in the text.

Beyond this, there have been endless serendipitous conversations at academic conferences over the years, particularly at Leeds, which have contributed to a greater or lesser degree to the book as a whole.

At this point, of course, I have to make the traditional scholarly disclaimer, and absolve all my readers and supporters of any blame for the errors which, in such a wide-ranging book, will inevitably remain.

I was very fortunate to be able to enlist a number of other readers who looked at the book from different angles. Lynda Edwardes-Evans gave the draft text a very close and professional reading, raising many important points. For a start, she declared that the title of what I had written should be 'Male Magnificence'. I hope that my response in chapter 6 both explains that difficulty and atones for the failings of the first draft. And two fellow-publishers and good friends appraised the text with considerable skill, Sue Bradbury, lately editorial director of the Folio Society, and Kevin Crossley-Holland, as a very successful interpreter of the middle ages for younger readers, and whose poetic work as a 'wordsmith' of great elegance throws down the gauntlet to a mere retailer of plain prose. Other readers included Kate Charlton-Jones, who encouraged me to think that non-scholarly readers would not be too daunted by the book. Elaine Barber has helped with problems in Greek and Latin, and with the text in general.

Klára Petříková made me very welcome in Prague, and organised a private visit to Karlstejn Castle, where Kryštof Buchal was an ideal guide, ready to discuss ideas and admirably well informed. She also read the relevant text and helped to find the excellent photographs by Radovan Bocek.

On translations, I have been able to call on the late David Preest, a seasoned classicist, who did sterling work with Giles of Rome's prolix Latin, which Professor Rod Thomson has rechecked and enlarged. Noel Fallows helped with letters in medieval Catalan.

The bulk of my scholarly research has been done through the London Library, whose help has always been exemplary and amazingly prompt. Living in Suffolk, I fear I have kept their postal service busy. Gosia Lawik was especially helpful with some obscure Continental titles (I was somewhat surprised by the arrival of one text scan from the libraries in Liechtenstein). The British Library and Cambridge University Library have been my other major sources, together with the library of the Society of Antiquaries.

The illustrations make a vital contribution to this book. Professor Beat Brenk kindly provided two really excellent images of the Palermo mosaics, which are a challenge to any photographer. Sian Phillips of Bridgeman Images managed to supply many of the items that I could not immediately track down. Mais Edwards used her understanding of Spanish working habits to track down photographs from an otherwise unresponsive organisation (which shall be nameless).

Good images are often difficult to find, and they are a vital element in the present book.

In practical terms, Judith Everard has done an excellent job in tackling a text which suffered the accidental repetitions and the failure to cut and paste neatly that writing on a computer brings. Catherine Larner eliminated a large number of problems in the course of her careful scrutiny as proofreader. Marie-Pierre Evans was responsible for the excellent index, no easy task with a multifarious text such as this. Simon Loxley has made a major contribution to the book by producing a design worthy of its title, using the many possibilities presented by four colour printing throughout. He has also remained cheerful despite the somewhat disorderly delivery of the text and illustrations for typesetting. And I must thank Ian Jacob, for underlining the word 'magnificence' in an earlier book of mine, and unwittingly starting the whole thing off.

Above all, though she appears at the end when she should be at the beginning, my loving thanks to Gay Edwards. Her dedication to the improvement of my style and the tireless hunt for the *mot juste* have been a wonderful co-operative exercise, while her appreciation and tolerance of my (hopefully temporary) obsession with the subject have been equally a marvel.

RICHARD BARBER

The following passages were reprinted with the permission of the publishers:

By permission of Arizona Center for Medieval Studies: Terence Scully, Du fait de cuisine/*On Cookery* of Maistre Chiquart,: pp. 243, 262-3.

By permission of The Boydell Press:
Richard Vaughan, *Philip the Bold*, pp. 83, 200-1
Richard Vaughan, *Charles the Bold*, pp. 194-5, 294

Because of the wide range of this book, I have reused some material which has appeared in previous books of my own. The preliminary version mentioned in the preface was published for the members of the Folio Society under the title *Splendour at Court*. There are also passages based on *Edward III and the Triumph of England* and *The Penguin Guide to Medieval Europe*.

# ✳ INDEX

References to illustrations are indicated in italics with page numbers for captions in brackets if placed on a different page. References to endnotes consist of the page number followed by the letter 'n' followed by the number of the chapter followed by the number of the note. When the author or subject mentioned in the endnote is not directly identified in the main text, the text page is added in brackets, e.g. 312n7/15 (112) refers to endnote 15 under chapter 7 on page 312, and the note number is to be found in the main text on p. 112.